The Encyclopedia of
MAGIC and ALCHEMY

For William G. Fellows

The Encyclopedia of
MAGIC and ALCHEMY

Rosemary Ellen Guiley

FOREWORD BY
Donald Michael Kraig

✓ Facts On File
An imprint of Infobase Publishing

Facts On File, Inc.
An imprint of Infobase Publishing
132 West 31st Street
New York NY 10001

Library of Congress Cataloging-in-Publication Data
Guiley, Rosemary.
The encyclopedia of magic and alchemy / Rosemary Ellen Guiley.
p. cm.
Includes bibliographical references and index.
ISBN 0-8160-6048-7 (hc : alk. paper)
1. Magic—Encyclopedias. 2. Alchemy—Encyclopedias. I. Title.
BF1588.G85 2006
133.4'303—dc22   2005027036

Facts On File books are available at special discounts when purchased in bulk quantities for businesses, associations, institutions, or sales promotions. Please call our Special Sales Department in New York at (212) 967-8800 or (800) 322-8755.

You can find Facts On File on the World Wide Web at http://www.factsonfile.com

Text design by Cathy Rincon
Cover design by Salvatore Luongo

Printed in the United States of America

VB FOF 10 9 8 7 6 5 4 3 2 1

This book is printed on acid-free paper.

CONTENTS

FOREWORD

by Donald Michael Kraig

In the 16th century, Pierre Charron, the famous Roman Catholic philosopher, moralist, preacher, and friend of Michel de Montaigne, wrote, "The true science and the true study of man is man." Poet Alexander Pope repeated this belief in the 18th century with his better-known statement, "The proper study of mankind is man." If these two eminent gentlemen are correct, the study of magic and alchemy should be at the forefront of the investigations of all educated persons.

And yet, quite obviously, they are not. In the world of knowledge, magic and alchemy usually lie overlooked and ignored, discarded and hidden like a polyester "leisure suit" we are too embarrassed to admit that we ever purchased and would be even more embarrassed to admit that we wore. We are, after all, far too enlightened to have ever believed in anything so quaint and crackpot. Certainly today only the uneducated, the gullible, and the cranks would ever waste their time studying such foolishness. Magic? Alchemy? Don't make me laugh.

The story of magic and alchemy, however, is the story of humanity. It is filled with hope and ecstasy, failure and despair. It is the greedy and self-centered search for terrestrial power and the spiritual striving for transcendence and a glimpse of the very person of God. Whether it is the seeking of gold to amass personal wealth, the creation of a golem to defend a people against oppression, or a magician of the East meditating to achieve advanced levels of spirituality, virtually every aspect of humanity—the same ones revealed in the plays of Greece and Shakespeare, the Bible, the Koran, and the Mahabharata and in the works of Freud and his metaphoric progeny—was exhibited by those who studied and practiced these ancient arts and sciences.

And indeed, sciences they are! The basic technique of experimental science, commonly called the scientific method, was originated by the alchemists of centuries past (much to the chagrin of many scientists, as well as debunkers and those who have usurped the term *skeptic* to represent their rationalization for an obsessive need not just to denounce, but to attempt to silence any who dare to have a philosophy other than their own übermaterialism). They would logically plan out their experiments and carefully record their results. They would eliminate other potential causes of their results, repeat experiments, and share results with others to see if their experiments could be reproduced. The famous mathematician and physicist, Sir Isaac Newton, creator of the famous three laws of motion studied by students of physics all over the world, wrote more on alchemy than any other subject (more than a million words).

If a person sees a movie or reads a novel about vampires, he or she may think, "That's scary," or "That's fun," but they know that it is just a fiction and not true. However, most of our knowledge of magic and alchemy are not derived from a study of mages and alchemists themselves but from those who would denounce them or use them as little more than a "plot point" in a novel or film. Curiously, rather than thinking that these interpretations of the subjects are "just a fiction and not true," we accept the myths and misunderstandings as valid representations. If magic and alchemy were individuals, they could sue in court for libel and slander.

Is it any wonder, then, that most people who come to study magic today do so with the false expectation that they can use these methods to obtain power quickly and easily over others or to have a miracle when all other hopes have failed? And when their brief explorations do not give them the results that they saw in a film or comic book, is it any wonder that they become disappointed and turn away? Society has built a massive false image, a factual straw man, blithely declaring of the misrepresentation, "This is magic!" And when this false image is revealed to be nothing but straw, incapable of achieving anything, disenchantment is the inevitable result.

I remember, as a youth, receiving a chemistry set for my birthday. I tried an experiment from the all-too-brief booklet that came with it, and did not experience the result that was described in the book. My mother told me, "You did something wrong." Most people who attempt magic today, with skills based on bad books or silly films, also do not end with the desired results. But their conclusion is not that they did something wrong. Rather, they conclude that magic does not work. But what if it does? What if magic is not the straw man that is assembled by the media, supported by many religions, and denounced by the materialists to defend their rapidly crumbling, thought-limiting paradigm? What if magic and alchemy are real?

Magic today is studied and practiced by many tens of thousands of people all over the world. Those who get past the aforementioned desire for power over others or for a miracle cure for their problems discover magic's ultimate secret: As I have written many times, "Magic isn't something you do. Magic is something you are." Real magic is not about gaining power over others: it is about gaining power over yourself. And you are doing it 24 hours a day, seven days a week. Magic is a way to learn how to control all of your normal, conflicting desires, thoughts, and actions and unite them with the power of the universe—some might call it the Will of God—to act like a thousand people working in harmony to achieve a desired end. With power like that, who needs to control others?

Note, however, that this does not occur outside of the real world. This means that magic is not supernatural. With proper training, knowledge, and practice, you could easily perform magic to improve your finances. But this does not mean, as shown in films and fiction, that a pile of gold coins would suddenly appear at your feet. That would be supernatural, something magic is not. Instead, it would harness your own abilities, and that of the universe, to improve your financial situation. Perhaps a relative would send you a gift in the mail. Maybe you would receive a raise at work or a better-paying job.

Magic is in harmony with the universe. It has its own set of natural rules or laws that are as invariable as the law of gravity. The question is, how do you learn such harmony? The journey to find a satisfying answer to this question eventually leads a student to move practices and studies of magic from being mere physical actions combined with memorized data to a quest for something more spiritual, the ultimate quest of all mystics, to unite, if only for a moment, with the Divine. In the mystical traditions of India, it is taught how to achieve magical powers (*siddhis*), but that they may get in the way of spiritual advancement.

This is, perhaps, one of the keys as to why, when it is not mocked, magic is hated and feared. After all, if you have direct communications with the Divine, why would you need an intercessor in the form of priest or prelate,

rabbi or imam? For religions to exist and survive, magic must be forbidden or strictly controlled.

Profane sources such as governments traditionally forbade magic, too, although today they simply mock the science. If you have the power to achieve any goal and the spiritual wisdom to know that you are free to do whatever you will, and if at the same time you are responsible for your actions, then governmental threats no longer have an effect on you. True magicians are threats to both religions and governments not for what they do but for who they are: liberated, responsible, independent people.

Most of the famous fathers of the science of astronomy from ages past were actually astrologers. Astronomy was simply a sideline to help them in their calculations. Similarly, many of the famous scientists of the past were also alchemists. Already mentioned was Sir Isaac Newton. Other famous alchemists include Roger Bacon, Tycho Brahe, and the father of toxicology and modern allopathic medicine, Paracelsus.

Alchemy is even more hidden than magic, but it is alive and thriving today. For years there were classes available in San Jose, California, for members of the AMORC Rosicrucians. One of those students, Dr. Albert Richard Riedel, took the name "Frater Albertus," wrote several books on the subject, and actually led a school that taught many hundreds of people, including the late Dr. Israel Regardie (who is described, referred to, and quoted in the body of this book).

Traditionally there were two basic themes in alchemy. Curiously the most famous is perhaps the least being currently explored, the conversion of base metals into gold. With modern advances in science, however, such amazing magic may not be so unusual. Already, precious gems that are indistinguishable from natural ones are being created in laboratories. Why not metals? The other direction was the creation of the universal panacea—the cure for all diseases and the source for the extension of life. Even as you read this, people are working in modern laboratories to find cures for pharmaceutical companies, as well as in alchemical laboratories to create more magical remedies.

In living alchemy, there are three major trends. The first could be called the literal or traditional path. Researchers are literally interpreting classical texts to see what they can create. The second is the mystical trend. People who follow this path see the classical texts as metaphoric. The concept of turning base metals to gold is taken as a metaphor for turning our base and materialistic selves into more spiritual persons. Its formulae include a type of deconstruction of the ancient texts to describe breathing, meditative, and other practices to achieve the spiritual ecstasies usually left to the descriptions of the mystical philosophers of India and Asia.

The third trend may be the most controversial. Like the mystical, it reinterprets the ancient alchemical texts, but instead of looking at them as metaphors for mystical practices, the instructions are seen as codes for sexual practices that are similar to some of the mysticomagical sexual practices of the Indian Tantrics and Chinese Taoists.

Magic and alchemy have evolved in different ways in virtually every culture on this planet. In cultures that actively forbade the practices, magic and alchemy flourished, either in hidden grottos or in the back rooms of the wealthy and powerful. Thousands of volumes have been written on the history and practices of these two sciences. All are highly incomplete, no matter how complete they may claim to be.

That is why the book you have in your hands can be such a valuable resource. As with any encyclopedic book, entries, by necessity, are brief. They can only give an overview and a glimpse of a topic as if seen through a glass darkly. Other books end here, but Ms. Guiley has included resources for further reading after her entries. Because of this design, this should not be "just another book" on the subject. Rather, it should be the first resource for discovering the essence of magic and alchemy, the beginning from which you can expand your study to any level of expertise you desire.

And what is it you desire? There is a tradition in both Tantric and Taoist philosophy that one of the ulti-mate forms of magic is the ability to have whatever you need before you realize you need it. But there is a secret to this concept. It is not about acquisition. Rather, it is about changing yourself so that as you become more and more spiritualized, the need for things or "attachments" becomes less and less. You have all you desire because you find happiness, joy, and bliss with what you have.

Can you imagine a world where people were filled with happiness, joy, and bliss? How would it be different? Certainly, there would be no wars as there would be no need for them. Such a world may not be immediately possible. But can you imagine a world where your life is filled with happiness, joy, and bliss? How would your life be different? Would you like that?

Then I invite you to explore that world. In my experience, happiness, joy, and bliss are attainable on a personal basis. From that we can expand to a global consciousness that can change the world. Take a moment to imagine what could be rather than being unhappy with what is. To this end I invite you to explore magic and alchemy.

—Donald Michael Kraig
Author, *Modern Magick*

❧ INTRODUCTION ❧

by Rosemary Ellen Guiley, Ph.D.

Every day, human beings around the world make use of a natural power without realizing they are doing so. That power is magic, a natural and real force woven into the very fabric of all creation. Magic is about manifestation. Making things happen. Achieving desired goals and results. Shaping events. Putting forces in motion. Influencing people and opportunities. Achieving enlightenment and self-mastery.

If you have

- made a prayer
- said an affirmation
- visualized a goal
- directed your thoughts
- carried a lucky charm
- taken any action for luck

then you have performed an act of magic.

People have been doing magic for thousands of years, and they do it still today in hopes of improving their circumstances and lives. However, most people do not think of such activities as "magic." Prayer and some affirmations are religious or spiritual in context. Visualization and direction of thought are principles of self-help and business achievement. Lucky charms and acts are folklore or "harmless" superstitions. Call them by whatever label, the fundamental power behind them, however, is magic.

Magic is the intense marshaling of thought, will, and imagination, in conjunction with appeals to higher forces, to manifest a desired goal. At one end of that spectrum are material things. At the other end are the virtues that lead to enlightenment. One end serves humankind's lower nature; the other end serves cosmic balance and harmony.

Demonstrations of magic are prominent in the Bible, even though passages warn against wizards. Moses and Aaron take on the pharaoh's magicians and win. They produce better magic, though it is couched in different language, that of miracles and the intervention of God in the world. Jesus performs miraculous feats which, if done by a "wizard," would be called magic. He proclaims that "He who believes in me will also do the works that I do; and greater works than these will he do" (John 14:12). His apostles believe it and perform "wonder-working" after Jesus's resurrection—but the use of the power dies with them and does not spread to the masses, who probably could not grasp that natural power is everywhere and available to anyone who seeks to master it.

Since magic is a power that is available everywhere to everyone, it is no surprise that organized religion has sought to demonize it and suppress it. Throughout Western history, even in pagan times, magic has belonged to "specialists," that is, certain trained and privileged persons, who strictly control the use of magic. Such efforts at suppression never succeed, for there is always some "upstart" group or order that keeps the knowledge and practice of magic alive.

The suppression of magic includes its continual association with evil: cursing, low spell-casting, sorcery, and witchcraft. Literary arts and the media have reinforced this negative image to the point where magic is widely regarded de facto as an evil power. Magic also is portrayed as a silly power involving the waving of a wand, strange clothing, marching brooms, enormous supernatural abilities, and so forth.

Magic deserves to be rehabilitated and restored to its respected state as a natural power. Power is neutral and is colored by those who use it. Like any power, magic can be used for good or for ill. Take prayer, for example. It is no secret that not all prayer is for benefit. People pray daily against their enemies. A prayer against someone is the equivalent of a magical curse. A prayer for someone is the equivalent of a magical blessing.

The restoration of magic as a natural power is especially important to spiritual development. As long as magic stays in a basement of demonization, it will not be appreciated, understood, and used in positive ways. Today in Western research of consciousness and alternative healing, "intentionality" is the latest darling. *Intentionality* means that the direction of your thought and intent has a direct bearing on things that happen to you and around you. Personal intentionality has a more limited effect, while collective intentionality has a greater, even global effect. Intentionality is a form of magic, a politically correct word for a very old power.

Research into psychical phenomena and quantum physics also demonstrates the validity of magic. Psychokinesis, or the ability to influence physical objects with intentional thought, has been well demonstrated in scientific experiments. So have other psychic phenomena such as clairvoyance ("remote viewing") and telepathy. These abilities seemed magical in ages past, but today the average person has had at least one experience with them. Quantum physics shows us that all things in the universe are connected in mysterious ways and that things exist only as probabilities until they are observed. These concepts are not new to magic. In the universe of the magician, everything in creation is interconnected. Consciousness affects matter, acts at a distance, and moves backward and forward in time. Magic exerts forces on probabilities, manifesting or fixing them into the realm of matter.

Magic is usually associated with elaborate and secret rituals, clothing, tools, trappings, and so forth. Some practices of magic do involve such elements, but magic can be practiced quite effectively without them. In fact, there are many forms of magic, good and bad, high and low, complex and simple. The highest form of magic is mystical, a path of illumination and enlightenment that adepts pursue with as much intensity as adepts in traditional religions.

The underlying principles of magic can be found in alchemy, which also has a long and universal history on this planet. Alchemy is about perfection—taking an imperfect thing and making it perfect. According to alchemy, all things in creation have within them the seed of perfection. Imperfect things naturally evolve toward their highest state. Alchemy involves processes that speed up perfection. Just like magic, however, alchemy has gotten a bad reputation. It is most commonly associated with attempts—usually fraudulent—to turn base metals such as lead into perfect metals such as gold or silver. Granted, a great deal of fraud has been committed in this type of alchemy. But in a spiritual sense, alchemy is about the perfection of the human being, purifying flaws so that one becomes closer to the Godhead. Purification and enlightenment are the goals of religion and spiritual practice, couched in morals, ethics, sacred laws, right living, and so forth. Human alchemy is inner work.

Magic and alchemy lie at the heart of the purpose of life. We are born into an amazing universe, and we spend our lives trying to comprehend it and our purpose in it. We strive to become better, to perfect ourselves, and to enhance our place in the scheme of things. We try to make the opportunities and events work for us, not against us. We are a long way from perfection and even adeptness in these efforts, and so life for most of us is a struggle, with victories and setbacks.

This is not to say that magic offers a panacea, an effortless way to having whatever one wants. Far from it. The forces at play in the world and the cosmos are complex and even unfathomable. We can spend a lifetime studying magic and become quite proficient at it without ever achieving all that we desire. Nonetheless, we are likely to accomplish far more with the conscious practice of magic than without it, and thus we contribute to the overall alchemical evolution of humankind.

Magic is a real and valuable resource. Misused, it creates imbalance and havoc; used properly, it contributes to the holistic balance of all things.

This encyclopedia is an exploration of magic and alchemy, the bad and the good, the low and the high. The intertwined history of both magic and alchemy is deeply imbedded in our culture, in our religious and spiritual views, and even in our approach to science. While magical practices are universal, I have kept largely to their Western history and development. Some of the accounts of misused and low magic and alchemy are shocking, while accounts at the opposite end of the spectrum fall into the realm of mysticism. Magic and alchemy have so often been condemned, dismissed, and stereotyped. It is my hope that this work will contribute to an open and honest examination of them so that we may better understand and use our natural powers for the advancement of all.

—Rosemary Ellen Guiley

ENTRIES
A–Z

Abano, Peter of (1250–1316) Italian physician condemned by the Inquisition for his alleged infernal knowledge and magical practices. Peter of Abano wrote on ASTROLOGY and GEOMANCY but was not likely to have been a magician. His fate at the hands of the Inquisition made him "one of the moral martyrs of Magic," according to ARTHUR EDWARD WAITE.

Peter of Abano was born in 1250 in Abano, Italy, a small town near Padua. He established his medical practice in Paris, where he gained fame for his work to reconcile different medical systems. He said that astrology was essential to medicine, and he introduced ideas from Arab doctors, primarily Ibn-Rushd (Averroës). Jealous peers accused him of heresy, and he fled back to Abano.

A chair was created for him at the University of Padua, but the accusations of heresy continued to hound him. Some said he denied the existence of DEMONS, while others said he kept seven IMPS in a bottle from whom he gained his medical and magical knowledge. The accusations twice drew the attention of inquisitors. In his first trial, he was acquitted, but in the second trial he was condemned to death by burning at the stake. Prior to the carrying out of his sentence, Abano died. He left behind a testament affirming his belief in Christianity.

Peter of Abano was buried on sacred ground, which infuriated the Inquisition tribunal. The tribunal ordered the Padua magistrates to exhume the body or to face excommunication. The corpse was removed by a faithful servant and was secretly buried in another churchyard. Still the tribunal wanted the sentence carried out, but in the end, inquisitors had to be content with the burning Peter of Abano in effigy. A century later, Abano's memory

Ideal portrait of Peter of Abano, in Liber Chronicarum, *by Hartmann Schedel, 1493.* (Author's collection)

1

was rehabilitated with the placement of a bust of him in the town hall in Padua. A statue of him also was erected in Urbino, Italy.

Peter of Abano wrote a respected medical work, *Conciliator Differentium*, published in 1303.

FURTHER READING:
Waite, Arthur Edward. *The Book of Black Magic and of Pacts.* 1899. Reprint, York Beach, Maine: Samuel Weiser, 1972.

ablution   Bathing or washing the body as a means of purification, in preparation for a RITUAL. An ablution is undertaken for an INITIATION and certain magical rites. Ablutions also are often done in conjunction with other purifications such as fasting and abstinence from sex.

See also BATH.

abracadabra   Magical word, especially popular in medieval times in CHARMS and SPELLS for the ridding of illness, misfortune, or DEMONS. Abracadabra makes something disappear.

Most commonly, *abracadabra* is inscribed on an AMULET in the shape of a magical inverted triangle. One letter of the word is dropped in each succeeding line, until one letter forms the point of the triangle. The evil is supposed to fade away just as the word does. The diminishing-word technique is used in many other spells for the same purposes.

In medieval times, *abracadabra* was believed to ward off the plague. The triangle was written on a piece of paper, which was tied around the neck with flax and worn for nine days and then tossed backward over the shoulder into a stream of water running toward the east.

The word's origin is unknown; most likely, it is a corruption of another word or phrase. Various explanations have been put forward, among them:

- It was invented by Quintus Serenus Sammonicus, a third-century C.E. physician to the Roman Emperor Severus, as a cure for fever.
- It derives from the old Aramaic phrase, *abhadda kedhabhra,* "disappear like this word," or the Hebrew phrase, *abreq ad habra,* "hurl your thunderbolt even unto death."
- It derives from the name Abraxas, the Gnostic god who appears on charms against the EVIL EYE.
- It is a corruption of the name of some long-forgotten demon.

The Puritan minister Increase Mather dismissed *abracabadra* as a "hobgoblin word" empty of power. But ALEISTER CROWLEY considered it to possess great power; he said its true form is *abrahadabra.*

Abracadabra has been diminished as a magical word of power by overuse in stage magic and illusion.

Abraham the Jew   See ELEAZAR, ABRAHAM; FLAMEL, NICHOLAS.

Abra-malin the Mage   See GRIMOIRES; MATHERS, SAMUEL LIDDELL MacGREGOR.

adept   A person who has advanced through levels of learning to become a master. In MAGIC, an adept commands considerable secret magical knowledge and is proficient in RITUALS, DIVINATION, psychic powers, communication with spirits, and perhaps the casting of SPELLS. In addition to skill and knowledge, an adept also has achieved an enlightened consciousness. Without enlightenment one cannot be considered an adept. A magus is an enlightened adept especially skilled in the magical arts.

In ALCHEMY, an adept describes a person who has learned the secret of making the PHILOSOPHER'S STONE, but more from the perspective of spiritual, rather than physical and literal, transmutation. For the true adept, the transmutation of metals is a secondary pursuit—even a by-product of the spiritual pursuit. The Hermetic ideal man, or divine man, is raised up from the material, sensual man. The adept acquires True Knowledge, the perfect knowledge of Self, which is required to attain knowledge of God. This spiritual path is reflected in the Hermetic concept of the universe, that the microcosm is a reflection of the macrocosm. Thus, by gaining perfect knowledge of the Self—the microcosm—one attains knowledge of God—the macrocosm. A male adept is called an *artifex,* and his female partner a *soror mystica* (mystical sister).

The adept also aspires to a greater and higher good. In the HERMETIC ORDER OF THE GOLDEN DAWN, one of the aims of the adept is "regeneration of the Race of the Planet." The term *magus* describes initiates in the higher orders of the the Golden Dawn.

The spiritual qualities of the adept are emphasized repeatedly in alchemical and magical literature. For example, the alchemical adept is urged to fully trust in God, lead a righteous life, subdue falsehood, be patient and not ambitious, and not engage in sinful activities—the same qualities of sainthood. The adept must especially avoid the pitfalls of egotism, and even spiritual egotism, which leads to self-righteousness.

According to FRANZ BARDON, an adept knows and appreciates the truth in all religions of all eras. He does not believe in a personified God but adheres to universal laws, upon which all religions are based. He may belong to a religion if it aids his work with others. An adept does not believe anything he cannot convince himself of, and he is able to competently answer questions put to him about esoteric matters.

The Islamic alchemist JABIR IBN HAYYAN wrote that alchemists who are preoccupied only with making GOLD out of base metals will be denied the secrets of alchemy by God himself:

Our art is reserved in the Divine Will of God, and is given to, or withheld from, who he will; who is glorious, sublime, and full of all Justice and Goodness. And perhaps, for the punishment of your sophistical work [that which is intended just for material transmutation and gain], he denies you the Art, and lamentably thrusts you into the by-path of error, and from your error into perpetual felicity and misery: because he is most miserable and unhappy, to whom (after the end of his work and labor) God denies the sight of Truth. For such a man is constituted in perpetual labor, beset with all misfortune and infelicity, loseth the consolation, joy, and delight of his whole time, and consumeth his life in grief without profit.

In the literature of the Golden Dawn, the path of adeptness is related to alchemical allegory:

The Heart of man is as the Sun, the reception organ for the Divine Ray of spiritual initiation descending unto Man. The Brain of Man is as the Moon,—the source of human intellect. The Body of Man is the Earthly vehicle.

Let the sun impregnate the Moon, or let Spiritual Fire prompt the human intellect—and let the rest fructify in the womb of a purified Body, and you will develop the Son of the Sun, the Quintessence, the Stone of the Wise, True Wisdom and Perfect Happiness.

In *The Magus* (1801), FRANCIS BARRETT stated:

An adept . . . is one who not only studies to do God's will upon earth, in respect of his moral and religious duties; but who studies, and ardently prays to his benevolent Creator to bestow on him wisdom and knowledge from the fullness of his treasury; and he meditates, day and night, how he may attain the true *aqua vita*—how he may be filled with the grace of God; which, when he is made so happy, his spiritual and internal eye is open to a glorious prospect of mortal and immortal riches . . . he is filled with the celestial spiritual manna. . . . Therefore, to be an adept . . . is to know thyself, fear God, and love thy neighbor as thyself; and by this thou shalt come to the fulfilment of thy desires, O, man; but by no other means under the scope of Heaven.

The apprenticeship and levels of training may require many years of study and INITIATION, depending upon the order, fraternity, lodge, or system to which the magician belongs.

FURTHER READING:
Bardon, Franz. *Frabato the Magician*. Salt Lake City: Merkur Publishing, 1979.
Barrett, Francis. *The Magus*. 1881. Reprint, Secaucus, N.J.: The Citadel Press, 1967.
Holmyard, E. J. *Alchemy*. New York: Penguin Books, 1957.
King, Francis (ed.). *Ritual Magic of the Golden Dawn*. Rochester, Vt.: Destiny Books, 1997.

aethyrs   See CHORONZON; CROWLEY, ALEISTER; ENOCHIAN MAGIC.

Agla   In MAGIC, an acronym for *Ate Gebir Leilam Adonai*, which is Hebrew for "Thou art mighty forever, O Lord." Agla also is used as the NAME of an ANGEL invoked in magic. Agla appears in numerous CHARMS and AMULETS for invoking divine protective power against fever, misfortune, and evil.

The *Lemegeton*, a handbook of magic (see GRIMOIRES), refers to Agla as a "great and mighty" name of God. ARTHUR EDWARD WAITE gave it great importance for divine protection that should be invoked in the making of magical TOOLS for RITUALS. *Agla* is inscribed on swords and knives.

Agrippa, Heinrich Cornelius (1486–1535)   Important occult philosopher whose seminal work, *Occult Philosophy*, had a profound impact on the development of Western occultism and MAGIC. Heinrich Cornelius Agrippa—also known as Heinrich Cornelius Agrippa von Nettesheim—wrote extensively on Neoplatonic philosophy and kabbalistic magic, and sought to unite the two.

Agrippa had a difficult life. Far ahead of his time and contemptuous of other intellectuals, he was misunder-

Heinrich Cornelius Agrippa von Nettesheim, in Das Kloster, *vol. I by J. Scheible, 1845. (Author's collection)*

stood by his contemporaries, and he angered authorities of church and state.

He was born on September 14, 1486, in Cologne, and in 1499 entered the university there. He probably adopted the name "von Nettesheim," or "of Nettesheim," himself, after the founder of Cologne.

Agrippa had a quick and inquiring mind. He learned eight languages and engaged in a deep study of ALCHEMY, the HERMETICA, and the KABBALAH. His personal aim was to achieve a spiritual union with the Godhead.

His first job was an appointment as court secretary and then soldier to Maximilian I, king of Rome and Germany. He was sent to Paris, where mixed with scholars and the nobility, founding a secret society with them. His love of intrigues and secrecy would continue throughout his life.

In 1509, Agrippa went to Dôle, where he lectured on the kabbalah at the university and earned a doctorate of divinity. He tried to win the patronage of Maximilian's daughter, Margaret of Austria, with a flattering work, *The Nobility of Women,* but the clerics denounced him as a heretic and prevented publication of the work. Margaret did not come to his aid. Agrippa abandoned his efforts and went to England and then Cologne. His arrogance created strained relationships even with his admirers.

Agrippa collected a vast store of occult knowledge and made notes for what would become his most important work, the three-volume *Occult Philosophy,* a summation of all the magical and occult knowledge of the time. In 1510, he sent the manuscript to Abbot JOHANNES TRITHEMIUS, at the monastery of St. Jakob in Würzburg, for approval. Trithemius was impressed and responded with this advice:

> I have only one more admonition to give you. Never forget it: to the vulgar, speak only of vulgar things; keep for your friends every secret of a higher order; give hay to the oxen and sugar to the parrot. Understand my meaning, lest you be trod under the oxen's feet, as oftentimes happens.

Occult Philosophy remained unpublished until 1531 because of efforts to block it by Dominican inquisitors. The first edition was followed by the complete work in 1533. By then Agrippa had been "trod under the oxen's feet" many times over and had even recanted the material in his manuscript.

During the intervening years between 1509 and 1531, he drifted around Europe, forming secret societies and working at various jobs. He was frequently at odds with the church, for he considered many monks to be ignorant and narrow-minded. He was unlucky in marriage and money: two wives died and the third ruined him emotionally and financially.

In 1515, Agrippa went to Italy with Maximilian's army. He was knighted on the battlefield. The cardinal of St. Croix sent him to Pisa on church business, but the church council disbanded, prematurely ending any ecclesiastical career Agrippa might have entertained.

He then went to Turin and Padua, lecturing on alchemy and HERMES TRISMEGISTUS, and gaining fame for his knowl-edge. In 1516, the Lords of Metz named him advocate, syndic and orator of the city. That job lasted only two years. Agrippa successfully defended a country woman against charges of WITCHCRAFT, which embroiled him in a dispute with the inquisitor of Metz. The chief evidence against the woman was that her mother had been burned as a witch. Agrippa destroyed the case against her—and the credibility of the inquisitor—with the theological argument that man could be separated from Christ only by his own sin, not that of another. The humiliated inquisitor threatened to prosecute Agrippa for heresy. Agrippa returned to Cologne and then moved on to Geneva and Fribourg, where he practiced medicine.

In 1524, he went to Lyons and was appointed physician to Duchesse Louise of Savoy, the mother of the King Francis I of France. The post secured him a long-sought-after pension. But the duchess wanted him to tell her fortune by ASTROLOGY, which he considered beneath his vast talents. She was slow to pay him and kept him confined to Lyons, impoverished, until 1526, when she left Lyons.

In 1529, Agrippa had four sponsors: King Henry VIII of England, the chancellor of the emperor of Germany, an Italian marquis, and finally Margaret of Austria, who made him historiographer. He accumulated enough money to spend his time studying alchemy.

Agrippa's work *On the Vanity of Arts and Sciences* was published. In it he declared that all human thought and activity are vain—a complete contradiction of his championship of magic in his yet-unpublished manuscript *Occult Philosophy.* Agrippa's pension was canceled, and he was jailed for debt in 1531. His friends released him, but only a year later, his writings caused him to be accused of impiety. The Dominicans attempted to block publication of some of his work. Emperor Charles V demanded that he recant many of his opinions. In 1535, the emperor condemned him to death as a heretic. Agrippa fled to France but was imprisoned. Sprung free by friends once again, he set out for Lyons but fell sick along the way and died.

During his life, Agrippa attracted many pupils. One of the most famous was Johann Weyer, who wrote extensively on demonology. Agrippa wrote numerous other works, which he collected together with his letters toward the end of his life and published as *Opera.*

In *Occult Philosophy,* Agrippa said that magic is powerful, full of mystery, and comprises a profound knowledge of the most secret things. Magic is philosophy, physics, mathematics, and theology. It has nothing to do with the devil or SORCERY, but it depends on natural psychic gifts such as second sight. He believed in the ultimate power of WILL and IMAGINATION to effect magic, and he understood the power that the mind has over the body. Man achieves his highest potential by learning the harmonies of nature. The ASTRAL BODY is the "chariot of the soul" and can leave the physical body like a light escaping from a lantern. The greatest and highest wonder-working name is Jesus.

Occult Philosophy is comprised of three books. Book one covers natural magic in the elementary world, including stones, herbs, metals, and so forth. Agrippa agrees with the Neoplatonic idea that the ELEMENTS exist everywhere throughout the universe, even in spirits and ANGELS, in varying states of purity. The elements birth natural virtues. The world soul, or ANIMA MUNDI, infuses things with occult virtues through the agent of ideas. Occult virtues can be known and studied through "resemblances"—the sympathetic and antipathetic relationships between things.

Book two covers the celestial or mathematical world and discusses the magical properties of celestial bodies and NUMBERS. Resemblances also occur among the planets, and provide a source of magical power to the magus. All things below are inferior to and influenced by all things above. Favorable influences can be obtained from the stars, "good demons," and even from God. Resemblances also govern DIVINATION and AUGURY.

Numbers and mathematics govern the order, structure, natural virtues, and harmony of all things. Knowledge of numbers is necessary to understand musical harmony, which reflects the harmony of the cosmos. Agrippa discusses the work of PYTHAGORAS, concerning sacred numbers dedicated to the elements and planetarian gods.

Book three covers the intellectual world of pagan gods and spirits—including angels and demons—and gives magical procedures for invoking and communicating with them, as well as with God. Agrippa gives instructions for making SIGILS and AMULETS, working with angelic scripts (see MAGICAL ALPHABETS), and working with sound and fumes (see PERFUMES). The kabbalistic TREE OF LIFE is explained, including the hierarchies of angels and demons associated with each sephirot.

Agrippa says that religion is necessary to every act of magic. His concept of religion was not traditional or orthodox but a mixture of Christianity, Neoplatonism, and kabbalism. He states:

> Religion is the most mysterious thing, and one about which one should keep silent, for Trismegistus says that it would be an offense to religion to confide it to the profane multitude.

Agrippa equates angels to INTELLIGENCES and spirits in that they all are nonphysical entities, are immortal, and wield great influences over things in creation. There are three kinds in the traditions of the magicians. The first kind are the supercelestial angels, intellectual spheres focused on worshiping the one and only God. They infuse the lower angelic orders with the light they receive from God, and they instruct the orders in their duties.

The second kind are the celestial angels, or worldly angels, who are concerned with the spheres of the world and for governing "every heaven and star." The celestials are divided into orders, as many as are there heavens and as there are stars in the heavens. All of these angels have NAMES and SEALS that are used in ceremonial magic operations.

The third kind of angels are ministers who govern the daily affairs of Earth and people. They can help procure success and happiness—and also inflict adversity. The orders of ministers fall into four categories that are aligned with the characteristics of the four elements, which govern different faculties of mind, reason, imagination, and action.

There are nine orders of demons, according to Agrippa. They wander the Earth, enraged and fomenting trouble, but they have the potential for redemption if they repent. The orders are, from the most important to the least:

- False Gods, who are ruled by Beelzebub and who usurp the name of God and demand worship, sacrifices, and adoration;
- Spirits of Lies, who are ruled by Pytho and deceive oracles, diviners, and prophets;
- Vessels of Iniquity, also called Vessels of Wrath, who invent evil things and the "wicked arts" such as card games and gambling, and who are ruled by Belial;
- Revengers of Evil, who are ruled by Asmodeus and cause bad judgment;
- Deluders, who are ruled by Satan and imitate miracles, serve wicked conjurers and witches, and seduce people by their false miracles;
- Aerial Powers, who are ruled by Meririm and cause pestilence and terribly destructive storms, and who are personified by the Four Horsemen of the Apocalypse in the book of REVELATION;
- Furies, who are ruled by Abbadon (Apollyon) and wreak war, discord, devastation and evil;
- Accusers, who are ruled by Astaroth and lie and slander; and
- Tempters and Ensnarers, who are ruled by Mammon and inspire covetousness and "evil genius."

A spurious *Fourth Book* of *Occult Philosophy* appeared in 1567 but was denounced by Weyer. (See GRIMOIRES.) An English translation of *Occult Philosophy*, published in 1651, was plagiarized by FRANCIS BARRETT, who published a truncated version of it as his own book, *The Magus*, in 1801. The HERMETIC ORDER OF THE GOLDEN DAWN used *Occult Philosophy* as a key source.

FURTHER READING:
Morley, Henry. *The Life of Henry Cornelius Agrippa.* London: Chapman and Hall, 1856.
Seligmann, Kurt. *The History of Magic and the Occult.* New York: Pantheon Books, 1948.
Three Books of Occult Philosophy Written by Henry Cornelius Agrippa of Nettesheim. Trans. by James Freake. Ed. and anno. by Donald Tyson. St. Paul, Minn.: Llewellyn Publications, 1995.

Aiwass (Aiwaz)   Imposing entity who dictated to ALEISTER CROWLEY *The Book of the Law,* Crowley's most significant magical work. Crowley considered Aiwass to be his HOLY GUARDIAN ANGEL, or divine Higher Self, acting as intermediary for higher beings such as the Secret Chiefs, superhuman ADEPTS of the HERMETIC ORDER OF THE GOLDEN DAWN.

Occultists have debated whether Aiwass was an entity in its own right or part of Crowley himself. For Crowley, the Holy Guardian Angel was a discrete entity and not a dissociated part of his own personality. Crowley originally spelled the entity's name *Aiwaz* but then later changed the spelling to *Aiwass* for numerological reasons.

Aiwass made his entrance in April 1904 through the mediumship of Crowley's wife, Rose, while the couple was on honeymoon in Cairo. Rose described Aiwass as an emissary of the Egyptian god Horus, son of ISIS and OSIRIS. Crowley envisioned Aiwass as a male entity, one distinctly different and more unfathomable than other entities he had encountered. Answers to questions posed by Crowley indicated that Aiwass was:

> . . . a Being whose mind was so different from mine that we failed to converse. All my wife obtained from Him was to command me to do things magically absurd. He would not play my game: I must play His.

On April 7, 1904, Aiwass commanded that the drawing room of the Cairo apartment leased by the Crowleys had to be turned into a temple. Aiwass ordered Crowley to enter the temple precisely at noon on the next three days and to write down exactly what he heard for precisely one hour.

Crowley followed the instructions. Inside the "temple," he sat alone at a table facing the southern wall. From behind him came the voice of Aiwass, which Crowley described as "a rich tenor or baritone . . . deep timbre, musical and expressive, its tones solemn, voluptuous, tender, fierce, or aught else as suited the moods of the message." The voice was "the Speech in the Silence," he said. Later he called Aiwass "the minister of Hoor–Paar–Kraat" or "the Lord of Silence," an aspect of Horus that was the equivalent of the Greek Harpocrates.

During the dictation, Crowley did not see a visual apparition of Aiwass, though he did have a mental impression of the entity. Aiwass had

> . . . a body of "fine matter" or astral matter, transparent as a veil of gauze or a cloud of incense-smoke. He seemed to be a tall, dark man in his thirties, well-knit, active and strong, with the face of a savage king, and eyes veiled lest their gaze should destroy what they saw.

Further, Aiwass seemed dressed in the garb of an Assyrian or a Persian.

Crowley took Aiwass's dictation for three hours on April 8–10, scribbling in longhand to keep pace with the voice. The sessions lasted exactly one hour each. The 65 pages of handwritten material comprised the three chapters of *The Book of the Law*, which Crowley saw as the herald of the New Aeon or a new religion. Each chapter carried the voice of an Egyptian deity: Nut, the goddess of the heavens; and two aspects of Horus, Ha-Kadit, a solar aspect, and Ra-Hoor-Kuit, or "Horus of the Two Horizons."

For years Crowley remained in awe of Aiwass. In *The Equinox of the Gods,* he acknowledged that he never fully understood the nature of Aiwass. He alternately called the entity a God or Demon or Devil; a praeterhuman intelligence; a minister or messenger of other Gods; his own Guardian Angel, and his own subconscious (the last he rejected in favor of the Holy Guardian Angel). Crowley also said he was permitted from time to time to see Aiwass in a physical appearance, inhabiting a human body, as much a material man as Crowley was himself.

C.S. Jones, who ran the Vancouver, B.C., lodge of the ORDO TEMPLI ORIENTALIS, said he underwent a series of magical INITIATIONS that revealed to him that Aiwass was in truth an evil DEMON and the enemy of humanity. Others considered Jones to have gone mad.

FURTHER READING:
Sutin, Lawrence. *Do What Thou Wilt: A Life of Aleister Crowley.* New York: St. Martin's Griffin, 2000.

akasha (akasa)   In Eastern mysticism and occultism, the all-pervasive life principle or all-pervasive space of the cosmos. The term *akasha* is derived from the Sanskrit term for "sky." The akasha is known by various other names in Western occultism and MAGIC.

In Hinduism, the akasha is the substance ether, a fifth ELEMENT and the subtlest of all elements. The akasha permeates everything in the universe and is the vehicle for all life and SOUND. In yoga, the akasha is one of three universal principles along with *prana,* the universal life force, and creative mind. These three principles are immanent in all things throughout the universe and are the sources of magical and psychic power. From the akasha comes WILL, an important component of magic, which enables all manner of feats to be accomplished.

In Buddhism, the akasha is not ether but space, of which there are two kinds. One is space that is limited by the material, from which springs the manifestation of the elements of nature. The second is space that is unlimited, unbounded by the material and beyond description.

The concept of the akasha was introduced to Western occultism in the early 20th century by HELENA P. BLAVATSKY, founder of the THEOSOPHICAL SOCIETY. Blavatsky said the akasha forms the ANIMA MUNDI and constitutes the soul and astral spirit of man. It produces mesmeric, magnetic, and psychic phenomena and is a component in all magical operations of nature. Blavatsky compared the akasha to the "sidereal light" of ROSICRUCIANISM, THE ASTRAL LIGHT of ELIPHAS LEVI, and the odyle or odic force of Baron Karl von Reichenbach. It is the equivalent of the Hebrew *ruah,* the wind, breath, air in motion, or moving spirit, and is identical with the spirit of God moving on the face of the waters. FRANZ BARDON described the akasha as incomprehensible, non-created, and undefinable. Akasha creates everything and keeps everything in balance—it is the "all in all."

Akashic Records

Everything that ever happens throughout the universe— every thought, sound, emotion, action, and so forth—is recorded permanently upon the akasha. The Akashic

Records exist as impressions in the ASTRAL PLANE and can be accessed by magical means, through CLAIRVOYANCE and by ASTRAL TRAVEL. The Akashic Records are consulted for information about past lives, lost civilizations, and other planes of existence. Spiritual beings—perceived by some as ANGELS—provide assistance in accessing the records.

The American trance psychic Edgar Cayce frequently consulted the Akashic Records to obtain past-life information that explained clients' health, personal, and marital problems in their current lives. Cayce sometimes referred to the Akashic Records as "The Universal Memory of Nature" and "The Book of Life." The astral repository was like a great temple filled with books, he said.

Rudolph Steiner called the records the Akashic Chronicle. He consulted them to produce his detailed descriptions of the lost civilizations of Atlantis and Lemuria.

See also TATTVAS.

FURTHER READING:
Blavatsky, H.P. *The Secret Doctrine.* London: The Theosophical Publishing Co., Ltd., 1888.
———. *Isis Unveiled.* Pasadena, Calif.: Theosophical University Press, 1976.
Langley, Noel. *Edgar Cayce on Reincarnation.* New York: Castle Books, 1967.
McDermott, Robert A. *The Essential Steiner.* San Francisco: Harper & Row, 1984.

Albertus Magnus, St. (c. 1206–1280) Dominican scholar, theologian, and scientist with interests in ALCHEMY. Albertus Magnus ("Albert the Great") is better known for his theological career; St. THOMAS AQUINAS, who became the preeminent theologian of the Catholic Church, was among his pupils.

Albertus Magnus was born Albert de Groot, Graf von Bollstädt, in Swabia, Germany, in about 1206. In later years, he took the surname "Magnus" ("the Great"), which is the Latin equivalent of his family name. ARTHUR EDWARD WAITE described him as having a reputation for "excessive stupidity" in his youth, but his devotion to the Virgin Mary led to a vision in which he received a divine favor of intellectual illumination.

He entered the Dominican order in 1223, advancing until he was named bishop of Ratisbon in 1260, but resigned in 1262 in order to teach. He wrote extensively on Aristotle. In his later years, his brilliance faded.

He is credited with a number of firsts in alchemy: the production of arsenic in free form; the discovery of the chemical composition of cinnibar, minium, and whitelead; and the preparation of caustic potassium. He believed in the transmutation of base metals into GOLD. In *Secretum Secretorum*, published in 1508, he described his own experiments, including the testing of gold and SILVER produced by an alchemist. The "transmuted" metals proved to be false. Nonetheless, Albertus Magnus believed in the possibility of transmutation in accordance with the principles of nature.

In *On Alchemy,* he advised other alchemists to live a life of isolation, patience, and discretion and to have enough money to support themselves in case their experiments to create gold failed. He advised discretion because once word of success leaked out, especially to the royalty and nobility, the alchemist's work could be destroyed.

Albertus Magnus was not a magician, as he was described by demonologists later on. In fact, he said that "stories of DEMONS prowling the air" were "absurdities which can never be admitted by sober reason." A spurious GRIMOIRE attributed to him, *Le Admirables Secrets d'Albert le Grand ("The Admirable Secrets of Albertus Magnus"),* covers the magical properties of herbs and stones, DIVINATION by physiognomy, and the preparations of various medicines.

Stories of incredible magic are attributed to Albertus Magnus. He supposedly had a PHILOSOPHER'S STONE, though there is no such record in his own writings. According to MICHAEL MAIER, the disciples of St. Dominic gave him the secret of the stone, and Albertus Magnus in turn gave it to Aquinas. Albertus Magnus also reportedly had a magical stone marked with a serpent, which had the ability to force other serpents out of their hiding places.

According to one tale, he once invited some guests, including William II, the count of Holland, for dinner at his home on New Year's Day, 1249. The count owned a piece of land which Albertus Magnus wanted to purchase for a monastery; the count did not want to sell. When the guests arrived, they were astonished to see that Albertus Magnus had set up a meal in the garden outdoors. Everything was covered with snow and the temperature was freezing. He assured them that everything would be all right. Despite their misgivings, the guests sat down to eat. As soon as they had done so, the snow melted, the sun came out, flowers burst into bloom and birds flew about and sang. When the meal was over, the summery scene vanished, and the shivering guests had to go inside to warm by the fire. The impressed count agreed to sell Albertus Magnus the land he wanted.

In another legend, Albertus Magnus, using natural magic and ASTROLOGY, created a HOMUNCULUS which could talk and function as his servant. But its jabbering so disturbed Thomas Aquinas in his studies that Aquinas smashed it to pieces.

Albertus Magnus died on November 15, 1280, and was buried in Cologne. He was beatified in 1622, and was canonized in 1932 by Pope Pius XI.

FURTHER READING:
Guiley, Rosemary Ellen. *The Encyclopedia of Saints.* New York: Facts On File, 2002.
Waite, Arthur Edward. *Alchemists Through the Ages.* Blauvelt, N.Y.: Rudolph Steiner Publications, 1970.

alchemy The ancient art of transmutation, and the precursor of modern chemistry and metallurgy. Alchemy is more than 2,000 years old.

An alchemist praying in his laboratory, in Amphitheatrum sapientiae aeternae, *by Heinrich Khunrath, 1602.* (Author's collection)

The word *alchemy* is derived from the Arabic word *alkimia. Al* means "the." The meaning of *kimia* is less certain. It may derive from *kmt* or *chem,* the ancient Egyptian term for "Egypt," the "black [fertile] land." It may also be related to the Greek word *chyma,* which refers to the fusing or casting of metal.

PARACELSUS coined the term *spagyric* art, from the Greek terms for "to tear" and "to bring together," to describe alchemy.

Initially, alchemy was a physical art related to metallurgy, chemistry, perfumes, dyes, embalming, and so forth. Alchemy is associated with the quest to turn base metals such as lead into perfect metals such as SILVER and GOLD. The heart of alchemy, however, is spiritual: a means of personal transformation, purification, and perfection into a state of prolonged life or immortality. Alchemy was practiced by the ancient Egyptians, Greeks, Arabs, Indians, and Chinese. Western and Eastern systems have comparable elements, although Western alchemy later gave more emphasis to the physical transformation of metals.

Western Alchemy

Western alchemy is based on the Hermetic tradition, a syncretism of Egyptian metallurgy and Neoplatonism, Gnosticism, and Christianity. The core text is the EMERALD TABLET, a mystical tract attributed to the legendary HERMES TRISMEGISTUS ("thrice greatest Hermes"). The central tenet of the Emerald Tablet is "as above, so below": humanity is a microcosm of the macrocosm of heaven, and CORRESPONDENCES exist between the two. One reflects the other. Other Hermetic works of importance, which were published much later, are known as the *CORPUS HERMETICUM* and the HERMETICA.

The Egyptians developed one of the basic fundamentals of alchemy, that of "first matter," that is, that the world was created by divine force out of a chaotic mass called *PRIMA MATERIA,* or First Matter. All things can be reduced to first matter through *solve et coagula,* "dissolve and combine," and transmuted to something more desirable. This transmutation was accomplished through the joining of opposites. The entire chemical process was based on the assumption that all things in nature evolve into their purest and highest form. Thus imperfect base metals eventu-

The impending union of opposite represented by the king and the queen, Sol and Luna. In the vessel are the lady (the Mercury of the Philosophers) and the youth (the Sulphur of the Philosophers). In Anatomia auri, *by Johann Daniel Mylius, 1628.* (Author's collection)

ally become gold on their own. Alchemy merely speeds up the process.

According to early alchemy, all things have a hermaphroditic composition of two substances: SULPHUR, which represents the soul and the fiery male principle, and MERCURY, which represents spirit and the watery female principle. Later European alchemy added a third ingredient, SALT, which corresponds to body. The transmutation process involves separating these three essentials and recombining them into a different form. The process must be done according to astrological auspices.

By the third century C.E., alchemy was widely practiced, and had replaced many of the disintegrating mystery traditions. Of note is ZOSIMOS (c. 250–300), a Greek author of numerous alchemical texts. Zosimos traced alchemy to biblical origins, an idea that gained popularity as alchemy reached its peak in medieval times. Zosimos also emphasized the transmutation of metals in his treatise *The Divine Art of Making Gold and Silver.*

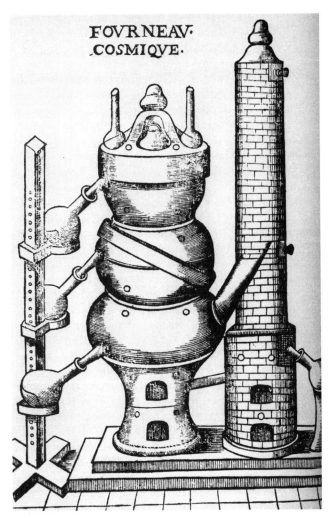

Alchemical apparatus, in La theotechnie ergocosmique, *by Annibal Barlet, 1653.* (Author's collection)

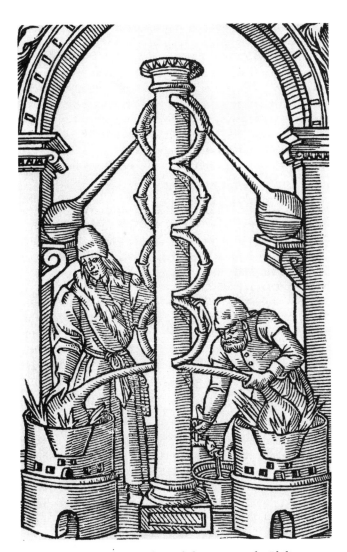

Alchemists at work, in Coelum Philosoporum, *by Philippus Ulstadius, 1544.* (Author's collection)

Western alchemy suffered a setback in 296, when the Roman emperor Diocletian ordered the burning of Egyptian and Hermetic alchemical texts, thus destroying a great deal of knowledge.

However, the Emerald Tablet had by then passed into Arabic culture, where it continued to evolve. It was a highly respected science, practiced by adepts who wrote their treatises and manuals in deliberately obscure language. The term *gibberish* is derived from the name of a medieval alchemist, JABIR IBN HAYYAN, known as Geber (c. 721–815), whose writings were difficult to comprehend. Alchemy thrived in Moorish Spain, where from the 12th century on it spread throughout Europe.

By the 15th century, alchemy was a thriving, but not always reputable, practice; Prague became one of the capitals of alchemy. Alchemy also took hold in England. Some European rulers and nobles became obsessed with transmuting metals into gold in order to increase their personal wealth and their war chests, especially for the expensive Crusades, and hired alchemists to produce gold. Fraudulent alchemists criss-crossed Europe, promising results in time to make personal gains and then flee when patience with them was exhausted. Some made no escape and were imprisoned or executed by irate patrons.

The transmutation of metals was accomplished with the PHILOSOPHER'S STONE, a mysterious and elusive substance that was never described in direct terms. The Philosopher's Stone also was the ELIXIR OF LIFE that would bestow immortality. The process of creating the Philosopher's Stone is the Great Work, or Magnum Opus. The Philosopher's Stone is both the beginning of the Great Work, the *Prima Materia*, and the end result.

Base metals are first reduced to a formless mass by melting or by placing them in a bath of mercury, the "Universal Solvent." The first stage is called the nigredo, characterized by blackness. Through recombining, other stages are reached: citrinas, a yellowing; albedo, a whiteness; and rubedo, a redness. Sometimes a stage of all possible colors, called the "peacock's tail," was said to occur between albedo and rubedo. Sometimes the red and white appeared simultaneously. The final stage yielded gold as well as the Philosopher's Stone. The stone was highly concentrated, and when added into the alchemist's furnace of molten metals, it encouraged the rapid transmutation to gold.

Alchemists jealously guarded their secrets, and alchemical texts were written in obscure terms, as well as images and symbols that had to be interpreted intuitively by the individual alchemist. The *MUTUS LIBER*, or "Silent book," is perhaps the best example of alchemy explained only through images. The hermaphroditic nature of alchemy was often expressed in erotic art, though there is no evidence that actual sexual rites were practiced (unlike some Eastern alchemical traditions). Alchemists were primarily male, but some worked with a female partner, usually a wife, who served as the *SOROR MYSTICA*, or "mystical sister"—the feminine component of the Great Work.

The ability to make gold out of lead was more legendary than factual, but numerous stories circulated about the alleged successes of some alchemists. In the course of their pursuits, alchemists were responsible for many discoveries important in metallurgy, chemistry, and medicine. However, in the early 19th century, alchemy was discredited by the discoveries of oxygen and the composition of water. Alchemy was reduced to the level of pseudoscience and superstition and was replaced by physics.

Modern Western interest in alchemy was revised by CARL G. JUNG, who saw both the spiritual and physical dimensions in alchemy. Despite Jung's pioneering work uniting depth psychology and alchemy, interest in alchemy remained low until about the second half of the 20th century. A revival of interest led to alchemy schools and products for cosmetics, herbal medicines, beverages and wines, perfumes, and so forth.

In addition, modern alchemists pursue the Elixir or Philosopher's Stone that will restore youth and lengthen life. One of the chief substances believed to accomplish these goals is a form of gold called monoatomic gold, or

the "gold of Isis," created through various chemical procedures. Monoatomic gold is available for sale. Claims are made that when ingested in sufficient quantity, physical youthfulness is restored.

Eastern Alchemy

The immortality sought by the Chinese was the attainment of a state of timelessness spent with the Immortals, in which one had supernormal powers. Ancient Chinese alchemy focused on meditation and breathing techniques and also various elixirs, which were purified by combining ingredients and repeatedly heating them in various vessels.

The legendary mystic, Lao Tzu (Laozi) is credited as the father of alchemy in ancient China. Little is known about Lao Tzu. According to lore, he was born around 604 B.C.E., and he is famous for writing the *Tao Teh Ching* (*Daodejing*), or *Classic of the Way of Its Virtue*, the mystical work upon which Taoism (Daoism) is based. Initially, the book was called the Lao Tzu. The name was changed to the *Tao Teh Ching* sometime during the Western Han dynasty, which lasted from 202 B.C.E. to 9 C.E.

But whether or not Lao Tzu was a real person is debated by scholars. According to biographer Ssuma Ch'ien (Sima Qian; 145–86 B.C.E.), Lao Tzu came from the southern state of Ch'u (Chu), which is now the provinces of Hunan and Hupei (Hubei). He worked as custodian of the imperial archives of the (Zhou) Chou dynasty in the city of Loyang. He reportedly granted an interview to Confucius, who was some 50 years younger, and came to him with questions about rituals.

Lao Tzu's cultivation of Tao (Dao) allegedly enabled him to live for more than 200 years, outliving Confucius by 129 years, according to Ssuma Chi'en. He retired from his job when the Chou dynasty began to decline. He traveled west and went through a pass known as Hsin Yi (Xinyi). The warden of the pass, asked him to write a book for his enlightenment. Lao Tzu agreed, and the result was the *Tao Teh Ching*. More than 1,000 commentaries have been written on Lao Tzu's work.

"Tao" means "the Way." It is the impersonal absolute truth, which is expressed through the masculine and feminine principles of yang and yin, respectively. These principles are in constant flux and ebb in an eternal flow of the Way. "Teh" (De) is the virtue or power of the Tao, which is experienced by *wu-wei,* or non-interference, that is, being "in the flow" of the Tao. The earliest written description of yin and yang is in the I CHING (Yijing). According to the *I Ching,* the Great Primal Beginning generates the two primary forces, which in turn generate four images, which in turn generate the eight trigrams upon which the *I Ching* is based. Lao Tzu is said to have been inspired by the *I Ching* in his writing of the *Tao Teh Ching*.

Like Hermetic philosophy, Taoism views humanity as a microcosm of the macrocosm. The external workings of nature have internal counterparts. There are correspondences between the basic elements of nature and the internal workings of the human body. In Chinese medicine, this is expressed in five elements: wood, air, fire, metal, earth, and water.

The alchemical process of spiritual purification comes through purity of heart and avoidance or elimination of desires, which enables the seeker to embrace the One. The best way to accomplish this is through meditation. Taoist meditation is characterized by several features: concentration, breath control, purification of heart and mind, practice of *wu-wei* in daily life, and the ability to play the female, or yin, role during mystical union with Heaven, the yang principle.

Breath control is of great importance. Meditation and breathing techniques circulate *chi (yi)* the universal life force, through the body, purifying it. *Chi* is created when the nutritious elements of food are combined with secretions from glands and organs. This forms blood and sexual energy (ching[*xing*]). Heat in form of breath transforms the sexual energy to *chi,* which circulates up and down psychic channels along the spine, from the crown to the abdomen, somewhat akin to the kundalini energy of yoga. The *chi* passes through 12 psychic centers located along the channels. After many cycles, the *chi* becomes refined. It reaches the crown in a highly concentrated state, where it can be manipulated or else sent back down to the abdomen. The *chi* can be stored for future use.

Lao Tzu favored natural breathing, which induces tenderness, the essential characteristic of life (as opposed to rigidity, the characteristic of death). Lao Tzu considered the infant to be the perfect symbol of Tao, and said it was highly desirable to breathe as an infant does. Later Taoist alchemists advocated "fetus breathing," which is so faint that it is nearly extinguished, and which when done precedes the mystical state of *samadhi.*

(It is interesting to note that fetus breathing is similar to *hesychasm,* an alchemica/mystical breathing that emerged in monastic practice in Eastern Orthodox Christianity, and probably evolved from Buddhist influences. Its chief advocate was St. Gregory Palamas (c. 1296–1359). *Hesychasm* comes from *hesychia,* which means "stillness" or "light." It is a method of prayer that combines extremely shallow, controlled breathing with yoga-like posture to induce a vision of light that is supposed to be comparable to the light seen at Jesus transfiguration on Mt. Tabor. There are dangers involved in the shallow breathing of both fetus breathing and *hesychasm:* damage to both the physical body and psychological/mental state.)

The return to a newborn state as a way to Tao is expressed in Taoist yoga, which advises (for men) the sublimation of the vital male force at age 16, when it is at its apex of strength, into *hsien t'ien (xian tian),* the prenatal vital force, which leads to spiritual immortality.

Lao Tzu's approach to alchemy was primarily spiritual. Later Chinese alchemists looked for physical alchemy, and added elixirs to their pursuits.

According to lore, the first Daoist pope, Chang Tao-Ling (Zhang Daoling; b. 35 C.E.), pursued alchemy in his remote mountain abode. By supernatural means, Lao Tsu gave him a mystical treatise that enabled him to attain the Elixir of Life.

In India, alchemy traces its roots to earlier than 1000 B.C.E. in the development of Ayurvedic ("the wisdom of life") medicine, where it continues to play a role in the present. Indian alchemy is a union of male (*shiva*) and female (*parvati*) principles, which creates *jivan,* an enlightened being.

Meditation, breath control, and posture are important elements of Indian alchemy. Immortality also may be achieved through Tantra, a sexual yoga, which is either prolonged abstinence or coitus without ejaculation. Tantra is believed to intensify the life force (*prana,* or *xi*) and produce physiological changes.

The Importance of Alchemy

As noted earlier, alchemists made significant contributions to the physical sciences and medicine. In the Western tradition, the Hermetic philosophy became the basis for magical practices. GRIMOIRES, or magical handbooks, contained many principles of correspondences for the casting of SPELLS. The traditions of ceremonial magic, or high magic are paths of enlightenment based on the balancing of the masculine and feminine principles, and the perfection of the whole being.

See also MAGIC.

FURTHER READING:
Cockren, A. "History of Alchemy." Available online. URL: http://www.alchemylab.com/history_of_alchemy.htm. Downloaded January 8, 2006.
Gray, Ronald D. *Goethe the Alchemist: A Study of Alchemical Symbolism in Goethe's Literary and Scientific Works.* Mansfield Centre, Conn.: Martino Publishing, 2002.
Hall, Manly P. *The Secret Teachings of All Ages.* 1929. Reprint, Los Angeles: The Philosophic Research Society, 1977.
Jung, C. G. *Psychology and Alchemy.* Rev. ed. Princeton, N.J.: Princeton University Press, 1968.
Lash, John. "Parting of the Ways," *Gnosis* 8 (Summer 1988): 22–26.
Melodini, Jim. "The Age of Gold," *Gnosis* 8 (Summer 1988): 8–10.
Nintzel, Hans. "Alchemy Is Alive and Well," *Gnosis* 8 (Summer 1988): 11–15.
Zolla, Elemire. "Alchemy Out of India," *Gnosis* 8 (Summer 1988): 48–49.

alembic In alchemy, a glass flask used for the process of distillation to obtain purified substances. The term *alembic* comes from the Arabic term for a still, *al-anbiq.* The alembic has two sections. Liquids are heated in the bottom section, and the resulting vapors rise into the top section where they condense and are channeled into a long spout.

One type of alembic is called the pelican because of its long, downward-pointing spout.

Alfarabi (d. 954) Arab alchemist second to JABIR IBN HAYYAR (Geber) in repute during his lifetime.

Alfarabi was a learned man who led a wandering life in search of the secrets of ALCHEMY. He entertained at court but never accepted invitations to stay. He said he would never rest until he discovered the PHILOSOPHER'S STONE. In Syria he entertained the Sultan Seiffeddoulet and the same evening set out on a journey through the desert. He was set upon by thieves and murdered.

Alfarabi is said to have authored several manuscripts on alchemy and the sciences, but none survive.

alkahest   Term coined by PARACELSUS for a mysterious "universal solvent" in alchemical transmutation. Alkahest also is known as the ELIXIR and "the water which does not wet the hands." The exact origin of the term is unknown.

Paracelsus made his first mention of alkahest in *Members of Man,* saying, "There is also the spirit alkahest, which acts very efficiently upon the liver: it sustains, fortifies, and preserves from the diseases within its reach. . . . Those who want to use such a medicine must know how the alkahest is prepared."

JEAN BAPTISTA VAN HELMONT gave great credence to alkahest, describing it as "Fire Water" or "Hell Water" that is able to dissolve all bodies "as warm water dissolves ice." Van Helmont said, "It is a salt, most blessed and most perfect of all salts; the secret of its preparation is beyond human comprehension and God alone can reveal it to the chosen."

During the 17th and 18th centuries, alchemists searched for alkahest in order to dissolve substances to find the PRIMA MATERIA. Some considered the word *alkahest* as an anagram of its true name. Some said the name really meant "alkali est," or "It is alkali," or else "All-Geist," German for "universal spirit." Various recipes were given for making alkahest; the best ingredient was held to be BLOOD, plus worms, sweat, and SPITTLE.

Interest in alkahest ended in the mid-18th century when the German alchemist Kunckel pointed out that if alkahest were a true universal solvent, then it would dissolve even the vessel that held it. Kunckel disdainfully said the alkahest was really *"Alles Lugen ist,"* German for "All that is a lie."

Alkahest is used in MAGIC to clear away fog and obstruction so that a desired thing can manifest. In spiritual alchemical processes, alkahest is the dark water of the unconscious in which the ego is dissolved.

FURTHER READING:
Seligmann, Kurt. *The History of Magic and the Occult.* New York: Pantheon Books, 1948.

altar   See TOOLS.

Aluys, Albert (18th c.)   French fraudulent alchemist. Albert Aluys (also given as Alnys) was stepson to the alchemist JEAN DELISLE.

Little is known about Aluys's life prior to the involvement of his mother with Delisle, whom she met in a road-side cabaret. She left her husband and departed with Delisle, remaining with him for five or six years and eventually marrying him. Some sources say that Albert Aluys was Delisle's illegitimate son, but Delisle took on the role of stepfather.

Aluys learned the fraudulent alchemical trade from Delisle and spoke the jargon with the best of them. Upon Delisle's death in about 1711–12, Aluys let it be known that he had inherited the secret of the PHILOSOPHER'S STONE. His mother helped him commit fraud. Their goal was to deceive wealthy patrons into supporting them in a lavish lifestyle.

Aluys and his mother left Provence, France, and traveled about Europe sponging off credulous victims, and performing phony transmutations with the help of double-bottomed crucibles. By 1726 the mother was dead, and Aluys journeyed to Vienna, where he presented himself to the Duke of Richelieu, the French ambassador. Richelieu was duped, witnessing on several occasions the apparent transmutation of lead into GOLD. He even made an IRON nail turn into SILVER. The duke boasted of his deeds but disappointed Aluys by not giving him funds. Rather, the duke expected Aluys to transmute all of his base metals, including every common tool and implement, into precious metals, simply for the pleasure of it.

Aluys decamped for Bohemia, taking with him a student and a girl who was in love with him and whom he married. There he successfully deceived a number of nobles by presenting them with a gift of transmuted metal and promising them riches, if only they would provide lodging, meals, and expenses.

He returned to France, but in Marseilles he was arrested and imprisoned on charges of coining, or counterfeiting. He ingratiated himself with the daughter of the jailer and after a year was able to make his escape, leaving the jilted girl behind.

Joined by his wife, Aluys went to Brussels, where he set up a laboratory and publicized that he knew the secret of the Stone. People flocked to him and believed him. Aluys duped a wealthy man for a year, and when the man discovered that Aluys was a fraud, he demanded his money back. Aluys refused and was taken to court. But the case was never prosecuted because the patron died suddenly. Rumor had it that he had been poisoned by Aluys. Sentiment turned against the alchemist, and he fled the city for Paris. There he lived quietly. His fate is not known.

FURTHER READING:
Mackay, Charles. *Extraordinary Popular Delusions and the Madness of Crowds.* New York: Farrar, Straus & Giroux, 1932.

amulet   An object, inscription, drawing, or SYMBOL imbued with magical protective power against bad luck, accidents, illnesses, supernatural attack, the EVIL EYE, and other misfortunes. The term *amulet* is derived either from the Latin *amuletum* or the Old Latin *amoletum* for "means of defense."

The simplest amulets are natural objects whose unusual shapes, colors, or markings indicate their supernatural properties. Precious and semiprecious stones all are considered to have amuletic properties. Vegetables and fruits can be amulets: garlic is said to be a protection against evil and illness. Peach wood and stones are ancient amulets in Chinese lore. Many amulets are made from certain materials that are considered powerful—such as IRON, GOLD, SILVER, and copper—and are imbued with their magical properties. Making an amulet creates the power, especially if done ritualistically or during certain times.

Amulets are worn, engraved on buildings and objects, buried under thresholds, and hung in windows and doorways. Written amulets are CHARMS or PRAYERS and the NAMES of God, deities, angels, and other spirits whose benevolent powers are invoked for protection. Some inscriptions are nonsensical names and words containing distorted Latin, such as this formula for protection against arrows:

Write these words on a piece of paper:
"Araba Omel alifal Cuttar uden et amoen
Trol Coblamot Fasteanus."
Carry these words with you.

See also TALISMAN.

FURTHER READING:
Budge, E. A. Wallis. *Amulets and Superstitions*. 1930. Reprint, New York: Dover Publications, 1978.
Cavendish, Richard. *The Black Arts*. New York: Perigee Books, 1967.
Rustad, Mary S. (ed. and translator). *The Black Books of Elverum*. Lakeville, Minn.: Galde Press, 1999.

angel   A supernatural being who mediates between God and mortals. Angels minister over all living things and the natural world and also over all things in the cosmos. They play an important role in MAGIC.

The term *angel* comes from the Greek *angelos,* which means "messenger." Similarly, the Persian term *angaros* means "courier." In Hebrew, the term is *malakh,* which also means messenger. The name refers to one of the angel's primary duties, to shuttle back and forth between realms, bringing human prayers to heaven and returning with God's answers. Angels also mete out the will of God, whether it be to aid or to punish humans. Angels are specific to Judaism, Christianity, and Islam; however, they derive from concepts of helping and from tutelary spirits that exist in mythologies the world over.

Angels evolved from the mythology of the Jews, influenced by the mythologies of Babylonians, Persians, Sumerians, Egyptians, and others with whom the Jews had contact. The Jewish angel passed into Christian and Islamic mythology.

The Bible presents angels as representatives of God. They exist in a celestial realm and are numberless. They are incorporeal but have the ability to assume form and pass as mortals. They also appear as beings of fire, lightning, and brilliant light, sometimes with wings and sometimes not. Various classes of angels are mentioned in the Bible; by the sixth century these were organized into hierarchies.

The church fathers of Christianity gave extensive consideration to the duties, nature, numbers, abilities, and functions of angels. This theological interest peaked by the Middle Ages and began to decline in the Renaissance.

Angels are prominent in Jewish magic and preside over every aspect of creation. They are featured in KABBALAH-based magic, which forms a significant part of the Western magical tradition. Angels, along with demons, are involved in RITUALS given in magical books and GRIMOIRES. They are invoked by sacred NAMES, SYMBOLS, SEALS, and so forth, and their names are inscribed on magical TOOLS, MAGIC CIRCLES, AMULETS, and TALISMANS.

angel alphabets   See MAGIC ALPHABETS.

angel magic   See ASHMOLE, ELIAS; DEE, JOHN; ENOCHIAN MAGIC; MAGIC.

Anima Mundi   The Soul of the World. The *Anima Mundi* is the feminine creative power of God who turns

Anima Mundi, *the soul of the world, in* Utriusque Cosmi Historia, *by Robert Fludd, 1617. (Author's collection)*

the sphere of the stars and disperses planetary influences to nourish the material world. She is comparable to the Shakti creative force in Hinduism.

The *Anima Mundi* appears in *The History of the Macrocosm and the Microcosm* of ROBERT FLUDD, who described her as a "supreme intelligence" of "an angelic nature." As man has a soul, so must the macrocosm have a soul, Fludd said. The engraving of the *Anima Mundi* shows a virgin joined to God by a chain that descends through the levels of the hierarchy of existence. Fludd describes:

> On her breast is the true Sun; on her belly the Moon. Her heart gives light to the stars and planets, whose influence, infused in her womb by the mercurial spirit (called by the philosophers the Spirit of the Moon), is sent down to the very center of the Earth. Her right foot stands on earth, her left in water, signifying the conjunction of sulphur and mercury without which nothing can be created.

The description bears a strong resemblance to the passage in chapter 12 of the Book of Revelation of the "woman clothed in the sun":

> And there appeared a great wonder in heaven; a woman clothed with the sun, and the moon under her feet and upon her head a crown of twelve stars.

Fludd's depiction of the *Anima Mundi* received a great deal of criticism in his day, and was among the reasons why his opponents called him a heretic. Critics were especially angered by his statement that Christ and DEMONS were of the same soul. Marin Marsenne, French physician, complained:

> Compounded from God and this ethereal Spirit is the *Anima Mundi*. The purest part of this Soul is the Angelic nature and the Empyrean heaven, which is understood to be mixed in all things. The Demons are part of the same essence, but joined to evil material. All souls, whether of men or of brutes, are none other than particle of this same Soul. This Soul is also the Angel Michael or *Misattron* [Metatron]. What is more, the same Soul is the true Messiah, Savior, Christ, *cornerstone* and *universal rock,* on which the Church and all salvation is founded.

Fludd defended himself, stating that the principles are not on the same level of being, as Marsenne seemed to think, but are different manifestations of the same principle in different worlds.

FURTHER READING:
Godwin, Joscelyn. *Robert Fludd: Hermetic Philosopher and Surveyor of Two Worlds.* Grand Rapids, Mich.: Phanes Press, 1979.

ankh   Egyptian symbol of life, the universe, and IMMORTALITY; important in MAGIC. *Ankh* means both "life" and "hand mirror." It is in the shape of a tau, or looped, CROSS.

The ankh is a SYMBOL of regeneration, an AMULET against bad luck, and a TALISMAN for good fortune. It also represents the alchemical union of the male principle (the staff) and the female principle (the closed loop).

In ancient Egypt, the House of Life was a building or group of buildings that housed the temple library, the repository of all magical lore available to the magicians, priests, and laymen. Egyptian art shows the ankh being carried as a scepter in the right hand of deities and being applied to the nostrils of the dead in order to bring them back to life. Ankh amulets were made of faience, semiprecious and precious stones, wax, metal, and wood. The pharaoh Tutankhamen had a hand MIRROR in the shape of an ankh.

Egyptians who converted to early Christianity used both the ankh and the Christian cross as their spiritual signs.

Apollonius of Tyana (first c. C.E.)   One of the most reputed ADEPTS of the Roman Empire, skilled in healing, MAGIC, and ALCHEMY. A romantic but unreliable account of his life, *The Life of Apollonius of Tyana,* was written by Philostratus in the third century C.E. Though little is known about his life for certain, it is evident that Apollonius was a popular hero, at least by the second century. He is some-

Ideal portrait of Apollonius of Tyana, in De Divinatione et Magicis, *by Jacques Boissard.* (Author's collection)

times identified with another figure of the same period, Balinas.

Apollonius was born on an unknown date in the first century in Tyana, Cappadocia, now part of Turkey. He may have studied with the neo-Pythagorean branch of philosophy. A charismatic, he gained fame throughout Asia Minor as a magician or miracle worker and a teacher. He wrote at least one book, *On sacrifices,* though other books are attributed to him, including a four-volume work titled *On astrology* and a work on PYTHAGORAS and his doctrines.

Philostratus, a Greek sophist born circa 170 C.E., sought to portray Apollonius as a champion of Greek culture. According to Philostratus, Apollonius traveled widely throughout the ancient world with his disciple and traveling companion, Damis, and had numerous adventures. He learned the Hermetic knowledge. Apollonius had regular contact with the Magi and influenced the king of Babylonia. In India, the sages taught him magical and mystical arts. He visited Pergamum, the shrine of Asclepius, and Troy, and conversed with the ghost of Achilles. He saved a pupil, Menippus, from his VAMPIRE bride and banished DEMONS. In Rome, Apollonius fell in and out of favor with the emperor Nero. In Alexandria, he advised the new emperor Vespasian. Traveling on to Ethiopia, he spent time with the gymnosophists, who he considered to be inferior in wisdom to the Indians. The tyrannical emperor Domitian, whom Apollonius opposed, had him imprisoned and put on trial. Apollonius was acquitted at the trial and miraculously disappeared from the court. Later while in Ephesus, he observed by CLAIRVOYANCE or remote viewing the murder of Domitian in Rome. He declined the request of the succeeding emperor, Nerva, to act as his adviser, sending Damis instead. After his death, Apollonius appeared in a DREAM to a young man to confirm the immortality of the soul. According to Philostratus, throughout this action-filled life, Apollonius performed numerous healings and miraculous acts.

Letters of Apollonius is a collection of more than 100 letters allegedly written by him. Most are known to be written anonymously. Some are older than Philostratus's account and seem to be based on information known about Apollonius. In two letters, Apollonius acknowledges being a "magician."

In the 19th century, magician ELIPHAS LEVI attempted to conjure the spirit of Apollonius in a NECROMANCY ritual. A spirit appeared and terrified Levi, but he never acknowledged whether or not it was indeed Apollonius.

FRANCIS BARRETT described Appollonius as "one of the most extraordinary persons that ever appeared in the world."

FURTHER READING:
Flinterman, Jaap-Jan. "Summary of Philostratus' *Life of Apollonius.*" Available online. URL: http://www.livius.org/apark/apollonius/apollonius_life.html. Downloaded January 10, 2005.

apples   This seemingly innocent fruit, cultivated by the Romans and Britons as early as 3000 B.C.E., has had a long association with MAGIC, WITCHCRAFT, and goddess worship. Apples represent immortality and fertility. They also serve as the principal ingredient in love potions and CHARMS and act as healing agents for a variety of ailments. Apple TREES were sacred to the ancient Celts and Druids, and chopping one down brought the death penalty under old Irish law. The apple was so vital to daily life and the success of the community that the tasty fruit received as much magic as it helped to create.

The word *apple* derives from the Latin *pomum,* meaning fruit; its botanical classification is a pome, or a fruit with many tiny seeds in its core. The Roman goddess Pomona is the patroness of fruit trees. Early apples were more like modern crabapples—small, hard and sour—but Roman farmers discovered that grafting cuttings, called scions, of different cultivars onto hardy rootstock produced about seven dependable varieties that were delicious and thrived in a variety of climates. Apples were so ubiquitous that seeds and cuttings of exotic fruit plants brought to Europe by early explorers and travelers were called apples until a better name was agreed upon. Some of the foods that were originally "apples" include melons, avocados, cashews, cherimoyas, dates, eggplants, lemons, oranges, peaches, pineapples, pine nuts, pomegranates, potatoes, quinces, and tomatoes.

In Celtic lore, apples represented regeneration, eternal life, and fertility; apples also symbolized the SUN, the source of all life. Apple trees grew in the Celtic underworld, where they provided food for the dead during the bleak winter before resurrection by the goddess Olwen in the spring—a story similar to the Greek myth of Hades and Persephone. Possession of the Silver Bough, an apple branch that bore flowers, buds, and ripe fruit simultaneously, allowed the owner to enter the land of the gods. After the battles with Mordred, Morgana spirited King Arthur away to the Isle of Avalon, or "Apple Land," ruled by the goddess MORGAN LE FAY. Arthur's knight Lancelot fell asleep under an apple tree and was spirited away by FAIRY queens. And the king's bride Guinevere unfortunately gave an apple to St. Patrick before he died and was condemned to burn as a witch. The mythical unicorn lived under apple trees. In ancient Ireland, an apple tree was one of only three objects that could be paid for with living things; the other two were the hazel bush and the sacred grove.

Throughout the medieval period—and even up to the present day—apple growers perform magical ceremonies to help ensure a bountiful harvest. At Christmastime in Somerset and the West Country of England, tradition called for villagers to go "apple-wassailing," also called "apple-howling." On Twelfth Night (Epiphany, or January 6) townspeople entered the village orchards and selected one tree to represent the rest. First they made as much noise as possible by firing guns into the air, blowing horns, and beating pots and pans to ward off evil spirits. Then they sang hymns to the tree and danced around it, toasted the tree three times, and threw cider (wassail) over the tree's roots. The final stage involved asking the tree to bear abundantly and then making it an offering of a cider-soaked piece of bread or hotcake in its branches. Burying 13 apple leaves after harvest also guaranteed a good crop next year, as did seeing the sunlight through apple tree branches on Christmas Day. In Germany, if a woman with many children sleeps under an apple tree, the tree will bear abundantly also.

Divination and Love Charms

Apples—all parts of the fruit, blossoms, and wood—form the main ingredient in love potions and spells that are used to divine one's intended spouse or lover. They may be added to brews, incenses, and sachets; to pink wax for candles; or simply used in their natural form. Apple cider may be substituted for BLOOD in old spell recipes.

In the 15th and 16th centuries, apples were especially popular in love charms. Apples were prescribed to make someone fall in love, as in the following charms from medieval manuscripts. The basic formula called for inscribing the names of angels and spirits on apples and giving them to a person to eat.

> Pick an apple from the tree and use a sharp knife. Write on the apple Aleo + Deleo + Delato and say, "I conjure thee, apple, by these names which are written on thee, that what woman/man/virgin [select the appropriate term] toucheth and taste thee, may love me and burn in my love as fire melteth in wax." Give the apple to the object of your desire to eat.

> Write on an apple Guel + Bsatirell + Gliaell +, and give it to her/him to eat.

> Write on an apple Raguell, Lucifer, Sathanus and say, "I conjure thee apple by these three names written on thee, that whosoever shall eat thee may burn in my love."

> Write on an apple your names and these three names, Cosmer + Synady + Heupide, and give it to eat to any man/woman that thou wouldst have and he/she shall do as thou wilt.

> Cutt [sic] an apple in IV parts, and on every part write Sathiel + Sathiel + Obing + Siagestard and say, "I conjure thee apple by the Holy God, by the IV Evangelists and gospels, and by Samuel and by Mary, that thou shall not stand still until I have the love of the woman/man which shall eat of thee."

Other successful prognostications involved selecting an apple with skin colored both red and green on the third day into the waning MOON. The diviner breathed on the green area and polished it with a red cloth while chanting, "Fire sweet and fire red, warm the heart and turn the head." Then the red part of the skin was kissed and the apple given to the intended. Some young women cut up apples in front of a MIRROR in a dark room just before midnight, accompanied by

a single CANDLE. They then tossed one piece over their right shoulders and ate the rest while brushing their hair. At midnight, their lovers' reflections would appear in the mirror.

Peels and seeds also served as diviners. Peeling an apple in an unbroken strip and then throwing it over the left shoulder revealed the initials of the beloved when the strip fell to the ground. Sticking an apple seed on one's forehead and then reciting the alphabet could work also: The seed fell off at the initial of the beloved. In Austria, throwing the seeds into a fire while reciting, "If you love me, pop and fly; if you hate me lay and die," is an apple variant on "He loves me, he loves me not."

Some of the maidens waited for the pagan feast of Samhain to learn their lovers' identities. To learn whether love lay ahead, young people would cut an apple into nine pieces at midnight on Halloween while standing before a mirror. The spell required each piece to be speared with the knife (preferably one of SILVER) and held over the left shoulder, one piece at a time. Upon stabbing the ninth piece, the intended's reflection appeared.

Halloween party games like bobbing for apples have their roots in Samhain celebrations. Each unmarried woman in the community cut an identifying mark into an apple and dropped it into a tub of water, where it floated. The local swains then went "apple-bobbing" (or "apple-dooking" in Scotland); whichever apple they successfully sank their teeth into revealed the mark of their prospective bride. Snap Apple—in which the apples were hung from strings suspended from the ceiling—held that the first one to bite an apple would be the next to marry.

Healing Arts

Apples appear as an ingredient in the recipes for many herbal treatments. The fruit reputedly clears the liver, tones the gums, and cures constipation (a property still true—witness the old adage "An apple a day keeps the doctor away"). Baked apples may be applied as a poultice for sore throats and respiratory inflammation, while cooked apples in general work as a laxative. Eating peeled, raw apples stops diarrhea. A modern variant on the fruit's antidiarrheal properties is the B.R.A.T. diet given to children with sick stomachs: the *A* stands for applesauce. The other elements are banana, rice, and toast.

In the second century C.E., drinking two-year-old cider reportedly cured everything. Three to four cups of cider a day corrects the intestinal flora, reduces acidity and gas, and helps the kidneys. An application of equal parts vinegar and water can restore hair growth and improve scalp and skin (if one is blonde, make sure to use white vinegar). At least two teaspoons of vinegar in a glass of water with honey improves digestion.

Cutting an apple into three pieces and rubbing the pieces on a sick person, then burying the pieces, draws the illness out and deposits it into the soil instead. This procedure supposedly works especially well to remove warts, particularly if one recites the incantation "Out warts, into apple" during the rubbing process.

Gods, Goddesses, and Witchcraft

Deities from many traditions beside the Celts hold the apple sacred. In Norse mythology, Idun (Idhunn or Iduna), the goddess of youth, guarded an apple orchard for the gods. The apples kept the gods from aging. When Thiassi stole Idun's apples and hid them, the gods grew old; they regained their youth when Idun found the stolen fruit. The fertility god Froh won the beautiful giantess Gerda by offering her 11 golden apples. Apples also symbolized the Norse goddesses Freya and Hel, queen of the Underworld.

In ancient Sumeria, the god Eriki offered the goddess Uttu an apple as a marriage proposal. Apple trees occupied the center of heaven in Iroquois tradition. And in Greek and Roman mythology, apples were associated with the goddesses Gaea, Artemis/Diana, Hera/Juno, Athena, and especially Aphrodite/Venus. Apples still on the bough were a major part of the feast of Diana, celebrated each August 13. Gaea, goddess of the Earth, guarded Greece's golden apples, much like Idun did for the Norse gods. The Greeks, like the Celts, considered apples to be the food of the immortals. As proof, they noted that an apple cut crosswise revealed a five-pointed star (later demonologists suspected the star was a PENTACLE). The followers of the mathematician PYTHAGORAS did not eat apples because they saw the star as a Pythagorean pentagram.

Perhaps the most famous golden apple was the one given to Aphrodite by Paris. The goddesses Aphrodite, Athena, and Hera tested Paris by making him decide which of them was superior. As recounted by Homer in the epic poem *The Iliad*, Paris chose Aphrodite for her beauty and allure. In return, she gave him the gorgeous Helen, wife of Menelaus of Sparta, and precipitated the Trojan War.

In Western, Judeo-Christian tradition, apples became synonymous with the temptation of Adam by Eve and the serpent in the Garden of Eden. In the second century C.E., Aquila of Pontus first identified the fruit of the Tree of Life (knowledge and immortality) as an apple, leading the church to equate apples with sin. In fact, while most people ate apples, many feared that such a pure fruit harbored devils and DEMONS. To avoid ingesting such evil spirits, eaters would vigorously rub the skin of the apple before taking a bite—a practice that has survived as polishing the fruit. Such scrubbing often proved worthless, however, as witches were reputedly fond of using the seemingly innocent apple as a means of bewitching or even poisoning their victims. The evil witch queen in the story of Snow White enticed the princess to take her sleeping poison by giving her an apple.

In 1657, neighbors of Richard Jones, a 12-year-old boy in the village of Shepton Mallet, county Somerset, England, became convinced that Jane Brooks, a young girl, had bewitched Richard by giving him an enchanted apple. The young man suffered fits, and the villagers testified that they had seen him fly over his garden wall. Brooks was condemned as a witch and was hanged on March 26, 1658.

Henri Boguet, a renowned demonologist and presiding judge in witchcraft trials in 17th-century France, believed without question that apples, already tainted by their association with Eve, raised no alarm and therefore were perfect for the transmission of evil. In Boguet's book, *Discours des sorciers* (1602), he related an incident that took place in Annecy, Savoy, in 1585 in which the townspeople reportedly heard strange and confusing noises emanating from an apple. Convinced that the apple was full of devils and that they were averting a demonic possession, the citizens marched the apple to the river and dropped it into the water to drown.

FURTHER READING:

Cavendish, Richard, and Brian Innes, eds. *Man, Myth and Magic,* revised ed. North Bellmore, N.Y.: Marshall Cavendish Corp., 1995.

Guiley, Rosemary. *The Encyclopedia of Witches and Witchcraft.* 2d ed. New York: Facts On File Inc., 1999.

"Herb Uses." Available online. URL: www.jksalescompany.com/dw/herbsandoil2.html. Downloaded August 16, 2004.

"The Magi's Magic Garden: Apple." Available online. URL: www.angelfire.com/de/poetryperso/Flower/Apple.html. Downloaded August 16, 2004.

"Pyre of the Phoenix." Available online. URL: www.pyreofphoenix.com/herb/herbsa.shtm#apple. Downloaded August 16, 2004.

Thompson, C. J. S. *The Mysteries and Secrets of Magic.* New York: Barnes & Noble, 1993.

Aquinas, Thomas (1225–1274) Dominican saint, philosopher, and arguably the greatest theologian of the Christian church. St. Thomas Aquinas, a student of ALBERTUS MAGNUS, was knowledgeable about ALCHEMY but avoided the subject in his writings. Thomas Aquinas is known as Doctor Angelicus and Doctor Communas for his great teachings. His revolutionary philosophy had an important impact on the witch hunts of the Inquisition and was cited by demonologists and inquisitors for centuries as a basis for their persecutions.

Thomas Aquinas was born Tomasso Aquino into the central Italian local gentry in Roccasecca near Aquino. At the age of six, he was sent to study at the famous Benedictine monastery at Montecassino. When he was 14, he entered the University of Naples, a school known for being innovative and for being one of the first conduits of Aristotle's complete works, which had only recently entered the Western world via Arabic translations. At 18 Aquinas joined the Dominicans, a new order of mendicant monks especially committed to study, teaching, and preaching. His family attempted to foil this decision by detaining him for almost two years, but they failed to deter him.

He rejoined his Dominican brethren and soon was sent to Paris, where he transcribed the lectures of Albertus Magnus. From 1248 to 1252, Aquinas lived at the priory of the Holy Cross in Cologne, studying with Albert especially the works of Aristotle, impressing his teachers and superiors. Tradition says he was called the dumb ox because he was physically heavy and had a silent, reserved manner. Albertus reportedly told his classmates: "We call this lad a dumb ox, but I tell you that the whole world is going to hear his bellowing!"

In 1256, Aquinas was licensed to teach Dominicans and was named professor of theology in 1257. He achieved fame for his superior intelligence and mental capacity. He taught in Paris and in cities in Italy. Aquinas favored Aristotelan philosophy and made it the foundation for his theological and philosophical writings. He produced numerous great writings, the most famous and important of which is *Summa Theologica,* a sweeping examination of the entire body of the church's theology. Begun in 1266, *Summa Theologica* remained unfinished at his death. He intended it to be a simple manual for students; it turned into the greatest theological document ever written in the church. Organized into three parts, it contains 38 treatises, 612 questions, 3,120 articles, and about 10,000 objections.

In December 1273, Aquinas suffered some sort of breakdown—probably the result of exhaustion—and suddenly abandoned his usual routine and writing. He set out on a journey to Lyons the same month but fell ill on the way. He never recovered. After two months, he was taken to a nearby Cistercian monastery, where he died in a guest room on March 7, 1274. He was canonized in 1323 by Pope John XXII and was declared Doctor of the Church and Doctor Angelicus in 1567 by Pope Pius X.

Aquinas's only comment on alchemy was that "it is not lawful to sell as good gold that which is made by Alchemy." Nonetheless, several spurious works on alchemy are attributed to him: *Thesaurus Alchemiae,* which is addressed to "Brother Regnauld" and discusses the creation of the PHILOSOPHER'S STONE; *Secreta Alchymiae Magnalia; De Esse et Essentia Mineralium;* and *Comment on the Turba.* Whoever wrote these treatises coined or recorded for the first time terms still in use in chemistry today—for example, the term *amalgam,* a compound of MERCURY and other metals.

Aquinas's philosophy had a major impact upon the church's view of WITCHCRAFT and in the transformation of SORCERY into the heresy of witchcraft. Heresy, even if the product of ignorance, was a sin because ignorance is the product of criminal negligence. Aquinas also stated that the practice of magic was not virtuous and was practiced by "men of evil life."

He believed in the devil as a tangible person with the senses of man. While he did not believe in formal PACTS with the devil, he did believe in implicit pacts. A heretic, just by virtue of being a heretic, could be assumed to give himself or herself over to the Devil, whether or not the thought had even crossed his or her mind. He also believed in the witches' alleged powers of transvection (flying through the air), metamorphosis (see SHAPE-SHIFTING), storm-raising, and other castings of malevolent SPELLS.

DEMONS, Aquinas said, do assail people and do so with the explicit permission of God. Demons and the devil tempt with pseudo-miracles and are responsible for all sin and sexual impotence. Witchcraft, he declared, is permanent in the world, not to be remedied by more witchcraft, but only by the cessation of sin and sometimes by EXORCISMS performed by the church.

According to lore, Aquinas mastered certain feats of MAGIC himself. Such stories were commonly attributed to persons who had knowledge of the supernatural, and Aquinas's association with Albertus Magnus probably encouraged them. Aquinas is said to have assisted Albertus in the creation of a HOMUNCULUS, an animated, humanoid brazen statue that could talk. The statue worked as a servant but chattered so much that Aquinas smashed it to pieces with a hammer.

According to another legend, Aquinas became greatly annoyed by the clatter of horses' hooves outside his study window every day as grooms led their animals on daily exercises. He created a TALISMAN of a small bronze statue of a horse, inscribed with kabbalistic SYMBOLS, and buried it at midnight in the middle of the road. The next morning, the horses refused to pass over the spot where the statue was buried, rearing up on their hind legs and showing great fright. The grooms were forced to find another place for daily exercises, and Aquinas was left in peace.

FURTHER READING:

Guiley, Rosemary Ellen. *The Encyclopedia of Saints.* New York: Facts On File, 2002.
———. *The Encyclopedia of Witches and Witchcraft.* 2d ed. New York: Facts On File, 1999.
Waite, Arthur Edward. *Alchemists Through the Ages.* Blauvelt, N.Y.: Rudolph Steiner Publications, 1970.

Artephius (12th c.)   Mysterious Hermetic philosopher and alchemist alleged to have lived more than 1,000 years, thanks to the secrets of the PHILOSOPHER'S STONE. Artephius was among the most respected of medieval alchemists.

His disciples attempted to prove that he was APOLLONIUS OF TYANA. Scholars disagree over whether he was an Arab or a Jew; some have identified him with the Arab poet and alchemist, al-Tughrai, who was executed sometime between 1119 and 1122. Adding weight to the Arab argument is the title of his earlier book, *Artefeii Arabis liber secretus artis occultae* (*The Secret Book of the Occult Art of Artefius the Arab*). However, all of Artephius's writings were in Latin, not Arabic.

Artephius wrote three works on ALCHEMY. Besides the one aforementioned, they are *Tractate de vita propaganda* (*Tractate about the prolongation of life*), which he claims in the preface to have written at the astonishing age of 1,025; and *Liber qui clavis majoris sapientiae dicitur* (*The Book Called the Key of Major Wisdom*), about the Philosopher's Stone and other subjects.

The "three vases of Artephius" is a DIVINATION method attributed to Artephius, combining the magic MIRROR, hydromancy (divination by water), and oinomancy (divination by wine). According to the method, a wooden table is prepared that is pierced with holes to receive the rays of the SUN and the MOON. Three vases are placed on it: an earthenware vase containing oil of myrrh; a green eathenware vase containing wine; and a white earthenware vase containing water. Substitutions of copper and glass vases may be made for the second and third vases, respectively. A lighted CANDLE is placed by each vase. The diviner also has three TOOLS: a poplar wand half stripped of its bark; a knife; and a pumpkin root. According to an anonymous manuscript:

> [B]y the earthenware vase the past is known, by the copper vase the present, and by the glass vase the future. He [Artephius] arranges them in yet another fashion; that is to say, in place of the earthenware vase a silver vase full of wine is set, and the copper one is filled with oil, and the glass with water. Then you will see present things in the earthen vase, past things in the copper, and future things in the silver. . . . All must be shielded from the sun; and the weather must be very calm, and must have been so far for at least three days. By day you will work in sunny weather, and by night in the moonlight and by the light of the stars. The work must be done in a place far from any noise, and all must be in deep silence. The operator is to be garbed all in white, and his head and face covered with a piece of red silken stuff or fine linen, so that nothing may be visible but the eyes. . . . In the water the shadow of the thing is seen, in the oil the appearance of the person, and in the wine the very thing itself; and there is the end of this invention.

FURTHER READING:
Grillot de Givry, Emile. *Witchcraft, Magic and Alchemy.* New York: Houghton Mifflin, 1931.
Patai, Raphael. *The Jewish Alchemists.* Princeton, N.J.: Princeton University Press, 1994.

artifex See ADEPT.

Ashmole, Elias (1617–1692) English historian and scholar with an intense interest in ALCHEMY. Elias Ashmole is best known as the founder of the Ashmolean Library in Oxford.

Ashmole was born in 1617 to a Lichfield saddler. He studied law and then served as a Royalist in the Civil War. In 1673, he was elected a Fellow of the Royal Society and was one of its founding members. He was one of the first "speculative Masons" accepted into the London guild of "working Masons." (See FREEMASONRY.)

Ashmole was intensely interested in alchemy, ASTROLOGY, Hermetic philosophy, MAGIC, ANGEL magic, and other esoteric topics. William Backhouse, his adoptive father, was an alchemist who one day took Ashmole aside and revealed to him the secret of the PHILOSOPHER'S STONE.

In 1652, Ashmole published *Theatricum chemicum Brittanicum,* a substantial opus on the study of alchemy. In it, he expounds on Hermetic and Neoplatonic principles. The EMERALD TABLET—that which is above is like that which is below—contains the true cosmology, expressing the CORRESPONDENCES binding the celestial world and the earthly

world together. The true alchemist is one in whom the spiritual descends into the material, creating a unity, or *vinculum,* which has the power to hold all celestial influences.

Ashmole believed in the transmuting powers of the Stone but held that its true power and purpose lay in spiritual transmutation, not changing base metals into GOLD and SILVER. He said:

> And certainly he to whom the whole course of Nature lies open, rejoyceth not so much that he can make Gold and Silver, or the Divells to become Subject to him, as that he see the Heavens open, the Angells of God Ascending and Descending, and that his own Name is fairely written in the Book of Life.

He upheld the principles of natural magic. He considered medicine to be an Hermetic art linked to SOLOMON and MOSES, who, along with HERMES, are the only ones ever to have fully understood the nature and powers of the Stone. The Stone, he said, bears a relationship to SCRYING crystals, such as the one used by JOHN DEE and EDWARD KELLY for contacting angels. Ashmole believed in an invisible angel scrying stone that:

> hath a Divine Power, Celestiall and Invisible, above the rest; and endowes the possessor with Divine Gifts. It affords the Apparition of Angells, and gives the power of conversing with them, by Dreams and Revelations: nor dare any Evill Spirit approach the Place where it lodgeth.

Ashmole believed strongly in practical astrology—he kept a horoscope of Backhouse—and in the efficacy of magical TOOLS, SIGILS, SEALS, and so forth.

Ashmole also translated *Fasciculus chemicus* by Arthur Dee, published in 1650, a work aimed at ADEPTS. For his own name, he used an anagram, James Hasolle.

astral body An etheric double that is the exact duplicate of the physical body. The astral body is the vehicle for consciousness when projected out of the body (ASTRAL PROJECTION). It also is used in sleep for the experience of dreams.

The astral body has been called by different names. Sylvan Muldoon, who developed an expertise in ASTRAL TRAVEL, called the astral body the soul body and said that it is "the condenser of cosmic energy [which is] the breath of life, omnipresent in every living thing. . . ." In *The Projection of the Astral Body,* Muldoon said:

> The Astral Body, belonging to every person, is an exact counterpart of the perfect physical body of the person. It is composed of fine ethereal matter, and is usually encased in the physical body. In ordinary cases, the detachment of the astral body from its physical counterpart is accomplished only with great difficulty, but in the case of dreams, great mental stress, and under certain conditions of occult development, the astral body may become detached and sent on long journeys, traveling at a rate of speed only less than that of light-waves.

Robert A. Monroe, who became famous for his journeys out of the body, called the astral body the second body. He said that the second body begins as a duplicate of the physical body, but as the astral travel goes on, it begins to deteriorate in form (probably to its essence as energy) but can be rehabilitated into a physical duplicate by thought. His own second body appeared as a bright, glowing outline duplicating the physical and which recorded the sensation of touch and moved according to his thought.

The astral body stays connected to the physical body by a silver cord that resembles an elastic, silver-gray umbilical cord of infinite length. The astral cord has been described by such terms as "a coil of light," "a luminous garden-hose," "a strong ray of light," "a lighted cord," and "a tail of light." When the physical body dies, the cord breaks, and vice versa. The cord possesses its own energy and seems to be alive itself. Australian aborigines liken it to a snake. Muldoon said that severance of the cord results in instant death but that such an occurrence "is almost unheard of" under ordinary circumstances.

The astral body plays a role in vitalizing the physical body. In his own experiences, Muldoon observed that breath travels from the astral to the physical via the astral cord. "You breathe in the Astral, and your heart beats in the Astral. . . . Your physical heart beats because within it the Astral heart beats," he said. "Each breath taken in the Astral can be seen pulsing over the 'cord' and causes a duplicate breath to be taken by the body."

Magical work is performed in the astral body, enabling the consciousness of the magician to access the ASTRAL PLANE and other realities.

FURTHER READING:
Crookall, Robert. *Psychic Breathing: Cosmic Vitality from the Air.* Wellingborough, England: Aquarian Press, 1979.

Monroe, Robert A. *Journeys Out of the Body.* Garden City, N.Y.: Doubleday, 1971.

Muldoon, Sylvan, and Hereward Carrington. *The Projection of the Astral Body.* London: Rider, 1929.

astral guardian   An entity, ghost, or THOUGHT-FORM that guards a place, especially of a sacred nature. An astral guardian is usually invisible but may be perceived psychically.

An astral guardian can be summoned by RITUAL when a sacred place is consecrated. Astral guardians may be spontaneously attracted to a place on their own accord. For example, the ghost of someone who had a strong personal connection to a place while alive may linger to guard and "haunt" the place after death. Thought-form guardians can be created by MAGIC ritual.

ANGELS and FAIRIES also act as guardians of places.

astral light   An all-permeating subtle fluid that interpenetrates all things and is the magical agent of the Formative World. The concept of the astral light was developed primarily by ELIPHAS LEVI.

Levi described the astral light as:

. . . an agent which is natural and divine, material and spiritual, a universal plastic mediator, a common receptacle of the vibrations of motion and the images of form, a fluid and a force, which may be called in some way the Imagination of Nature. . . . The existence of this force is the great Arcanum of practical Magic.

ISRAEL REGARDIE said of the astral light:

Vibrating at another rate of motion than does the gross substance of the physical world, and thus existing on a higher plane, the Astral Light contains the builder's plan or model, so to speak, projected downwards by the Ideation or Imagination of the Father; the plan on which the external world is constructed, and within whose essence lies latent the potentiality of all growth and development.

The astral light has electric, magnetic, and radioactive properties. It is represented in various SYMBOLS, such as the girdle of Isis, the bull-headed SERPENT, the goat- or dog-headed serpent, the OUROBOROS, the emblem of Prudence, the symbol of Saturn, the winged DRAGON of Medea, the double serpent of the CADUCEUS, the serpent in the Garden of Eden, the brazen serpent of Moses entwined around the TAU CROSS or the generative lingam, the Hyle of Gnosis, the double tail that forms the legs of the Gnostic deity Abraxas, the goat of the witches' sabbats, and BAPHOMET.

Madame HELENA P. BLAVATSKY, a founder of the THEOSOPHICAL SOCIETY, associated the astral light with the *ANIMA MUNDI*, or World Soul, in her work *Isis Unveiled:*

The Astral Light or anima mundi, is dual or bi-sexual. The male part of it is purely divine and spiritual, it is the *Wisdom*; while the female portion (the spiritus of the Nazarenes) is tainted in one sense, with matter, is indeed matter, and therefore is evil already. It is the life-principle of every living creature, and furnishes the astral soul, the fluidic *perispirit* to men, animals, fowls of the air, and everything living.

Regardie said that every thought is impressed upon the astral light and that "tradition has it that it coalesces with one of the creatures of that plane and then passes away from our immediate control into this pulsating ocean of vitality and feeling to influence other minds for good or for ill."

Regardie drew correspondences between the concepts of ether and the collective unconscious and the astral light. The astral light also corresponds to the Akashic Records, the records of all things, for all acts, thoughts and emotions of all forms, become impressed upon it for eternity.

Levi said that life can be destroyed by the sudden congestion or withdrawal of the astral light.

FURTHER READING:
Blavatsky, H. P. *Isis Unveiled.* Pasadena, Calif.: Theosophical University Press, 1976.

Levi, Eliphas. *The History of Magic.* 1860. Reprint, York Beach, Maine: Samuel Weiser, 2001.

Regardie, Israel. *The Tree of Life: A Study in Magic.* York Beach, Maine: Samuel Weiser, 1969.

astral plane   A plane of existence that lies next to the physical realm. The astral plane has a high or divine level and a low level. The divine level is solar in nature and contains the blueprint for all things, archetypes, and the living entities formed by thought, ideas, SIGILS, SYMBOLS, NUMBERS, and so forth. The divine level reflects the emotional nature of individuals and the collective and is the realm of the collective unconscious. The low level is lunar in nature, is the abode of certain entities, and is the first sphere of existence reached by the soul after death.

The astral plane is important in magical work. In kabbalistic terms, it corresponds to Yetzirah, one of the Four Worlds. The astral plane is connected to the physical plane (Assiah, another of the Four Worlds) via the subconscious and intuition. EVOCATIONS can be done on the astral plane; some magicians work strictly at this level.

The astral plane has no natural landscape of its own but is white and formless. It consists of astral matter, which can be magically manipulated like a form of proto matter to create THOUGHT-FORMS. Duplicates of everything in the physical world exist on the astral plane and pre-exist everything on the physical plane. In magic, nothing can exist on the physical plane without existing first on the astral plane. Things can be created magically on the astral plane; they eventually will manifest on the physical plane. Things are constantly created on the astral plane by VISUALIZATION, goal-setting, meditation, affirmation, PRAYER, and so on. Without sustained intensity, however, such thought-forms do not last long enough to manifest on the physical plane.

Low-level entities inhabit the astral plane, such as those personalities who often are evoked through talking boards, planchettes, and automatic writing. These entities may engage in masquerades, passing themselves off as something that appeals to the person on the other end.

FURTHER READING:

Ashcroft-Nowicki, Dolores, and J. H. Brennan. *Magical Use of Thought Form: A Proven System of Mental and Spiritual Empowerment.* St. Paul, Minn.: Llewellyn Publications, 2001.

Kraig, Donald Michael. *Modern Magick: Eleven Lessons in the High Magickal Arts.* 2d ed. St. Paul, Minn.: Llewellyn Publications, 2004.

astral projection   The nearly complete separation of consciousness from the physical body in a secondary vehicle, the ASTRAL BODY. Astral projection is used in magical work. Another term for astral projection is *out-of-body experience.*

The leaving of the physical body is often preceded by strong and high-frequency vibrations. Individuals leave through their head or solar plexus or by rising up and floating away. Reentry is accomplished by returning through the head or solar plexus or by melting back into the body.

During astral projection, the physical body appears to be sleeping or in a coma-like state. Consciousness remains connected to the body via the astral cord, which allows the astral body to range anywhere in the universe. The closer the astral body is to the physical body, the thicker the cord. The astral cord is the primary means for return of consciousness to the physical body. According to lore, the cord is severed at death; also, severing the cord causes physical death.

Knowledge that consciousness can separate from the body is ancient and universal. Descriptions are nearly universal and contain many similarities. The ancient Egyptians described a *ba*, or a soul-like essence that manifested itself outside the body during sleep and after death. It was often portrayed as a bird with a human head. The *ka* was the vital essence, more of a collective energy but part of every individual and which could be projected outward. In the Eastern mystical traditions, existence of the astral body is acknowledged, and techniques are taught in the yogas for mastering it. In the West, Plato held that the soul could leave the body and travel. Socrates, Pliny, and Plotinus gave descriptions of experiences that resemble astral projections; Plotinus wrote of being "lifted out of the body into myself" on many occasions. Plutarch described an astral projection that occurred to Aridanaeus in 79 C.E. Saints and mystics recorded astral projection and ASTRAL TRAVEL.

Magical work such as RITUALS can be done on the astral plane by astral projection, using IMAGINATION, VISUALIZATION, and breathing techniques. A SYMBOL, such as one of the TATTVAS, an *I CHING* hexagram, or a TAROT card, is concentrated upon until it turns into a doorway to the astral plane. Such work is never to be undertaken if a person is feeling angry or fearful, for those feelings will be magnified.

Astral projection can be undertaken for the purpose of CLAIRVOYANCE.

FURTHER READING:

Crookall, Robert. *Out-of-the-Body Experiences: A Fourth Analysis.* New York: University Books, 1970.

———. *Psychic Breathing: Cosmic Vitality from the Air.* Wellingborough, England: Aquarian Press, 1979.

Fox, Oliver. *Astral Projection: A Record of Out-of-the-Body Experiences.* Secaucus, N.J.: The Citadel Press, 1962.

King, Francis (ed.). *Ritual Magic of the Golden Dawn.* Rochester, Vt.: Destiny Books, 1997.

Kraig, Donald Michael. *Modern Magick: Eleven Lessons in the High Magickal Arts.* 2d ed. St. Paul, Minn.: Llewellyn Publications, 2004.

Muldoon, Sylvan, and Hereward Carrington. *The Projection of the Astral Blody.* London: Rider, 1929.

astral travel   The ability to visit other and distant locations following an ASTRAL PROJECTION. Astral travel can take place on the earth plane, the ASTRAL PLANE, and other planes of existence. Astral travel is a skill to be mastered in

MAGIC. *Astral travel* is a term sometimes used interchangeably with *astral projection*.

Systematic experimentation in astral travel began in the 19th century. Yram, born Marcel Louis Forhan (1884–1917), was a Frenchman who believed everyone capable of astral travel in a variety of bodies of various densities and dimensions, which he recorded in his book, *Practical Astral Travel*. Yram paid astral visits to a woman whom he later married; the two traveled astrally together and experienced ecstatic astral sex.

Sylvan Muldoon, an American, researched astral travel from 1915 to 1950 as a result of his spontaneous experiences beginning at age 12. Muldoon was a sickly youth who spent a good deal of time in bed. As his health improved, his astral travel became less frequent. Muldoon traveled about in his ASTRAL BODY. He remained on the earth plane. Muldoon believed that DREAMS of falling and flying corresponded to movements during astral travel.

Like Muldoon, Englishman Oliver Fox, born Hugh G. Callway in 1885, was a sickly child. However, he did not experience astral travel until adulthood when he succeeded in inducing it with lucid dreaming. He experimented between 1902 and 1938. Fox's "Dream of Knowledge" was an effort to remain awake mentally while sleeping physically. He published his account in 1920 in the *English Occult Review;* it was later published as a book, *Astral Projection*.

Fox viewed his lucid dreamworld as comparable to the ASTRAL PLANE described in Theosophy. He experienced false awakenings, or waking up in the dream thinking that he was really awake; telepathy with others; religious visions, such as the figure of Christ (which he decided was a THOUGHT-FORM); and precognition (he viewed a test prior to his taking it and correctly saw two questions that would be asked). Fox initially believed that the dream state was essential to have his astral experiences. Eventually he discovered that he could project himself out-of-body without going to sleep but by staying in the hypnagogic state, a drowsy state that marks descent into sleep, which is often filled with fleeting imagery and voices.

Englishman J. H. M. Whiteman claimed to have more than 2,000 episodes of astral travel between 1931 and 1953, which he described in *The Mystical Life* (1961). He had his first experience at age 12 in 1919 without realizing what had happened. Whiteman considered his astral travels as mystical experiences. He sometimes found himself in the form of a child or a female.

In 1958, an American radio and television executive named Robert A. Monroe began to travel astrally spontaneously while relaxed and near sleep. Monroe had incredible experiences not limited to the earth plane but to realms in which he visited the afterlife transition plane. He had contact with discarnate humans and a variety of nonhuman beings. Like Fox, he conducted his own research, which eventually led to several books and the establishment of the Monroe Institute in Faber, Virginia. Monroe began to work with inducement techniques using guided meditation and sound.

Monroe's initial experiences began when he would lie down to go to sleep. Before he reached sleep—when he was in the hypnagogic stage—he would experience a buzzing and a vibrating and feel himself lift out of his body. Like an explorer touching the shores of an unknown land, Monroe explored and mapped this state of being.

He described an astonishing range of experiences, both pleasant and unpleasant, in which he encountered: other intelligences, some of whom provided assistance; demonic or subhuman entities and THOUGHT-FORMS who attacked him; an energy presence of overwhelming magnitude (he does not say whether or not it was "God"); the astral bodies of other humans; sexual experiences on the astral level which produced intense shocks by a seeming interflow of electrons (comparable to Yram's experience). He occasionally had difficulty reentering his body, and on one occasion entered a corpse by mistake.

Monroe identified various levels of reality:

- Locale I is the here-and-now earth plane, people and places in the physical world.
- Locale II is the infinite astral plane, the place where dreams occur and which incorporates our ideas of heaven and hell. Many of the places in this level seem familiar, he said, for they are the creations of consciousness and have been mapped and visited by countless souls. Here are the dead as well as nonhuman entities, many of whom are intelligent and can communicate. The lower reaches are closest to Earth and are populated by unpleasant, demonic entities obsessed with emotional and sexual gratification.
- Locale III transcends time and space and appears to be a parallel universe located on the other side of a hole in the space-time continuum. According to Monroe, there are yet unidentified, higher realms beyond our ability to comprehend.

Monroe observed what many others have before him: that the relaxed state of presleep, the hypnagogic state, is an ideal medium for astral traveling. The key is developing the ability to hold onto lucidity, or awareness, instead of falling asleep. He called this "mind awake body asleep." Monroe later patented a soundwave system called Hemi-Sync (for hemispheric synchronization), which balances the right and left hemispheres of the brain and which is used in the Monroe training systems. While a bodily vibration seemed to be intrinsic to Monroe's own experiences, it does not occur to everyone. Monroe also found that heightened sexual energy often facilitated his ability to astral travel. Monroe noted that fear is the biggest barrier to being able to astral travel: fear of what might happen, fear of death, fear of not being able to reenter the body. Although Monroe did have some experiences with unpleasant entities and a few episodes of difficulty getting back into his body, he believed that overall the astral travel posed no real hazards.

FURTHER READING:

Crookall, Robert. *Out-of-the-Body Experiences: A Fourth Analysis.* New York: University Books, 1970.

Fox, Oliver. *Astral Projection: A Record of Out-of-the-Body Experiences.* Secaucus, N.J.: The Citadel Press, 1962.

Guiley, Rosemary Ellen. *Dreamwork for the Soul*. New York: Berkley Books, 1998.

King, Francis (ed.). *Ritual Magic of the Golden Dawn*. Rochester, Vt.: Destiny Books, 1997.

Monroe, Robert A. *Journeys Out of the Body*. Garden City, N.Y.: Doubleday, 1971.

Muldoon, Sylvan, and Hereward Carrington. *The Projection of the Astral Body*. London: Rider, 1929.

astral vision In MAGIC, a vivid and controlled type of day-dream in which contact is made with the ASTRAL PLANE and the collective unconscious, or the ANIMA MUNDI (World Soul). An astral vision has a three-dimensional reality and is not like a mental picture.

The astral vision is created by concentrating on a SYMBOL. As the astral vision unfolds, the magician sees a figure walking, then sees himself as the figure, and then sees through the figure's eyes and feels sensations through the figure's form. The figure is then controlled and directed to visit places in the astral plane and to meet with other entities.

astrology An ancient system in which the positions of the planets and stars are used for PROPHECY and DIVINATION and which plays an important role in MAGIC and ALCHEMY. Of all the occult arts, astrology is the most enduringly popular, despite attempts by scientists to discredit it.

Astrology is based on a principle attributed to HERMES TRISMESTIGUS: "as above, so below." The ancients viewed Earth and man as microcosms of the universe, a belief that endured through the Renaissance. Astrology holds that the celestial bodies exert forces and exhibit personalities that influence people and events below in the microcosm. These influences may be determined by mapping positions in the sky at various times. The influences also are used to determine the most auspicious times to undertake magical work and alchemical processes.

Historical Overview

The Chaldeans were the first to develop astrology as a divination and magical system in about 3000 B.C.E. Chaldean astrologer-priests observed the heavens from towers called ziggurats. The Babylonians also practiced astrology; either they or the Chaldeans formalized the zodiac, a band of 12 constellations through which the SUN, the MOON, and the planets appear to journey from the perspective of the Earth. The band is the ecliptic, the middle of which is the plane of the Earth's orbit around the Sun. The term *zodiac* was applied later by the Greeks, meaning "circus of animals."

The ancients especially used astrology to forecast auspicious times for matters of state, including war, and to predict weather and natural disasters. Two types of astrology evolved: horary, which determines auspicious times for action, and mundane, which predicts disasters and other great happenings and is concerned with countries, races, and groups of people.

Astrological arts have been practiced around the world. Chinese astrology was documented as early as 2000 B.C.E. The emperor was considered the high priest of the heavens and made sacrifices to the stars to stay in harmony with them. The four corners of the emperor's palace represented the cardinal points in space, the equinoxes and the solstices, and he and his family moved from one corner to another as the seasons changed. The ancient Indians also used astrology, and the ancient Mayans calculated the times for BLOOD sacrifices based on the stars. The Chinese and the Indians provided the sources for Tibet to create its own system of astrology and the devising of astrological almanacs. The ancient Egyptians did not practice a Chaldean form of astrology, though they gauged seasons by the stars. Egyptian astrologer-priests maintained mythological calendars that instructed people in how to behave.

The Greeks loved astrology and democratized it, moving it out of the exclusivity of the royal court and into the hands of the masses. The Chaldeans actually were the first to observe relationships between the positions of stars and planets at the time of birth and a person's subsequent destiny. The horoscope, the celestial picture of the moment of birth, was used extensively by the Greeks for personal matters. Thus a third type of astrology, natal, evolved. PYTHAGORAS, Plato, and Aristotle were among the many great philosophers who accepted the influence, but not the rule, of the stars upon life on Earth below. The Greeks believed that astrology could reveal favorable and unfavorable times for taking certain actions but could not guarantee success.

The Romans imported astrology from Greek slaves circa 250–244 B.C.E., contributing the names of the planets still used in modern times. Astrologer fortunetellers, many of them fraudulent, became so popular in the Roman Empire that they were driven out by decree in 139 B.C.E. by Cornelius Hispallus. But astrology was already too popular, and it regained its influence in all classes of Roman society. Augustus was the first emperor to become an open believer in astrology.

One of the most important astrological books in history was written by Ptolemy, a Greco-Eygptian astronomer who lived circa 140–200 C.E. and devised the Earth-centered Ptolemaic system of the universe. *Tetrabiblios* (*Four Books on the Influence of the Stars*) created the foundation on which astrology still rests.

Astrology suffered under Christianity, despite the lore that the three magi, Persian astrologer–wise men, were guided by a star to find the infant Jesus. In 333, Emperor Constantine, a Christian convert, condemned astrology as a "demonic" practice. St. Augustine, one of the early fathers of the church and the bishop of Alexandria, also denounced it. The church replaced astrology and other pagan seasonal practices with Christian festivals.

While astrology withered in the West, it continued to flourish in the East and the Islamic world. IBN SINA (Avicenna), 10th-century Persian alchemist and philosopher, refuted it, however, but it remained firmly entrenched in royal courts and society.

Beginning in about the 12th century, Arab astrology found its way back into the West through Spanish kabbalists. By the time of the Renaissance, most great scientists, alchemists, astronomers, physicians, and philosophers studied and accepted astrology. PARACELSUS related astrology to alchemy and medicine, advising that no prescriptions be given without consulting the heavens. He believed that the human body is a constellation of the same powers that forms the stars. He associated certain metals with the planets and formulated TALISMANS out of metal disks, which were stamped with planetary SYMBOLS and forged under astrologically auspicious times. Astrology was taught in universities and was tolerated by the church.

The Renaissance was astrology's last association with science in the West. In 1666, the prestigious Academy of Sciences was created by Jean-Baptiste Colbert, minister to Louis XIV, and it omitted astrology from the disciplines. The discoveries of science in the ensuing centuries widened the gap between science and the occult, and astrology fell permanently into the latter—but never out of public favor. It remains a favored tool for prediction, personal fortune, and relationships, and it is even used on past-life regression and in counseling.

The Horoscope

The horoscope (Greek for "I look at the hour") is the chief component of natal astrology, which predicts the general course of a person's character and destiny throughout life based upon the positions of stars and planets at the exact time and place of birth. The oldest-surviving horoscope is Babylonian, circa 410 B.C.E.; another found in Uruk, Chaldea (now Iraq), dates to 263 B.C.E.

The Greeks believed astrology should be available to all, not just the royalty. Greek astrologers used the time, the date, and the place of birth to cast a chart of the heavenly configurations at that moment. Their system is still in use.

The most important factor in a horoscope is the sun sign, which is the constellation or sign of the zodiac occupied by the Sun at the time of birth. The sun sign indicates overall personality traits. Each sign is ruled by one or two planets and is ascribed certain positive and negative personality and character traits. The beginning of the zodiac is figured from the sign in which the Sun rises on the first day of spring. Some 2,000 years ago, the beginning sign was Aries. Due to precession, a gradual shift of the Earth's axis, a slippage of one sign occurs approximately every 2,000 years, and the vernal equinox is now in Pisces.

The second most important feature in a horoscope is the ascendant or rising sign, which reveals character, abilities, the manner of self-expression, and one's early environment. The third most important factor is the moon sign, which reveals one's emotional nature.

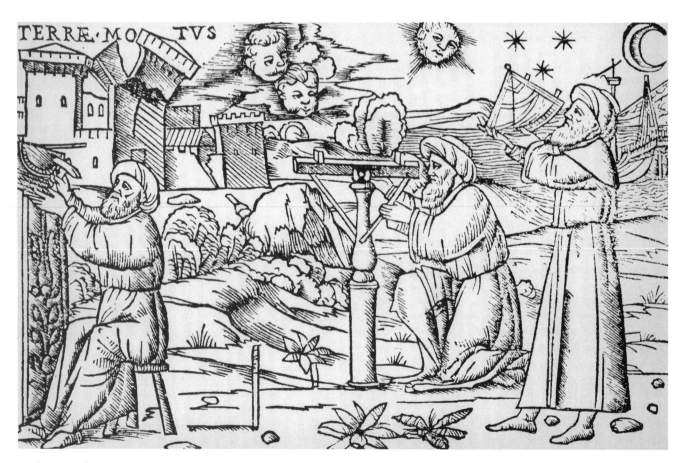

Arabian astrologers, in In Somnium Scipionis, *by Macrobius, 1513. (Author's collection)*

Astrologer casting a horoscope, in Utriusque Cosmi Historia, *by Robert Fludd, 1619. (Author's collection)*

The horoscope is divided into 12 houses, each of which governs a different facet of life, such as money, relationships, career, creative expression, intellect, and so on. The position of the Sun, the Moon, and the planets at the time of birth determines the celestial influences that act on each of these houses, creating a host of strengths and weaknesses.

Most astrologers say a horoscope is not predestination but is a guide to potentials, opportunities, and timing. It does not determine career and marriage choices but points out tendencies and abilities that may be maximized or changed. Astrologer Dane Rudhyar called astrology "the algebra of life" and said that "The stars impel, they do not compel."

While anyone can draw up a horoscope from a birth date, a time, a place, and an astonomical ephemeris, skill and knowledge are required to properly interpret the chart. An astrologer considers hundreds of planetary configurations and relationships. Many astrologers use psychic abilities in their work.

Most Eastern astrologers and an increasing number of Western astrologers use the actual positions of the zodiac as the basis for their computations; they are called sidereal astrologers or siderealists. Those who prefer to use the ancient positions are called tropical astrologers or tropicalists.

Astrology and Jung

Astrology interested CARL G. JUNG, who sometimes consulted the horoscopes of his patients to search for insights into their inner potentials and latent problems. Jung believed that astrology, like alchemy, springs from the collective uncon-

scious, a layer of consciousness deep below waking thought which unites all human beings and is a symbolic language of psychological processes that unites the inner and outer worlds. Astrology is synchronistic, Jung said. Whatever is born or done has the quality of that moment in time.

Jung's curiosity about astrology especially was aroused by astrological and alchemical correspondences to marriage. When astrologers examine the horoscopes of two individuals for signs of compatibility, they look closely at the relationships among the positions of the Sun, the Moon, and the ascendant, that is, the sign that is rising on the horizon at the time of a person's birth. Conjunctions—the proximity of two planetary bodies, usually in the same sign—can signal harmonies that will help a relationship thrive through the years. Thus, if one partner's sun sign is Taurus and the other's moon sign is Taurus, that means their sun and moon conjunct. Other signs for happy relationships are conjunctions of both moons and conjunction of the moon and the ascendant. Unless there are astrological peculiarities, these conjunctions indicate a harmonious, complementary balance between the partners. An astrological tradition dating to the time of Ptolemy holds that at least one of these conjunctions—Sun/Moon, Moon/Moon, or Moon/ascendant—is required for an enduring marriage.

Jung undertook a study of the horoscopes of 483 married couples, randomly collected, to see how often these conjunctions appeared. The results showed an unusually high number of all three possible conjunctions. Jung examined the horoscopes in batches. The first batch of 180 marriages (360 horoscopes) revealed 10.9 percent with Sun/Moon conjunctions—a probability of 1 in 10,000. The second batch of 220 marriages (440 horoscopes) revealed 10.9 percent of Moon/Moon conjunctions—another probability of 1 in 10,000. The third batch of 83 marriages (167 horoscopes) revealed 9.6 percent Moon/ascendant conjunctions, or a probability of 1 in 3,000.

The probability that all three conjunctions would show up in the horoscopes studied was 1 in 62,500,000. Jung said that marriage is such a complex relationship that one would not expect it to be characterized by any one or several astrological configurations. Nonetheless, the improbability of the high incidence of these three conjunctions in the sample group being due to mere chance was so enormous that it necessitated taking into account the existence of some factor responsible for it: perhaps synchronicity, or "meaningful coincidence." Somehow, persons who were compatible according to their horoscopes had found each other and married. (Jung offered no comment upon the happiness or stability of the marriages in his astrological study.)

Although his results appeared to validate astrology, Jung said they did not. In his monograph, *Synchronicity: An Acausal Connecting Principle* (1960), he said that the astrological correspondences simply existed "like any other agreeable or annoying accident, and it seems doubtful to me whether it can be proved scientifically to be anything more than that."

Astrology and Science

Astrology usually fails scientific tests. Astrologers asked to match people to birth charts usually score no better than chance, sometimes worse. In tests where false birth information is given, the horoscopes produced often describe the individuals in question just as well as their real charts.

One scientific anomaly in support of astrology is the "Mars effect," discovered by Michel Gauquelin, a French psychologist. In 1949, Gauquelin began work to disprove astrology. While he did disprove much of traditional astrology, some of his findings proved to be startling in their support of astrology. He examined the horoscopes of 576 French physicians and found, to his surprise, that more were born within the two hours of the rise and culmination of Mars, Jupiter, and Saturn than could be explained by chance. Intrigued, Gauquelin extended his research to sports champions and found that they tended to be born after the rise and culmination of Mars. His findings became known as the Mars effect.

Gauquelin's findings were replicated by other researchers, much to the dismay of some scientists. A petition of protest signed by 192 persons, including Linus Pauling, Sir Francis Crick, Fred Hoyle, and B. F. Skinner, appeared in the *Humanist*. The petition asserted that acceptance of astrology "only contributes to the growth of irrationalism and obscurantism." It called for a challenge to "the pretentious claims of astrological charlatans." The controversy helped spawn the formation of the Committee for the Scientific Investigation of Claims of the Paranormal (CSICOP) in Buffalo, New York. In 1981, CSICOP attempted to replicate Gauquelin's work with the intent of proving it false. Instead, CSICOP validated it. The organization allegedly then falsified results and published them. A scandal erupted when the matter was exposed by Dennis Rawlins, a former CSICOP member, in *FATE* magazine.

Gauquelin pursued further research, collecting more than 50,000 character traits of successful persons in 10 occupations. Results were similar to the Mars effect. He concluded that the findings do not demonstrate that planets and stars directly influence a person but that a sort of cosmic biology is at work, including genetic heredity. He observed, as did French astrologer Paul Choisnard at the turn of the 20th century, that children often are born with the same sun, moon, or rising sign as a parent. The effect is doubled if both parents share the same attributes. Furthermore, Gauquelin theorized that the unborn child may be reacting to cosmic influences when it chooses the moment of birth. The increase of Caesarian birth and artificial inducement of labor obliterates this cosmic biology.

The Mars effect does not seem to apply to ordinary people, however, only to superachievers. Since charts show only potential, only the very successful exhibit the typical traits ascribed to planets and signs, Gauquelin opined. He also found there are no "typical" astrological profiles of the insane and criminal types.

FURTHER READING:
Gauquelin, Michel. *Birth-Times*. New York: Hill and Wang, 1983.

———. *Dreams and Illusions of Astrology*. Buffalo, N.Y.: Prometheus Books, 1979.
Jung, C. G. *Synchronicity*. From *Collected Works* vol. XIII. 1952. Reprint, Princeton, N.J.: University of Princeton Press, 1973.
Rudhyar, Dane. *The Astrology of Personality*. 2d ed. Garden City, N.Y.: Doubleday, 1970.

AUGMN A mantra created by ALEISTER CROWLEY that he said was the magical formula of the universe. Crowley believed that the sound vibrations of AUGMN were so powerful that a magician who mastered them would be able to control the forces of the universe.

AUGMN is an expansion of the most sacred Hindu mantra, Om, which is an expression of the Supreme Reality and is the sound from which the universe was created. The Buddhist mantra "Om mani padme hum," meaning "O, Jewel of the Lotus, Amen," or "The Supreme Reality (is the) lotus jewel of Oneness," is an AMULET against evil and bad luck, as well as for religious and spiritual purposes.

Augurello, John Aurelio (1441–1524) Italian alchemist who tried to impress Pope Leo X with his knowledge of ALCHEMY.

John Aurelio Augurello was born in Rimini, Italy, in 1441. He distinguished himself as a professor of belles lettres in Venice and Trevisa. Fascinated by alchemy, Auguerello prayed earnestly to God to be given the secret of the PHILOSOPHER'S STONE. He spent all of his money on alchemical equipment and supplies but failed in his efforts. When he had no more money with which to continue his work, he conceived of an idea to extract a grant of funds from Pope Leo X. He composed a mediocre poem, "Chryospeia," in which he pretended to know the secret of transmutation, and dedicated it to the pope. Leo, being an astute judge of poetry, was most unimpressed by the poem, and he also disapproved of alchemy in general. When Augurello petitioned him for money, Leo—with great ceremony—presented him with an empty purse.

Augurello never achieved his dream and died in extreme poverty at age 83 in 1524.

augury A type of DIVINATION involving the interpretation of signs in nature. Augury is based on the belief that spirits or the divine inhabit everything in the natural world and can reveal divine will concerning human decisions and actions.

Augurs study and interpret cloud formations, eclipses, weather conditions, the behavior of animals and birds, and other things found in the natural world. Sometimes the behavior of people are augured as well. Such signs are called auspices, which reveal divine favor.

Augury was especially important in ancient Rome, where it was viewed as a science. The Romans adopted augury from the Etruscans. At first an oral tradition handed down through generations grew in importance and became institutionalized. During the Roman Republic, augurs taught and practiced at formal colleges. They were instrumental in determining the auspices for matters of state such as elections, ceremonies, and war declarations. Their readings were kept in secret archives. The augurs assisted priests in conducting ceremonies. They were responsible for keeping the Sibylline books, a collection of prophecies made by ORACLES.

Roman weather augurs were blindfolded to do readings and thus relied on their intuition and psychic ability. They would travel to a site with a magistrate and listen as the magistrate described what he saw in nature. They would then give their interpretation.

One of the most important auspices was lightning, which the Romans considered to be direct communication from the primary god, Jupiter. Where lightning appeared in the sky determined whether the auspices were good or bad. The most auspicious lightning appeared in the northwest, followed by the east. Lightning in the west was a bad sign, and the worst of all was the northwest.

Roosters were favored for animal augury. A circle was drawn in the dirt and marked into pie sections, with a letter of the alphabet in each section. Feed was scattered over the circle. The augur asked a question and then watched as a rooster ate his way around the circle, thus spelling out the answer.

Roman augurs eventually were superseded in importance by haruspices, diviners who examined the entrails and livers of sacrificed animals.

Many people in modern times practice informal augury when they look to signs in nature to help them with decisions and for validation. The flight of a certain bird overhead, the appearance of a certain animal—these may have personal meaning for the individual. Such auspices today are often regarded as synchronicity, but in earlier times were forms of divination.

Types of Augury
Dozens of methods of augury have been developed, involving everything imaginable in natural phenomena and objects—even features of the human body. Some common and unusual ones are:

Aeromancy: the observation of atmospheric phenomena

Alectromancy: the eating patterns of roosters

Aleuromancy: the swallowing of special wheat or barley cakes by the guilty

Alphitomancy: the swallowing of special wheat or barley cakes by the guilty

Amniomancy: the condition of a child's caul at birth

Anthropomancy: the behavior of dying sacrificial humans

Apantomancy: the meeting of animals

Armomancy: haphazard appearances of objects

Aspidomancy: trance utterances while sitting on a shield in a magic circle

Astragalomancy: the casting of marked knucklebones

Austromancy: the observation of winds

Axinomancy: the balancing of a stone on a red-hot axe

Belomancy: the observation of the flight of arrows

Bibliomancy: random consultation of biblical passages

Botanomancy: the burning of briar or vervain branches

Capnomancy: the observation of smoke in the wind

Catoptromancy: staring into a lens or a magic mirror

Causimomancy: the casting of objects into a fire

Cephalomancy: the boiling of a donkey's head

Ceromancy: the shapes formed by melted wax dripped into water

Chalcomancy: the tones made by striking copper or brass bowls

Cheiromancy: the study of the lines on the hands and the shapes of the hands

Chresmomancy: the utterances of a person in a frenzied state

Cleidomancy: a pendulum of a key on a string suspended from a virgin's third finger

Coscinomancy: the spinning of a suspended sieve

Cromniomancy: the growth of special onions

Crystallomancy: the appearance of images on a crystal or shiny surface

Cylicomancy: the appearance of images on water in a vessel or hole

Cubomancy: the use of thimbles

Dactylomancy: the use of rings made according to planetary auspices

Daphnomancy: the sound of burning laurel leaves

Empyromancy: observation of objects placed in sacrificial fires

Felidomancy: the behavior of cats

Floromancy: the study of flowers and plants

Gastromancy: the reflections of lighted torches on a round glass filled with water

Geomancy: the patterns of dirt, sand, or pebbles cast on the ground

Gelomancy: the interpretation of hysterical laughter

Gyromancy: the mutterings of people exhausted by wild dancing

Halomancy: the casting of salt into a fire

Haruspicy: the examination of the entrails and livers of sacrificed animals

Hepatoscopy: "Liver gazing," the examination of the livers of sacrificed animals

Hippomancy: the gait of horses in ceremonies

Hydromancy: the appearance of images on still water

Ichthyomancy: the examination of living and dead fish

Lampodomancy: the observation of the flames of lamps

Lecanomancy: the whistling of precious stones dropped into water

Libanomancy: the observation of the smoke of incense

Lithomancy: the reflection of candlelight in precious stones

Macharomancy: the observations of swords, daggers, and knives

Margaritomancy: the use of enchanted pearls

Metopomancy/metoposcopy: the examination of lines in a person's forehead

Moleoscopy: the examination of moles on the human body

Molybdomancy: the noises of drops of molten lead cast into water

Myomancy: the sounds, actions, and sudden appearances of rats or mice

Nephelomancy: the movements and shapes of clouds

Oenomancy: the color, appearance, and taste of wine

Oenisticy: the observation of the flight of birds

Oinomancy: the use of wine

Omphalomancy: the study of one's own navel

Oneiromancy: the interpretation of dreams and night visions

Onychomancy: the reflection of sunlight on fingernails

Ophiomancy: the study of serpents

Ovomancy: the shapes formed by egg whites dropped in water

Pegomancy: the examination of spring water

Phrenology: the examination of the contours of the human skull

Phyllorhodomancy: the sound of rose leaves clapped against the hands

Physiognomy: the examination of facial features

Podomancy: the examination of soles of the feet

Pyromancy: the patterns of smoke and flames of a fire

Scapulomancy: the markings on the shoulder bones of animals

Sciomancy: the size, shape, and changing appearance of shadows of the dead

Selenomancy: the phases and appearances of the Moon

Sideromancy: the shapes formed by dropping dry straw onto a hot iron

Splanchomancy: the entrails of sacrificed humans

Sycomancy: the drying of fig leaves

Tasseomancy/tasseography: the patterns of tea leaves in the bottom of a teacup

Transataumancy: the events seen or heard accidentally

Tyromancy: the coagulation of cheese

Uromancy: the inspection of urine

Xylomancy: the appearance of fallen tree branches or the positions of burning logs

Zoomancy: the reports of imaginary animals and monsters

FURTHER READING:
Grillot de Givry, Emile. *Witchcraft, Magic and Alchemy.* New York: Houghton Mifflin, 1931.
Mysteries of the Unknown: Visions and Prophecies. Alexandria, Va.: Time-Life Books, 1988.
Spence, Lewis. *The Magic Arts in Celtic Britain.* Van Nuys, Calif.: Newscastle Publishing, 1996.

Avicenna   See IBN SINA.

Awenydhon   See ORACLE.

Azoth   In ALCHEMY, a name for MERCURY, especially the hypothetical "mercury of the philosophers," or the spiritual essence of mercury. Azoth is a corruption of the Arabic word for mercury, *al-zauq.* It was considered to have great occult powers because it contains both the first and last letters of the Greek, Roman, Hebrew, and Arabic alphabets.

Azoth also is a name for CELESTIAL DEW.

A woodcut of PARACELSUS shows him holding a round-headed staff bearing the name Azoth.

Babako In Vodoun, the feared loa or spirit who is regarded as the chief of evil MAGIC. Babako is considered to be extremely difficult to control once evoked, and he is not reliable to follow instructions. His TALISMAN features two broken crosses and a bolt of lightning.

Babalon See CROWLEY, ALEISTER; PARSONS, JOHN WHITE-SIDES.

Bacon, Roger (1214–1292) The earliest alchemist in England, known as Doctor Mirabilis. Roger Bacon was a philosopher, a genius, and a scientist far ahead of his time, anticipating by centuries the inventions of airplanes, automobiles, powered ships, and suspension bridges. He reconciled the Julian calendar, though the changes were not instituted until much later. Though his work influenced the development of gunpowder, spectacles, and the telescope and led to advancements in astronomy, his unusual gifts earned him persecution. His importance in ALCHEMY may be inflated, for many of his ideas were derivative or vague, and Bacon was seldom mentioned among great alchemists through at least the 17th century.

Bacon was born in 1214 near Ilcester in Somerset, England. He was a quick student. He entered the Order of St. Francis and studied at Oxford and in Paris, applying himself especially to mathematics and medicine. He returned to England and continued his studies, learning several languages—Hebrew, Latin, and Greek—and philosophy.

In about 1247, Bacon read *The Secret of Secrets,* a spurious work on the occult attributed to Aristotle. Prior to that, Bacon had evidenced skepticism about alchemy, stating in lectures that transmutation of metals was not possible based on philosophical grounds. *The Secret of Secrets* stimulated his interest in medicine, ASTROLOGY, alchemy, and MAGIC, and he began a search for a universal science that would integrate all things.

His interest in alchemy was philosophical, and he especially saw it as important to religion and salvation. Medicine combined with morality and alchemy could increase longevity by several centuries. Astrology explained the correspondences among the body, the humors, the ELEMENTS, the stars, and the PLANETS. All this ultimately was significant to religion, for it could explain the composition of human bodies before the Fall of Adam and Eve and also explain how the souls of the damned would be tortured in hell. In a commentary on *The Secret of Secrets,* Bacon said that God wishes for humanity to be saved and provides through revelation the knowledge by which salvation can be obtained. Christian morality is key to longevity and to the success of science.

Bacon was interested in showing that natural materials could be employed to create what appeared to be magic, that is, the marvelous inventions of future machines that he envisioned. He said that a person who has purified his or her body by alchemy could create a magical MIRROR for PROPHECY and DIVINATION. He called this mirror *Almuchefi* and said that it had to be made under the proper astrological auspices.

He was critical of ALBERTUS MAGNUS, saying he lacked the proper perspective to understand the whole of things and was fundamentally ignorant of the principles of alchemy.

Despite Bacon's religious convictions, his contemporaries reacted to his unorthodox views by shunning him and his works; his own Order of St. Francis banned his books from their library. In 1278 Bacon was imprisoned and was forced to repent and to leave his order. In 1292 he was set free, and he returned to Oxford. He died soon thereafter and was buried at the Greyfriars Church of the Franciscans in Oxford.

Several centuries later, the demonologist Johann Weyer accused Bacon of practicing black magic and collaborating with DEMONS. Bacon's enchanted mirrors, said Weyer, would be used by the Antichrist to perform lying MIRACLES.

Many of Bacon's works were never published and remain in manuscript form. His most important alchemical work, *Speculum Alchimiae,* was published posthumously in Lyons, France, in 1557. Like other great scientists and alchemists of his and later times, spurious works were attributed to Bacon's authorship. Among them is *Radix Mundi,* which makes a case that the secret of Hermetic philosophy can be found in the four ELEMENTS.

FURTHER READING:

Brehm, Edmund. "Roger Bacon's Place in the History of Alchemy," *AMBIX,* vol. 23, part 1, March 1976. Available online. URL: http://www.levity.com/alchemy/rbacon.html. Downloaded March 30, 2005.

Holmyard, E. J. *Alchemy.* New York: Penguin Books, 1957.

Waite, Arthur Edward. *Alchemists Through the Ages.* Blauvelt, N.Y.: Rudolph Steiner Publications, 1970.

Baka   An evil loa or god in Vodoun who can only be evoked and commanded by the most powerful magical adepts, a *houngan* or *mambo.* Baka is summoned to CURSE others with misfortune, havoc, and death. He is appeased by BLOOD SACRIFICES of a black rooster or a black goat or sexual play with a virgin. In such appeasement RITUALS, the priest takes the role of the *loa.*

Banishing Pentagram   See PENTAGRAM.

Baphomet   The SYMBOL of the satanic goat. Baphomet is portrayed as a half-human, half-goat figure, or a goat head. It is often misinterpreted as a symbol of WITCHCRAFT. Baphomet has also been called the Goat of Mendes, the Black Goat, and the Judas Goat.

The origin of the term *Baphomet* is unclear. It may be a corruption of *Mahomet* or *Muhammed.* The English occult

Baphomet, by Eliphas Levi, in Ritual of Transcendental Magic. (Author's collection)

historian Montague Summers suggested that it was a combination of two Greek words, *baphe* and *metis,* or "absorption of knowledge."

In the Middle Ages, Baphomet was believed to be an idol, represented by a human skull, a stuffed human head, or a metal or wooden human head with curly black hair. The idol was said to be worshiped by the ORDER OF THE KNIGHTS TEMPLAR as the source of fertility and wealth. In 1307 King Philip IV of France accused the Order of the Knights Templar of heresy, homosexuality, and worshiping this idol and anointing it with the fat of murdered children. However, only 12 of the 231 knights interrogated by the church, some under torture, admitted worshiping or having knowledge of the Baphomet. Novices said they had been instructed to worship the idol as their god and savior, and their descriptions of it varied: It has up to three heads and up to four feet; it was made of either wood or metal or was a painting; it was gilt.

In 1818 idols called heads of Baphomet were discovered among forgotten antiquities of the Imperial Museum of Vienna. They were said to be replicas of the Gnostic divinity, Mete, or "Wisdom."

The best-known representation of Baphomet is a drawing by the 19th-century French magician, ELIPHAS LEVI, called The Baphomet of Mendes. Levi combined elements of the TAROT Devil card and the he-goat worshiped in antiquity in Mendes, Egypt, which was said to fornicate with its women followers—just as the church claimed that the devil did with witches. Levi's Baphomet has a human trunk with rounded, female breasts, a CADUCEUS in the midriff, human arms and hands, cloven feet, wings, and a goat's head with a PENTAGRAM in the forehead and a torch on top of the skull between the horns. The attributes, Levi said, represented the sum total of the universe—intelligence, the four ELEMENTS, divine revelation, sex and motherhood, sin, and redemption. White and black crescent moons at the figure's sides represent good and evil.

ALEISTER CROWLEY named himself Baphomet when he joined the ORDO TEMPLIS ORIENTIS, a sex magic order formed in Germany at the turn of the 20th century.

The Church of Satan, founded in 1966 in San Francisco, adopted a rendition of Baphomet to symbolize satanism. The symbol is a goat's head drawn within an inverted PENTACLE, enclosed in a double circle. In the outer circle, Hebraic figures at each point in the pentagram spell out *Leviathan,* a huge water serpent associated with the devil.

See also BARDON, FRANZ.

baptism A SYMBOL of an INITIATION or death and rebirth, especially of a spiritual nature. Baptisms also may represent becoming aware of one's own "dirt" and removal of projections of the Shadow. Baptisms are featured in some magical RITUALS of initiation to a new state of consciousness, power, and being.

Baptisms have different meanings according to the ELEMENTS:

- Baptism by water represents an immersion in the unconscious and emotions. This is a cleansing and dissolving process. In myth, baptism by water is the creation of a new personality on a higher plane. In ALCHEMY, it is dissolution: a rejuvenation of spirit, energy, and viewpoint that transcends the ego. (See BATH.)
- Baptism by wind (air) represents a blowing away of chaff; air represents the involvement of the intellect.
- Baptism by fire represents a purging or burning away of what is no longer needed.

Baptism by BLOOD is comparable to baptism by fire since both blood and fire are symbols of intense purging. Blood has the additional dimension of redemption, as seen in Christ's sacrifice of his own blood in order to redeem humanity. Psychologically, baptisms by either fire or blood refer to the ordeal of enduring intense affect that taxes the ego. Successfully enduring this ordeal results in a refinement.

barbarous names Corrupted NAMES of deities used in magical INVOCATIONS and EVOCATIONS. Barbarous names sound like the originals and carry the same magical force.

Barbarous names have been used since ancient times, especially in INCANTATIONS in which the original language was not understood.

Some barbarous names originated in Hellenistic Egyptian magic. An example of barbarous names comes from a Graeco–Egyptian magical text called the *Harris Magical Papyrus:*

> Adiro–Adisana! Adirogaha–Adisana. Samoui–Matemou–Adisana!
> Samou–Akemoui–Adisana! Samou–deka! Arina–Adisana! Samou–dekabana–adisana! Samou–tsakarouza–Adisana! Dou–Ouaro–Hasa! Kina! Hama! (Pause.) Senefta–Bathet Satitaoui–Anrohakatha–Sati–taoui! Nau–ouibairo–Rou! Haari!

Barbarous names were integrated into Jewish, Hellenistic, Gnostic Essene, and Christian lore and magic. They acquired importance in the Western magical tradition, appearing in the ENOCHIAN MAGIC of JOHN DEE and EDWARD KELLY.

Barbarous names were especially emphasized by ALEISTER CROWLEY for their power to raise the consciousness of the magician in performing a RITUAL. Crowley said that "long strings of formidable words which roar and moan through so many conjurations have a real effect in exalting the consciousness of the magician to the proper pitch. . . ."

FURTHER READING:
Crowley, Aleister. *Magic in Theory and Practice.* 1929. Reprint, New York: Dover Publications, 1976.

Barbault, Armand See VEGETABLE GOLD.

Bardon, Franz (1909–1958) Czech occultist, Hermetic ADEPT, and magician whose work has influenced magical methods and practices. Franz Bardon is widely regarded as one of the most knowledgeable occultists of the West.

Life
Bardon was born on December 1, 1909, in Katherein, near Opava, Czechoslovakia. His father, Viktor, was a devout Christian mystic. Bardon's devoted student and secretary, Otti Votavova, encouraged the legend that Bardon was not born as an infant but was a highly evolved Hermetic adept who entered the Earth plane in 1924 by coming into the body of the 14-year-old boy known as Franz. In popular New Age terminology, this would make him a "walk-in." His purpose was to aid and initiate his father, who was stuck in his spiritual development.

As Franz Bardon, he was the oldest of 13 children. He attended public school and then apprenticed as an industrial mechanic in Opava. He married a woman named

Marie. In the 1920s and 1930s, he gained recognition as a stage magician in Germany; his stage name was Frabato the Magician.

His ordinary life masked a remarkable occult life. Bardon formulated his own system of magic and developed alchemical recipes for medicine purported to have amazing powers of healing. His work shows influences by ALEISTER CROWLEY, FRANCIS BARRETT, ELIPHAS LEVI, and the Tibetan occultism of ALEXANDRA DAVID-NEEL.

After the Nazis gained power, they persecuted members of FREEMASONRY, the ORDO TEMPLI ORIENTIS, and other MAGICAL LODGES and orders. Hitler and some of his friends reportedly were members of the Thule Order, the external organization of some Tibetan black magicians. According to Votavova, they also were members of the FOCG or 99 Lodge, which Bardon later described in his autobiographical novel, *Frabato the Magician*. Bardon maintained that he was never a member in any magical lodge or order; however, according to some sources, he was a member of the Fraternity of Saturn, a German order important in the early 20th century.

To avoid notice by the Nazis, Bardon urged a student and friend, Wilhelm Quintscher, to destroy all their correspondence. Quintscher failed to do so, and in late 1941 or 1942, he and Bardon were discovered and arrested. In prison, they were tortured and whipped. Quintscher broke down and uttered a kabbalistic formula to immobilize the torturers. The Nazis were able to break the SPELL and then shot him to death in retaliation.

Hitler offered Bardon a high position in his Third Reich in exchange for Bardon's magical help to win World War II. Hitler also wanted Bardon to reveal the identities and locations of the lodges that were part of the legendary 99 Lodge of adepts. Bardon refused and was severely tortured. He was subjected to operations without anesthesia and was confined in iron balls and chains.

Bardon was interred in a Nazi concentration camp for three and a half years. In 1945, he was sentenced to death, but the prison was bombed to ruins before the sentence could be carried out. Russian fellow prisoners helped him escape from the ruins. Bardon hid until the end of the war, when he made his way back to Opava.

According to Votavova, Bardon used his magical abilities when the war was over to discover that Hitler had survived and fled the country into hiding. He said Hitler underwent magical operations to alter his appearance so that no one would ever recognize him.

After the war, Bardon worked as a naturopath and graphologist and resumed his occult study and writing. He is said to have cured cancer. His work was published beginning in 1956, which drew attention to him, and people sought him out for healing. He also came to the attention of the repressive communist Czech regime, which discouraged occult work.

Bardon was arrested in Opava on March 28, 1958, during a communist purge. According to Votavova, he was accused of being a spy for the West; however, other accounts say he was accused of making illegal medicines, that he was accused of not paying taxes on the alcohol used for his medicines, or that he said treasonous things about his country in a letter he sent to Australia.

He was imprisoned for about four months and then suddenly died on July 10, 1958, under "unusual circumstances" in a prison hospital in Brno, Czechoslovakia. It has been speculated that he committed a sophisticated suicide. Bardon was severely ill for the last years of his life, suffering from obesity, blood pressure problems, and pancreatitis. Supposedly he could not use his advanced powers of healing and psychic ability to heal himself because doing so was forbidden by karmic laws. Three days before his death, he asked his wife Marie to send to him "speck," or fat bacon, which could have compromised his health because of his pancreatic condition.

He was rumored to have discovered the ELIXIR OF LIFE. His body was dissected twice, adding fuel to those rumors. Bardon's occult, magical, and alchemical books and manuscripts, along with his magical talismans, amulets, and rings, were confiscated by authorities and were never returned to his family.

Works

Bardon is renowned for four books. His first, *Initiation into Hermetics,* published in 1956, is his most impressive, comprehensive, and influential. In it, he puts forth an energetic model of the magical universe, drawing on Hermetic and Eastern philosophies. In Part I he presents his theory, and in Part II he presents a 10-step program of mental, physical, and psychic training. He called all of his disciples *magicians*, the word being "a symbol of the deepest initiation and the highest wisdom."

According to Bardon, the cause of all things existing is the AKASHA, an Eastern term for what the alchemists called the QUINTESSENCE, or fifth ELEMENT or power. In Bardon's universe, electric and magnetic fluids are comparable to yin and yang. Electric fluids (masculine, or yang) are warm, positive, and red in color, and magnetic fluids (feminine, or yin) are cool, negative, and blue in color. Together they make up the vital power or life force, which Baron Karl von Reichenbach earlier called the "od" or "odyle" force. Bardon occasionally used von Reichenbach's term *od*. According to Bardon, every part of the body is governed by either electric or magnetic energy or is neutral. Disease arises when imbalances occur.

Bardon said that the human being is superior to all spirits, including ANGELS and DEMONS, because a human is tetrapole, or four-pole—that is, composed of all four elements. Each element has its own energetics, and a magician must learn how to balance his or her own elements before proceeding any further in magical training. Failure to learn this results in failure in magical work and is hazardous to the magician. The harmonizing and balancing of inner elements is accomplished through self-observation, meditation, recording of one's strengths and weaknesses, and remedial measures. This enables the magician to have control over the beings of the elements and ELEMENTAL realm.

Other instructions address proper concentration and breathing, including a special breathing through the skin; VISUALIZATION and element manipulation; RITUALS; levitation; ASTRAL TRAVEL; development of psychic abilities, such as CLAIRVOYANCE and clairaudience; use of magic MIRRORS for astral travel and healing; gaining access to higher spiritual levels; and the preparation and use of FLUID CONDENSERS, magical TOOLS for the manipulation of electric and magnetic forces. Bardon provides instructions for "loading" tools with magical energy.

Bardon's second book, *The Practice of Magical Evolution,* is a monumental ceremonial magic GRIMOIRE on the making and use of magical tools, the proper EVOCATIONS of numerous spirits, and the dangers of PACTS with spirits. To evoke a spirit, the magician works in a proper magical environment to create a sphere hospitable to the entity. He enters a trance and projects his consciousness into the sphere and then calls it back. Bardon said that he contacted all of the named spirits himself and omitted many more because he thought they were unsuitable for beginners.

Bardon's third work is *The Key to the True Kabbalah,* in which he gives a unique system based on the SOUNDS of letters of the alphabet. He presents a method of empowering letters and combining them using magical keys to create magical effects.

His fourth work, *Frabato the Magician,* is a novel that at the time of his death was incomplete and consisted mostly of notes. It was fleshed out and finished by Votavova and was revised by the publisher, Dieter Ruggeberg. Votavova vouched that the story was Bardon's own spiritual autobiography, and Ruggeberg vouched for Votavova. According to Votavova, Bardon's prior past life was as Mahum Tah-ta, a Tibetan wise man who lived in the mountains. He also was connected to APOLLONIUS OF TYANA, HERMES TRISMEGISTUS, Lao Tzu (see I CHING), ROBERT FLUDD, NOSTRADAMUS, and COMTE DE SAINT-GERMAIN. According to Ruggeberg, two portraits in the book, of Hermes Trismegistus and Lao Tzu, were painted by Bardon with the help of a magic MIRROR.

The title is Bardon's stage magician name. The story describes his arrival into the body of a 14-year-old boy, his stage magic work, his secret life as an adept in the Brethren of Light BROTHERHOOD, his magical battles with the FOCG black LODGE, his escape from Germany before World War II, and his spiritual mission to provide instruction on Hermetic wisdom. In the novel, Frabato is a great adept who demonstrates feats of real magic in his hugely popular stage magic show. He has refused INITIATION into the FOCG lodge, a black-magic order serving BAPHOMET, whose members gain riches and power with the help of their own personal demon assigned to them. There are 99 members in the lodge and 98 other secret lodges around the world, each with 99 members, all in pacts with demons.

The riches come at great price, for upon death, the magicians must serve the demons. Also, lots are drawn every year, and a member of the lodge is sacrificed to Baphomet. Members who break their oaths of secrecy are executed by magic, as are enemies of the lodge. The FOCG lodge tries to magically destroy Frabato by sending out death rays using a magical instrument called the tepaphone, but he outwits them.

Evocative of the novels of DION FORTUNE—which also contain descriptions of real magic—*Frabato the Magician* has been published with added commentaries and notes.

In 1998, another work, *Questions and Answers,* was published, giving Bardon's thoughts on 185 spiritual questions. The book was compiled by Czech students from his oral teachings.

FURTHER READING:
Allen, Paul. "Did Franz Bardon Commit Suicide?" Franz Bardon Research Website. Available online. URL: http://www.geocities.com/franzbardon/bardonsend.html. Downloaded June 1, 2006.
Bardon, Franz. *Frabato the Magician.* Salt Lake City: Merkur Publishing, 1979.
———. *Initiation into Hermetics: A Course of Instruction of Magic Theory and Practice.* Wuppertal, Germany: Dieter Ruggeberg, 1971.
———. *The Key to the True Kabbalah.* Salt Lake City: Merkur Publishing, 1996.
———. *The Practice of Magical Evocation.* Albuquerque, N.Mex.: Brotherhood of Life, 2001.
"The Hermetic Magick of the Great Magus Franz Bardon." Available online. URL: http://www.glassbeadgame.com/magic.htm. Downloaded June 1, 2006.
Scott, Tim. "Who Was Franz Bardon?" Franz Bardon Research Website. Available online. URL: http://www.geocities.com/franzbardon/timscott.html. Downloaded June 1, 2006.

Barrett, Francis (19th c.) English magician and occultist. Little is known about Francis Barrett beyond his authorship of *The Magus,* a compendium of occult and magical information, published in London in 1801.

A self-described Rosicrucian, Barrett taught chemistry, metaphysics, and natural occult philosophy. He gave lessons in the magical arts from his apartment in Marlebourne. Most of his occult knowledge probably came from books rather than personal experience as a magician. *The Magus* borrows heavily from *Three Books on Occult Philosophy* written by HENRY CORNELIUS AGRIPPA. Barrett also borrowed extensively from the works of PETER OF ABANO, JEAN BAPTISTE VON HELMONT, and other alchemists and occultists. Barrett added new illustrations, portraits of important DEMONS that he may have seen while SCRYING.

Francis Barrett, in The Magus *by Francis Barrett, 1801. (Author's collection)*

Despite its lack of originality, *The Magus* stimulated a revival of interest in occultism; the great occultist ELIPHAS LEVI was influenced by it.

FURTHER READING:
Barrett, Francis. *The Magus.* 1801. Reprint, Secaucus, N.J.: The Citadel Press, 1967.
Encyclopedia of Occultism & Parapsychology. 5th ed. J. Gordon Melton, ed. Detroit: Gale Group, 2001.

basilisk Mythological creature with a fowl's head and serpentine body, important as a SYMBOL in ALCHEMY and in MAGIC.

There are three types of basilisks:

- The first and most deadly is hatched from a hen's EGG by a SERPENT; it has the head of a cock with a toad mouth and the body of a DRAGON with chicken feet, as well as Gorgon eyes that can kill with a glance. This basilisk is about the size of a chicken, has no wings, and has short feathers on its head, neck, and back. The only way to kill it is to make it stare at its own reflection in a MIRROR preferably made of steel.
- The second type of basilisk is made magically with herbs and is venomous.

- The third type is harmless and exists in mines. It has the head and feet of a chicken, a serpent's tail, and beautiful eyes. It is coal black and has shining wings, upon which can be seen veins. Its oil and water are valuable to alchemists, who sometimes find gems inside its head.

The basilisk is a symbol of wisdom and is often shown devouring a human. To the ancients, to be devoured by wisdom means enlightenment, gnosis, and INITIATION into the mysteries. The basilisk also is related to the all-powerful Gnostic god Abraxas, ruler of magic and spiritual powers in the universe, who is portrayed in art as having the head of a cock or lion and the body of a man with legs that end in serpents or scorpions.

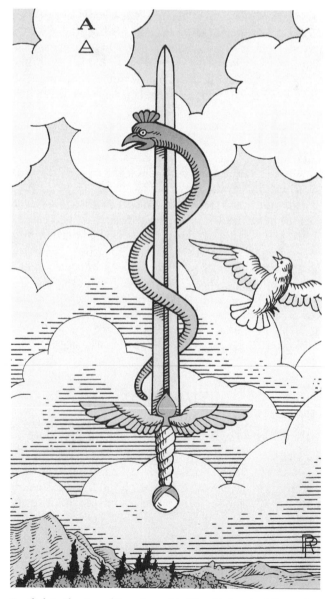

Basilisk in the Ace of Swords card in The Alchemical Tarot, *by Rosemary Ellen Guiley and Robert Michael Place.* (Copyright by and courtesy of Robert Michael Place)

Christianity demonized the basilisk as a SYMBOL of the devil.

bath In ALCHEMY, a simmering heat that is part of the process of creating the PHILOSOPHER'S STONE. The bath is also called the *Bain Marie,* named after MARIA PROPHET-ESSA, who is credited with developing the warming apparatus. The bath is related to BAPTISM.

In alchemical art, naked men and women, SYMBOLS of opposites, are shown together in a bath: Sol and Luna or the King and the Queen, representing the masculine and the feminine, the volatile and the fixed, GOLD and SILVER, or MERCURY and SULPHUR. The bath is cleansing, perfecting, and purifying; the water is rejuvenating and redemptive.

bell See TOOLS.

Bennett, Allan (1872–1923) English occultist and a principal member of the HERMETIC ORDER OF THE GOLDEN DAWN. Allan Bennett was regarded by his peers as having exceptional magical skill, and he was an early teacher of ALEISTER CROWLEY. Bennett's father died when he was young, and he was raised in the Catholic faith by his widowed mother. An asthmatic, he trained as an analytical chemist and worked as an electrical engineer.

Bennett was attracted to occultism and MAGIC and joined the Golden Dawn, rising to the rank of Adeptus Minor by the age of 23. His MAGICAL MOTTO was *Yehi Auor,* "Let there be light." Charismatic, he radiated intense spiritual energy and power to others. He was renowned for his skill in ceremonial magic, notably the EVOCATION of the spirit Taphtharatharath to visible form, a RITUAL that involved used of a pickled snake's head in a "hell broth" of ingredients.

He possessed a BLASTING ROD, a glass rod taken from a chandelier and consecrated with magical power. The rod was mounted in a wooden handle painted with words of power. Bennett changed the words in accordance with the purpose of his magical operations. A Theosophist acquaintance once ridiculed the idea of a blasting rod and found himself paralyzed for 14 hours—an apparent lesson from Bennett.

Bennett helped SAMUEL LIDDELL MacGREGOR MATHERS, one of the founding chiefs, to organize the order's materials, some of which were published later by Crowley as *Liber 777.*

In spring 1899, Bennett met Crowley when the latter was brought to a Golden Dawn meeting by C. G. Jones. Both were impressed with the other. Bennett believed Crowley to be under black magic PSYCHIC ATTACK from a jealous WILLIAM BUTLER YEATS, and the two devised a magical defense.

The friendship with Crowley led to Bennett moving in with Crowley in his London flat on Chancery Lane. While there, Bennett taught Crowley magical skills and shared with him Golden Dawn material—a violation of his INI-TIATION oath, for Crowley had not yet reached Adeptus Minor. It is possible that Mathers may have given Bennett his tacit permission to do so.

Toward the end of 1899, Crowley said that Bennett would die of his asthma unless he moved to a warmer climate. Crowley had ample funds to pay for such a move, but Bennett declined to do so, believing that magical knowledge should be a gift and not purchased. Instead, Crowley evoked the DEMON Buer, whose powers reputedly included healing "all distempers in man." Crowley was assisted in the ritual by Jones. Buer made an appearance but was visible only as a helmeted head and a leg. The ritual failed to aid Bennett's health. Crowley then persuaded one of his former mistresses to give Bennett the money he needed.

Bennett turned to Buddhism and left England to study in the East. He gave up all his possessions and joined a *sangha,* a spiritual community, taking the spiritual names of Swami Maitrananda and then Ananda Metlaya. He traveled to Burma. Years later, he returned to England as a missionary, founding a Buddhist lodge.

Bennett eventually tired of Buddhism and returned to Western occultism. He retired to a small room that was unfurnished save for a table, his blasting rod, a few books, and machinery with which he hoped to establish communication with the ASTRAL PLANE.

Living again in England proved disastrous to Bennett's health, and his asthma worsened, aggravated by his austere and poor lifestyle. He traveled to Liverpool and sought passage on a ship bound for a warmer climate, but the captain refused him because of the severity of his poor health.

Bennett was sent into a fatal tailspin of asthmatic spasms and convulsions. In his final days, he resigned from his Buddhist lodge. He died in 1923, leaving the locations of his manuscripts and other writings known only to a few close friends and associates.

FURTHER READING:
"Allan Bennett." Available online. URL: http://www.golden-dawn.org/biobennett.html. Downloaded June 29, 2005.
King, Francis. *Megatherion: The Magickal World of Aleister Crowley.* New York: Creation Books, 2004.

Bernard of Trèves (1406–1490) Alchemist also known as Bernard Trèvisan, who spent a fortune and endured a life of hardship and poverty in search of the PHILOSOPHER'S STONE. According to lore, Bernard of Trèves finally succeeded in his last years, though he acknowledged that he had wasted much of his life pursuing fruitless experiments. Many of the experiments were bizarre; Bernard was credulous and easily swayed by others. Popular lore held that he had a "devil's bird" as a FAMILIAR. His story is one of the strangest in ALCHEMY, and demonstrates the absurd measures undertaken by many alchemists in their obsession to find the Stone.

Accounts of his life differ. Bernard was born in 1406 in Trèves; some sources say Padua, Italy. His father was distinguished and wealthy and may have been a physician;

some accounts say he was a nobleman, the count of the Marches of Trèves, a title inherited by Bernard. His father died and left Bernard with a large estate, which he applied to alchemy.

Bernard was 14 years old when he began his serious studies of alchemy. With the consent of his family and a grandfather's help, he immersed himself in Arabic alchemical works and was especially enamored with a book written by RAZI, through which he believed he could make GOLD. Bernard set up an alchemical laboratory and followed Razi's work in his efforts. After four years, he had produced nothing and had spent the large sum of 800 crowns (another account claims the cost was 3,000 crowns). He turned next to the works of JABIR IBN HAYYAN (Geber) and spent another two years in his laboratory. Meanwhile, other alchemists and pretenders, attracted to his fortune, insinuated themselves in his good graces to obtain funds. Bernard was generous to a fault, earning the nickname "the good Trèvisan."

Bernard next turned to the dubious works of JOHN DE RUPECISSA and Archelaus Sacrobosco. One of his followers was a Franciscan monk, whose name is not known. The monk cultivated a close friendship with him and shared in the reading of alchemical works. The two became convinced that highly rectified spirits of wine were the ultimate ALKAHEST (dissolvent) needed for the process of transmutation. They set about rectifying alcohol 30 times, until the liquor was so strong that it broke the glass vessels in the laboratory. The effort cost them 300 crowns, took three years, and resulted in nothing. The two then worked with human excrement, spending two years mixing it with various ingredients such as MERCURY, SALT, and lead. This effort also failed.

The monk became disillusioned and drifted away. Bernard took up with a magistrate of the city of Trèves, who was as obsessed as he about finding the Stone. This man assured Bernard that the ocean was the mother of all gold and that sea salt would change base metals into gold and SILVER. Bernard, ever credulous, moved his alchemical laboratory to a house on the Baltic Sea, where he worked for more than a year with salt in various forms and drank salty concoctions. He rectified a sea-salt concoction 15 times during the course of a single year and found no alteration in its substance. None of the experiments succeeded, but the magistrate never became discouraged.

The magistrate then advised dissolving silver and mercury in aquafortis. The dissolutions were performed separately and left for a year; then they were combined and reduced to two-thirds over hot ashes. Twenty-two vials of the concentrated remains were exposed to the SUN and then air in the hopes that they would crystalize. They did not. In all, five years were wasted.

Bernard was not completely disillusioned but pulled back from the work. He was by then 46 years old and desired to travel around Europe. Still, he contacted alchemists wherever he went. In Citeaux, France, he met a monk named Geoffrey Leuvier (also given as Master Geof-frey de Lemorier) who was convinced that the essence of eggshells was crucial to the Great Work. Bernard launched himself into another round of experiments. The two men purchased 2,000 chicken eggs, hard boiled them in water, removed the shells and burned them in a fire, and removed the yolks, which they putrified in horse manure. The putrified yolks were distilled 30 times in an effort to obtain a white and red water. The efforts were unsuccessful, but the two men kept trying variations, giving up after eight years of effort.

Bernard then was persuaded by an attorney from Bergheim (or Bruges), Flanders, that there was a better idea: use vinegar to extract the Stone from copperas (sulphate of IRON). Bernard duly proceeded and nearly poisoned himself in the process. The experiments began with three months of calcining the copperas and then soaking it in vinegar that had been distilled eight times. This mixture was poured into an ALEMBIC and distilled 15 times a day for a year. Bernard's handling of this resulted in a severe quartan fever that lasted for 14 months, nearly killing him.

But his brush with death did not deter him. Upon recovery, Bernard heard that a Master Henry, the confessor to Emperor Frederic III of Germany, had discovered the secret of the Stone. He set off for Vienna, accompanied by five of his acolytes. When he arrived, he invited Master Henry to meet him, and the man came with nearly all the alchemists of the city. Bernard lavishly entertained them all, after which Master Henry confessed that he did not possess the secret, though he had searched for it all of his life and would do so until he died. Bernard immediately saw him as a kindred soul and vowed eternal friendship with him.

The alchemists present agreed to raise 42 marks of gold, which Master Henry said he could increase fivefold in his alchemical laboratory. Bernard, being the richest among them, would of course contribute the most, 10 marks of gold. Master Henry would contribute five, and the others one or two marks each. Bernard's acolytes, who were poor and dependent upon him, would have to borrow their share from Bernard.

The 42 marks of gold were put into Master Henry's furnace along with salt, copperas, aquafortis, eggshells, mercury, lead, and dung. But after three weeks nothing happened, and they gave up. The gold that remained was worth only 16 marks.

Another account says that the alchemists attempted to multiply 42 marks of silver, with Bernard putting up the lion's share of 10 marks. Master Henry assured that the silver would be increased by at least one-third. The silver, along with mercury, olive oil, and sulphur, were dissolved together over a fire while being continually stirred. After two months, the mixture was placed in a glass vial and covered with clay and hot ashes. After three weeks, lead was dissolved in a crucible and added on top, and the entire mixture was refined. But the final results were disappointing, for the silver had not increased at all; it was reduced to one-fourth of its original mass.

Regardless of whether it was gold or silver, Bernard finally became disillusioned. He left Vienna, vowing to give up his alchemical pursuits, but like a gambler addicted to the game, he could not stay away from them for more than two months. He resolved to find an ADEPT who had truly found the secret and would be willing to give it to him.

For eight years, Bernard wandered through Europe, northern Africa, the Mediterranean, and the Middle East. He went to England for four years. His travels cost him most of his remaining inheritance—13,000 crowns. He was forced to sell an estate which provided him with an income of 8,000 florins a year. Besides his travel expenses, he shoveled more money into his furnaces, and he continued to lavish money on alchemists who claimed to have the secret but did not.

Bernard was about 62 by the time he returned home to Trèves, exhausted and nearly penniless. His relatives avoided him, and he was regarded as a madman. Though Bernard had generously given away much of his money, he was too proud to ask for help. He still entertained the dream that someday he would find the Stone and be rich beyond imagination.

He decided to retire to Rhodes and live in anonymity, concealing his poverty. There he met a poor monk. They could afford no equipment, but together they read alchemical treatises. After a year, Bernard met a wealthy man who lent him 8,000 florins, provided he put up as collateral the last remaining property in his estate. This Bernard happily did and resumed once again his alchemical experiments. So obsessed was he that for three years he lived and worked in his laboratory, rarely leaving it and rarely taking the time to keep himself clean. He burned away all of his money but persisted to the end, dying in 1490 in Rhodes.

According to lore, he was 82 (some accounts say 73) when he at last discovered the Stone and spent his remaining years enjoying his wealth. More likely, he died in poverty.

Bernard is credited with writing *La Philosophie Naturelle des Metaux*, his major work, and *Book of Chemistry, Verbum dimissum*, and *De Natura Ovi*. He advocated that alchemists spend much time in meditation and have great patience. Gold, he said, is quicksilver coagulated by sulphur. The secret of the Great Work is dissolution accomplished with the help of mercury.

FURTHER READING:

Mackay, Charles. *Extraordinary Popular Delusions and the Madness of Crowds.* New York: Farrar, Straus & Giroux, 1932.

Waite, Arthur Edward. *Alchemists Through the Ages.* Blauvelt, N.Y.: Rudolph Steiner Publications, 1970.

bewitchment The condition of being under the influence of a SPELL. People, animals, and even objects can be bewitched to behave in certain ways. In folk MAGIC, love bewitchments are common, as are bewitchments to cause farm animals to be unproductive, such as for cows to stop giving milk or chickens to stop laying eggs.

An example of an AMULET spell for protection against bewitchment is the following from Norwegian folk magic:

> Write on a piece of paper the following words:
> "Porto Hamsias F Emanuel F dorenus."
> Carry this with you, always.

Another Norwegian spell for breaking the bewitchment of a love spell is the following:

> In secret, take or clip hair from his or her head [of the one who has caused the bewitching]. Put the hair in your left shoe and walk on it for a time. The unnatural, bewitched feeling usually goes away.

See also ENCHANTMENT; FASCINATION.

FURTHER READING:

Rustad, Mary S. (ed. and translator). *The Black Books of Elverum.* Lakeville, Minn.: Galde Press, 1999.

bilocation The ability to be in two places simultaneously by projecting one's double or astral self to another location. To others, the double may appear as a solid physical form or an apparition but may not behave "normally" or speak.

Bilocation can occur spontaneously or at will. Bilocation at will is a magical skill learned by ADEPTS, and also it is an ability ascribed to spiritually advanced persons such as saints and mystics. For example, Saint Anthony of Padua, Saint Ambrose of Milan, Saint Severus of Ravenna, Padre Pio, Philip Neri, and Alphonsus Maria de' Ligouri are among the many Christian saints said to bilocate. In 1774, Saint Alphonsus Maria de' Ligouri was seen at the beside of the dying pope Clement XIV in Rome; at the same time he was in his monastery cell, a four-day journey away.

Catholicism considers bilocation to be the appearance of a phantasm, a spiritual body that can be in many places simultaneously. In Eastern traditions such as yoga, bilocation is one of the advanced supernormal powers of the adept, acquired through meditation and the channeling of *prana,* the universal life force, through the chakras of the body and its aura.

Magical adepts learn how to bilocate by using the force of WILL and mental thought to project out of the body, usually to a specific location. RITUALS invoking astrological auspices and spiritual forces may be part of the bilocation process.

In occult folklore, a spontaneous bilocation may be considered a harbinger of death—the imminent separation of the soul from the physical form.

In psychical research, a bilocation observed by others falls into the category of "collective apparition." If there is interaction with others, it is a "reciprocal apparition."

FURTHER READING:

Guiley, Rosemary Ellen. *The Encyclopedia of Saints.* New York: Facts On File, 2002.

Hart, Hornell, and Ella B. Hart, "Visions and Apparitions Collectively and Reciprocally Perceived," *Proceedings of the Society for Psychical Research,* vol. 41, part 130, 1932–33, pp. 205–249.

Myers, F. W. H. *Human Personality and Its Survival of Bodily Death.* 1903. Reprint, New York: Longmans, Green and Co., 1954.

binding spell   See CURSE.

black book   A magical book. In folklore, a black book provides instructions for trafficking with spirits, DIVINATION, and acquiring and using supernatural powers. In some cases, possession of the black book itself bestows supernatural powers, wealth, or luck upon its owner. However, use of a black book usually backfires with serious consequences. Some black books are said to be written in BLOOD as a PACT with the devil.

According to a German tale, a black book of unknown origin was passed down through inheritance and came into the possession of some peasants. Its magical powers were released by reading it forward and backward. If anyone failed to read the book backward, the devil was able to take control of them. Once activated, the book enabled people to acquire great wealth and to do terrible things to others without punishment. However, there were consequences to using the black book that caused its owners grief. They tried to get rid of the book but could not do so. They sought

Reading the black book, by van der Wyngaert, 17th century. (Author's collection)

help from a minister, who successfully nailed the book into a drawer. Such a tale serves to demonstrate the power of Christianity over both occult powers and pagan folk magic.

Black books are more than mysteriously empowered things of folklore, however. In practice, many people and families kept black books as guides for living. They included magical cures and healing recipes, PRAYERS, CHARMS, INCANTATIONS, blessings, RITUALS for burial, seasonal and agricultural rites, techniques for divination, and ways to ward off evil and bad luck and attract good luck. The material is a mixture of old folk ways and lore and Christian elements. Some black books credit their origins to Cyprianus of Antioch (Saint Cyprian), who lived in the fourth century C.E. in Turkey. According to lore, Cyprian was a SORCERER who escaped the domination of DEMONS and the devil by making the sign of the CROSS. He converted to Christianity and became a bishop. He ended his life as a martyr.

GRIMOIRES are a type of black book, sets of instructions for ceremonial magical rituals for dealing with demons, ANGELS, and other powers. The *Key of Solomon,* which calls these powers the Animals of Darkness, gives instructions for making a black book. It should be made of virgin paper. The magician should write in it the conjurations of spirits that will summon them at any time. The book should be covered with SIGILS and a plate of SILVER and engraved with PENTACLES. The book can be used on Sundays and Thursdays.

In other lore, sorcerers, witches, and others who possess magical powers are said to keep the secrets of their powers and their SPELLS in black books. In Wicca, the book is called the BOOK OF SHADOWS.

See also SIXTH AND SEVENTH BOOKS OF MOSES; WHITE BOOK.

FURTHER READING:

Butler, E. M. *Ritual Magic.* Cambridge: Cambridge University Press, 1949.

Rustad, Mary S. (ed. and translator). *The Black Books of Elverum.* Lakeville, Minn.: Galde Press, 1999.

black magic   See MAGIC.

Black Mass   A perversion of a Christian Mass for magical or diabolical purposes. Accounts of perverted Christian masses and rituals are documented, though it is questionable how much is fact versus fiction. The church used accusations and torture-induced "confessions" of diabolical rites to persecute heretics and witches. The Black Mass also became a staple of demonic novels and films.

There is no one, definitive Black Mass ritual. Elements include performing the traditional Catholic Mass or parts of it backward; inverting, stepping on, or spitting on the CROSS; stabbing the Host; substituting URINE for holy water or wine; substituting rotten turnip slices, pieces of black leather, or black triangles for the Host; using black CANDLES; and so forth. The service may be performed by a defrocked priest, who wears vestments that are black or the color of dried BLOOD and are embroidered with an inverted cross, a goat's head, or magical symbols.

The magical significance of the Black Mass derives from the MIRACLE of the Holy Mass, the transubstantiation of the bread and wine into the body and blood of Christ. This miraculous or magical power theoretically could be used by a priest for other purposes.

Magical uses of the Mass and alleged perversions of it are almost as old as Christianity itself. In the second century Saint Irenaeus accused the Gnostic teacher Marcus of perverting the Mass. The Gelasian Sacramentary (circa sixth century) documents Masses to be said for a variety of magical purposes, including weather control, fertility, protection, and love DIVINATION. Masses also were said with the intent to kill people; these were officially condemned as early as 694 by the Council of Toledo. Magical uses of the Mass were especially prevalent in the Middle Ages.

In 1307, the ORDER OF THE KNIGHTS TEMPLAR was accused of conducting blasphemous rites—though not called a "Black Mass"—in which Christ was renounced and idols made of stuffed human heads were worshiped (see BAPHOMET). The Templars also were accused of spitting and trampling upon the cross and worshiping the devil in the shape of a black cat. The order was destroyed.

In 1440, the French baron Gilles de Rais was convicted and executed for allegedly conducting Black Masses in the cellar of his castle to gain riches and power. The baron was accused of kidnapping, torturing, and murdering more than 140 children as SACRIFICES.

During the European witch hunts, witches were accused of conducting obscene rites that parodied Christian rites, but they were called sabbats and not Black Masses. The descriptions came either from tortured victims or from zealous witch-hunters, and their veracity must be held in doubt. Historian Jeffrey Burton Russell in *A History of Witchcraft* (1980) states that "the black mass is unknown in historical European witchcraft. . . ."

The first mention of a sabbat in a witch trial was in 1335 in Toulouse. By the 15th and 16th centuries, tales abounded of these infernal rites, said to include roasting and eating of babies, kissing the devil, dancing wildly, fornication, PACTS with the devil, sermons by the devil, and obscene Masses using black or red hosts, urine, and so on. Most of these tales were undoubtedly wildly distorted or entirely fictionalized.

The "Black Mass" reached its organized peak in France in the 17th century during the reign of Louis XIV—a place and time of increasing popularity of magical texts known as GRIMOIRES. Black Mass scandals in France resulted in the execution of dozens of people, including priests. Some of the scandals revolved more around sex and love magic than actual worship of the devil.

Other cases of Black Masses date to the 18th and 19th centuries, but the evidence is unreliable. The Black Mass became romanticized in fiction and film.

Accounts of the Black Mass, whether from historical record or fiction, have inspired fantasy-prone individuals to copy what is supposed to take place. When Anton LaVey founded the Church of Satan in 1966, he did not include the Black Mass among its rituals, as he believed it to be "outmoded."

FURTHER READING:
Guiley, Rosemary Ellen. *The Encyclopedia of Witches and Witchcraft.* 2d ed. New York: Facts On File Inc., 1999.
Russell, Jeffrey Burton. *A History of Witchcraft.* London: Thames & Hudson, 1980.

Black Moon   See MOON.

blacksmiths   Men associated with magical powers. Blacksmiths may have gained their reputation for possessing supernatural powers because of their ability to work with IRON. In African lore, blacksmiths can at will shapeshift into wild animals, especially hyenas, and rob graves at night.

See also SHAPESHIFTING.

Blake, William (1757–1827)   English poet, engraver, artist, and printer whose works reflect his interests in ALCHEMY, MAGIC, and mysticism. William Blake created some of the most beautiful, unusual, and revolutionary art and literature of the early Romantic period. His iconoclastic positions on equality of the sexes and classes, the existence of magic and mysticism, and the right to unfettered sexual expression not only separated him from most of his peers but mark him as still quite controversial today. Blake relied on a mystical knowledge that transcended his era's reliance on reason and Newtonian certainties. Through his visions of angels and the art they inspired, Blake viewed his world as a magical place.

Blake was born to James and Catherine Blake on November 28, 1757, the third of eight children. The Blakes were Dissenters (perhaps Baptists or Moravians), providing the young William with a basis for his mistrust of established religion. A quiet child, he spent much of his time sketching. He also claimed to see ANGELS. William's parents encouraged his artistic talent and apprenticed him to an engraver, Henry Basire. During his apprenticeship Blake copied art and funerary sculpture from many of London's Gothic churches. He finished his apprenticeship in 1779, at which time Blake enrolled at the Royal Academy, but his dislike of the influence of such painters as Sir Joshua Reynolds caused Blake to go it alone. He struggled until 1782, when his friend John Flaxman became his patron, providing Blake with enough support to open his own engraving business and even to marry. Catherine Boucher was five years younger than Blake and illiterate. He taught her to read and write, to color his drawings and engravings, and to sew the bindings. They had no children.

Blake's true vocation was not engraving, however, but writing poetry, which he illustrated. His first small book, *Poetical Sketches* (1783), was published through a conventional printer, but he self-published all his succeeding works. In 1788 Blake developed a process he called Illuminated Printing whereby he could print text and engravings simultaneously, and in 1789 he published *Songs of Innocence* and *Songs of Experience*. The latter contains one of Blake's most famous poems, "Tyger," the first verse of which is familiar to nearly every student of English literature:

> Tyger, Tyger, burning bright,
> In the forests of the night;
> What immortal hand or eye,
> Could frame thy fearful symmetry?

Blake also published *The Book of Thel* that same year.

With *The Marriage of Heaven and Hell* (1790–93), Blake began to define and illustrate his own mythological world, one that reinforced his intense dislike and mistrust of the prevailing orthodoxies of his time: organized religion, divisions by class and gender, and stultification of social conventions. He and his wife Catherine joined the New Church of Emanuel Swedenborg in 1789. Blake was naturally drawn to Swedenborg's gentler, mystical form of Christianity in which truth came from personal revelation, not priestly academics and arguments.

Swedenborg's mystical revelations also influenced— and perhaps abetted—Blake's desire for what the 20th century called free love and the right for adults to engage in sex unfettered by ideas of sin or social ostracism. Additionally, Swedenborg subscribed to the kabbalist belief that God was composed of dynamic sexual potency and that true, perfect union with the Divine was akin to orgasmic intercourse. However, for the true adept such intercourse was an exercise of the mind featuring concentration on the male and female characteristics of Hebrew letters and leading to intense arousal without release, thereby pushing the adept into a trance. (Swedenborg also reportedly enjoyed more conventional sex and had a mistress in London.)

Blake subscribed to the idea of sex as sacred communion, perhaps joining his friend Richard Cosway and other Moravians in ritual nudity and orgiastic ceremonies. Cosway, a painter as well as a magician and a mesmerist, combined his erotic pursuits with drug experimentation and the search for alchemical transmutation. Blake felt that intercourse should be pursued often and gladly as an example of divine union, and he often included sexual imagery—some more explicit than others—in his poetry and art. Blake illustrated that point in *The Four Zoas* (1795–1804), in which he drew a naked woman whose genitals resembled an altar or a chapel with a phallus superimposed like a statue. Blake's libido reportedly

created discord early in his marriage to Catherine; when they could not have children, Blake supposedly proposed bringing a concubine into their home, much as an Old Testament patriarch might have done. But he backed down when Catherine tearfully objected; from all accounts, their marriage was happy thereafter.

One other anecdote about Blake's casual approach to nudity and sex: In 1790 Blake and Catherine moved from London to a house in Lambeth that was graced with a garden and summerhouse. One day when Blake's friend and most important patron Thomas Butts, a government official, called, he found the couple sitting in the summerhouse, "freed from those troublesome disguises" that man had worn since the Fall, according to Butts. Blake heartily welcomed Butts into the garden, saying, "Come in! It's only Adam and Eve, you know!" Before Butts's arrival, Blake and Catherine had been reciting passages from Milton's *Paradise Lost*.

His friendship with Richard Cosway illustrated many of Blake's associations and pursuits. He was a Freemason, as were most of the English intellectuals of the late 18th century, and was an admirer of COUNT CAGLIOSTRO, the flamboyant con artist and Rosicrucian. He sought the alchemical transmutation of base metal into GOLD but came to believe that true transformation meant the release of the illuminated soul from the darkness of matter. He was a Neo-Platonist, a Paracelsian, and an astrologer. He saw visions of angels and imputed contradictory characteristics to them as sacred beings or indifferent bystanders. He studied MESMERISM, magnetism, demonic POSSESSION and EXORCISM, and the healing effects of electricity, even suggesting that electric therapy would cure Catherine's rheumatism. Superstitious, he subscribed to the notion that his ill luck resulted from magical interference. He was a radical and a libertarian, once risking conviction as a traitor for angrily refusing to kowtow to a drunken English soldier during the wars with Napoleon. He chafed against authoritarianism of any kind.

Blake refined his mythology in several more books, such as *Visions of the Daughters of Albion* (1793); *The Book of Urizen* (1794), in which he recasts the Book of Genesis; *The Book of Los* (1795); and his epic poem *Jerusalem*, which he wrote and illustrated from 1804 to 1820. He was profoundly affected by the American and French Revolutions and their democratic ideals and wrote *The French Revolution* in 1791 and *America: A Prophecy* in 1793. He illustrated the Old Testament of the Bible, most memorably the Book of Job, and wrote and illustrated *Milton* (1808). His was a vision of Everyman reborn in freedom and equality.

But his work sold poorly, and when he died in London on August 12, 1827, he was placed in an unmarked grave. Blake's mystical explorations and defiance of authority only really became widely accepted in the latter part of the 20th century to generations that shared his vision of Christianity recast and the lure of a spiritual, philosophical, psychological, and sexual renaissance. Blake summed up the enlightenment of a single, beautiful revelation in the poem *Songs of Innocence:*

> To see a World in a Grain of Sand
> And a Heaven in a Wild Flower,
> Hold Infinity in the Palm of your Hand
> And Eternity in an Hour.

FURTHER READING:

Ackroyd, Peter. *Blake: A Biography*. New York: Alfred A. Knopf, 1996.

"Blake's Life and Times." Available online. URL: www.newi. ac.uk/rdover/blake/blakes_1.htm. Downloaded July 8, 2004.

Guiley, Rosemary Ellen. *The Encyclopedia of Angels*. 2d ed. New York: Facts On File Inc., 2004.

"The Resources of William Blake." Originally published in *Manas*, September 6, 1978. Available online: URL: www. theosociety.org/pasadena/sunrise/28-78-9/ph-mana.htm. Downloaded July 8, 2004.

Schuchard, Marsha Keith. "Why Mrs. Blake Cried: Swedenborg, Blake and the Sexual Basis of Spiritual Vision." Available online. URL: www.esoteric.msu.edu/VolumeII/BlakeTextOnly.html. Downloaded July 8, 2004.

blasting   In folk MAGIC, the power to interfere with or destroy the fertility of man, beast, and crop. According to lore, witches blast as acts of revenge or unprovoked malice. They cause sexual dysfunction, impotency, barrenness, miscarriages, stillbirths, and deformities. Their power to wreak such havoc comes from the devil, who grants it in exchange for service and soul. The destruction of fertility, growth, and abundance is practiced in SORCERY traditions around the world.

In ceremonial magic, blasting is a means of coercing a DEMON to appear and perform tasks on command. Blasting is done with a magical wand called a BLASTING ROD.

blasting rod   According to the *Grand Grimoire*, a rod or wand used by a magician to control spirits, especially unruly ones. The blasting rod is held to have terrible powers over demons that will cause them to obey the magician.

The *Grand Grimoire* describes the blasting rod as a hand wand with forked ends that are capped with magnetized steel. It

> . . . causes the spirits to tremble; which God also used to arm his Angel when Adam and Eve were driven out of the Earthly Paradise; wherewith, finally, he smote the rebellious Angels, precipitating their ambitions into the most appalling gulfs by the power of this very Rod—of this Rod which collects the clouds, disperses tempests, averts the lightning, or precipitates each and all upon any portion of the earth at the pleasure of its director.

In conjuring spirits, the magician threatens to smite Lucifer and all his race with the blasting rod, sending them into the bottomless abyss, if the spirit fails to appear in the MAGIC TRIANGLE without noise or evil smell and answer the magician's questions in a clear voice. If the spirit still refuses to appear, the magician is to:

> . . . smite all the spirits by plunging the forked extremities of your rod into the flames, and be not alarmed in so doing at the frightful howls which you may hear, for at this extreme moment all the spirits will manifest.

If the spirit still refuses, further threats of smiting with the blasting rod are made, along with increasingly powerful INCANTATIONS.

See also BENNETT, ALLAN; GRIMOIRES.

FURTHER READING:

Butler, E. M. *Ritual Magic*. Cambridge: Cambridge University Press, 1949.

Blavatsky, Helena Petrovna (1831–1891)   Author, occultist, psychic, and cofounder of the Theosophical Society. Known as Madame Blavatsky or HPB, she introduced many Western mystics to the Eastern religions and promoted the influence of Hinduism and Buddhism on Hermetic philosophy. By redefining evolution as a multistage spiritual quest for perfection with the One instead of the mechanistic system many believed it to be, Madame Blavatsky gave wisdom seekers a way to reconcile religion and science.

Helena Petrovna was born in Ekaterinoslav (now Dnepropetrovsk, Ukraine), Russia, on July 31, 1831, the daughter of Colonel Peter von Hahn and Helena Andreyevna de Fadayev. Helena Andreyevna wrote novels about the constricted lives of Russian women and was called the George Sand of Russia. She died in 1842 at age 28, and 11-year-old Helena Petrovna and her brother and sister were packed off to live with their maternal grandparents. Helena's grandmother was Princess Helena Pavlovna Dolgorukov de Fadayev, an eminent botanist. Both women exerted tremendous influence on young Helena, supplementing her own tendencies for stubbornness, fiery temper, and nonconformity.

The peasants who served in her grandmother's house regaled Helena Petrovna with stories of the supernatural, and accounts tell of the girl's early psychic abilities. She read the occult books in the library of Prince Pavel Dolgorukov, her great-grandfather, who had been initiated into Rosicrucian Freemasonry under the Rite of Strict Observance in the 1770s. The rite, founded by German baron von Hund around 1754, claimed that its legitimacy came from Unknown Superiors, later identified as descendants of the fabled ORDER OF THE KNIGHTS TEMPLAR; higher degrees involved study of ALCHEMY, MAGIC, and the KABBALAH. Prince Pavel reputedly had met the flamboyant COUNT CAGLIOSTRO, who introduced Egyptian

FREEMASONRY to Europe, and the enigmatic COMTE DE ST. GERMAINE, who allegedly began life in Atlantis and had reincarnated through the lives of many of history's greatest adepts. Freemasonry provided the model for Madame Blavatsky's later conception of the Masters, combining secret societies with a select group of wise teachers.

In 1849 at age 17, reportedly to spite her governess, Helena Petrovna married 40-year-old Nikifor (also spelled *Nicephor*) Vassilievitch Blavatsky, the vice-governor of Erivan province in Armenia. The new Madame Blavatsky abandoned her husband on their honeymoon, never consummating the marriage, and took the advice of an old family friend: travel the world and seek wisdom.

From 1849 through 1858, HPB traveled to Turkey, Greece, North America, and back to the Middle East, sometimes accompanied, sometimes alone—an extraordinary act for a woman in the Victorian age. One of her favorite fellow travelers was Albert Rawson (1828–1902), a young American explorer, artist, and author. Together they studied with a Coptic magician in Cairo. Rawson made many trips to the Middle East, writing about the region's history, geography and language; he also joined several secret Masonic lodges with ties to Muslim groups and was initiated by the Druze sect in Lebanon into the ways of the Sufi. Madame Blavatsky met with her first adept "Master" while visiting London in 1851. She and Rawson toured North and South America, then India, in 1852 but could not enter Tibet, the home of the Masters. She went to America in 1854 before returning to India, and this time traveled to Tibet, Kashmir, and Burma.

Russia beckoned at Christmas 1858 but only long enough to collect Hungarian opera singer Agardi (Agadir) Metrovitch. Rumors had circulated for years that while HPB may not have slept with Monsieur Blavatsky she certainly had lovers and perhaps a son Yuri, who was deformed. Madame Blavatsky apparently adored the boy, who died at age five, but maintained that he was the son of her friends, the Metrovitches. Now she and Agardi were traveling companions, with Metrovitch singing and HPB giving piano recitals in Serbia and Transylvania during 1865. The two also joined Garibaldi's Italian campaign to overthrow the Hapsburgs. In 1868, while visiting Florence, HPB supposedly heard from her future Master, Morya, to meet him in Constantinople and go with him to Tibet. HPB allegedly became a disciple (*chela*), studying with Morya and the other Masters near the grand monastery of Tashi Lhunpo at Shigatse from 1868 until late 1870.

In 1871, HPB and Metrovitch planned a return to Cairo when an explosion on the boat killed Metrovitch. Madame Blavatsky continued on, and in 1872 she and colleague Emma Cutting established the Societé Spirite for the study of occult phenomena. The Societé closed in 1873 under charges of fraud.

At Master Morya's suggestion, HPB traveled to the United States in 1873. She quickly acquainted herself with the occult community in New York, impressing her hosts with some of the psychic phenomena that she used

to perform in Russia: mediumship, levitation, out-of-body projection (see ASTRAL TRAVEL), telepathy, CLAIRVOYANCE, clairsentience, and clairaudience. But the real success of her New York stay was meeting Colonel Henry Steel Olcott (1832–1907), a lawyer, agricultural expert, and journalist, in 1874. Olcott was investigating seances that had purportedly produced material spirits at a farm in Vermont, and initially Blavatsky loyally defended the notion of Spiritual materialization, claiming she had spoken with the spirit "John King." She dropped King soon thereafter, however, concentrating on Masters Serapis Bey and Tuitit Bey. Olcott and HPB became lifelong friends, living together in an apartment dubbed the "Lamasery."

William Quan Judge (1851–96), an Irish-born New York lawyer, frequently joined Olcott and HPB at the Lamasery during the summer of 1875 to discuss occultism. HPB and Olcott often sponsored lectures at the apartment, and after hearing noted Freemason and kabbalist George Henry Felt on September 7, Olcott proposed forming a society for esoteric studies. The group chose the name *Theosophical* (Greek for "wisdom concerning God") because of its Western and neo-Platonist emphasis. The Theosophical Society officially organized on November 17, 1875.

Other, more mundane matters intruded on HPB's pursuits in 1875, however. She received word that her long-forgotten husband, Nikifor Blavatsky, had died, legally freeing her to marry. She quickly wed Russian peasant Michael C. Betanelly but claimed this marriage too was unconsummated. In any case they divorced when HPB learned that Blavatsky was inconveniently alive.

With the formation of the Theosophical Society, HPB settled down with Olcott and wrote *Isis Unveiled* (1877), her first attempt to explain not only Theosophy but the Brotherhood of the Great White Masters, Freemasonry, ROSICRUCIANISM, the kabbalah, Hinduism and Buddhism, and Gnostic Christianity. She explained that all faiths derived from an ancient wisdom-religion: a Hermetic guide to the cosmos, human life, and all of nature, ageless and containing the "alpha and omega" of universal science. HPB posited that each of us contains a "divine spark" from the Great One and that this "spark" descends into the dense matter of a human spirit to the darkest, densest point. At this juncture the divine spark starts its ascension, aided by the teachings of the Masters, until it rises to the highest level and is joined with the One.

The brilliance of this explanation is that there is development both down and up for the soul's enlightenment—an idea not much different from the theory of evolution put forth by Charles Darwin. Madame Blavatsky managed to combine mechanized, cold science with the embracing warmth of religion.

By 1878, the popularity of *Isis Unveiled* had eclipsed the society, which was in danger of collapse. In July, Madame Blavatsky became the first Russian woman to acquire United States citizenship, primarily to keep the British Raj from suspecting her as a spy. She and Olcott returned to India in December, where they gained support for their work and theories from journalist A. P. Sinnett, statesman Allen O. Hume, and various high-caste Indians who applauded HPB's positions on their religions in the face of Western missionary efforts. HPB hooked Sinnett completely, arranging for him to receive letters from the Masters Morya and Koot Hoomi. When Sinnett returned to London in 1883, he became president and secretary of the London lodge of the society.

Olcott and HPB, reveling in their success, moved the socety's international headquarters to Adyar, near Madras, in December 1882 to be nearer the Masters. HPB did not travel throughout most of 1883 but stayed in India writing for the journal *The Theosophist* and honing her philosophies. She and Olcott returned to Europe in 1884 where Theosophical Society lodges were opening in England and Germany.

Then disaster struck. Madame Blavatsky's previous friend Emma Cutting, now Coulomb, and her husband claimed in the press that the Madame was a fraud and had manufactured the Masters' letters and manipulated the various appearances by the adepts. Counteraccusations placed the Coulombs's motivation for exposure on bribes offered by Christian missionaries who were determined to discredit Theosophy. Richard Hodgson, head of the London Society for Psychical Research (SPR), traveled to Adyar and prepared a damning report, accusing HPB of fraud. The Theosophical Society, afraid of further bad publicity, forbade HPB to pursue redress in the courts, and she left India for good in 1885 in poor health and demoralized.

Madame Blavatsky devoted her last years to writing. She began her major work, *The Secret Doctrine,* in 1885 while living in Würzburg, Germany, accompanied by the Swedish countess Constance Wachtmeister. She moved to London in 1887 for the last time, where she released *The Secret Doctrine* in 1888.

This enormous, two-volume work encompassed all of HPB's theories on the evolution of the soul, the source of all religions, karma and reincarnation, and the birth of the cosmos. The first volume, "Cosmogenesis," outlines in detail how a new cycle of the universe begins, descending from spirit to matter and back again. Like human ascension to perfection with the One, the cosmos also must take a seven-stage evolutionary journey to go from matter to spirit. The second volume, "Anthropogenesis," describes people's similar passage, although unlike the universe, people must compensate for their mistakes through karmic reincarnations until they have attained enlightenment. HPB claimed that the process of the soul, from its descent into darkest matter to its ascension to spirit, was not outlined in *Isis Unveiled* because she had later learned these teachings from an ancient Chaldean *Book of Numbers.* Other passages supposedly came from a manuscript called *The Book of Dyzan.* Nevertheless, HPB stressed that the final purpose of a person is the emancipation of his or her soul, and that by many reincarnations and much study, humans can be gods.

ARTHUR EDWARD WAITE, the occultist and head of the HERMETIC ORDER OF THE GOLDEN DAWN after 1903, was attracted to Theosophy but did not always trust HPB's sources or methods. Author and researcher Paul Johnson presented findings in his books *In Search of the Masters: Behind the Occult Myth* (1990) and *The Masters Revealed: Madame Blavatsky and the Myth of the Great White Lodge* (1994) that most of HPB's philosophy was a mash of Freemasonry, Rosicrucianism, the kabbalah, Sufism, and any other esoteric idea that she encountered. And while Hodgson's damaging report from the SPR was retracted years later, a cloud surrounded HPB and the Society.

Madame Blavatsky wrote two more books in 1889: *The Key to Theosophy* and *The Voice of the Silence.* She continued making converts, attracting a young woman activist named Annie Wood Besant. Besant and her friends, supporters of progressive causes, reinvigorated the society when she became its president after Olcott's death in 1907.

By the end of 1890, HPB's health had declined so badly that she could no longer walk and rode in a conveyance that resembled a giant baby's perambulator. She suffered from Bright's disease, heart disease, and rheumatism and had survived influenza. Madame Helena Petrovna Blavatsky died at her London home on May 8, 1891, and was cremated. One-third of her ashes remained in Europe, William Judge took one-third to America, and Annie Besant scattered the remaining third in the Ganges River. Theosophists commemorate her death each May 8 as White Lotus Day.

Madame Blavatsky and Theosophy introduced the West to the ancient Eastern religions and managed to blend their ideas with Western occult thought. Her support of Indian religions and culture energized the Indian nationalist movement; both Gandhi and Nehru looked to Theosophy as a means to rediscover their heritage. Finally, with the assertion that spiritual knowledge could coexist with natural science, Madame Blavatsky was a major voice ushered in the emerging New Age.

See also BROTHERHOODS.

FURTHER READING:

Goodrick-Clarke, Nicholas. *Helena Blavatsky.* Part of the Western Esoteric Masters Series. Berkeley, Calif.: North Atlantic Books, 2004.

Guiley, Rosemary Ellen. *Harper's Encyclopedia of Mystical & Paranormal Experience.* San Francisco: HarperSanFrancisco, 1991.

blood   In MAGIC, a source of considerable power that is unleashed in a RITUAL of SACRIFICE, usually the killing of an animal or a fowl but sometimes a human. Blood shed in a ritual is believed to have magic powers to appease deities and spirits, cause spirits to appear, ensure good harvests and good luck, and to provide a source of magical power to the magician.

Blood sacrifices are part of most GRIMOIRES, derived from ancient Hebrew rituals calling for animal sacrifices to please God.

Animal Blood

Animal blood is used in folk CHARMS and SPELLS. The blood of a black cat is said to cure pneumonia. A black hen beat to death with a white cane will provide blood that can be used in sympathetic magic: Smear the blood on a victim or his clothing to CURSE the victim with a death as agonizing as that of the hen.

ALEISTER CROWLEY sacrificed animals in his magical rituals. In 1909, while working with his assistant, Victor Neuberg, Crowley had a formidable encounter with a DEMON named CHORONZON. The demon was evoked (see EVOCATION) in a ritual that involved slitting the throats of three pigeons and pouring their blood upon the sand.

Human Blood

Some sources of blood are considered to be more powerful than others. Human blood is identified with the soul and carries the greatest power. Ingesting human blood is believed to confer the powers and strengths of the victim upon the conqueror. Possessing few drops of a person's blood gives a witch or a magician power over that person or enables the magician to harness that person's emotional state. By the principles of sympathetic magic, a person may be bewitched or cursed.

The blood of executed criminals is said to be a powerful protector against disease and bad luck because of the energy of resentment and fury that is released on execution. Spectators at public executions such as beheadings sought to obtain the victims' blood on handkerchiefs or bits of cloths for later use in magical rituals.

Human blood also is used to seal PACTS of oath and brotherhood. During the European witch hunts of the Inquisition, it was believed that witches signed blood pacts with the devil to pledge servitude and obedience to him. The magical power of a witch could be neutralized or destroyed by burning her blood in fire—hence the common European method of execution by burning at the stake—or a practice called blooding. The witch was scored above the breath (the mouth and nose) and allowed to bleed, sometimes to death.

Human blood was believed to strengthen the foundations of buildings, and sometimes sacrificial victims were walled up in temples, forts, and other structures.

Menstrual Blood

Menstrual blood, which is linked to the phases of the MOON, is particularly potent. The blood of the Goddess, also called wine, milk, mead, and wise blood, appears universally in mythologies; it is drunk as a charm for wisdom, fertility, regeneration, immortality, and healing. The blood of ISIS, symbolized in an ambrosia drink, conferred divinity on pharaohs. According to ancient Taoism, red yin juice, as menstrual blood was called, conferred long life or immortality.

Menstrual blood has a long history of being feared by men, and proscriptions have been given against associating with, touching, or having sex with menstruating women, for their blood has the power to harm. Ancient Romans believed the touch of a menstruating woman could blunt knives, blast fruit, sour wine, rust IRON, and cloud MIRRORS. In the Old Testament, Leviticus 18:19 states, "You shall not come near a woman while she is impure by her uncleanness to uncover her nakedness." The Talmud instructs that husband and wife are to be sexually separated during menstruation and for a week later to ensure cleanliness.

In Christianity, menstrual blood was believed to spawn DEMONS and to defile altars. Up to the late 17th century, menstruating women were forbidden to partake in communion or in some cases even to enter church.

In folk magic, menstrual blood is believed to be a powerful ingredient in love potions and CHARMS. A few drops of menstrual blood mixed in a man's meal supposedly will secure his undying love. Conversely, menstrual blood also is used in charms to cause impotency.

In many modern magical ceremonies, menstruating women are barred from participation because it is believed their flux interferes with the raising of psychic power and the effectiveness of spells.

FURTHER READING:
Cavendish, Richard. *The Black Arts*. New York: G.P. Putnam's Sons, 1967.
Guiley, Rosemary Ellen. *The Encyclopedia of Witches and Witchcraft*. 2d ed. New York: Facts On File Inc., 1999.

bloodstone   A semiprecious stone once said to be important in ceremonial MAGIC. According to ancient lore, anyone who possesses and carries a bloodstone will be given whatever he asks for. GRIMOIRES instruct a magician to carry a bloodstone, called an *ematille* and purchased from a druggist, as protection against unruly DEMONS they seek to invoke. The *Grand Grimoire* specifies that the magician should use his bloodstone to inscribe his MAGIC TRIANGLE.

See also PACTS.

bocor   A Vodoun witch doctor who specializes in herbal MAGIC. The bocor is sought for counterspells to break CURSES and for protective magic.

Böhme, Jakob (1575–1624)   Bohemian shoemaker and mystic, whose works are important to a spiritual interpretation of ALCHEMY. Jakob Böhme (also spelled Jacob Boehme), called the German Theosopher, was famous in his lifetime and for generations that followed. His works influenced theological and philosophical thinking, espe-

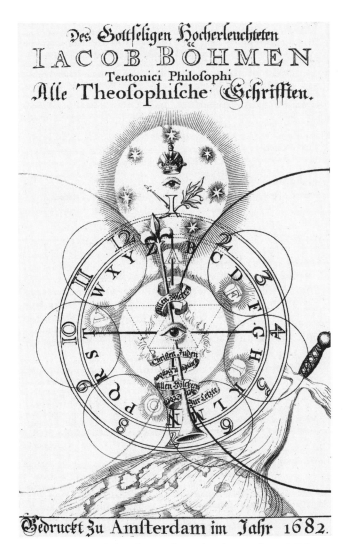

Des Gottfeligen Hocherleuchteten
IACOB BÖHMEN
Teutonici Philofophi
Alle Theofophifche Schrifften.

Gedruckt zu Amfterdam im Jahr 1682.

Frontispiece to Jakob Böhme's Thesophische Werken, *1682.*
(Author's collection)

One day a mysterious man came to the shoemaker's shop while Böhme was there alone. The stranger asked the price of a pair of shoes. At first Böhme was reluctant to give a figure, fearing he would displease his master, but the stranger insisted, and finally the youth gave a price. The man bought the shoes and left. He had gone a short distance down the street when he stopped and called out in a loud voice, "Jakob, Jakob, come forth." Frightened, Böhme ran out in the street.

The stranger looked at him with compelling eyes that seemed to radiate divine light. The man took hold of Böhme's right hand and said, "Jakob, thou art little, but shalt be great, and become another man, such a one as at whom the World shall wonder. Therefore be pious, fear God and reverence his Word. Read diligently the Holy Scriptures, wherein you shall have comfort and instruction. For thou must endure misery and poverty, and suffer persecution, but be courageous and persevere, for God loves and is gracious to thee."

This experience left a deep impression upon Böhme, and he followed the man's instructions. After much study and contemplation, he had a seven-day-long extraordinary experience in which the mysteries of the invisible world were shown to him. The visionary experience was alchemical in nature, cooking within him for years before unfolding in written form. Böhme wrote this description of his vision:

> I saw the Being of all Beings, the Ground and the Abyss; also the birth of the Holy Trinity; the origin and the first state of the world and of all creatures. I saw in myself the three worlds—the Divine or angelic world; the dark world, the original of Nature; and the external world, as a substance spoken forth out of the two spiritual worlds. . . . In my inward man I saw it well, as in a great deep; for I saw right through as into a chaos where everything lay wrapped, but I could not unfold it. Yet from time to time it opened itself within me like a growing plant. For twelve years I carried it about within me, before I could bring it forth in any external form; till afterwards it fell upon me, like a bursting shower that kills where it lands, as it will. Whatever I could bring into outwardness I wrote down. The work is none of mine; I am but the Lord's instrument, with which He does what He wills.

Böhme was a master shoemaker when he began to write philosophical and theological works. He studied with a Lutheran pastor of mystical leanings, Martin Moller of Görlitz. Böhme joined a mystical meditative group organized by Moller called The Conventicle of God's Real Servants. The group and Moller himself encouraged Böhme to explore his own spiritual knowledge obtained through his visionary experiences. He kept careful records.

The experiences would come upon him spontaneously. Böhme would be working away and suddenly would feel the spirit move him. He set aside his work and went into a back room of his cobbler's shop. He waited quietly for the next stage, which was a shift in his consciousness and an out-of-body experience. First the walls became

cially during the late 17th and early 18th centuries. More than any other alchemist, he systematized the SYMBOLS of alchemy. His admirers include ISAAC NEWTON, the English theologian William Law, German philosopher Friedrich W. J. von Schelling, and poets WILLIAM BLAKE and Samuel Taylor Coleridge.

Böhme was born in Altsteidenberg (Old Seidenberg), Upper Lusatia, to a peasant family. In childhood he tended his family's sheep and briefly attended school. At age 13 he went to Görlitz, where he learned the shoemaking trade and became a master by 1599. He married Katharina Kantzschmann, the daughter of a butcher.

According to MANLY PALMER HALL, Böhme's innate CLAIRVOYANCE was opened in a major way one day when he was a young man. Böhme was standing in his kitchen when sunlight struck a pewter plate and temporarily blinded him. From then on, he was able to see all the beings of the invisible universe. Another story tells that Böhme's mystical life was initiated while he was still a young cobbler's apprentice.

dim and then transparent, and the air took on an opaque cloudiness. When the cloudiness cleared, Böhme was in a mystical state surrounded by light. He could see various beings, including ANGELS, and could flow through mysterious vistas. He could look back on his own body sitting in his shop. In this state, Böhme received teachings from the beings through TELEPATHY. After receiving teaching, he heard a voice say, "Jakob, return to your house." Böhme found himself back in his body in his shop. The walls around him turned gray and back to normal.

Another type of experience was his ability to merge with another life-form through his willpower. He could focus on something, such as a plant, and will himself to become one with it, feeling its life force and presence.

Böhme's first work, a philosophical treatise titled *The Aurora,* was completed in 1612. It was immediately popular and was passed among scholars without Böhme's permission. By then, Moller was gone and replaced by a new pastor, Gregory Richter, who was almost the complete opposite of Moller: conservative and orthodox. Richter whipped up heresy charges against Böhme. The Lutheran Church publicly denounced Böhme and had him temporarily banished from Görlitz. The town council seized the original manuscript and forbade him to write. For seven years Böhme complied, keeping his experiences and knowledge to himself.

Böhme resumed writing by 1618. He met his next mentor, Balthasar Walter, a physician and Paracelsian alchemist and probably a Rosicrucian. Walter introduced Böhme to the KABBALAH and alchemy and encouraged him to write. Böhme discovered that the kabbalah was a mirror of his visionary experiences and used it to describe his inner experiences. Through Walter, Böhme met other alchemists.

For the remainder of his life, Böhme worked privately on his writings, producing more than works, including:

The Three Principles of the Divine Essence

The Signature of All Things

Mysterium Magnum

Concerning the Election of Grace

Forty Questions Concerning the Soul

The Way to Christ

The Threefold Life of Man

Publication of these works was hindered by Richter, who continued to hound Böhme as a heretic. Böhme was denounced by the church again and decided to leave town for Dresden to meet with a group of his supporters. While there he fell fatally ill with fever and was carried back home, where he died.

Böhme's supporters wasted no time in getting his works into print throughout Europe and into England. Böhme's entire body of work was translated into English in the 18th century by William Law, an English minister and mystic.

Böhme's principal works concern study of God, the structure of the world and humanity, and theological speculations. He saw the threefold nature of God in the triune components of alchemy, MERCURY, SALT, and SULPHUR. He made a major contribution to the evolution of spiritual alchemy and the departure from emphasis on physical alchemy. He did not claim to communicate with ANGELS, spirits, or saints or to perform MIRACLES that were attributed to him.

His best-known work is *Mysterium Magnum.* To help others understand the salient points in his philosophy, he composed *The Clavis,* or key, a primer to his deeper works.

CARL G. JUNG considered Böhme a modern Christian Gnostic. He noted that Böhme's life cycle, which moves through seven "Forms" or "properties" of Nature, creates a Gnostic mandala holding threefold "hellish" or dark elements (attraction, expulsion, and the wheel of anguish) and "heavenly" or light elements (light or love, intelligible sound, and the all-embracing Reality) in balance with lightning sparking between them, much like the Gnostic deity Abraxas.

In Böhme's visionary scheme, all seven Forms are found within all things, even in God's name. The same forces operating above in the celestial world also operate below, in stones, earth, and plants. The shapes of individual beings are ruled by the angels, who represent the formed powers of God's Word and his Thoughts. Angels help God rule the world. They are brethren to human in looks because they were created in the image of God, with hands, feet, mouth, nose; they eat paradisiacal fruit of the divine power of God's Word.

All of life is endowed by an imprint. The kabbalah calls it Tav, the mark of the Shekinah, or divine presence in the world. Böhme calls it *Signatura rerum,* the seal or signature of the eternal within things.

FURTHER READING:
Hall, Manly P. *Sages and Seers.* Los Angeles: The Philosophical Research Society, 1959.
The "Key" of Jacob Böhme. Translated by William Law. Grand Rapids, Mich.: Phanes Press, 1991.
Stoudt, John Joseph. *Jacob Böhme: His Life and Thought.* New York: Seabury Press, 1968.
Weeks, Andrew. *Böhme: An Intellectual Biography.* New York: State University of New York Press, 1991.

boning   See POINTING.

Book of Shadows   In Wicca, a personal and secret book of RITUALS, SPELLS, Wiccan spiritual laws and beliefs, and magical lore. Material is added as a Wiccan advances in rank. For some practitioners, a Book of Shadows is a magical diary.

According to tradition, covens have a master copy of the coven Book of Shadows, which serves as a guidebook for all members. Personal Books of Shadows are supposed to be destroyed upon a Wiccan's death, but many are kept and passed on as inheritances.

See also BLACK BOOK.

Bornless Ritual   One of the most important God INVOCATIONS in ceremonial MAGIC. The Bornless Ritual is based on Graeco-Egyptian magical writings.

The RITUAL was published in 1852 as *Fragment of a Graeco-Egyptian Work Upon Magic* by Charles Wycliffe Goodwin for the Cambridge Antiquarian Society. E. A. Wallis Budge included part of it in *Egyptian Magic* in 1899. Different versions of it have been written and used in rituals.

The original intent of the Bornless Ritual was EXORCISM. It shows Jewish influence, referring to Moses and the "ceremonies of Israel." It employs BARBAROUS NAMES to command all spirits of the firmament, ether, and the ELEMENTS.

Wycliffe's translation is as follows; some of the original text is missing:

An address to the god drawn upon the letter.

I call thee, the headless one, that didst create earth and heaven, that didst create night and day, thee the creator of light and darkness. Though art Osoronnophris, whom no man hath seen at any time; though art Iabas, though art Iapos, though has distinguished the just and the unjust, though didst make female and male, though didst produce seeds and fruits, though didst make men to love one another and to hate one another. I am Moses thy prophet, to whom thou didst commit thy mysteries, the ceremonies of Israel; though didst produce the moist and the dry and all manner of food. Listen to me: I am an angel of Phapro Osoronnophris; this is thy true name, handed down to the prophets of Israel. Listen to me, ...
.... hear me and drive away this spirit.

I call thee the terrible and invisible god residing in the empty wind,.................... thou headless one, deliver such an one from the spirit that possesses him......................
.... strong one, headless one,
deliver such an one from the spirit that possesses him
....
deliver such an
one..
This is the lord of the gods, this is the lord of the world, this is whom the winds fear, this is he who made voice by his commandment, lord of all things, king, ruler, helper, save this soul
.... angel of
God ....
.... I am the headless spirit, having sight in my feet, strong, the immortal fire; I am the truth; I am he that hateth that ill-deeds should be done in the world; I am he that lighteneth and thundereth; I am he whose sweat is the shower that falleth upon the earth that it may teem: I am he whose mouth ever burneth; I am the begetter and the bringer forth (?); I am the Grace of the World; my name is the heart girt with a serpent. Come forth and follow.—The celebration of the preceding ceremony.—Write the names upon a piece of new paper, and having extended it over your forehead from one temple to the other, address yourself turning toward the north to the six names, saying: Make all spirits subject to me, so that every spirit of heaven and of the air, upon the earth and under the earth, on dry land and in the water, and every spell and scourge of God, may be obedient to me.—And all the spirits shall be obedient to you. . . .

Budge opined that the barbarous names were corruptions of Egyptian words: Osoronnophis was "Answer Unnefer," the god of the dead, and Paphro was "per-aa," or "great house," or "pharaoh." The Greek version of the manuscript contains more barbarous names than are in the early English translations.

Golden Dawn Usage

The Bornless Ritual (the "headless one" became the "Bornless One") was adapted by the HERMETIC ORDER OF THE GOLDEN DAWN but was never an official ritual of the order. Probably it appealed to members who were interested in the initiatory aspects of Egyptian magic drawn from the Egyptian Book of the Dead. When ALEISTER CROWLEY joined the order in 1898, he shared his London flat for a time with member ALLAN BENNETT, who most likely introduced Crowley to the ritual. Crowley was immediately taken with it, and it became an integral part of his magical philosophy and practice.

In 1903 Crowley included a version of the Bornless Ritual with more barbarous names, as the Preliminary Invocation to *The Goetia—The Lesser Key of King Solomon*, an edition of the GRIMOIRE that he commissioned and financed. Crowley used the translation of the *Goetia* done by SAMUEL LIDDELL MacGREGOR MATHERS, though he denounced MacGregor Mathers in his introduction.

In the 1920s Crowley took the Preliminary Invocation and edited and expanded it into the *Liber Samekh*, which later appeared in his book *Magick in Theory and Practice*. Crowley placed a great deal of emphasis on sexual interpretation and on the use of barbarous names of EVOCATION. Crowley's version of the Bornless Ritual invokes the Higher and Divine Genius, or HOLY GUARDIAN ANGEL, and elevates the magician's consciousness to align it with Truth, Light, and the Resurrection and the Life. By performing the ritual, the magician enters a POSSESSION of sorts by the Holy Guardian Angel. The ritual was designed to take place within a Golden Dawn Temple for the Neophyte Grade.

The ritual is intended to deliver an ecstatic experience in which one realizes that he is and always has been the Bornless Spirit. At the end of the ritual, the aspirant realizes he no longer needs to invoke the Bornless Spirit because he is identified with it.

Performing the Bornless Ritual requires a six-month withdrawal from the world. Crowley recommended 11 lunar months in an increasing schedule of devotion that taxes even the most dedicated student:

> Let the Adept perform this Ritual aright, perfect in every part thereof, once daily for one moon, then twice, at dawn and dusk, for two moons, next thrice, noon added, for three moons. Afterwards, midnight, making up his course, for four moons four times every day. Then let the eleventh Moon be consecrated wholly to this Work; let him be instant in continual ardor, dismissing all but his sheer needs to eat and sleep.

ISRAEL REGARDIE, who was Crowley's companion for a time, published the Bornless Ritual in a simple form in his book *The Tree of Life* and another version in his book *The Golden Dawn*. Regardie called the Bornless Ritual "the most devastating and the most rewarding experience of the life-time."

FURTHER READING:

Budge, Wallis. *Egyptian Magic.* 1899. Reprint, New Hyde Park, N.Y.: University Books, n.d.

Regardie, Israel. *Ceremonial Magic: A Guide to the Mechanisms of Ritual.* London: Aeon Books, 2004.

———. *The Golden Dawn.* 6th ed. St. Paul, Minn.: Llewellyn Publications, 2003.

Bottinger, Johann F.   See PUFFER.

Boyle, Robert (1627–1691)   Irish physicist, chemist, and alchemist. Robert Boyle was of noble birth, the 14th child of the earl of Cork who owned Lismore Castle in Ireland. Boyle enjoyed a privileged upbringing and education that included Eton College in England and extensive travel on the Continent.

Unlike most alchemists who carefully guarded their experiments and knowledge, Boyle believed in the free sharing of information. He associated with a group of intellectuals known as the Invisible College, which eventually became the Royal Society of London for Improving Natural Knowledge.

Boyle especially disliked the deliberately obscured language of ALCHEMY and considered it an obstacle to scientific progress. He sarcastically said that the most open statement ever made by an alchemist was *"ubi palam locuti sumus, ibi nihil diximus"* ("where we have spoken secretly, there we have said nothing").

Boyle accepted the conclusion of JEAN BAPTISA VAN HELMONT that water was the PRIMA MATERIA for plants, but he rejected Helmont's extension to minerals and inorganic materials.

Boyle's most famous work is *The Sceptical Chymist* (1661), in which he offered a new definition of the ELE-MENTS to replace the Aristotlean concept of four and the Paracelsian concept of three (see TRIA PRIMA). Rather, he described elements as "certain primitive and simple, or perfectly unmingled bodies; which are not being made of any other bodies, or of one another," and which were of varying sizes and shapes. These independent bodies mixed together to form the "One Catholic Matter" or the PRIMA MATERIA.

Boyle believed in the transmutation of base metals into GOLD and spent years in experimentation of that. In 1676, he presented a paper to the Royal Society about his work with a special form of refined MERCURY that he believed had great powers of transmutation. He also said that he transmuted pure rainwater into white earth through a process of distillation. He reasoned that the agitation of the water caused a sticking together of particles that formed knots and sank to the bottom in a "Powder," or white earth. Boyle further reasons that the same principle applied to the transmutation of base metals into gold. His theories were an inspiration to ISAAC NEWTON.

Boyle's interests in transmutation led him to persuade Parliament to repeal a ban on "multiplying gold" that had been in force since the days of Henry IV.

FURTHER READING:

Coudert, Allison. *Alchemy: the philosopher's stone.* London: Wildwood House Ltd., 1980.

Brahan Seer   See ODHAR, COINNEACH.

Brahe, Tycho (1546–1601)   Danish astronomer and alchemist. Tycho Brahe is best known for his astronomical observations that led to the establishment of a correct model of the solar system. In MAGIC, he is known for a magical calendar of unlucky days, compiled from his astrological work for Holy Roman Emperor Rudolph II.

Brahe was born Tyge Brahe (Tycho is the Latinized form of his first name) to a noble family at Knutsstorps Castle in Skåne. By prior arrangement, his father had agreed to entrust Tycho to his brother, Tycho's uncle, to be raised. But the father reneged, and later the uncle kidnapped Tycho.

The uncle wished Tycho to become a lawyer and sent him at age 13 to the University of Copenhagen to study law and philosophy. While there, Tycho witnessed a partial eclipse of the Sun, and became interested in predicting the motions of the planets. At the time, the Earth-centered model of the solar system endorsed by the Catholic Church was the prevailing view.

At 16, Tycho was sent to study law in Leipzig, but he became obsessed by astronomy instead. He invented equipment that helped him make more accurate observations of the planets and stars.

A quarrel with a student resulted in a fight in which part of Tycho's nose was cut off with a rapier. He had a GOLD and SILVER piece made that he kept pasted over his ruined nose for the rest of his life; it became one of his unusual trademarks.

In 1570, Tycho returned to Denmark and continued his star gazing. In 1572, he observed a nova that enabled him to refine his system of astronomical measurements. His fame spread, and to keep him in Denmark, King Frederick II offered him an entire island, Hveen (Ven), where he could build an observatory and castle. The observatory was named Uraniborg ("Castle of the heavens"). Brahe entertained a constant stream of royal visitors and became rather arrogant, often abusing his tenants. King Frederick died in 1588, and his successor, Christian IV, was not enamored with Brahe. Feeling the chill, Brahe gathered up his equipment, family, and servants and departed in 1597 to travel around Europe. In Prague, Emperor Rudolph II employed him at a handsome salary and offered him the castle of his choice.

Brahe was an adherent of ASTROLOGY as well as astronomy and followed the medical astrology of PARACELSUS. He believed in the CORRESPONDENCES between heavenly bodies and material things and advocated the study of astrology and ALCHEMY together.

Brahe's model of the solar system fell between Ptolemy and Copernicus, but had the Earth at its center. The astronomer Kepler went to Prague to study with Brahe and used his data to confirm a Sun-centered model for the solar system.

On October 13, 1601, Brahe dined with guests at the home of Baron Peter Vok von Rosenberg in Prague. There were numerous toasts of wine. Brahe, out of respect for his host, held his bladder to the point of pain, at which he had to go home. He contracted a severe bladder infection that led to his death on October 24. He was buried as a nobleman in Prague.

During the course of his astrological work for Rudolph II, Brahe compiled a list of extremely unlucky days—so unlucky that the best course of action would be to do nothing at all on those days. The unlucky days are

January: 1, 2, 4, 6, 11, 12, 19	July: 17, 21
February: 17	August 2, 10
March: 1, 4, 14, 15	September: 1
April: 10, 17, 18	October: 6
May: 7, 15, 18	November: 16, 18
June: 6	December: 6, 11, 18

Another calendar, *The Magical Calendar of Tycho Brahe*, is a document of magical and occult symbolism and CORRESPONDENCES, important in the Rosicrucian movement. *The Magical Calendar of Tycho Brahe* was designed by the engraver Theodor DeBry, who worked with ROBERT FLUDD, MICHAEL MEIER, and other alchemists. ELIPHAS LEVI considered the calendar to be one of the most important occult documents of the 17th century.

Brodie-Innes, J. W. (1848–1923) Scottish occultist, lawyer, and author, noted for his involvement in the HERMETIC ORDER OF THE GOLDEN DAWN and the THEOSOPHICAL SOCIETY.

John Williams Brodie-Innes was born in Morayshire, Scotland. He went to Cambridge to study law and then went to Edinburgh to practice as a lawyer after graduation. He participated in Masonic and occult activities in Edinburgh, and in 1884 he founded the Scottish Lodge of the Theosophical Society, of which he became president.

In 1890, Brodie-Innes joined the Golden Dawn, whose MAGICAL MOTTO was *Sub Spe*, "With hope." By 1893, he was Adeptus Minor and had founded the Amen-Ra Temple of the order in Edinburgh. When the Golden Dawn broke apart around the turn of the 20th century, Brodie-Innes sided with SAMUEL LIDDEL MACGREGOR MATHERS. He worked to save the Amen-Ra Temple by joining it to Golden Dawn splinter orders—first the Stella Maututina and then the Alpha et Omega.

In 1911, Brodie-Innes became president of the Sette of Odde Volumes, a bibliophile group in London.

Brodie-Innes's occult interests extended to WITCHCRAFT, Gypsy lore, Celtic lore, and mystical Christianity. He wrote several novels on witchcraft and MAGIC. His book on Christian mysticism, *The True Church of Christ*, was published in 1893. He also wrote numerous articles on occultism.

According to some sources, he taught DION FORTUNE how to use occult power. In turn, Fortune used him as the model for her soul doctor in her fictional work *The Secrets of Dr. Tavener* (1926). Other sources say that the model was Dr. Theodore Moriarty, an occultist and fellow Mason with whom Fortune studied.

FURTHER READING:

Gilbert, R.A., ed. *The Sorcerer and His Apprentice: Unknown Hermetic Writings of S. L. MacGregor Mathers and J. W. Brodie-Innes*. Wellingborough, England: Aquarian Press, 1983.

Richardson, Alan. *Priestess: The Life and Magic of Dion Fortune*. Wellingborough, England: The Aquarian Press, 1987.

brotherhoods Groups of highly evolved entities, both discarnate and incarnate, whose missions are to provide spiritual growth and teachings to mankind throughout Earth's history. Brotherhoods are dedicated to selfless service and manifesting the law of divine love. They carry on most of their work invisibly, contacting only those persons who have advanced to a sufficiently high level of spiritual awareness. When necessary, they incarnate themselves.

One of the best-known brotherhoods is the Great White Brotherhood, the Brotherhood of the Cross of Light within the Circle of Light. The teachings of this brotherhood were publicized by Grace Cooke, a British spiritualist, with the help of her spirit guide, White Eagle, a master of the brotherhood.

According to White Eagle, the Great White Brotherhood has sent messengers to Earth in different ages to teach secret wisdom and help human beings in their search for truth. They come from more advanced planets, incarnating on

Earth as priests and ADEPTS. They have been called Sun-gods, Sun-men, the Illumined Ones, and Ascended Masters.

The Great White Brotherhood is said to exist all over the world and has been present throughout the history of the human race. They were responsible for the great, lost civilizations of Atlantis and Lemuria, the survivors of which went to Egypt, the Americas, Britain, and elsewhere. In the Americas, the brotherhood was given to the Indians. The Master of the Great White Brotherhood is the Christ, also known as Quetzacoatl, who pours out love from the Sun in his heart. The symbol of the brotherhood is a cross within a circle, the SYMBOL of sacrifice and suffering within God's eternal love.

FRANZ BARDON was said to be a high-ranking ADEPT in the legendary Brethren (Brotherhood) of Light, as he claimed in his novel *Frabato the Magician*, which his secretary said was actually his spiritual autobiography. In the novel, the brethren have 99 secret lodges around the world, each of which has 99 members, all of whom are the highest initiates in the cosmic system and masters of the highest state of magical perfection. They are led by a Prime Initiator who has the rank of a mahatma and who possesses knowledge of all cosmic secrets. The Prime Initiator has held his post since the beginning of the world and seldom materializes in a physical body. He does so only when it is of utmost importance and when he wishes to give advice to members. Second in rank are 12 adepts who have taken on the most difficult spiritual tasks. These adepts also seldom materialize in bodies and work in the "Earth Girdle Zone," or ASTRAL PLANE. On average, they may incarnate once every 100,000 years or so. The Prime Initiator and the 12 adepts form a "Council of the Old," which meets regularly to decide the fate of people. Each of the 12 has subordinate to them 72 wise men or illuminated men, each of whom in turn has 360 masters reporting to him. All of these adepts report to a general assembly when one is convened.

FURTHER READING:
Bardon, Franz. *Frabato the Magician*. Salt Lake City: Merkur Publishing, 1979.
Cooke, Grace. *The Illumined Ones*. New Lands, England: White Eagle Publishing Trust, 1966.

Bruno, Giordano (1548–1600)   Italian Hermetic philosopher. Giordano Bruno was influenced by the works of HENRY CORNELIUS AGRIPPA, Pico de Mirandola, and Marsilio Ficino, and he presented a new vision of cosmology during the Renaissance. He was persecuted by the Inquisition.

Bruno was born in Nola, Italy, near Mount Vesuvius, in 1548. At age 15, he entered a Dominican monastery near Naples but had difficulty conforming to their dogmatic ideas. In 1576 he was forced to leave under a cloud of heresy for his unorthodox ideas on the magical art of memory, cosmology, and MAGIC. He traveled around Europe, giving lectures. He was not always welcome.

In 1581 he moved to Paris, where he attracted the favor of King Henri III, who, as a patron of NOSTRADAMUS, appreciated revolutionary thinking. Bruno became known for his knowledge of Egyptian religion and philosophy and soon was the advocate of a reformed religion based on the Egyptian mysteries. He claimed he received divine revelations. He wrote two books on the magical art of memory, including one dedicated to the king, *De umbris idearum* (*On the shadow of ideas*), published in 1582.

In 1583 Bruno went to England to lecture at Oxford. His ideas were not universally well received—for example, he favored a heliocentric solar system, not because it was mathematically correct, but because it fit his magical scheme of things. He wrote, "We are no *more* the center than any other point in the universe." This was a dangerous view during a time when the Ptolemaic view prevailed—that the Earth was the center of the universe, around which all things revolved. He held that humans could enter into a "cooperation" with nature through the power of NUMBERS; geometric figures are numbers made visible.

Like PARACELSUS, Bruno was known for bombast and arrogance, and his satires of fellow academics earned him animosity. He openly argued against the "tyranny of the pope."

Bruno left England and traveled to Germany. From there he returned to Italy. In 1592 the Inquisition arrested him in Venice on charges of heresy. He was imprisoned and interrogated, and finally in 1600 he was condemned to death and burned at the stake.

FURTHER READING:
Yates, F. A. *Giordano Bruno and the Hermetic Tradition*. London: Routledge and Kegan Paul, 1972.

Builders of the Adytum (BOTA)   Mystery school founded by PAUL FOSTER CASE, an American member of the HERMETIC ORDER OF THE GOLDEN DAWN and an authority on the TAROT and the KABBALAH. The Builders of the Adytum (BOTA) is based in Los Angeles.

BOTA has an outer school and an inner school. Students are dedicated to live by following a spiritual path that recognizes kinship with all life, a brotherhood of humanity, and oneness with God. They adhere to seven values:

• Universal peace
• Universal political freedom
• Universal religious freedom
• Universal education
• Universal health
• Universal prosperity
• Universal spiritual unfoldment

The kabbalah and the Tarot are the foundation of BOTA's ceremonial MAGIC. Students pursue transformation of the personality, which enables them to make desired changes in their physical environment.

caduceus A wand entwined by two snakes and topped by wings or a winged helmet. The caduceus is associated with MAGIC, spiritual enlightenment, wisdom, immortality, and healing. The T shape of the caduceus is derived from the tau cross, a T-shaped cross used in the ancient Egyptian and Mithraic mysteries initiations.

The caduceus is most strongly associated with HERMES, the Greek messenger god of magic who flies as fleet as thought. Hermes carries his magical wand when escorting souls to the underworld. Hermes's caduceus is made of olive wood, symbolic of peace and the continuity of life. The wand's shaft represents power; the SERPENTS represent wisdom or prudence; the wings represent diligence; and the helmet represents high thoughts. With a touch of his caduceus, Hermes puts mortals to sleep or raises the dead. He cures any illness and changes whatever the wand touches into GOLD. The Romans, who called Hermes Mercury, viewed the caduceus as a symbol of moral conduct and equilibrium.

The association of the caduceus with GOLD and the powers of transmutation made it a symbol of the PHILOSOPHER'S STONE in ALCHEMY. In alchemy the entwined serpents take on the additional symbolism of masculine and feminine forces, which must be in balance for transmutation to occur.

The caduceus appears in Mesopotamian cultures in about 2600 B.C.E. where its serpents signified a god who cured illness. The association of the caduceus with medicine and health was passed from the Middle East to the Greek culture. Asklepios, the Greek god who heals in dreams, possesses a staff entwined by a single serpent.

In ancient India, the caduceus appeared in temples as a symbol of the four ELEMENTS: the wand (earth), the serpents (fire and water), and the wings (air).

In Yoga, the caduceus represents the transformation of spiritual consciousness through the vehicles of the body's pranic energy system. The wand is the spine, and the serpents are the kundalini force, or serpent power, which resides in the earth and at the base of the spine. When stimulated either through spiritual study or sometimes emotional shock, the kundalini entwines up the spine and flowers with wings at the top of the head. The wings signify the rise of the consciousness through higher planes of awareness.

In FREEMASONRY, the caduceus represents the harmony and balance between negative and positive forces, the fixed and the volatile, the continuity of life and the decay of life.

FURTHER READING:

Guiley, Rosemary Ellen, and Robert Michael Place. *The Alchemical Tarot*. London: Thorsons/HarperCollins, 1995.

Hall, Manly P. *The Secret Teachings of All Ages*. 1928. Reprint, Los Angeles: The Philosophic Research Society, 1977.

Waite, Arthur Edward. *A New Encyclopedia of Freemasonry*. Combined ed. New York: Weathervane Books, 1970.

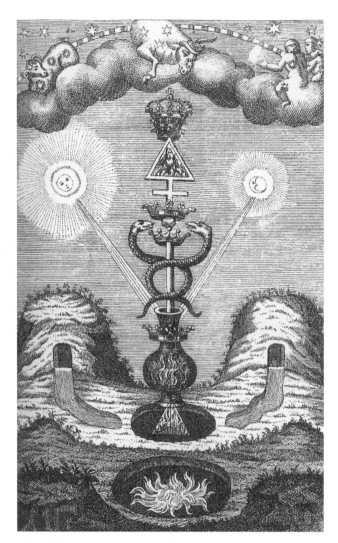

The Philosopher's Stone, symbolized by a bird in a triangle, rests atop the caduceus of Mercury in Le Triomphe hermetique, *by A. T. de Limojon de Saint-Didier, 1765. (Author's collection)*

Cagliostro, Count Alessandro (1743–1795) Italian occultist and alchemist, reputed to be one of the most celebrated magicians of his time. A friend and successor of COMTE DE SAINT-GERMAINE, Count Alessandro Cagliostro was a glamorous figure in the royal courts of Europe, where he practiced MAGIC, psychic healing, ALCHEMY, SCRYING, and other occult arts. He has been called both a fraud and a genuine ADEPT.

Cagliostro was born Guiseppe Balsamo in 1743 in Palermo, Italy, to a poor Sicilian family. Whether or not he was born with psychic talent, he learned as a child how to operate a lucrative fortune-telling business. At 23, he went to Malta, determined to make a name and fortune for himself. There he was initiated into the Order of the Knights of Malta and studied alchemy, the KABBALAH, and the occult. He changed his name to Count Alessandro Cagliostro, borrowing the surname from his godmother. Later, he joined

the Freemasons in England, who had a great influence on his metaphysical beliefs.

Cagliostro spent most of his adult life circulating among royalty in Europe, England, and Russia. In Rome, he met and married Lorenza Feliciani, who became his partner in various occult ventures. According to lore, they practiced crystal gazing, healing by a laying on of hands, conjuring spirits, and predicting winning lottery numbers. They also sold magic potions, the ELIXIR OF LIFE, and the PHILOSOPHER'S STONE. They held seances, transmuted metals, practiced NECROMANCY—Moses was among the spirits of the dead invoked—and cast out DEMONS, and hypnotized people. Cagliostro gained a reputation for accurate fortune-telling, which led to a new name: "The Divine Cagliostro." He also went by the title Marquis di Pellegrini.

His RITUALS were colorful, dramatic, and steeped in a mix of traditions: alchemy, Masonic rites, the Egyptian Cult of the Dead, the KABBALAH, Roman magic, and the Greek Eleusinian mystery cult.

Perhaps because of his success, Cagliostro fell out of favor with the medical community and the Catholic Church. In 1875, he and his wife were victimized in an infamous fraud, the "Queen's Necklace Affair." The two were set up by countess de Lamotte, who swindled 1.6 million francs for a diamond necklace—ostensibly for Marie Antoinette—and accused Cagliostro and his wife of stealing the necklace.

Cagliostro and Lorenza were among those jailed and tried for the fraud. Cagliostro purportedly won freedom for himself and his wife by telling a fantastic story of his life. He said he had been raised in Medina, Arabia, by a man, Althotas, who taught him his occult knowledge. He explained his wealth as coming from the Cherif of Mecca, who mysteriously set up open bank accounts for him wherever he went. He denied being a 300-year-old Rosicrucian and said that he had prophesied that the countess de Lamotte was a dangerous woman.

After they were freed, Cagliostro and Lorenza went to England, where he predicted the French Revolution. But a London newspaper published an expose of Cagliostro's true personal history, and his glittering reputation was destroyed.

Humiliated, he and his wife went to Rome where Cagliostro attempted to create an "Egyptian Freemasonry" order. The church had him arrested and imprisoned for 18 months in Castel San Angelo. Brought before the Inquisition, he was found guilty of "impiety, heresy, and crimes against the church" and was sentenced to death on April 7, 1791. Lorenza was sentenced to life imprisonment in a convent in Rome where she is believed to have died in 1794.

Pope Pius VI commuted Cagliostro's sentence to life imprisonment. He was sent to San Leo where he spent four years in solitary confinement in a subterranean cell. Shortly after being moved to a cell above ground, he died, allegedly of apoplexy, on March 6, 1795. Rumors that he lived and miraculously escaped persisted for years in Europe, Russia, and America.

In the 19th century, a controversial Genevese medium, Helene Smith (real name Catherine Elise Muller), claimed to channel the spirit of Cagliostro while in trance. When the spirit of Cagliostro appeared, Smith's appearance changed markedly to drooping eyelids and a double chin. The spirit used her vocal chords, speaking in a deep bass voice. Most likely, "Cagliostro" was one of Smith's secondary personalities.

FURTHER READING:

Dumas, F. Ribadeau. *Cagliostro*. London: George Allen and Unwin, 1967.

Flournoy, Theodore. *From India to the Planet Mars: A Study of a Case of Somnambulism with Glossolalia*. New York: Harper & Bros., 1900.

McCalman, Iain. *The Last Alchemist: Count Cagliostro Master of Magic in the Age of Reason*. New York: HarperCollins, 2003.

Seligmann, Kurt. *The History of Magic and the Occult*. New York: Pantheon Books, 1948.

Wilson, Colin. *The Occult*. New York: Vintage Books, 1971.

candles   In MAGIC and folklore, lights to attract certain spirits and dispel others. Candles also are associated with ghosts and the dead, DIVINATION of the future, and the finding of buried treasure.

The origin of candles is not known. Beeswax candles were used in Egypt and Crete as early as 3000 B.C.E. Other early candles consisted of tapers made of a fibrous material, such as rushes, that were saturated with tallow.

Ancient peoples observed that candle flames revealed mysterious things. By staring into a flame, one could enter an altered state of consciousness and see gods and spirits or see the future. The late Egyptians of about the third century C.E. used lamps and possibly candles in a magic RITUAL for "dreaming true," or obtaining answers from dreams, especially about the future. The individual retired to a dark cave facing south and sat and stared into a flame until he or she saw a god. He or she then lay down and went to sleep, anticipating that the god would appear in his or her dreams with the sought answers.

Ancients used candles and lamps in religious observances, a practice which the Roman Christian theologian Tertullian vehemently protested as "the useless lighting of lamps at noonday." By the fourth century, both candles and lamps were part of Christian rituals, but it was not until the latter part of the Middle Ages, from the 12th century on, that candles were placed on church altars. The Catholic Church established the use of consecrated holy candles in RITUALS of blessings and absolving sins and in exorcizing DEMONS.

Witchcraft

During the witch hunts of the Middle Ages and Renaissance, inquisitors' handbooks such as the *Malleus Malefi-carum* (1486) prescribed holy candles as among those consecrated objects "for preserving oneself from the injury of witches." Farmers used holy candles to protect their livestock from danger and bewitchment.

According to the prevailing lore during the witch-hunts, witches were said to light candles at their sabbats as offerings of fealty to the devil, who was often portrayed as wearing a lighted candle between his horns. The witches lit their candles from the devil's candle; sometimes he lit the candles and handed them to his followers. Witches also put lighted candles in the faggots of their brooms, which they rode through the air to their sabbats.

It was believed that witches made perverse use of holy candles in putting curses on individuals. According to an English work, *Dives and Pauper* (1536), "it hath oft been known that witches, with saying of the Paternoster and dropping of the holy candle in a man's steps that they hated, hath done his feet rotten of."

Black Magic

Candles made of human fat were believed to contain life energy and supposedly were used in the Black Mass in the 17th century and in other black magic rituals. The *Petit Albert,* an 18th-century GRIMOIRE, claims that a "Magic Candle" made of human tallow would disclose buried treasure. The treasure seeker took the candle into a cave or other subterranean location. When the candle began to sparkle brightly and hiss noisily, treasure was at hand. The nearer the treasure, the more intensely burned the candle, until it went out at the exact spot. Treasure hunters were advised to carry along lanterns with consecrated candles, not only for light but to conjure the spirits of dead men who were said to guard buried treasure. The spirits were to be summoned in the name of God and promised anything to help them find "a place of untroubled rest."

At the turn of the 19th century, FRANCIS BARRETT, author of *The Magus* (1801), wrote that candles made of "some saturnine things, such as a man's fat and marrow, the fat of a black cat, with the brains of a crow or raven, which being extinguished in the mouth of a man lately dead, will afterwards, as often as it shines alone, bring great horror and fear upon the spectators about it."

In Vodoun, black candles rubbed down with the sperm of a black goat are considered to be the most powerful objects for casting a HEX.

The Dead

In folklore, candles have a strong association with the dead. A Jewish custom of lighting candles for the dying and the dead was absorbed into Christian practice. A lit candle placed by the bedside of a dying person is believed to frighten away demons. One Jewish custom calls for keeping a lit candle for a week in the room where a person died, perhaps to purify the air. In American folklore, however, a candle burning in an empty room will cause the death of a relative. Superstitions about candles hold that a guttering candle means that someone in the house is about to die, and a candle that burns blue means that a ghost is nearby.

Wicca and Practical Magic

In some Wiccan rituals, consecrated white candles are placed on altars and at the four quarters of a MAGIC CIRCLE. If a ritual calls for it, candles are placed at the points of a PENTAGRAM. Colored candles are used in many magical SPELLS; each color has its own symbolism and influences.

As part of the preparation for casting a spell, rub a candle with anointing oil while concentrating on the purpose of the spell. The formula of the oil will be determined by the purpose of the spell, or a spell is written on a candle, which is burned.

The following are some of the magical uses of colored candles:

White: Spiritual truth and strength; purity and purification; meditation; attract benevolent spiritual forces; break curses; feminine principle (in ALCHEMY).

Pink: Love and friendship; harmony; entertaining; morality; domestic tranquility; the sign of Cancer.

Red: Sexuality; strength; physical health and vigor; passion; protection; the signs of Scorpio and Aries; masculine principle (in alchemy).

Orange: Courage; communication; solving of legal problems; concentration; encouragement; the sign of Taurus.

Yellow: Persuasion; confidence and charm; aid to memory and studying; the signs of Virgo and Gemini.

Green: Healing; money and prosperity; luck; fertility; the sign of Sagittarius.

Blue: Psychic and spiritual awareness; peace; prophetic dreams; protection during sleep; the signs of Aquarius and Virgo.

Purple: Ambition; ruling authority; reversing a curse; speeding healing in illness; extra power; the sign of Pisces; lavender for the sign of Libra.

Gold: Protection; enlightenment; masculine principle; the Sun; the sign of Leo.

Silver: Intuition; subconscious; feminine principle; the Moon.

Brown: Protecting pets; solving household problems; attracting help in financial crises; the sign of Capricorn.

Gray: Stalemate; neutrality; cancellation.

Black: Loss; sadness; discord; releasement; negativity.

Angel Magic

Colored candles are used in spells involving ANGELS, among them:

Haniel—red and pink
Michael—gold and yellow
Gabriel—white and silver
Raphael—green and orange
Uriel—ice white and ice blue

Case, Paul Foster (1884–1954)   American occultist and founder of the Builders of the Adytum. Paul Foster Case was a gifted musician and charismatic teacher of the Western mystery tradition. He was an advanced member of the HERMETIC ORDER OF THE GOLDEN DAWN and one of the greatest authorities on the TAROT and the KABBALAH.

Case was born in Fairport, New York, on October 3, 1884. His mother was a teacher, and she gave birth to him in the town library where his father worked as head librarian. It was a fitting symbolic beginning, for Case soon exhibited a tremendous thirst for knowledge, especially hidden knowledge, and he learned to read at an early age. At age three, Case exhibited a talent for music, and by age nine was the organist at the Congregational church where his father was a deacon.

Case began to have extraordinary experiences in early childhood, which seemed to him to be real and not imaginary. He also had a marked ability for lucid dreaming and manipulating his dreams. When he was seven, he wrote to author Rudyard Kipling about these "fourth dimensional" experiences. Kipling responded that they were real and not imaginary.

At age 16, Case got the first of what he called directives, cues from the spiritual world for directions that he was to follow. At a charity event where he performed, Case met the occultist Claude Bragdon, who asked Case his opinion about the origin of playing cards. This led Case into a study of the Tarot, and in a short time he had amassed a large collection of books and decks on the subjects. He was fascinated by the archetypal and alchemical symbolism of the cards. His work with the cards opened a distinct inner voice that awakened him to the deeper meanings of the symbols.

Case's reputation for occult knowledge spread, and in New York he was invited to join the Thoth–Hermes Temple of the Golden Dawn (Alpha et Omega) by Michael Whitty, the Praemonstrator. Case accepted and sped through the Esoteric Order. He was initiated into the Second Order on May 16, 1920. His MAGICAL MOTTO was *Perservantia,* "Perserverance." He continued a rapid advancement and within a year succeeded Whitty as Praemonstrator.

Given the political history of the Golden Dawn, it was perhaps only inevitable that Case would run afoul of members. He was widely regarded as the most knowledgeable occultist in New York, but some of his teachings drew criticism. He did not like ENOCHIAN MAGIC and concluded that it was demonic, not angelic. He also discussed sex magic, which was not part of the Golden Dawn curriculum. Case felt that sexual energy had to be redirected to higher centers of the brain in order for expansions of consciousness to occur.

On July 18, 1921, MOINA MATHERS wrote to him about complaints she had received about him. Members complained about his teachings on sex magic and also about his personal relationship with a female member, Lilli Geise. (Case defended the propriety of their relationship. Later he married Geise, and she died several years after.) Mathers asked Case to resign as Praemonstrator, which he did.

Case established his own school, the School of Ageless Wisdom, but it failed within a few years. He left New York for Los Angeles, where he established the BUILDERS OF THE ADYTUM (BOTA), still in existence. Meanwhile, the Golden Dawn suffered from his departure.

Case remarried. He died in 1954 while vacationing in Mexico with his second wife, Harriet.

Case's best known work is *Book of Tokens* (1947) about the Tarot. He also wrote *The True and Invisible Rosicrucian Order, The Masonic Letter G,* and numerous articles.

MANLY PALMER HALL called Case the leading American authority on the Tarot. In his book *The Tarot: A Key to the Wisdom of the Ages* (1947), Case describes the Tarot as "a pictorial text-book of Ageless Wisdom. From its pages has been drawn inspiration for some of the most important works on occult science" beginning with ELIPHAS LEVI'S revival of interest in magic in 1854.

FURTHER READING:
Case, Paul Foster. *The Tarot: A Key to the Wisdom of the Ages.* Richmond, Va.: Macoy Publishing Co., 1947.
"Paul Foster Case." Available online. URL: http://www.golden-dawn.org/biocase.html. Downloaded June 29, 2005.

celestial dew Condensed moisture with alchemical properties. Dew is considered a gift of heaven or the gods, sent down to Earth, and thus has a special purity. In ALCHEMY, dew gathered in the morning is PRIMA MATERIA for the process of making the PHILOSOPHER'S STONE.

PARACELSUS used dew in his medical treatments. He captured dew on plates of glass under various astrological auspices, which he believed imbued themselves into the dew itself. He gave the dew to patients to ingest.

FURTHER READING:
Hall, Manly P. *Paracelsus: His Mystical and Medical Philosophy.* Los Angeles: The Philosophic Research Society, 1964.

ceremonial magic See MAGIC.

Chaldean Oracles Fragmentary Greek magical texts comprising revelations from the gods. The Chaldean Oracles were among the texts important to the HERMETIC

Celestial dew, enriched by the rays of the Sun and the Moon, is collected in dishes, in the Mutus Liber, *attributed to Altus, 1677. (Author's collection)*

ORDER OF THE GOLDEN DAWN and other Western magical traditions.

The texts were written in the second century C.E. by Julianus the Theurgist. They purport to reveal magical teachings based on Platonism, and they were important to Platonic scholars of the day.

chalice See GRAIL; TOOLS.

chaos magic See MAGIC.

charm In MAGIC, a SPELL or object made for a specific magical purpose.

A spoken charm is a "little prayer," usually composed in verse. For example, the following charm is for mending lovers' quarrels and would be spoken in a RITUAL invoking an ANGEL or spirit for assistance:

Love has no room
For spats and fights

Heal these wounds
At once tonight

Many charms in folklore blend pagan and Christian elements. The following charm that protects against marsh fever has pagan Norse origins that were Christianized. The charm calls for three horseshoes to be nailed to one's bedpost. The charm is recited while the work is done. The Holy Crok refers both to the hammer of the thunder god Thor and to the crucifix of Christianity; Wod is Wotan, the chief of gods; and Lok is Loki, the TRICKSTER god.

Father, Son, and Holy Ghost
Nail the Devil to this post.
Thrice I smite with Holy Crok,
With this mell I thrice do knock,
One for God, and one for Wod, and one for Lok.

Charms also are magical objects, such as POPPETS, good luck pieces, AMULETS, and so forth.

FURTHER READING:
Ashley, Leonard R. N. *The Amazing World of Superstition, Prophecy, Luck, Magic & Witchcraft.* New York: Bell Publishing Company, 1988.
Guiley, Rosemary Ellen. *Angel Magic for Love and Romance.* Lakewood, Minn.: Galde Press, 2005.

charm lamps   See LAMPES DE CHARM.

Charnock, Thomas (1526–1581)   English alchemist. Thomas Charnock was born in 1524 in Faversham, Kent. In his early twenties, he became fascinated by ALCHEMY and traveled all over England in search of knowledge of it. In Oxford he met an ADEPT named "James S." who took him on as apprentice and then bequeathed to him the secret of the PHILOSOPHER'S STONE when he died in 1554. Charnock failed to write the secret down and lost it when the laboratory burned down soon thereafter.

Fortunately for Charnock, he was able to learn the secret again from William Holloway, a prior of Bath. Holloway said he had hidden a flask of the Red Elixir in a wall at Bath Abbey, but when he had gone to look for it, he could not find it. He was so upset that he thought he would go mad. Holloway was old and blind when Charnock met him. Holloway swore him to secrecy and then gave him the secret.

Charnock worked for months and finally felt that he was nearing success. But his work was halted in 1557 when he was drafted into the militia to fight for the duke of Guise in his attack on Calais, France. The war was won by the English in 1558, and Charnock returned to England. In 1562, he married Agnes Norden of Stockland, Bristol; they had two children, a son who died in infancy and a daughter.

Charnock moved his family to Combwich, near Edgewater. He set up an alchemical laboratory where he worked until his death in 1581.

In 1556, he wrote *A Book of Philosophie,* dedicated to Queen Elizabeth I. In it, Charnock boasted that he could make GOLD at risk of losing his head if he failed. The queen never put him to the test; the book eventually vanished from her possession.

About 100 years later, a roll of parchment was discovered in the wall of Charnock's last home. It dealt with alchemy. According to Charnock, he finally succeeded in making the Stone in 1579, after laboring away at the task for 24 years.

FURTHER READING:
Holmyard, E. J. *Alchemy.* New York: Penguin Books, 1957.

Cheiro (1866–1936)   Professional name of famed Irish palm reader "Count" Louis Hamon. Cheiro was a charismatic and flamboyant personality who demonstrated a genuine skill in DIVINATION, and he left a lasting impression upon the art of PALMISTRY. His professional name Cheiro means "hand" in Greek.

Cheiro wrote his autobiography in his book *Confessions,* which probably features some exaggerated accounts of his feats and circumstances. By his own account, he was born William Warner on November 1, 1866, in Ireland to Count William de Hamon and Mademoiselle Dumas. He said his family lineage descended from Normans before the time of William the Conqueror. He was forced to drop out of school when his family was reduced to poverty. He acquired his interest in the occult from his mother.

Cheiro went to London to seek his fame and fortune. On the train from Liverpool to London, his destiny as a fortune-teller was sealed. Cheiro sat reading a copy of an English translation of the first textbook on palmistry, *Die Kunst Chiromantie,* published in Germany in 1485. His traveling companion remarked that it was a strange interest. Cheiro read his palm and foretold that the man would be a great leader, but his career would be cut short by a woman. The stranger was Charles Stewart Parnell, a politician who advocated Irish home rule. Several years later, Parnell's career was cut short when he was named as a correspondent in a divorce suit.

After a brief stay in London, Cheiro traveled as a stowaway to Bombay, India, where he developed his skill in palmistry with the help of a Hindu priest. It is likely that during this time he developed a psychic gift; he said later that the lines on a hand did not directly provide information but that they stimulated his "occult consciousness." He also traveled to Egypt.

Cheiro returned to London and opened a salon on the pricey and elegant Bond Street and furnished it in elegant style. His first client was Arthur Balfour, who was active in the new Society for Psychical Research and who went on to become one of its presidents. The SPR was actively investigating all kinds of psychic phenomena. Balfour went away impressed with his reading; word of mouth did the rest, and soon Cheiro was famous among London's upper crust. He was known for his accurate predictions. His fame spread to Europe and America. Cheiro was so much in demand that in one year alone he read for 6,000 clients. His advice was sought by royalty, politicians, artists, and writers. Among his clients were American President Grover Cleveland, Oscar Wilde, England's king Edward VII, Belgium's king Leopold, Lord Randolph Churchill, Sarah Bernhardt, and others.

One of Cheiro's clients was the American author Samuel Clemens (Mark Twain). According to Cheiro, Clemens was mightily impressed with his reading and said that his fortunes changed as a result of it. Clemens visited Cheiro in London in the early 1890s. He was on the brink of financial ruin late in his life and was despondent about the future. He found Cheiro's explanations of palmistry fascinating. From this session, Clemens was inspired to write a book, *The Tragedy of Pudd'nhead Wilson,* in which fingerprints were important to the plot. The book provided much-needed income, as did a lecture series in Europe.

Cheiro traveled extensively, visiting China, Russia, and the United States as well as Europe, where he lectured to large audiences. In *Confessions,* he claimed to have joined in a battle of skills with GRIGORI RASPUTIN. Each tried unsuccessfully to hypnotize the other. Cheiro said he predicted Rasputin's death in the Neva River and the fall of the Romanoff dynasty—prophecies also claimed to have been made by Rasputin.

It is not certain if Cheiro ever worked for British intelligence; according to lore, he did so during World War I and was a lover of the famed spy Mata Hari.

In 1920, Cheiro married one of his clients, a woman much younger than himself and who had irresistible small hands.

Cheiro wrote about a dozen books on the occult, including one on ASTROLOGY in which he claimed to have worked out an astrological system for winning roulette. He also developed a complicated NUMEROLOGY system that he called Fadic numbers that he used in conjunction with his palm-reading skills.

Cheiro went to Hollywood where he wrote film scenarios and hoped to make a film of the life of CAGLIOSTRO, a goal he never achieved. By then he had amassed a fortune. He started a private banking house and made investments for clients. He was charged with skimming about $500,000 in funds and was sent to prison for a short term.

In about 1930, his powers suddenly failed, and his friends and clients deserted him. He fell into depression and suffered setbacks. He wrote books to make a meager living. In 1936, he was found by Hollywood police babbling incoherently on a sidewalk. They took him to a hospital, but he died enroute.

Cheiro made no innovations to palmistry, but he did dramatically raise its visibility and popularity.

FURTHER READING:

Cheiro [Count Louis Harmon]. *Mysteries and Romances of the World's Greatest Occultists.* New Hyde Park, N.Y.: University Books, 1972.

Mysteries of the Unknown: Visions and Prophecies. Alexandria, Va.: Time-Life Books, 1988.

Choronzon DEMON of Dispersions and of the Abyss, summoned in an EVOCATION by ALEISTER CROWLEY and VICTOR NEUBERG. The account of the evocation is full of drama; it is not known whether the events happened as objective experiences or were experienced as visions. Crowley claimed to have conquered Choronzon to become a full Master of the Temple and Secret Chief.

The evocation was performed in 1909. In November, Crowley and Neuberg went to Algiers on holiday and walked south through the desert to Aumale. There Crowley was summoned by the voice of AIWASS, the entity who had dictated to him *The Book of the Law,* to "call Me." He had with him the Enochian Keys of JOHN DEE and EDWARD KELLY and felt that he had received a divine message to use them. Crowley had successfully used the 19th Key or Call, the most difficult, to access two of the 30 aethyrs or aires of expanded consciousness. He decided to access the remaining 28 aethyrs.

Crowley and Neuberg went out into the desert to a mount and ascended it. To make the Call, Crowley held a vermilion-painted Calvary Cross with an engraved topaz set in its axis. The topaz was engraved with a rose of 49 petals. When his clairvoyant visions unfolded, Crowley dictated to Neuberg. They did one aethyr a day, except for one day when they did two aethyrs. They started with the last numbered aethyr and worked backward toward the first.

Most of Crowley's visions were apocalyptic in nature. In the 15th aethyr, he underwent an INITIATION to the magical grade of Master of the Temple, a title that could be fully realized only by accessing the other aethyrs. However, Crowley experienced great difficulty in trying to access the next and 14th aethyr. After making several attempts, he stopped.

He and Neuberg were on their way down the mount when Crowley suddenly was seized with the inspiration to perform a homosexual magic RITUAL with Neuberg and dedicate it to the Greek god of nature, Pan. They went back to the top of the mount, inscribed in the sand a MAGIC CIRCLE protected with NAMES and words of power, and made a crude stone altar. Crowley took the submissive role in the sexual act as a way of eliminating ego. The ritual marked a turning point for him in his view of the importance of sex in MAGIC; he now saw it as a beneficial sacrament.

The ritual also led to a breakthrough in consciousness, for later that evening Crowley gained access to the 14th aethyr. In his vision he was informed that to attain his cherished goal of becoming a Secret Chief and Master of the Temple, he had to undergo the complete death of his ego and unite his spirit with the ocean of infinity. Only this way could he cross the Abyss, the gulf that separates ordinary mortals from the Secret Chiefs.

Crowley was able to resume his explorations of the other aethyrs, where he received revelation after revelation, laden with symbolism. In the 11th aethyr, he was told that in the 10th aethyr he would have to make a conscious crossing of the Abyss, which was inhabited by a single entity, the demon Choronzon, the "first and deadliest of all the powers of evil," a being comprised of "complete negation."

The ritual for crossing the Abyss took place on December 6, 1909, outside of the town of Bou Saada. Crowley and Neuberg walked out into the desert until they found a valley that had a suitable floor of fine sand. They formed a circle of rocks, drew around it a MAGIC CIRCLE, and then drew a MAGIC TRIANGLE. The demon would be invoked into the triangle. The circle would protect Neuberg, who would sit within it armed with a magical knife and a notebook for recording what happened. Crowley intended to enter the triangle, a dangerous act for a magician. He thus became perhaps the first magician in the Western magical tradition to offer his own body ritually as a vehicle for manifestation of a demon.

Before the start of the ritual, Neuberg took an oath that he would defend the magic circle "with thoughts and words and deeds," and would use the knife to attack anything that entered it, even Crowley himself.

Crowley apparently was not in the triangle when he invoked the aethyr but was in a "secret place" out of the sight and hearing of Neuberg. After the invocation, Crowley entered the triangle. To help the demon materialize, he sacrificed three pigeons at the points of the triangle and sprinkled their BLOOD. He took care not to let a drop fall outside the triangle, for that would enable Choronzon to manifest in the universe. When all the blood had soaked into the sand, he secretly recited the Call of the aethyr. He was in full trance.

Neuberg records that he heard a voice, simulating Crowley's voice, call out BARBAROUS NAMES and then blasphemies. Visions appeared within the triangle. First Neuberg saw the form of a woman prostitute he had known in Paris. The "woman" tried to seduce him, but Neuberg resisted, figuring it was Choronzon in a shape-shifted form. The "woman" then offered submission, which he also rejected. The demon next turned into an old man, then a snake, and then into Crowley, who begged for water. Neuberg held fast within the circle.

Neuberg ordered Choronzon to declare his nature. The demon replied that he spat upon the name of the Most High. He was Master of the Triangle who had no fear of the PENTAGRAM. He would give Neuberg words that the magician would take as "great secrets of magic" but would be worthless, a joke played by the demon.

Neuberg invoked Aiwass. Choronzon said he knew the name of the ANGEL and that "all thy dealings with him are but a cloak for thy filthy sorceries."

Ordered again to declare his true nature, Choronzon said his name was *Dispersion* and he could not be bested in argument. He uttered a rapid string of blasphemies that taxed Neuberg's ability to write them down. While distracting the magician with blasphemies, Choronzon threw sand onto the magic circle. When the outline was sufficiently blurred, he took the form of a naked man and leaped into it, throwing Neuberg to the ground. The two fought furiously. The demon tried to tear out Neuberg's throat with his froth-covered fangs. At last Neuberg was able to force Choronzon back into the triangle, and he repaired the magic circle.

Man and demon argued. Choronzon threatened Neuberg with all the tortures of hell, and Neuberg denounced the demon as a liar. After a long time at this, the demon suddenly vanished, leaving Crowley alone in the circle. Crowley traced the word BABALON in the sand, and the ritual was over. He and Neuberg built a fire for purification and ritually destroyed the circle and triangle.

Neuberg maintained that he had literally wrestled with Choronzon and not with Crowley possessed by the demon. Some occultists have posited that Crowley somehow exuded an ectoplasm that enabled the demon to make a form tangible enough to fight with Neuberg. Another explanation advanced is that the entire experience was visionary. Whatever the truth, both Crowley and Neuberg felt that Crowley had beaten the demon and achieved the status of Master of the Temple and Secret Chief. Crowley's new vision of himself was as teacher and prophet who was to indoctrinate the world with the philosophy of *The Book of the Law.*

Associates of Crowley said that the ritual permanently damaged him and that he was possessed by Choronzon for the rest of his life.

FURTHER READING:
King, Francis. *Megatherion: The Magickal World of Aleister Crowley.* New York: Creation Books, 2004.

Christ   See *ANIMA MUNDI;* FLUDD, ROBERT; JUNG, CARL G.; PHILOSOPHER'S STONE.

Christian Rosenkreutz   See ROSENKREUTZ, CHRISTIAN.

cinnabar   Red sulphide of MERCURY important in ALCHEMY. Cinnabar is called dragon's blood and also has importance in MAGIC.

When heated, cinnabar releases fumes of mercury, which condense in a silver magic MIRROR. Cinnabar is an ingredient in numerous formulae for the ELIXIR, a form of the PHILOSOPHER'S STONE.

circle   A SYMBOL of oneness, completion, perfection, the cosmos, eternity, and the SUN. A feminine symbol, the

The circle, a symbol of unity, represented in the alchemical axiom, "Make of man and woman a circle, from that a square, then a triangle, then another circle, and you will have the philosopher's stone." In Atalanta fugiens, *by Michael Maier, 1618. (Author's collection)*

circle appears in sacred art and architecture and plays an important role in various religious and magical RITUALS. According to Pascal, God is a circle, in which the center is everywhere and the circumference is nowhere.

A MAGIC CIRCLE demarcates a holy space which protects one from negative forces on the outside and facilitates communion with spirits and deities. Within the circle, one may ritually achieve transcendent levels of consciousness. Magic circles are constructed or drawn according to instruction provided in magical texts and are purified and consecrated. If temporary, they are ritually dissembled. If permanent, their sacred power is periodically ritually renewed. To step outside the circle during a ritual, or even to cross the boundary with an arm or leg, is to invite magical disaster. (See CROWLEY, ALEISTER.)

In folk magic, circles drawn around the beds of the sick and of new mothers protect them against DEMONS.

In Wicca, all worship and magical rites are conducted within a circle, which provides a sacred and purified space and acts as a gateway to the gods. The circle symbolizes wholeness, the creation of the cosmos, the womb of Mother Earth, and the Wheel of Rebirth, which is the continuing cycle of the seasons in birth-death-rebirth.

FURTHER READING:
Levi, Eliphas. *The History of Magic*. 1860. Reprint, York Beach, Maine: Samuel Weiser, 2001.

clairaudience   The hearing of sounds, music, and voices not audible to normal hearing. The term *clairaudience*

comes from French for "clear hearing." In yoga, it is an astral sense, which is experienced when the fifth chakra, located at the throat, is activated. Clairaudience is a psychic ability used in the practice of MAGIC.

Clairaudience manifests as an inner sound or voice that is clearly distinguishable from one's own inner voice. Sometimes it seems to be external, emanating from the space around a person. It may be recognized as the voice of a dead relative or interpreted as the voice of a spirit, such as an ANGEL, a guide, a disembodied ADEPT, or even God. It occurs in dreams, especially when important messages are given, and in the mystical and trance experiences of ORACLES, shamans, priests, prophets, mystics, saints, and others. In the late 17th and early 18th centuries, practitioners of MESMERISM observed that magnetized subjects experienced clairaudience, particularly the voices of the dead, as well as other psychic phenomena. Messages from the dead, received by a medium clairaudiently, became an integral part of many seances.

In magical work, clairaudience is employed in travels to the ASTRAL PLANE and in communication with various spirits. According to FRANZ BARDON, advanced beings existing on the MENTAL PLANE use clairaudience to communicate.

FURTHER READING:
Bardon, Franz. *Questions & Answers*. Salt Lake City: Merkur Publishing, 1998.
Butler, W. E. *How to Develop Clairvoyance*. 2nd ed. New York: Samuel Weiser, 1979.

clairvoyance   The psychic ability to see the unseen, such as spirits, auras, ghosts, otherworldly dimensions, and distant locations. *Clairvoyance* comes from the French term for "clear seeing." It is experienced in different ways, such as externalized visions, inner visions, and impressions. Clairvoyance overlaps with other psychic faculties and phenomena, such as clairaudience (psychic hearing), clairsentience (psychic sensing), telepathy (thought transfer), precognition (seeing the future), retrocognition (the past), psychometry (obtaining information by handling objects), and remote viewing (a modern term for "traveling clairvoyance" or seeing distant locations).

Clairvoyance has been a valued skill in DIVINATION, PROPHECY, and MAGIC since ancient times. Some individuals are born with marked abilities for clairvoyance; others can cultivate it through training, sometimes through the use of psychedelic agents such as drugs and herbs, and also by techniques to induce altered states of consciousness. In folklore, clairvoyance is a gift sometimes bestowed upon humans by FAIRIES or deities. Magical objects, such as a RING or hat, also confer the gift of clairvoyance.

In magical practice, clairvoyance is used to visit and work on the ASTRAL PLANE and to evoke and communicate with entities.

In Irish lore, the *thumb of knowledge* is a term for clairvoyance, or supernatural sight. When a SORCERER desired "the sight," he pressed one of his teeth with his thumb. The origin of the thumb of knowledge is in the saga of Fionn, or Finn MacCoul, who injured his thumb when he jammed it into the door of a fairy knoll. He sucked on his thumb to ease the pain and discovered that he suddenly possessed supernatural sight.

Robert Kirk, a 17th-century Scottish minister who perceived the fairy world, said that seers continually have a beam of light around them that enables them to see the atoms in the air. He described ways to acquire the second sight in *The Secret Commonwealth*. In one method, a man takes hair that bound a corpse to a bier and runs it in a helix around his middle. Then he bows his head down and looks back through his legs until he sees a funeral approach, or he looks backward through a knothole in a fir tree. But if the wind changes while the hair is still tied around him, his life is in danger.

Kirk said that a way to gain temporary clairvoyance—especially for seeing fairies—is for a man to put his foot on the foot of a seer, and the seer put his hand on the head of the man. The man looks over the seer's right shoulder. The sudden appearance of multitudes of swarming fairies will strike people breathless and speechless, Kirk said.

See also IMAGINATION; ORACLE.

FURTHER READING:
Guiley, Rosemary Ellen. *Harper's Encyclopedia of Mystical & Paranormal Experience.* San Francisco: HarperSanFrancisco, 1991.
Spence, Lewis. *The Magic Arts in Celtic Britain.* Van Nuys, Calif.: Newscastle Publishing, 1996.
Stewart, R. J. *The Living World of Faery.* Lake Toxaway, N.C.: Mercury Publishing, 1995.

Clavicle of Solomon   See GRIMOIRES.

Coeur, Jacques (15th c.)   French fraudulent alchemist. Jacques Coeur was a flamboyant man who enjoyed prestige in the court of King Charles VII of France. He attempted to disguise his ill-gotten riches by pretending to have created them through ALCHEMY.

Coeur was born in Bourges in the early 15th century. His father was a goldsmith. The family had no money to pay for Coeur's training in goldsmithing, and in 1428 he went to work in a low-level job at the Royal Mint of Bourges. The young Coeur distinguished himself with his quick learning of metallurgy. He gained the patronage of Agnes Sorel, a mistress of the king. He advanced quickly in his career and was made Master of the Mint and Grand Treasurer of the royal household.

Coeur exhibited a skill in finances and with the advantage of his position, amassed a fortune. He bought stocks of grain, honey, wine, and other produce, creating short-ages and then sold them at maximum price. He became the richest man in France and was a trusted adviser of the king. In 1446, Charles sent him on diplomatic missions to Genoa, Italy, and to see Pope Nicholas V. His stellar performance earned him even more riches.

In 1449, war broke out between the French and the English over Brittany, and Coeur financed the French fighting. The French were victorious, which made Coeur nearly invincible against his critics and detractors.

At the close of the war, Coeur returned to business. He initiated trade with Genoa and bought up large estates throughout France. He procured for his religious son the office of archbishop of Bourges.

Coeur's jealous detractors circulated rumors that he had debased the currency and forged the king's signature to a document that fraudulently made him wealthy. Coeur attempted to dispel these rumors by letting it be known that he had in fact discovered the secret of the PHILOSOPHER'S STONE, which was not true. He built lavish houses in Bourges and Pontpellier, decorating both with alchemical SYMBOLS and invited foreign alchemists to live with him. Coeur wrote a treatise in which he stated that he knew how to transmute base metals.

His efforts in vain, Coeur was arrested in 1452. Of the several charges brought against him, he was acquitted of only one—that he had been an accessory in the poisoning death of his patronness, Agnes Sorel. He was found guilty of debasing the currency, forging the king's signature, and supplying the enemy Turks with arms and money. He was fined 400,000 crowns and was banished from France. King Charles VII believed him to be innocent of all charges but was able only to reduce his fine and have him imprisoned.

After some time, Coeur was released. It was said that Charles secretly gave him a handsome sum of money with which Coeur retired to Cyprus and lived an opulent life. Coeur died in about 1460.

FURTHER READING:
Mackay, Charles. *Extraordinary Popular Delusions and the Madness of Crowds.* New York: Farrar, Straus & Giroux, 1932.

conjuration   See EVOCATION.

consecration   A RITUAL for making something sacred. In MAGIC, the TOOLS and CLOTHING used for a ritual are consecrated prior to use to imbue them with supernatural power. Consecrated objects are used only for ritual purposes and not for everyday tasks. A magician also consecrates himself—an act of purification—prior to ritual.

An Egyptian papyrus from the first century C.E. specifies a ritual for a magician to consecrate himself:

> Keep yourself pure for seven days, and then go on the third day of the moon to a place which the receding Nile has just laid bare. Make a fire on two upright bricks with

olive-wood when the sun is half-risen, after having before sunrise circumambulated the altar. But when the sun's disk is clear above the horizon, decapitate an immaculate, pure white cock, holding it in the crook of your left elbow; circumambulate the latter before sunrise. Hold the cock fast by your knees and decapitate it with no one else holding it. Throw the head into the river, catch the blood in your right hand and drink it up. Put the rest of the body on the burning altar and jump into the river. Dive under in the clothes you are wearing, then stepping backwards climb on the bank. Put on new clothes and go away without turning around. After that take the gall of a raven and rub some of it with the wing of an ibis on your eyes and you will be consecrated.

Constant, Alphonse Louis   See LEVI, ELIPHAS.

Corpus Hermeticum   A collection of spiritual texts attributed to the legendary HERMES TRISMEGISTUS that expand on the teaching contained in the EMERALD TABLET.

The *Corpus Hermeticum* feature dialogues between Hermes Trismegistus and his teachers, son, and disciples. The collection includes 17 short texts, some of which are fragmentary and which probably were not originally together. The nucleus of them, 14 treatises written in Greek, were brought to attention in 1460 when a monk named Leonardo of Pistoia brought them to Florence. Leonardo had been dispatched by Florence's ruler, Cosimo de' Medici, to hunt for forgotten ancient writings. Leonardo's discovery was greeted with great attention, for HERMES, identified with the Egyptian god THOTH, was considered to be older than PLATO and Moses. The scholar Marsilio Ficino was assigned the task of translating them into Latin. His edition of the 14 texts was published in 1471. Later manuscripts by others added other texts.

For more than a century, the *Corpus* was held in high regard by scholars. It was taken for granted that the texts were ancient Egyptian wisdom written by the real Hermes who either instructed Moses or was instructed by him. The *Corpus* was so impressive that in 1481 a large figure of Hermes Trismegistus instructing men from both the West and the East was inscribed on the pavement of Siena Cathedral.

The first book, called *Poimandres to Hermes Trismegistus,* is a dialogue between Hermes and his teacher "Poimandres, the *Nous* [the invisible good, mind, imagination, or intuition] of the Supreme." Another teacher is Agathos Daimon, featured in book 12. In 13 books, Hermes teaches ASCLEPIUS, the Greek god of healing, and his own son Tat. In two books, 16 and 17, Asclepius and Tat are the teachers.

The fundamental principle of the *Corpus* is that there is an underlying unity to all things. The individual is the same as the Supreme. Man is made like God of life and light, and his destiny is ruled by the planetary administrators. When man was revealed to Nature, she fell in love with him and persuaded him to live on Earth. Through the spiritual path of *gnosis* (knowledge), man learns to apprehend God and thus himself, and he rises above all time and becomes eternal.

The *Corpus Hermeticum* works actually date to between the first and third centuries C.E. They were produced in Alexandria—then under Roman rule—and reflect the syncretism of the times of Egyptian, Greek, Roman, Jewish, Christian, and Gnostic thought. Most likely they were authored by several anonymous persons in succession. Even though not as old as purported, the texts reflect ancient wisdom.

In the early 17th century, the alleged antiquity and authorship of the *Corpus* were discredited. Isaac Casaubon, a Calvinist from Geneva, Switzerland, sought to prove that the *Corpus* were based on Platonic and biblical sources. In 1614 he disclosed the true dates of authorship of the texts and said that they were forgeries written by "semi-Christians." The prestige and authority of the *Corpus* were effectively eclipsed, and the works slipped into obscurity. They were kept alive in secret societies such as the FREEMASONS and the ROSICRUCIANS. When the Nag Hammadi texts were found in Egypt in 1945, interest in Hermetic writings was revived: it continues to the present.

See also HERMETICA.

FURTHER READING:

Hall, Manly P. *The Secret Teachings of All Ages.* 1928. Reprint, Los Angeles: The Philosophic Research Society, 1977.

Hauck, Dennis William. *The Emerald Tablet: Alchemy for Personal Transformation.* New York: Penguin/Arkana, 1999.

The Way of Hermes: New Translations of The Corpus Hermeticum *and* The Definitions of Hermes Trismegistus to Asclepius. Rochester, Vt.: Inner Traditions, 2000.

correspondences   Associations between objects, forces, SYMBOLS, and NAMES that are employed in magical RITUAL.

The idea of correspondences has existed since antiquity. In Hermetic thought, everything in the macrocosm corresponds to something in the microcosm. For example, in ASTROLOGY, the PLANETS correspond to certain characteristics and forces that exist in the physical plane.

In kabbalistic mysticism, every letter of the Hebrew alphabet corresponds to spirits, INTELLIGENCES, COLORS, gems, ideas, and PERFUMES. Thus, a name of a spirit can be translated into a recipe for a perfume to be used in ritual that will invoke that particular entity.

The elemental weapons used in magical rituals (see TOOLS) correspond to attributes of gods and spirits. When the magician uses a tool, he or she takes on the authority of that entity.

FURTHER READING:

Regardie, Israel. *The Tree of Life: A Study in Magic.* York Beach, Maine: Samuel Weiser, 1969.

cover name   See SYMBOL.

cross   An ancient AMULET, predating Christianity by many centuries. The cross is an important SYMBOL in magical work.

The most common cross has four equilateral arms. The cross has been associated with sun deities and the heavens and in ancient times may have represented divine protection and prosperity. Also it is the world-axis in the center of the universe, the bridge between the Earth and the cosmos, the physical and the spiritual. In MAGIC, an equilateral-armed cross represents the four ELEMENTS and the union of the physical with the spiritual.

In Christianity, the cross represents the suffering of Christ's crucifixion, but it also functions as an amulet, protecting against the forces of evil. Even before the crucifixion of Christ, the cross was a weapon against the dark forces. According to legend, when Lucifer declared war upon God in an attempt to usurp his power, his army scattered God's angels twice. God sent to his angels a Cross of Light on which were inscribed the names of the Trinity. Seeing this cross, Lucifer's forces lost strength and were driven into hell.

As the church grew in power, so did the cross. Its power is invoked by making the sign of the cross on the upper body, using hand motions to connect the forehead, the heart, and the two shoulders. According to tradition, nothing unholy can stand up to the cross. It exorcizes DEMONS, prevents BEWITCHMENT, and banishes evil presences and creatures. Inquisitors wore crosses or made the sign of a cross when dealing with accused witches to ward off any evil SPELLS the witches might cast against them.

In magical work, a white cross is placed on an altar. The Rose Cross is a cross with a rose at its intersection. The rose represents the unfolding of the soul and the evolution of spiritual consciousness.

See also KABBALISTIC CROSS; RITUAL OF THE ROSE CROSS.

FURTHER READING:
Guiley, Rosemary Ellen. *Harper's Encyclopedia of Mystical & Paranormal Experience.* San Francisco: HarperSanFrancisco, 1991.
Kraig, Donald Michael. *Modern Magick: Eleven Lessons in the High Magickal Arts.* 2d ed. St. Paul, Minn.: Llewellyn Publications, 2004.

crossing running water   A remedy against supernatural entities. According to widespread folklore beliefs, water is pure and holy and will reject the unholy. A person threatened or pursued by ghosts, FAIRIES, DEMONS, witches, VAMPIRES, and so forth can halt them in their tracks by crossing running water.

During the witch hunts of the Inquisition, one method of determining the innocence or guilt of accused witches was "swimming," in which they were tossed into deep water with their arms and legs bound. If the water rejected them and they floated, they were guilty. If they were innocent, the water accepted them and they sank. In either case, the witch usually was doomed. Sinking often meant drowning. Floating was a certain sentence to execution by hanging or burning.

crossroads   A place of change and great magical power. The junction of roads, where forces of energy cross, have been considered to have magical significance since ancient times.

Crossroads are haunted by demonic and negative forces and are where witches supposedly gather for sabbaths. FAIRIES who like to fool travelers haunt crossroads. Ghosts appear at crossroads at certain times, such as All Hallow's Eve.

Some magical RITUALS are performed at crossroads, such as NECROMANCY, the GOLD-FINDING HEN, conjurations of spirits and DEMONS, and sacrifices of animals.

Crossroads are unhallowed ground and according to folklore tradition are the places where suicide and murder victims, criminals, and the unbaptized should be buried. Restless ghosts and VAMPIRES can be prevented from walking among the living by burying corpses at crossroads.

crow   A messenger between heaven and Earth, an omen of death, and prophet of the hidden truth or the unconscious. Because of its black color, the crow is often associated with evil.

Like the raven, the crow in ALCHEMY represents the *nigredo*, the initial blackening and putrefaction that initiate the process of the Great Work.

Crowley, Aleister (1875–1947)   English magician and occultist and one of the most flamboyant and controversial figures in Western MAGIC. Aleister Crowley was a man of enormous ego, excess, and magical skill. He practiced outrageous magic of sex, drugs, and SACRIFICE; yet he made significant contributions to magic. Claiming to remember numerous past lives, Crowley considered himself to be the reincarnation of other great occultists: Pope Alexander VI, renowned for his love of physical pleasures; EDWARD KELLY, the notorious assistant to JOHN DEE in Elizabethan England; COUNT CAGLIOSTRO; and ELIPHAS LEVI, who died on the day Crowley was born. Crowley also believed he had been Ankh-f-n-Khonsu, an Egyptian priest of the XXVIth dynasty.

He was born Edward Alexander Crowley on October 12, 1875, in Leamington Spa, Warwickshire. His father was a wealthy brewer and a "Darbyite" preacher, a member of a Fundamentalist sect known as the Plymouth Brethren or Exclusive Brethren. Crowley's parents raised him in an atmosphere of repression and religious bigotry. He rebelled to such an extent that his mother christened him "the

Beast" after the Antichrist, a name he delighted in using later in life, calling himself the Beast of the Apocalypse.

Crowley was drawn to the occult and was fascinated by BLOOD, torture, and sexual degradation; he liked to fantasize being degraded by a "scarlet woman." He combined these interests in a lifestyle that shocked others and reveled in the attention he drew. He was in his teens when he adopted the name Aleister.

In 1887, Crowley's father died, and he was sent to a Darbyite school in Cambridge. His unhappy experiences there at the hands of a cruel headmaster made him hate the Darbyites.

Crowley studied for three years at Trinity College at Cambridge but never earned a degree. He wrote poetry, engaged in an active bisexual life style, and pursued his occult studies—the Great Work—the latter of which were inspired by *The Book of Black Magic and of Pacts* by ARTHUR EDWARD WAITE and *The Cloud Upon the Sanctuary* by Carl von Eckartshausen. In his first volume of poetry published in 1898, Crowley foreshadowed his occult excesses with his statement that God and Satan had fought many hours over his soul. He wrote, "God conquered—now I have only one doubt left—which of the twain was God?"

Crowley was in his third year at Trinity when he formally dedicated himself to magick—which he spelled with a *k* to "distinguish the science of the Magi from all its counterfeits." He also pledged to "rehabilitate" it. He saw magic as *the* way of life, a path of self-mastery that was achieved with rigorous discipline of the WILL illumined by IMAGINATION.

After leaving Trinity, Crowley took a flat in Chancery Lane, London. He named himself Count Vladimir and pursued his occult activities full-time. Stories of bizarre incidents circulated, perhaps fueled in part by Crowley's mesmerizing eyes and aura of supernatural power. A ghostly light reportedly surrounded him, which he said was his astral spirit. One of his flat neighbors claimed to be hurled downstairs by a malevolent force, and visitors said they experienced dizzy spells while climbing the stairs or felt an overwhelming evil presence.

In 1898, Crowley went to Zermatt, Switzerland, to mountain climb. He met Julian Baker, an English occultist, who in turn introduced Crowley back in London to George Cecil Jones, a member of the HERMETIC ORDER OF THE GOLDEN DAWN. At Jones's invitation, Crowley was initiated into the order on November 18, 1898. He took the MAGICAL MOTTO *Frater Perdurabo* ("I will persevere.") He used other names, among them *Mega Therion* ("the Great Wild Beast"), which he used when he later attained the grade of Magus.

Crowley was already skilled in magic when he joined the Golden Dawn, and its outer First Order bored him. He was intrigued, however, by the skill and knowledge of one its members, ALLAN BENNETT, whom he met in 1899. Bennett invited Crowley to live with him for a time in his London flat. Bennett taught Crowley Eastern mysticism and material from the Golden Dawn's inner Second Order.

SAMUEL LIDDELL MacGREGOR MATHERS, one of the founders of the Golden Dawn, taught Crowley Abremalin magic from an old manuscript, *The Sacred Magic of Abra-Melin the Mage,* which Mathers had translated. Mathers believed the manuscript was bewitched and inhabited by an entity. The magic prescribed a rigorous six-month program conducted in complete withdrawal from the world, after which the initiate would make TALISMANS that would bring money, great sexual allure, and an army of phantom soldiers to serve at his disposal. Crowley intended to undergo this rite beginning at Easter 1900 at Boleskin Manor, his house in Scotland.

His plans were disrupted by internal fighting in the Golden Dawn. In late 1899, Crowley was refused initiation into the Second Order because of his active homosexuality. Mathers, who was by then living in Paris, was incensed. In January 1900, he invited Crowley to Paris, and initiated him into Adeptus Minor grade of the Second Order in the at the Golden Dawn temple there.

The London temple was not pleased, and when Crowley appeared there to claim his rightful magical manuscripts accorded his new rank, he was dismissed empty-handed. The Golden Dawn, under the leadership of FLORENCE FARR, deposed Mathers.

Aleister Crowley as a young man in ceremonial magic garb. (Author's collection)

In April 1900, Crowley again went to Paris at the behest of Mathers, who threatened magical punishment of the London rebels. He authorized Crowley to go back to London as his official representative, install those loyal to Mathers as the new chiefs, and seize the ritual vault. However, Crowley was rebuffed again, and ADEPTS of the temple, which was now under the direction of WILLIAM BUTLER YEATS, marshaled an occult attack on Crowley.

Crowley broke into the temple and seized possession of it, but the rebels gained it back and changed the locks. Crowley reappeared the next day, dressed in full Highland garb and black mask. Yeats called the police and had him taken away.

Soon after this escapade, Crowley suddenly left for New York. The Golden Dawn expelled him. His relationship with Mathers ended badly as well; in 1910, Mathers sued him in court to try to stop him from publishing the secret Golden Dawn rituals in his magazine *Equinox*. Mathers lost.

From 1900 to 1903, Crowley traveled extensively, visiting the Far East and delving deeper into Eastern mysticism.

In 1903, he married Rose Kelly, the first of two wives. Kelly bore him one child, a daughter, Lola Zaza. Their honeymoon lasted several months. In 1904 they were in Cairo, where Crowley was attempting to conjure sylphs, the ELEMENTALS of the air. On March 18, 1904, Rose suddenly began to trance channel, receiving communications from the ASTRAL PLANE that the Egyptian god, Horus, was waiting for Crowley. The communicating entity was a messenger, AIWASS. For three days, Aiwass dictated information to Crowley. The result was *Liber Legis*, better known as *The Book of the Law*, Crowley's most important work. Central to it is the Law of Thelema: "Do what thou wilt shall be the whole of the Law." The law has been misinterpreted to mean doing as one pleases. According to Crowley, it means that one does what one must and nothing else. Perfect magic is the complete and total alignment of the WILL with universal will, or cosmic forces. When one surrenders to that alignment, one becomes a perfect channel for the flow of cosmic forces.

Besides the Law of Thelema, the book holds that every person is sovereign and shall be self-fulfilled in the Aeon. "Every man and every woman is a star," it states. However, the Aeon of Horus would be preceded by an era of great violence, aggression, and fire.

Aiwass told Crowley that he had been selected by the SECRET CHIEFS, the master ADEPTS behind the Golden Dawn, to be the prophet for the coming Aeon of Horus, the third great age of humanity. Crowley genuinely believed that the Aeon of Horus would spread around the world like a new religion—Crowleyanity—and replace all other religions. *The Book of the Law* remained a focus of Crowley's life for the rest of his years.

Crowley insisted that he never understood all of what was dictated. However, the style compares to some of his other writings, suggesting that the material may have originated in his subconscious. The promised self-fulfillment seemed to elude him. Throughout his life Crowley believed that he had the ability to manifest whatever he desired, including large sums of money, but after squandering his inheritance he was never able to do so.

After returning home to Scotland, Crowley informed the Golden Dawn that he was its new head, but he received no reply. He then determined that Mathers had launched a psychic attack against him, and he responded by summoning Beezlebub and his DEMONS to attack back. (See PSYCHIC VAMPIRE.)

Crowley had a prodigious sexual appetite and had numerous mistresses, some of whom he called "scarlet women" and some of whom bore him illegitimate children. He was fond of giving his women "serpent kisses," using his sharpened teeth to draw blood. He branded some of his women and eventually abandoned all of them to drugs, alcohol, or the streets. Crowley tried unsuccessfully to beget a "magical child." He fictionalized these efforts in his novel, *Moonchild* (1929).

Crowley believed he was irresistibly sexually attractive because he doused himself daily with "Ruthvah, the perfume of immortality." The perfume, a mixture of three parts civet, two parks musk, and one part ambergris, was rubbed into his hair and skin. The scent, he said, would cause others to obey his commands without realizing that they were doing so.

Rose descended into alcoholism, and in 1909, she divorced Crowley on grounds of adultery. The same year, Crowley began a homosexual relationship with the poet VICTOR NEUBERG, who became his assistant in magic. Their most famous workings together took place in 1909 in the desert south of Algiers, when they performed a harrowing conjuration of the demonic Dweller of the Abyss, CHORONZON. Crowley was inspired to incorporate sex into the RITUAL, and he became convinced of the power of sex magic. By 1910, he was involved with the ORDO TEMPLI ORIENTIS sex magic occult order and in 1912 was invited to head the organization in Britain. He took the magical name BAPHOMET.

From late 1914 to 1919, Crowley lived in the United States, where he was unsuccessful in rousing much interest in the Aeon of Horus. He kept a record of his prodigious sexual activities, which he titled *Rex de Arte Regia* ("The King of the Royal Art.") Many of the prostitutes whom he hired had no idea that he was actually involving them in sex magic. He and one scarlet woman of the moment, Roddie Minor, performed sex magic and drug rituals—by then he was addicted to heroin—for the purpose of communicating with an entity Crowley called the wizard Amalantrah who existed on the ASTRAL PLANE.

In 1916, Crowley initiated himself into the rank of Magus in a bizarre black magic rite involving a frog. The hapless creature was offered GOLD, frankincense, and myrrh, then was baptized as Jesus, and was worshiped as God incarnate. After a day of this, Crowley arrested the frog and charged it with blasphemy and sedition, sentencing it to crucifixion. The sentence was carried out. While the frog suffered, Crowley declared that its elemental spirit would enter his service as a guardian of his work, so that—incredibly—"men may speak of my piety and my gentleness and of all the virtues and bring to me love and service and all material things so ever where I may stand in need." He then stabbed the frog to death, cooked it, and ate its legs as a sacrament. The remainder of the frog was burned to ashes.

In 1918, Crowley met Leah Hirsig, a New York school teacher. They were instantly attracted to one another, and Hirsig became his most famous scarlet woman. He called her "the Ape of Thoth." They decided to found an Abbey of Thelema, a monastic community of men and women who would promulgate *The Book of the Law,* perform magic, and be sexually free.

In 1920, while driving through Italy, he had a vision of a hillside villa. He found the place in Cefalu, Sicily, took it over, and renamed it the Sacred Abbey of the Thelemic Mysteries. It served as the site for numerous sexual orgies and magical rites, many attended by his illegitimate children. Leah bore a daughter, Anne Leah, who died in childhood.

In 1921, Crowley decided that he attained the magical rank of Ipsissimus, equal to God.

He went to France in 1922 to try to end his heroin addiction but was only partially successful. He and Hirsig went to England, where Crowley earned money writing articles and books. His novel *Diary of a Drug Fiend* (1922) drew heavily upon his own experiences.

He discovered a 23-year-old Oxford student, Raoul Loveday and named him his magical heir. He took Loveday and his wife, Betty May, to Thelema where Loveday engaged in Crowley's practices of drugs, orgiastic sex, and self-mutilation. Betty May despised Crowley. Loveday's health declined, and he fell ill after drinking cat's BLOOD in a ritual. Crowley attempted to cure him magically, without success. On February 15, 1923, he told Loveday that he would die the following day. Loveday did. The official cause was enteritis, but Crowley believed Loveday had brought about his own demise by leaving a MAGIC CIRCLE during a ritual, thus exposing himself to evil forces.

The Loveday episode created a scandal, and in May 1923, Benito Mussolini expelled Crowley from Italy, forcing him to abandon the abbey. By the end of the year, Crowley and Hirsig parted ways.

In 1929, Crowley married his second wife, Maria Ferrari de Miramar, in Leipzig. Her reputed magical powers led him to name her the High Priestess of Voodoo. They separated in less than a year when Crowley took up with a 19-year-old girl. Maria entered a mental institution, enabling Crowley to divorce her.

Crowley's later years were plagued by poor health, drug addiction, and financial trouble. He kept himself barely afloat by publishing nonfiction and fiction writings. In 1934, desperate for money, Crowley sued sculptress Nina Hammett for libel. Hammett had stated in her biography,

Laughing Torso (1932), that Crowley practiced black magic and indulged in human sacrifice. The English judge, jury, spectators, and press were repulsed by the testimony that came out in the trial. The judge stated he had "never heard such dreadful, horrible, blasphemous and abominable stuff. . . ." The jury stopped the trial and found in favor of Hammett.

In 1945, Crowley moved to Netherwood, a boarding house in Hastings, where he lived the last two years of his life, asthmatic, dissipated, and bored, consuming amounts of heroin every day that would kill some addicts. During these last years, he met GERALD B. GARDNER, an English Witch, and shared ritual material with him. He was involved with JACK PARSONS, criticizing his attempts to create a "Moonchild" (see HOMUNCULUS).

In 1946, Cambridge professor E. M. Butler visited Crowley to interview him for her book *The Myth of the Magus.* She was repulsed by his sickly appearance and pretentious demeanor, and his squalid surroundings, the walls of which were covered with his grotesque drawings. Crowley spoke of himself in reverent terms and offered to prove his magical ability by making himself instantly invisible, but he was unable to do so. According to Butler:

> Yet there he sat, a wreck among ruins, living or rather dying in penury on the charity of friends, speaking of himself in all seriousness as an "instrument of Higher Beings who control human destiny."

Butler barely mentioned him in her book and in *Ritual Magic* (1949) dismissed him as a "failed Satanist."

Crowley died of cardiac degeneration and severe bronchitis on December 1, 1947. He was cremated in Brighton. At his funeral, a Gnostic Mass was performed and his "Hymn to Pan" was read. His ashes were sent to followers in the United States.

Numerous editions and collections of Crowley's writings have been published. Besides *The Book of the Law,* his other most notable work is *Magick in Theory and Practice* (1929), considered by many occultists to be a superb work on ceremonial magic. *The Equinox of the Gods* (1937) reflects back on *The Book of the Law. The Book of Lies* features 91 sermons and commentaries on each. *The Book of Thoth* (1944) presents his interpretation of the TAROT. The Thoth Tarot deck, inspired by Crowley, is one of the more popular decks in modern use.

Crowley's work continues to inspire people, and Thelemic organizations exist around the world. He has inspired artists of all kinds. Posthumously, Crowley has perhaps gained more fame and credibility than he had during his life. He remains controversial to the extreme, vilified as a "satanic occultist" and praised as a brilliant magician.

See also PARSONS, JOHN WHITESIDES.

FURTHER READING:
Crowley, Aleister. *The Holy Books of Thelema.* York Beach, Maine: Samuel Weiser, 1983.

———. *Magic in Theory and Practice.* 1929. Reprint, New York: Dover Publications, 1976.

King, Francis. *Megatherion: The Magickal World of Aleister Crowley.* New York: Creation Books, 2004.

Michaelsen, Scott (ed.). *Portable Darkness: An Aleister Crowley Reader.* New York: Harmony Books, 1989.

Stephenson, P. R., and Israel Regardie. *The Legend of Aleister Crowley.* St. Paul, Minn.: Llewellyn Publications, 1970.

Sutin, Lawrence. *Do What Thou Wilt: A Life of Aleister Crowley.* New York: St. Martin's Griffin, 2000.

Symonds, John, and Kenneth Grant (eds.). *The Confessions of Aleister Crowley, an Autobiography.* London: Routledge & Kegan Paul, 1979.

crystal ball   One of the best-known magical TOOLS for DIVINATION. The use of a crystal ball for SCRYING, the seeing of the future, is called crystallomancy, a method of divination in which shiny and reflective objects reveal images and visions of the future.

The crystal ball has become the stereotyped staple of the fortune-teller from GYPSIES to sorcerers, WIZARDS, witches, and magicians. According to tradition, the best crystal is natural. Crystal balls made of artificial glass and crystal are widely used in modern times. Glass fishing floats also work.

Magical tradition holds that a crystal ball, like other magical tools and TALISMANS, should be magically empowered. This can be done through magical RITUAL or by powers endowed by supernatural entities such as ANGELS. For example, the 16th-century scryer JOHN DEE claimed that he was given a crystal by the angel Uriel.

In earlier times, elaborate rituals were performed for scrying with a crystal ball, which would include invoking certain spirits and working only at auspicious times according to ASTROLOGY or the phases of the MOON. Modern practitioners vary in their rituals. At the least, the practitioner alters consciousness to facilitate the appearance of visions and the reception of information. Some may not see actual visions in a crystal but nonetheless receive information. The crystal itself is not considered to hold any magical power but to be a means for the practitioner to access psychic ability.

cube   The Earth, the material world, the four ELEMENTS, the foundation of the cosmos. Cubes represent wholeness and also Truth because the view is the same from every angle. Cubes also symbolize solidity and firmness and in allegories represent the persistence of the virtues. Chariots and thrones often are represented as cubes.

In ALCHEMY, the cubes is the squaring of the circle, or completion and wholeness. It also represents SALT.

curse   A malevolent SPELL or intent to punish, harm, or kill. Curses are part of all practices of MAGIC and SORCERY since antiquity. Catholic priests are empowered to curse.

The term *curse* comes from the Anglo-Saxon word *cursein,* the etymology of which is not known but which means "to invoke harm or evil upon."

How Curses Are Made

Curses are made or "thrown" by a variety of methods, some of them by magic and some by spontaneous act. In the broadest sense, wishing anyone ill is a form of cursing, for it projects a THOUGHT-FORM made of WILL and IMAGINATION upon a victim. Most ill wishing is transitory and has little or no effect (see WISH). The more concentrated the emotions and projection, the more powerful the curse. Most powerful of all is a deathbed curse, for the dying are believed to project the most intensity. Cursing survivors, successive generations, or even places may last for centuries, just as the curse made by a witch named Old Chattox (see below).

Curses are both spoken and written; an example of a formal written curse is an anathema proclaimed by the pope, which excommunicates a person from the church. The EVIL EYE is a curse both involuntary and deliberate, causing a victim to suffer misfortune and perhaps even death. POINTING with a finger or a bone, especially while uttering a malediction, is a universal method in WITCHCRAFT and sorcery. Magical objects such as dolls or POPPETS—a substitution for the victim—can be ritually cursed, burned, stabbed, or otherwise marked. A photograph of the victim works equally well, as do nail clippings, bits of hair, and personal belongings. Ordinary objects can become cursed through tragedy and misfortune and can affect the persons who own them.

The Egyptians wrote curses on magical papyri, a practice adopted by Greeks and Romans. From about the fifth century B.C.E. to the fifth century C.E., curse tablets (*tabellae defixonium*) were especially popular in the Hellenistic world. *Tabellae defixonium* refers to tablets that fix or pin down, especially in the sense of delivering someone over to the powers of the underworld. The curse tablets were thin pieces of lead (and sometimes other materials) on which were inscribed the victim's name, the curse, magical SYMBOLS and NAMES of various deities, or the more generic DAIMONES invoked to carry out the curse. The tablets were buried near a fresh tomb, a battlefield, or a place of execution, all of which were believed to be populated by spirits of the dead en route to the underworld. The curses gave the spirits the power to assault the victim. Curse tablets also were fixed with nails and were thrown into WELLS, springs, or rivers that were also said to be inhabited by spirits. Curses were made for all manner of purposes, including preventing rival athletes from winning competitions, as in this late Roman Empire curse for a chariot race found in Africa:

> I conjure you, daemon, whoever you may be, to torture and kill, from this hour, this day, this moment, the horses of the Green and the White teams; kill and smash the charioteers Clarus, Felix, Primulus, Romanus; do not leave breath in them. I conjure you by him who has deliv-

ered you, at the time, the god of the sea and the air: *Iao, Iasdo . . . aeia.*

Iao and *Iasdo* are variants of Yahweh, a Jewish name for God.

Curses in Witchcraft

During the witchcraft trials in Europe and Britain, witches were often accused of cursing victims and of causing blight, misfortune, illness, and even death. In 1612–13, about 20 persons were suspected of witchcraft in the Pendle Forest area in Lancashire, England; 11 were tried. Sixty-year-old Anne Whittle, known as "Old Chattox," confessed to having a PACT with the devil and to practicing malefic magic. When a farmer ordered her off his land, she urinated on it (see URINE) and said that the land was now cursed and that cattle would never be able to graze there. For centuries cattle died and could not thrive there. In the 1950s, a poisonous weed was found that was believed to be the cause. Though the weed seemed a natural reason for the problem, local residents noted that it was unusual that the weed grew in that particular field only and not in the surrounding area.

In numerous other witch trials, witches were accused of cursing people by sticking pins into poppets, by BLASTING, and by casting various spells.

Curses often are written or publicly proclaimed to maximize their effectiveness upon the victim. Many curses, however, are done in secret magical RITUALS. A widespread method of cursing is to pray against a victim, even to death. (See DEATH PRAYER; HEX.)

Curses among Magicians

In the Western magical tradition, cursing is done frequently among occultists and is not considered to be immoral. Arguments and disputes can result in cursing warfare. Famous cursing battles took place among members of the HERMETIC ORDER OF THE GOLDEN DAWN, involving the sending of vampiric entities. SAMUEL LIDDELL MacGREGOR MATHERS, and ALEISTER CROWLEY engaged in such mutual attacks. The magician WILLIAM G. GRAY was known to send powerful curses against most of his students.

Cursing is still done in magical lodges and circles in modern times, though practitioners often are secretive about it due to beliefs by younger generations that cursing is immoral and will backfire on the sender. In Wicca, Paganism, and many modern magical traditions, there is a belief that magic of any sort will return to the sender, sometimes threefold; hence a curse will be revisited on the sender with three times the effect. More acceptable to many practitioners is the "binding spell," which is intended to prevent another person from interfering or doing harm.

This moralistic view against cursing is not found in most magical and SORCERY practices outside the modern West.

Cursing Demons

In ceremonial magic, spirits or DEMONS who refuse to appear when evoked in ritual may be cursed to burn in fire by the magician. This threat is said to terrify the spirits into obedience. The *Key of Solomon* GRIMOIRE gives this curse:

> We deprive ye of all office and dignity which ye may have enjoyed up till now; and by their virtue and power we relegate you unto a lake of sulphur and of flame, and unto the deepest depths of the Abyss, that ye may burn therein eternally for ever.

Another curse is called "Curse of the Chains" or "The General Curse (called the Spirits Chains)," and involves ritual cursing and a sealing of the disobedient demon inside a box bound by IRON chains:

> O spirit N., who art wicked and disobedient, because thou hast not obeyed my commands and the glorious and incomprehensible Names of the true God, the Creator of all things, now by the irresistible power of these Names I curse thee into the depths of the Bottomless Pit, there to remain in unquenchable fire and brimstone until the Day of Wrath unless thou shalt forthwith appear in this triangle before this circle to do my will. Come quickly and in peace by the Names Adonai, Zebaoth, Adonai, Amioram. Come, come, Adonai King of Kings commands thee.

The magician then writes the demon's NAME and SEAL on parchment, which he or she places in a black wooden box that contains sulphur and other foul-smelling ingredients. He or she binds the box with iron chains, which imprison the demon. The magician hangs the box on the point of a sword and holds it over a fire, saying:

> I conjure thee, Fire, by Him who made thee and all other creatures of this world to burn, torture and consume this spirit N. now and for evermore.

The magician warns the demon that his name and seal will be burned in the box and then buried. If the spirit still does not appear, the magician works himself or herself up into a greater fury of cursing, calling down the wrath of all the company of heaven, the SUN, the MOON, the stars, and the light of the hosts of heaven. As a final measure, he or she drops the box into the fire. The demon will find this unbearable and will appear.

Cursed Objects

Any object can be ritually cursed to affect whoever owns it with bad luck, misfortune, and even death. Sometimes objects are cursed by circumstances. For example, the "screaming skulls" of England are said to be haunted by restless ghosts of the dead. Some skulls belong to victims of religious persecution during the 16th-century Reformation initiated by King Henry VIII. Others are from Oliver Cromwell's Roundheads during the English Civil War in the mid-17th century. Still other skulls are from people who lost their heads in various violent episodes, such as murders.

The victims often gave the same deathbed curse: If their remains were not buried within the walls of their house, their spirits would not rest in peace. The skulls reportedly act up whenever someone tries to remove them from their houses. The skulls are said to reappear mysteriously and then take revenge by causing bad luck or death. Violent storms or fires may destroy the property, or crops may fail and cattle dry up or die.

Protection against Curses

Numerous remedies against cursing exist universally. AMULETS protect against or deflect curses, whether a person has specific knowledge about them or not. Semiprecious stones and jewels have been used since ancient times as amulets against curses and other forms of dark magic, illness, and misfortune. For example, the ancient Egyptians inscribed spells on lapis lazuli. The early Greeks and Romans wore certain carved semiprecious and precious gems as RINGS and necklaces to ward off curses.

It is assumed in many cultures that one will be cursed by one's enemies for any reason. Spells, CHARMS, and petitions invoke the protection and intervention of benevolent spirits. An individual who has been cursed sometimes visits another witch or sorcerer to break the curse, and to curse the curser back.

The "Curse" of Tutankamen

Ancient Egyptians sought to protect their tombs by cursing anyone who broke into them. Such curses were written on the walls and sarcophagi in the tombs. The Egyptians believed that tomb desecration would render the spirit of the dead homeless.

The most famous story of an Egyptian tomb curse was that of the lavish burial place of the pharaoh Tutankamen, discovered in 1922 by Lord Carnavon and Howard Carter. According to lore, the Englishmen found a clay tablet inside the tomb with a curse written upon it: "Death will slay with his wings whoever disturbs the pharaoh's peace."

However, the existence of this tablet has never been proved. It was not photographed and supposedly disappeared from the collection of artifacts. According to Egyptologist Bob Brier, it is doubtful that the tablet existed. There are no reliable references to such a curse. Further-more, it was not typical Egyptian custom to write on clay tablets or to describe death as coming on wings.

Nonetheless, mysterious deaths affected some of the people involved in the tomb's opening and excavation. Carnavon, 56, died two months later. He cut his face shaving, and the cut became infected. He fell into a severe fever and delirium and repeated, "A bird is scratching my face." When he died, all the lights were said to go out in Cairo.

Others associated with the tomb also died. George Jay-Gould, American entrepreneur, visited the tomb and died soon thereafter. British industrialist Joel Woolf visited the tomb and on the way home to England via boat fell into a fever and died.

By 1929, 22 people associated with tomb had died, seemingly prematurely. Thirteen of them had been present at the opening of the tomb. In 1966 and 1972, two Egyptian directors of antiquities who were involved in exhibitions of the Tutankamen treasures died: One was killed when he was hit by a car, and the other fell dead when the Tutankamen gold mummy mask left Cairo for exhibition in England.

Howard Carter died of natural causes in 1939. He had maintained a strong skepticism of the power of curses throughout his life, thus lending support to the idea that belief in curses initiates self-fulfillment of them.

FURTHER READING:

Brier, Bob. *Ancient Egyptian Magic*. New York: William Morrow, 1980.

Butler, E. M. *Ritual Magic*. Cambridge: Cambridge University Press, 1949.

Cavendish, Richard. *The Black Arts*. New York: G.P. Putnam's Sons, 1967.

Gordon, Stuart. *The Book of Curses: True Tales of Voodoo, Hoodoo and Hex*. London: Brockhampton Press, 1994.

Guiley, Rosemary Ellen. *The Encyclopedia of Witches and Witchcraft*. 2d ed. New York: Facts On File Inc., 1999.

Luck, Georg. *Arcana Mundi: Magic and the Occult in the Greek and Roman Worlds*. Baltimore: Johns Hopkins University Press, 1985.

Robins, Joyce. *The World's Greatest Mysteries*. London: Hamlyn Publishing Group Ltd., 1989.

daimones In Greek mythology, a type of spirit or INTELLIGENCE between gods and humans. *Daimones* means "divine beings." They can be either good or evil in nature, though even good ones will act in a hostile fashion when angered. A good *daimon* is called an *agathodaimon*, and an evil *daimon* is called a *kakodaimon*. Christianity assigned all of them to the infernal ranks of DEMONS, along with all pagan deities.

Daimones include various classes of entities, such as guardian spirits of places, TUTELARY SPIRITS, GENII, ministering spirits, and demigods. They also have been associated with the souls of the dead and ghosts, and with stars and PLANETS, and with plants and minerals of the Earth. They are ministering spirits (resembling ANGELS), godlike beings, and souls of dead persons. *Daimones* can take over human bodies in the form of POSSESSION (especially for oracular prophecy) and also possess humans to cause physical and mental illness. Some are vampiric in nature.

GRIMOIRES for ceremonial MAGIC include instructions for evoking and commanding *daimones*.

FURTHER READING:
Guiley, Rosemary Ellen. *The Encyclopedia of Angels.* 2d ed. New York, Facts On File Inc., 2004.
Luck, Goerg. *Arcana Mundi: Magic and the Occult in the Greek and Roman Worlds.* Baltimore: Johns Hopkins University Press, 1985.

Damian, John (15th–16th c.) Scottish alchemist who assisted King James IV (1473–1513). John Damian apparently lacked great alchemical knowledge but made up for his deficiency in brashness and daring. He convinced James to set up an alchemical laboratory in Stirling Castle where Damian spent huge sums of money for years trying to make GOLD. James eventually tired of the expense and made Damian an abbot. Damian continued to borrow money from the king to supplement his abbot's salary. He was fond of elaborate clothing and whiskey and wine. Despite his lack of alchemical success, Damian remained on good terms with James and played dice and cards often with him.

Once while still at Stirling Castle, Damian attempted to fly by fastening wings made of feathers to himself and leaping off the castle battlements. He fell to the ground and broke a leg. He explained away his failure by the fact that some of the feathers were from barn-door birds who seldom flew much.

D'Apone, Pietro (b. 1250) Italian physician, alchemist, and reputed magician who met his demise in the Inquisition. Many of the feats of MAGIC and SORCERY attributed to Pietro D'Apone were probably more fiction than fact, but they were sufficient to secure his condemnation.

D'Apone was born in Apone, near Padua, Italy, in 1250. A physician, he knew ARNOLD DE VILLANOVA. He possessed enough knowledge about ASTROLOGY, ALCHEMY, and the magical arts to impress others. He lived in Paris for many years where he made his living by telling fortunes and practicing medicine; then D'Apone returned to Italy.

According to lore, his powers came from seven infernal FAMILIARS that he kept trapped in seven crystal vases. Each familiar functioned like a muse with its own area of expertise: philosophy, alchemy, astrology, medicine, poetry, music, and painting. Whenever D'Apone needed information, he let out a familiar and received instruction from it. It was said that with the help of the spirits, D'Apone could mimic the greatest artists and thinkers.

D'Apone reputedly made GOLD out of brass, but he used magic to keep it to himself. Whenever he gave out his gold, he said a CHARM over it that caused it to be returned magically to him. No locks or surveillance could keep the gold in place. This power extended to SILVER as well.

D'Apone thus had few friends and many enemies and compounded his unpopularity by making unwise statements about religion that came to the attention of the Inquisition. He was arrested and charged with heresy and sorcery and was brought before an Inquisition tribunal. He was tortured severely on the rack but continued to protest his innocence.

D'Apone died in prison before being brought to trial. He was found guilty posthumously. The Inquisition ordered his bones to be dug up and publicly burned. He was burned in effigy in the streets of Padua.

FURTHER READING:

Mackay, Charles. *Extraordinary Popular Delusions and the Madness of Crowds.* New York: Farrar, Straus & Giroux, 1932.

David-Neel, Alexandra (1868–1969)

French explorer, occultist, and Tibetan scholar. Alexandra David-Neel led an exotic life and was the first Western woman to enter Llasa, the forbidden capital of Tibet. She spent 14 years in Tibet and became one of the first Westerners to learn Tibetan secrets of MAGIC and mysticism. Her knowledge influenced the magical practices of other Western occultists, such as FRANZ BARDON. David-Neel loved adventure and said that the surest ELIXIR is not an alchemical formula but travel and intellectual activity.

Life

David-Neel claimed to be descended from Genghis Khan on her mother's side. She was born Louise Eugenie Alexandrine Marie David on October 24, 1868, in Paris. Her father, Louis David, was a Huguenot activist and friend of novelist Victor Hugo. At age five, she moved to Brussels with her parents.

From early childhood, David-Neel was odd and sickly, preferring solitude to the company of friends. She suffered from depression. She had a talent for music and singing. She longed to go off by herself to travel and explore distant lands—an unusual interest for women of her era. At age 15 she read a journal published by the Supreme Gnosis, an occult society in London, and became fascinated by occultism. Five years later, she was sent to London to study for a year; she boarded at the Supreme Gnosis quarters. David-Neel reveled in the occult activities and lectures of the THEOSOPHICAL SOCIETY, ROSICRUCIANISM, and spiritualism.

Upon completion of her studies in London 1889, she went to Paris to attend the Sorbonne. She lived with Theosophists in the Latin Quarter. She became interested in Buddhism and wrote articles on religion and occultism for various intellectual journals. Around the end of 1890 or early 1891, she was severely depressed and decided to commit suicide by shooting herself with her handgun. She changed her mind, deciding that suicide was a coward's way out that would incur bad karma in her next incarnation.

In 1891 David-Neel inherited money from a godmother, which enabled her to travel to India and Ceylon. She joined the cult of Sri Ananda Sarawati, where she was introduced to hashish. She reportedly smoked it only once, and for the remainder of her life she considered drugs useless for occult work.

Travel consumed her inheritance, and David-Neel returned to Paris to work as a singer under the pseudonym Mademoiselle Myrial, after one of Hugo's characters. In 1900, at age 32, she met Philip Neel, a bachelor and engineer seven years her senior. She became one of his many mistresses. David-Neel had resisted getting married because she did not want to lose her legal rights and be subjugated by a husband. Neel was persuasive, however, and the two were married in 1904 in Tunis. Two stormy years later, David-Neel left Neel and went to Belgium on the excuse of paying respects to a friend who had died. Her real reason probably was to avoid getting pregnant, for Neel was pressing her to have a child. David-Neel never returned to the marriage. They remained married but led separate lives. Neel supported her financially during most of her years of travel.

By 1904 David-Neel had gained recognition in occult circles in London and Paris for her articles and lectures on Buddhism. In 1911 she followed her husband's suggestion to return to India to study Eastern languages. She met the mystic Sri Aurobindo in 1911 and was deeply impressed by him.

In 1912 she met the man who opened the door to Tibet for her: Sidkeong Tulku, the Maharaj Kumar (Crown Prince) of Sikkim. He invited her to visit him in Gangtok, the capital of Sikkim, which lies at the border between India and Tibet. There she became romantically involved with the crown prince and became fascinated by Tibet. Sidkeong took her hiking through the mountains and introduced her to lamas of both the Red Hat (traditional) and Yellow Hat (reformed) branches of Tibetan Buddhism. Wherever she went, people treated her as an emanation of Queen Victoria, the Palden Llamo, or patron goddess of Tibet.

On April 15, 1912, David-Neel had the first of her two audiences with the Thirteenth Dalai Lama, held in

Kalimpong, India. He advised her to learn Tibetan. Shortly thereafter, she met a *naljorpa*, a WIZARD, who told her to enter Tibet and be initiated by a master. At the time, travel in Tibet was forbidden to foreigners, but the *naljorpa* told David-Neel she could do it by bypassing dangerous areas. Instead, she returned to Sikkim to resume her study of Sanskrit, believing that her destiny lay in writing a major comparative work on branches of Buddhism. Her circumstances changed radically in 1914, when the early death of Sidkeong cut off her access to royal courts and World War I prevented her return to her husband.

David-Neel became a disciple of the Gomchen (Great Hermit) of Lachen, whom she had met in 1912 and who lived as a hermit 12,000 feet high in the Sikkim Himalayas at De-Chen in the Cave of Clear Light. David-Neel pledged complete obedience to him. They agreed to teach each other English and Tibetan. If she proved worthy, he would also teach her secret Tantric wisdom. She took up residence as a hermit in a cave one mile below his. One of her servants was Aphur Yongden, a 15-year-old boy who later became her adopted son and a lama.

David-Neel and the Gomchem developed a telepathic rapport, considered the highest form of teaching but rarely attained because most pupils lacked the proper psychic development. She learned various psychic arts, such as *tumo* breathing, a technique that is used to raise body temperature during the severe winters and that prepares one for spiritual emancipation. During this time, David-Neel connected with a past life in which she was a nomad in central Asia.

The Gomchen is most likely the one who initiated David-Neel into the "Short Path" of Tibetan mysticism. The traditional path is to enter monastic life. The Short Path is free of the bondage of discipline, and the initiate may undertake whatever experiments he or she desires for advancement. The Short Path is the preferred path of Tibetan sorcerers and magicians. The Gomchen gave her the name of "Lamp of Wisdom" and probably gave her permission to reveal certain knowledge to the West.

In 1916 David-Neel secretly entered Tibet and settled in Shigatse in the monastery of the Panchen Lama, second in rank to the Dalai Lama. The British authorities found out, sacked her hermit's cave below the Gomchem, and expelled her from Sikkim. All of her servants except Yongden, who had a British passport, deserted her. Determined to reenter Tibet, David-Neel and Yongden went to Japan and then China. They secretly penetrated Tibet in a dangerous journey. They traveled to Kumbum, a monastery that probably served as the model for the Shangri-La in James Hilton's novel by the same name. There they spent two-and-a-half years, during which David-Neel translated rare Tibetan occult manuscripts into French and English and observed the magical and psychic feats of Tibetan ADEPTS.

In 1921 she, Yongden, and a new party of servants set out for Lhasa. She had no money and wore tattered clothing. She was beset by bandits but was never harmed, per-

haps because Yongden passed her off as a sorceress and as the wife of a deceased sorcerer. She also masqueraded as a *kamdora*, a FAIRYlike female spirit whose blessings are sought. This enabled her to obtain food from peasants wherever they went.

The journey to Llasa took her three years through rough territory. They made their way through deep snow and slept in icy caves. In the last stage they traveled across the uncharted and treacherous Po country, whose wild inhabitants were rumored to be cannibals. David-Neel used *tumo* breathing to stay alive during the severe winters. She also used *lung-gom*, a type of entranced movement that lightens the body and enables rapid traveling—even flying—without food, water, or rest. According to lore, entranced *lung-gom-pas* cannot be disturbed, or the god within them will depart prematurely and cause their death. David-Neel also had a frightening time with a *tulpa*, or THOUGHT-FORM, that she created, which went out of control.

The party reached Lhasa in February 1924. David-Neel retained her disguise as a beggar, which prevented her from engaging in the intellectual life she desired. A year later she and Yongden were back in Paris, where she was lauded for her exploits. She lectured and began a demanding schedule of writing books and articles. In 1928 she bought a small villa outside of Digne in southern France and named it Samten Dzong, the "Fortress of Meditation."

In 1937 David-Neel and Yongden went to Peking, where they intended to get help in translating old manuscripts. They never reached the capital, because of the outbreak of the Sino-Japanese War, but they stayed in the country until 1945. Meanwhile, her husband Philip died in 1941.

David-Neel and Yongden returned to France in 1946. With Philip gone, David-Neel publicly acknowledged participating in Tantric sexual rites. She also said she performed a mild version of the *chod* ("to cut up") ritual, designed to stir up occult forces and liberate one from all attachments. In the *chod*, the participant sacrifices himself of herself to dismemberment and devouring by hungry ghouls or spirits, and then renounces the sacrifice as illusion because he or she is nothing and therefore has nothing to give. David-Neel probably continued to practice the *chod* during her later years in France.

Yongden became an alcoholic and died of uremic poisoning in 1955. In 1958 David-Neel hired a secretary, Jeanne Denys, to look after her estate. But David-Neel's bad temper caused Denys to despise her, and the secretary spent many years trying to debunk David-Neel's work as fiction. In 1959 Denys was replaced by Marie-Madeleine Peyronnet, who looked after David-Neel until her death on September 6, 1969. True to her assertion that travel and intellectual activity constituted the elixir of longevity, David-Neel was nearly 101 when she died. Of all her adventures, she considered her stay in the hermit's cave in the Sikkimese Himalayas to be the summit of her life's dream.

Most of David-Neel's manuscripts and Tibetan artifacts went to museums or remained at Samten Dzong, which became a conference center and museum.

Works

David-Neel's works include more than 30 titles and contain descriptions of Tibetan magical and religious practices, rituals, and ceremonies. Her best-known books are *My Journey to Lhasa* (1927), an account of her three-year journey; *Magic and Mystery in Tibet* (1929), anecdotal accounts of magical and mystical practices; *Initiations and Initiates of Tibet* (1930), a more serious discussion of Tantric lore and mystical rites; and *Buddhism: Its Doctrines and Its Methods* (1936), a recapitulation of an earlier work on Buddhist doctrines.

FURTHER READING:

David-Neel, Alexandra. *Magic and Mystery in Tibet.* 1929. Reprint, New York: Dover Publications, 1971.
———. *My Journey to Lhasa.* 1927. Reprint, Boston: Beacon Press, 1986.
Foster, Barbara, and Michael Foster. *Forbidden Journey: The Life of Alexandra David-Neel.* San Francisco: Harper & Row, 1987.

Da Vinci Code, The Author Dan Brown's extraordinarily successful thriller novel, published in 2003, which proposes that for over 2,000 years, the Catholic Church has been trying to hide—and destroy—any evidence that would reveal the most explosive secret in world history: that Jesus and Mary Magdalene were married, that she was pregnant at the time of the crucifixion, and that descendants of this holy marriage have survived to the present day, faithfully documented and protected by the shadowy Priory of Sion and its Grand Masters, notably Leonardo da Vinci. The movie by the same name, starring Tom Hanks and Ian McKellen, was released in 2006.

The Da Vinci Code is Brown's fourth book and the second in a trilogy featuring Harvard professor of religious symbology Robert Langdon. He first appeared in *Angels and Demons* (2002), which takes place in Rome and concerns the ILLUMINATI. Brown's first book, *Digital Fortress*, was published in 1998, and the third, *Deception Point*, was released in 2001. The last of the Langdon books, *The Solomon Key* (2007), takes Langdon into the esoteric rites of FREEMASONRY.

Plot

The plot of *The Da Vinci Code*, full of SYMBOLS and coded riddles, begins with the murder of Jacques Saunière, a curator at the Louvre in Paris. His nude body is found posed like Leonardo da Vinci's famous drawing, *Vitruvian Man*, marked with a PENTAGRAM drawn in his own BLOOD. Next to the body is a cryptic message consisting of three ana-

grams: the first consists of the digits of the mathematical Fibonacci sequence, but out of order; the second and third are "O, draconian devil!" and "Oh, lame saint!," which when rearranged say, "Leonardo da Vinci" and "The *Mona Lisa.*" Additionally, there seems to be a postscript, "P.S.: Find Robert Langdon," which French police official Bezu Fache thinks is a clue to the murderer's identity.

Cryptologist Sophie Neveu realizes that the "P.S." refers to her, however, as Saunière was her grandfather and always called her "Princesse Sophie." He had raised Sophie after her family died in an auto accident, but they have been estranged for 10 years. Langdon is brought in to interpret the strange clues. Sophie warns him that he is in danger from Fache, and the two manage to elude Fache to solve the next puzzle. The *Mona Lisa* anagram reveals a secret message written on the protective glass over the painting that says "So dark the con of Man," which leads to da Vinci's *Madonna of the Rocks.* And behind that painting is the key to a box held in a Swiss bank.

Langdon and Neveu manage to escape Fache and open the box, which contains a cryptex, an encrypted cylinder that works like a Rubik's cube as a means of sending secret messages. This cryptex is the "keystone" that Saunière's murderer sought, and it holds a smaller cryptex with another code. After successfully dodging Fache yet again, Langdon and Neveu head for the chateau of Langdon's old friend Sir Leigh Teabing.

Meanwhile, Father Aringarosa of the Catholic Church organization Opus Dei and his associate, a fanatical monk named Silas who engages in self-flagellation and other mortifications of the flesh, are also heading for Teabing's along with Fache. Silas murdered Saunière. Before all parties collide, Teabing explains to Neveu about the search for the GRAIL (*san greal* in French), which is really a wordplay on *sang real*: royal blood. He tells her and Langdon that the figure to Jesus's right in da Vinci's *Last Supper* is not the apostle John but actually Mary Magdalene. The space between them is a "V," which represents both the male (the "blade") and the female (the "chalice"). Teabing asserts that Mary Magdalene was pregnant with Jesus's child at the time of His crucifixion, and that afterward she fled to what is now France and had a daughter, Sarah. Other descendants married into what became the Frankish Merovingian ruling dynasty, eventually overthrown in 751 C.E. by Charles Martel, the first Carolingian.

The tumult over the possibility of an important woman in the life of Christ supposedly led to the church's Council of Nicea in 325 C.E., during which the church fathers established what was orthodoxy and suppressed other early texts from the canon—including any that gave women a larger role or made mention of a marriage or children between Jesus and Mary Magdalene. But according to legend, documents of the sacred union were hidden in Jerusalem and discovered by knights on Crusade in the 11th century. These knights—who became the ORDER OF THE KNIGHTS TEMPLARS—vowed to preserve and protect the information, a promise they scrupulously kept until King Philip IV of France destroyed the Templars in 1307. After 1314, surviving Templars, forced into hiding, allegedly formed the Priory of Sion. The Priory's Grand Masters, including da Vinci, Sir Isaac Newton, and Alexander Pope, pledged their lives to saving the secret proof and protecting the "chalice" of the Holy Grail: Mary Magdalene's relics and the documents.

Teabing, who appears so genial, is double-crossing Langdon and Neveu. He takes them on his private jet to London with the intention of killing them and the Opus Dei priest Aringarosa so that he can reveal the great secret and reap all the glory. But he fails, enabling Langdon and Neveu to solve the rest of the puzzle, discover the location of the secret documents, and learn who is the current bearer of the holy blood.

That bearer is Neveu, and she is reunited with her protectors at Rossyln Chapel in Scotland. There is no tomb of Mary Magdelene there, however. Finally Langdon makes the intuitive discovery that Mary Magdelene is entombed in the Louvre.

Reaction

Many in the Catholic Church and other Christian groups and organizations have been outraged by the book and its allegations of a royal bloodline. Although Brown defends the book as fiction, he asserts that the descriptions of artwork, architecture, and RITUALS in it are accurate. Such claims are not easily proved but have convinced many of the book's fans. Some source material for Brown comes from *Holy Blood, Holy Grail* (1982) by Michael Baigent, Richard Leigh, and Henry Lincoln, in which the authors assert that evidence exists for a marriage between Jesus and Mary Magdalene, that there really is a Priory of Sion, that the members are dedicated to the reestablishment of the Merovingian dynasty as head of a Holy European Empire, and that all these secrets were found in the small French village of Rennes-le-Château. Baigent and Leigh sued Brown for plagiarism ("Teabing" is an anagram for "Baigent") but lost.

Overall, the story and its validation of what is called "the sacred feminine," an acknowledgment of the power and influence of women on both religion and humanity, appeals to readers looking for spiritual answers far from fundamentalism and paternalistic hierarchies. One of the rituals described in *The Da Vinci Code* is *hieros gamos*, or "sacred marriage": a formal sexual rite that preserved the purity of royal bloodlines and attempted to guarantee fertility and prosperity. It was Neveu's inadvertent witness to her grandfather's participation in the ritual that estranged them.

By early 2006, *The Da Vinci Code* had sold more than 60.5 million copies and had been translated into 44 languages, making it the sixth-best-selling book of all time. The much-anticipated and heavily publicized movie version premiered at the Cannes Film Festival on May 17, 2006. The film was released internationally the next day and in the United States on May 19. Earnings topped $224 million the first weekend.

Academy Award–winner Tom Hanks plays Langdon, and French actress Audrey Tautou plays Sophie Neveu. Two-time Oscar nominee Sir Ian McKellen is Sir Leigh Teabing. Alfred Molina plays Father Aringarosa, and Paul Bettany portrays the tortured monk Silas. Dan Brown co-wrote the screenplay with Akiva Goldsman; Oscar-winner Ron Howard directed.

The film adheres to the book fairly closely, although there are some differences in the ways the characters solve the riddles and eventually find the secret documents. Probably the main difference (and one that is unusual for Hollywood) is the very chaste parting at the end between Langdon and Neveu, who show no hint of sexual attraction. The book ends with the beginning of an affair.

Controversy erupted before the movie opened. Ordinary citizens who had not seen the film protested, while some church officials advocated actions from disclaimers to boycotts. The film was banned or severely restricted in several Asian and Middle Eastern countries. The National Organization for Albinism and Hypopigmentation expressed concern that Bettany's performance gives albinos a bad name.

Perhaps because of the overheated atmosphere surrounding the movie's release, the majority of critics were unimpressed. Even stars Hanks and McKellen expressed doubts about the story. But the idea that Jesus and Mary Magdalene begat a bloodline is deeply entrenched in esoteric lore. Unlikely ever to be proved or disproved, the romance it inspires will continue.

FURTHER READING:

Barlowe, Byron. "*The Da Vinci Code:* Of Magdalene, Gnostics, the Goddess and the Grail." Leadership University. Available online. URL: http://www.leaderu.com/focus/davinci code.html. Downloaded June 8, 2006.

Brown, Dan. *Angels and Demons.* New York: Doubleday, 2000.

———. *The Da Vinci Code.* New York: Doubleday, 2003.

death prayer   A CURSE done by RITUAL in which a victim is killed at a distance magically. The death prayer is especially prominent in the MAGIC of the Kahuna ("Keepers of the Secret") priests of Hawaii. A death prayer is done as punishment for a grievous offense or crime and also for revenge.

Unlike many other forms of cursing in which the victim knows she or he is being cursed, the victim of a Kahuna death prayer is given no warning. However, a sense of guilt over wrongdoing is important in the success of the curse.

The symptoms of the death prayer are a slow paralysis starting with the lower limbs and gradually creeping up the torso until the heart is stopped.

To perform a death prayer, a Kahuna must be able to control *uphili,* subconscious spirits. He inherits these from another Kahuna or captures and enslaves them by hypnosis. He orders them to absorb his own *mana,* or vital force, which is manipulated in many magical SPELLS. The Kahuna sends the spirits to the victim. They shock the victim with the force of the *mana* and then suck off the victim's own *mana,* initiating the creeping and fatal numbness.

Death prayers, or ritual cursing to death, exist in other forms as well.

FURTHER READING:
Long, Max Freedom. *The Secret Science Behind Miracles.* Los Angeles: DeVorss & Co., 1954.

Dee, John (1527–1608) Alchemist, mathematician, astronomer, and astrologer, sometimes called the last royal magician because of his astrological services to Queen Elizabeth I. Dee was a scholarly man—some say he was the most learned man in Euorpe of his time—who was fascinated by the occult and MAGIC. He was an adept in Neoplatonic, Hermetic, and kabbalistic philosophy. He devoted most of his life to trying to communicate with spirits, for which he had to rely on mediums due to his own lack of psychic ability.

Dee was born in London on July 13, 1527. His father, a Welshman, was a minor official in the court of Henry VIII. As a child Dee exhibited a quick mind. He entered St. John's College in Cambridge at age 15, vowing that he would spend the rest of his life studying for 18 hours a day, eating for two hours, and sleeping for four. It is not known how well he adhered to this rigorous schedule throughout his 81 years, but he did pursue a lifelong quest for mystical knowledge. After earning his bachelor's degree in 1545, he was given a fellowship at the college. In 1546, Trinity College opened, and Dee transferred there as one of the original fellows, teaching Greek. His intellect and imagination earned him the nickname of sorcerer.

Magic and ALCHEMY intrigued him; at that time, those fields were closely related to science. Dee found Cambridge boring, and from 1547 to 1551, he traveled in France and northern Europe, lecturing and teaching. He caused a sensation in Paris, delivering a series of brilliant lectures on the works of Euclid. Thousands came to hear him speak.

Dee was heavily influenced by the occult writings of HENRY CORNELIUS AGRIPPA and also by his meeting of Jerome Cardan, a self-professed WIZARD who apparently possessed genuine clairvoyant ability and could experience ASTRAL PROJECTION.

Dee was plagued with money problems and decided that alchemy could provide the solution. He was determined to contact spirit forces who would help him find the PHILOSOPHER'S STONE or discover buried treasure. He paid great attention to his dreams and tried SCRYING. Except for a few instances during his life, Dee was unable to see or hear spirits. Dee considered himself a resolute Christian; the spirits he sought were ANGELS, not DEMONS. He believed that the magic he pursued was pure and good and not demonic or evil. His intense desire to communicate with the spirit realm led him into gullible relationships with unscrupulous people.

In 1551, after the death of Henry VIII, Dee returned to England and was granted a pension by Henry's 10-year-old successor, Edward VI. Edward died at 16 and with him Dee's hopes for a financially secure future. His prospects brightened when Queen Mary gained the throne and asked him to cast her horoscope. He also visited Mary's younger sister, Elizabeth, whom Mary had imprisoned, and cast a horoscope for her to determine when Mary would die. For this, Dee was accused of attempting to murder Mary by black magic, and he was imprisoned. He was also accused of murdering children by SORCERY (for which he was acquitted) and for being "a companion of hellhounds and a caller and conjurer of wicked and damned spirits." He was found not guilty of treason and was released in 1555.

Dee's friendship with Elizabeth proved beneficial to him. Mary died in 1558, and Elizabeth ascended the throne. Much more superstitious and interested in ASTROLOGY than her sister, she consulted Dee for an auspicious day for her coronation in 1558. His horoscope casting gained favor in court, and he also gave Elizabeth lessons in mystical interpretations of his writings. But Elizabeth never granted him the generous pension he sought, and his income from horoscope casting was meager. He was able to buy a riverside home at Mortlake; once Elizabeth and her courtiers paid a visit to him there to see his famous scrying smoky quartz crystal.

Dee performed various tasks. He interpreted the appearance of a comet. But when called upon to exorcize some possessed children, he could do no more than to refer the family to preachers for help. On another occasion, he counteracted a death SPELL against the queen, which was discovered when a man found a POPPET of her stuck with pins in a field. Elizabeth afforded him protection against his detractors, who would have had him accused of WITCHCRAFT. According to lore, he spied for Elizabeth on his travels around the Continent.

Catherine de Médicis, the queen of France, was among Dee's regular and most important clientele. Catherine was a big believer in magic and the occult arts and made no personal or public decisions without consulting a host of diviners and magicians. Dee divined the future of her sons. It is likely that Dee shaped his predictions to suit her interests and did the same with other clients as well, especially royalty and nobility.

Dee's modest income still enabled him to collect thousands of occult and esoteric books. His library of 4,000 volumes became famous and may have been one of the largest such collections of the time. Most of the books were salvaged from monasteries and churches ransacked under the dissolution orders of Henry VIII. Other books came from his travels. In Antwerp in 1563, he found a rare copy of *Stenographia,* written about 100 years earlier by the German Benedictine abbot, JOHANN TRITHEMIUS, on magic, NUMBERS, cyphers, and SYMBOLS. This inspired Dee to write his own book on the subject, *Monas Hieroglyphia*. Dee wrote 79 manuscripts in all, but few were published by the time of his death.

Dee was married three times. His first marriage, to Katherine Constable, took place in 1565. Little is known about her, but evidently she died by 1575 when Dee married for the second time. His unknown second wife died in 1576 of the plague, and in 1578, he married Jane Fromond, much younger than he. She bore him eight children.

By 1580, Dee was thoroughly immersed in magic and alchemy and believed that he was in communication with angels and spirits. He dressed like an exotic WIZARD. He scried with both the smoky quartz and a disk of polished cannel coal.

In 1581, Dee had an experience that set his life on a new track. Late one autumn evening he knelt in prayer when, by his own account, "there suddenly glowed a dazzling light, in the midst of which, in all his glory, stood the great angel, Uriel." The angel gave him a crystal "most bright, most clear and glorious, of the bigness of an egg." Uriel told Dee that he could communicate with spirits by gazing into the crystal.

Dee was ecstatic at this prospect, but his scrying efforts were not fruitful. In his diary, he recorded his dreams, alleged spirit rappings, and the few times he thought he saw spirits. Frustrated, Dee hired others to help him. The assistant would scry while Dee took down notes. His first partnership was with a young man named Barnabas Saul, who got into trouble with the law after a few months.

Then in 1582 Dee met EDWARD KELLY, a rogue and opportunist who had lost his ears as punishment for forgery. Kelly said he could communicate with spirits. For seven years, the two had an uneasy partnership; Dee never saw through Kelly's charlatan ways. Kelly was hot tempered, impetuous, and opportunistic, and he wanted only to make a quick fortune in alchemy. Dee was low key, serious, and scholarly and an easy target for manipulation.

Kelly impressed Dee by gazing into Dee's crystal and claiming to see angels. According to Dee, Kelly said that "in the middle of the stone seemeth to stand a little round thing like a spark of fire, and it increaseth, and it seemeth to be as a globe of twenty inches in diameter, or there about." The glowing globe contained a host of angels who spoke in Enochian, their language and the language of Paradise. (See ENOCHIAN MAGIC.)

Kelly soon moved into the Dee house in Mortlake. Dee's wife took an instinctive and immediate dislike to Kelly, who was rumored to practice NECROMANCY and be inhabited by an evil spirit. But Kelly held the upper hand in his strange relationship with the studious Dee. Kelly would gaze into a crystal and summon spirits with INCANTATIONS, or "calls" in Enochian. He said he could see and hear the spirits, and he acted as intermediary for Dee, who would pose questions to them. Prominent among the spirits were Uriel, the angel of light in the KABBALAH, and

a childlike being named Madimi; Dee named one of his daughters after her.

Shortly after Kelly arrived on the scene, Dee was rewarded with one of his few psychic experiences in which he saw Uriel floating outside his window, holding a pale pink crystal about the size of an orange. Then the Archangel Michael appeared and told Dee to use it. This crystal, Dee's "magic MIRROR"—a black obsidian mirror from Mexico—and other of his magical instruments are on display in the British Museum.

Dee and Kelly provided their mediumistic services to a variety of nobles, including Count Albert Laski of Poland, who urged them to come to Poland. Laski had lost his fortune and was in hopes of recovering it quickly through alchemy. In 1584, Dee, Kelly, and their wives and families set off on a four-year journey around the Continent, performing for royalty and nobility but without much success. They stayed first at Laski's castle in Cracow, but when Dee and Kelly failed to produce GOLD, Laski sent them to Emperor Rudolf II in Prague. Rudolf was unimpressed. The pair managed to get an introduction to King Stephen of Poland. They staged a seance for him, but the king suspected them of fraud and sent them back to Prague. They were thrown out of the city because the pope accused Dee of necromancy. They went to Erfurt but were turned away by authorities. They had a short stay at Hesse-Cassel and then finally were invited by Count Rosenberg to his castle Tribau in Bohemia.

Dee and Kelly had numerous quarrels, and Kelly would quit scrying for periods of time. The breaking point came in 1587 when Kelly informed Dee that a female spirit had

John Dee, in A True and Faithful Relation of What Passed for Many Years between Dr. John Dee and Some Spirits, *by Meric Causabon, 1659. (Author's collection)*

ordered them to share wives, which Dee reluctantly agreed to do. Jane was hysterical but acquiesced, and the Dees signed a written contract with Kelly. It is not recorded whether or not Kelly actually slept with her, but shortly after that, the strange partnership between Dee and Kelly broke up, and in 1588 the Dees returned to England. Kelly remained in Europe and went to Prague. In 1595 he died from severe injuries suffered when he tried to escape from prison.

Back in England, Dee found his Mortlake house ransacked by his enemies and a good number of his books and scientific instruments destroyed. Elizabeth reimbursed him for some of the 2,000 pounds in damages he claimed, and he was able to salvage some 3,000 books, most of which are in British museums.

Elizabeth made him warden of Christ's College in Manchester in 1595, but Dee did not find the job fulfilling. Jane died of the plague. Elizabeth died in 1603, and her successor, James I, was a firm opponent of magic and witchcraft. Dee retired to Mortlake where he lived in poverty. He subsisted on a meager income from fortune-telling and was forced to sell some of his remaining precious books to eat.

He found a new scrying partner, Bartholomew Hickman, who said he could communicate with the angel Raphael. The spirit offered Dee vague murmurrings of discovering the secrets of God and the universe that he had pursued for so many years, but none were realized. Another scryer also proved to be dishonest.

Dee died in obscurity in 1608 and was buried at Mortlake church. His biographer, John Aubrey, described him in his last years as a beaten old man who had a "long beard as white as milke, tall and slender, who wore a gowne with hanging sleeves."

Dee's son, Arthur, became an alchemist and served as physician to the czar of Russia and to Charles I.

Only a small proportion of Dee's angel diaries survive; most were destroyed either by him or by a maid who used the pages as pie plate liners. In the mid-19th century, one of his private diaries was discovered, written in a small, nearly illegible script on the margins of old almanacs. The notes recount Dee's European adventures with Kelley and Dee's belief that Kelley had indeed unlocked the secret of the PHILOSOPHER'S STONE. In addition, five of his diaries from 1582–83 were discovered in an old chest and were published in 2003.

Dee's work influenced the HERMETIC ORDER OF THE GOLDEN DAWN, although ALEISTER CROWLEY described Dee as a humorless old man and expressed reverence for Kelly.

FURTHER READING:
Dee, John. *True and Faithful Relation of What Passed for Many Years Between Dr. John Dee and Some Spirits.* Whitefish, Mont.: Kessinger, 1999.
Halliwell, James Orchard. *Private Diary of Dr. John Dee and the Catalog of His Library of Alchemical Manuscripts.* Whitefish, Mont.: Kessinger, 1997.
Harkness, Deborah E. *John Dee's Conversations with Angels.* Cambridge: Cambridge University Press, 1999.
Holmyard, E. J. *Alchemy.* New York: Penguin Books, 1957.
Peterson, Joseph. *John Dee's Five Books of Mystery: Original Sourcebook of Enochian Magic.* York Beach, Maine: Samuel Weiser, 2003.
Suster, Gerald. *John Dee: Essential Readings.* London: Crucible, 1986.

Delisle, Alain (d. 1298) Flemish alchemist. Little is known about the life of Alain Delisle (also spelled Alain de Lisle) of Flanders, who was a contemporary of ALBERTUS MAGNUS. Delisle was called the universal doctor because of his extensive knowledge of all sciences. He was a friar at the abbey of Citeaux. He wrote a commentary on the prophecies of MERLIN.

According to lore, he discovered the PHILOSOPHER'S STONE at the age of 50, which enabled him to live another 60 years, dying at age 110.

FURTHER READING:
Waite, Arthur Edward. *Alchemists Through the Ages.* Blauvelt, N.Y.: Rudolph Steiner Publications, 1970.

Delisle, Jean (17th–18th c.) French blacksmith, fraudulent alchemist, and rogue. Jean Delisle—which may not have been his real Christian name—was born to a peasant family in Provence, France. Delisle was uneducated and never learned to read or write. He earned a living as a blacksmith. He developed a reputation for rudeness and fanaticism. His schemes earned him an unhappy ending to his life.

He is said to have learned the alchemical arts during service to an unknown gentleman who received the secret of the PHILOSOPHER'S STONE from LASCARIS. The master fell into disrepute with King Louis XIV and was forced to flee France. He went to Switzerland, taking Delisle with him. But at a mountain pass near Savoy, Delisle murdered his master and robbed him, allegedly stealing a large quantity of transmuting powder.

Delisle returned to France is disguise as a pilgrim. He spent the night at an inn, where he met a married woman whose surname was Aluys (or Alnys). According to lore, the two fell madly in love, and Aluys left her domestic life and went off with Delisle. They lived quietly together for five or six years in Provence, near Barjarumont in the parish of Sylanes. In about 1706, rumors circulated that Delisle was in possession of the Philosopher's Stone and was turning lead, IRON, and ordinary pumps and shovels into GOLD or SILVER. He was about 35 years of age.

In a letter written on November 18, 1706, by the prior of Chateauneuf, M. de Cerisy, to his cousin the vicar of St. Jacques du Hautpas, de Cerisy reported eyewitness accounts by the bishop of Senes and other esteemed citizens. They said that Delisle accomplished his transmutations by heating the ordinary metals and pouring over them his mysterious mixture of powder and oil. When he drew them out, they appeared to be a pale gold. Delisle also transmuted steel into gold and turned base metals into SILVER. Eyewitnesses, often initially skeptical, came away convinced that Delisle was not committing fraud. It was said that the oil was gold or was silver that was reduced to that state by Delisle who left it exposed to the rays of the SUN for long periods of time. Delisle told people that it took him six months to make his preparations. The powder, he said, was composed of simple substances, mostly the herbs Lunaria major and minor.

Some of Delisle's gold reportedly was refined in Paris, and three medals were struck from it. Jewelers in Lyons were said to be impressed by it, and a merchant in Digne bought 20 pounds of it.

Delisle was said to make nails that were part gold, part silver, and part iron. The prior said in his letter that he had been promised one and that he had seen a nail of gold reportedly made by Delisle; it was now possessed by the prior's brother-in-law, who had witnessed the transmutation. The prior also saw an ingot of gold made out of pewter, possessed by the baron and baronness de Rheinwald.

Delisle's unsuspecting clients did not realize that he accomplished his transmutations with the help of a double-bottomed crucible and a hollow wand.

The superintendent of the French royal court household sent some of Delisle's ingots to the king, who summoned Delisle to an audience. Delisle declined with an astonishingly rude answer: The climate was not right for his herbal preparations, he loved his liberty, he had no politeness, and he spoke French badly. He was ordered to appear in royal court in Paris. This time Delisle said he would comply willingly and would come in the spring; he needed time to collect his materials to make an experiment for the king of converting lead into gold.

On January 27, 1707, the prior de Cerisy wrote again to his cousin to report that with the help of Delisle, he had himself made a nail that was half iron and half silver and had used the oil-and-powder mixture to transmute a piece of lead into gold. The prior dined with Delisle and told him that if he would divulge his secret to King Louis, he could "humble all the enemies of France." De Cerisy described Delisle as "the miracle of art."

Meanwhile, Delisle, despite his summons to court, continued to defraud people. A local resident named de la Palu who had no money for dowries for his middle-aged daughters took him in to live in his chateau after Delisle promised to make the daughters the richest in the province before he left for the royal court.

Whether or not Delisle ever made good on that promise is not known; most likely, he did not. He succeeded, however, in delaying his trip to Paris for two years, despite being assured safe conduct.

Suspicious of fraud, the French minister of finance, Desmarets, wrote to the bishop of Senes to try to find out what was the truth. The bishop replied that initially he had suspected Delisle of fraud and for three years had tried to expose him but without success. He now believed him to be a genuine alchemist.

Delisle was summoned to court a third time, but again he delayed with one excuse or another. The bishop, who had personally guaranteed that Delisle would comply, now worried about repercussions against himself from the court. He arranged for Delisle to be arrested in June 1711. Delisle was taken away to Paris to be imprisoned in the Bastille.

Enroute, Delisle's guards plotted to extort the riches they thought he possessed. Delisle was led to believe that he would be allowed to escape. In fact, the guards meant to let him get away, then pursue him, and shoot him dead. They would then take the Stone to Paris and tell Desmarets that Delisle was killed trying to escape.

The plan nearly succeeded. Deslisle was allowed to run, and then one of the guards shot him in either the thigh or the head (accounts differ). They could not complete the killing because of the timely arrival of peasants. Instead, the guards had to carry Delisle, wounded and bleeding, on to Paris. He was placed in a dungeon in the Bastille. He went into frenzies and repeatedly tore his bandages off.

The bishop of Senes visited Delisle, who claimed he could not make the secret powder—he had only been given some by an Italian philosopher, and he had used it all up in Provence.

Some accounts say that Delisle never got up from his sick bed and died in prison. Others say that he was forced to perform his alchemical experiments in his cell. After a short period of time, Delisle refused to continue. His mental condition worsened, and after nearly a year in prison, he died from his wounds or, by some accounts, poisoned himself.

See also ALUYS, ALBERT.

FURTHER READING:
Mackay, Charles. *Extraordinary Popular Delusions and the Madness of Crowds.* New York: Farrar, Straus & Giroux, 1932.
Waite, Arthur Edward. *Alchemists Through the Ages.* Blauvelt, N.Y.: Rudolph Steiner Publications, 1970.

Delphi   Site of the most famous and powerful ORACLE of ancient Greece, located about 100 miles from Athens near the foot of Mount Parnassus. Hundreds of correct Delphic prophecies have survived history.

Two temples were built at Delphi: the Temple of Athena Pronaia, used for RITUALS, and further up the mountain the Temple of Apollo where the women oracles did their prophecy. The Temple of Apollo was built in the sixth century B.C.E. originally for the worship of the earth goddess, Gaia. The name *Delphi* comes from *Delphyne,* the great snake of the Mother. Snakes, associated with PROPHECY and wisdom, were in residence at the temple, and the sacred SERPENT was a spiraling python. Later, the earth goddess

The Delphi Pythia handling a snake, in Histoire de la magie, *by Paul Christian.* (Author's collection)

gave way to Apollo when, according to myth, he slew the sacred python.

Gaia, then Apollo, dispensed prophecy and advice through an entranced priestess, the Pythonness or Pythia. Enquirers were chosen by lots and paid fees. While the enquirer remained in an outer chamber, the Pythia descended into an inner sanctuary. Her trance ritual included drinking BLOOD, which was supposed to feed the ghosts of the temple and induce prophecy. According to some accounts, she may also have inhaled smoke or chewed laurel leaves. Ancient art depicts her as sitting upon a tripod, gazing into a flat dish (see also SCRYING), and holding a laurel branch. The Pythia's trance was often accompanied by frenzy and strange moanings and sounds. The sounds and cryptic answers that issued forth were interpreted by priests and turned into hexameter verses. Originally, the prophecies were given only on the seventh day in a month in spring but later were given once a month, except for three months in the winter.

One of the best-known Delphi prophecies was said to have been given to King Croesus of Lydia. After testing a number of oracles in various temples for accuracy, he asked the one at Delphi if he should wage war against the Persians. The answer was that if he attacked the Persians, a great army would be destroyed. Confident of victory, Croesus attacked the Persians, but the great army that was defeated was his own.

There is no evidence of a cave or subterranean room at Delphi, despite the belief of some that the Pythia did her work underground. By the fourth century C.E., the Greeks and the Romans believed the Pythia breathed vapors emitted from the rocks to enter a trance. However, geologists have determined that the rocks, which are limestone, could not produce hallucinatory vapors. No clefts have been discovered that might indicate the escape of gases from the Earth's interior. However, foliage, branches, or other substances, such as laurel leaves, could have been burned and inhaled.

After the fourth century B.C.E., oracles in parts of Asia Minor eclipsed the prominence of Delphi.

demon   A lesser spirit that can be invoked in MAGIC. Demons usually are regarded as malevolent or evil, in contrast to ANGELS, who are regarded as benevolent. Like angels, demons are numberless.

Demons are unruly; magicians must force them to obey commands for service. GRIMOIRES give the names, duties, SEALS, INCANTATIONS, and RITUALS for summoning and controlling demons. They are especially useful in DIVINATION, finding lost treasure and the casting of SPELLS. When evoked, demons are made to take form in a MAGIC TRIANGLE, a secured boundary from which they cannot threaten the magician, who is protected by a MAGIC CIRCLE.

Western concepts of demons evolved from various sources. The Greek DAIMONES are both good and evil according to their inherent nature, and include a broad range of beings from spirits to spirits of the dead to gods. The Christian church condemned as evil all pagan spirits whose purpose is to ruin souls so that they are condemned to hell.

Judaic demonologies evolved with influences from the lore of the Babylonians, the Persians, and the Egyptians. In Talmudic tradition, demons are ever-present enemies posing constant dangers to humanity. They were created by God on the first Sabbath eve at twilight. Dusk fell before God finished them, and thus they have no bodies. They have wings and exist between humans and angels—roughly between the Earth and the MOON—and are less powerful than angels. They frequent uninhabited and unclean places, and once they attach themselves to a person or family, bad luck follows. By the Middle Ages, rabbinic writings had elaborated upon demons, expanding their classes and duties.

In Christianity, demons are unrelentingly evil and are the minions of Satan, the devil. They live in hell but can prowl the world actively looking for souls to subvert. By the end of the New Testament period, demons were synonymous with fallen angels, the one-third of the heavenly host cast out of heaven along with Lucifer (later identified as Satan) who all descended into hell. As Christianity spread, the ranks of demons swelled to include the gods and demons of the ancient Middle Eastern and Jewish traditions, all pagan deities, and NATURE SPIRITS.

During the Inquisition, demons especially became associated with witches, who also were regarded as agents of the devil. Much was written about the specific ways demons tormented humans, especially by sexual assault. Male demons (incubi) and female demons (succubi) were believed to visit people in their beds at night to copulate with them. Monstrous births were explained away as the products of human–demon intercourse. Witches—as well as alchemists and other ADEPTS—were said to have demons as FAMILIARS.

See also CHORONZON.

Portraits of the dignitaries of hell, in the grimoire The Red Dragon, *1522. (Author's collection)*

FURTHER READING:

Flint, Valerie I. J. *The Rise of Magic in Early Medieval Europe.* Princeton, N.J.: Princeton University Press, 1991.

Guiley, Rosemary Ellen. *The Encyclopedia of Witches and Witchcraft.* Rev. ed. New York: Facts On File, 1989.

Russell, Jeffrey Burton. *A History of Witchcraft.* London: Thames and Hudson, 1980.

Thomas, Keith. *Religion and the Decline of Magic.* New York: Charles Scribner's Sons, 1971.

Trachtenberg, Joshua. *Jewish Magic and Superstition: A Study in Folk Religion.* New York: Berhman's Jewish Book House, 1939.

de Rupecissa, John (14th c.)   French monk and alchemist of dubious reputation. John de Rupecissa was a Franciscan who gained fame in about the mid-14th century, especially for his alleged prophecies. Pope Innocent VI found his prophecies so offensive that he had him arrested and imprisoned in the Vatican dungeons. According to lore, de Rupecissa died there.

His alchemical treatises are *De Confectione Lapidis,* his major work, and *Book of Light, Five Essences,* and *Heaven of Philosophers.* De Rupecissa was regarded as a pretender by other alchemists. BERNARD OF TRÈVES, however, took his work seriously.

dice   In magical lore, TOOLS of DIVINATION and chance. St. Cyrprian (200–258) said that dice were inspired by the devil, which encouraged lore that DEMONS lived inside of them. In Indian lore, dice made from a dead man's bones will always ensure a win.

Digby, Sir Kenelm (1601–1665)   English alchemist. Sir Kenelm Digby was a colorful character, though of modest achievement in ALCHEMY. He is best known for his cures based on sympathetic MAGIC. He was an original member of the Royal Society and was the first to note the importance of "vital air," or oxygen, to plants. His primary interests lay in alchemy and ASTROLOGY.

Born on July 11, 1603, Digby was the oldest son of Sir Everard Dibgy. His father was executed for conspiracy, and most of his fortune was confiscated by the Crown. Son Digby nonetheless retained enough to live well. He attended Worcester College and was reputed to learn 10 to 12 languages.

In 1625 he married his childhood sweetheart, Venetia Stanley, and enjoyed a happy marriage.

In 1627 he engaged in pirating on the Mediterranean and had some spectacular successes that earned him royal commendations and, undoubtedly, a financial reward. But the high days came to an end in 1633 when Venetia died and Digby, crushed, retired to Gresham College in London. There he immersed himself in medicine, chemistry, and alchemy. He collected manuscripts of purported alchemical secrets and conducted experiments.

His alchemical efforts met with little success, and some considered him to be credulous and deceitful. He had better success with medical "cures," including a weapon-salve (see also OINTMENTS) and a cure for toothache. The toothache remedy consisted of scratching the gums near the infected tooth with an IRON nail and then hammering the nail into a wooden beam.

After his death in 1665, one of his alchemy assistants, Georg Hartmann, published a collection of Digby's "rare chymical secrets."

FURTHER READING:
Holmyard, E. J. *Alchemy.* New York: Penguin Books, 1957.

divination   The use of psychic, magical, or supernatural power to foretell the future, find hidden and lost objects, know secrets, and uncover truth. Divination is universal throughout history and is traditionally performed by a priest, a prophet, an ORACLE, a witch, a shaman, a magician, a psychic, or another person who is reputed to have supernatural powers and skills.

Many divinatory, or mantic, methods exist, and diviners use the ones sanctioned by their cultures. *Mantic* comes from the Greek term *mantis,* which mean "diviner" or "prophet." Thus, the names of many techniques of divination end in *-mancy.*

Techniques fall into two broad categories: AUGURY, the interpretation of natural or artificial signs, OMENS, portents, and the casting of lots; and the direct communication with gods, ANGELS, and spirits through oracles, visions, trance, dreams, and POSSESSION. All divination is an attempt to communicate with the divine or supernatural to learn the will of the gods, and even in the interpretation of natural signs and lots it is assumed that the gods interfere to provide answers to questions. A skilled diviner also employs a keen sense of intuition and an innate understanding of human nature and often gives advice along with PROPHECY and prediction.

In early civilizations, divination was a royal or holy function, used for guidance in matters of state and war and to forecast natural disasters. Most courts employed royal diviners, whose lives often depended upon the accuracy of their forecasts. The Chaldeans and Babylonians had elaborate divinatory systems that were under the auspices of priests who saw portents in everything in nature around them. The ancient Chinese had court astrologers and other diviners who interpreted cast lots of yarrow sticks, bones, and other objects. Early Egyptian priests slept in temples in hopes of receiving divinatory information from the gods in dreams. In ancient Rome, a special caste of priests called augurs interpreted signs in nature that were believed to be messages sent by the gods. Augurs interpreted such natural phenomena as the flights of birds, the patterns of clouds and smoke, and the markings on the livers of sacri-

ficed animals (livers, rather than hearts, were believed the central organ of the body). The Greeks divined dreams and consulted special oracles, who went into trance to allow the gods to speak through them. The most famous oracle resided at Delphi, near the base of Mount Parnassus. The Greeks helped spread divination among the masses by popularizing ASTROLOGY.

SCRYING, the interpretations of images that appear on reflective surfaces, is one of the most widespread forms of divination. It requires a reflective surface on which visions form, such as CRYSTAL BALLS, MIRRORS, and pools of water and liquids.

Many divination methods involve the interpretation of artificial signs. The most common are types of sortilege, such as the casting of stones, bones, shells, and other objects that yield answers from the patterns of their fall. The TAROT and the I CHING are examples of sortilege divination.

In Western society, divination has been associated with SORCERY. The Old Testament contains proscriptions against consulting diviners. As early as 785, the Catholic Church forbade the use of sorcery as a means of settling disputes, but that did not prevent consultation of village WIZARDS and wise men and wise women. During the Middle Ages and the Renaissance, diviners who invoked demonic forces were punished by fines, humiliation in a pillory, or loss of property; some who were also convicted of witchcraft were put to death.

Despite the efforts of the church and the scientific community and the many laws against fortune-telling (widely considered a fraud), divination has never been eradicated; the average person has too great a desire to see into the future.

FURTHER READING:
Grillot de Givry, Emile. *Witchcraft, Magic and Alchemy.* New York: Houghton Mifflin, 1931.
Guiley, Rosemary Ellen. *Harper's Encyclopedia of Mystical & Paranormal Experience.* San Francisco: HarperSanFrancisco, 1991.
Thomas, Keith. *Religion and the Decline of Magic.* New York: Scribner, 1971.

divining rod   See WAND.

doll sorcery   See POPPET.

dowsing   A form of DIVINATION for locating lost and missing persons and animals and for detecting hidden objects and substances, such as water, oil, coal, minerals, cables, and pipes. Dowsing also is used in the mapping of archaeological sites. Many people dowse as a way of checking their intuition about decisions and choices for virtually any purpose.

Dowsing rods in use in mining, in Cosmographia universalis, *1522. (Author's collection)*

No one knows exactly how or why dowsing works. The tool responds to the user. For example, if a dowser is looking for underground water with rods, the rods will signal where the water is by moving up and down or back and forth. A pendulum will begin to whirl. Along with the signals from the tool, the dowser may also get intuitive visual impressions. Dowsers do not necessarily need to go on location to search for things. Many dowse maps in a type of remote viewing.

Dowsing is at least 7,000 years old; its exact origins are unknown. Rods of wood or metal (even coat hangars) are used as well as pendula. Ancient Egyptian art portrays dowsers with forked rods and headdresses with antennae. Ancient Chinese kings used dowsing rods. The Kalahari bushmen of Africa have long used dowsing to find sources of water.

During the Middle Ages, dowsing was used widely in Europe and Great Britain to locate underground water and coal deposits. It was associated with the supernatural, which gave rise to the terms *water witching* and *wizard's rod.* Among the first books on the subject were *The Diviners* by Gaspard Peucer, published in 1553, and *De Re Metallica* by Agricola, published in 1556 in Germany. Dowsing was transplanted to America by the early colonists.

Dowsing was widely used until the 19th century when scientists dismissed it as superstition. In the 20th century, dowsing made a comeback as an intuitive skill. It is used in archaeological digs, the search for gas, oil, minerals, and buried cables, and in medicine. During wartime, dowsers helped locate mines, unexploded shells, and buried mortars for the military.

Dowsers also have contributed research toward the understanding of mysterious earth energies, such as LEYS. Individuals dowse for personal matters and divination.

FURTHER READING:

Guiley, Rosemary Ellen. *Breakthrough Intuition: How to Achieve a Life of Abundance by Listening to the Voice Within.* New York: Berkley Books, 2001.
Lethbridge, T. C. *Ghost and Divining-Rod.* London: Routledge & Kegan Paul, 1963.
Wilson, Colin. *Mysteries.* New York: Perigee Books/G.P. Putnams' Sons, 1978.

dragon   A powerful SYMBOL of psychic transformation. Like the SERPENT, the dragon represents primordial consciousness, underworld powers, the feminine, the womb, the unformed PRIMA MATERIA, and wisdom and knowledge. The word *dragon* comes from the Greek term *drakos,* or "serpent."

A dragon also symbolizes the hero figure and, accompanied by treasure or by a cave and treasure, signifies an ordeal in the life of the hero. Slaying the dragon represents the battle between the forces of light and darkness: conquering one's own inner darkness to master the self. Rescuing a maiden from a dragon is the preservation of purity from the forces of evil.

In ALCHEMY, the dragon especially represents the treasure of the Great Work, the PHILOSOPHER'S STONE, and also the alchemical process from chaos to the Stone via countless transformations. A winged dragon represents volatile MERCURY, and a wingless dragon represents a fixed state. In alchemical art, the HERMAPHRODITE is often shown standing atop a winged and fire-breathing dragon.

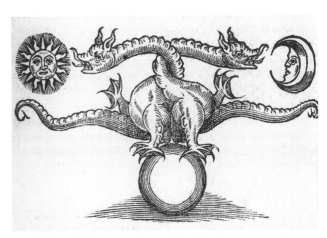

Double-headed dragon with symbols of the Sun and the Moon, in Theatrum chemicum Britannicum, *by Elias Ashmole, 1652. (Author's collection)*

The dragon also is related to the OUROBOROS, the tail-biting serpent of alchemy.

Also associated with sky gods, the dragon brings fertilizing rain (the waters of the unconscious), thunder, and lightning.

Other meanings of dragon are one's inner fears and the negative aspect of the Mother figure.

Drawing Down the Moon   See MOON.

dream sending   In MAGIC, the ability to enter another person's dreams to deliver a message, cause them to dream a certain dream, or influence their behavior and actions. Dream sending is an old magical art. The most common use of dream sending is for love SPELLS, to cause another person to fall in love with the dream sender.

Ancient Egyptians priests or magicians performed RITUALS to cause other persons to have a specific dream. A legend concerning Alexander the Great credits his divine origins to a sent dream. According to lore, Nectanebo, the last native king of Egypt, used dream magic to cause the Greek queen Olympias to dream that the Egyptian god Amun would make love to her and she would bear a god. Nectanebo accomplished this through sympathetic magic, by pouring the extracted juices of various desert plants over a wax effigy of the queen and reciting a spell.

Nectanebo then turned his attention to Philip of Macedon. He said a spell over a hawk, which flew to the sleeping Philip and told him to dream that Olympias was going to bear a child who was the son of a god. The magic was successful, and when Alexander was born, his divine origin was unquestioned.

The Greeks and the Romans, who also were very skilled in proactive and magical dreaming, had RITUALS for sending dreams by petitioning intermediary beings to serve as messengers. According to Greek magical papyri, they "extended the individual upward" by serving as "detectives of the heart's secrets."

Dream messengers include 12 spirits or ANGELS who govern the hours of the night and are under the control of Selene, the goddess of the MOON. The rituals were performed in the middle of the night, with the appropriate angel invoked for the hour in which the ritual was done. The *Papyri Graecae Magicae* states that the sender should invoke Selene to "give a sacred angel or a holy assistant who serves this very night, in this very hour . . . and order the angel to go off to her, NN ("so-and-so"), to draw her by her hair, by her feet; may she, in fear, see phantoms, sleepless because of her passion for me and her love for me, NN, come to my consecrated bedroom."

Persons who work with their dreams discover that they often can send a dream message to others successfully. However, though recipients may receive the messages, it is unlikely that they can be coerced to take actions that they do not want to do. The noted psychical researcher Harold Sherman found that he obtained the best results with both sending and receiving impressions when in a relaxed state bordering on sleep. He would visualize what he desired to achieve, such as meeting someone he needed to see. The subconscious mind would attract the elements needed to materialize the goal. He experimented doing these visualizations when he was certain that others would be asleep and therefore more likely to be receptive to his telepathic images.

According to lore, dream sending is best done during the waxing Moon. One can invoke Selene or Gabriel, the archangel who rules Monday and the Moon.

FURTHER READING:
Guiley, Rosemary Ellen. *Angel Magic for Love and Romance.* Lakewood, Minn.: Galde Press, 2005.
Luck, Georg. *Arcana Mundi: Magic and the Occult in the Greek and Roman Worlds.* Baltimore: Johns Hopkins University Press, 1985.

Druids   An exalted caste of priests of the Celts, renowned, according to the Romans, for their powerful MAGIC. *Druid* means "knowing the oak tree" in Gaelic.

The Celts were a barbaric, tribal people who spread through Gaul, Britain, Ireland, Europe, Asia Minor, and the Balkans by the fifth century B.C.E. In the first century C.E., the Romans launched a series of suppressions of the Celts, and their religion eventually was replaced by Christianity.

The RITUALS and teachings of the Druids were highly secret and passed on in an oral tradition. Little actually is known about the Druids, though much has been speculated about them since antiquarian times. Most of what is known comes from the writings of Greeks and Romans, the latter of whom, as the conquerors, must be viewed with some skepticism; and from archaeological evidence obtained from graves, shrines and temples, and iconography. The few writings span the second century B.C.E. to the fourth century C.E.

The exact role of the Druids in Celtic society has been described differently. Diogenes Laertius noted that the Druids were already an ancient institution in the fourth century B.C.E., during the time of Aristotle. Julius Caesar said the Gaulish Druids were one of the two highest castes, along with the knights, and were organized under a single titular head. In Ireland, the Druids were the second highest of three castes, below the nobility and above the plebes, or landless ones.

By most accounts, the Druids were the keepers of traditional wisdom who were concerned with moral philosophy, natural phenomena, and theology. They were skilled in DIVINATION, the interpretation of OMENS, the rites of SACRIFICE, the construction of a calendar, the magical medicine of herbs, the science of astronomy, and the composition of poems. They played a key role in the sacred and secular life of the Celts. They conducted religious ceremonies; served as mediator between the people and the gods; exercised influence over the moral, ethical, and spiritual fabric of Celtic society; and made political and judicial decisions. Ammianus, quoting Timagenes, said that Druids "are uplifted by searchings into things most secret and sublime." Gaulish Druids were said to administer law and justice, though it is unknown how they did so in consideration of tribal chiefs. Irish Druids were described as men of learning and art who included seers, wise men, bards, and jurists. The Druids of Gaul and Britain were said to be separate from others in the priesthood, including diviners, bards, and seers. There seemed to be overlap, as Druids were said to read OMENS and prophesy the future. Druids included both men and women, for women had a place of importance in Celtic society.

In the first century C.E., Dio Chrysostom equated the Druids with Hindu brahmins, Persian magi, and Egyptian priests. In more recent times, they have been described as shamans because of their practices of night fires, drumming, chanting and, ecstatic dancing/possession.

Certain TREES, plants, and animals were believed to be endowed with sacred and curative powers, and the Druids used them in religious ceremonies and for remedial purposes. The MISTLETOE, believed to be a sign from heaven, was used as a remedy against poisons and infertility even for animals. The robur oak tree was thought to have come from the sacred forest, and its foliage was used in ceremonies.

Ceremonies were conducted in sacred woods or oak groves which served as temples. These sacred enclosures were also assembly sites where the Druids made decisions and administered justice in civil and criminal disputes. Other meetings took place at river sources and lakes because the Celts worshiped water gods and believed water to be sacred.

The Druids practiced both animal and human sacrifices. Human victims were burned alive in wickerwork cages, stabbed, impaled on stakes, or shot with arrows. It was the sacrifice of humans that so outraged the Romans, who had outlawed it as barbaric by Senatorial decree in 97 B.C.E. The only extant detailed account of a Druid ceremony comes from Pliny and concerns the harvesting of mistletoe. On the sixth day of the MOON, a Druid who was garbed in a white robe climbed an oak tree and, with the left hand, cut the mistletoe with a GOLD sickle (more likely it was a gilded bronze sickle since gold is too soft to cut mistletoe). The mistletoe, not supposed to fall to the ground, was caught in a white cloth. Two white bulls were sacrificed, and a feast held.

In interpreting omens, the Druids observed the hare or such birds as the crow and the eagle to foretell events. They practiced divination by observing the death throes and entrails of their sacrificial victims. During religious festivals, the Druids divined by dreams. A man would be put to sleep with Druids chanting over his body. Awakening, the man would describe his dream, and the Druids would interpret it.

Classical writings make references to magic, including CHARMS with herbs and mistletoe, and to belief in a magical egg made from the SPITTLE of angry snakes, which would ensure success in court and guarantee favors from princes.

The Druids believed in the immortality of the soul and life after death, which some writers have equated with PYTHAGORAS's belief in metempsychosis. The dead were cremated with all their possessions. Sometimes relatives committed religious suicide by jumping into the fire and holding the corpses so as to be with them in the next world. The Celts wrote letters to the dead and advanced loans that would be repayable after death. Caesar said that this belief in immortality sustained the legendary Celtic courage in battle.

The Romans feared and were repulsed by the Celts, and in 43 C.E., Claudius banned Druidism throughout the empire. In 60 or 61, the Romans sacked and destroyed their holy stronghold on the island of Mona (also called Mon, and Anglesey). According to Tacitus, black-clad Druidesses leaped among the Celtic warriors, howling to the gods and screaming CURSES at the Romans. The Romans were victorious. They slew the warriors and the Druids and laid waste to the sacred groves. The loss sent Druidism into permanent decline; within several generations, the venerated and powerful priesthood was on a par with common sorcerers.

Druidic Revivals

In the 16th and 17th centuries, interest in the Druids revived. Translators of the classical texts romanticized them and turned them into folklore characters. John Aubrey, British antiquarian of the 17th century, suggested that the Druids had constructed Stonehenge, a theory which has since been refuted as false. Aubrey's views were endorsed in the 18th century, however, by William Stukeley, who became known as the "Arch Druid" and the founder of modern Druidism. A meeting of "British Druids" is said to have taken place in 1717, organized by John Tolan and led by Stukeley. In 1781 the Ancient Order of Druids was founded by Henry Hurle, a carpenter. This order was inspired by FREEMASONRY and also was a benefit society. The issue of charity split the organization in 1833. The United Ancient Order of Druids continued purely as a benefit society, while the Ancient Order of Druids retained its mystical underpinnings. By the early 20th century there were at least five modern Druidic organizations, including the Druidic Hermetists and the British Circle of the Universal Bond, but most did not survive more than a few decades. In 1963 the Order of Bards, Ovates, and Druids split away from the Ancient Order of Druids, drawing members away from that group and from the British Circle of the Universal Bond.

Before 1915 Stonehenge was privately owned, but modern Druids were allowed to assemble there. In 1900 a stone was knocked over, and the owner fenced the henge and began to charge admission. At the next solstice ceremony, some of the Druids objected to the fee. The police were called, and the Druids were thrown out. They ritually cursed the owner. In 1915 Stonehenge was sold to Cecil Chubb, who turned it over to the government. The modern Druids were allowed to hold festivals at Stonehenge until 1985 when the monument was placed off limits to all such festivals, due to vandalism by the spectators who were attracted to the gatherings. Since then, small groups, including Druids, have been given permission to conduct ceremonies and rituals inside the henge.

Druidism is the second-largest tradition within the Pagan movement. Followers reinterpret what is known about the Druids and construct a spiritual path of devotion, ritual, and magic.

dybbuk   In Jewish demonology, an evil spirit or a doomed soul that possesses a person body and soul, speaking through the person's mouth and causing such torment and anguish that another personality appears to manifest itself. The term *dybbuk* (also spelled *dibbuk*) was coined in the 17th century from the language of German and Polish Jews. It is an abbreviation of two phrases: *dibbuk me-ru'ah* ("a cleavage of an evil spirit"), and *dibbuk min ha-hizonim* ("dibbuk from the demonic side" of man). Prior to the 17th century, the dybbuk was one of many evil spirits that were called *ibbur.*

In early folklore, dybbukim were thought only to inhabit the bodies of sick persons. Possessive evil spirits are referenced in the Old Testament. For example, Samuel I describes the possession of Saul and how David exorcized the spirit by playing the harp. In the Book of Tobit, the archangel Raphael instructs Tobit in ways of exorcisms. In the rabbinical literature of the first century, exorcisms called for the ashes of a red heifer, or the roots of certain herbs, that were burned under the victim, who was then surrounded with water. Other methods included incantations in the name of SOLOMON, repetition of the Divine Name of God (see NAMES), reading from Psalms, and the wearing of herbal AMULETS.

By the 16th century, the concept of possessive evil spirits changed. Many Jews believed that the spirits were transmigrated souls that could not enter a new body because of their past sins and so were forced to possess the body of a living sinner. The spirits were motivated to possess a body because they would be tormented by other evil spirits if they did not. Some thought the dybbukim were the souls of people who were not properly buried and thus became demons.

The KABBALAH contains RITUALS for exorcizing a dybbuk; many are still in use in modern times. The exorcism must be performed by a *ba'al shem,* a miracle-working rabbi. Depending on how the exorcism is done, the dybbuk either is redeemed or is cast into hell. It usually exits the body of its victim through the small toe, which shows a small, bloody hole as the point of departure.

effigy See POPPET.

egg A SYMBOL of genesis, beginnings, and growth. The egg, properly fertilized with the creative force and incubated, germinates new life. In a dream, this might be a new project, a new phase in life, or a new sense of self.

The egg also is a universal symbol of fertility. In mythology, the egg represents the primordial cosmos, the life principle, the undifferentiated totality, wholeness, and the womb of the Mother Goddess. This Cosmic Egg is often represented by an egg entwined by a snake (see SERPENT/SNAKE) or OUROBOROUS.

In ALCHEMY, the egg is the *PRIMA MATERIA,* or hermetically sealed vessel, in which the PHILOSOPHER'S STONE is created. Its white color lends it the association of perfection. MICHAEL MAIER, in *Atalanta fugiens* (1617), depicts a knight with sword poised to strike an egg. Maier explains that the knight is Mars (IRON) and fire (Vulcan's sword) and that the egg represents both GOLD and SULPHUR and *albedo,* the whitening stage of the Great Work. States Maier:

> There is a bird in the world, more sublime than all,
> Let it be your only care to find its egg.
> Attack it cautiously with a fiery sword, (as is the custom),
> Let Mars assist Vulcan; the bird arising from it
> Will be conqueror of iron and fire.

Other meanings of eggs are spiritual nourishment, hope, and resurrection.

See also LAM.

Alchemist poised to strike the alchemical egg to divide it into its elements, in Atalanta fugiens, *by Michael Maier, 1617.* (Author's collection)

egregor A term in Western MAGIC applied to the collective energy or force of a group of individuals, especially when the individuals are united toward a common purpose. An egregor forms in a magical LODGE and becomes a reservoir of magical and spiritual power that influences RITUALS, the lodge itself, and the individuals within the lodge. DION FORTUNE referred to this energy as "a great thought-form in the group-mind of the Lodge." The term *egregor* is said to have originally been used for an ELEMENTAL magically created by a group to guard it.

An egregor evolves from the thoughts, emotions, and awareness of a collective. It can be either positive or negative. A negative example would be mob violence, and a positive example would be a healing circle.

A magical lodge egregor takes time to develop. Lodges that have been in existence for a long time have powerful egregors. Everything that takes place within a lodge—meetings, activities, INITIATIONS, and various rituals—contributes to and energizes the egregor. In addition, the individual thoughts, intentions, emotions, virtues, and actions of the members feed the egregor as well. An egregor takes on a synergistic life of its own. This is one reason that lodges are careful about who they admit to membership, for if the egregor loses power or turns negative, the lodge ultimately will fail.

A newly chartered lodge will build its egregor in part from its chartered tradition, by drawing upon the SYMBOLS, teachings, deities, myths, rituals, and INNER PLANES CONTACTS used by other lodges.

See also THOUGHT-FORM.

FURTHER READING:
Fortune, Dion. *Esoteric Orders and Their Work and The Training and Work of the Initiate.* London: The Aquarian Press, 1987.
Greer, John Michael. *Inside a Magical Lodge: Group Ritual in the Western Tradition.* St. Paul, Minn.: Llewellyn Publications, 1998.

Egyptian magic   See MAGIC.

Eleazar, Abraham (14th c.?)   Mysterious Jewish alchemist, associated by some with NICHOLAS FLAMEL.

Nothing is known about the life of Abraham Eleazar other than what is contained in his book *Uraltes Chymishces Werck (Age-Old Chymical Work)*. Scholars have debated the verity of the work and the existence of Eleazar, some contending the work is spurious and was written as late as the 17th century, while others say the work dates to the early 14th century and may or may not have been written by one "Abraham Eleazar." A distinguishing characteristic of the book is its emphasis on the Jewish religion and the plight and suffering of Jews, elements usually not found in purely alchemical manuscripts, even those written by Jewish alchemists.

Age-Old Chymical Work was printed in German in 1735. The book has two parts. The title pages describe Eleazar as "A Prince, Priest, and Levite, Astrologer and Philosopher, born of the Stock of Abraham, Isaac, Jacob and Judah." The book is a "gift of God of Samuel Baruch," an unknown person but supposedly—according to the second title page—a rabbi, astrologer, and philosopher, born of the same stock as Eleazar. The book purports to teach "the great Secret of the great Master Tubal-Cain, from his tablet, found by the Jew Abraham Eleazar." Julius Gervasius, another unknown figure, is credited with publishing the book and adding illustrations, indices, and so forth. Of all of these names, the only one known is the mythical Tubal-Cain.

According to Gervasius's preface, Eleazar lived prior to the time of Flamel, or before the 14th century; he "flourished quite some time after the destruction of Jerusalem." Eleazar was concerned about the plight of the Jews in his community under the oppression of the Roman Empire, whom he witnessed in great suffering and believed that the suffering was the results of the sins of their forefathers. He said he would teach the secrets of ALCHEMY so that his people could benefit and pay their required taxes to the empire.

Gervasius equates the manuscript with the mysterious book of alchemical hieroglyphs acquired by Flamel, the so-called book of Abraham the Jew. He says that in *Age-Old Chymical Work*, Eleazar explains the hierogylphs that were originally made by Tubal-Cain.

Eleazar's book contains alchemical recipes and mysticism and discusses alchemical SYMBOLS. The second part, which is attributed to the unknown Samuel Baruch, is an alchemical commentary on Genesis. Eleazar explains that he found the secret writings of Baruch on copper tablets and copied them into tree bark—another apparent link to Flamel's book, which Flamel said was written on pages made of tree bark and covered with a thin sheet of copper.

Some scholars have speculated that Gervasius is the true author of the book, which is not likely. He is critical of the Jews in his preface, calling them a "miserable people" who are cursed by their condemnation of Jesus. Nonetheless, he has respect for Jewish alchemical ADEPTS.

It is difficult to know whether *Age-Old Chymical Work* is a genuine text that preceded Flamel or whether it was inspired by Flamel as a spurious work. Most likely, it is not older than the 14th century.

FURTHER READING:
Patai, Raphael. *The Jewish Alchemists.* Princeton, N.J.: Princeton University Press, 1994.

elementals   Beings created from the four ELEMENTS of nature. Elemental spirits are evoked in magical rites.

The classes of elemental spirits and their elements are:

Earth: Gnomes or pigmies

Water: Undines or nymphs

Fire: Salamanders

Air: Sylphs

PARACELSUS included giants and dwarfs among elementals.

Characteristics of Elementals

According to Paracelsus, all elementals have human form and can mix with humans; yet they have no relationship to humans and are not descended from Adam and Eve. They are not spirits per se but are made in the image of man, with flesh, bones, and BLOOD. However, they are higher than man, for they are both of the physical and spirit worlds. They are mortal but have no soul as do humans, and thus they lack a moral character. They do not worship God and live according to instinct and reason. Because they are soulless, they have no afterlife.

Humans and elemental spirits can mate and produce hybrid offspring (see FAIRIES) that would belong more to the human race than to the elementals.

Elementals can enter the human world, but humans cannot enter the realms of the elementals because the physical body is too coarse. Some elementals are generous to humans, helping them in tasks and chores and bestowing gifts such as treasures upon them.

Organization of Elementals

Each class of elemental stays strictly within its element. They do not mingle with other elementals, though they all mingle with humans. They wear clothing suitable to their forms and element. They are organized into societies with leaders and laws, as are humans. They live according to the keeping of time.

The different classes vary in their ability to interact with humans. The undines or nymphs have the most interaction, followed by the sylphs. Gnomes and salamanders, both of whom are gifted in PROPHECY, rarely interact with people. This is especially true of the elusive salamanders, said Paracelsus.

Evoking Elementals

GRIMOIRES, books of magical instruction, provide information on the powers of elemental spirits and how to command them. The *Key of Solomon* gives this description of the elemental spirits:

> Some are created from Water.
>
> Others from the Wind, unto which they are like.
> Some from Earth.
> Some from Clouds.
> Others from Solar Vapors.
> Others from the keenness and strength of Fire; and when they are invoked or summoned, they come always with great noise, and with the terrible nature of fire.
>
> When the Spirits which are created of Water are invoked, they come with great rains, thunder, hail, lightning, thunderbolts, and the like.
>
> When the spirits which are created of Clouds are invoked, they come with great deformity, in a horrible form, to strike fear into the Invocator, and with an exceeding great noise.
>
> Others which are formed from the wind appear like thereunto and with exceeding swift motion, and whensoever those which are created from Beauty appear, they

will show themselves in a fair and agreeable form; moreover, whensoever thou shalt call the Spirits created from Air, they will come with a kind of gentle breeze.

> When the spirits which are created from the Vapors of the Sun are invoked, they come under a very beautiful and excellent form, but filled with pride, vanity and conceit. They are clever. . . . They show great ostentation and vainglory in their dress, and they rejoice in many ornamentations and decorations. Thou shalt only invoke them in serene, mild, and pleasant weather.

Commanding the elemental spirits requires that the magician be free of common weaknesses and vices and be "fortified by the grace and favor of the superior world," said ARTHUR EDWARD WAITE. According to ELIPHAS LEVI in *The Doctrine and Ritual of High Magic:*

> To overcome and subjugate the elementary spirits, we must never yield to their characteristic defects. . . . In a word, we must overcome them in their strength without ever being overcome by their weaknesses.

Creating Elementals

A magician can create an elemental from a substance on the MENTAL PLANE for the purpose of fulfilling a certain task. Such an elemental has no astral form and remains on the mental plane. It can perform only a single task and cannot do anything that its magician creator cannot do. The magician creates it from the elements and gives it attributes that are appropriate to the task. The magician imparts some of his own consciousness into the elemental, gives it a NAME by which it can be summoned and controlled, and determines a finite life span for it. He assigns the task to the elemental and then detaches himself from it. The elemental sustains itself from the mental essence of the magician. If the elemental is assigned to work for other humans, it can draw sustenance from the universe.

JACK PARSONS, a follower of ALEISTER CROWLEY, used magic to make an elemental summoning, who came in the form of a woman.

FURTHER READING:
Bardon, Franz. *Questions and Answers.* Salt Lake City: Merkur Publishing, 1998.
Butler, E. M. *Ritual Magic.* Cambridge: Cambridge University Press, 1949.
Hall, Manly P. *Paracelsus: His Mystical and Medical Philosophy.* Los Angeles: The Philosophic Research Society, 1964.
Waite, Arthur Edward. *The Book of Black Magic and of Pacts.* 1899. Reprint, York Beach, Maine: Samuel Weiser, 1972.

elemental weapons   See TOOLS.

elementaries   Artificial beings similar to THOUGHT-FORMS.
PARACELSUS said elementaries are not part of the natural order but are evil beings created in the invisible realms

by excesses of human thought and emotion, corruption of character, degeneration of faculties, and misuse of powers (see LARVAE).

Elementaries are dependent on humans for existence and initially for survival. If they are nourished enough by human negativity, they gain an independence and can turn on their creators, draining them of their life force and vitality. Examples of elementaries are vampiric entities (see VAMPIRES) and sexual predators such as the incubus and succubus. Mental disorders, such as obsession, and negative physical actions such as anger, aggression, and corruption, can be explained as effects of parasitic elementaries.

According to Paracelsus, most physical ailments and diseases could also be explained by the attachment of elementaries. Fear, depression, self-pity, and feelings of victimization stimulate the IMAGINATION in a wrong way to open the door for attachment of elementaries, he said. Recovery is accomplished through a reversal of thoughts and emotions to the positive, which literally starves the elementaries and forces them away.

Paracelsus did not believe that a person's elementary can be sent to another person, such as by MAGIC. Rather, an elementary can only feed off of its creator.

FRANZ BARDON defined elementaries as astral beings created consciously by a magician out of a particular ELEMENT. They are like elementals but exist on the ASTRAL PLANE and not the MENTAL PLANE. The magician imbues an elementary with some of his own consciousness, gives it a NAME and life span, and assigns it tasks. During its life span, the elementary is nourished by the astral substance of the magician. When the tasks are completed, the elementary dissolves back into the astral matrix. However, elementaries are intelligent, and if not strictly controlled they can become independent of the magician. If they go out of control, they will cause problems for which the magician will be responsible.

FURTHER READING:

Bardon, Franz. *Questions and Answers.* Salt Lake City: Merkur Publishing, 1998.

Hall, Manly P. *Paracelsus: His Mystical and Medical Philosophy.* Los Angeles: The Philosophic Research Society, 1964.

elements   The building blocks of the material world. In Western thought, there are four primary elements: earth, air, fire, and water; the esoteric tradition describes a fifth and spiritual element, the QUINTESSENCE.

Each element has its unique properties and characteristics, which in MAGIC and ALCHEMY as well as in ancient traditions of medicine, function on both physical and spiritual levels. In addition, there are beings called ELEMENTALS that live in each element and embody its essence.

Associations of the elements are:

Earth: physical; the body; health; personal resources such as money, time, energy; solidity; fertility.

Water: emotions; intuition; the unconscious; vitalizing fluids and forces; rhythms of nature.

Air: mental effort; thought; rationality; communication; intellectual activities; decisions.

Fire: action; exploration; purification.

According to HENRY CORNELIUS AGRIPPA in *Occult Philosophy,* the four elements exist through the universe in everything, even spirits and ANGELS, and occur in three types. On Earth they are mixed and impure; in the stars they are pure. A third type are composite elements which are mutable and are the vehicles for all transformations.

In kabbalistic thought, the four elements are represented by the four rivers that flow out of the Garden of Eden, described in Genesis.

The four elements are associated with the four fixed signs of the zodiac, the four apostles of the New Testament, and the four directions of the world:

ELEMENT	ZODIAC SIGN	DIRECT-ION	APOSTLE
Earth	Taurus the Bull	North	Luke
Water	Scorpio the Scorpion	West	Matthew
Air	Aquarius the Water-bearer	East	John
Fire	Leo the Lion	South	Mark

PARACELSUS distinguished two types of substances, Adamic and non-Adamic. Adamic flesh, from which all human beings are made, is composed of the four elements, each of which rule different aspects of health and being. The body has a physical or mineral component, a vegetative or humid component, a fiery or warmth and motion component, and an airy or intellectual component.

FURTHER READING:

Bardon, Franz. *Initiation into Hermetics: A Course of Instruction of Magic Theory and Practice.* Wuppertal, Germany: Dieter Ruggeberg, 1971.

Hall, Manly P. *Paracelsus: His Mystical and Medical Philosophy.* Los Angeles: The Philosophic Research Society, 1964.

Melville, Francis. *The Secrets of High Magic.* Haupaugge, N.Y.: Barron's, 2002.

elf arrows   See FAIRIES.

Elixir/Elixir of Life   In ALCHEMY, frequently used names for the PHILOSOPHER'S STONE. The Elixir has healing proper-

The Emerald Tablet, in Amphitheatrum sapientiae aeternae, *by Heinrich Khunrath, 1602.* (Author's collection)

ties, healing the deficiencies and imperfections of base metals so that they can be transmuted into the perfect metals of GOLD and SILVER. The Elixir also heals the imperfections in humans, creating longevity and potentially immortality. PARACELSUS developed hundreds of elixirs for treating various medical conditions, disorders, and illnesses; his most famous was *aurum potabile,* or "potable gold."

Elixirs for immortality are more common in Eastern alchemy than in Western alchemy. MERCURY and cinnabar are frequently named ingredients.

Emerald Tablet

Emerald Tablet   The central teaching of the *CORPUS HERMETICUM,* the foundation of Western esotericism, MAGIC, and ALCHEMY. The Emerald Tablet may be the oldest surviving alchemical text.

Origins of the Emerald Tablet

The Emerald Tablet (or Emerald Table), held by HERMES TRISMEGISTUS in art, is said to be inscribed with the whole of the Egyptians' philosophy, including the magical secrets of the universe. It is cited as the credo of ADEPTS, particularly the alchemists, who interpreted it as a description of the transmutation process.

The true origins of the Emerald Tablet are not known. No original text survives, only translations. The text has been attributed to early Arabic alchemy in the seventh century, to Chinese alchemy, and even to Atlantean origins.

According to one legend, the Emerald Tablet was found clutched in the hand of the body of Hermes Trismegistus in his cave tomb. Another version has it that Hermes Trismegistus's body was mummified and interred in the Great Pyramid of Giza.

The Tablet probably first appeared in the West in editions of the psuedo-Aristotlean *Secretum Secretorum,* a translation of the *Kitab Sirr al-Asrar,* a book of advice to kings which is thought to date to the ninth century and was translated into Latin by Johannes Hispalensis in about 1140 and by Philip of Tripoli in about 1243. Similarities are found between the Tablet and the Syriac *Book of Trea-*

sures written by Job of Odessa in the ninth century, and the Greek writings of the bishop Nemesius of Emesa in Syria from the mid-fourth century. Of particular importance to the Western magical tradition are three Latin translations, the earliest of which dates to circa 1200.

Was the Emerald Tablet literally made of emerald? The Greeks and Egyptians used the term translated as *emerald* for emeralds, green granites, and possibly green jasper.

The Text and Commentaries
The text of the Emerald Tablet states:

> True, without falsehood, certain, most certain. What is above is like that which is below, and what is below, like that which is above, to make the miracle of One Thing. And as all things were made from contemplation of One, so all things were born from one adaptation. The father is the Sun, its mother is the Moon. The wind carried it in its womb, the earth breast fed it. It is the father of all works of wonder in the world. Its power is complete if turned towards earth, it will separate earth from fire, the subtle from the gross. With great capacity (Wisdom) it ascends from earth to heaven. Again it descends to earth, and takes back the power of the above and the below. Thus you will receive the glory of the distinctiveness of the world. All obscurity will flee from you. This is the most strong strength of all strength, for it overcomes all subtle things, and penetrates all solid things. Thus was the world created. From this comes marvelous adaptations of which this is the procedure. Therefore I am called Hermes Thrice-Crowned because I have three parts of the Wisdom of the whole world. And complete is what I had to say about the work of the Sun.

Numerous analyses of these statements have been made by scholars. Some interpretations are as follows:

1. *True, without falsehood, certain, most certain.* The Emerald Tablet speaks a universal truth on many levels. If the text cannot be perceived as truth, the fault lies with the individual, not with the text.

2. *What is above is like that which is below, and what is below, like that which is above, to make the miracle of One Thing.* The One Thing is an infinite continuum of upwardness and downwardness. Since the continuum is infinite, any point along it is at the center. The One Thing symbolizes the Self.

3. *And as all things were made from contemplation of One, so all things were born from one adaptation.* The One is the Universal Mind, which contemplates or meditates all things into being. All things mirror its power and can create by adapting the creative process of the One.

4–6. *The father is the Sun; its mother is the Moon. The wind carried it in its womb; the earth breast fed it. It is the father of all works of wonder in the world.* The father/sun is the archetype of light/fire and downward creative process of light piercing darkness. The mother/moon is the archetype of in-forming/water,

taking the light of the father/sun and reflecting it to the earth. The wind/womb is air, which mediates between fire and water. The earth/breast fed is the archetype of form. It is the element of earth, created by the combination of the other three elements. The father of all works of wonder in the world is the four elements combined with the fifth element of the QUINTESSENCE, the conscious awareness of the One or creator, which is independent life.

7. *Its power is complete if turned toward earth, it will separate earth from fire, the subtle from the gross.* The Quintessence is clothed in physical form and is divine conscious awareness as expressed through human beings.

8. *With great capacity (Wisdom), it ascends from earth to heaven. Again it descends to earth and takes back the power of the above and the below.* Conscious awareness rises and falls through the continuum in a constant process of integration and unison.

9. *Thus you will receive the glory of the distinctiveness of the world. All obscurity will flee from you.* The constant process of integration creates a new level of enlightenment.

10. *This is the most strong strength of all strength, for it overcomes all subtle things, and penetrates all solid things.* The new Father/Light, or new level of enlightenment, is completely realized Self-awareness. There is a constant cycle of recreation, where each level of Father/Light creates a new level of Father/Light.

11. *Thus was the world created.* Everything in the world is imbued with the power of Father/Light.

12. *From this comes marvelous adaptations of which this is the procedure.* Everything in the world is the seed of its future self.

13–14. *Therefore I am called Hermes Thrice-Crowned because I have three parts of the Wisdom of the whole world. And complete is what I had to say about the work of the Sun.* There is personal knowledge and experience of the process of enlightenment, which is to be done physically, mentally, and astrally. The triple crown expresses the power of the center within the infinite continuum, for it can be anywhere and everywhere; it is the Sun and the Moon and everything that lies between. Thus, the Emerald Tablet describes the process of enlightenment as force into form.

Examples of Translations
Numerous translations have been made of the Emerald Tablet. No two are the same. Below are three examples of other translations:

Jabir ibn Hayyan (Geber)

0. Balinas mentions the engraving on the table in the hand of Hermes, which says:

1. Truth! Certainty! That in which there is no doubt!

2. That which is above is from that which is below, and that which is below is from that which is above, working the miracles of one.

3. As all things were from one.

4. Its father is the Sun, and its mother the Moon.

5. The Earth carried it in her belly, and the Wind nourished it in her belly,

7. as Earth which shall become Fire.

7a. Feed the Earth from that which is subtle, with the greatest power.

8. It ascends from the earth to the heaven and becomes ruler over that which is above and that which is below.

14. And I have already explained the meaning of the whole of this in two of these books of mine.

Isaac Newton

1. Tis true without lying, certain & most true.

2. That wch is below is like that wch is above & that wch is above is like yt wch is below to do ye miracles of one only thing.

3. And as all things have been & arose from one by ye mediation of one: so all things have their birth from this one thing by adaptation.

4. The Sun is its father, the moon its mother,

5. the wind hath carried it in its belly, the earth its nourse.

6. The father of all perfection in ye whole world is here.

7. Its force or power is entire if it be converted into earth.

7a. Seperate thou ye earth from ye fire, ye subtile from the gross sweetly wth great indoustry.

8. It ascends from ye earth to ye heaven & again it desends to ye earth and receives ye force of things superior & inferior.

9. By this means you shall have ye glory of ye whole world & thereby all obscurity shall fly from you.

10. Its force is above all force, pfor it vanquishes every subtile thing & penetrates every solid thing.

11a. So was ye world created.

12. From this are & do come admirable adaptations whereof ye means (Or process) is here in this.

13. Hence I am called Hermes Trismegist, having the three parts of ye philosophy of ye whole world.

14. That wch I have said of ye operation of ye Sun is accomplished & ended.

Madame Helena P. Blavatsky

2. What is below is like that which is above, and what is above is similar to that which is below to accomplish the wonders of the one thing.

3. As all things were produced by the mediation of one being, so all things were produced from this one by adaption.

4. Its father is the sun; its mother the moon.

6a. It is the cause of all perfection throughout the whole earth.

7. Its power is perfect if it is changed into earth.

7a. Separate the earth from the fire, the subtle from the gross, acting prudently and with judgment.

8. Ascend with the greatest sagacity from earth to heaven, and unite together the power of things inferior and superior;

9. Thus you will possess the light of the whole world, and all obscurity will fly away from you.

10. This thing has more fortitude than fortitude itself because it will overcome every subtle thing and penetrate every solid thing.

11a. By it the world was formed.

FURTHER READING:

Clark, Rawn. "Commentary on the Emerald Tablet of Hermes." Available online. URL: http://www.alchemywebsite.com/rawn_cla.html. Downloaded April 12, 2005.

"Emerald Tablet of Hermes." Available online. URL: http://www.levity.com/alchemy/emerald.html. Downloaded May 11, 2005.

Hauck, Dennis William. *The Emerald Tablet: Alchemy for Personal Transformation.* New York: Penguin/Arkana, 1999.

Encausse, Gerard   See PAPUS.

enchantment   A magical SPELL. An enchantment places a person—or even an animal—under the influence of another person. Enchantments especially refer to love spells and to spells in which pleasurable, alluring illusions are cast. For example, FAIRIES enchant humans to fool them. *Enchantment* can be used synonymously with BEWITCHMENT and FASCINATION.

Enchiridion of Pope Leo III   See GRIMOIRES.

Enochian magic   A system of MAGIC involving communication with ANGELS and spirits and travel through various planes, or aethyrs, of consciousness. Enochian magic originated with JOHN DEE and EDWARD KELLY in the 16th century. Dee, who was royal astrologer to Elizabeth I, joined in an odd partnership with Kelly in attempts to communicate with the spirits through SCRYING. Dee is said to have recorded their proceedings and RITUALS, thus creating the Enochian system of magic.

The communication was done in the Enochian language, reputedly a real and complex language of unknown origin with a melodic sound similar to Sanskrit, Greek, or Arabic. Kelly, who had a reputation for fraud, may have invented Enochian; he told Dee that it was the language of angels and was spoken in the Garden of Eden. Lore holds that he and Dee may have used it as a secret code for espionage activities for Queen Elizabeth I.

Dee and Kelly conjured the angels with the Nineteen Calls or Keys of Enochian, or INVOCATIONS. The first two keys conjured the element Spirit, and the next 16 keys conjured the four ELEMENTS, each subdivided into four. The 19th key invoked any of 30 "aethyrs" or "aires" which have never been precisely defined; the HERMETIC ORDER OF THE GOLDEN DAWN said they represent new dimensions of consciousness.

When the angels appeared in Kelly's crystal, he communicated with them in Enochian, using a complicated procedure. He set up charts of squares either filled with letters or left blank. The angels spelled out messages by pointing with a rod to various squares. Kelly claimed to see the angels with CLAIRVOYANCE, and he dictated the messages to Dee.

Kelly said the messages were always dictated backwards because communicating directly with angels would unleash dangerous and powerful forces beyond control. When the messages were finished, he and Dee rewrote them reverse order.

The complete Enochian material produced by Dee and Kelly included:

- Nineteen invocations (Calls or Keys)
- Translations of the Calls
- An Enochian alphabet comprised of 21 letters
- More than 100 large squares, each divided into smaller squares (2,401 in number), containing letters
- Instructions for using the squares in concert with the Calls
- Occult teachings

Following the deaths of Dee and Kelly, Enochian magic sank into obscurity. It was revived in the late 19th century by the Golden Dawn, which credited it with great importance. Some occultists said it was the lost tongue of Atlantis. In the Golden Dawn view, the lower 18 Keys invoked angels of various MAGIC SQUARES. The 19th Key invoked one or other of 30 aethyrs into unexplored dimensions of consciousness. In Enochian, the 19th Key is:

Madriaax Ds Praf [name of the aethyr] Chis Macaobz Saanir Caosgo Od Fisis Babzizras Iaida! Nonca Gohulim: Micma Adoian Mad, Iaod Bliorb, Soba Ooaona Chis Luciftias Piripsol. Ds Abraassa Noncf Netaaib Caosgi. . .

Dee and Kelly translated this as:

The Heavens which dwell in [name of the aethyr] Are Mighty in the Parts of the Earth And execute the Judgment of the Highest! Unto you it is said: Behold the Face of Your God, The Beginnings of Comfort, Whose Eyes are the Brightness of the Heavens, Which Provided You for the Government of Earth . . .

The Enochian Keys were studied at length by ALEISTER CROWLEY, who explored all of them and pronounced them genuine. In his autobiography, *The Confessions of Aleister Crowley,* he states that ". . . anyone with the smallest capacity for Magick finds that they work." Even beginners in magic get results with Enochian calls, he said. Crowley's most extensive commentary on the magic of the Keys was published in his book *The Vision and the Voice* in 1911.

Crowley subscribed to the definition of the aethyrs—or aires—as "'Dominion extending in ever widening circles without and beyond the Watch Towers of the Universe,' these Watch Towers composing a cube of infinite magnitude." He said only properly initiated ADEPTS could invoke all of the 30 aethyrs in the 19th Key. The results produced visions of spirits and astral beings, and Crowley recorded his communications with them. In 1900 he accessed the two outer aethyrs, 29 and 30, while on a trip to Mexico. His next experience of them came in 1909 in North Africa when he and his assistant VICTOR NEUBERG invoked the DEMON CHORONZON.

Despite the importance given the Keys by the Golden Dawn, which taught them to all adepts, there is no evidence that anyone but Crowley ever actually worked with them; they were appreciated in theory but not in practice.

Enochian magic has been revived and is practiced in more recent times by other occultists. The adept reaches various aethyrs through travel in the ASTRAL BODY, the mental body, and mystical states of consciousness akin to *samadhi,* a high state of consciousness in yoga that transcends thought. Some of the aethyrs have sexual energies. Many involve an initiatory experience, such as death of the old personality/ego and rebirth of the new.

Although some doubt that Enochian is a genuine language, it has been demonstrated that English can be translated into it. Crowley took the INVOCATIONS of the GRIMOIRE the *Lesser Key of Solomon* and translated them into Enochian.

Claims of antiquity have been made for Enochian magic, even stretching back to the fabled continent of Atlantis, but there is no basis for it existing prior to the partnership of Dee and Kelly.

FURTHER READING:
King, Francis. *Megatherion: The Magickal World of Aleister Crowley.* New York: Creation Books, 2004.
King, Francis (ed.). *Ritual Magic of the Golden Dawn.* Rochester, Vt.: Destiny Books, 1997.
Laycock, Donald. *The Complete Enochian Dictionary: A Dictionary of the Angelic Language as Revealed to Dr. John Dee and Edward Kelley.* York Beach, Maine: Samuel Weiser, 2001.
Peterson, Joseph. *John Dee's Five Books of Mystery: Original Sourcebook of Enochian Magic.* York Beach, Maine: Samuel Weiser, 2003.

evil eye   The supernatural or magical power to cause disaster, calamity, illness, and even death with a glance or lingering look. The evil eye is also called FASCINATION, over-looking, *mal occhio*, and *jettatura*. AMULETS are worn to ward it off; RITUALS such as spitting (see SPITTLE) can nullify it.

The evil eye is one of the most feared supernatural powers. In earlier times it was believed that the eye emitted powerful beams of energy that could be used by malevolent people to cause harm. Records of the evil eye date back to 3000 B.C.E. in the cuneiform texts of the Sumerians and Assyrians. The Babylonians believed in it, as did the ancient Egyptians and Greeks. The Romans were afraid of it. It is even mentioned in the Bible.

The evil eye is an inherent power possessed by certain people. For example, a person may be cursed with evil eye from birth and not know it. Their envious or admiring glances are harmful to others. Consequently, individuals must be on constant guard against the inadvertent malevolent glance. The evil eye is most likely to strike when one is at the peak of prosperity and happiness. Women, children, and animals are particularly vulnerable.

Deliberate evil eye is cast by a person who possesses magical powers, such as a witch or a sorcerer, and is used to wreak magical harm. The death-dealing evil eye appears frequently in Native American folklore. The fatal look may be used in conjunction with the POINTING of the shaman's finger, stick, or wand, which sends negative energy streaming toward the victim.

Amulets and gestures are the primary defenses against the evil eye. The ancient Egyptians protected their possessions, dwellings, and tombs against the evil eye with an amulet called the *udjatti*, also called the Two Eyes or the Eye of the Sun and the Eye of the Moon. The *udjatti* were worn and were also painted on objects, coffins, and structures. Sometimes a single *udjat* was used, but the amulet was most powerful if both eyes reflected the baleful glance of evildoers. Grotesque heads of DEMONS or monsters, such as Medusa, also repel the evil eye.

The most common amulets are two phallic symbols: the *corno*, a curved horn, and the "fig," a clenched hand with thumb stuck through middle and fourth fingers. The ancient Romans used phallic amulets after their phallic god, Priapus, also called Fascinus, from which comes "fascination" or BEWITCHMENT. Other amulets include eyes, bells, brass, red ribbons, garlic, IRON, horseshoes, objects made of rowan or juniper, and shamrocks.

If an unprotected person is hit with the evil eye, immediate action must be taken to avoid disaster. In Italy, some men grab their genitals. Spitting will nullify the evil, as will making the signs of the *corno* or fig with the hand. Some victims consult a witch, a wise woman, or a sorcerer for a counterspell.

A widespread belief about peacock tail feathers associates the eye in the feathers with the evil eye; thus peacock feathers should not be kept in a house.

FURTHER READING:
Elworthy, Frederick Thomas. *The Evil Eye: An Account of This Ancient and Widespread Superstition*. New York: OBC, Inc., 1989.

Gordon, Stuart. *The Book of Curses: True Tales of Voodoo, Hoodoo and Hex*. London: Brockhampton Press, 1994.

evocation   In RITUAL, the calling forth of a spirit, entity, or deity. The spirit may be either an external, independent force or the physical manifestation of a force within the magician. According to FRANCIS BARRETT, "gods and hierarchies of spirits may be reasonably supposed to be but previously unknown facets of our own consciousness."

In MAGIC, SORCERY, and WITCHCRAFT, an evocation is a command to an entity to appear and do the bidding of the magician. In ceremonial magic, spirits are evoked to appear in a MAGIC TRIANGLE outside the magician's protective MAGIC CIRCLE, lest they cause him harm. Evocation is an elaborate ritual, and various procedures for it are detailed in the many magical GRIMOIRES.

Before the ritual, the magician must map out exactly what he desires to accomplish and how he intends to do so. He must carefully choose the spirit or INTELLIGENCE that he will summon to aid in the purpose of his work. He must know the ritual thoroughly and be able to perform it smoothly and flawlessly without break or pause.

The magician purifies himself through fasting and PRAYER, dons his garb, purifies his magical TOOLS, and casts the circle and triangle. To evoke the spirit, he must have perfect knowledge of it and the purpose it is to serve. The correct SIGILS, PERFUMES, and NAMES must be used. He must visualize the spirit, for once evoked, the spirit will reappear in the same form in subsequent evocations. The evocation comprises words and gestures with ritual tools. The magician speaks in a commanding tone of voice and may even shriek the evocation to intimidate unruly spirits.

FRANZ BARDON said that evocation is the most difficult magic to understand. In his second book, *The Practice of Magical Evocation* (1956), he gives one of the first detailed public descriptions of evocation in the Western tradition. Bardon said that the powers of astral seeing and hearing—psychic senses of CLAIRVOYANCE and CLAIRAUDIENCE—are essential to evoking spirits. He said it does not matter where a spirit is evoked—triangle, magic MIRROR, FLUID CONDENSER—as long as the magician creates an artificial atmosphere akin to the environment of the spirit. The magician must transfer his consciousness into the atmosphere in order to be noticed by the spirit.

See also INVOCATION.

FURTHER READING:
Bardon, Franz. *The Practice of Magical Evocation*. Albuquerque, N.Mex.: Brotherhood of Life, 2001.
Barrett, Francis. *The Magus*. 1801. Reprint, Secaucus, N.J.: The Citadel Press, 1967.
Regardie, Israel. *The Tree of Life: A Study in Magic*. York Beach, Maine: Samuel Weiser, 1969.

Excalibur   King Arthur's magical SWORD that was given to him by VIVIANE, THE LADY OF THE LAKE. After Arthur's fatal encounter against Mordred, Excalibur was thrown in the lake and returned to the Lady.

Contrary to popular belief, Excalibur is not the weapon pulled out of the stone which established Arthur as heir to King Uther Pendragon. That sword broke in battle, after which MERLIN arranged for Arthur to accept a new, elven-made sword, the magical Excalibur, from the Lady of the Lake. Merlin took Arthur to the lake's edge and pointed to the arm extended out of the water holding a sword. Amazed, Arthur then saw a beautiful woman rowing a small boat to the shore, and he asked who she might be. Merlin replied that it was Viviane, who lived on a rock in the lake's mists—in other words, at Avalon. At first the Lady refused to give Excalibur to Arthur but finally gave in, requesting that Arthur present her with a gift at some future time. The king agreed and sailed on a barge out to the middle of the lake to claim the weapon. The arm then disappeared beneath the water's surface.

Excalibur itself was unbreakable, and its scabbard protected Arthur when he wore it. *Excalibur* is the French version of the sword's name, which was originally called *Caladfwich,* a Welsh word derived from the Gaelic *Calad-Bolg,* which means "hard lightning." Viviane defines the name as meaning "cut-steel." Geoffrey of Monmouth, an early storyteller, called the sword Caliburn, which eventually became *Excalibur.* In the great Irish epic poem *An Tain Bo Cuailgne (The Cattle Raid of Cooley),* the hero Cu Chulainn also possesses a sword named *Caladbolg.*

In his study of weapons and warfare in J. R. R. TOLKIEN'S THE LORD OF THE RINGS, author Chris Smith remarks that a sword is designed for no other purpose than as a weapon, whereas an axe, a spear, or a knife can be used for hunting food or clearing land. Swords, therefore, symbolize rank and privilege: To own a sword meant one had enough money to spend on something that had no secondary use. Sword blades and hilts were beautifully made and engraved, while the scabbards might be decorated or even contain jewels. Such treasures were cared for lovingly, like a member of the family. To give the sword a name conferred power, which emboldened the owner and frightened his enemies.

The legends relate that MORGAN LE FAY, half-sister to Arthur and a skilled enchantress, stole Excalibur and gave it to her lover, Sir Accolon of Gaul. Viviane retrieved the sword and gave it back to Arthur, but Morgan threw the scabbard in the lake. After Mordred, Arthur's illegitimate son, challenged Arthur in the Battle of Camlann and destroyed them both, the dying king requested that Sir Bedivere (Bedwyr or Girflet) throw the sword back in the lake. At first Bedivere tried to keep Excalibur for himself, but Arthur—who realized Bedivere still had the sword—commanded that the knight try again. This time Bedivere threw Excalibur far into the lake, where the mysterious arm and hand caught the sword and immediately sank into the murky water.

In the film version of *The Mists of Avalon,* based on Marion Zimmer Bradley's book of the same name, Morgaine (Morgan) rows Arthur across the lake to Avalon but has lost the ability to part the mists that hide the ancient temple. Arthur surmises the Goddess requires an offering and suggests Morgaine give Excalibur to her. When Morgaine throws the sword, it becomes a bright light in the sky, changing from a sword with hilt to a Christian cross. The mists successfully part but only for a moment, and then Arthur dies.

FURTHER READING:
Bradley, Marion Zimmer. *The Mists of Avalon.* New York: Knopf, 1983.
"Excalibur and the Sword in the Stone." The Camelot Project at the University of Rochester. Available online. URL: www.lib.rochester.edu/camelot/swrdmenu.htm. Downloaded October. 17, 2004.
Ford, David Nash. "Excalibur: A Discussion of the Origins of King Arthur's Sword." Available online. URL: www.britannia.com/history/arthur/excalibur.html. Downloaded October 17, 2004.
Smith, Chris. *The Lord of the Rings: Weapons and Warfare.* New York: Houghton Mifflin, 2004.
"Welcome to Camelot, Home of King Arthur and His Court." Available online. URL: www.geocities.com/Athens/Acropolis/2025/art.htm. Downloaded October 17, 2004.

excrement   In ALCHEMY, a SYMBOL of the *nigredo,* the stage of putrefaction that begins the Great Work. Human and animal excrement were employed in various alchemical procedures aimed at creating the PHILOSOPHER'S STONE.

Excrement also symbolizes the darkness of the unconscious from which enlightenment arises. It is the power of a person, the essence of one's being. It associated with gold and riches and is the fertilizer of new growth and beginnings.

See also URINE.

exorcism   The expulsion of spirits believed to be possessing a human being or disturbing a place that humans frequent. Exorcisms range from friendly, persuasive conversations to elaborate RITUALS commanding the entity to leave in the name of God or a god.

The word *exorcism* comes from the Greek *exorkizein,* meaning oath, and translates as *adjuro,* or "adjure," in Latin and English. To "exorcise" does not mean to cast out so much as it means "putting the spirit or demon on oath," or invoking a higher authority to compel the entity to act in a way contrary to its wishes.

Exorcisms of spirits, DEMONS, ghosts, poltergeists, ELEMENTALS, and unwanted or negative spirits, energies, or THOUGHT-FORMS are commonplace around the world. Traditionally, they are performed by qualified persons of religious or magical skill. Magical GRIMOIRES contain instructions for exorcism rituals.

Literature of the HERMETIC ORDER OF THE GOLDEN DAWN provides information for performing exorcisms. In a record of a personal experience, Frater Sub Spe said that he concluded that he and his wife were possessed by a vampirizing elemental after his wife's bout of influenza left both of them in a state of inexplicable exhaustion. Frater Sub Spe at first thought to consult a fellow ADEPT, but during a state of intense concentration he was instructed by a nonphysical guide to perform the exorcism himself with the guide's instructions. A vision of a stately man in black magical robes appeared and responded to the secret Golden Dawn salutes given him by Frater Sub Spe. The magician merged with the body of Frater Sub Spe, taking possession of it and giving instructions via words and impressions.

Frater Sub Spe was told to do the following: Turn down the gas; burn incense; trace an invoking PENTAGRAM of Fire toward the East; trace the SIGIL of Leo in the center of the pentagram; vibrate the NAME of Power "Adni ha Aretz"; return the coal to the fire; and face East and make the qabalistic cross; and trace an invoking Pentagram of Earth.

Frater Sub Spe did as instructed, and at the end of the ritual he ordered the possessing spirit to appear before him:

> As I did so a vague blot, like a scrap of London fog, materialized before me. At the same time I sensed my guide, standing close to my right hand, raising his hand in the attitude of the 1=10 sign [a grade of the Golden Dawn]. I felt him (my guide) mentally order me to command the appearance of the obsessing entity, using the Names JHVH, ADNI, AGLA, AHIH. I did so and the mist thickened and formed a kind of nucleus. My guide then instructed me, "Use the Name of the Lord Jesus." I did so, commanding in that name a fuller manifestation. I saw, at first dimly, as "in a glass darkly," and then with complete clarity, a most foul shape, between a bloated big-bellied toad and a malicious ape. My guide spoke to me in an audible voice, saying Now smite it with all your force, using the "Name of the Lord Jesus." I did so gathering all the force I possessed into, as it were, a glowing ball of electric fire and then projecting it like a lightning flash upon the foul image before me.
>
> There was a slight feeling of shock, a foul smell, a momentary dimness, and then the thing was gone; simultaneously my Guide disappeared. The effect of this experience upon me was to create a great tension of nerves and a disposition to start at almost anything. Afterwards, when going upstairs, I saw floating balls of fire; this may have been hallucination.

> Both my wife and myself rapidly recovered our full health. Afterwards, a message came to me that "the unclean spirit is gone out, but it remains to purge away his traces from the house of life."

The Christian church has formal exorcism rites for expelling demons, such as the Catholic *Rituale Romanum*. Protestant rites also are performed. In June 2005 an exorcism ritual was taken to an extreme in Tanacu, Romania, when a 23-year-old nun died during a Russian Orthodox exorcism at the Holy Trinity monastery. A schizophrenic, the nun's behavior convinced her sister nuns that she was possessed by the devil. Father Daniel ordered the nun to be chained to a cross in a mock crucifixion. Her mouth was stuffed with a towel. Denied food and water, she was found dead after three days of hanging on the cross. Father Daniel and several nuns were arrested on murder charges.

A Jewish exorcism ritual concerns the DYBBUK, an evil spirit or doomed soul that enters the body of a person, latches onto the victim's soul, and causes mental illness and a personality change. The exorcism ritual calls for expelling the dybbuk through the victim's small toe and either redeeming it or sending it to hell. Pamphlets describing famous cases once were published; the last appeared in 1904 in Jerusalem.

Modern versions of the dybbuk are found in the treatments of personality and mental disorders. Dr. Carl Wickland, American physician and psychologist (1861–1945), and his wife, Anna, believed that possessing spirits were the dead who were not evil but trapped on the Earth plane and confused. The Wicklands said that the possessing dead caused multiple and dissociated personalities, and insanity. The practice of "spirit releasement," a modern definition of exorcism, continues the Wicklands' work with applications for the stresses and setbacks of daily life.

FURTHER READING:

"Crucified nun dies in exorcism." Available online. URL: http://news.bbc.co.uk/1/hi/world/europe/4107524.stm. Downloaded June 21, 2005.

Frater Sub Spe. "Flying Roll XXXIV: An Exorcism." Available online. URL: http://www.golden-dawn.org/gd_fr34.htm. Downloaded June 29, 2005.

Martin, Malachi. *Hostage to the Devil*. New York: Harper & Row, 1976.

Wickland, Carl. *Thirty Years Among the Dead*. 1924. Reprint, N. Hollywood, Calif.: Newcastle Publishing Co., 1974.

fairies   Magically empowered beings who occupy a middle realm between Earth and the heavenly planes. The term *fairy* comes from the Latin word *fata,* or fate, which refers to the Fates of mythology: three women who spin, twist and cut the threads of life. *Fairy* came into usage in medieval times and was often used to refer to women who had magical powers. *Fairy* originally meant *faerie,* or a state of ENCHANTMENT. According to lore, fairies themselves do not like the word but prefer such labels as *the Good Neighbours, the Gentry, the People of Peace, the Strangers, Themselves, The Seely (Blessed) Court* and similar terms. Fairies are often referred to as "the Little People."

Origins of Fairies

Fairy beliefs are universal and, despite their variations, are strikingly similar. While their lore can be found around the world, fairy beliefs are particularly strong in the British Isles and in Europe. Fairy lore is older than Christianity, but much of it has acquired Christian elements. The major explanations for the origins of fairies are:

- They are the souls of the pagan dead. Those who were not baptized Christian became at death trapped between heaven and Earth.
- They are the guardians of the dead. Their realm is a between-place between the realm of the living and the realm of the dead.
- They are themselves the ghosts of venerated ancestors.

- They are fallen angels who were cast out of heaven with Lucifer but condemned by God to remain in the elements of the Earth.
- They are nature spirits who are attached to particular places or to the four elements.
- They are supernatural creatures who are monsters or half-human, half-monster.
- They are small-stature human beings, a primitive race that went into hiding to survive.

In all likelihood, there is no one origin or explanation of fairies. Some may be NATURE SPIRITS or ELEMENTALS, others belong to the realm of supernatural forces, others are associated with the land of the dead, and still others have a distant relationship to humans.

Contemporary popular Western beliefs about ANGELS link fairies to angels as a subordinate class of beings, in accordance with the idea of ministering angels—everything in nature has its guiding, or ministering, angel. In folklore tradition, however, fairies are not a type of heavenly angel but a separate class of beings that exist between the human realm and the realm of spirits. They are more closely tied to and associated with the concerns of Earth than are angels, demigods, and gods.

Fairies also have been compared with sightings of extraterrestrials; many descriptions of the latter are similar to older descriptions of fairies. UFO researcher Jacques Vallee has made compelling comparisons between ETs and fairies and elves and DEMONS and emphasizes the similarity between ETs and the fairy-faith Celtic folklore. Supporters of this view argue that ETs are a modern way of explaining encounters with certain types of otherworldly beings. Opponents say that the lack of modern fairy traditions, especially in the United States, causes many experiencers to explain beings as ETs instead of fairies.

Descriptions of Fairies

Fairies have many names and descriptions. They usually are invisible save to those with clairvoyant sight. Fairies are elusive, and many prefer to keep to themselves. They can make themselves visible to humans if they so desire. They are best seen at twilight.

Some fairies are diminutive, even tiny, while others are huge, larger than humans. Some are beautiful, and some are ugly. Some resemble humans, while others are spirit-like, with wings. WILLIAM BUTLER YEATS said of fairies, "Do not think the fairies are always little. Everything is capricious about them, even their size. They seem to take what size or shape pleases them."

Traditionally, fairies are feared more than courted. They are supernaturally endowed and can do MAGIC, and for that reason people throughout the ages have sought their help and favors despite the dangers of dealing with them.

Some fairies are morally ambivalent, while others are always benevolent, and still others are believed to be always malevolent, such as those that guard places in nature or who like to trick the unwary traveler.

Some fairies are solitary, especially those that inhabit the wild. Others live as a fairy race or nation, usually said to be underground and accessed through mounds, caves, burrows, holes in the ground, and under piles of stones and rocks. The Land of Fairy, also called Elfland, has characteristics of the land of the dead. Time is altered so that a day in human life might stretch into years in fairyland. There is no day or night but a perpetual twilight.

The subjective nature of perception of fairies is amply illustrated in the variety of anecdotal accounts recorded for centuries. For example, in 1556 a Dorset, England, man accused of WITCHCRAFT, John Walsh, said that fairies were divided into three types: white, green, and black. They could be contacted between the hours of 12 and 1 day and night, but great care had to be taken with the black fairies, for they were "the worst."

More than a century later, a detailed description of fairies and their realm was written in 1691–92 by Robert Kirk, a Scottish Episcopalian minister who lived near Stirling in the Aberfoyle region. Kirk, a SEVENTH SON, may have inherited the gifts of second sight (CLAIRVOYANCE) and healing from his mother. Kirk's handwritten manuscript, *The Secret Commonwealth*, still ranks as one of the most significant documents of personal knowledge of fairies. According to lore, Kirk's relationship with fairies was so strong that he did not die physically but passed directly into the fairy realm through a hill at Aberfoyle now named after him. He remains in fairyland and will help humans who seek him out.

According to Kirk, fairies are real and intelligent beings with supernatural powers. He described some fairies as having light, changeable bodies of congealed air or condensed clouds, while others have grosser bodies and feed on corn, liquor, and grain. Their clothing and manner of speech follow the customs of the land in which they live.

W. Y. Evans-Wentz, who collected anecdotal accounts of fairies and fairy lore in the 19th and early 20th centuries, recorded many descriptions of them given by eyewitnesses. This one of "the gentry" came from a man who had contact with them:

> The folk are the grandest I have ever seen. They are far superior to us, and that is why they are called the gentry. They are not a working class, but a military–aristocratic class, tall and noble-appearing. They are a distinct race between our own and that of spirits, as they have told me. Their qualifications are tremendous. "We could cut off half the human race but would not," they said, "for we are expecting salvation.". . . Their sight is so penetrating that I think they could see through the earth. They have a silvery voice, quick and sweet. The music they play is most beautiful. They take the whole body and soul of young and intellectual people who are interesting, transmuting the body to a body like their own. I asked them once if they ever died, and they said, "No; we are always kept young." Once they take you and you taste the food in their palace you cannot come back. You are changed to one of them, and live with them for ever. They are able to appear in different forms. Once one appeared to me, and seemed only four feet high, and stoutly built. He said, "I am bigger than I appear to you now. We can make the old young, the big small, the small big. . . . Besides the gentry, who are a distinct class, there are bad spirits and ghosts, which are nothing like them. My mother once saw a leprechaun beside a bush hammering. He disappeared before she could get to him, but he also was unlike one of the gentry.

Another description of fairies given to Evans-Wentz came from "a cultured Irish woman" who had frequent visions of fairies and had divided them into five classes:

> (1) There are the Gnomes, who are earth–spirits and who seem to be of a sorrowful race. I once saw them distinctly on the side of Ben Bulbin. They had rather round heads and dark thick-set bodies, and in stature were about two and one-half feet. (2) The Leprechauns are different, being full of mischief, though they, too, are small. I followed a leprechaun from the town of Wiclow out to the Carraig Sidhe, "Rock of the Fairies," a distance of a half a mile or more, where he disappeared. He had a very merry face, and beckoned to me with his finger. (3) A third class are the Little People, who, unlike the Gnomes and Leprechauns, are quite good-looking; and they are very small. (4) The Good People are tall beautiful beings, as tall as ourselves, to judge by those I saw at the rath in Rosses Point. (5) The Gods are really the Tuatha de Danaan, and

they are much taller than our race. There may be many other classes of invisible beings which I do not know.

Modern concepts of fairies divide them into four main groups aligned with the four ELEMENTS of nature:

Earth fairies are associated with gardens, woodlands, nature, flora, animals, minerals, places in nature, mines, caves, and so on. Earth fairies also include those who work in human households, such as brownies. Dwarfs, gnomes, elves, pixies, trolls, and knockers are Earth-oriented fairies.

Water fairies inhabit lakes, rivers, ponds, and other bodies of water, including seas and oceans. Sprites, nymphs, selkies, and mermaids are among the many kinds of water fairies.

Air fairies, often called sylphs, govern the winds, the clouds, and the weather. They are especially associated with storms and tempests.

Fire fairies live in wild fires, volcanoes, bonfires, the fires of the home hearth, and electricity.

Activities of Fairies

Kirk said that the fairy realm is the MIRROR opposite of the human world. Fairies are organized into tribes and orders and live as humans do: They marry, have children, work, and so forth. The fairy world is underground, where the spirits of the dead also reside. Fairies take care of and guard the world of nature. The interactions of fairies with humans depend upon the kind of fairy and its purpose. For example, a fairy of a river will not have as much interaction with humans as a fairy who looks after human tools.

It is bad luck to disturb a known fairy dwelling or any place where fairies might live, such as under piles of stone. The fairies will be angry and take revenge. Fairies travel along lines or tracks called fairy paths. The fairies travel along their paths at night at all costs to humans. For example, if someone is unfortunate enough to build a house atop a fairy path, bad luck will follow, for the fairies will march right through it. The occupants will sicken, the animals will die, and the crops will not grow or will become blighted. Doors and windows, especially those right along the path, will not stay closed.

In addition to their night marches, fairies move their lodgings on the Quarter Days, the times of the equinoxes and solstices. They are restless folk and move constantly "until doomsday," according to Kirk. During these mass relocations, people who possess second sight can have terrifying encounters with them. Tradition holds that it is advisable not to travel on those days, and to attend church to pray for protection against fairy attacks.

Traditionally, the existence and activities of fairies explain the reasons for illnesses, deformities, and untimely deaths among children; epidemics among livestock, and various disasters of weather. Fairies cause sudden, mysteri-ous and sometimes fatal illnesses in animals and people by attacking with elf arrows, soft flint barbed arrowheads that are flung with great force like darts. Elf arrows have the ability to penetrate deep into bodies and mortally wound vital organs without ever breaking the skin. Cattle are said to be particularly vulnerable to being "elf-shot."

They control crops; problems with harvests are blamed upon them. On All Hallows Eve, fairies blight blackberries and sloes; eating them on this night results in serious illness.

Fairies like to lead travelers astray. In Cornwall, where fairies are called piskeys, a person is said to be "piskey-led" if he or she becomes confused, disoriented, and lost. Fairies bewitch both animals and people.

Fairies steal human women for wives. They steal human babies and substitute their own sickly children, or changelings, in their place. Fairy women like to spin.

Fairies especially love to dance at night, forming circle dances that leave marks in grass or rings of mushrooms called fairy rings. The grass beneath them withers and is called a briza or dawdle. If a person walks across one of these dance rings, he is likely to become drowsy and fall into a permanent sleep. Offerings of cheese left in fairy rings will gain the favors of fairies.

Another favored activity of fairies is to eat food at human funeral banquets. Men who have second sight can see these dining fairies; hence they refuse to touch the meat served, lest they be poisoned by the fairies.

Fairies bestow the gift of prophecy and second sight upon certain individuals—usually men according to folklore tradition—and use their own powers to convey information about the future through these seers. Fairies possess their own books of magical CHARMS and counter-charms and teach witches magical arts of BEWITCHMENT and SPELL-casting.

To stay in the good graces of fairies, humans should keep clean houses and leave out food and drink. In return, fairies will bestow gifts, luck, fertility, and money and will help humans with their chores. Fairies also are given offerings at sacred WELLS, fountains, lakes, tree groves, and other places said to be "fairy haunts" so that humans can ward off illness and misfortune.

IRON weakens and repels fairies. Thus, iron implements should not be left in places frequented by fairies. Iron weapons can be used successfully against them.

The folk concept of benign or malignant fairies is often ambiguous. Whatever the disposition of a particular fairy or group of fairies, human respect for them is essential. Many folk tales illustrate the desirability of kindness, politeness, observance of taboos, and correct etiquette in dealing with the fairies.

Fairy Abductions

Fairies are fond of kidnapping people and carting them off to Elfland. They kidnap people who displease them and people who deliberately or accidentally manage to see them. Sometimes they take people just because it is in their nature to do so. A victim may remain in fairyland an hour or two, a day, or if longer, in years in multiples of seven: seven years, 14 years, 21 years, and so on. Those who are released by the fairies—or who manage to escape—often have no recollection of their time spent in fairyland. People who go into trancelike states are said to be off in fairyland enjoying a festival.

One of the oldest oral accounts of about being taken away by a fairy is *The Ballad of Thomas Rhymer,* which dates to 13th-century Scotland. Thomas Rhymer (Thomas of Erceldoune or Earlston) was sleeping under a tree on a grassy bank when the queen of Fair Elfland came riding up on a milk-white horse. At first Rhymer thought she was the queen of heaven, but she corrected him with her true identity. She ordered him to come with her and to serve her for seven years "through good or ill as chance may be." Rhymer obeyed and got on the horse behind her. The steed took off faster than the wind. For 40 days and nights they rode, going through knee-deep BLOOD, seeing neither SUN nor MOON. Rhymer could only hear the sound of roaring sea. Eventually they came to a garden tree, and Rhymer offered to pick some fruit for the fairy queen. She warned him not to touch it, "for all the plagues that are in hell are upon the fruit of this country." Instead, she produced bread and wine in her lap. After Rhymer ate, the fairy queen told him to lay his head on her knee. She showed him THREE roads: the road to wickedness, which looked inviting; the road to righteousness, which was narrow and full of thorns; and the road to Elfland, which was beautiful. The queen warned Rhymer that once they got to Elfland, he was not to speak a single word, or he would never return to his own land. Rhymer obeyed, and vanished for seven years. When he returned, he had the gift of prophecy and also was given green velvet shoes and a woven cloth coat.

The place where Rhymer met the queen of fairies is in the Eildon Hills in the Borders of Scotland. The Rhymer's Stone, on the old road between Melrose and St. Boswells, marks the spot where the Trysting Tree, also called the Eildon Tree, originally stood. The tree is where Rhymer was sleeping when he was summoned by the fairy queen and is where he made his prophecies after returning from his stay in Efland. The stone is modern and replaces an original stone, the historical details of which are not known.

Magical Work with Fairies
In earlier times, people usually avoided fairies and sought not to draw their attention and certainly not their ire. However, their magical abilities of healing, protection, and prophecy enticed some persons to seek them out. A 15th-century English manuscript prescribed a magical way to summon fairies at will with the help of a crystal, hen's blood, hazel wands, and other ingredients:

> First get a broad square christall or Venus glasse, in length and breadth three inches; then lay that glasse or chrystall in the blood of a white Heene, three Wednesdays or three Fridays, then take it out and wash it with Holy Water and

fumigate it [with incense]. Then take three hazels sticks or wands of a years growth, peel them fayre and white and make them so long as you write the spirits or fayries which you call three times on every sticke, being made flatt on one side. Then bury them under som hill, wheras you suppose fayries haunt, the Wednesday before you call her, and the Friday following, take them up and call her at 8, 3, and 10 of the clocke which he good planets and hours, but when you call, be of cleane life and turn thy face towards the east, and when you have her, bind her to the stone or glasse.

In modern times, attitudes have shifted toward seeking out fairies for communication and magical and spiritual work. Wiccan and Pagan interests often use the spelling *faery* to distinguish modern magical work from old fairy folklore.

Magical work with fairies includes communing with them via meditation, clairvoyance, telepathy, and work with dreams and magical RITUALS, as well as shamanic journeys to the fairyland Underworld. The purposes of magical work include spiritual growth and enlightenment; service to Nature; healing; and spell-casting. A fairy altar (see TOOLS) may be constructed in a home or garden as a place to focus fairy magic work.

FURTHER READING:
Briggs, Katherine Briggs. *The Vanishing People.* New York: Pantheon Books, 1978.
———. *An Encyclopedia of Fairies: Hobgoblins, Brownies, Bogies, and Other Supernatural Creatures.* New York: Pantheon Books, 1976.
Evans-Wentz, W. Y. *The Fairy Faith in Celtic Countries.* 1911. Reprint, New York: Carroll Publishing Group, 1990.
Guiley, Rosemary. *Fairy Magic.* London: Element/Thorsons, 2004.
Stewart, R. J. *The Living World of Faery.* Lake Toxaway, N.C.: Mercury Publishing, 1995.
Vallee, Jacques. *Passport to Magonia: From Folklore to Flying Saucers.* Chicago: Henry Regnery Co., 1969.

familiar   A shape-shifted spirit, usually in the form of an animal, who assists a magical practitioner in the performance of spell-casting and RITUALS. The familiar is found in magical traditions around the world.

Familiars are acquired in INITIATION or the attainment of a certain level of magical skill. They may keep one form or may have the ability to shapeshift into different animal forms. They serve only the persons to whom they are bonded. A practitioner can have multiple familiars, each with its own function and specialty.

Familiars offers advantages of being able to do things and go places that humans cannot, but animals can. They are dispatched on magical errands, such as to deliver BEWITCHMENTS.

In Western lore, the familiar gained unfortunate notoriety as a supposedly evil, demonic entity during the antiwitch hysteria that began in the Middle Ages. Witches were said to use their cats, a common household resident, as well as dogs, toads, farm animals, and wild creatures to carry out their alleged evil intents.

The *Malleus Maleficarum,* the Dominican inquisitors' handbook written in Germany in 1486, offers no instructions concerning familiars in the interrogation and trial of witches, but it does acknowledge that an animal familiar "always works with her [the witch] in everything." The familiar hysteria was greater in England and Scotland than in Europe. In England, the Witchcraft Act of 1604 made it a felony to "consult, covenant with, entertain, employ, feed, or reward any evil and wicked spirit to or for any intent or purpose." In witch trials, animals alleged to be familiars were cited as evidence against accused witches and sometimes were even put on trial and executed. Familiars were less significant in witch trials in the American colonies.

In contemporary magical practices, familiars have a special psychic attunement and rapport that makes them valuable participants in raising power, setting and clearing space, spell-casting, SCRYING, healing, and other rituals and magical activities.

Farr, Florence Beatrice (1860–1917)

English actress, occultist, and an important member of the HERMETIC ORDER OF THE GOLDEN DAWN.

Florence Farr was born on July 7, 1860. Her father was a physician and named her after his friend, the famous nurse Florence Nightingale. According to Farr's horoscope, her sun was in the 12th house, which presaged psychic abilities and an interest in the occult. Both proved to be true.

In her teens, Farr became friends with the daughter of Jane Morris, May Morris, who served as a model in pre-Raphaelite paintings. Farr and May Morris modeled for "The Golden Stairs," painted by Sir Edward Burne-Jones.

Farr was intelligent and gifted with a beautiful voice. She was not content with the traditional role expected of Victorian women—to marry and have children and be obedient to a husband. She attended Queen's College, the first woman's college in England. After college she taught, but the job failed to hold her interest. She turned to acting and was modestly successful. She fell in love with an actor, Edward Emery, and married him, but after marriage he treated her like a possession and demanded that she stay home and fulfill her traditional domestic duties. Farr rebelled, and a few years later they separated. Emery went to America. Farr never remarried, though she had numerous lovers.

In 1890 Farr moved in with her sister in Bedford Park, London, and the two entered a bohemian subculture of artists, political radicals, and free thinkers. Here she felt at home, on an equal footing with men. Her stage performances as a high priestess drew the admiration of George Bernard Shaw and WILLIAM BUTLER YEATS, both of whom envisioned her as the perfect woman to perform in their plays. Both men wrote plays entirely for her: Yeats did *The Countess Cathleen,* and Shaw did *Arms and the Man.* With the help of the wealthy Annie Horniman, Farr helped Yeats and Shaw have their plays produced.

Also in 1890 Farr joined the Golden Dawn, taking the MAGICAL MOTTO *Sapientia Sapienti Dono Data,* "Wisdom is a gift to be given to the wise." Shaw was dismayed, believing occultism to be far beneath her talents. But Farr treated her magical career quite seriously, seeking to transform her very body into an instrument for the receipt of divine wisdom. She was determined to be dominated by no man ever again, not even the adoring Shaw and Yeats. She advanced quickly through the grades and was initiated as Adeptus Minor in 1891, the second person to achieve the rank. In 1892 she became Praemonstratrix (leader of the order) and worked to improve the Golden Dawn's RITUALS. Her skill as an actress lent her a commanding presence in the performance of ceremonial magic.

Farr became skilled in ENOCHIAN MAGIC and DIVINATION with the I CHING. She was particularly skilled in SCRYING. She contacted the spirit of an Egyptian priestess of the Temple of Amon-at-Thebes, Nem Kheft Ka. The authenticity of the contact was validated by SAMUEL LIDDELL MacGREGOR MATHERS, one of the three founding Chiefs of the Golden Dawn. Mathers encouraged Farr to learn the temple's rituals for use in the Golden Dawn. As a result, Farr attempted an EVOCATION of the Spirit Taphthartharath with ALLAN BENNETT and two other members. Farr took the dangerous role of becoming THOTH and then commanding the spirit, rather than using the traditional magical approach of using WILL and magical TOOLS.

Under Farr's leadership as Praemonstratrix, the Golden Dawn grew rapidly. She eased the examinations for advancement by eliminating written tests and substituting oral ones. She also made it easier for gifted students to become ADEPTS, as she desired to have them join "The Sphere," a Second Order group that specialized in scrying. But rather than benefiting the Golden Dawn, the easing of requirements only served to fuel petty intrigues and jealous bickering, which escalated over time.

When WILLIAM WYNN WESTCOTT resigned as Chief Adept in Anglia in 1897, Farr assumed the position. By then, rifts were widening, and scandals and infighting ensued. Farr rejected ALEISTER CROWLEY for INITIATION as Adeptus Minor, citing his "sex intemperance" as a major reason. Farr resigned, but Mathers refused to accept it. He revealed to her that Westcott had forged letters pertaining to an alleged lineage of occult tradition for the Golden Dawn, which Farr made public to members. After Crowley made his famous but failed attempt to storm the London temple, Mathers was expelled, and the Golden Dawn reformed initiation for Adeptus Minor, enabling candidates to bypass the entire Outer Order. By that time, the Golden Dawn was riddled with rifts and factions. Farr, exhausted by them all, broke all connection with the Golden Dawn in 1902.

She returned to her acting career and cowrote and produced two plays about Egyptian mysteries. In 1907 she toured America, but by 1912 her acting career faded along with her youthfulness and beauty. She took a teaching job in Ceylon and became a Buddhist nun. A few years later she developed breast cancer and had a mastectomy. She wrote to Yeats about it, and he knew she was near her end. Two months after sending the letter, Farr died alone in a hospital in Colombo on April 29, 1917. Her body was cremated, and her ashes were scattered in a river.

Throughout her magical life, Farr was a prolific writer, authoring numerous articles on occultism as well as two novels based on her own experiences. She was especially interested in ALCHEMY and Egyptian magic and wrote on the parallels between Egyptian magic, alchemy, Hermetic, Kabbalistic, and Rosicrucian thought. For the Golden Dawn, she wrote "flying scrolls"—study materials for the Second Order—on ASTRAL TRAVEL and Hermetic love and higher MAGIC.

FURTHER READING:
"Florence Beatrice Farr." Available online. URL: http://www. golden-dawn.org/bioffarr.html. Downloaded June 29, 2005.
Greer, Mary K. *Women of the Golden Dawn: Rebels and Priestesses.* Rochester, Vt.: Inner Traditions, 1995.

fascination   A BEWITCHMENT that enables a magician or a witch to affect the behavior or life of another person.

HENRY CORNELIUS AGRIPPA defined fascination as a "binding." Fascination is accomplished through the eyes. The magician or witch projects a SPELL through the eyes of the victim. It enters the heart and takes effect. Making direct eye contact with a bewitcher enables fascination to occur.

Agrippa said that the instrument of fascination is the spirit, "generated of the purer blood, by the heat of the heart," which is sent forth in rays through the eyes. In fascination, a corrupted BLOOD is involved, which makes the eyes of the bewitcher appear red.

In MAGIC, fascination is especially used to procure love, but it also can be used to cause a person to suffer misfortunes and illness.

Dr. Edward Berridge, a homeopathic physician who was a member of the HERMETIC ORDER OF THE GOLDEN DAWN, counseled people who believed they were under a spell of fascination. One of his cases involved a woman who said she was under the unnatural fascination of a man. She did not like him but could not stop thinking about him. Berridge discovered that the man was knowledgeable about Voodoo magic. He then performed a RITUAL to break the spell:

I imagined they stood facing each other and that he had thrown out currents of odic fluid [universal life force], which had entangled her in their meshes. Then I imagined a sword in my hand with which I severed them, and

then with a torch burnt up the ends of the filaments still floating around her.

According to Berridge, several months later the fascination came to an end.
See also EVIL EYE.

FURTHER READING:
King, Francis (ed.). *Ritual Magic of the Golden Dawn.* Rochester, Vt.: Destiny Books, 1997.

Father   See SULPHUR.

fetish   An object that holds spirits, gods and magical powers. Fetishes can be POPPETS or images of gods, animal teeth, snake bones, beautiful stones, and so forth. They are often worn or carried as AMULETS.

African wooden doll fetishes, called *juju*, were brought to the New World during the slave trade. Possession of a fetish by a slave was punishable by death and sadistic torture.

In Vodoun, fetishes act as TALISMANS as well as amulets. They are sewn into RED flannel bags or leather pouches, and are worn about the neck. The more fetishes, the more protection one has from anything harmful or evil.

First Matter   See PRIMA MATERIA.

fith-fath   See INVISIBILITY.

Flamel, Nicholas (1330–1416)   French scribe, bookseller, and adept who, according to legend, became one of the most successful alchemists ever. With the help of an ANGEL and a mystical book, Nicholas Flamel and his wife Pernelle reputedly found the PHILOSOPHER'S STONE and converted base metals into SILVER and GOLD. Unlike the COMTE DE SAINT-GERMAIN or other adepts with uncertain heritages, Flamel and his wife were real people, registered citizens of Paris.

Nicholas Flamel was born in Pontoise, 18 miles north of Paris, in 1330 to a poor but respectable family. After completing his schooling, which included the study of classical language, he set up a tiny bookstall against the walls of the Cathedral of St. Jacques de la Boucherie in Paris, where he copied and illustrated books for sale. He met and married Madame Pernelle (also called Perenelle or Petronella) Lethas, an older woman, twice widowed, who had inherited some property, and they settled into a comfortable but unremarkable life.

But Flamel's real interest became ALCHEMY. The search for the Philosopher's Stone—the way to turn base metal into gold—obsessed many of the scientists and intellectuals of Flamel's day. More than mere riches, the mastery of alchemical transmutation revealed the essential secrets of Nature and the Divine. Flamel had some knowledge of the hermetic arts, and he no doubt copied some alchemical manuscripts. He was convinced that the answers lay in a book but had no idea where to find it. One night Flamel dreamed that an angel stood before him and held out an old, strange, and beautiful book. The angel said, "Look well at this book, Nicholas. At first you will understand nothing in it—neither you nor any other man. But one day you will see in it that which no other man will be able to see." When Flamel stretched out his hand to take the book, the angel disappeared in a golden cloud.

Intrigued, Flamel often thought about the book but could not guess its whereabouts. Then in 1357 a man desperate for money accosted him in his bookstall and offered to sell a rare book for two florins. Flamel recognized the book from his dream and paid the man his price without quibbling. The book did not have parchment pages but instead had leaves made of tree bark inscribed with a steel point. The binding was quite old and made of copper that was covered in strange SYMBOLS. There were only 21 pages, divided into three sets of seven. The seventh page of each set contained no writing, only pictures that Flamel could not understand. The first drawing showed a CADUCEUS with intertwined serpents, the second a SERPENT crucified on a cross, and the third a desert covered with snakes and a beautiful mountain in the middle. The first page of the book identified the author as ABRAHAM ELEAZAR (the Jew): "prince, priest, Levite, astrologer and philosopher," and described the CURSES that would befall anyone who tried to read the book who was not a priest or scribe. The word *maranatha* appeared throughout the manuscript, adding to its mystery. Other drawings illustrated winged HERMES with Saturn holding an hourglass and a scythe and a rose with a blue stem and red and white flowers blowing in the winds on a mountain.

Flamel decided that as a scribe he was immune from the curses and began to try to read the strange tome. He and Pernelle studied the book for 21 years, comparing it to the texts of Almasatus and other learned alchemists, but to no avail. Since the author was Jewish and some of the manuscript was in ancient Hebrew, Flamel decided that he needed the help of a rabbi—preferably a kabbalist—to help him decipher his treasure. Unfortunately, the Jews had been driven out of France, so Flamel undertook a trip to Spain where many of the Jews had migrated to the lands occupied by the Moors. He told his friends that he was making a pilgrimage to San Diego de Compostela. Flamel copied some of the precious pages and set out, only to be rebuffed by Jews suspicious of a French Christian with such a story.

But Flamel persisted and after about two years met an old Jewish physician named Maitre Canches (or Cauches) in Leon who joyously recognized the renderings as part of a legendary kabbalist manuscript called the *Asch Mezareph,* written by a Rabbi Abraham and long believed lost. Canches wanted to see the book so badly that he offered to

return to Paris with Flamel—even convert to Christianity so he could enter France—and help him translate the secret text. The two set out, but the old rabbi fell ill at Orleans and died. Flamel returned to Paris alone, but his conversations with Canches had given him enough clues to decipher the book on his own. Even so, he and Pernelle labored to create a Philosopher's Stone for another three years.

In January 1382, Flamel wrote that he had successfully used the Philosopher's Stone to transmute lead (or perhaps mercury) into silver and then gold. His own description of it was follows:

> . . . I made projection of the Red Stone upon half a pound of mercury, . . . the five-and-twentieth day of April following, the same year [1382] about five o'clock in the evening; which I transmuted truly into about the same quantity of pure gold, most certainly better than ordinary gold, being more soft and more pliable. . . . I had indeed enough when I had once done it, but I found exceeding

Illustration from the mysterious book of Nicolas Flamel. Saturn (antimony) and Mercury fix the dragon, the philosopher's vitriol. In Uraltes chymisches Werk, *by Abraham Eleazar, 1760. (Author's collection)*

great pleasure and delight in seeing and contemplating the admirable works of Nature.

Flamel reportedly made three projections, or batches, of gold—enough to make donations to 14 hospitals, build three chapels, enable repairs to various churches, and richly endow the Cathedral of St. Jacques de la Boucherie, whose wall had supported his bookstall. The Flamels also donated to religious institutions in Bologne, Pernelle's birthplace.

At age 80, Flamel remained in excellent health. He made no changes to his lifestyle, preferring that his wealth be distributed for the glory of God rather than his enrichment. Stories of his success reached the ears of neighbors, alchemists, and even King Charles VI, but Flamel never revealed his knowledge of the Philosopher's Stone—nor did he make any more gold. He and Pernelle were satisfied with their accomplishments. He did provide seekers with one tantalizing clue, painting some of the drawings from his mystical book as frescoes in an archway at the Cemetery of the Holy Innocents in Paris. These renderings allegedly depicted the Great Secret and were the subject of intense scrutiny for years.

Pernelle died in 1397, although some accounts place her death in 1414. Flamel died on November 22, 1416 (or maybe 1417 or 1418), at 116 years and was buried with great pomp and ceremony in the Cathedral St. Jacques de la Boucherie. His tombstone had already been carved and featured a sun above a key and a closed book. Treasure hunters ransacked the Flamels's home many times but never found anything, including one who tore the house apart on the pretext that he was repairing it. At least two accounts reported that vials of reddish powder were found in the house; they were dismissed as worthless, but they might have been the Philosopher's Stone.

The alchemist supposedly gave some of his precious powder to Pernelle's nephew, Perrier, who gave it to a Dr. Perrier. Upon the doctor's death his grandson Dubois found the magic agent—and possibly the book—in his grandfather's effects. He arrogantly claimed to King Louis XIII that he could transmute base metal and actually managed to change a few balls of lead into gold. The king's adviser, Cardinal Richelieu, demanded Dubois repeat his feat and when he could not had the hapless pretender imprisoned. Discovering that Dubois had committed other offenses in the past, Richelieu condemned him to hang and confiscated his property—including, it was rumored, the book of Abraham Eleazar.

Legend persisted that Flamel and his wife did not really die. In the 17th century, King Louis XIV sent an archaeologist named Paul Lucas on a mission to the Middle East to bring back scientific and historical artifacts to France. Lucas was an early Indiana Jones: a soldier, an adventurer, a scholar, a lover. In the port of Broussa, Turkey, Lucas met a philosopher who admitted that he was one of seven sages who traveled the world seeking wisdom and then gathered every 20 years to tell their stories. He remarked that anyone possessing the ELIXIR OF LIFE could live a thousand years and that Flamel was such a person. He also told Lucas about the secret book and how Flamel had obtained it.

According to the philosopher, Abraham Eleazar was a member of this select group of ADEPTS. He had traveled to France to see friends, and while there made the acquaintance of a rabbi anxious to find the Philosopher's Stone. Abraham explained the alchemy to the rabbi but was repaid by treachery and murder. The rabbi was convicted of the crime and burned alive; not long afterward France expelled the Jews. Abraham's book was sold to Flamel by someone who did not know its worth. Even more astonishing, wrote Lucas in his memoir *Voyage dans la Turquie,* was the philosopher's assertion that the Flamels were both still living and in India.

The truth behind Flamel's alchemy may never be known. He was a scribe; he and his wife did leave a fortune to charity; and he did pay for the alchemical symbols to be inscribed at the Church of the Holy Innocents.

Texts purporting to be written by Flamel appeared in later centuries and are forgeries. One, the *Testament of Flamel* outlines the alchemist's procedures and processes. Attributed to the first-person authorship of Flamel and addressed to his nephew, it more likely was written by an anonymous author in the late 18th century, when interest in Flamel's work was in revival. In the *Testament,* "Flamel" describes the preparation of MERCURY using animal and astrological symbols and language commonly understood to practitioners of the day. For instance, the author rarely identifies the metals used in transmutation, instead calling them Saturnia, the Sun and the Moon, or the Voracious Wolf; the wolf refers to antimony. Other parts of the process, either in the crucible or under heat, are often disguised as appearances by the toad or the RAVEN (blackening), the coming of the white swan (whitening during burning), the peacock's tail (iridescence), a pelican feeding its young with its own BLOOD (reddening), and the Phoenix arising from the ashes (the final result).

Another forgery is his *Exposition of the Hieroglyphicall Figures which he caused to bee painted upon an Arch in St. Innocents Church-yard, in Paris,* published in London in 1624. It supposedly is a first-person autobiographical account of Flamel's life, the discovery of the book and its alchemical secrets, and an explication of alchemical figures painted upon the church arch.

Flamel enjoyed renewed fame in best-selling fiction: *The Da Vinci Code,* in which author Dan Brown portrays Flamel as one of the past Grand Masters of the Priory of Sion, and in the HARRY POTTER books by J. K. Rowling. In the first book, *Harry Potter and the Sorcerer's Stone* (the British version is *Harry Potter and the Philosopher's Stone*), Harry and his friends Ron and Hermione learn that Flamel did possess the magic powder and Elixir of Life. Albus Dumbledore, the fictional headmaster of the Hogwarts School of Witchcraft and Wizardry, says that his considerable abilities as a wizard are due to his association with Flamel. Harry's nemesis, Lord Voldemort, attempts to steal the Stone, hidden somewhere at Hogwarts, but is thwarted by Harry's magic. Whether dead or alive, if Nicholas Flamel can still weave his magic more than 600 years later, his reputation as an adept is assured.

FURTHER READING:

Coudert, Allison. *Alchemy: The Philosopher's Stone.* London: Wildwood House Ltd., 1980.

"Flamel's Hieroglyphics." Available online. URL: http://www.levity.com/alchemy/flam_h0.html. Downloaded December 21, 2004.

Guiley, Rosemary Ellen. *An Encyclopedia of Angels.* 2d ed. New York: Facts On File Inc., 2004.

Holmyard, E. J. *Alchemy.* New York: Penguin Books, 1957.

Mackay, Charles. *Extraordinary Popular Delusions and the Madness of Crowds.* New York: Farrar, Strauss & Giroux, 1932.

McLean, Adam. "Animal Symbolism in the Alchemical Tradition." Available online. URL: www.levity.com/alchemy/animal.html. Downloaded July 5, 2004.

Merton, Reginald. "A Detailed Biography of Nicholas Flamel." Available online. URL: www.flamelcollege.org/flamel.htm. Downloaded July 5, 2004.

"Nicholas Flamel: The Real-Life Wizard Behind 'Harry Potter.'" Available online. URL: http://wiccanet.tv/articles/03/06/22/1837230.shtml. Downloaded July 5, 2004.

"Testament of Flamel." Available online. URL: www.levity.com/alchemy/testment.html. Downloaded July 5, 2004.

Fludd, Robert (1574–1637)

Brilliant English physician and alchemist. Robert Fludd was one of the most preeminent scholars of his day. He was a strong supporter of ROSICRUCIANISM.

Fludd was born in Bearsted, Kent, in 1574 to a military administrator, Sir Thomas Fludd, who was in the good graces of Queen Elizabeth I. Fludd was raised a devout Christian and exhibited an unusual piety early in life; he viewed sex as the true cause of humanity's fall from grace. At age 17, he entered St. John's College in Oxford, where he excelled in studies.

Sometime between 1596 and 1598, Fludd graduated with bachelor of arts and master of arts degrees and embarked on a six-year sojourn on the European Continent as a tutor. His interests were wide and eclectic, embracing ASTROLOGY, metaphysics, ALCHEMY, chemistry, physics, natural history, theology, and medicine. He was especially interested in the works of PARACELSUS, though he proved to be more conservative than other Paracelsians of the day.

By the time he returned to Oxford, Fludd was 31. He entered school at Christ Church and by 1605 had earned a bachelor of medicine and a doctor of medicine degrees. However, his arrogance and his unusual ideas countered the university's traditional teachings that were based on the Greek physician Galen, who lived in the second century C.E. Perhaps because of his views, it took Fludd nearly four years to become a fellow in the College of Physicians.

Robert Fludd, in Morborum Integrum Mysterium, *by Robert Fludd, 1631.* (Author's collection)

As a doctor, Fludd enjoyed a thriving practice. He mixed mysticism and astrology with medicine. He believed illness was caused by DEMONS; he gave great weight to diagnosis based on the color of URINE. He consulted horoscopes for diagnosis and treatment. People flocked to him for care. He earned enough to maintain his own apothecary and a laboratory where he carried out his alchemical experiments.

Fludd was highly creative, writing works on a wide range of subjects and designing props for stage dramas. His special interest, however, was alchemy, especially its high spiritual principles—which he called the invisible parts of man—and he denigrated the efforts to transmute metals as base and vulgar.

He was drawn to the philosophy of Rosicrucianism, especially the concept that the greatest human aspiration is to know God. Fludd may have been a Rosicrucian—he wrote in defense of the order—but he never publicly admitted so. He was knowledgeable about the KABBALAH and attempted to reconcile Aristotelean and kabbalistic philosophies as expressed in the 10 spheres of Aristotle and the 10 *sephirot* of the kabbalistic Tree of Life.

Fludd appreciated the fact that many could not comprehend the lofty philosophical and spiritual ideas of alchemy. To demonstrate alchemical principles, he devised an experiment to distill the PRIMA MATERIA and the QUIN-

TESSENCE from wheat. To his surprise, some of the quintessence became filled with strange white worms when it became accidentally filled with rainwater. Fludd concluded that the worms could only have come from spontaneous generation due to the vital nature in the quintessence of the wheat.

Fludd's interest in astrology and alchemy led him into frequent clashes with his contemporary physicians, theologians, and others. For example, he said that it was natural for BLOOD to circulate throughout the body because the heavenly bodies circulated through the macrocosm. He believed in sympathetic MAGIC and defended Paracelsus's weapon-salve therapy involving magical OINTMENT, which critics called WITCHCRAFT.

Despite his unorthodox views, Fludd remained highly respected throughout his life, though he had to answer charges of heresy from some of his critics. He became an accomplished musician. He was celibate and never married; he prided himself on his "unstained virginity" and emphasized sexual desire as the cause of man's Fall from Paradise.

Fludd died on September 8, 1637, of unknown causes; it is speculated that years of intense work may have been contributing factors. He evidently knew he was dying, as he arranged his affairs and had a tombstone prepared for his grave. He was buried in Bearsted Church near Maidstone, England.

Fludd's best-known work is *The History of the Macrocosm and the Microcosm,* which explains the interrelationships between man and the heavens. The two-volume work was never completed. The first part was published in 1617, and the last part of it was written in 1624. The work created a stir as a bible of Rosicrucian and alchemical philosophy.

Fludd saw God in all things; everything is created out of the Light of God. Everything is both a macrocosm and a microcosm. He describes hierarchies of ANGELS and demons—he placed Christ among the angels—and the elemental world of men, plants and minerals. All partake of the Light of God, the degree of which depends on their place in the hierarchy of creation. At the midpoint is the SUN, the "Tabernacle of God." Fludd endorsed the Pythagorean concept of the MUSIC of the spheres: The music created by the movement of heavenly bodies turns the universe into a single musical instrument of harmony. He endorsed the doctrine of CORRESPONDENCES: Every level of the hierarchy of creation reflects the next higher realm. Without reflection there can be no creation.

One of his chief critics was a French scientist, Marin Marsenne, who accused Fludd of being a magician, a heretic, and an atheist—serious charges in Fludd's day. Marsenne especially objected to Fludd's alchemical interpretation of creation and felt that alchemy should remain separate from theology. He also objected to Fludd's equation of Christ with the ANIMA MUNDI, the feminine creative force of God, and to angels.

Fludd defended his cosmology in writing and reasserted his religious faith. Fortunately, King James remained his patron, and he had friends among the bishops of the Church of England.

FURTHER READING:
Godwin, Joscelyn. *Robert Fludd: Hermetic Philosopher and Surveyor of Two Worlds.* Grand Rapids, Mich.: Phanes Press, 1979.
M. W. Sharon. "Doctor Robert Fludd. (1574–1637)." Available online. URL: http://www.levity.com/alchemy/fludd1.html. Downloaded on March 14, 2005.
Seligmann, Kurt. *The History of Magic and the Occult.* New York: Pantheon Books, 1948.

fluid condenser   In the magical system of FRANZ BARDON, a special TOOL that concentrates, stores, and manipulates the electric and magnetic fluids of the universal life force. Bardon defined three types of fluid condensers: solid, liquid, and aerial. He created various alchemical recipes for fluid condensers. He said their "charge," or power, could be increased significantly by the addition of GOLD or gold tincture. The magician's own BLOOD or sperm also increases the charge.

Solid fluid condensers are made of resins and metals. Liquid ones are tinctures, oils, lacquers, and extracts composed from resins produced by plants. Aerial ones are fumigations, flavors, selling waters, and evaporations; Bardon considered these the least important in magical work.

When properly made and stored, fluid condensers can keep their power for long periods of time, even indefinitely. They are used in magical RITUALS and are manipulated by the magician through WILL and IMAGINATION to affect other things, including the body, and thus physical health. A liquid fluid condenser can be added to potions or incense compounds or placed in bowls to concentrate energies.

Bardon said that the ELIXIR OF LIFE, the elusive alchemical formula for longevity and immortality, is a magically loaded fluid condenser that influences the physical, mental, and astral bodies.

FURTHER READING:
Bardon, Franz. *Initiation into Hermetics: A Course of Instruction of Magic Theory and Practice.* Wuppertal, Germany: Dieter Ruggeberg, 1971.

folk magic   See MAGIC.

Fortune, Dion (1891–1946)   English magician, occultist, and expert on PSYCHIC ATTACK. Dion Fortune—her magical and pen name were created taken from her MAGICAL MOTTO—was born Violet Mary Firth. She exhibited mediumistic abilities by her teens.

Fortune became an expert on psychic attack through her own experience, which she described in her book *Psychic Self-Defence* (1930). As a young working woman in her twenties, she was subjected to mind manipulation by her female boss who, Fortune said, attempted to break her WILL. Fortune departed her job mentally shattered and physically exhausted. It took her three years to recover.

As a result, Fortune became interested in occultism, in an attempt to understand what had happened to her and to defend herself against any future such attacks. Her research led her to conclude that damage had been sustained by her etheric double, a nonphysical replica of the body which is attached to it and helps channel the universal life force to it. Fortune believed that the damage to her etheric double, caused by her boss, created a leak in her life force. Fortune's interest in psychic attack remained a focal point throughout her entire life and especially through her magical career. She worked as a psychiatrist, and attributed many of the symptoms in cases she saw to psychic attacks.

In 1919, she took INITIATION into the Alpha et Omega Lodge of the Stella Matutina, an outer order of the HERMETIC ORDER OF THE GOLDEN DAWN which by then had splintered into various groups. The Alpha et Omega Lodge was created by SAMUEL LIDDELL MacGREGOR MATHERS, one of the original founders of the Golden Dawn, and his wife, MOINA MATHERS. Fortune took as her magical motto *Deo Non Fortuna* ("By God, not chance"). She was talented as a magician. She participated in psychic warfare and believed that Moina attacked her psychically.

Fortune had numerous dramatic magical experiences, including materializing a THOUGHT-FORM WEREWOLF. The materialization happened spontaneously one night, and Fortune later concluded that it was the by-product of her hateful thoughts about revenge against a person. The werewolf seemed to emerge from the solar plexus area of her auric field. At first Fortune thought she could control the thought-form with her own WILL, but her magical teacher advised her to reabsorb the thought-form before it went out of control.

In 1924, Fortune departed Stella Matutina and founded her own order, the Community (later Society) of the Inner Light. Initially, the order was part of the Golden Dawn, but later it separated.

Fortune authored a number of fiction and nonfiction books about the occult. *Psychic Self-Defence* is considered the definitive work on psychic attack and psychic vampirism.

Fortune was married to Dr. Thomas Penry Evans. She died in January 1946. The Society of the Inner Light is based in London and continues to offer teachings in the Western occultism.

FURTHER READING:

Fortune, Dion. *Psychic Self-Defence.* 1939. Reprint, York Beach, Maine: Samuel Weiser, 1957.

Guiley, Rosemary Ellen. *The Encyclopedia of Vampires, Werewolves and Other Monsters.* New York: Facts On File, Inc., 2004.

Knight, Gareth. *Dion Fortune and the Three-Fold Way.* London: S.I.L. (Trading) Ltd., 2002.

Richardson, Alan. *Priestess: The Life and Magic of Dion Fortune.* Wellingborough, England: The Aquarian Press, 1987.

Fourth Book See GRIMOIRES.

Freemasonry A fraternal organization that bases its principles and teachings on many great streams of philosophical wisdom and incorporates a system of degrees that emulates the ancient mystery schools of the historical golden periods of Egypt, Israel, and Greece. Freemasonry's mysteries incorporate these ancient philosophic teachings, along with lore of the building of King Solomon's temple (see SOLOMON), as described in the Holy Bible, which Freemasonry refers to as the "Sacred Volume of Law." The rituals of the York Rite, which include the first three degrees, known as the Blue Lodge, are allegorically based on the building and sacred construction of Solomon's temple. Freemasonry is also called the Brotherhood or the Craft, the latter of which encompasses the skilled process of transforming one's soul or temple into a work befitting a Master Mason. Achieving the higher degrees of Freemasonry demonstrates that the Mason has sought esoteric knowledge and enlightenment. In present times, there are different Grand Lodges, or organizational Orders of Freemasonry. There are several different Orders, Organizations, or Grand Lodges of Speculative Masonry that are designated for men only, but there are also co-Masonic organizations that foster both men's and women's membership in the Masonic lodge. Several small Freemasonic Grand Lodges or organizations have only women for their membership.

History

Researchers of Freemasonry do not agree on its origins. There are three main theories:

- Freemasonry originated in ancient Egypt. Freemasonic SYMBOLS, TOOLS, and implements have been found in ruins and temples. One of the best examples is that of the obelisk, "Cleopatra's Needle," which is in New York City's Central Park. When it was excavated for transport to the United States, the symbolic working tools of a Master Mason—the square, compass, plumb, level, and master apron—were found buried beneath it.
- Modern Freemasonry descended from the ORDER OF THE KNIGHTS TEMPLAR. Many Masonic rituals and degrees are related to the Knights Templar and their rites.

- Modern Speculative Freemasonry may have descended or found inspiration from the operative builder and stone craft guilds of the Middle Ages. The operational mason guilds had an organizational structure that could be a foundation for modern speculative freemasonry, but the individuals who formed the modern Grand Lodges generally had great learning and education and were leading citizens. Many of them were founding members of or played a part in the Royal Society, which is beyond operative guilds.

Whatever the exact origins, Masonry is connected to building. Architects and builders traditionally occupied places of honor in societies dating back to those that constructed the pyramids of Egypt and the temples and monuments of Greece and Rome. To erect a building symbolized creation and the glorification of the gods. To the ancient builders, King Solomon's temple exemplified all the knowledge and talent of their craft. The legends of the temple's construction and its proportions form the cornerstone of Masonry, but avoiding any Judaic or Christian overtones, the story concentrates on Hiram Abiff, the builder/architect.

In I Kings 7:13–45, the Bible related that King Hiram of Tyre sent a man who was highly skilled in bronze work, also named Hiram, to make all the pillars, vessels, and decorative objects for the temple. This story was repeated in II Chronicles 2:13, but Hiram's talents expanded to work in gold, silver, iron, wood, engraving, and textiles. The biblical accounts ended there, but in Masonry the story concluded with Hiram Abiff's murder at the hands of three workmen when he would not divulge the secret Name of God hidden in the temple structure. Ritually, petitioners "die" as Hiram died and are reborn in Masonry.

The philosopher and Freemason MANLY P. HALL compared the Hiramic legend to the death and dismemberment of Osiris by Set and the resurrection of Osiris by Isis (although she never could find his phallus) to the search for the lost Name of God. The secrets of the Egyptian mystery schools provided a foundation for Freemasonry as they had for Rosicrucianism. Followers of the Isis cult were called "widow's sons," and Masons are called "sons of the widow."

Muslims maintained that the builders of King Solomon's temple were not Jews but Sufi mystics who incorporated the holy Word of God into the temple measurements, making Masonry Arabic in origin. If so, then the first man to introduce Masonry to the West was Saxon king Aethelstan (894–939), who brought the society to England after studying with the Spanish Moors.

None of these accounts can be proven, however. What is true is that itinerant master builders and masons traveled across Europe in the Middle Ages seeking work. Often illiterate, these craftsworkers hired local labor and communicated the necessary instructions by means of crude drawings and universally accepted proportions to ensure that the height and length of walls and roofs could be adequately supported. This knowledge was especially important in the construction of cathedrals, which by the 12th century had become soaring monuments to God with flying buttresses, windows, towers, and other Gothic details. To protect the builders' knowledge, craft guilds formed with strict rules regarding contracts, wage scales, work hours and seasons, support by those commissioning the work, advancement, and apprenticeships. Additionally, guild members were required to be devout. The builders' secret wisdom was often passed down orally to the next generation. How these craft guilds began to accept unskilled, or speculative, members remains a mystery, but eventually those with more interest in the study of the secrets than in the construction of buildings became the majority. The guilds may have been covers for more esoteric pursuits or those with radical political or religious leanings.

Masonic historians consider ELIAS ASHMOLE, a 17th-century astrologer, antiquarian, and officer of the Restoration court of Charles II, to have introduced Freemasonry into England. Ashmole studied ALCHEMY, Rosicrucian philosophy, and the KABBALAH; he shared his age's fascination with scientific experiment and was friends with Sir Francis Bacon and the other founders of the Royal Society. Ashmole's diary recorded his initiation in 1646, by which time there were hardly any actual craftsworkers left in Masonry.

By the 18th century, nearly every public house and tavern in England and Scotland hosted a Masonic lodge. To standardize ritual, four London lodges merged in 1717 to become the Grand Lodge of England, with Anthony Sayer as its first Grand Master. Between 1751 and 1753, Scottish and Irish Freemasons separated from the Grand Lodge and founded the Antient Grand Lodge, but both groups merged again in 1813 as the United Grand Lodge of England.

Freemasonry attracted royalty and commoners alike. The king of England serves as grand patron, although Queen Elizabeth II is the grand patroness. Wolfgang Amadeus Mozart was a Mason and incorporated Masonic and Rosicrucian symbolism into his opera *The Magic Flute*. Christopher Wren, architect of St. Paul's Cathedral in London, was most likely a member, as was Sir Francis Bacon. Nearly all the intelligentsia of 18th-century Europe—including the COMTE DE SAINT-GERMAIN—belonged to a lodge, often pursuing the higher esoteric degrees. British Masonry functions much like an old school network, with strong ties to the brotherhood in law, jurisprudence, police, government, and the armed forces. Winston Churchill was a Freemason.

Eight signatories of the Declaration of Independence—including Benjamin Franklin and John Hancock—were Masons, leading proponents of the craft to give Freemasonry credit as a spiritual foundation of the United States. George Washington joined the Brotherhood in 1752, but not wanting to be identified in any way with an English monarch declined the position of leader of all Freemasonry in the United States; consequently, each state has a Grand

Lodge and a Grand Chapter. Washington's aide, the Marquis de Lafayette, was a Mason, as were Presidents Madison, Monroe, Jackson, Polk, Buchanan, Andrew Johnson, Garfield, McKinley, Theodore Roosevelt, Taft, Harding, Franklin Roosevelt, Truman, Lyndon Johnson, Ford, Reagan, George H. W. Bush, Clinton, and George W. Bush. Former perennial Democratic candidate Adlai Stevenson was a Freemason, as was Vice President Hubert Humphrey. More recently, Vice Presidents Al Gore and Dick Cheney are "widow's sons," as are former senators Bob Dole and Jack Kemp and Secretary of State Gen. Colin Powell.

Tenets and Symbols
Speculative Masonry inherited seven fundamental principles from the medieval craft guilds:

- an organization composed of three grades: Entered Apprentice, Fellow of the Craft, and Master Mason
- a chapter unit called a lodge
- strict rules of secrecy
- secret means of member identification
- histories of the brotherhood contained in about 100 manuscripts called the Old Charges, particularly the *Regis Manuscript* (1390)
- a tradition of fraternal and benevolent relations among members
- a thorough grounding in Christianity

But by 1723 all references to Christianity—or any other organized religion—had been removed. Members were required to believe in a Supreme Being, who became known as "The Great Architect of the Universe," or T.G.A.O.T.U.

Besides the three initial degrees (also known as the Blue Lodge), Hiram Abiff's three murderers symbolize thought, desire, and action. Masons strive to transmute these baser responses into spiritual thought, constructive emotion, and labor. Petitioners for membership are known as rough ashlars, or uncut stones.

The tools of the builder's craft are the symbols of Masonry: the square, the compass, the plumb line, and the level. Members wear white leather builders' aprons. The order's colors are blue and gold, and the capital letter *G* within the compass most likely means God. The floors of meeting lodges or temples are black-and-white checkered to represent man's dual nature. Masonic symbolism also uses the Great Pyramid of Giza, always drawn with a flat top to represent man's incompleteness and showing only 72 stones—a number that equates to the 72 combinations of the four-letter secret Name of God (called the Tetragrammaton, or YHVH in Hebrew). Floating above the pyramid is the All-Seeing Eye of God, also associated with the Egyptian god Horus. America's Masonic Founding Fathers placed the Pyramid of Giza and the All-Seeing Eye of Horus on the one-dollar bill and the reverse of the Great Seal of the United States.

Members of the Ancient Grand Lodge added a fourth degree, the Holy Royal Arch, but after reunification with the Grand Lodge in 1813 the Holy Royal Arch became an "exalted" level of Master Mason. Holders of the Holy Royal Arch claim intense spiritual consciousness and oneness with the Great Architect. They no longer belong to a Lodge but affiliate with a Chapter, which is overseen by a Grand Chapter. Exalted Master Masons may remain at that level or strive for true mystic union by pursuing the Antient and Accepted Rite of the 33rd Degree. A Supreme Council administers these degrees; in the United States, the Supreme Council in Charleston, South Carolina, awards each level separately. In Britain, degrees four through 17 are bestowed with 18 and then 19 through 29 with 30. Awarded individually are 31, 32, and 33. Some of the degree names cross over into Rosicrucianism. The Higher Degrees, in order, are:

4. Secret Master
5. Perfect Master
6. Intimate Secretary
7. Provost and Judge
8. Intendant of the Buildings
9. Elect of Nine
10. Elect of Fifteen
11. Sublime Elect
12. Grand Master Architect
13. Royal Arch of Enoch
14. Scottish Knight of Perfection
15. Knight of the Sword, or of the East
16. Prince of Jerusalem
17. Knight of the East and West
18. Knight of the Pelican and Eagle Sovereign Prince Rose Croix of Heredom
19. Grand Pontiff
20. Venerable Grand Master
21. Patriarch Noachite
22. Prince of Libanus
23. Chief of the Tabernacle
24. Prince of the Tabernacle
25. Knight of the Brazen Serpent
26. Prince of Mercy
27. Commander of the Temple
28. Knight of the Sun
29. Knight of St. Andrew
30. Grand Elected Knight Kadosh Knight of the Black and White Eagle
31. Grand Inspector Inquisitor Commander
32. Sublime Prince of the Royal Secret
33. Grand Inspector General

Controversy and the Popular Imagination
The Catholic Church takes the structure of Freemasonry very seriously, forbidding membership by any Catholic. The Vatican issued its first papal condemnation in 1738, decreeing excommunication for any Catholic Freemason. Many Catholics were originally Masons, including Vatican prelates, and church officials often turned a blind eye,

especially in England. The Greek Orthodox Church condemned Masonry in 1933 as a heathen mystery religion. Stephen Knight, author of *Operative Masonry*, claimed that during the ritual for the Holy Royal Arch candidates learn the secret name of God—*Jahbulon: Jah* for Yahweh, *Bul* for the Canaanite fertility god Baal, and *On* for OSIRIS. Such references, he contended, proved devil worship.

Freemasonry, as well as ROSICRUCIANISM, received a boost in popularity with the 2003 international bestselling novel *The Da Vinci Code*. Author Dan Brown ties Rosicrucianism and Freemasonry to the legends of the so-called Priory of Sion, a secret order descended from the lost Knights Templar, to prove that Mary Magdalene is the real HOLY GRAIL.

FURTHER READING:
Duncan, Malcom C. *Duncan's Ritual of Freemasonry.* New York: Crown Publishers, n.d.
Heywood, H. L. *The Newly-Made Mason: What He and Every Mason Should Know about Masonry.* Richmond, Va.: Macoy Publishing and Masonic Supply Co., 1973.
Pike, Albert. *Morals and Dogma of the Ancient and Accepted Scottish Rite of Freemasonry.* Richmond, Va.: L. H. Jenkins, 1871.
Roberts, Allen E. *The Craft and Its Symbols: Opening the Door to Masonic Symbolism.* Richmond, Va.: Macoy Publishing and Masonic Supply Co., 1974.

frith   In Scottish magical lore, an important SPELL for seeing someone's situation at a distance. The *frith* was probably of Norse origin.

The spell could only be performed by a *Frithear* on the first Monday of the quarter before sunrise. The *Frithear* fasted in advance and performed the RITUAL with bare feet. He walked sunwise around a house with closed eyes until he reached the doorstep. He made a circle with his thumb and forefinger and looked through it. The first thing he saw was an OMEN, which he interpreted. A sacred SYMBOL, such as two straws crossed, meant that all was well, while a man standing meant a sign of recovery. A woman standing was a bad sign.

FURTHER READING:
Spence, Lewis. *The Magic Arts in Celtic Britain.* Van Nuys, Calif.: Newscastle Publishing, 1996.

fumigations   See PERFUMES.

Gardner, Gerald Brousseau (1884–1964) English Witch and founder of the modern religion of WITCHCRAFT, more commonly called Wicca to differentiate it from folk MAGIC and SORCERY.

Gerald B. Gardner was born into a well-to-do family in Blundellsands, near Liverpool, England, on Friday, June 13, 1884. His father was a merchant and a justice of the peace, a member of a family that had made money in the timber trade. Gardner claimed that an ancestor, Grissell Gairdner, was burned as a witch in 1610 in Newburgh and that other members of the family had possessed psychic gifts.

The middle of three sons, Gardner was raised primarily by the family's nurse and governess, Josephine "Com" McCombie. He lived and worked in Ceylon, Borneo, and Malaysia, where he became fascinated by Eastern RITUAL daggers and weapons and magical beliefs and practices. From 1923 to 1936 Gardner worked as a civil servant for the British government as a rubber-plantation inspector, a customs official, and an inspector of opium establishments. He made a considerable sum of money in rubber. In 1927 he married an Englishwoman, Donna. The two returned to England on his retirement from government work in 1936.

They lived in the New Forest region where Gardner became involved with the Fellowship of Crotona, an occult group of Co-Masons, a Masonic order established by Mrs. Besant Scott, daughter of Theosophist Annie Besant. The group had established "The First Rosicrucian Theater in England," which put on plays with occult themes. Within

the Fellowship of Crotona was another, secret group, which drew Gardner into its confidence. The members claimed to be hereditary Witches, who practiced a craft passed down to them through the centuries, unbroken by the witch hunts of the Middle Ages and Renaissance. The group met in the New Forest. Gardner was initiated into the coven in the home of old Dorothy Clutterbuck in 1939.

Gardner became intensely interested in magic and witchcraft and invested much time in extending his network of contacts in occultism. He collected material on magical procedures, especially ceremonial magic, which he put together in an unpublished manuscripted entitled *Ye Bok of ye Art Magical.*

In 1946 Gardner met Cecil Williamson, an occultist and owner of a museum of witchcraft. He later acquired the museum from Williamson and operated it in different locations.

In 1947 Gardner was introduced to ALEISTER CROWLEY by one of Gardner's own initiates, Arnold Crowther. Crowley made Gardner an honorary member of the ORDO TEMPLI ORIENTIS (OTO), a Tantric sex magic order at one time under Crowley's leadership in Britain, and granted Gardner a charter to operate an OTO lodge.

Gardner was especially interested in gleaning whatever he could from Crowley, who by then was in poor health and only months away from death. Gardner obtained magical material from Crowley. From this and other sources, he compiled his BOOK OF SHADOWS, a collection of rituals and Craft laws. Gardner claimed to have received a fragmentary Book of Shadows from his New Forest coven. At the time witchcraft was against the law in England, and he disguised his Book of Shadows in a novel, *High Magic's Aid,* published in 1949 under the pseudonym Scire. When the law was repealed in 1951, Gardner left the New Forest coven and established his own group.

In 1953 Gardner initiated Doreen Valiente, who substantially reworked his book of shadows, taking out most of the Crowley material because his "name stank" and giving more emphasis to the Goddess. From 1954 to 1957 Gardner and Valiente collaborated on writing ritual and nonritual material, a body of work which became the authority for what became known in Wicca as the Gardnerian tradition. Valiente and others in the coven departed in 1957 over disapproval of the media attention that Gardner received, much of which was negative. Valiente persuaded Gardner to destroy his papers.

Gardner engaged in magical warfare; in 1956 he enlisted the help of AUSTIN OSMAN SPARE against KENNETH GRANT.

Gardner was a voyeur and naturalist and required coven meetings and magical work to be done in the nude, or "skyclad." He claimed that this was an old tradition; whether or not it was, it suited his interests. He advocated raising magical power through an "eightfold path" that includes dancing; chants, SPELLS, and INVOCATIONS; trance and ASTRAL PROJECTION; incense, wine, and drugs; meditation and concentration; use of cords for BLOOD control and KNOT magic; scourging; and sex, as performed in the Great Rite, a ceremony conducted by a coven high priestess and high priest.

In 1963 Gardner set sail for Lebanon. He died aboard ship on his return home on February 12, 1964, suffering heart failure at breakfast. He was buried ashore in Tunis on February 13.

Gardner's nonfiction book on the craft, *Witchcraft Today* (1954), and *The Meaning of Witchcraft* (1959) remain in print and are considered authoritative works on Wicca, though few Wiccans today believe his assertion that a religion of Witchcraft has existed unbroken since ancient times. This claim, put forward in the 1930s by anthropologist Margaret A. Murray, has been debunked by scholars.

After his death much of the contents of his museum were sold to the Ripley organization, which dispersed the objects to its various museums. Some of the items have since been resold to private collections.

FURTHER READING:
Gardner, Gerald B. *Witchcraft Today.* London: Rider & Co., 1954, 1956.
———. *The Meaning of Witchcraft.* 1959. Reprint, New York: Magickal Childe, 1982.
Guiley, Rosemary Ellen. *The Encyclopedia of Witches and Witchcraft.* 2d ed. New York: Facts On File Inc., 1999.
King, Francis. *Megatherion: The Magickal World of Aleister Crowley.* New York: Creation Books, 2004.

Geber   See IBN HAYYAR, JABIR.

gematria   One of three kabbalistic systems for discovering the secret and mystical truths of words and the NAMES of God and ANGELS and for interpreting biblical words and passages, all by analyzing their numerical values. Each letter of the Hebrew alphabet has a numerical value and a certain spiritual, creative power; God creates everything in the universe by uttering certain words. The values of words and names are totaled and then equated with other words and names that have the same numerical values, and then analyzed within the context of Scripture and other factors.

Gematria was developed into a sophisticated system by German kabbalists during the 13th century but was known and used much earlier by other cultures. King Sargon II, who ruled Babylonia in the eighth century B.C.E., used the numerical value of his name to determine that the wall of Khorsabad should be built to the same equivalent, or 16,283 cubits. The ancient Greeks, Persians, Gnostics, and early Christians used gematria for a variety of purposes. The Greeks applied it to dream interpretation, and the Gnostics to the names of deities. Early Christians arrived at the dove for the symbol of Christ because the Greek letters of alpha and omega (the Beginning and the End) and the Greek term for dove (*peristera*) add up to the same number, 801.

The kabbalistic system of gematria derived from Near Eastern Gnostic and Helenistic cultures. It is more complex than merely tallying up numerical values of letters; it involves various methods of analysis by which the mystical purposes of the Scriptures, buildings, and objects may be determined. Not only are the numerical values considered but also the size and strokes of the letters. The kabbalists of the 13th century, most notably Eleazar of Worms, applied gematria to the Scriptures, which were held to have been inspired by God and written in code. Thus, "And lo, three men" from Genesis 18:2 is interpreted as referring to the archangels Michael, Gabriel and Raphael, for "And lo, three men" and "Elo Michael Gabriel Ve-Raphael" each have the same numerical value of 701.

Gematria was used to ascertain the secret, ineffable, and indescribably powerful names of God. These names were incorporated into the incantations of ceremonial MAGIC, which were used for conjuring and controlling DEMONS. Some names of angels also are secret names of God, such as *Azbogah.*

Different systems of gematria were developed; the Kabbalist Moses Cordovero said there were nine. Gematria spread into alchemical and esoteric Christian works. Hebrew words—with or without gematria—took on greater importance for their mystical power or hidden meanings and connections.

Lesser known than gematria are notarikon and temurah, two other systems of decoding and analyzing mystical truths. Various methods exist in both systems. In notarikon, the first letter of words may be extracted and combined to form new words, or the first, the last, and sometime the middle letters of words are combined to create new words or phrases. Names of God and angels are revealed in this fashion. In temurah, letters are organized in tables or mathematical arrangements, which are then substituted for the letters in words, or letters are rearranged into anagrams. For example, such tables can be used to discover the names of the good and evil angels of the planets and signs of the zodiac.

genii In Roman mythology, guardian spirits of people, places or things. A genius presides over the birth of a person, a place, or a thing and shapes its character and destiny. Like a guardian ANGEL, it remains with a person throughout life and becomes the person's living soul after death. The genius of a place is the living spirit that animates a locale and gives it its unique powers and atmosphere.

Genii can be evoked and commanded in ceremonial MAGIC.

See also *DAMIONES*.

geomancy A method of DIVINATION involving the Earth. Geomancy also is called the art of little dots, but it is not to be confused with cartomancy. *Geomancy* comes from the Greek words *ge*, "earth," and *manteia*, "PROPHECY."

Geomancy may have originated in northern Africa under Muslim influences and by the Middle Ages had spread to Europe. It was a popular alternative to ASTROLOGY because it requires no special equipment or books.

A handful of dirt, sand, seeds, or pebbles is cast on the ground or on a smooth tabletop or a sheet of paper. The resulting figures and dots are interpreted. Other methods of geomancy are the making of random marks on the earth with a stick or on a piece of paper with a pencil or a pen. The tossing of coins or sticks also are forms of geomancy (see *I CHING*). Regardless of form, geomancy involves the interpretation of 16 figures, called tetragrams.

Geomancy was one of the main divinatory arts taught by the HERMETIC ORDER OF THE GOLDEN DAWN. The chief method taught was the generation of random dots on paper with a pen. Sixteen tetragrams are possible. Each tetragram is a four-part figure comprised of four lines, each of which is comprised by one or two dots. The geomancer generates 16 random numbers; odd numbers have one dot and even numbers have two dots. The 16 numbers become the Four Mothers, from which other tetragrams are created, until there are a total of 16. The tetragrams are used for yes/no answers. More information can be divined with astrological associations by placing the first 12 tetragrams on a square chart of zodiac signs.

In Golden Dawn magic, geomancy tetragrams can be used for SCRYING and to create SIGILS for TALISMANS.

See also AUGURY.

FURTHER READING:
Cicero, Chic, and Sandra Tabatha Cicero. *The Essential Golden Dawn*. St. Paul, Minn.: Llewellyn Publications, 2004.

glamour A type of BEWITCHMENT in which things or people are made to seem better than they are. In Celtic magical lore, a SPELL for glamour is called *glamourie*, or *sian* in Gaelic. Glamour spells are cast by FAIRIES, WITCHES, SORCERERS, and deities.

A glamour spell creates illusions: Rags look like elegant clothing, ugly people look handsome, hovels look like castles, and worthless objects look like treasures. Animals look like beautiful people. Glamour spells end suddenly. For example, in the fairy tale about Cinderella, a glamour spell makes her appear elegantly dressed, and a pumpkin pulled by mice appears to be a fine carriage drawn by horses. The spell ends at midnight on the night of a ball.

Glastonbury Ancient, sacred site in England's West Country, identified with the GRAIL and the mythical Avalon of Arthurian legends. For centuries, Glastonbury has drawn spiritual pilgrims, including many practitioners of MAGIC.

Glastonbury is located on the plains of Somerset Levels, not far from the Bristol Channel. It comprises an abbey, a town, and Glastonbury Tor, a terraced volcanic rock with the remains of an old church tower at its apex. The area around the town was once almost an island surrounded by marshlands—it was not dry until the 16th century—and is thought to have been inhabited by humans since Mesolithic times. There is evidence that it may have been a sacred site of the Druids. The ruins of lake villages found at Glastonbury and neighboring Meare most likely date from the third or fourth century B.C.E. and are believed to have been deserted shortly before the Roman occupation. North Somerset was a Roman settlement, and excavations have uncovered pottery and coins in and around the Glastonbury area, near the abbey, at Chalice Well, and on the Tor.

The Tor

From the 500-foot summit of Glastonbury Tor, one can see 50 to 60 miles in all directions. The terraced slopes (three of which are steep) suggest the Tor once was farmed. Another theory holds that the terraces are the remnants of a three-dimensional maze dating to the first Christian settlements and serving as a path for pilgrims.

At one time, there was a stone circle atop the Tor. In the Middle Ages, monks built St. Michael's there; it was later destroyed during an earthquake. The remains standing today are those of a later church built on the site. A six-day fair dedicated to the saint was held at the foot of the Tor each year from 1127 to 1825.

According to legend, the summit of the Tor is said to have been the location of a stronghold belonging to King Arthur and also purported to be the entrance to Annwn, the secret, underworld kingdom of Gwyn ap Nudd, king of the FAIRIES. The sixth century Saint Collen is said to have visited Gwyn by entering through a hidden entrance. Finding himself inside a palace, Saint Collen sprinkled holy water around, and the palace vanished, leaving the saint standing alone on the top of the Tor.

Geomantic figures, in The Magus, *by Francis Barrett, 1801. (Author's collection)*

The Tor also is the site of strange lights that hover about it, perhaps the effects of a mysterious magnetic earth energy or, as some UFO watchers believe, connected to extraterrestrial spacecraft.

Modern practitioners of magic, Paganism, Wicca, and other spiritual traditions hold rites and RITUALS on the Tor.

The Abbey

Legend has it that Joseph of Arimathea, the rich man who wrapped the body of Jesus and carried it to his tomb, later came to Glastonbury and built England's first Christian church, "the Old Church," below the Tor. Legend also has it that St. Patrick lived among the monks there and was buried there.

King Ine is believed to have founded a monastery on the site circa 705, which became a Benedictine house in the 10th century. The abbey's 12th century Lady Chapel replaced a former church on the site that was destroyed by fire in 1184, which itself had replaced the "Old Church." The standing remains are said to be from the structure built in the 13th or 14th century and destroyed in the 16th century during the reign of King Henry VIII. In the abbey ruins blooms the Glastonbury Thorn at Easter and Christmas. According to tradition, Joseph arrived by boat on Wearyall Hill and while leaning on his staff in prayer, the staff took root and the Thorn was seeded.

The abbey grounds also are the alleged burial sites of King Arthur and Queen Guinevere—one of many mentioned in legend. Arthur's sword, EXCALIBUR, which in legend was tossed into a lake by Sir Bedivere on the dying king's instructions, may have been thrown into the now drained mere at Pomparles Bridge near Glastonbury. A Welsh bard is said to have revealed the secret burial site to King Henry II. The abbey was destroyed by fire in 1184; during rebuilding, monks searched for the remains of Arthur and Guinevere. In 1190, they claimed to find them in a hollow log coffin nine feet below a stone slab. The man measured eight feet in height and had a damaged skull; a bit of blonde hair was found with the woman's remains. A lead cross was inscribed, "here lies buried the renowned King Arthur in the Isle of Avalon." The bones were reinterred in 1278 in a black marble tomb. Though investigations in the 20th century confirmed discovery of the graves, it has been impossible to identify them conclusively as those of Arthur and his queen.

Chalice Well

At the foot of the Tor stands Chalice Well, believed to be the hiding place where Joseph of Arimethea threw the chalice that had been used by Jesus at the Last Supper. The Holy Grail reportedly had magical powers, and it figures in the popular legend of the Knights of the Round Table failing to recover it after its disappearance.

According to legend, the Chalice Well was built of large blocks of stone by the DRUIDS. Also referred to as Blood Spring, some 25,000 gallons of reddish IRON oxide spring water, said to have magical properties, flow through the well each day.

The Bond Excavations

In 1907, the Church of England took over the ruins of Glastonbury and began excavations under the direction of Frederick Bligh Bond. Bond located unknown chapels and parts of the abbey and concluded that the abbey had been constructed according to an ancient, sacred geometry known to the builders of the Egyptian pyramids and the Masons. He attributed his brilliant success to automatic writing, in which mediums communicated with the spirits of monks and received directions from them. A scandal ensued, and Bond was fired. Decades later, his findings were reinvestigated and appreciated in a new light.

Bond had intuited a connection between Glastonbury and Stonehenge and Avebury, which has been borne out. A LEY is said to pass through the Tor linking it to Stonehenge. The ley runs along an old road called Dod Lane (from the German word for *dead, tod*), or "Dead Man's Lane." In folklore, Dod Lane is the path of spirits; the alleged gravesite of King Arthur is on an extension of this ley. Also, the Sun rises exactly in line with Avebury about 40 miles away. And, Glastonbury Abbey is said to have been built according to the same secret geometry as Stonehenge.

The Glastonbury Zodiac

The Glastonbury Zodiac, an ancient Temple of the Stars, is believed to have been the human attempt to understand the world (the microcosm) by studying the stars and the PLANETS (the macrocosm). The 12 signs of the zodiac are laid out in patterns in the Earth south of Glastonbury. First discovered by the late 16th-century physician and astrologer to Queen Elizabeth I, JOHN DEE, the zodiac was rediscovered in 1929 by Katherine Maltwood. Maltwood, a sculptress, was illustrating the *High History of the Holy Grail,* written circa 1200 in Glastonbury, when she discovered the patterns made by natural earth formations, roads, ditches, paths, and earthworks, covering a circle measuring 10 miles in diameter. In her book, *The Glastonbury Temple of the Stars,* she linked the figures to Arthurian legends. Arthur is Sagittarius, Merlin is Capricorn, and Guinevere is Virgo. Glastonbury itself is Aquarius, the sign of the New Age of Enlightenment.

Goethe, Johann Wolfgang von (1749–1832)   German writer, poet, and alchemist. Johann Wolfgang von Goethe's works are heavy in alchemical symbolism, especially his most famous work, *Faust,* considered one of the world's greatest literary achievements.

Goethe was born at Frankfurt-on-the-Main on August 28, 1749. His father was a lawyer. At an early age, he demonstrated an ability to draw and was interested in drama. By his early teens he was writing and also was learning several languages: Italian, Greek, Latin, English, and Hebrew.

Goethe entered the university at Leipzig intending to become a lawyer, but instead he was drawn to the classics and to writing prose and verse. In 1771 he returned to Frankfurt where he wrote poems and critiques for the newspapers. The publication of his love poems for Lilli Schonemann, the daughter of a local banker, made him instantly famous, and Duke Carl August invited him to court at Weimar. He performed numerous administrative duties and founded a court theater. He maintained a rigorous schedule of writing, producing some of his best works.

In 1795 Goethe met the noted poet and playwright Frederich von Schiller and entered into a collaboration with him to produce a literary magazine that was intended to educate the masses. He wrote plays. His work impressed Napoleon Bonaparte, who decorated him with the cross of the Legion of Honor.

Goethe was famous for his love affairs, but in 1806 he settled down and married. He enjoyed a celebrated life and met other famous people, such as Beethoven and William Makepeace Thackeray. In his later years his health declined, and he died on March 22, 1832.

Goethe was fascinated by ALCHEMY, and he had an alchemical laboratory in the attic of his father's house where he conducted long experiments in search of the ELIXIR OF LIFE. He began his experiments in 1768 on his return, ill, from Leipzig University. First he immersed himself in the writings of alchemists, notably PARACELSUS, BASIL VALENTINE, JEAN BAPTISTA VAN HELMONT, GEORGE STARKEY, and others. In addition to alchemy, he studied PALMISTRY, ASTROLOGY, and NUMEROLOGY, as well as other occult sciences.

Goethe even had his own SOROR MYSTICA in his explorations, the Pietist Fraulein von Klettenberg. His interest in alchemy was further bolstered by his own cure, aided by a "Universal Medicine" given him by a Dr. Metz, who was a friend of Fraulein von Kletterberg.

In his experiments, Goethe sought to create the Liquor Silicum, a transparent glass that melted on contact with air and took a clear liquid form. The Liquor Silicum would in turn lead him, he hoped, to Virgin Earth from which he would be able to create other magical substances. Goethe also tried to create Airy Salt, another substance that melted on contact with air and combined with other "superterrestrial things" to create a substance of great magical power. Though he experimented for nearly two years, Goethe was unable to produce anything of magical import and created only a fine powder that had no wondrous properties whatsoever.

In 1770 Goethe met J. G. Herder, who criticized his occult pursuits and influenced Goethe to turn gradually away from alchemy toward science. From 1771 to 1775, Goethe turned to the works of Swedish mystic Emanuel Swedenborg, who mixed both occultism and science. Goethe never completely deserted alchemy and MAGIC but looked for a bridge that would join them to science.

Faust

Goethe began *Faust* in 1774 and worked on it for 60 years, leaving parts of it to be opened posthumously. The story is of a genius who sells his soul to the devil, then sins, repents, dies, and is redeemed. *Faust* is an aspect of Goethe himself and shows Goethe's knowledge of religion and alchemy and his mystical speculations.

The Prologue in Heaven was probably influenced by Goethe's reading of *Paradise Lost* by John Milton. It presents God with the archangels Michael, Raphael, and Gabriel. Mephistopheles, the devil, enters as a court jester and asks God about humankind's wretchedness. God mentions Faust, "my serf," and agrees to let Mephistopheles try to sway him. Faust is "doctor" of all knowledge of all the realms but has no solace. He projects a noble aspiration of the human spirit, despite his sinister side. He serves as the focal point for the struggle between good and evil as a necessary part of evolution. In Goethe's view, the seeds of good can lie hidden in evil, but at the same time there can be something satanic in the most lofty feeling, or the satanic can even grow out of it.

In Part I, Faust is in despair with weariness and emptiness. He deplores the limitations of book learning and decides to seek real power through magic, but both his immense knowledge and his magical power have been rebuffed by the Earth Spirit, the lesser deity that dwells in the Earth. He is miffed that he, "godhead's likeness," "more than cherub," has been "withered" by the Earth Spirit's rejection. Faust is about to commit suicide when Easter bells and a chorus of ANGELS interrupt him. Mephistopheles—a SYMBOL of the libido's greed for GOLD and lust—arrives on the scene with attendant spirits he calls "my airy cherubim." The seduction of Faust through his limitations begins, and Faust sells him his soul. His youthful vigor restored by a witch, he descends into sensuality, which destroys Gretchen, an innocent woman who loves him. Faust attends a witches' sabbat. He watches Gretchen die and pray to the heavenly hosts for protection. A heavenly voice proclaims that she is redeemed while Mephistopheles insists that she is damned.

As Part II opens, it seems lifetimes later. Faust wakes in a charming landscape with FAIRIES and Ariel (the same spirit of the air from Shakespeare's play). Mephistopheles next takes Faust to Greece for an inside view of an emperor, lovemaking with Helen of Troy, and frolicking among the gods, the satyrs, the fauns, and the nymphs. His steady movement to damnation contrasts with the glories of knowledge and sensuality. After Faust dies, he is buried by angels and DEMONS.

In Act V, the heavenly angels confront Mephistopheles and his devils to seize Faust's soul and carry it off. In the epilogue male and female saints and blessed children sing of God's plan as the ranks of angels comment on the ascent of Faust's immortal essence. Gretchen is heard among the chorus of penitent women, and Faust's soul is received by a Sophia-like "Woman Eternal."

FURTHER READING:
Goethe, Johann Wolfgang von. *The Autobiography of Johann Wolfgang von Goethe,* vols. 1 & 2. Chicago: University of Chicago Press, 1976.

———. *Faust.* Ed. Cyrus Hamlin. Trans. Walter Arendt. New York: Norton, 1976.

Gray, Ronald D. *Goethe the Alchemist: A Study of Alchemical Symbolism in Goethe's Literary and Scientific Works.* Mansfield Centre, Conn.: Martino Publishing, 2002.

Lukacs, Georg. *Goethe and His Age.* New York: Grosset and Dunlap, 1969.

gold   The most precious metal that is the goal of ALCHEMY. Gold has ruled the fates of empires and nations. It is so valued and so rare that if all gold in existence from the time the Earth began were melted into a single cube, it would measure less than 19 yards square.

During the height of alchemy in the Renaissance, European nobility and royalty hoped that alchemy would provide a magical means of unlimited wealth. Alchemists were hired to transmute base metals such as lead and copper into gold or even SILVER—sometimes under threat of death if they failed. Much counterfeit "alchemical gold" was circulated, but some alchemists reportedly were successful.

According to PARACELSUS, there are three types of gold in alchemy: astral gold, elementary gold, and vulgar gold. Astral gold "has its center in the sun, which communicates it by its rays to all inferior beings. It is an igneous substance, which receives a continual emanation of solar corpuscles that penetrates all things sentient, vegetable, and mineral." Elementary gold "is the most pure and fixed portions of the elements, and of all that is composed of them. All sublunary beings included in the three kingdoms contain in their inmost center a precious grain of this elementary gold." Vulgar gold "is the most beautiful metal of our acquaintance, the best that Nature can produce, as perfect as it is unalterable in itself."

Paracelsus said that the PHILOSOPHER'S STONE is elementary gold, or "living philosophical gold," "living sulphur," and "true fire."

Gold is the metal of the SUN, solar MAGIC, the male principle, light, power, divine intelligence, purity, and spiritual enlightenment. In spiritual alchemy it represents the attainment of a refined and high level of consciousness. Chrysaor, the magic sword of gold, is symbolic of supreme spiritual determination.

Gold also symbolizes all that is superior. Since ancient times, it has been prized for its healing properties and power in AMULETS. The ancient Chinese used gold leaf in unguents, believing it to be a restorative to the entire body.

FURTHER READING:
Paracelsus. "Alchemical Catechism," in *Hermetic and Alchemical Writings of Paracelsus,* A. E. Waite, trans. 1894. Available online. URL: http://www.sacred-texts.com/tschoudy.htm. Downloaded January 10, 2005.

Golden Dawn   See HERMETIC ORDER OF THE GOLDEN DAWN.

Gold-Finding Hen   A magical hen that can find GOLD, according to RITUAL instructions in a magical GRIMOIRE written in about 1740, *The Black Pullet.*

The ritual tells how to hatch a magical hen by placing certain aromatic woods in a chafing dish mixed with oil and incense. The mixture is poured into a golden EGG container and covered with a black cushion. A chicken egg is placed on the cushion and covered with a bell glass made of faceted rock crystal. The egg is left in the sun and INCANTATIONS are spoken over it. The egg disappears and a black pullet appears. The pullet can be commanded with certain magical words and will search out hidden gold and other treasures.

An alternate method of creating the magical bird is to find a black hen, pluck out any nonblack feathers, and then find an unspotted egg. Put a black hood over the hen, place it in a black box, deprived of all light, and set it to hatch the egg. Feed it only at night, and minimize disturbances. According to the grimoire, the bird's imagination will be overwhelmed by the blackness and will hatch the perfect black pullet.

Another version of the ritual appeared in a later grimoire, *Red Dragon,* which involves the EVOCATION of a DEMON. Secure a black hen that has never mated, and do so without making the hen cackle. Take it to a CROSSROADS at midnight and trace a MAGIC CIRCLE around you with a cypress rod. Say THREE times, *"Eloim, Essaim, frugativi et appellavi."* After making ritual movements, a demon will appear in a scarlet overcoat, a yellow vest, and pale green breeches. His head will be that of a dog, his ears those of an ass, his head will have two horns, and he will have the legs and hooves of a calf. The demon will ask for your orders, which he must obey at all costs. You can direct the demon to find treasures.

FURTHER READING:
Wright, Elbee. *The Book of Magical Talismans/The Black Pullet.* Minneapolis: Marlar Publishing Co., 1984.

golem   In kabbalistic lore, an artificial living creature, usually a human, created with the sacred NAMES of God. *Golem* means "shapeless" or "lifeless."

The creation of living beings from images and idols by MAGIC appears in many cultures, including the ancient Egyptians, Greeks, and Arabs. Popular legends about the golem as a magician's slave were widespread in Europe during the Middle Ages.

In Talmudic usage, the term *golem* refers to something imperfect and unformed. In the Old Testament, Adam is called golem, meaning that he has a body without a soul. The concept of the golem that developed during the Middle Ages is tied to interpretations of the Sefer Yezirah, the "Book of Creation," the central text of the KABBALAH dealing with cosmology and cosmogony. According to the legends that gained favor, ancient Talmudic mystics gained the power to create a golem after intense study of the mysteries of the Sefer Yezirah. For example, one legend tells of two rabbis who met every Friday to study the book and create a three-year-old calf, which they ate. They did so by combining the letters of the Name (the most sacred name of God) by which the universe was created. This was not considered to be forbidden magic because all works were brought forth into being through the name of God.

The humanoid golem symbolized the highest level of achievement. In the 13th century, German hasidim—the pietists and mystics—were interested in creating a humanoid from the magical INVOCATION of names. Numerous legends on into the 17th century sprang from their writings. The golem had no independent mind, usually could not speak, and was dominated by his master.

In one legend, Rabbi Samuel created a golem to accompany and serve him on his travels; the golem could not speak. In another legend, Elijah of Chelm made a golem from clay and animated it by inscribing the name of God upon its forehead. It, too, could not speak, but it grew to enormous size and strength, which alarmed the rabbi. He tore the name of God from the golem's forehead, and the golem crumbled to dust. According to another version, Elijah's golem ran amok and had to be destroyed.

Various formulae were given for the creation and destruction of a golem. Besides clay, it could be made from soil, wood, wax, metal, or pieces of corpses sewn together. It was given life by the carving into its forehead of the name of God, the word *emet* ("truth") or "the seal of the Holy One." The mystics walked around it in a circle while reciting the secret and powerful names of God. Walking around the golem in the opposite direction took the life away from it. A golem could also be destroyed by erasing the first letter of *emet*, the *alef*, which left *met*, or "dead."

Eleazar of Worms, one of the most esteemed German mystics, recorded an elaborate formula for golem-making. It was to be made from "virgin soil, from a mountainous place where no man has ever dug before." The INCANTATION comprised "the alphabets of the 221 gates" and had to be recited over every organ. Eleazar's formula called for inscription of *emet* on the forehead to animate, and its alteration to *met* to destroy.

The golem legends are related to other legends, such as those popular in Italy from about the 10th century on that tell of corpses being resurrected from the dead with the secret names of God and with the artificial beings of natural magic and ALCHEMY, such as the HOMUNCULUS of PARACELSUS. In the 13th century, ALBERTUS MAGNUS was said to have created a talking man–android. In the 16th century, the Rabbi Elijah of Chelm was said to have a golem, as was Rabbi Judah Loew of Prague in the same century. In some versions of the Loew legend, the golem aided the Jews by discovering plots against them.

The golem is said to have inspired Johann Goethe's *The Sorcerer's Apprentice* and Mary Shelley's *Frankenstein,* among other literary creations.

FURTHER READING:

Scholem, Gershom. *Kabbalah.* 1974. Reprint, New York: Dorset Press, 1987.

Trachtenberg, Joshua. *Jewish Magic and Superstition: A Study in Folk Religion.* New York: Berhman's Jewish Book House, 1939.

Grail   Spiritual mystery in the Western esoteric tradition. The Grail is a pagan story which became Christianized but retained much of its pagan imagery and symbolism. The Grail is a gateway to Paradise, a point of contact with a supernatural and spiritual realm. It possesses unlimited healing power and makes possible a direct apprehension of the Divine.

As a pagan image, the Grail is a cup of regeneration, the vessel in which the life of the world is preserved and which symbolizes the body of the Goddess or Great Mother. In its Christianized form, the Grail is the chalice used by Christ at the Last Supper and which held his BLOOD following the crucifixion. It is not known whether such an object truly existed or exists, and there is no definitive image of it. As a spiritual mystery, the Grail represents regeneration through Christ's teachings; in medieval belief, blood embodied the soul and in Christ's case, even his divinity.

Various versions of the Grail legend exist. The first written texts appeared toward the end of the 12th century and were popular through the 14th century, though it is likely that the story existed earlier in oral pagan tradition. An account attributed to the sixth-century Celtic bard Taliesin but appearing 400 years after his life tells of a magic cauldron in Annwn, the Otherworld. The cauldron, guarded by nine maidens, is sought by King Arthur's men. As versions of the core story proliferated, elements of classical and Celtic mythology, Christian iconography, Arabic poetry, and Sufi teachings were incorporated. The Grail was first identified with the Last Supper in about 1190.

The Grail was never fully accepted in Catholic apocrypha, but neither was it denied nor labeled as heretical. Probably it was never fully accepted because it could not be identified with a relic, although lore held that the Grail cup was kept hidden by the ORDER OF THE KNIGHTS TEMPLAR in the castle of Muntsalvaesch (thought to be Montsegur). The Grail became widely popular in medieval chivalric lore. Its symbolisms were absorbed into ROSICRUCIAN esoterica.

According to a Christian version of the Grail Story, Joseph of Arimathea is charged with preparing Christ's body for the tomb. He has obtained the cup used by Christ at the Last Supper, and while he washes the body, he uses the cup to catch blood which flows from the wounds. When the body of Christ disappears from the tomb, Joseph is accused of stealing it and is jailed without food. Christ appears to him, puts the cup in his care, and teaches him various mysteries, including the Mass. Joseph remains alive in prison by a mysterious dove which appears every day and leaves a wafer in the cup. After his release in 70, according to one version, Joseph travels to Britain, where he founds the first Christian church at GLASTONBURY, dedicated to Mary, mother of Christ. He enshrines the Grail in the church. The Chalice Well at Glastonbury also is associated with the Grail. Its IRON and mineral-laced waters have been considered a sacred healing spring.

In another version, Joseph passes the Grail to Bron, his sister's husband, who becomes the Rich Fisher when he feeds many from the cup with a single fish. The company goes to Avaron (perhaps Avalon, the Otherworld of Arthurian lore) and waits for a new Grail keeper.

The Grail is housed in a temple on Muntsalvaesch, the Mountain of Salvation. It is guarded by an Order of Grail Knights. The grail keeper, who is king, is wounded in the thighs or genitals by a spear (associated with the spear wounds of Christ). The causes of the wound are varied, but the result is that the kingdom withers and becomes the Waste Land; it can only be restored when the king is restored to health (a motif common in folk and fairy tales).

Thus begin the Arthurian quests for the Grail. At Pentecost, the Grail appears floating in a sunbeam to the Knights of the Round Table, who pledge to find it. The quests are INITIATIONS.

Galahad the pure, Perceval the fool, and Bors the humble are the only knights to find the Grail. Lancelot, stained by his impure love for Queen Guinevere, fails. Perceval finds the wounded king and is asked the ritual question that can heal him: "Whom does the Grail serve?" The answer is not given, but it is the king. Perceval answers correctly, the king heals and is permitted to die, and the Waste Land is restored.

The three knights then travel East to Sarras, the Heavenly City, where they celebrate the mysteries of the Grail, and a Mass is said using the Grail. Galahad dies in sanctity and the Grail ascends to heaven. Perceval takes the king's place, and Bors returns to Camelot.

Early origins of the Grail legend may be found in the ancient and universal motif of sacred vessel as a SYMBOL of power and the source of MIRACLES. Such vessels, feminine symbols, are in Vedic, Egyptian, classical and Celtic mythology, and various mystery traditions as cups or cauldrons of inspiration, rebirth, and regeneration. In Tibetan Buddhism, a corollary is found in the human skulls that represent vessels of transformation.

In ALCHEMY, the Grail is represented by the PHILOSOPHER'S STONE, a symbol of unification with God.

The Grail also is represented by other feminine symbols, such as a dish, a womb, or another stone. One version of the legend, *Parzival,* finished in 1207 by Wolfram von Eschenbach, said the Grail was an emerald that fell from Lucifer's crown during his battle with God and was brought to Earth by ANGELS.

CARL G. JUNG said that the story of the Grail remains psychically alive in modern times, coming to the fore in times of collective need.

The Grail quest is a search for truth and the real Self and may be seen as a paradigm of the modern spiritual journey to restore the Waste Land and become whole again. There are many paths to the Grail. According to lore, the Grail may be seen only by those who have attained a certain spiritual consciousness, who have raised themselves above the limitations of the senses.

FURTHER READING:
Hall, Manly P. *The Secret Teachings of All Ages.* 1928. Reprint, Los Angeles: The Philosophic Research Society, 1977.
Jung, Emma, and Marie-Louise von Franz. *The Grail Legend.* 1960. Reprint, Boston: Sigo Press, 1986.
Matthews, John. *The Grail: Quest for the Eternal.* New York: Crossroad, 1981.
Matthews, John (ed.). *At the Table of the Grail: Magic and the Use of Imagination.* 1984. Reprint, London: Arkana, 1987.

grave   In ALCHEMY, a SYMBOL of the *nigredo,* the blackening phase that represents the death and destruction of the old to make way for new spiritual growth.

Graves also symbolize the past that is dead and buried, the dying of something to the world, and spiritual or emotional withdrawal. Rising from a grave in alchemical art symbolizes rebirth and resurrection.

graveyard dirt   A powerful ingredient in magical SPELLS, especially of an evil nature.

A 19th-century account from rural America records a man's testimony that he believed that he was the victim of a spell cast with the help of graveyard dirt and other ingredients combined in a CHARM BAG buried under the threshold of his front door. To break the spell, he spread red pepper around his home to purify it and immediately consulted a root doctor, a man skilled in herbal MAGIC. The man said:

> I opened the bag and found some small roots about an inch long, some black hair, a piece of snake skin, and some graveyard dirt, dark-yaller, right off some coffin. . . . Only root doctors can git the graveyard dirt, they know what kind to git and when, the hants [ghosts] won't let everybody get it, they must git it through some kind of spell, for the graveyard dirt works trouble 'til it gits back into the ground, and then [the spell] wears off. It must git down to the same depth it was took from, that is as deep as the coffin lid was from the surface of the ground.

See also WANGA.

Gray, William G. (1913–1995)   English RITUAL magician, occultist, and founder of the Sangreal Sodality.

William G. Gray was born in Harrow, Middlesex, England, on March 25, 1913. His grandfather, William Gray, was a rector in a lineage tracing to Archbishop Walter de

Gray of York. His father, John McCammon Trew Gray, worked as a theatrical business manager. His mother, Christine Ash, a Scottish-American and a Catholic, became a well-known astrologer and introduced Gray to occult ideas at an early age. Christine Gray was naturally clairvoyant, and encouraged her son to explore and accept the paranormal. The young Gray was fascinated by Catholic ritual and persuaded his mother to have him rebaptized in the Catholic faith. When he was nine, his mother became ill and entered a sanitorium in Montreal. Gray also went to Montreal to enter the care of relatives. Upon Christine's recovery, the family moved to Southampton, England.

During a bout with measles, Gray had a visionary experience that altered the course of his life. He found himself in a perfect place where everything was made of light, called into being by pure thought. The experience was permeated by wonder and ecstasy. Gray became interested in MAGIC and experimented with rituals. In time Gray drifted away from the Catholic Church, alienated by its emphasis on sin.

Christine's involvement in occult circles brought numerous visitors to the house, among them ALEISTER CROWLEY and his assistant VICTOR NEUBERG. Gray liked Neuberg, whom he later described as "one of the gentlest men I ever met." Crowley's visits were brief; on one occasion, he presented Christine with a signed copy of his book 777. Christine burned it, feeling it to be a source of direct, bad influence from Crowley, but not before Gray had secretly copied it for himself.

Gray met Theosophists and Rosicrucians and was an avid reader—as was his mother—of the magazine *Occult Review*. It was through the magazine that Gray met his spiritual mentor, "ENH," a Rosicrucian who was an associate of "Papus," a French occultist whose real name was Gerard Encause. ENH wrote to Gray concerning a letter of Gray's published in the magazine that dealt with ROSICRUCIANISM. Their resulting relationship lasted many years until ENH died of liver cancer. Gray credited him with much of his magical and spiritual development.

At age 18, Gray joined the Royal Corps of Signals of the British Army and was sent to Egypt, where he learned local magical and occult lore. He returned to England and in World War II served in active duty in France. He was evacuated during the battle at Dunkirk. After the war, Gray suffered a breakdown of health and was released from the army. He moved to Gloucester and worked as a chiropodist. He met his future wife, Bobbie, at a meeting of occultists and science-fiction afficionados. Bobbie became a professional astrologer and assisted Gray in his esoteric work. The couple had no children.

Gray circulated with occultists and self-professed Witches, the latter of whom included Doreen Valiente and Patricia Crowther, close associates of GERALD B. GARDNER. Gray briefly joined the Society of the Inner Light, founded by DION FORTUNE; he was not impressed with the society's rituals.

William G. Gray in ceremonial dress. (Courtesy of Alan Richardson)

At about this time, Gray suffered poor health from an abscessed tooth but made no marked recovery after the extraction of the diseased tooth. His health was restored by a magical healing circle ritual conducted by Robert Cochrane (Roy Bowers), who claimed a lineage of hereditary witches and was the founder of the Clan of Tubal Cain, known in America as the "1734" tradition of modern witchcraft. Cochrane told him to be asleep by midnight on a certain night, to take no sleeping aids, and not to be surprised by any dreams he might recall. Gray did as instructed. He described the results:

> At some unknown hour I had the distinct feeling of being tossed from one person to another in a peculiar pattern as they chanted or sang amongst themselves. I seemed to be something like a ball or small parcel which they handed quite freely and easily between them. Suddenly I became conscious of lying in bed on my stomach with a piercing point of agony somewhere under my lower right ribs. Slowly it moved to my left side, then back again, after which it went in a downward direction and finally faded out entirely leaving me exhausted but entirely free from any pain. I felt so utterly relieved at this I straightway slipped back into sleep with intense gratitude.

In the late 1960s, Gray began to write about occultism and magic, starting with an essay on the KABBALAH that he intended to circulate only among friends. The essay was so well received that he expanded it to a book, published as *The Ladder of Lights,* still considered a classic in Western occult literature. Gray wrote eight more books about the kabbalah and the Western Inner Tradition and four books on the Sangreal Sodality, an esoteric brotherhood he founded. Some of Gray's work was published with the help of a wealthy America patron, Carr Collins.

The Sangreal Sodality resulted from inspirations Gray experienced while on a visit to South Africa at the invitation of Jacobus Swart, an occultist interested in Gray's work. Gray and Swart worked Gray's Rite of Light—which became Gray's signature ritual—and Gray formed the Sangreal concepts. The basis is that all humans possess divine BLOOD, brought to Earth long ago by star people, and which contains the potential for perfection. It is vital that humans recognize that they are all part of the same Being.

On his return to England, Gray wrote lessons and rituals which Collins backed for publishing in a series of books. Sangreal Temples were established in England by Gray, in South Africa by Swart, in Albany, New York, by Marcia Pickands, and in Brazil. To Gray's keen disappointment, the sodality did not attract interest in Britain, and there was little rapport between the American and South African temples. In his waning years, Gray "passed the rod" of authority to Swart, his third choice.

Gray had strong opinions and was often scathing in his criticism of his peers. He ritually cursed others, including some of his students.

In his personal memoirs, Gray said that in his later years he finally discovered the meaning of the literal GRAIL:

> It was really too simple and yet too obvious. The real Holy Grail of historical significance had been the recognition and acknowledgment of a Feminine quotient to Deity as an equal and complementary Energy within the Christian Godhead. In other words, it was an objective of those who wanted the old Goddess worship restored to its proper place in their religious lives and practices.

Gray died in England in 1995.

FURTHER READING:
Gray, William G. *Western Inner Workings.* York Beach, Maine: Samuel Weiser, 1983.
Richardson, Alan, and Marcus Claridge. *The Old Sod: The Odd Life and Inner Workings of William G. Gray.* London: ignotus press, 2003.

Greater Key of Solomon   See GRIMOIRES.

Greatrakes, Valentine (1629–1683)   Irish healer called "Mr. Greatrix," "Mr. Greatraks," and the "stroker," who cured maladies by a laying on of the hands. Valentine Greatrakes's abilities compared to the magical powers of the cunning men/women, witches, and WIZARDS of his time.

The SEVENTH SON of an Irish gentleman in County Cork, Greatrakes reputedly suffered from "melancholy derangement" early in life. He served in Cromwell's army and then in the government, retiring when he lost his office of county magistrate. Shortly thereafter, he had a spiritual awakening that God had given him the power to heal the "king's evil" by touching. He tested himself by curing a Saltersbridge man of the king's evil in his eyes, cheek, and throat. He launched a new career as a healer and attracted a huge audience of satisfied customers. He cured epilepsy, ulcers, lameness, and other sicknesses and had the ability to cause and cure fits and cast out evil spirits, which he said were the cause of various afflictions. As word of his ability spread, so many persons sought him out that he worked from six in the morning until six at night, stroking everyone who came to see him.

In 1661 Greatrakes was summoned to the trial of Florence Newton to help determine that she was a witch. In 1666 he went to England where he effected more cures, but he failed to cure the chronic headaches of Anne, Viscountess Conway. He also failed in a demonstration to Charles II and soon returned to Ireland.

Greatrakes always invoked the name of God when he worked and accepted no fees other than reimbursement for travel. He rejected cases that appeared to be incurable. His stroking powers apparently were limited to physical ills, for he was unable to help an earl's butler who was possessed by FAIRIES and made to levitate off the ground.

The Puritan minister and witch hunter Increase Mather dismissed Greatrakes as a fraud, claiming he attempted to effect cures by using MAGIC, specifically "that hobgoblin word, *Abrodacara*" (ABRACADABRA).

grimoires   Handbooks of MAGIC that provide instructions for RITUALS, the casting of SPELLS, the procuring of treasure and love, the procuring of FAMILIARS, and the EVOCATION and control of spirits to perform various tasks. *Grimoire* is a French term for "grammar book."

Although any handbook of magic could be called a grimoire, the term usually applies to specific texts that purport to descend from the magical knowledge of King SOLOMON. The material in grimoires is heavily derivative of Hebrew magical and mystical lore, involving the NAMES, powers, and duties of spirits—DEMONS and ANGELS—and the powerful names of God. Other sources are Hellenistic Greek and Egyptian magical texts, and Latin lore.

Though grimoires claimed to date to ancient sources, most were written in the 17th and 18th centuries and were popular well into the 19th century. In his book *The Book of Black Magic and of Pacts* (1899), ARTHUR EDWARD WAITE said that "back-dating and imputed authorship are the two crying bibliographical sins of Grimoires and magical handbooks" and that "there never was a literature so founded in forgery as that of Magic, except the sister science of Alchemy."

Printed on cheap paper, grimoires circulated primarily in France and Italy. The best were a composite of kabbalistic magic and folk magic, but many were full of fictitious material aimed at the popular interest in magic. For the most part, Christian elements are absent. The old grimoires are still consulted, but modern magicians have written their own textbooks of magic (see BLACK BOOK; BOOK OF SHADOWS; WHITE BOOK).

Grimoires give instructions for rituals to conjure and control spirits and cosmic forces for protection, wealth, luck, supernatural power, CURSES on enemies, and so forth. They instruct the magician on what to wear, what TOOLS to use, how to purify himself, and what PRAYERS and INCANTATIONS to recite at precise astrological times and various hours of the day and night, according to the ruling ANGELS and INTELLIGENCES. They give recipes for fumigations (see PERFUMES); descriptions of the creation of MAGIC CIRCLES, MAGIC TRIANGLES, PENTACLES, AMULETS, TALISMANS, SEALS, and SIGILS; instructions on the slaughtering and SACRIFICES of animals; and ways to deal with unruly DEMONS, including rites of EXORCISM. Some of the prescriptions call for bizarre ingredients, such as bat's BLOOD and human body parts. Some modern occultists say that these terms were blinds for other, less gruesome ingredients and that the coding was a way of keeping the true rituals secret among ADEPTS. Blood sacrifices were traditional in ancient times, however, and it is unlikely that a reference to blood in a grimoire meant anything other than blood.

W. E. BUTLER said that magicians themselves were to blame for the dubious nature of many purported grimoires. According to tradition, written accounts of magical rituals had to be executed with consecrated paper and pens; a magician had to make his or her own copy by his or her own hand. The desire for magical textbooks stimulated the production of false texts, some of which were based on real texts, while others contained bogus material. Waite wrote extensively on the grimoires in *The Book of Black Magic and of Pacts*, and his opinions of many of the texts are withering.

Some grimoires are devoted to theurgy, or white magic, while others concern goetia, or black magic. Some include both. The attainment of treasure and love and the ability to harm one's enemies are prominent throughout the grimoires. Some were printed in red ink and were said to burn the eyes if gazed at too long.

The following are the grimoires of significance:

Key of Solomon

The most important grimoire is the *Key of Solomon*, also called the *Greater Key of Solomon* and the *Clavicle of Solomon*, for this text is the source for most other grimoires. The book is attributed to the legendary King Solomon, who asked God for wisdom and commanded an army of demons to do his bidding and build great works. In the first century C.E., the Jewish historian Josephus mentioned a book of incantations for summoning and thwarting demons that was attributed to the authorship of Solomon. Josephus said that a Jew named Eleazar used it cure cases of POSSESSION. Josephus may have been referring to the *Key,* but some historians believe it was the *Testament of Solomon* (see below) or, more likely, a different text altogether.

It is mentioned in literature throughout the centuries, growing in size and content. So many versions of this grimoire were written that it is virtually impossible to ascertain what consisted the original text. A Greek version which dates to 1100–1200 C.E. is part of the collection in the British Museum. From the 14th century, Solomonic magical works took on increasing importance. In about 1350, Pope Innocent VI ordered a grimoire called *The Book of Solomon* to be burned; later, in 1559, Solomon's grimoire was condemned by the Inquisition again as dangerous. The *Key of Solomon* was widely distributed in the 17th century. Hundreds of copies of the *Key,* in differing versions, still exist. Supposedly the original manuscript was written in Hebrew, but no such text is known.

The *Key of Solomon* was especially important to the HERMETIC ORDER OF THE GOLDEN DAWN. In 1889 SAMUEL LIDDELL MacGREGOR MATHERS translated a version from seven codices held in the British Museum: one in Latin, one in Italian, and five in French. The material may date to the 14th or 15th centuries and is primarily kabbalistic in nature mixed with folk magic that is probably from a variety of sources.

Two of the codices used by Mathers have pseudo-historical introductions, based on Solomon's biblical dream in which he prayed to God for an understanding heart and was granted great wisdom and riches. One introduction says that the *Key* was buried with Solomon in his tomb, in accordance to his instructions to his son, Roboam. The text was discovered much later by Babylonian philosophers, who could not understand it until one prayed to God and was enlightened by an angel. In the other codice, Solomon warns Roboam:

> If thou dost not intend to use for a good purpose the secrets which I here teach thee, I command thee rather to cast this Testament into the fire, than to abuse the power thou wilt have of constraining the Spirits, for I warn thee that the beneficent Angels, wearied and fatigued by thine illicit demands, would to thy sorrow execute the commands of God, as well as to that of all such who, with evil intent, would abuse those secrets which He hath given and revealed to me.

Mathers believed the work to be white magic contaminated by black magic from other sources. Unfortunately, he purged some of the content that he considered to be black magic, especially involving blood. In so doing, he ignored or overlooked Solomon's alleged admonition that failure to follow the instructions precisely as given would result in failure. Instead, Mathers said that working evil would rebound on the magician:

I must further caution the practical worker against the use of blood; the prayer, the pentacle, and the perfumes, rightly used, are sufficient; and the former verges dangerously on the evil path. Let him who, in spite of the warnings of this volume, determines to work evil, be assured that the evil will recoil on himself and that he will be struck by the reflex current.

Waite considered the *Key* to be a composite magical work of both white and black magic. Both Waite and Mathers deplored the emphasis on blood sacrifices in the grimoire's rituals and to rituals devoted to hatred and destruction, which in Waite's terms were "distinctive marks of Black Magic." The *Key* places great importance on the magical finding of treasure with the help of spirits and also to interfering in the free will of others, such as in forcing a person to fall in love. Waite concluded that the *Key* was "a grotesque combination of the pompous and the ridiculous; it is, in fact, the old story of the mountain and the mouse, but so great is the travail that, in this case, the mouse is brought forth dead."

Lemegeton

Another grimoire attributed to Solomon is the *Lemegeton*, or *Lesser Key of Solomon*. The origin and meaning of *Lemegeton* is not known. The book also was known as *Liber Spirituum* (see below) and *Liber Officiorum*. Claims were made that the *Lemegeton* was originally written in Chaldean and Hebrew, but these are doubtful. Waite called it "a work of far more exalted pretensions" than the *Key of Solomon* and that "deploys all the hierarchies and evokes spirits by the milliards."

Like the *Key*, the *Lemegeton* claims to have been written originally in Hebrew, but the earliest perfect examples of it are in French. Part of the *Lemegeton* was published in Latin by the demonologist Johann Weyer in 1563, entitled *Pseudomonarchia Daemonum (Pseudo-Monarchy of Demons)*. MICHAEL SCOT translated some of it into English in his work *Discoverie of Witchcraft* in 1584, and Waite condensed and reproduced part of it, taken from a manuscript in the British Museum dated 1676.

The material in the *Lemegeton* probably is derived in part from the *Testament of Solomon* (see below) and also the apocryphal book of *Enoch*.

The book is divided into four parts: Goetia, Theurgia, the Pauline Art, and the Almadel. The Almadel was mentioned in writing in about 1500. Goetia is devoted to evil spirits. Theurgia (or Theurgia-Goetia as it is also called) is devoted to both good and evil spirits and all aerial spirits. The Pauline Art concerns the spirits who govern the planets, the signs of the zodiac, and the hours of the day and night. The Almadel concerns 20 chief spirits who govern the four quarters and the 360 degrees of the zodiac. Goetia is the part published by Weyer. Waite speculated that Goetia is the original *Lemegeton* and that the other three parts were unknown to Weyer and were added at a later time.

The *Lemegeton* lists 72 fallen angels, their titles, seals, duties, and powers and the angels who can thwart them. (Curiously, Weyer listed only 69, and Scot listed only 68.) The number 72 may have been inspired by the Schemhamphorae, 72 angels who bear the Names of God, which are given in Hebrew Scripture and are expressed at the end of every verse. The verses are used in INVOCATION and in magic. The Schemhamphorae function as names of power.

The 72 demons in the *Lemegeton* possess teaching skills for the sciences and art, as well as the ability to cause terrible diseases and disasters. Few have any healing ability. Waite described them as "two-and-seventy methods of accomplishing all abominations . . . Satanism undiluted, *plus* all the mysteries of the undiluted Venus."

Testament of Solomon

The *Testament of Solomon* is a Greek text in the pseudepigrapha written between the first and third centuries C.E. It tells the story about how King Solomon built the Temple of Jerusalem by commanding demons. The text is rich in demonology, angelology, and lore about medicine, astrology, and magic. The author probably was familiar with the Babylonian Talmud.

The text says that stellar bodies are demonic, wielding destructive power over the affairs of humanity. The 36 decans, or 10-degree portions of the zodiac, are called heavenly bodies and likewise are ruled by demons, who cause mental and physical illnesses. There are seven "world rulers" who are equated with the vices of deception, strife, fate, distress, error, power, and "the worst," each of whom is thwarted by a particular angel (with the exception of the worst).

The testament provides a significant contribution to the legends of Solomon's magical powers and the magical handbooks attributed to Solomon. It is not a grimoire of magical instruction, however.

Grand Grimoire

This French grimoire was probably authored in the 17th or 18th century. The earliest edition of it bears no date or place of publication; one version of it claims to date to 1522. Its full title is *The Grand Grimoire, with the Powerful Clavicle of Solomon and of Black Magic; or the Infernal Devices of the Great Agrippa for the Discovery of all Hidden Treasures and the Subjugation of every Denomination of Spirits, together with an Abridgment of all the Magical Arts*. The editor, Venitiana del Rabina, said that he translated the work from the writings of Solomon himself, which came into his possession.

The *Grand Grimoire* is a text of black magic, which Waite described as "one of the most atrocious of its class." It has the same chief demons as the *Grimorium Verum* and nearly the same subordinate officers, but it describes different duties for them. The book is especially significant for its feature of a specific PACT between the magician and Lucifuge Rofocale, the Prime Minister of Lucifer, who makes his only appearance in this grimoire alone. How-

Lucifuge Rofocale, in the grimoire Grand Grimoire. *(Author's collection)*

ever, his last name Rofocale may be an anagram of Focalor, a demon named in the *Lemegeton*.

The book also includes instructions for NECROMANCY that "only a dangerous man-iac or an irreclaimable criminal" would attempt, according to Waite. The rite calls for, among other things, creating a disturbance during a midnight Mass on Christmas Eve.

Grimorium Verum

Drawn on the *Greater Key of Solomon* and written in French, this book probably was written in the mid-18th century. Claims were made that it was translated from Hebrew by a Dominican Jesuit named Plaingiere and was published by "Alibeck the Egyptian" in 1517. Its full title is *Grimorium Verum, or the Most Approved Keys of Solomon the Hebrew Rabbin, wherein the Most Hidden Secrets, both Natural and Supernatural, are immediately exhibited, but it is necessary that the Demons should be contented on their part.* Waite classified this work as one of black magic.

The *Grimoirium Verum* nearly copies the *Key of Solomon* in instructions for preparation of the magician and his tools, but it provides different instructions for the preparation of the virgin parchment and for the evocation and dis-

missal of spirits. There is an entirely different hierarchy of demons, who number 30 and who report to three leaders, Lucifer, Beelzbeub, and Astaroth, who have among them six deputy chiefs.

The material also shows influences from *Lemegeton*. It includes the "Admirable Secrets" of the pseudo-Albertus Magnus, or *Little Albert* (see below), which appear in other later grimoires.

The *Grimorium Verum* covers the "Genuine Sanctum Regnum," or the true method of making pacts.

Fourth Book

Authorship is attributed to HENRY CORNELIUS AGRIPPA, but the book, supposedly the fourth volume of Agrippa's monumental three-volume *Occult Philosophy,* was written by an unknown author. It is also known as the *Liber Spirituum* and is in the opening of the *Lemegeton*. The *Fourth Book* appeared after the death of Agrippa in 1535 and rehashes in an informal way much of the material in *Occult Philosophy.* Weyer, a student of Agrippa, rejected it as a forgery, as did other occultists.

Like the *Lemegeton*, the *Fourth Book* gives instructions for communicating with evil spirits. It covers the names of spirits associated with the planets and their characters, sigils, and pentacles. There are rituals for evoking both good and evil spirits and for practicing necromancy.

Waite called the *Fourth Book* "muddled" and said that its lack of precision rendered it ineffective as a manual of magic.

Grimoire of Honorius

Also called the *Constitution of Honorius,* this text may have been authored in the 16th century but was first published in Rome in 1629. It gained wide circulation during the 17th century. The authorship is attributed to Pope Honorius III (r. 1216–1227), who is credited with rites of exorcism. The book shows influences from the *Lemegeton* and claims to be based on the Practical Kabbalah, but this connection is tenuous. Rather, it is the only grimoire to introduce significant Christian elements, which earned it the reputation of the blackest of black magic texts. The grimoire is cast as a papal bull in which the pope decrees that the authorities of the church, from cardinals to secular clerks, should have the power of invoking and commanding spirits of all sorts. This power had been vested with the papal office as the successor to Saint Peter. (See POPES AND SORCERY.) Waite opined that the *Grimoire of Honorius* "may be a perversion of the orthodox conjurations, and if not that, it is a reprisal; it is Sorcery revenging herself on a Pope who casts out devils by representing him as the prince of those who dealt with them."

The rituals in *Honorius* combine kabbalistic elements such as the 72 sacred names of God and Christian elements such as confessions, litanies, masses of the Holy Ghost and angels, the Office of the Dead, the Gospel of Saint John, and various PRAYERS, with gruesome sacrifices of animals. The effect is more like a BLACK MASS than anything sacred.

Figures from the title page of the grimoire Grand Honorius.
(Author's collection)

The devil bearing treasure, in the grimoire Grand Honorius,
1823. (Author's collection)

The 1670 edition of *Honorius* includes a rite of exorcism for both humans and animals. The 1800 edition calls for using holy water in human exorcisms. In animal possessions it prescribes the use of SALT that has been exorcized with blood drawn from a bewitched animal.

As a magical text it is viewed as having little foundation and probably was written for commercial appeal. It is not to be confused with *The Sworn Book of Honorius,* credited to the authorship of Honorius of Thebes, master magician. Waite said that the grimoire "must be avoided, were it necessary at the present day to warn any one against practices to which no one is likely to resort, which belong to the foolish mysteries of old exploded doctrines, and are interesting assuredly, but only as curiosities of the past."

Arbatel of Magic

The *Arbatel of Magic* is slim text written in Latin and published in Basel, Switzerland, in 1575. It was translated into German in 1686. The authorship is not known, but it is speculated the person may have been Italian, due to several obscure references to Italian history. Waite said that *Arbatel* is probably the name of an instructing or revealing angel. The book refers to "Theophrastic Magic," indicat-

ing influences of PARACELSUS. It has no connection to the Solomonic writings and does not even mention Solomon; rather, it has strong Christian elements. Waite considered it representative of "transcendental magic."

The *Arbatel* purports to be a nine-volume work of instructions on the magical arts, but only the first volume, or tome, is extant. It is uncertain whether the other eight tomes were ever written; perhaps the anonymous author intended to write them but failed to follow through. The first tome is called Isagoge, which means "essential or fundamental instruction." The missing tomes are:

- Microcosmical Magic, about spiritual wisdom
- Olympic Magic, concerning the evocation of the OLYMPIC SPIRITS
- Hesiodiacal and Homeric Magic, about the operations of *kako-daimones* (see DAIMONES)
- Roman or Sybilline Magic, concerning TUTELARY SPIRITS
- Pythagorical Magic, concerning the genii of the arts (see GENII)
- Magic of Apollonius, concerning the power over people (see APOLLONIUS OF TYANA)
- Hermetic or Egyptian Magic (see HERMETICA)
- Prophetical Magic, about the Word of God (see DIVINATION)

Isagoge comprises Seven Septenaries of aphorisms of a moral and spiritual nature that cite the sources of occult wisdom: God; angels; learned men; nature (stones, herbs, and so forth); apostate spirits; ministers of punishment in hell (comparable to the avenging classical gods); and the spirits of the ELEMENTS. The wisdom obtainable from these sources ranges from the low magic of finding treasures to alchemical transmutations to mystical knowledge of God. Meditation, love of God, and living in accordance to the virtues are emphasized as the best means for practicing the magical arts.

The book features the Ritual of the Olympic Spirits, INTELLIGENCES who rule the natural and magical operations in the world. Unlike Solomonic grimoires, the *Arbatel* places no emphasis on the importance of the correct pronunciation of the spirits' names but instead recommends working magically with them according to their offices and without their names.

Theosophia Pneumatica

Also known as *The Little Key of Solomon*, this grimoire was published in 1686 in German. It possibly was included in the German edition of the *Arbatel of Magic*, a work it follows closely. Of anonymous authorship, the *Theosophia Pneumatica* makes no claims to ancient origins. Like the *Arbatel*, it is Christian in orientation and holds that the exaltation of prayer is the end of the Mystery. The Hebrew term *Talmid*—derived from the verb for "to learn"—is used to describe the aspiring magician. The author also was knowledgeable about ALCHEMY and included references to it. Waite included this book in his classification of transcendental magic.

The only section of the *Theosophia Pneumatica* that differs significantly from the *Arbatel* is the appendix, which contains strong Christian elements and terminology used by Paracelsus. It affirms that all things are threefold in nature after the model of the Father, the Son, and the Holy Ghost. The human being is threefold, having a body, a soul, and a rational spirit. The body is of the earth. The soul is of the ELEMENTS derived through the stars, is the seat of understanding, and is the genius for arts and sciences. The rational spirit is from God and is the medium through which divine inspiration enters the physical body. The soul and the rational spirit are joined in marriage by God to reside in the body. Regeneration is achieved when the rational spirit overcomes the soul. There are two kinds of death: deterioration of the body and destruction of the soul via poisoned stellar influences. In either case, the rational spirit departs; it may also depart at the will of God. It is not possible to cure certain diseases by which God has chosen to afflict humankind. The unicorn, QUINTESSENCE, AZOTH, and the PHILOSOPHER'S STONE are all useless. All other diseases can be cured with natural magic and alchemy.

Heptameron

Also called *Magical Elements*, this book is attributed to PETER OF ABANO, an Italian physician who died in 1316 after being condemned to death by the Inquisition. Abano is not believed to be the author. The *Heptameron* probably was written in the 16th century and may have been intended as a supplement to the *Fourth Book*.

The grimoire is a composite work of white and black magic that deals with finding treasure, procuring love, detecting secrets, opening locks, fomenting hatred and evil thoughts, and so on. It is divided into two parts: the evocation of the Spirits of the Air, who are demons, and a set of angelic evocations for each day of the week. Waite described the *Heptameron* as "an attempt to . . . offer the neophyte a complete wizard's cabinet."

Little Albert

Also titled *Marvelous Secrets of the Natural and Cabalistic Magic of Little Albert,* this text was published in 1722. Material from it appears in various grimoires. (See INVISIBILITY.)

The Enchiridion of Pope Leo

This book is technically not a grimoire, although Waite included it in *The Book of Black Magic and of Pacts*. The *Enchiridion of Pope Leo* offers no instructions for magical rituals but is a collection of CHARMS turned into prayers, accompanied by mysterious figures supposedly taken from rare old manuscripts. ELIPHAS LEVI gave it more importance than it merits, claiming that it had never been published with its true figures, an assertion that cannot be proven.

According to the story of the book's alleged origins, Pope Leo III (r. 795–816) gave the Roman emperor Charlemagne a collection of prayers following his coronation in Rome in 800. The collection had special properties: Whoever carried it about on his or her person with the proper attitude—respect for the Scriptures—and recited it daily in the honor of God would have divine protection for his entire life. He would never be defeated by his enemies and would escape all dangers without harm. The text claims that Charlemagne, who enjoyed great fortune, wrote a letter of thanks in his own hand to Pope Leo III, which is still preserved in the Vatican Library.

This collection of prayers was published as the *Enchiridion* for the first time in Rome in 1523. A second edition is said to have been issued in 1606, and a final edition in 1660. The book was probably composed in the 17th century and given the legend to lend it authenticity. Charlemagne may not have been literate, and no letters of his are extant.

The *Enchiridion*'s charms are dressed up as prayers, but few are spiritual in nature and are instead concerned with material things such as acquiring wealth, happiness, and advantage, and protecting one's self against all kinds of dangers, misfortunes, natural disasters, and evils. The text denies any association with magic, but in the fashion of magic, it describes a ritual for its proper use. The book must be kept clean in a bag of new leather. It must be carried on the person, and at least one page of it must be read with devotion every day. Specific pages can be read for various needs. To read from the book, one must face east and get down on the knees, for this, claims the *Enchiridion,* is what Charlemagne did.

Alberti Parvi Lucii Liber de Mirabilibus Naturae Arcanis

Attributed falsely to the authorship of ST. ALBERTUS MAGNUS, this grimoire was published in Lyons, France, with the kabbalistic date of 6516. It gives instructions for making PHILTRES, interpreting dreams, discovering treasure, making a HAND OF GLORY, making a RING that confers invisibility, and other magical acts.

The following texts were written in the 18th and 19th centuries and are often called grimoires:

The Book of Sacred Magic of Abra-Melin the Mage

Authorship is attributed to Abra-Melin (also spelled *Abramelin*), a Jewish kabbalistic mage of Wurzburg, Germany, who supposedly wrote the grimoire for his son in 1458. The manuscript, written in French in the 18th century, claims to be a translation of the original Hebrew manuscript. The book was a major influence in the 19th-century occult revival carried out by the Golden Dawn. Mathers translated it into English. Crowley borrowed from it for his own rituals to master demons.

The book comprises three books, all derivative of the *Key of Solomon.* According to lore, Abra-Melin said that he learned his magical knowledge from angels, who told him how to conjure and tame demons into personal servants and workers and how to raise storms. He said that all things in the world were created by demons, who worked under the direction of angels, and that each individual had an angel and a demon as familiar spirits. The basis for his system of magic, he said, may be found in the kabbalah.

The magical system is based on the power of numbers and sacred names and involves the construction of numerous MAGICAL SQUARES for such purposes as invisibility, flying, commanding spirits, necromancy, and SHAPE SHIFTING. Rituals for conjuring spirits, creating magic squares, and making seals and sigils are elaborate and must be followed exactly in accordance with astrological observances.

True Black Magic

Also called *The Secrets of Secrets,* this black magic grimoire purportedly was written in the 1600s by a magician named Toscraec, who claimed that it was based on a centuries-old manuscript written in an unknown language. Toscraec said that he was only able to translate the manuscript with the help of angel. It probably was written in the 18th century.

True Black Magic is a goetic adaptation of the *Key of Solomon.* In the book, claims were made that the manuscript was found in the tomb of Solomon and that it was translated from the Hebrew in 1750 by the MAGUS Iroe–Grego. It includes 45 talismans, their properties and uses, and "all magical characters known unto this day."

The grimoire quotes Solomon as saying that divine love must come first before magical wisdom can be acquired. Solomon allegedly stated:

The beginning and key of my Wisdom are the fear of God, to do Him honor, to adore Him with great contrition of heart, and to invoke His aid in all our intentions and aspirations; which fulfilling, God will lead us into the good way.

Waite described the text as "exceedingly confused."

The Black Pullet

According to lore, this grimoire was published in Egypt in 1740, but it was probably authored in the late 18th century in Rome or in France. *The Black Pullet* is one of the few grimoires that does not claim to be a manuscript of antiquity. It does not link itself to Solomonic magic but shows influences of the spurious *Fourth Book.* It places particular emphasis on 20 magic talismans and 20 corresponding magic RINGS, plus two talismans of a magic circle and a magic rod or wand. It disavows all connections to black magic. It has appeared in altered versions as *Treasure of the Old Man of the Pyramids* and *Black Screech Owl.* The 22 talismans have been linked to the 22 trumps of the TAROT.

The Black Pullet tells a colorful story about itself and its alleged origins. The original—and ambitious—French title of the grimoire was *The Black Pullet, or the Hen with the Golden Eggs, comprising the Science of Magic Talismans and Rings, the Art of Necromancy and of the Kabbalah, for the Conjuration of Aerial and Infernal Spirits, of Sylphs, Undines, and Gnomes, for the acquisition of the Secret Sciences, for the Discovery of Treasures, for obtaining power to command all beings, and to unmask all Sciences and Bewitchments, The whole following the Doctrines of Socrates, Pythagorus [sic], Zoroaster, Son of the Grand Aromasis, and other philosophers whose works in the MS escaped the conflagration of the Library of Ptolemy, Translated from the language of the Magi and that of the Hieroglyphs by the Doctors Mizzaboula-Jabamia, Danhuzerus, Nehmahmiah, Judahim, and Eliaeb, Rendered into French by A.J.S.D.R.L.G.F.*

The Black Pullet claims it is the narrative of an unnamed man who was a member of Napoleon's armed forces that were sent to Egypt. With several companions, he went to the pyramids outside of Cairo where they all stopped for lunch. They were attacked by Arabs, and all but the author were killed. He was left for dead. When he regained consciousness, he assumed that he would soon be dead due to his abandonment in the desert, and he delivered a farewell to the setting sun.

Suddenly a stone rolled back in the Great Pyramid, and a man came out. The soldier could tell by his turban that he was a Turk. As luck would have it, the soldier knew the Turkish language and could communicate. The Turk revived him with a liquor and took him inside the pyramid, which was revealed to be the magical home of the mysterious man.

The soldier was astonished to find vast halls, endless galleries, subterranean chambers, and piles of treasures, all ministered by spirits. There were blazing lamps and magic suppers. A genius or FAMILIAR named Odous was the special attendant of the Turk. The soldier was also shown *The Black Pullet,* a text that was like a version of Aladdin and the magic lamp but with an inner meaning by the demon Astaroth. The magical power was created with talismans embroidered on silk and rings made of bronzed steel.

The Turk said that he was the only heir to this magic, which was based on Egyptian hieroglyphs. He told the soldier that he was near death. He possessed a magic talisman that enabled him to be fluent in 22 languages. The Turk conveyed to the soldier all the secrets of the book, and then immediately died on his sofa. The soldier fell into a swoon.

When he recovered, the soldier left the pyramid, accompanied by Odous, who was now under his command, and took with him *The Black Pullet,* the ashes of the Turk, and piles of treasures. He sailed for Marseilles and settled in Provence, where he spent the rest of his days experimenting with the secrets of the book. He published the book and created a magic talisman that would afflict anyone who pirated it with ears six inches longer than Midas.

The talismans of *The Black Pullet* are, in more modern times, embroidered onto silk but are best engraved on SILVER or GOLD or on metals resembling them. They are sometimes used alone rather than in conjunction with the rings.

Once armed with the talismans and rings, the spirits can be commanded. The EVOCATION for Odous is: "Thomatos, Benesser, Flianter," which first summons 37 spirits. Address them by saying "Litan, Izer, Osnas," and they will bow down before you. Say "Nanther" as each one does. The command "Soutram Urbarsinens" will cause the spirits to transport you through the air wherever you wish to go, and they will return you home upon the command "Rabiam."

A major section of *The Black Pullet* tells how to procure a GOLD-FINDING HEN.

Red Dragon
Published in 1822 but reported to date back to 1522, this is nearly identical to the *Grand Grimoire.* Later editions of *Red Dragon* incorporated the instructions for the Gold-Finding Hen from *The Black Pullet.*

Transcendental Magic
This book comprises Eliphas Levi's own system of magic and was published in 1896. Waite called it a grimoire of "absolute science." Levi based his system on the *Key of Solomon,* adding his own views based upon his experiences in magic and alchemy.

The Book of Black Magic and of Pacts
Written in 1898 by Waite, the book discusses other grimoires and provides a "Complete Grimoire of Black Magic."

Waite draws upon and compares different grimoires in discussing rituals and the fundamentals of magic.

FURTHER READING:

Butler, E. M. *Ritual Magic.* Cambridge: Cambridge University Press, 1949.

Cavendish, Richard. *The Black Arts.* New York: G.P. Putnam's Sons, 1967.

Grillot de Givry, Emile. *Witchcraft, Magic and Alchemy.* 1931. Reprint, New York: Dover Publications, 1971.

Leitch, Aaron. *Secrets of the Magical Grimoires: The Classical Texts of Magick Deciphered.* St. Paul, Minn.: Llewellyn Publications, 2005.

Levi, Eliphas. *Transcendental Magic.* 1896. Reprint, York Beach, Maine: Samuel Weiser, 2001.

Mathers, S. L. MacGregor. *The Book of the Sacred Magic of Abra-Melin the Mage.* Wellingborough, England: The Aquarian Press, 1976.

Thompson, C. J. S. *The Mysteries and Secrets of Magic.* New York: Barnes & Noble, 1993.

Waite, Arthur Edward. *Alchemists Through the Ages.* Blauvelt, N.Y.: Rudolph Steiner Publications, 1970.

———. *The Book of Black Magic and of Pacts.* 1899. Reprint, York Beach, Maine: Samuel Weiser, 1972.

Wright, Elbee. *The Book of Magical Talismans/The Black Pullet.* Minneapolis: Marlar Publishing Co., 1984.

gris-gris In Vodoun, a special CHARM or AMULET to ward off bad luck, ill health, property loss, financial ruin, and any other misfortune. The origin of the word *gris-gris* is not certain, but may have evolved from *juju,* a West African term for FETISH. *Gris-gris* are also called *gri-gri.*

The original *gris-gris* were probably POPPETS or images of the gods. Most modern *gris-gris* are small cloth bags filled with herbs, oils, stones, small bones, HAIR AND NAIL CLIPPINGS, pieces of clothing soiled with perspiration, and/or other personal items, gathered under the direction of a particular god and designed to protect the owner.

A *gris-gris* is ritually made at an altar and consecrated with the four ELEMENTS of earth (salt), air (incense), water, and fire (a candle flame). The number of ingredients is always either one, three, five, seven, nine, or 13. Ingredients can never be an even number, nor more than 13. Stones and colored objects are selected for their occult and astrological properties, depending on the purpose of the *gris-gris.* Once made, they are buried on property, hung over doorways and onto doors, and even worn on the person.

Gris-gris also have other functions. They are TALISMANS to attract love, money, and other desired things, and they can be used to cause someone else ill luck, known as "putting a gris-gris" on a person.

hair and nail clippings Important ingredients in many magical SPELLS. Hair and nail clippings provide a personal, sympathetic link and are sometimes used in conjunction with BLOOD, URINE, SPITTLE, and feces in many kinds of spells, including BEWITCHMENT and NECROMANCY. The ancient Egyptians believed that a potion made of hair, nail clippings, and human blood would give a person absolute power over another.

Hair is associated with strength, and in folklore magical power is bound in hair. Shaking hair increases the power of a spell; cutting hair diminishes magical power. Pubic hair is considered an especially potent ingredient in love CHARMS. Nails have been associated with DEMONS, who can live under long nails and unkempt nails. For centuries practices have existed for the safe disposal of hair and nail clippings so that they cannot be used for magical purposes. Ideally, they should be buried, according to Zoroastrian lore from the mid-fifth century B.C.E. ALEISTER CROWLEY secretly disposed of his hair and nail clippings throughout his life so that others could not use them in magical spells against him. In Ozark lore, hair combings are buried, never thrown out. French peasants bury hair; Turks and Chileans stuff hair clippings into walls.

A bewitched victim's hair thrown into a fire supposedly projects the pain of the flames back onto the witch or sorcerer. In German lore, a small bag of smooth human hair placed on the stomach will tell someone if they have been bewitched. The answer is yes if the hair is tangled after three days. An old charm tells how to reverse a spell cast by a witch who has used a person's hair or nail clippings by using the urine of the person who is under bewitchment:

> To House the Hag, you must do this:
>
> > Commix with Meale a little Pisse
> > Of him bewitcht: then forthwith make
> > A little Wafer or a Cake;
> > And this rawly bak't will bring
> > The old Hag in. No surer thing.

FURTHER READING:
Ashley, Leonard R. N. *The Amazing World of Superstition, Prophecy, Luck, Magic & Witchcraft.* New York: Bell Publishing Company, 1988.
Guiley, Rosemary Ellen. *The Encyclopedia of Witches and Witchcraft.* 2d ed. New York: Facts On File Inc., 1999.

Hall, Manly Palmer (1901–1990) Philosopher, metaphysician, author, and founder of the PHILOSOPHICAL RESEARCH SOCIETY. Manly Palmer Hall was a prolific writer and lecturer and was renowned for his knowledge of esoteric wisdom. He is best known for his comprehensive work *The Secret Teachings of All Ages.*

Hall was born on March 18, 1901, in Peterborough, Ontario. His family moved to the United States in 1904, and he was raised by his maternal grandmother. An early interest in the occult, metaphysics, religion, and philosophy led Hall to join FREEMASONRY, ROSICRUCIANISM, the

THEOSOPHICAL SOCIETY, and the American Federation of Astrologers. He believed that all religious and philosophies point to a universal wisdom.

At age 20, Hall delivered his first public lecture, on reincarnation. His first publications were two booklets, *The Breastplate of the High Priest* and *Wands and Serpents,* both of which were later incorporated into a booklet, *Symbolic Essays.* His first books were *The Lost Keys of Freemasonry* and *The Ways of the Lonely Ones.*

In 1923 he moved to Los Angeles and became minister of a metaphysical church, the Church of the People. He began to publish a magazine, *The All-Seeing Eye.* During 1923 and 1924, he traveled throughout Egypt, Europe, and Asia, researching esoteric subjects. Material he collected became part of his eventual magnum opus, *An Encyclopedic Outline of Masonic, Hermetic, Qabalistic, and Rosicrucian Symbolical Philosophy,* published in 1928 and better known as *The Secret Teachings of All Ages.* It took Hall six years to write it and to raise $100,000 to have it published. The book is a monumental work, made all the more remarkable because of Hall's young age and lack of higher education. *Secret Teachings* remains a classic in esoteric literature.

In his preface to the 1975 Golden Anniversary Edition of the encyclopedia, Hall emphasized the importance of SYMBOLS as a means of communicating the great mysteries. Symbolism should be restored to world education, he said, noting that "symbols that help us to grow are precious things for they open the doors to life everlasting." The encyclopedia itself is "a symbol made up of many symbols gathered from rare sources," inviting the reader to arrive at his own intuitive understanding of their meanings.

In 1934 Hall founded the Philosophical Research Society in Los Angeles, which he envisioned as a center of esoteric studies for all of North America. He dedicated it "to the ensoulment of all arts, sciences, and crafts, and devoted to the one basic purpose of advancing the brotherhood of all that lives, to meet all lovers of wisdom on a common ground." He collected thousands of books and manuscripts for its library, including many rare works.

Hall wrote more than 200 books and hundreds of essays and articles on a wide range of esoteric topics. During the six decades of his career, he delivered 8,000 lectures. Among his other well-known books are *The Mystical Christ* and *Meditation Symbols in Eastern & Western Mysticism* (1988), his last work.

In 1990 Hall was recognized as a 33rd-degree Mason, the highest rank in the Scottish Rite. He died in Los Angeles on August 29, 1990.

FURTHER READING:

Hall, Manly P. *The Secret Teachings of All Ages.* 1928. Reprint, Los Angeles: The Philosophic Research Society, 1977.
"Manly P. Hall." Available online. URL: http://www/prs.org/mphbio.htm. Downloaded August 29, 2005.

Hamon, "Count" Louis   See CHEIRO.

hand of glory   In European MAGIC folklore, the severed and preserve hand of a criminal, used in SPELL casting. According to lore, the hand of glory renders people afraid and powerless and makes people fall into a deep sleep, thus enabling thieves to break into homes and steal their possessions and money.

The term *hand of glory* is believed to be derived either from the French *main de glorie* or *mandrogore,* or mandrake plant, which is associated with gallows. The hand was linked to WITCHCRAFT in trials of accused witches during the Inquisition. Belief in the hand persisted into the 19th century.

RITUALS in GRIMOIRES for making a hand of glory specify that the right hand of a murderer should be cut off during an eclipse of the MOON. Failing an eclipse—few and far between—one can chop off a murderer's hand on any night while the corpse still hangs on the gallows.

The hand is wrapped in a piece of the corpse's burial shroud and squeezed dry of BLOOD. It is then placed in an earthenware pot and pickled for two weeks in a mixture of saltpeter, salt, and peppers. The hand is wrapped in vervain and either dried in the August sun or baked in an oven. The dried hand is either dipped in wax so that the fingers can be burned as CANDLES, or else the hand is fitted with one or more candles placed between the fingers. The candles should be made out of the fat of the hanged man, of another executed murderer, or of a pony, along with sesame and virgin wax. The dead man's hair or the pony hair is used for the wick.

The hand of glory is burned to cast the sleeping spell. If the thumb does not light, it is a sign that someone in the house cannot be bewitched.

Magical lore holds that the only thing capable of extinguishing a lit hand of glory is milk. The 16th-century Dutch Jesuit demonologist Martin Del Rio wrote of the milk remedy in his study of witchcraft, *Disquisitionum magicarum libri VI* (1599). Del Rio told of a servant girl who discovered a thief breaking into her employer's home with a hand of glory. She tried to extinguish the candle with water and beer, which failed. Out of desperation, she tried milk, which put out the flame. The bewitched family immediately awoke and caught the thief.

The story probably is based on folk tales which tell of similar circumstances: a servant girl rescuing a household in danger from a thief armed with a hand of glory. In some versions of the tale the girl uses milk, and in others she blows out the candles herself.

A magical antidote to the hand of glory calls for smearing thresholds, chimneys, window sashes, and other potential places of entry with OINTMENTS made from the blood of screech owls, the fat of white hens, and the bile of black cats. The ointments would prevent anyone from bewitching occupants with a hand of glory.

The hand of glory is similar to other magic lights used by thieves in folklore. See RAVEN STONES; THIEVES' LIGHTS.

FURTHER READING:

Ashiman, D. L. (ed.) "The Hand of Glory and other gory legends about human hands." Available online. URL: http://www.pitt.edu/~dash/hand.html. Downloaded December 22, 2004.

Guiley, Rosemary Ellen. *Moonscapes: A Celebration of Lunar Astronomy, Magic, Legend and Lore.* New York: Macmillan, 1991.

"The Hand of Glory." Available online. URL: http://www.themystica.com/mystica/articles/h/hand_of_glory.html. Downloaded December 22, 2004.

"The Hand of Glory and Witchcraft." Available online. URL: http://www.shanmonster.com/witch/wards_tools/hand.html. Downloaded December 22, 2004.

Masello, Robert. *Raising Hell: A Concise History of the Black Arts—and Those Who Dared to Practice Them.* New York: Berkley Books, 1996.

hands   SYMBOLS of strength, authority, and power, a meaning perhaps dating to the ancient Egyptians, whose term for the hand also related to pillar and palm. In ALCHEMY, the right hand signifies the masculine principle and rational, conscious thought, and the left hand signifies the feminine principle and intuitive, unconscious thought. Thus clasped hands in alchemy symbolize the mystic marriage of opposites to create wholeness and also the communication between the conscious and unconscious.

heart   The seat of the soul, the seat of intelligence, and the locus of all emotion and of WILL.

In MAGIC, the heart is the seat of the emotions. Some CURSES against love, such as to break love or prevent love, involve sticking pins or thorns in the heart of a POPPET or in the heart of an animal, such as a sheep or pig.

In ALCHEMY, the heart is the SUN, or illumination, within a person. The heart also signifies mystical or spiritual love, the mystic center, and the temple of God.

Helmont, Jean Baptista van   See VAN HELMONT, JEAN BAPTISTA.

Helvetius, John Frederick Schweitzer (1625–1709)
Dutch court physician and alchemist who said he successfully transmuted LEAD into GOLD.

Helvetius was born John Frederick Schweitzer in 1625 in Kothen in the Duchy of Anhalt. He excelled in medicine and became the court physician to William of Orange.

By his own account, Helvetius was skeptical of MAGIC, and he exposed false medicines of the day that were reputed to have magical curative powers. He especially was critical of SIR KENELM DIGBY's "Sympathetic powder," which he termed a "gigantic hoax." But an encounter with a strange visitor caused him to reconsider his views and to plunge into an exploration of ALCHEMY in a quest for the PHILOSOPHER'S STONE.

According to Helvetius, on the morning of December 27, 1666, a man dressed like a Mennonite paid an unexpected visit to him at his residence in The Hague. The man identified himself as Elias, an artist and brass founder from North Holland. He appeared to be in his midforties. Elias quizzed Helvetius on his skepticism about magic, suggesting that surely there must be a universal medicine or ELIXIR such as claimed by ancient sages. Helvetius agreed that such a substance would be desirable but that he had never found any evidence

A heart bearing the fruit of life in the Ace of Vessels card in The Alchemical Tarot, *by Rosemary Ellen Guiley and Robert Michael Place. The fish is a messenger from the unconscious.* (Copyright by and courtesy of Robert Michael Place)

that a Philosopher's Stone ever existed, nor had he ever attempted the Great Work himself.

Helvetius wrote that Elias then

> . . . took from his bag an ivory box of cunning workmanship in which there were three large pieces of a substance resembling glass or pale sulphur and informed me that here was enough of the Tincture to produce twenty tons of gold.
>
> When I held the treasure in my hands for some fifteen minutes listening to an account of its curative properties, I was compelled to return it, not without a certain degree of reluctance. After thanking him for his kindness I asked why it was that his Tincture did not display that ruby color which I had been taught to regard as characteristic of the Philosophers' Stone. He replied that the color made no difference and that the substance was sufficiently mature for all practical purposes. He refused somewhat brusquely my request for a piece of his substance, were it no larger than a coriander seed, adding in a milder tone that he could not do so for all the wealth which I possessed; not indeed on account of its preciousness but for another reason that it was not lawful to divulge. Indeed, if fire could be destroyed by fire he would cast it rather into the flames. Then after a little consideration he asked whether I could not shew him into a room at the back of the house, where we should be less liable to observation. Having led him into the state parlor, he requested me to produce a gold coin, and while I was finding it he took from his breast pocket a green silk handkerchief wrapped about five medals, the gold of which was infinitely superior to that of my own money. Being filled with admiration, I asked my visitor how he had attained this most wonderful knowledge in the world, to which he replied that it was a gift bestowed upon him freely by a friend who had stayed a few days at his house, who had taught him also how to change common flints and crystals into stones more precious than rubies, chrysolites and sapphires.
>
> "He made known to me further," said the artist, "the preparation of crocus of iron, an infallible cure for dysentry; of a metallic liquor, which was an efficacious remedy for dropsy, and of other medicines."
>
> To this, however, I paid no great heed as I, Helvetius, was impatient to hear about the Great Secret of all.

According to Elias, his master instructed him in the drinking of this metallic liquor, giving him a glass of warm water to which white powder and an ounce of SILVER were added. The silver melted like ice. Drinking it, Elias discovered that it tasted like fresh milk and that its effect was "most exhilarating."

On further instructions from the master, Elias melted a piece of lead water pipe. The master cut off a bit of crystal and tossed it in. After exposing the compound to a fierce fire, the master poured out a great mass of liquid gold upon the floor of the kitchen. He gave one-sixteenth of the gold to Elias to keep and told him to distribute the rest to the poor. Elias gave a large sum of money in trust to the Church of Sparrendaur. The master taught Eliza the Divine Art and then left.

Elias refused to give Helvetius any of t[...] said that he would return in three weeks a[...] tius something that would open his eyes.

Helvetius had secretly collected fingerna[...] one crystal, and in the meantime he attem[...] mute molten lead into gold. He produced on[...] and had to wait for the return of Elias. Acc[...] vetius:

> He [Elias] returned punctually on the promi[...] invited me to a walk, in the course of whic[...] profoundly on the secrets of Nature in fir[...] noticed that my companion was exceedingly [...] the subject of the Great Secret. When I prayed him, however, to entrust me with a morsel of his precious Stone, were it no larger than a rape seed he delivered it like a princely donation. When I expressed a doubt whether it would be sufficient to tinge more than four grains of lead he eagerly demanded it back. I complied, hoping that he would exchange it for a larger fragment, instead of which he divided it with his thumb, threw half in the fire and returned the rest, saying "It is yet sufficient for you."

Helvetius revealed his failed experiment. Elias, amused at his theft of some of the crystal, said that he would have succeeded had he wrapped the crystal substance in yellow wax to protect it from the fumes of the lead. The philosopher's stone would have sunk to the bottom and transmuted into gold. This simplistic explanation sounded fraudulent to Helvetius.

The next day, January 19, Helvetius's wife urged him to try a projection. Working with her, he melted half an ounce of lead and dropped in the wax-covered crystal. The mixture hissed and glowed in iridescence, then turned brilliant green and then blood red as it cooled. Within 15 minutes, Helvetius had an ingot of "the best and finest gold." He wrote, "Yea, could I have enjoyed Argus's eyes, with a hundred more, I could not sufficiently gaze upon this so admirable and almost miraculous a work of nature."

Helvetius took the ingot to an assayer, who tested it and affirmed that it was "the most excellent gold in the whole world," and offered to buy it at 50 florins per ounce.

Word of Helvetius's achievement spread, and the next day he was visited by numerous illustrious persons and students who were curious to learn more. Even the Assayer-Master of the Mint came and tested the gold. Helvetius and others went to a silversmith, where Helvetius successfully transformed six drams and two scruples of lead and silver into "most pure gold."

Helvetius wrote that this experience convinced him of the wisdom of the sages and that there existed a spiritual alchemy as well. He said that "through metals and out of metals, purified by highly refined and spiritualized metals, there may be prepared the Living Gold and Quicksilver of the Sages, which bring both metals and human bodies to perfection."

In 1664, Helvetius was said to witness the projection of a pound of lead into part gold and part silver in The Hague by a silversmith named Gril. The silversmith used a tincture received from an alchemist, John Caspar Knoettner.

FURTHER READING:
Helvetius, John Frederick. *The Golden Calf, Which the World Adores and Desires: In which is handled The most Rare and Incomparable Wonder of Nature, in Transmuting Metals; viz. How the intire Substance of Lead, was in one Moment Transmuted into Gold-Obrizon, with an exceeding small particle of the true Philosophick Stone. At the Hague. In the year 1666. Written in Latin by John Frederick Helvetius, Doctor and Practitioner of Medicine at the Hague, and faithfully Englished.* London, 1670.
Holmyard, E. J. *Alchemy.* New York: Penguin Books, 1957.
Waite, Arthur Edward. *Alchemists Through the Ages.* Blauvelt, N.Y.: Rudolph Steiner Publications, 1970.

herbal magic   See MAGIC.

hermaphrodite   In ALCHEMY, the figure of a merged man and woman, symbolizing the conjunction or marriage of opposites. The hermaphrodite is also known by its Latin name, *rebis,* meaning "double thing." In Greek mythology, Hermaphrodite is an *androgyne* (man and woman) that was born to HERMES and Aphrodite.

Alchemical emblems represent the hermaphrodite as the product of the union of the king and the queen, representing SULPHUR and MERCURY, who merge in a BATH. Sol and Luna (SUN and MOON) also are representations of alchemical opposites. The hermaphrodite is the culmination of the Great Work: the PHILOSOPHER'S STONE. The hermaphrodite combines all the characteristics of the opposites, spirit and matter, soul and body, masculine and feminine. It is whole and perfect, complete unto itself, and able to reproduce itself. It is the "one in all" and the "all in one."

CARL G. JUNG said the alchemical symbol of the crowned hermaphrodite represents the self, which transcends ego consciousness.

Hermes   The Greek messenger god, known as Mercury in the Roman pantheon, represents wisdom, cunning, MAGIC, spiritual illumination, skill with words, and mischief. He is the initiator, the god of beginnings, and the god of travel, commerce, and sales. Wings on Hermes's feet and helmet sped him on his way as the communicator between the gods or between the gods and mortals. He is messenger to the gods in heaven and psychopomp of the souls of the dead to the underworld. His swift-footedness makes him the god of speed and running and of athletics.

Hermaphrodite on The Devil card in The Alchemical Tarot, by Rosemary Ellen Guiley and Robert Michael Place. The hexagram is another symbol of the unification of opposites. The fire-breathing dragon represents the devil, a symbol of the alchemical stage of coagulation. Inspired by Johann Daniel Mylius's Philosophia reformata, *1622. (Copyright by and courtesy of Robert Michael Place)*

Hermes is the gatekeeper, the patron of the traveler; his image often appeared at CROSSROADS in ancient times. As a god of healing, Hermes carries a CADUCEUS, the SERPENT-entwined staff that symbolizes the reconciliation of opposites and is associated with doctors and medicine; he uses it as his magic wand. He is clever, crafty, and sly—the trickster who deceives with eloquent words. He is a consort of Aphrodite, goddess of love, with whom he unites to form the hermaphrodite of ALCHEMY. Wily and playful, he delights in his role as Trickster, bedeviling mortals and immortals alike. The son of Zeus and Maia, one of Atlas's daughters, Hermes is a thief, a scoundrel, a guide, and a magician.

To protect homes and to ensure that Hermes facilitates access to the other gods, households placed small figurines

Hermes as The Magician card in The Alchemical Tarot, *by Rosemary Ellen Guiley and Robert Michael Place. Hermes is the alchemical prima material. Inspired by Altus's* Mutus Liber, *1677.* (Copyright by and courtesy of Robert Michael Place)

the underworld as well, acting as the recorder of divine judgments on the souls of the deceased. Besides clerking, Thoth sometimes weighs the souls of the dead himself (a job usually performed by Anubis) in a giant scale that is counterbalanced by a feather of Truth from the goddess Maat, sister to Queen ISIS. If the soul, heavy from sin and degradation, sinks lower than the feather, it is immediately fed to a slathering monster named Ammit, who waits impatiently under the scales.

Hermes and Thoth together comprise aspects of the legendary HERMES TRISMEGISTUS, or "thrice-greatest Hermes," the greatest of all philosophers, kings, and priests.

FURTHER READING:
Guiley, Rosemary Ellen. *The Encyclopedia of Witches and Witchcraft.* 2d ed. New York: Facts On File Inc., 1999.
"Thoth: Egyptian Moon God." Available online at http://osiris.colorado.edu/LAB/GODS/throth.html. Downloaded August 18, 2004.

Hermes Trismegistus   Legendary figure who is the author of the EMERALD TABLET, the foundation of Western MAGIC and esoteric tradition. Hermes Trismegistus is a composite of the Greek god HERMES and the Egyptian god THOTH.

The Greeks who settled in Egypt identified Thoth and Hermes with one another. Thoth ruled mystical wisdom, magic, writing, and other disciplines and was associated with healing. Hermes was the personification of universal wisdom and patron of magic; a swift, wing-footed messenger, he carried a magic wand, the CADUCEUS. Both were associated with the spirits of the dead: Thoth weighed their souls in the Judgment Hall of OSIRIS; Hermes escorted shades to Hades. Both were credited with writing the sacred books of science, healing, philosophy, magic, and law and revealing the wisdom to mankind.

Thrice greatest refers to Hermes Trismegistus as the greatest of all philosophers, the greatest of all kings, and the greatest of all priests. The legend that developed around him held him to be a mythical king who reigned for 3,226 years. He carried an emerald, upon which was recorded all of philosophy, and the caduceus, the symbol of mystical illumination. He vanquished Typhon, the dragon of ignorance and mental, moral, and physical perversion. He is credited with writing 36,525 books on the Principles of Nature. Iamblichus reported the number at 20,000, and Clement of Alexandria at 42.

The biblical prophet Enoch is identified with Hermes Trismegistus.

representing Hermes, called herms, throughout the house and grounds. As communicator, messenger, and jester to the gods, Hermes shares characteristics with gods of other traditions. The Hellenistic Greeks and Romans associated Hermes most closely with THOTH, the ibis-headed god of wisdom, magic, music, medicine, surveying, drawing, and writing. Hermes, too, loved music; to apologize to Apollo for stealing his prized heifers, Hermes created the lyre as a present for the god. Hermes also closely resembles the TRICKSTER GODS of West Africa, the *Eshus,* and the animal deities of Native American peoples.

Thoth's association with drawing and writing corresponds with Hermes's role as a bringer of language. Some myths claimed that Hermes invented the alphabet. Both gods function as arbitrators in disputes between the gods or between the deities and humankind. Thoth works in

Hermetica   The spiritual wisdom that, along with the KABBALAH, forms the foundation of the Western esoteric tradition, including MAGIC and ALCHEMY. The Hermetica are early writings that were attributed to the Egyptian sage HERMES TRISMEGISTUS. Some are short treatises, and others

Ideal portrait of Hermes Trismegistus, in De Divinatione et Magicis, *by Jacques Boissard.* (Author's collection)

are collections of aphorisms that are meant to be learned and put into practice. The most famous Hermetic work is the EMERALD TABLET.

Most Hermetic writings were done during the first four centuries after Christ; some were written even later. They are a syncretism of Hellenistic and Judeo-Christian thought. Hermetism is not a philosophy or teaching but a way to spiritual progress. Humanity is created by God like God and lives under the aegis of Nature. Destinies are ruled by the heavenly bodies; the microcosm, or Earth, is a reflection of the macrocosm, or heaven. Through the spiritual path, a human can know God and thus himself or herself and realize his or her immortal nature. This is accomplished by developing three faculties:

- *Gnosis,* or knowledge, which is a spiritual awakening to the realization that God wants to be known;
- *Logos,* or reasonable speech, which is education on the structure and nature of creation;
- *Nous,* or mind, which is enlightenment achieved through the development of intuition, IMAGINATION, and mystical INITIATION.

According to lore, Hermes Trismegistus is credited with the writings of 36,525 books on the Principles of Nature. Iamblichus reported the number at 20,000, and Clement of Alexandria at 42. Most were said to have been lost in the destruction of the library at Alexandria where they were housed. Legend says that surviving texts were buried in the desert by initiates.

Key Hermetic texts, known as the CORPUS HERMETI-CUM, were rediscovered in 1461 and were translated and published throughout Europe to an enthusiastic audience of scholars and scientists. They fell into disrepute in the 17th century but regained significance in the 20th century, especially with the discovery of the Nag Hammadi literature in Egypt in 1945.

Hermetic Order of the Golden Dawn The most influential secret society in the Western magical tradition. Though short-lived in the last years of the 19th century, its teachings, RITUALS, and organization continue to influence the practice of ceremonial MAGIC, a path of enlightenment.

During its height, the Hermetic Order of the Golden Dawn possessed the greatest repository of Western magical knowledge—despite the fact that its original intent was not to be a magical lodge. The key purpose of the order was "to prosecute the Great Work: which is to obtain control of the nature and power of my own being." Some of the texts included Christian elements, such as the establishing of a closer relationship with Jesus, the "Master of Masters." Members circulated various Catholic and Anglican writings and sermons. These were omitted from the materials eventually published by ISRAEL REGARDIE. Elements of Golden Dawn rituals, ROSICRUCIANISM, and FREE-MASONRY have been absorbed into the rituals of modern WITCHCRAFT.

History
The history of the Hermetic Order of the Golden Dawn—usually known simply as the Golden Dawn—is colorful and explosive and involves some of the most esteemed occultists of the time. It was formed in England during a renaissance of interest in magic that began in the early 19th century and picked up steam with the advent of Spiritualism, Theosophy, and the New Thought movement. This renaissance built on a foundation already established by ALCHEMY, the occult arts, Freemasonry, Rosicrucianism, the KABBALAH, and other secret societies.

The original intent of the Golden Dawn founders was to have a secret society that would instruct a small number of initiates and ADEPTS in a complete course of training for spiritual growth. Three principal figures were all both Rosicrucians and Freemasons: WILLIAM WYNN WESTCOTT, a London coroner; SAMUEL LIDDELL MacGREGOR MATHERS, an occultist and author; and WILLIAM ROBERT WOODMAN, a retired physician and horticulturist who was Supreme Magus of the Rosicrucian Society of Anglia. Woodman also brought a strong interest in and knowledge of the kabbalah, which he had introduced to Rosicrucian studies. Westcott conceived the idea for the Golden Dawn and invited Woodman and Mathers to cofound it with him. Woodman was old enough to be the "gentleman" of the society and lend it an air of Victorian respectability.

Traditionally, secret societies have a legacy linking them to older or ancient groups or teachings, thus demonstrating an inherited stream of esoteric knowledge and a link to an established authority. It can only be presumed that Westcott felt a need to produce the same, knowing that serious kabbalists, Rosicrucians, and Masons would not otherwise be attracted to the new organization. He fabricated a legacy: the Cipher Manuscript, a mysterious document that served as the basis for Golden Dawn rituals and teachings.

Westcott's story was that in 1887 he acquired part of an apparently old manuscript written in brown ink cipher that contained fragments of rituals. Westcott said that thanks to his Hermetic knowledge, he was able to decipher the manuscript. He discovered that it concerned fragments of rituals for the "Golden Dawn," an unknown organization that apparently admitted both men and women. Inserted in the manuscript was another document, also written in cipher, that provided the name, the address, and credentials of a woman in Germany, "Fraulein Sprengel" (Anna Sprengel) whose MAGICAL MOTTO was *Soror Sapiens Dominabitur Astris,* or "the wise person shall be ruled by the stars." Westcott said he wrote to Sprengel and was informed that she was an adept of an occult order called *Die Goldene Dämmerung,* or The Golden Dawn. Westcott said that Sprengel authorized him to set up a new temple of the order in England and to sign her name to any documents. Thus in the spring of 1888 Westcott created a Charter of Warrant for the Isis-Urania Temple No. 3 of the Order of the Golden Dawn in London, with himself, Mathers, and Woodman as the three Chiefs.

The true authorship of the Cipher Manuscript has never been disclosed. Westcott is believed by many to be the author. Other candidates put forward are Lord Edward Bulwer-Lytton, who wrote the occult novel *Zanoni, A Strange Story;* Frederick Hockley, a Rosicrucian who transcribed old manuscripts; and Kenneth Mackenzie, a Rosicrucian and Freemason and author of *The Royal Masonic Encyclopedia.* A good case can be made for Mackenzie, who knew ELIPHAS LEVI and another high-grade Mason, Frederick Holland. Holland founded the occult Society of Eight in 1883, and Mackenzie wrote the ritual outlines of the Cipher Manuscript for it. After Mackenzie's death, Westcott acquired the manuscript.

Westcott probably wrote the additional document about Sprengel and their correspondence himself as a means to obtain an "official" charter. The magical motto that he claimed was hers actually belonged to Anna Kingsford, a Theosophist and the founder of the Hermetic Society, who died in 1888. The Hermetic Society was formed in 1885 in London to promote Western esoteric teachings, and Westcott and Mathers had lectured to its members. Perhaps it was there that Westcott conceived the idea for his own secret society.

With the establishment of the Isis-Urania Temple No. 3, Westcott asked Mathers to flesh out the fragments of the Cipher Manuscript into full-scale rituals. The secret society quickly caught on. By the end of 1888, the temple had 32 members, nine of whom were women. Three more temples were established: Osiris Temple No. 4 in Weston-super-Mare; Horus Temple No. 5 in Bradford; and Amen-Ra Temple No. 6 in Edinburgh.

Membership continued to grow rapidly. Woodman died in 1891 before the order reached its peak. From 1888 to 1896, 315 INITIATIONS took place.

From 1888 to 1891, the order taught Outer Order theoretical magic. One advanced through the ranks of the Outer Order by examination. Initially, Westcott, Mathers, and Woodman were the only members of the Second Order, and they claimed to be under the direction of the SECRET CHIEFS of the Third Order, who were beings that manifested only on the ASTRAL PLANE. Mathers's rituals were based largely on Freemasonry.

After Woodman's death, Mathers became the primary Chief and created an initiation ritual based on the legend of Christian Rosenkreutz for a fully functional Second Order that was open by examination and invitation. He renamed the Second Order the *Ordo Rosae Rubeae et Aureae Crucis,* or the Order of the Rose of Ruby and Cross of Gold (R.R. et A.C.). In the initiation ritual, Christian Rosenkreutz symbolized the buried, sleeping Higher Self. The ritual required an impressive reconstructed tomb, a circular altar, and a coffin containing the preserved body of Rosenkreutz.

Mathers revised the curriculum and added practical magic. Initiates into R.R. et A.C. were required to make their own magical TOOLS: a Rose Croix lamen, a magical sword, and a lotus wand, plus tools that corresponded to the ELEMENTS—a dagger (air), a pentacle (earth), a cup (water), and a wand (fire). The dagger-and-wand associations were said to be reversed in a blind to foil noninitiates. Second Order studies centered on the kabbalistic Tree of Life. Three magical systems were taught: the *Key of Solomon* (see GRIMOIRES); Abra-Melin magic (see ABRA-MELIN THE MAGE); and ENOCHIAN MAGIC. Materials also were incorporated from the Egyptian *Book of the Dead,* William Blake's Prophetic Books, and the CHALDEAN ORACLES, fragmentary ancient texts. Instruction was given in ASTRAL TRAVEL, SCRYING, ALCHEMY, GEOMANCY, the TAROT, and ASTROLOGY.

However, Mathers's curriculum was so rigorous that few people could ever complete it.

As the Golden Dawn was rising, Mathers's own fortunes were in eclipse. Near penniless, he and his wife, Moina, also a Golden Dawn member, were forced to rely on the benefaction of ANNIE HORNIMAN, a wealthy member who gave support to several Golden Dawners. In 1892 the Matherses moved to Paris, ostensibly to set up a lodge there, but in actuality they could no longer afford to live in London.

Horniman expected Mathers to devote himself fully to the Golden Dawn, but instead he spent most of his time translating occult manuscripts and pursuing Celtic politics. In 1896 Horniman cut off her financial support. To shore up his failing hold on authority, Mathers claimed that the Secret Chiefs had initiated him into the Third Order, and he demanded complete obedience from all adepts in the First and Second Orders and also from Horniman. When she refused and disputed his claim, he expelled her, upsetting many members. The Golden Dawn had reached its peak.

In 1897 Westcott resigned from both the First and the Second Orders. Possibly members began to discover the truth about the fallacious legacy of the Golden Dawn, but more likely he resigned due to threats from Mathers to expose him. Westcott was succeeded by FLORENCE FARR. Irreparable schisms formed within the Golden Dawn.

By 1900 Farr had grown weary of dealing with Mathers and suggested to him that the entire Golden Dawn be dissolved. Thinking that she was really plotting to bring back Westcott, Mathers revealed to Farr that the letters to Sprengel were falsified by Westcott. The disclosure rocked the membership. Even more unsettling, Westcott declined to comment when confronted.

More trouble came from ALEISTER CROWLEY, who had been initiated in 1898 and had risen rapidly up the ranks. In 1899 he went to Paris and insisted on being initiated into the Second Order. Mathers complied. The London lodge, under Farr, rejected his initiation. In 1900 Mathers declared the Second Order to be nullified and sent Crowley back to England as his "Envoy Extraordinary" to take control of the quarters of the Second Order. Crowley appeared wearing a black mask, Highland dress, and a gilt dagger. He staged a dramatic attempt but was rebuffed.

The Crowley-Mathers alliance was an uneasy one. Crowley considered himself a superior magician to Mathers. Supposedly, the two engaged in magical warfare. Mathers sent an astral VAMPIRE in a PSYCHIC ATTACK on Crowley, who responded with an army of DEMONS led by Beelzebub. After the fiasco by Crowley on the Second Order quarters, the London lodge expelled both Crowley and Mathers. Crowley planned revenge by publishing the Golden Dawn's secret rituals. In 1910 Mathers went to court and successfully obtained an order to prevent Crowley from doing so. Crowley appealed and used magic to win a reversal of the order. He used a TALISMAN that had been taken from Mather's translation of *The Sacred Magic of Abramelin:*

ALMANAH
L
MARE
AALBEHA
N

AREHAIL
HA

Following his court victory, Crowley retaliated by publishing some of the Golden Dawn's secret rituals in his magazine, *The Equinox.*

WILLIAM BUTLER YEATS took over the Second Order. He attempted to restore unity by restructuring the order, but the Golden Dawn broke into independent groups. Farr and others even had a secret group going, with the tacit consent of Yeats. By 1901 Yeats gave up trying to hold the Golden Dawn together and resigned.

Followers of Mathers formed the Alpha et Omega Temple. In 1903 ARTHUR EDWARD WAITE and others left, forming a group with the name Golden Dawn but with more of an emphasis on mysticism than magic. In 1905 another splinter group was formed, the Stella Matutina, or "Order of the Companions of the Rising Light in the Morning." The Isis-Urania Temple No. 3 became defunct. In 1917 it was resurrected as the Merlin Temple of the Stella Matutina. The Stella Matutina went into decline in the 1940s, following the publication of its secret rituals by a former member, Israel Regardie, Crowley's one-time secretary.

Waite's group, which retained the Golden Dawn name and some of its rituals, declined after 1915 with Waite's departure. Some distant offshoots of the Golden Dawn continue in existence. Golden Dawn rituals and teachings continue to be widely used and adapted.

Organization

The Golden Dawn's hierarchy of three orders is organized around the Tree of Life of the kabbalah: 10 degrees correspond to the 10 *sephiroth*, plus an 11th degree for neophytes. The degrees are:

OUTER ORDER	
Neophyte	0 = 0
Zelator	1 = 10
Theoricus	2 = 9
Practicus	3 = 8
Philosophus	4 = 7

SECOND ORDER	
Adeptus Minor	5 = 6
Adeptus Major	6 = 5
Adeptus Exemptus	7 = 4

THIRD ORDER

Magister	8 = 3
Magus	9 = 2
Ipsissimus	10 = 1

In the column to the right, the numbers on the left signify the number of initiations symbolically taken on the Tree to attain the grade, and the second numbers signify the *sephirah* represented by that grade.

The Outer Order is governed by three Greatly Honored Chiefs of the Second Order, who assume godforms of Egyptian deities and act as the inner planes contacts with the nonphysical Third Order. Each temple also has its own Temple Chief, who answers to the Greatly Honored Chiefs. In addition, there are other officers who perform specific duties.

The Golden Dawn has three degrees, which are not the same as the three orders, and they do not overlap with the *sephiroth* of the Tree of Life. The First Degree is the entire Outer Order, and represents the stage of purification, in which the student dedicates himself or herself to the Hermetic path and undergoes the initiations of the psychic four elements. The Neophyte chooses the magical motto that will set the stage for his or her magical career. The Second Degree is the Portal grade, a probationary stage between the First Order and Second Order that focuses on consecration and charging of the purified psychic elements. The Third Degree is the entire Second Order and represents union, in which the initiate prepares for initial contact with the Higher Self. These three degrees occur repeatedly and cyclically in magical integration.

FURTHER READING:

Cicero, Chic, and Sandra Tabatha Cicero. *The Essential Golden Dawn.* St. Paul, Minn.: Llewellyn Publications, 2004.

Howe, Ellic. *Magicians of the Golden Dawn: A Documentary History of a Magical Order 1887–1923.* York Beach, Maine: Red Wheel/Weiser, 1978.

Gilbert, R. A. *The Golden Dawn: Twilight of the Magicians.* San Bernardino, Calif.: Borgo Press, 1963.

Regardie, Israel. *The Golden Dawn.* 6th ed. St. Paul, Minn.: Llewellyn Publications, 2003.

hex   A SPELL or BEWITCHMENT, usually of a negative nature. The term *hex* comes from Pennsylvania Dutch folklore and is derived from the German word *hexe,* which means "witch."

In Pennsylvania Dutch folk MAGIC, a hex can be either good or bad. Ideally it is cast by a professional witch whose services are sought out and paid for with a "voluntary" contribution. Witches also are consulted to break and protect against hexes.

A "hex death" is magically induced death from a CURSE, or from breaking a TABOO.

In Vodoun, a *ranger* is a secret RITUAL for casting evil hexes intended to bring about great misfortune and death.

See also WANGA.

hexagram   Six-pointed star comprised of two intersecting triangles. The hexagram represents the union of opposites: fire and water; masculine and feminine; heaven and earth; light and dark; the macrocosm and the microcosm. Hexagrams are sometimes called the Star of David.

The hexagram also represents the perfected human being, and the penetration of human's higher nature and lower nature. In MAGIC, hexagrams are used to invoke and banish planetary and sephirotic forces. Hexagrams are traced in the air with a RITUAL tool such as a dagger. They are used in the creation of MAGIC CIRCLES, SIGILS, and SEALS.

ALEISTER CROWLEY developed a unicursal hexagram that can be traced in the air without making a break.

See also SEAL OF SOLOMON.

Holy Guardian Angel   Presence invoked in MAGIC, especially in the BORNLESS RITUAL. The Holy Guardian Angel is not an independent ANGEL but the Higher Self of the magician. It is the equivalent of the HERMETIC ORDER OF THE GOLDEN DAWN's concept of the Higher and Divine Genius, the Gnostic concept of Logos, and the THEOSOPHICAL SOCIETY's concept of the Higher Self.

The Holy Guardian Angel is the mediator between the aspirant and the Unknown Glory. It takes a form recognizable as the Holy Guardian Angel to each person, but it is also different in that it is shaped according to the contents of the unconscious. Hence, no two practitioners of the Bornless Ritual experience the Holy Guardian Angel in exactly the same way.

The Holy Guardian Angel is derived from *The Book of Sacred Magic of Abra-malin the Mage,* which was translated from French by SAMUEL LIDDELL MacGREGOR MATHERS of the Golden Dawn.

ALEISTER CROWLEY considered the Holy Guardian Angel to be an entity in its own right and not just an aspect of a magician's mind. He stated in a letter, written toward the end of his life, that:

> . . . the Angel is an actual individual, with his own Universe, exactly as a man is; or, for the matter of that, a bluebottle. He is not a mere abstraction, a selection from, an exaltation of, one's own favorite qualities. . . . He is something more than a man, possibly a being who has already passed through the stage of humanity, and his peculiarly intimate relations with his client is that of friendship, of community, of brotherhood or fatherhood.

See also AIWASS.

FURTHER READING:

King, Francis. *Megatherion: The Magickal World of Aleister Crowley.* New York: Creation Books, 2004.

Regardie, Israel. *Ceremonial Magic: A Guide to the Mechanisms of Ritual.* London: Aeon Books, 2004.

homunculus An artificial human created by MAGIC. A homunculus does the bidding of its creator.

A homunculus can be created as an astral THOUGHT-FORM in a RITUAL using a POPPET made of clay or wax. It is given physical features and the ability to speak. Such thought-forms usually have a temporary life span. However, according to magical lore, homunculi can be dangerous because they can go out of control and may not cease to exist when ordered to do so.

See also ALBERTUS MAGNUS; ASTRAL GUARDIAN; AQUINAS, THOMAS; GOLEM.

FURTHER READING:

Ashcroft–Nowicki, Dolores, and J. H. Brennan. *Magical Use of Thought Form: A Proven System of Mental and Spiritual Empowerment.* St. Paul, Minn.: Llewellyn Publications, 2001.

Horniman, Annie (1860–1937) Wealthy tea heiress, dramatist, and member of the HERMETIC ORDER OF THE GOLDEN DAWN.

Annie Horniman was born on October 3, 1860, in Forest Hill, England, to a Congregationalist family and was raised in Surrey. Her father served in Parliament. Her grandfather, a Quaker, was a tea merchant who invented the tea bag and made a fortune.

Horniman entered art school in 1882, and met MOINA MATHERS (then Mina Bergson); they became close friends. Mina married SAMUEL LIDDELL MacGREGOR MATHERS, and the two introduced Horniman to the Golden Dawn. Horniman was initiated in 1890 and took the MAGICAL MOTTO *Fortiter et Recte,* "Bravely and justly." Advancing quickly, in 1891 she became the first person to be initiated into the Second Order. In 1893 she became sub-Praemonstratrix under FLORENCE FARR.

Horniman received her inheritance in 1893, and she became benefactor to Golden Dawners. She helped Farr and WILLIAM BUTLER YEATS produce plays, and she supported the perpetually penniless Matherses. She secured for Mathers a job as curator of the Horniman Museum, and she financed their move to Paris in 1892. In 1896 she took a stand against member Dr. Edward Berridge, who championed the sexual theories of an American commune leader, Thomas Lake Harris. Horniman felt the theories were immoral. Mathers disgareed, and Horniman, angered, resigned as sub-Praemonstratrix. She also became dissatisfied with the amount of time Mathers was spending on Golden Dawn affairs; she expected more of him in exchange for her patronage. She cut off her support and in 1903 made a final break with Mathers. In return he had her expelled from the order.

Horniman returned to the theater world. In 1921 she joined the Quest Society, formed by Theosophist George R. S. Mead. She died on August 6, 1937.

FURTHER READING:

Greer, Mary K. *Women of the Golden Dawn: Rebels and Priestesses.* Rochester, Vt.: Inner Traditions, 1995.

horse Important sacred animal associated with fertility, MAGIC, CLAIRVOYANCE, and OMENS.

In Britain and throughout Europe, the eating of horse flesh was taboo, except during an October horse feast. In ancient Rome, the feast was begun on October 15 with a chariot race on the Field of Mars; the right-hand horse of the winning chariot was killed as a sacrifice to the god by being stabbed to death with a spear. The head was severed, decorated with a string of loaves, and fought over by two wards in a RITUAL battle to determine which side would get the head as a TALISMAN. The tail was severed and taken to the king's hearth where the BLOOD was dripped on the hearth. The rest of the blood was preserved and, the following spring, mixed with other blood by the Vestals and given to shepherds to be burned as a purifying agent for their flocks. The entire festival was a fertility rite to ensure good crops, with the horse representative of the corn spirit. In Denmark, the October horse feast was marked by the sprinkling of horse's blood toward the east and the south by a priest, in observance of the incarnation of the horse as Spirit of the Solar Year. The feast was banned in the Middle Ages by the church.

The horse as corn spirit appears in other pagan crop fertility rites. In Hertsfordshire, England, the reaping of crops was ended with a ceremony called crying the Mare. The last blades of standing corn were tied together as the Mare. The farmers threw their sickles at it, and the one who succeeded in cutting through it won blessings.

The Gallic Celts worshiped the Greek fertility goddess, Demeter, as the Mare Goddess under the name *Epona,* or *the Three Eponae,* associated with the Triple Goddess. Epona was adopted by the Roman army, which considered her the protector of horses; the goddess enjoyed a widespread cult throughout Europe. A cult which survived in Ireland until the 12th century performed a ritual in which a petty king undergoes a symbolic rebirth from a white mare. He imitated a foal by crawling toward the mare naked and on all fours. The mare was slaughtered, cut into pieces, and boiled in a cauldron. The king got into the cauldron and ate the pieces and broth. Then he stood on an inauguration stone and received a stright white wand, which he held while turning three times left and three times right in honor of the Trinity.

Other Greek deities with horse aspects include Athena, Aphrodite, and Cronus.

Poseidon, Greek god of the sea, whipped horses out of the waves, symbolizing the blind, primeval forces of chaos. The horse is associated with the burial rites of ancient chthonian cults. It was dedicated to Mars, god of war; an unexpected appearance of a horse was an omen of war. The horse also is linked to thunder, which it creates with its hooves.

The Celts believed that their souls traveled on horseback to the land of the dead.

Dreams of horses, especially white, are universal omens of good luck.

CARL G. JUNG believed horses represented the magical, intuitive side of humankind. Throughout history, horses have been believed to possess a clairvoyant power that enables them to sense unseen danger. Consequently, they have been considered especially vulnerable to BEWITCHMENT. According to lore, witches borrowed them at night to ride to sabbats, driving them hard and returning them at daybreak exhausted and covered with sweat and foam. To prevent "hag riding," bewitchment and the EVIL EYE, horse owners placed CHARMS and AMULETS in their stables and attached brass bells to halters. During the witch hunts of the Inquisition, the devil and witches were believed to have the power to shapeshift into horses (see SHAPESHIFTING).

ibn Sina (980–1037) Persian philosopher and physician who argued against the possibility of transmutation in ALCHEMY. Born Abu Ali al-Husain ibn 'Abdallah ibn Sina, he was known by his Latinized name, Avicenna, for centuries. He is one of the most important of Islamic philosophers. He enjoyed royal patronage that earned him the title "Prince of Physicians."

Ibn Sina was born in Kharmaithen near Bukhara (Bokhara), now part of Uzbekistan. His father was a village governor for the sultan of Bukhara. Ibn Sina was a quick student and at a young age was tutored in the Koran, poetry, Aristotlean and neo-Platonic philosophies, metaphysics, and logic. By age 13 he was studying medicine, and by age 16 he was doing charitable medical work with the sick. At age 17 he demonstrated his medical skill by curing the sultan of a serious colic illness that the sultan's own physicians were unable to treat. In exchange for the service, ibn Sina was given access to the sultan's royal library.

Seven years later the sultan was defeated by invading Turks, and ibn Sina's father died. With his royal patronage gone, he wandered from place to place, working as a physician and writing. He also indulged his passions for wine and women.

In Hamadan (now in Iran) the prince made ibn Sina court physician and appointed him twice as vizier. He was not an astute politician, and his enemies had him jailed as a political prisoner. He escaped prison disguised as a Sufi.

In 1022 ibn Sina again lost his royal patronage with the death of the prince, and he left Hamadan and joined the royal court in Isfahan as the prince's physician. He completed his major works and wrote additional ones. While accompanying the prince on a military march to Hamadan, he was stricken with colic and died, despite his attempts to minister to himself. According to some sources, he may have been poisoned by a servant. On his deathbed he repented his licentious ways, freed his slaves, and gave all his belongings to the poor.

Ibn Sina is credited with authoring more than 450 works, of which about 240 have survived. Of those, 150 are on philosophy, and 40 are on medicine, the two topics on which he wrote most frequently. His greatest works are *Qanun fi al-Tibb* (*Canon of Medicine*), an encyclopedic text that influenced medicine for centuries, and *Kitab al-Shifa*, an encyclopedic work on philosophy, science, metaphysics, and Muslim theology. He also composed works on alchemy, philosophy, theology, philology, astronomy, MUSIC, physics, and mathematics. In medicine and pharmacology especially, he was ahead of his time.

Ibn Sina acknowledged being a student of an alchemical ADEPT known only as Jacob the Jew, a man of "penetrating mind," he said. Jacob the Jew impressed upon him the desirability of understanding philosophies outside of one's own religion and of following the moral precepts found in the Ten Commandments and other religious doctrines.

Ibn Sina's comments on alchemy are in his *Book of the Remedy*, written while he was still in Hamadan, probably in about 1021. In medieval times it was translated into Latin as *De Mineralis* ("On Minerals") and was even attributed to the authorship of Aristotle.

His most important alchemical work is *Tractatulus Alchimia* ("Treatise on Alchemy"). Like JABIR IBN HAYYAN, ibn Sina believed that all metals are produced by combinations of SULPHUR and MERCURY in varying grades of purity. Mercury is the grand ELIXIR. The *PRIMA MATERIA* has spiritual powers far beyond nature.

However, he said that alchemists cannot truly change metals or their inherent natures, but they can produce imitations; for example, they can whiten a red metal so that it resembles SILVER, or they can tint it so that it resembles GOLD. Such imitations might fool even the shrewdest expert, ibn Sina said. His dismissal of alchemy received little support at the time, for the alchemists of his day either believed in literal transmutation or at least in the theoretical possibility of it.

Ibn Sina is cited as an authoritative source for some of the material found in various GRIMOIRES, handbooks of MAGIC.

FURTHER READING:

Holmyard, E. J. *Alchemy.* New York: Penguin Books, 1957.

Morewedge, Parvis. *The Mystical Philosophy of Avicenna.* Binghamton, N.Y.: Global Publications at SUNY Binghamton University, 2001.

Patai, Raphael. *The Jewish Alchemists.* Princeton, N.J.: Princeton University Press, 1994.

Waite, Arthur Edward. *Alchemists Through the Ages.* Blauvelt, N.Y.: Rudolph Steiner Publications, 1970.

I Ching (Yijing)   An ancient system of Chinese wisdom, often consulted for oracular DIVINATION. The *I Ching,* which means "Book of Changes," consists of 64 hexagrams of solid and broken lines. A hexagram is determined by the tossing three times of three coins or 50 yarrow sticks. Each hexagram has a meaning, which must be interpreted.

The *I Ching* expresses an entire philosophy based upon the concept of a unified and cyclical universe, in which the future develops according to fixed laws and NUMBERS. There is no "coincidence" or "chance" but causality, CARL G. JUNG's concept of synchronicity. The toss of the coins or sticks creates a synchronous event with the search for guidance. The *I Ching* shows what is possible when the mature "Superior Man" is in harmony with the flow of yin-and-yang energy. Its symbols reveal a high moral, social, and political code.

The *I Ching* does not give definitive answers but forces the inquirer to look within for answers. It reflects a moment in time and shows probable outcomes if various alternatives are undertaken. As a teacher, it instructs the pupil in how the Superior Man would respond to situations. Like the TAROT, the *I Ching* requires intuitive thought and an awareness of the flow and flux of energy throughout the universe.

The foundation of the *I Ching* dates back thousands of years in Chinese history, the evolutionary product of thought that pondered humankind's relationship to the tai chi, the Universal Principle. The hexagrams are composed of two trigrams that according to tradition, were developed by Emperor Fu-hsi (Fuxi) in about 2852 B.C.E. The solid lines represents the yang, or male/active/creative energy, and the broken lines represent the yin or female/passive/ receptive energy. Initially, Fu-hsi developed eight trigrams which represented the eight components of the universe: heaven, earth, thunder, water, mountain, wood and wind, fire, and marsh and lake.

The trigrams were doubled into 64 hexagrams in about 1143 B.C.E. by King Wen, a founder of the Chou (Zhou) dynasty. Wen organized the hexagrams and gave a name and a summary text of attributes and advice to each one. A commentary on the symbolism and meaning of the lines was added by the king's son, the duke of Chou.

The *I Ching* inspired Lao Tzu (Laozi; 604–531 B.C.E.), who drew upon it in the writing of *Tao te Ching,* the central text of Taoism. Confucius (c. 551–c. 479) also was inspired by it in his later years and added 10 commentaries, now called the Ten Wings appendices.

The *I Ching* did not reach the West until the 19th century when it was translated by James Legge and Richard Wilhelm. Wilhelm's translation—first into German and then into English—includes a foreword by Jung, who saw the *I Ching* as a way to tap into the collective unconscious through meditation upon the SYMBOLS.

The hexagrams are used in magical work as doorways for ASTRAL PROJECTION.

See also GEOMANCY; MAGIC SQUARE.

FURTHER READING:

Legge, James (trans.). *The I Ching.* New York: Dover Publications, 1963.

Lowe, Michael, and Carmen Blacker, *Oracles and Divination.* Boulder, Colo.: Shambala, 1981.

Wilhelm, Richard, and Cary F. Baynes (trans.). *The I Ching.* Princeton, N.J.: Princeton University Press, Bollingen Series XIX, 1969.

Illuminati   An order of adepts that is said to possess "light" from direct communication with a higher source. The term *Illuminati* was first used in 15th-century Europe. It was associated with various occult sects and secret orders, including the Rosicrucians and the Freemasons.

The most highly organized sect, the Bavarian Order of Illuminati, was founded in Bavaria in 1776 by Adam Weishaupt, a 28-year-old professor of law. Weishaupt may have created the order because he aspired to join the Masons. In 1780 he was joined by Baron von Knigge, a respected and high-level Mason, which enabled him to incorporate Masonic elements into his organizational structure and rites. The order failed to obtain official Masonic recognition, however, at a Masonic conference in 1782.

The Order of Illuminati was antimonarchial, and its identification with republicanism gained it many members throughout Germany. In 1784 Masonry was denounced to the Bavarian government as politically dangerous, which led to the suppression of all secret orders, including the Masons and the Illuminati. Later, the name *Illuminati* was given to followers of Louis Claude de St. Martin (1743–

1803), French mystic, author, and founder of the Martinist sect in 1754.

The Order of Illuminati included such luminaries as COUNT CAGLIOSTRO and FRANZ ANTON MESMER. Cagliostro was initiated in 1781 at Frankfurt to the Grand Masters of the Templars, the name used by the order there. Cagliostro supposedly received money from Weishaupt to be used on behalf of Masonry in France. Cagliostro later connected with the Martinists.

Following its suppression in Bavaria, the order was revived in 1880 in Dresden under the aegis of Leopold Engel. At the turn of the 20th century, Engel's order was resurrected as the Ordo Templi Orientis (Order of the Temple of the Orient, or OTO), with elements of Tantric mysticism and sex magic. Famous members included the ADEPT ALEISTER CROWLEY and Franz Hartmann, a Theosophist who had studied with a secret sect of Rosicrucians in his Bavarian hometown.

In 1906 Rudolph Steiner, philosopher, one-time Theosophist, and founder of Anthroposophy, accepted a charter from the OTO to establish a lodge named Mysteria Mystica Aeterna. It is unlikely that Steiner ever practiced the OTO's sex magic; nevertheless, his involvement in the OTO brought Anthroposophy much criticism. In his autobiography, Steiner refers to the OTO only as the order and describes it as "an institution of FREEMASONRY of the so-called higher degrees." He said he had "no intention whatever of working in the spirit of such a society" but had always respected what had arisen throughout history. "Therefore I was in favor of linking whenever possible, the new with what exists historically. . . . I took over nothing, absolutely nothing from this society except the merely formal right to carry on in historical succession my symbolic-ritualistic activity," he said.

In esoteric lore, the Illuminati are said to be a secret order of adepts who are the enemies of the Catholic Church.

FURTHER READING:

Steiner, Rudolph. *An Autobiography.* Blauvelt, N.Y.: Rudolph Steiner Publications, 1977.

Waite, Arthur Edward. *A New Encyclopedia of Freemasonry.* New York: Weathervane Books, 1970.

ill wishing   See WISH.

imagination   The creative faculty of the mind, which in MAGIC is the formative power for bringing things into manifestation. Imagination is an orderly and intentional mental process. It is distinguished from daydreaming and fancy, which consist of random thoughts and desires. It is not unreal but is a powerful creative force that becomes reality, especially when stimulated in deliberate ways by RITUAL. Imagination is the power of self-healing and MIRACLES, PROPHECY, and CLAIRVOYANCE.

Imagination works in tandem with WILL as a team of the two most potent forces employed by the magician. Iamblichus, writing in *The Mysteries,* said that the imagination is:

. . . superior to all nature and generation, and through which we are capable of being united to the Gods, of transcending the mundane order, and of participating in eternal life, and the energy of the supercelestial Gods. Through this principles, therefore, we are able to liberate ourselves from fate.

Imagination creates THOUGHT-FORMS on the ASTRAL PLANE or higher planes, which are as objective and real to the entities existing on those planes as are earthly surroundings to humans. The thought-forms created by imagination must be vitalized, powered, and directed by the will, otherwise they will be transient.

An example of how imagination is employed in occult practice comes from the writings of Dr. Edward Berridge, a homeopathic physician and member of the HERMETIC ORDER OF THE GOLDEN DAWN. Berridge's occult name was *Frater Resurgam.* Berridge was consulted by a man who said that several years prior, he had been in the frequent company of a man who made constant use of a certain profane expression. The words had stuck in his mind, and he could not rid himself of them. Berridge believed that the words were like a mantram and had the effect of vitalizing an ELEMENTAL entity that had attached itself to the man. He prescribed a magical remedy:

I advised him the next time the phrase troubled him— first to imagine he saw before him some horrible creature as the embodiment of the profanity itelf—next to hold this creature firmly before him, and then to send forth an occult dynamite shell, penetrating into the elemental, and then exploding and blowing it to atoms.

The man did as instructed. He said that he had not succeeded in destroying the elemental, but he did manage to send it away, though not permanently. However, he was seldom bothered by it.

See also TAROT; TATTVAS.

FURTHER READING:

King, Francis (ed.). *Ritual Magic of the Golden Dawn.* Rochester, Vt.: Destiny Books, 1997.

Regardie, Israel. *The Tree of Life: A Study in Magic.* York Beach, Maine: Samuel Weiser, 1969.

imp   A small DEMON that is kept inside a bottle or RING. An imp is like a FAMILIAR and is evoked for SPELLS, DIVINATION, and CHARMS. Imps are both good and evil.

As a familiar, imps can take the shape of animals, insects, and birds that are sent out on tasks at the command of a witch or magician. Witch hunters during the Inquisition accused witches of rewarding their imps for evil deeds by suckling them with their own BLOOD, which the imps sucked from fingers, warts, breasts, or any protuberance on the skin.

See also ABANO, PETER OF; GRIMOIRES.

incantation   A formula of words that are spoken or sung for a specific magical purpose. Incantations are part of the casting of SPELLS.

Many folk magic incantations have Christian elements, such as the following for stopping a snake:

> "Woman the seed shall thread, snake the seed in until fall. I command! Snake, I stop you, with God's words so powerful, that you shall lie paralyzed for me until I release you again. With Christ and Paul's hand, freeze! You cannot injure! In the name of the Trinity." Then say the Lord's Prayer.

Some incantations invoke both holy NAMES and the names of DEMONS, such as the following for protecting hidden goods:

Magical incantation according to the grimoire The Key of Solomon, *in Das Kloster, vol. 1, by J. Scheible, 1845. (Author's collection)*

> "In Jesus's name! These goods that lie here concealed and that are hidden by people, I claim them with three bands that have three names: the Father, the Son and the Holy Spirit. Yes! I have the power with the word of God. I compel and exhort you, Hells' eight princes, who are: Lucifer, Belsebub, Astaroht, Satanas, Anubes, Dyrttianus, Drakeus, Belial, that you depart from here with all your company. Let these goods come into human hands. After saying this, I stamp my foot. Jesus! who is God's and Mary's son. I strengthen my courage to take these goods in the holy and blessed name of God. I now take these goods with my hand, in the holy and blessed name of God. In the name of the Holy Trinity." Then say the Lord's Prayer.

In ceremonial MAGIC, incantations are to be spoken or vibrated with as much intensity as possible so that the magician feels the words in the body and visualizes them as well. The incantations are projected into etheric space.

FURTHER READING:
Rustad, Mary S. (ed. and translator). *The Black Books of Elverum.* Lakeville, Minn.: Galde Press, 1999.

incense   See PERFUMES.

initiation   A rite or RITUAL that marks the psychological or spiritual crossing of a threshold into new territories, knowledge, and abilities. Initiation brings a sense of attainment and accomplishment and effects subtle changes deep within the psyche in terms of how an individual perceives herself or himself. The central theme to initiation is suffering, death, and rebirth. The initiate undergoes an ordeal, symbolically dies, and is symbolically reborn as a new person, possessing new wisdom.

In MAGIC, initiation marks entry into a closed and secret society and opens the door to the development of magical powers and advanced consciousness. In its highest sense, initiation marks a spiritual transformation, in which the initiate begins a journey into Self and to reaching toward the divine. Many traditional initiation rites exist. Initiation may be experienced in a group or alone. It may be formal or informal. It may be done in an old ritual or a new one; it may come as a spontaneous spiritual awakening, in meditation, or in dreams. A person prepares for initiation through purification, such as fasting, bathing, BAPTISM, and meditation.

There are two main types of esoteric and magical initiation: physical and nonphysical. DION FORTUNE noted that they are usually done together, though one can be experienced without the other. A physical initiation marks entry into study in accordance with the structure and purpose of a group or LODGE. A nonphysical initiation is a spiritual experience in which an initiate gains INNER PLANES CONTACTS.

Fortune described initiation as "the dawning of the Inner Light, or coming into manifestation on the physical planes of the Augoeides, or Body of Light." The initiate is someone whose higher self has entered the personality, facilitating enlightenment.

A traditional format in magical orders is initiation by the four ELEMENTS in a series of trials. Magical lodges—as well as organizations of Wiccans and Pagans—have series of initiations that mark the progress of an individual's knowledge and skill.

FURTHER READING:

Fortune, Dion. *Esoteric Orders and Their Work and the Training and Work of the Initiate*. London: The Aquarian Press, 1987.

Gray, William G. *Magical Ritual Methods*. York Beach, Maine: Samuel Weiser, 1980.

Greer, John Michael. *Inside a Magical Lodge: Group Ritual in the Western Tradition*. St. Paul, Minn.: Llewellyn Publications, 1998.

inner planes contacts   In Western MAGIC, highly evolved discarnate ADEPTS, ascended masters, and gods who work with initiates. A magical LODGE's collective THOUGHT-FORM, or EGREGOR, also serves as an inner plane contact. Such contacts are sources of spiritual and magical power, as well as guidance and direction.

Sometimes inner planes contacts seek out initiates, responding to their spiritual and magical work with RITU-ALS, SYMBOLS, and sacred NAMES.

intelligences   Astral powers that rule all things in the celestial and natural worlds and that also can act as intercessors between humans and the divine. Intelligences can be compared to ANGELS and to the archons of Gnosticism. They are prominent in neo-Platonic philosophy.

HENRY CORNELIUS AGRIPPA said intelligences are forces governing all things. In *Occult Philosophy*, he described them as "an intelligible substance, free from all gross and putrifying mass of a body, immortal, insensible, assisting all, having influence over all; and the nature of all intelligences, spirits and angels in the same." GRIMOIRES of instruction for ceremonial magic include working with intelligences.

invisibility   The ability to become unseen or to render another person, animal, or object unseen is one of the most important SPELLS in MAGIC. In myths and folk tales, invisibility is sometimes conferred by TALISMANS, such as magical RINGS, hats, and wands.

RITUALS for making oneself invisible are provided in GRIMOIRES, magical handbooks. The *Grimorium Verum* specifies that the ritual must be begun on a Wednesday before sunrise. Take seven beans and the head of a dead man, and put one bean in the mouth, two in the eyes, and two in the ears. The other two beans probably are intended for the nostrils, though the grimoire does not say. Trace a pattern of your own design on the head with your fingers; then bury the head facing up. Water it with brandy every morning before dawn. On the eighth day, a spirit should appear and demand to know what you are doing. The correct reply is, "I am watering my plant." The spirit will want to water the head himself, but you must refuse, no matter how persistent he is. Finally the spirit will show you the pattern you traced on the head; this is proof that he is the true spirit of the head itself. Then let the spirit water the head. On the ninth day, the beans will sprout. Put the beans in your mouth. You will be invisible as long as they are in your mouth. Do not ingest them. Take them out when you want to become visible again.

Grimoires give instructions for attaining invisibility by means of a magical ring. According to the *Little Albert*, take a tuft of hair from the upper head of a hyena and plait it into a ring. Place the ring in a pewit's nest for nine days. "The perfumes of Mercury must be used in a like manner," the *Little Albert* states. Whoever wears this ring will be invisible and will reappear by removing the ring from the finger.

Another method from the *Little Albert* calls for a ritual to be performed on a Wednesday in spring under the auspices of Mercury when it is conjoined to other favorable PLANETS, such as the MOON, Jupiter, Saturn, and the SUN. Fashion a ring from the metal MERCURY for the middle finger. Place on it a small stone from a pewit's nest while intoning, "Jesus passing through the midst of them disappeared." Place the ring on a palette of fixed mercury. Compose the PERFUME of mercury and expose the ring to it. Wrap the ring in taffeta the color of the planet. Place the ring in the pewit's nest where the stone was obtained and leave it for nine days. Remove it and fumigate it as before. Store the ring in a box made of fixed mercury. To use it in ritual, place the ring on the middle finger with the stone outwards. It will fascinate people so that you seem invisible. To become visible, turn the ring so that the stone faces inward on the hand, and place the other hand over it. (See FASCINATION.)

In Celtic lore, the invisibility spell is called the *fith-fath* or *fath-fith*. The *fith-fath* (pronounced fee-fa) also transforms people into an animal. The *fith-fath* was especially important in Irish lore. It was said to have been given to the Tuatha De Danaan by the god Manannan, governor of the sea who had power over shifting fogs and illusions. Hunters and smugglers were said to favor using the *fith-fath*, which enabled hunters to leave forests with their kills invisible to enemy eyes and smugglers to travel with their invisible stolen goods undetected.

The *fith-fath* was written in various CHARMS, such as the following example:

A magic cloud I put on thee,
From dog, from cat,
From cow, from horse,

From man, from woman,
From young man, from maiden,
And from little child.
Till I again return.

Celtic lore also holds that invisibility can be conferred by fern seed, an invisible plant that becomes visible only on Saint John's Eve at the very moment that Saint John the Baptist was born. This is the only time that fern seed can be harvested. However, anyone who attempts to pick it will be attacked by FAIRIES.

FURTHER READING:

Cavendish, Richard. *The Black Arts*. New York: G.P. Putnam's Sons, 1967.

Spence, Lewis. *The Magic Arts in Celtic Britain*. Van Nuys, Calif.: Newscastle Publishing, 1996.

Waite, Arthur Edward. *The Book of Black Magic and of Pacts*. 1899. Reprint, York Beach, Maine: Samuel Weiser, 1972.

Invisible College   See BOYLE, ROBERT.

invocation   An invitation to a spirit, deity, or entity to be present and use its powers to grant requests. Invocations also are called conjurations.

An invocation uses the magical properties of SOUND, sacred and magical words, and sacred NAMES to align and harmonize the consciousness with spiritual forces. Invocations are carefully composed. To attract a particular deity or spirit, the invocation must address their powers, virtues, and attributes and offer the right praise.

Iamblichus wrote in *The Mysteries* that invocation

is the *divine key* which opens to men the penetralia of the Gods; accustoms us to the splendid rivers of supernal light; and in a short time disposes them for the ineffable embrace and contact of the Gods; and does not desist till it raises us to the summit of all.

An invocation must be spoken and not thought silently; both breath and sound carry magical properties. All senses and faculties must be employed in an invocation. ELIPHAS LEVI said that the magical idea of a RITUAL "must be translated into light for the eyes, harmony for the ears, perfumes for the sense of smell, savors for the mouth, and shapes for the touch."

Furthermore, an invocation must be spoken or "vibrated" with as much intensity as possible. ISRAEL REGARDIE noted that the secret of every invocation, as well as every act of magic, is to invoke often and inflame one's self with PRAYER.

In MAGIC, an invocation is done during the casting of a magic CIRCLE to ask specific entities to be present to protect and witness a ritual. Entities also can be invoked to temporarily possess a person, such as in mediumship, channeling, and trance rituals. Magical GRIMOIRES contain numerous invocations, as well as instructions for rituals. Among the most common purposes are procuring love, becoming pregnant, finding treasure or acquiring wealth, protection against enemies, misfortune and evil magic, and healing.

An invocation can be offered privately in which a deity or spirit is invited, praised, and beseeched for favors. The following invocation to HERMES comes from a Greek magical text from Hellenistic Egypt. It invites Hermes to bestow grace, material wealth, and protection against evil magic. It also asks for "might" and "form," a request for the strengthening and empowering of the *ka,* or soul. The DAIMONES mentioned are low-level spirits; the "black dog-ape" probably refers to the Egyptian god Anubis, lord of death. (Note: There is no verse 5.)

1. Come unto me, Lord Hermes, O thou of many names, who know'st the secrets hidden both beneath the poles [of heaven] and underneath the earth!

2. Come unto me, Lord Hermes, thou benefactor, who doest good to all the world!

3. Give ear to me, [and] give me grace with all that are on earth; open for me the hands of all that give like thee; [and] make them give me what their hands contain!

4. Even as Horus, if e'er he called on thee, O greatest of all gods, in every trial, in every space, 'gainst gods, and men, and daimones, and things that live in water and on earth—had grace and riches with gods, and men, and every living thing beneath the earth; so let me, too, who call on thee! So give me grace, form, beauty!

6. Hear me, O Hermes, doer of good deeds, thou the inventor of [all] incantations, speak me good words!

7. Hear me, O Hermes, for I have done all things [that I should do] for thy black dog-ape, lord of the nether ones!

8. O, soften all [towards me], and give me might [and] form, and let them give me gold, and silver [too], and food of every kind continually.

9. Preserve me evermore for the eternity from spells, deceits, and witchery of every kind, from evil tongues, from every check and every enmity of gods and men!

10. Give unto me grace, victory, success, and satisfaction!

11. For thou art I, and I am thou; thy Name is mine, and mine is thine; for that I am thy likeness.

12. Whatever shall befall me in this year, or month, or day, or hour—it shall befall the Mighty God, whose symbol is upon the holy vessel's prow.

The Great Magical Papyrus of Paris, a Coptic document, contains many invocations, SPELLS, CURSES, and AMULETS. The following is a syncretic invocation for the power of revelation. It combines Egyptian and Jewish elements, which perhaps made the author feel more secure or confident about success. The invocation opens with a string of words of power which are intended to call forth the right spiritual properties. Sacred names and words of power are sprinkled through the text. The invocation names Greek, Jewish/Christian, and Egyptian entities: Zeus, the king of gods; the archangel Michael; and Osiris the king of the underworld, THOTH the god of learning and magic, and Anubis:

SAPHPHAIOR

BAELKOTA SHAMAI ARABENNAK ANTRAPHEU
BALE
SITENGI ARTEN BENTEN AKRAB ENTH OUANTH
BALA SHOUPLA SRAHENNE DEHENNE KALASHOU
CHATEMOKK BASHNE BALA SHAMAI,
    on the day of Zeus, at the first hour,
    but on the (day) of deliverance, at the fifth hour,
    a cat;
    at the eighth, a cat.

Hail, Osiris, king of the underworld,
    lord of embalming,
    who is south of Thinis
    who gives answers in Abydos,
    who is under the noubs tree in Meroe,
    whose glory is in Pashalom.
Hail, Althabot;
    bring Sabaoth unto me.
Hail, Althonai, great Eou, very valiant;
    bring Michael unto me,
    the mighty angel who is with god.
Hail, Anubis, of the district of Hansiesi,
    you who are upon your mountain.
Hail, goddesses,
    Thoth the great, the great, the wise.
Hail, gods,
    Achnoui Acham Abra Abra Sabaoth.
For Akshha Shha is my name,
Sabashha is my true name,
Shlot Shlot very valiant is my name.
So let the one who is in the underworld
    join the one who is in the air.
Let them arise, enter and give answer to me
    concerning the matter about which I ask them.
    The usual.

In the Western magical tradition, a magician sacrifices his ego to invoke into him a god as a form of divine POSSESSION. An experienced magus delivers a spontaneous invocation. ALEISTER CROWLEY said that invocations should never be read, for they would lack the proper magical force for the invocation to be successful.

See also EVOCATION.

FURTHER READING:
Crowley, Aleister. *Magic in Theory and Practice.* 1929. Reprint, New York: Dover Publications, 1976.
King, Francis (ed.). *Ritual Magic of the Golden Dawn.* Rochester, Vt.: Destiny Books, 1997.
Mead, G. R. S. *Thrice Greatest Hermes: Studies in Hellenistic Theosophy and Gnosis.* York Beach, Maine: Samuel Weiser, 1992.
Meyer, Marvin W., and Richard Smoth (eds.). *Ancient Christian Magic: Coptic Texts of Ritual Power.* Princeton, N.J.: Princeton University Press, 1999.
Regardie, Israel. *The Tree of Life: A Study in Magic.* York Beach, Maine: Samuel Weiser, 1969.
Three Books of Occult Philosophy Written by Henry Cornelius Agrippa of Nettesheim. James Freake, trans. Ed. and annotated by Donald Tyson. St. Paul, Minn.: Llewellyn Publications, 1995.

Invoking Pentagram See PENTAGRAM.

iron A universal AMULET against evil spirits; BEWITCHMENTS by witches, FAIRIES, and sorcerers; and the EVIL EYE. According to lore, iron not only repels evil but drains the powers of evil spirits and people. Fairies have a particular dread of iron and are said to be weakened in its presence.

Iron is employed in countless folk MAGIC practices for protection. In Celtic lore, women who have just given birth and their infants are especially vulnerable to predatory spirits and can be protected by a row of iron pins around their bed or by an iron reaping hook. Children, also especially vulnerable, can be protected by the sewing of iron into their clothing or the wearing of iron pins and brooches. Horses, cattle, and other livestock are protected by the nailing of an iron horseshoe over the stable door; the horseshoe should have its ends pointed upwards in imitation of the crescent MOON and should be nailed with its own nails.

A favorite bewitchment of witches was to prevent butter from churning. This SPELL could be nullified by heating a smoothing iron until red hot and plunging it into water while repeating certain magical CHARMS and then pouring some of the treated water into the churn. The result would be a large quantity of butter.

FURTHER READING:
Spence, Lewis. *The Magic Arts in Celtic Britain.* Van Nuys, Calif.: Newscastle Publishing, 1996.

Isis Egyptian Mother Goddess who also rules MAGIC and SORCERY, and is important in the Hermetic tradition. The name *Isis* is the Greek word for the Egyptian hieroglyphic for "throne." Isis is identified as the Virgin in the constellation Virgo. In Christianity, she has been absorbed by the Virgin Mary. Her image is used in association with magical arts, the occult, thaumaturgy, and sorcery.

The Mythology of Isis
In Egyptian mythology, Isis is the sister and wife of Osiris, god of the underworld. She is associated with Sirius, the Dog Star, the rising of which signals the vernal equinox. Her symbol is the MOON. She is often shown crowned with a lunar orb nestled between the horns of a bull or ram. The worship of Isis was adopted by the Greeks, the Romans, and the Druids.

Isis originally was mortal and skilled in sorcery. She desired to become immortal like the gods and accomplished that by tricking the sun god, Ra, into revealing his secret and sacred NAME. She obtained some of his SPITTLE, made a snake from it, and left the snake in his path. Ra was bitten and in great agony. Isis offered to relieve the pain if he would tell her his secret name, and he relented.

When Osiris's treacherous brother, Set, murdered and dismembered him, Isis scoured the land to find the body parts and used her magical skills to reassemble them. She breathed life into the body so that she and Osiris could be together one last time before he left to rule the underworld.

A son, Horus, was born of this union posthumously and in a virgin birth. After the child was born, Set returned and cut the body of Osiris into 14 pieces, which he scattered along the Nile. Once again, Isis went in search of them, but this time she buried each piece where she found it so that it would fertilize the land. Isis protected the child against Set until Horus was old enough to fight. In art she was often depicted holding Horus in her arms.

Isis of the Mysteries and Hermetic Wisdom

According to Plutarch, Isis was believed to be the daughter of HERMES, while others said that she was the daughter of Prometheus. Plutarch said that her name meant "wisdom." She was known as the goddess of 10,000 appellations. In the Egyptian mysteries, Isis represents the female aspect of the Deity to humankind; she is the Universal Mother of all that lives; she symbolizes wisdom, truth, and power. Statues of her were decorated with stars, the moon, and the sun. Her girdle was joined together with four golden plates which signify the four ELEMENTS of nature. Her priests were adept at controlling and using the Unseen Forces.

According to the Hermetic wisdom, Isis, the Goddess of Women, was educated by Hermes. With him, she invented the writings of all nations, caused men to love women, invented sailing, gave humankind its laws, ended cannibalism, made justice more powerful than GOLD or SILVER, instructed humankind in the mysteries, and caused Truth to be considered beautiful. An inscription at her temple at Sais read: "I am that which is, which hath been, and which shall be; and no man has ever lifted the veil that hides my Divinity from mortal eyes." The Isis of the mysteries is completely veiled by a scarlet cloth. To initiates who learn her mysteries, she lifts her veil, and they are to remain forever secret about what they have seen.

The Bembine Table of Isis

In 1527, after the sacking of Rome, a bronze tablet measuring 50 by 30 inches and decorated with silver and enamel inlay came into the possession of a locksmith or ironworker, who sold it to Cardinal Bembo of Italy. The Bembine Table of Isis, or "Isaic Table," is covered with hieroglyphics and inscriptions concerning mystical knowledge and an occult system of sacrifices, rites, and ceremonies. It apparently was once used an as altar, perhaps in the chambers where the mysteries of Isis were revealed to initiates. ELIPHAS LEVI believed the tablet was a key to the Book of Thoth, or the TAROT. The tablet is in the Museum of Antiquities at Turin.

Isis as Goddess of Magic and Healing

Isis possesses such powerful magic that even Anubis, god of death, is subject to her whims. People have prayed to her on behalf of the sick and dying. She is goddess of healing and childbirth. At night, she visits the sick, brushing them gently with her wings as she intones magical INCANTATIONS to heal them.

Isis, in *Oedipus Aegyptiacus* by *Athanasius Kircher, 1652.* (Author's collection)

FURTHER READING:

Hall, Manly P. *The Secret Teachings of All Ages.* 1928. Reprint, Los Angeles: The Philosophic Research Society.

Jabir ibn Hayyan (c. 722/723–c. 815) One of the most important Islamic alchemists. Jabir ibn Hayyan, known in the West as Geber (also Giaber or Yeber), made significant contributions to ALCHEMY that were expanded upon by his followers. The term *gibberish* comes from his Latinized name.

Little is known about the early life of Jabir. His true name was Abu Moussah Djafar al Sofie, probably was born in 722 or 723 in Haman, Mesopotamia. According to some sources, he was a Persian born in Tus. His father, a druggist of Kufa, was a Shiite who became involved in political intrigue to overthrow the ruling Umayyad Caliphate. The successors, the Abbasids, turned on the Shiites and executed many of them, including Jabir's father. Jabir was sent from Kufa—a town on the banks of the Euphrates River—to Arabia, where he probably was raised by relatives in the Azd Bedouin tribe.

The next records of Jabir's life are from his middle age, when he served as a favored alchemist in the court of Caliph Harun al-Rashid. He also was a personal friend of the sixth Shi'ite Imam Ja'far al-Sadiq and was favored by the Barmecides, the powerful ministers of the caliph. By 803 the power of the Barmecides had grown so that Harun al-Rashid felt threatened by them, and he banished them. Jabir returned to Kufa, where he set up an alchemical laboratory. He lived in Kufa in seclusion for the rest of his life. The date of his death is uncertain but probably fell in about 815. About 200 years after his death, his Kufa laboratory was rediscovered when houses were demolished. Among the objects found was a GOLD mortar weighing two-and-a-half pounds.

During his days as an alchemist, Jabir was a prolific writer. However, many of the 500 or so works attributed to him probably were written in the 10th century by the Ismaelites, who were proponents of Jabir's work. Even if some of the actual treatises were not written by Jabir himself, they probably contain his ideas. The most important collections of treatises are *The Hundred and Twelve Books, The Seventy Books, The Ten Books of Rectifications,* and *The Books of the Balances.* In addition, Jabir is credited with writing on MAGIC SQUARES, TALISMANS, astronomical tables, medicine, philosophy, and other topics.

One of Jabir's most significant alchemical contributions is his theory of balance. The four ELEMENTS of fire, air, water, and earth each have qualities of hot, cold, dryness, and moisture. Fire is hot and dry; air is hot and moist; water is cold and moist; and earth is cold and dry. Metals have two natures, one internal and one external. For example, gold is hot and moist externally and cold and dry internally, while lead is cold and dry externally and hot and moist internally.

According to Jabir, all metals are formed under the influence of the PLANETS by the union of SULPHUR and MERCURY in the earth. The different metals come from the varying degrees of purity of sulphur and mercury. The source of this idea may have been APOLLONIUS OF TYANA, but Jabir's development of it was accepted by alchemists and chemists for generations following him.

Jabir recognized seven metals: gold, SILVER, lead, tin, copper, IRON, and *khar sini*. The latter is uncertain. *Khar sini* means "Chinese iron." It may have been an alloy of nickel, zinc, and copper.

Furthermore, metals all have 17 powers. The number 17 was highly important to Jabir; he said that everything in the world is governed by it. He also placed great importance on the NUMBERS that add up to 17—1, 3, 5, and 8—and also the number 28. Jabir used NUMEROLOGY and the qualities of the elements to explain the constitution of metals.

FURTHER READING:
Holmyard, E. J. *Alchemy.* New York: Penguin Books, 1957.
Waite, Arthur Edward. *Alchemists Through the Ages.* Blauvelt, N.Y.: Rudolph Steiner Publications, 1970.

jinx   Continual or repeated bad luck, usually due to a fatal accident. A jinx is not the same as a CURSE, which is deliberate. Objects such as cars, ships, or personal possessions can become jinxed when they are involved in tragic deaths. The jinx affects other people who come into contact with or ownership of the objects.

Jewels and precious stones, long reputed to have supernatural properties and powers, and some famous jewels have been associated with jinxes. For example, the Hope Diamond became jinxed in the 17th century when its owner, Madame de Montespan, the mistress of France's king Louis XIV, was said to conduct BLACK MASSES. A century later, King Louis XVI gave the diamond to Marie Antoinette, who loaned it to her friend, Princesse de Lamballe. Both were executed during the French Revolution. Subsequent owners also suffered tragic or untimely death. The jewel acquired its name from an English banker, Henry Thomas Hope. His descendant Lord Thomas Hope inherited it. When his marriage failed, his wife—who died in poverty—prophesied that everyone who owned the diamond would have bad luck.

FURTHER READING:
Gordon, Stuart. *The Book of Curses: True Tales of Voodoo, Hoodoo and Hex.* London: Brockhampton Press, 1994.

John XXII (r. 1316–1334)   Pope who opposed the ORDER OF THE KNIGHTS TEMPLAR and also condemned ALCHEMY. Nonetheless, alchemical ADEPTS believed that he secretly supported and practiced alchemy, perhaps out of a desire by alchemists to connect their art to the highest religious figure.

Born in 1249, Pope John XXII was educated by Dominicans. He became chancellor to Charles II of France and took up residence in Avignon. He remained there when he was chosen pope in 1316.

John XXII avidly followed the political and religious activities of many countries. He delivered legal opinions that aided the suppression of the Templars. He was aghast at the activities of alchemists, whose counterfeit gold pieces caused him to issue an edict against them. He depicted alchemists as frauds who should be branded in "perpetual infamy" and subjected to fines and even imprisonment. He also said that those who supported alchemy or attempted to use alchemical GOLD or SILVER as money should be punished as well. The text of his edict is as follows:

Poor themselves, the alchemists promise riches which are not forthcoming; wise also in their own conceit, they fall into the ditch which they themselves have digged. For there is no doubt that the professors of this art of alchemy make fun of each other because, conscious of their own ignorance, they are surprised at those who say anything of this kind about themselves; when the truth sought does not come to them they fix on a day for their experiment and exhaust all their arts; then they dissemulate their failure so that finally, though there is no such thing in nature, they pretend to make genuine gold and silver by a sophistic transmutation; to such an extent does their damned and damnable temerity go that they stamp upon the base metal the characters of public money for believing eyes, and it is only in this way that they deceive the ignorant populace as to the alchemic fire of their furnace. Wishing to banish such practices for all time, we have determined by this formal edict that whosoever shall make gold or silver of this kind or shall order it to be made, provided the attempt actually ensues, or whoever shall knowingly assist those actually engaged in such a process, or whoever shall knowingly make use of such gold or silver either by selling it or giving it in payment of a debt, shall be compelled as a penalty to pay into the public treasury, to be used for the poor, as much by weight of genuine gold or silver as there may be of alchemical metal, provided it be proved lawfully that they have been guilty in any of the aforesaid ways; as for those who persist in making alchemical gold, or, as has been said, in using it knowingly, let them be branded with the mark of perpetual infamy. But if the means of the delinquents are insufficient for the payment of the amount stated then the good judgment of the justice may commute this penalty for some other (as for example imprisonment or another punishment, according to the nature of the case, the difference of individuals and other circumstances). Those, however, who in their regrettable practice go so far as not only to pass monies thus made but even despise the precepts of the natural law, overstep the limits of their art and violate the laws by deliberately coining or casting or causing others to coin or cast counterfeit money from alchemical gold or silver, we proclaim as coming under this animadversion, and their goods shall be confiscated, and they shall be considered as criminals. And if the delinquents are clerics, besides the aforeside penalties they shall be deprived of any benefices they shall hold and shall be declared incapable of holding any further benefices.

John Dastin, an eminent alchemists of the time, wrote to John XXII in defense of alchemy but probably to no effect. Alchemists held to the belief that this bull was directed not against all alchemists but against the fraudulent ones.

John XXII left behind a considerable fortune of 18 millions florins, seven million florins' worth of jewels, and numerous consecrated vessels. Alchemists said that he made his fortune with the help of the PHILOSOPHER'S STONE and asserted that he had made 200 gold ingots in a single day. According to lore, the pope learned alchemical secrets from ARNOLD DE VILLANOVA, supposedly his friend and teacher, and also RAYMOND LULLY.

A spurious alchemical treatise, *The Elixir of the Philosophers, or the Transmutatory Art of Metals,* is attributed to John XXII. In 1557 it was translated from Latin into French. According to the treatise, the ingredients of the Stone are vinegar, SALT, URINE, sal ammoniac, and a mysterious substance called sulphur vive.

FURTHER READING:
Holmyard, E. J. *Alchemy.* New York: Penguin Books, 1957.
Waite, Arthur Edward. *Alchemists Through the Ages.* Blauvelt, N.Y.: Rudolph Steiner Publications, 1970.

Jung, Carl G. (1875–1961) Swiss psychiatrist who founded analytical psychology and almost single-handedly revived modern interest in ALCHEMY. Carl Gustav Jung's exploration of people's inner realms was fueled to a large extent by his own personal experiences involving dreams, visions, mythological and religious symbolism, and paranormal phenomena. A pupil of Sigmund Freud, he took Freud's work concerning the unconscious and brought it into spiritual realms.

Jung was born on July 26, 1875, in Kesswil, Switzerland. When he was four, his family moved to Klein-Huningen near Basel. Jung's entry into mystical and mysterious realms began early in childhood in dreams. As a boy, he began to feel that he had two personalities; besides himself was a wise old man who stayed with him and had increasing influence on his thought throughout his entire life. He experienced precognition, CLAIRVOYANCE, psychokinesis, and hauntings. Perhaps his psychic sensitivity was an hereditary gift: His mother and maternal grandmother both were known as "ghost seers." His grandmother, Augusta Preiswerk, once fell into a three-day trance at age 20 during which she communicated with spirits of the dead and gave prophecies. Jung's mother, Emilie, kept a personal journal of paranormal occurrences that took place in the house in which Jung grew up.

In 1898, Jung's interest in occult phenomena turned serious. A 16-year old cousin who was a practicing medium performed spiritualistic experiments for Jung's study. His notes later became the basis for his doctoral thesis and first published paper, "On the Psychology and Pathology of So-Called Occult Phenomena" (1902). Meanwhile, he decided to become a psychiatrist and in 1900 did his medical training at Basel.

Jung became interested in mythology around 1909, and a year later published a paper, "The Psychological Foundations of Belief in Spirits," in the *Journal of the Society for Psychical Research* in London. Jung did not believe in literal spirits but said that there are three main sources for the belief in spirits: the seeing of apparitions, mental disease, and dreams, the most common of the three. He said that spirits of the dead are created psychologically upon death: Images and ideas remain attached to relatives and are activated to form spirits by intensity of emotion.

Also in 1909, he resigned a post at Burgholzki Mental Clinic where he had been practicing for nine years. He traveled to the United States with Freud and received an honorary degree from Clark University in Worcester, Massachusetts. (Jung also received an honorary doctorate from Harvard in 1936, from Oxford in 1938, and from the University of Geneva in 1945.) In 1910, he was appointed permanent president of the International Congress of Psycho-Analysis.

Jung worked closely with Freud from 1907 to 1913 but broke with his mentor due to significant disagreements, among them Freud's emphasis on sexuality, his dismissal of spiritual aspects of the psyche and of the paranormal, and the meaning of SYMBOLS. In 1914, Jung resigned from his position at Burgholzki Mental Clinic, and in 1915, he resigned a professorship at the University of Zurich.

After these breaks with the establishment, Jung delved deeply into dreams, mythology, and ultimately alchemy. He suffered a six-year-long breakdown during which he had psychotic fantasies. He was labeled a "mystic" and was shunned by his peers. He experienced numerous paranormal phenomena. He became immersed in the world of the dead, which led to his *Seven Sermons to the Dead,* written under the name of the second-century Gnostic writer, Basilides, and published in 1916. He described the spirits of the dead as "the voices of the Unanswered, Unresolved, and Unredeemed."

After his recovery, Jung developed more fully his own theories: the psychological types, the anima (feminine principle) and animus (masculine principle), the collective unconscious, and archetypes. Of symbols, Jung said that they should be understood as "an intuitive idea that cannot yet be formulated in any other or better way." Concerning dreams, he said that they are the private property of the dreamer in terms of their meanings but said that some dreams come from the collective unconscious and belong to all humankind.

Jung was intensely interested in Gnosticism, particularly its Sophia, or wisdom, the desirable elements once rejected by the church along with its heretical elements. His explorations of Gnosticism, joined with his interest in alchemy, paved the way for a modern revival of interest in the spiritual dimensions of both subjects.

In 1944, Jung had a near-death experience (NDE) following a heart attack. He felt he was floating high over the

Earth and could see from the Himalayas across the Middle East to a part of the Mediterranean. He became aware that he was leaving the earth. Then he saw near him a huge block of stone that had been hollowed out into a temple. To the right of the temple entrance, a black Hindu was sitting in a lotus position. Jung knew that he was expected inside the temple. As he drew closer, he felt his earthly desires and attitudes fall away from him, and he became aware that inside he would understand the meaning of his life. At that moment, his earthly doctor appeared in the form of the basileus of Kos, the healer at the temple of Aesculapius, the Roman god of healing (Aesclepius in Greek), telling him that he had to return to Earth. Jung did so but most unhappily and with great resentment against his doctor.

After the death of his wife, whom he had married in 1903, Jung began to build a castle of stone on his newly acquired property in Bollingen, Switzerland. He carved numerous alchemical and mystical symbols into the stone. The ongoing building and altering of his tower signified for him an extension of consciousness achieved in old age. The tower and its symbolic role in his life is a leitmotif in Jung's writings. During his retirement at Bollingen, Jung reworked many earlier papers and developed further his ideas on many topics that are now of intense interest, including mandala symbolism, the I CHING, alchemy, synchronicity, and especially the phenomenology of the self, the latter culminating in the major work *Aion* in 1951. In *Aion,* Jung summarized the roles of the "archetypes of the unconscious" and commented especially on the Christ image as symbolized in the fish.

Jung believed in reincarnation and was influenced by *The Tibetan Book of the Dead.* He believed his own incarnation was not due to karma, however, but to a passionate drive for understanding in order to piece together mythic conceptions from the slender hints of the unknowable. He feared greatly for the future of humankind and said that the only salvation lay in becoming more conscious. He said he believed that his work proved that the pattern of God exists in every person.

Jungian principles have been found to be applicable to nearly all academic disciplines from mythology to religion to quantum physics and to nearly all aspects of modern life. His prolific writings have been collected into 20 volumes plus a supplement.

Jung and Alchemy

Jung's interest in alchemy grew out of his intense interest in Gnosticism and his desire, as early as 1912, to find a link between it and the processes of the collective unconscious that would pave the way for the reentry of the Gnostic Sophia into modern culture. He found such a link in alchemy.

Jung also was prompted to research alchemy by his dreams (see below). He collected a vast body of works on alchemy and immersed himself in study of the subject.

His first work on alchemy was a lecture on alchemical symbolism in dreams, entitled "Dream Symbols and the Individuation Process," delivered in 1935 at Villa Eranos. A year later, also at Eranos, he lectured on "The Idea of Redemption in Alchemy." His first book on the subject was *Psychology and Alchemy* (1944). *Aion, Alchemical Studies, Psychology and Alchemy,* and *Mysterium Coniunctionis* also deal with alchemy. In *Mysterium Coniunctionis* (1955–56), his last masterpiece, he states that he was satisfied that his pyschology was at last "given its place in reality and established upon its historical foundations." Jung's knowledge of alchemy is exemplified throughout all of his later writings.

Jung saw alchemy as a spiritual process of redemption involving the union and transformation of *Lumen Dei,* the light of the Godhead, and *Lumen Naturae,* the light of nature. The alchemists' experimental procedure of *solve et coagula* (dissolve and coagulate) symbolized the "death" and "rebirth" of the substances they used. The alchemists were part of the process themselves and transmuted their own consciousness into a higher state through symbolic death and rebirth. The alchemists' "projection," or transmutation of base metals into GOLD and SILVER, takes place within the psyche as the process of individuation, or becoming whole.

Jung's Alchemical Dreams

Jung had alchemical dreams and visions long before he knew what alchemy was about. Once he became immersed in it, he was able to understand dreams and visions from a new perspective, and he also was able to develop his theories on the personality. Alchemy led to one of his most important concepts, individuation, which is the process of becoming whole. Through our experiences in life, we are challenged to integrate pieces of ourselves. Each one of us has a feminine side, called the anima, and a masculine side, called the animus, which must be brought into harmony with each other. In addition, we have the shadow, parts of us that are repressed. Individuation enables us to become conscious of both our smallness and our great uniqueness in the grand scheme of things.

Like many of his contemporaries, Jung considered alchemy as "something off the beaten track and rather silly." But between 1926 and 1928, he had a series of dreams that changed his mind and his life.

In the first dream in 1926, he finds himself in South Tyrol during wartime. He is on the Italian front, driving back from the front lines in a horse-drawn carriage with a little peasant man. Shells explode all around them; the journey is very dangerous. They cross a bridge and then go through a tunnel whose vaulting has been partially destroyed by the shelling. At the other end is a sunny landscape, and the radiant city of Verona. The landscape looks lush and green. Jung notices a large manor house with many annexes and outbuildings. The road leads through a large courtyard and past the house. They drive through a gate and into the courtyard. Another gate at the far end opens onto the sunny landscape. Just as they are in the middle of the courtyard, the gates at both ends clang shut. The little peasant leaps down from his seat and announces,

"Now we are caught in the seventeenth century." Jung thinks to himself, "Well, that's that! But what is there to do about it? Now we shall be caught for years." He is then consoled by another thought: "Someday, years from now, I shall get out again."

The dream was prophetic: Jung would spend much of the rest of his life looking into alchemy, which peaked in Europe in the 17th century. He searched through works on history, religion, and philosophy to try to illuminate this puzzling dream but to no avail.

Other dreams occurred with the same theme. In them, he sees a previously unknown annex to his own house. He wonders how he could not have known about it. Finally, he enters the annex and finds that it contains a wonderful library, full of large 16th- and 17th-century books, hand-bound with pigskin, and illustrated with strange symbolic copper engravings. He has never before seen such symbols.

In 1928, a turning point came when his friend Richard Wilhelm gave him a copy of *The Secret of the Golden Flower,* a Chinese mystical and alchemical tract. *The Secret of the Golden Flower* revealed to Jung the bridge between Gnosticism and the psychology of the unconscious. In comparing the Chinese tract with Latin alchemical works, Jung found that the alchemy systems of both East and West essentially dealt with transformation of the soul.

Jung asked a bookseller to send him anything he obtained on the subject of alchemy. Soon he received a copy of a collection of classic 16th-century alchemical texts, *Artis Auriferae Volumina Duo.* But the book and its strange symbols still looked like nonsense to him, and Jung left it largely untouched for two years. Finally he realized that the language of alchemy *is* symbols, and he set about to decipher them. He then understood his dreams.

In the house dreams, the house represented his own consciousness, and the annex represented something that belonged to him but of which he was just emerging into his conscious. The library with its old books represented alchemy itself. Within 15 years, Jung had assembled a library similar to the one in his dream.

Jung had long sought to find a way to bridge the present and the past, to relate analytical psychology to myth through a historical context, and now he found that bridge in alchemy. The intellectual thread of Western alchemy extended back to the Gnostics, whom Jung had studied. He saw that the Gnostics and the alchemists were concerned with the same inner landscape as he.

Jung also recognized the archetypal nature of alchemical symbols and observed them in the dreams of his patients, who knew nothing about alchemy. He was able to understand certain dream motifs that had previously puzzled him. For example, one of his patients had a dream of an eagle flying into the sky. In this dream, the eagle begins to eat his own wings and then drops back to earth. Jung interpreted the dream on a personal level as a reversal of a psychic situation. He then discovered an alchemical engraving of an eagle eating its own wings, and thus saw the image in the dream as archetypal as well.

Three days before he died, Jung had the last of his visionary alchemical dreams and a portent of his own impending death. In the dream, he had become whole. A significant symbol was tree roots interlaced with gold, the alchemical symbol of completion. When he died in his room in Zurich on June 6, 1961, a great storm arose on Lake Geneva, and lightning struck a favorite tree of his.

Christ as Lapis

Much of Jung's efforts concerned relating analytical psychology to Christianity. In alchemical terms Jung saw the Christ figure as the lapis or PHILOSOPHER'S STONE, the agent that transforms the impure into the pure, the base metal into gold. Thus in its highest mystical sense, alchemy represents the transformation of consciousness to love, personified by the hermaphrodite, the union of male-female opposites (physicality and spirituality) who are joined into a whole.

One night Jung awakened from sleep to see a startling vision at the foot of his bed: a brightly lit figure of Christ on the Cross, not quite life-size, and breathtakingly beautiful. Christ's body was greenish gold. Jung was no stranger to powerful dreams or visions, but he was shaken by this one.

In interpreting the vision, Jung saw that Christ represented the *aurum non vulgi* ("not the common gold") of the alchemists. This referred to the more serious, esoteric purpose of alchemy, to produce not just ordinary gold, but *aurum philosophicum,* or philosophical gold—a transmutation of a spiritual nature.

The green-gold of Christ's body represented the living essence in all matter—the ANIMA MUNDI or World Soul or World Spirit that fills everything in existence. Thus, the alchemical Christ is a union between the spiritual and the physical.

See also GRAIL.

FURTHER READING:

Fodor, Nandor. *Freud, Jung and the Occult.* Secaucus, N.J.: University Books, 1971.

Hall, Calvin S., and Vernon J. Nordby. *A Primer of Jungian Psychology.* New York: New American Library, 1973.

Jung, C. G. Aion. 2d ed. Princeton, N.J.: Princeton University Press, 1968.

———. *Memories, Dreams, Reflections.* New York: Vintage Books, 1965.

———. *Mysterium Coniunctionis.* 2d ed. Princeton, N.J.: Princeton University Press, 1970.

———. *Psychology and Alchemy.* Rev. ed. Princeton, N.J.: Princeton University Press, 1968.

Pagel, Walter. "Jung's View on Alchemy." Available online. URL: http://www.compilerpress.atfreeweb.com/Anno%20PAgel%20Jung%20on%20Alchemy.htm. Downloaded April 12, 2005.

kabbalah (cabala, kabala, qabalah)   The mysticism of classical Judaism, and part of the foundation of the Western magical tradition.

Kabbalah is derived from the Hebrew word *QBL (Qibel),* meaning "to receive" or "that which is received." It refers especially to a secret oral tradition handed down from teacher to pupil. The term *kabbalah* was first used in the 11th century by Ibn Gabirol, a Spanish philosopher, and has since become applied to all Jewish mystical practice. The kabbalah is founded on the Torah but is not an intellectual or ascetic discipline. It is a means for achieving union with God while maintaining an active life in the mundane world.

In its role in Western MAGIC, the kabbalah is the science of letters, the universal language from which all things are created. This science of letters is used to create words and SOUNDS in RITUAL. According to FRANZ BARDON, the kabbalist is one who is connected to God and has realized the God within himself. He is a perfect embodiment of the universe in miniature, the microcosm. The kabbalist is the highest initiate, magically trained to use the science of letters, whose spoken word becomes reality. "To speak Kabbalistically means to create something out of nothing," Bardon said in *The Key to the True Kabbalah.* This is the greatest mystery that can ever be revealed to a human being.

Branches of the Kabbalah
There are four main, overlapping branches of the kabbalah:

- *The Classical, or Dogmatic, Kabbalah* concerns the study of the Torah and the central texts of the kabbalah, such as the *Sefer Yetzirah* and the *Sefer Zohar* (see below).
- *The Practical Kabbalah* concerns magic, such as the proper ways to make talismans and AMULETS.
- *The Literal Kabbalah* concerns the relationship between the letters of the Hebrew alphabet and NUMBERS. It features the deciphering of relationships and CORRESPONDENCES through GEMATRIA, a system for determining the numerical values of words and names; the finding of acronyms through *notarikon,* in which the first letters of words are used to make new words; and an encryption system called *temurah,* in which letters are transposed into code. *Temurah* plays a role in interpreting the Torah and in the making of talismans.
- *The Unwritten Kabbalah* concerns the study of the Tree of Life (see below).

Of the four branches, the Practical Kabbalah, the Literal Kabbalah, and the Unwritten Kabbalah are the most important to the Western magical tradition. Joined with Hermetic principles and philosophy, these part of the kabbalah create a philosophical, mystical and magical system for the practice of ceremonial magic. This system, sometimes called the western kabbalah or western qabalah, also plays a role in practical magic for the casting of SPELLS.

History of the Kabbalah

According to lore, God taught what became the kabbalah to ANGELS. After the Fall, angels taught the knowledge to Adam to provide people with a way back to God. The knowledge was passed to Noah and then to Abraham and Moses, who in turn initiated 70 Elders. Kings David and SOLOMON were initiates. Influenced by Gnosticism and neoplatonism, the oral tradition was passed on into the tradition and literature of the Merkabah mystics (c. 100 B.C.E.–1000 C.E.).

Merkabah means "God's Throne–Chariot" and refers to the chariot of Ezekiel's vision. The goal of the Merkabah mystic was to enter the throne world and perceive God sitting upon his throne. The throne world was reached after passing through seven heavens while in an ecstatic trance state. The passage of the mystic was dangerous, impeded by hostile angels. Talismans, SEALS, the sacred NAMES of angels, and INCANTATIONS were required to navigate through the obstacles.

The historical origin of the true kabbalah centers on the *Sefer Yetzirah* ("Book of Creation") attributed to Rabbi Akiba, whom the Romans martyred. The book's exact date of origin is unknown. It was in use in the 10th century, but it may have been authored as early as the third century.

The *Sefer Yetzirah* presents a discussion on cosmology and cosmogony and sets forth the central structure of the kabbalah. It also is reputed to contain the formula for creation of a GOLEM, an artificial human.

In 917 a form of practical kabbalism was introduced by Aaron ben Samuel in Italy; it later spread through Germany and became known as German kabbalism or early Hasidim. It drew upon the Merkabah practices, in that it was ecstatic, had magic rituals, and had as primary techniques PRAYER, contemplation, and meditation. The magical power of words and names assumed great importance and gave rise to the techniques of gematria, notarikon, and temurah.

The Classical Kabbalah was born in the 13th century in Provence, France, and moved into Spain where it was developed most extensively by medieval Spanish Jews. The primary work from which classical kabbalah developed is the *Sefer Zohar* ("Book of Splendor"), attributed to a second-century sage, Rabbi Simeon bar Yohai, but actually written between 1280 and 1286 by the Spanish kabbalist Moses de Leon. According to lore, the book comprises the teachings given to Rabbi Simeon by divine revelation.

The teachings of the *Zohar* became known as the Spanish kabbalah and spread into Europe in the 14th and 15th centuries. After the expulsion of Jews from Spain in 1492, kabbalah study became more public. Isaac Luria Ashkenazi (1534–72), called the Ari Luria, a student of the great kabbalist Moses Cordovero (1522–70), conceived of bold new theories which gave the kabbalah a new terminology and complex new symbolism. Luria emphasized letter combinations as a medium for meditation and mystical prayer.

In the 14th century, a practical kabbalah developed involving magical techniques for making amulets and talismans and for invoking spirits. The practical kabbalah is complex and features the use of MAGICAL ALPHABETS, secret codes of communication with angels.

The Hasidic movement emerged from the Lurianic kabbalah, and made kabbalah accessible to the masses. The Hasidim are the only major branch of modern Judaism to follow mystical practices. Interest in the kabbalah among Jews declined after the 18th century. The Reconstructionist movement, founded in 1922 by Rabbi Mordecai M. Kaplan, borrows from Hasidic traditions and espouses a more mystical Judaism. Interest in kabbalah enjoyed a cross-cultural renewal beginning in the late 20th century as part of a broad interest in esoteric subjects.

Western occult interest in the kabbalah grew first out of German kabbalism and then Lurianic kabbalism. Christian occultists were attracted to the magical amulets, incantations, demonology, angelology, seals, and letter permutations and used these as the basis for ritual magical texts (see GRIMOIRES). The TETRAGRAMMATON was held in great awe for its power over all things in the universe, including DEMONS, a subject of intense fear and interest.

In the late 15th century, the kabbalah was harmonized with Christian doctrines, which supposedly proved the divinity of Christ. CORNELIUS AGRIPPA VON NETTESHEIM included kabbalah in his monumental work, *Occult Philosophy* (1531). Also in the 16th century, alchemical symbols were integrated into the Christian kabbalah.

Interest in the kabbalah received renewed attention in the 19th century from non-Jewish occultists such as FRANCIS BARRETT, ELIPHAS LEVI, and Papus. Levi's works were especially important in the occult revival that spread through Europe in the 19th century. As did some of his contemporaries, Levi related the kabbalah to the TAROT and NUMEROLOGY and drew connections to FREEMASONRY, in which he saw a fusion of Judaic kabbalism and neoplatonic Christianity. The kabbalah, he said in *The Book of Splendours,* is one of three occult sciences of certitude; the other two are magic and Hermeticism. Of the kabbalah, Levi said:

> The Qabalah, or traditional science of the Hebrews, might be called the mathematics of human thought. It is the algebra of faith. It solves all problems of the soul as equations, by isolating the unknowns. It gives to ideas the clarity and rigorous exactitude of numbers; its results, for the mind, are infallibility (always relative to the sphere of human knowledge) and for the heart, profound peace.

The kabbalah, along with ENOCHIAN MAGIC, Egyptian magic, and Abremalin magic, was made a center of the teachings of the HERMETIC ORDER OF THE GOLDEN DAWN. In 1888 Golden Dawn founder SAMUEL LIDDELL MacGREGOR MATHERS published the first English translation of a Latin translation of the kabbalah, *Kabbala Denuda,* by Knorr von Rosenroth. In his introduction, Mathers describes the kabbalah as the key that unlocks the mysteries of the Bible.

Central Concepts of the Kabbalah

God is *Ain Soph* ("without end" or "unending"), who is unknowable, unnameable, and beyond representation.

God created the world out of himself but is not diminished in any way through the act of creation; everything remains within him. The aim of humanity is to realize union with the Divine. All things are reflected in a higher world, and nothing can exist independently of all else. Thus, people, by elevating their souls to unite with God, also elevate all other entities in the cosmos.

One of the mysteries of the kabbalah is why God chose to create imperfect, lower worlds, though it is held that he did so because he wished to show the measure of his goodness. He created the world by means of 32 secret paths of wisdom, which are formed of letters and numbers: the 22 letters of the Hebrew alphabet and 10 sephirot (from the Hebrew word for "sapphire"), which are vessels bearing the emanations of God or are expressions of God. They form a language that substitutes for God. The sephirot are the source from which all numbers emanate and by which all reality is structured.

The sephirot comprise the sacred, unknowable, and unspeakable personal name of God: YHVH (Yahweh), the Tetragrammaton. So sacred is the Tetragrammaton that other names, such as Elohim, Adonai, and Jehovah, are substituted in its place in scripture. The letters YHVH correspond to the Four Worlds that constitute the cosmos:

- Atziluth is the world of archetypes and emanation from which are derived all forms of manifestation. The sephirot themselves exist here. Atziluth is the realm of contemplation.
- Briah (also Beriyah) is the world of creation, in which archetypal ideas become patterns. The Throne of God is here, and God sits upon it and lowers his essence to the rest of his creation. It is the realm of meditation.
- Yetzirah is the world of formation, in which the patterns are expressed. It is the world of speech, and also the realm of ritual magic.
- Assiah is the world of the material. It is the realm of action in daily life.

The Tree of Life
The sephirot form the central image of kabbalistic meditation, the Tree of Life, a ladder map that depicts the descent of the divine into the material world, and the path by which a person can ascend to the divine while still in the flesh. The sephirot channel streams of divine light become denser and coarser as they near the material plane. The divine light flows both down to the material world and up to God along these paths.

Organization of the Tree. Each sephirah is a state of consciousness and a level of attainment in knowledge: mystical steps to unity with God. The 10 sephirot are arranged in different groups that facilitate the understanding of their meanings. The first sephirah, Kether (Crown), is the closest to Ain Soph and is the source of all life and the highest object of prayer. Malkuth (Kingdom) penetrates the physical realm and is the only sephirah in direct contact with it. The lower seven sephirot are associated with the seven days of creation. Another division splits them into two groups of five, the upper ones representing hidden powers and the lower five representing manifest powers.

In another division, the top three—Kether, Chockmah (Wisdom), and Binah (Intelligence)—are associated with the intellect; the middle three—Chesed (Love), Geburah (Strength), and Tipareth (Beauty)—are associated with the soul; and the lower three—Netzach (Victory), Hod (Splendor), and Yesod (Foundation)—are associated with nature.

The sephirot are ineffable and descriptions of them cannot begin to approach their true essence. They can be reached only through the second sephirah, Chockmah (Wisdom), which is nonverbal consciousness. Binah (Intelligence) is verbal consciousness. One must learn to oscillate between Chockmah and Binah states of consciousness to grasp the sephirot.

The Tree is split into three pillars. The Right Pillar, masculine, represents Mercy and includes the sephirot Chockmah, Chesed, and Netzach. The Left Pillar, feminine, represents Severity and includes Binah, Geburah, and Hod. The Middle represents Mildness or Moderation and includes Kether, Tipareth, Yesod, and Malkuth. The Middle Pillar alone also is called the Tree of Knowledge.

Sometimes an 11th sephirah is included, Daath (Knowledge), located on the Middle Pillar below Chockmah and Binah, and mediates the influences of the two; it is also considered to be an external aspect of Kether. Daath made its appearance in the 13th century. When represented on the Tree, it is depicted as a sort of shadow sphere. Daath cannot be a true sephirah, for the Sefer Yetzirah, the key text of kabbalistic philosophy, states that there can be only 10 sephirot, no more, no less.

The pathways linking the sephirot have become more complex over time. Illustrations in the early 16th century, for example, depict only 16 pathways. By the 17th century, there were 22 pathways, each of which was assigned a letter of the Hebrew alphabet. Thus, God's creation is made through the essences of numbers and letters.

Together the sephiroth of the Tree of Life comprise a unity and create a five-dimensional continuum: the three dimensions of the physical world, plus time, plus the spiritual realm. Like the Akashic Records, they serve as a permanent record of everything that has ever taken place and ever will take place—the memory of God. The sephirot also serve as a means of communication with the unknowable God. The totality of the sephirot is expressed in the Tetragrammaton.

Following are the names and associations of the sephirot, as given in Agrippa's *Occult Philosophy:*

Kether

Number: One

Titles: The Crown; The Ancient One; The Aged; The Most Holy Ancient One; The Ancient of the Ancient Ones; The Ancient of Days; The Concealed of the Concealed; The Primordial Point; The Smooth Point; The White Head; The Inscrutable Height; The Vast Countenance (Macroprosopus); The Heavenly Man

Divine Name: Eheieh (I Am)

Archangel: Metatron

Angelic Order: Hayyoth (The Holy Living Creatures)

Archdemons: Satan, Moloch

Demonic Order: Thamiel (The Two Contenders)

Heavenly Sphere: Primum Mobile

Part of Man: Head

Chockmah

Number: Two

Titles: Wisdom; Divine Father; The Supernal Father

Divine Names: Jah; Jehovah (The Lord); Yod Jehovah (given by Agrippa)

Archangel: Raziel

Angelic Order: Ophanim (The Wheels)

Archdemon: Beelzebub

Demonic Order: Ghogiel (The Hinderers)

Heavenly Sphere: Zodiac

Part of Man: Brain

Binah

Number: Three

Titles: Intelligence; The Mother; The Great Productive Mother

Divine Names: Elohim (Lord); Jehovah Elohim (The Lord God)

Archangel: Tzaphkiel

Angelic Order: Aralim (The Thrones)

Archdemon: Lucifuge

Demonic Order: Ghogiel (The Concealers)

Heavenly Sphere: Saturn

Part of Man: Heart

Chesed

Number: Four

Titles: Love; Greatness

Divine Name: El (The Mighty One)

Archangel: Tzadkiel

Angelic Order: Hasmallim (The Shining Ones)

Archdemon: Ashtaroth

Demonic Order: Agshekeloh (The Smiters or Breakers)

Heavenly Sphere: Jupiter

Part of Man: Right arm

Geburah

Number: Five

Titles: Strength; Judgment or Severity; Fear

Divine Names: Eloh (The Almighty); Elohim Gabor (God of Battles)

Archangel: Camael

Angelic Order: Seraphim (The Fiery Serpents)

Archdemon: Asmodeus

Demonic Order: Golohab (The Burners or Flaming Ones)

Heavenly Sphere: Mars

Part of Man: Left arm

Tiphareth

Number: Six

Titles: Beauty; Compassion; The King; The Lesser Countenance (Microprosopus)

Divine Names: Eloah Va-Daath (God Manifest); Elohim (God)

Archangel: Raphael

Angelic Order: Malachim (Kings or Multitudes)

Archdemon: Belphegor

Demonic Order: Tagiriron (The Disputers)

Heavenly Sphere: Sun

Part of Man: Chest

Netzach

Number: Seven

Titles: Firmness; Victory

Divine Name: Jehovah Sabaoth (Lord of Hosts)

Archangel: Haniel

Angelic Order: Elohim (Gods)

Archdemon: Baal

Demonic Order: Nogah (The Raveners)

Heavenly Sphere: Venus

Part of Man: Right leg

Hod

Number: Eight

Titles: Splendor

Divine Name: Elohim Sabaoth (God of Hosts)

Archangel: Michael

Angelic Order: Bene Elohim (Sons of Gods)

Archdemon: Adrammelech

Demonic Order: Samael (The False Accusers)

Heavenly Sphere: Mercury

Part of Man: Left leg

Yesod

Number: Nine

Titles: The Foundation; Eternal Foundation of the World

Divine Names: Shaddai (The Almighty); El Chai (Mighty Living One)

Archangel: Gabriel

Angelic Order: Cherubim (The Strong)

Archdemon: Lilith (The Seducer)

Demonic Order: Gamaliel (The Obsecene Ones)

Heavenly Sphere: Moon

Part of Man: Genitals

Malkuth

Number: Ten

Titles: The Kingdom; The Diadem; The Manifest Glory of God; The Bride (of Microposopus); The Queen

Divine Names: Adonai (Lord); Adonai Malekh (Lord and King); Adonai he-Aretz (Lord of Earth)

Archangel: Metatron in manifest aspect; also Sandalphon

Angelic Order: Issim (Souls of Flame)

Archdemon: Nahema (The Strangler of Children)

Demonic Order: Nahemoth (The Dolorous Ones)

Heavenly Sphere: Elements

Part of Man: Whole body

Magical Work with the Tree of Life. DION FORTUNE, a Golden Dawn initiate, called the kabbalah the Yoga of the West. In spiritual and magical study, the Tree of Life is used to achieve union with God. The pathways between the sephirot are avenues of navigation on the ASTRAL PLANE. WILLIAM G. GRAY described the Tree of life as a living entity that changes in accordance to use. The Tree is an "alphabet of symbols" for constructing a spiritual language that can be understood on both sides of the veil, by humans, gods and angels alike.

In magical training, the occultist must learn the associations of each sephirah and path, such as magical TOOLS, colors, planets, chakras, virtues, vices, sounds, PERFUMES, and tarot cards, in addition to the associations given above. SYMBOLS are used as magical images for constructing specific visions. The symbols are not understood consciously but are used to evoke images from the subconscious.

Communication with the Tree is accomplished through PRAYER, meditation, contemplation, and ritual magic. Some traditional meditations of arrays of numbers and Hebrew letters take days to complete.

The sephirot are contemplated by visualizing them vibrating with color (which represent various qualities), together with images of their corresponding Hebrew letters of the divine names of God, and the planets, angels, metals, parts of the body, and energy centers. Breath and sound also are utilized to raise consciousness. Mantras of arrays of Hebrew letters, having specific numerical properties, are employed.

Bardon's unique hermetic approach to bring the kabbalah and magic together involves the keys, or meanings, and the sounds of each letter of the alphabet, and the couplings of two, three, and four letters. These combinations have associated affects in the four planes of akasha, mental, astral, and matter, and the four ELEMENTS, fire, water, air, and earth. According to Bardon, this system has been in existence for thousands of years as an oral teaching. The actual power and might of esoteric societies, including FREEMASONRY, stemmed from their knowledge of how to use the key of the Tetragrammaton.

FURTHER READING:

Bardon, Franz. *The Key to the True Kabbalah.* Salt Lake City: Merkur Publishing, 1996.

Fortune, Dion. *The Mystical Qabalah.* York Beach, Maine: Samuel Weiser, 1984.

Gray, William G. *The Ladder of Lights.* York Beach, Maine: Samuel Weiser, 1981.

Kraig, Donald Michael. *Modern Magick: Eleven Lessons in the High Magickal Arts.* 2d ed. St. Paul, Minn.: Llewellyn Publications, 2004.

Levi, Eliphas. *The Book of Splendours: The Inner Mysteries of the Qabalah.* 1894. Reprint, York Beach, Maine: Samuel Weiser.

———. *Transcendental Magic.* 1896. Reprint, York Beach, Maine: Samuel Weiser.

Mathers, S. L. MacGregor. *The Kabbalah Unveiled.* London: Routledge and Kegan Paul, 1926.

Scholem, Gershom. *Kabbalah.* New York: New American Library, 1974.

Three Books of Occult Philosophy Written by Henry Cornelius Agrippa of Nettesheim. Trans. James Freake. Ed. and annot. by Donald Tyson. St. Paul, Minn.: Llewellyn Publications, 1995.

Kabbalistic Cross   In the magical tradition of the HERMETIC ORDER OF THE GOLDEN DAWN, a RITUAL that is performed at the beginning and the end of all magical workings. The ritual draws down divine power using the Kabbalistic Tree of Life so that the practitioner becomes a cross of light.

There are four components to the Kabbalistic Cross:

1. Touch the forehead while vibrating Ateh (thou art)
2. Touch the breast while vibrating Malkuth (the Kingdom)
3. Touch the right shoulder while vibrating Ve-Geburah (and the power)
4. Touch the left shoulder while vibrating Ve-Gedulah (and the Glory)

While performing these actions, the magician visualizes his hand drawing a line of white light through the crown of his head so that the light pours through his body to the solar plexus and then through to the feet, which are associated with the sephirah of Malkuth. The hand also draws a line of light from the right shoulder to the left shoulder. Thus the body becomes a cross of light. The magician visualizes in the center of the cross a rose or a rose-cross, while saying Le-Olam, Amen.

FURTHER READING:
King, Francis, and Stephen Skinner. *Techniques of High Magic: A Manual of Self-Initiation.* Rochester, Vt.: Destiny Books, 1976.

Kelly, Edward (1555–1595)   Fraudulent alchemist, best known for his turbulent partnership with JOHN DEE. Edward Kelly's name was also spelled *Kelley;* he used the alias surname of Talbot as well.

Kelly was born in Worcester, England, in 1555. He served as an apprentice to an apothecary, where he probably learned enough about chemistry to develop his fraudulent schemes later. He attended Oxford but left suddenly

Edward Kelly, in A True & Faithful Relation of What Passed for Many Years Between Dr. John Dee and Some Spirits, *by Meric Causabon, 1659.* (Author's collection)

without earning a degree. In London he earned a reputation as a fraudulent lawyer. He moved on to Lancaster where he engaged in forgery and counterfeiting, for which he was punished by having his ears lopped off in a pillory. He also was accused of practicing NECROMANCY with a corpse that he dug up himself.

Evidently Kelly heard about Dee and his occult interests. In 1582 he covered up his ear holes with a black skull cap and paid a visit to Dee at his home in Mortlake. He introduced himself as a serious student of the occult and asked Dee for instruction. Initially, Dee did not acknowledge his interest in MAGIC and SCRYING, but Kelly persuaded him to bring out his smoky quartz crystal for a scrying session with the spirits. While Kelly scried, Dee waited to take notes.

Not surprisingly, Kelly produced incredible results. He said the archangel Uriel appeared and gave instructions for invoking other spirits. Uriel also said that an evil spirit named Lundrumguffa was harmful to Dee and should be banished. Furthermore, Uriel instructed Dee to engage Kelly as scryer and to work with him always. Dee did as told, and Kelly moved in to the Dee household. He and Dee engaged in alchemical research as well as sessions with the spirits. The angels spoke in Enochian, according to Kelly. He could understand it and translated it for Dee. (See also ENOCHIAN MAGIC.)

Kelly easily fooled the credulous Dee. Once they took a trip to the abbey ruins at GLASTONBURY, where Kelly managed to "find" a supply of the PHILOSOPHER'S STONE that had been allegedly made by St. Dunstan.

Their work caught the attention of nobility, including the Polish count Albert Laski, who was looking for alchemists to restore his lost fortune. Laski invited Kelly and Dee to Europe, and they and their wives set off in 1584. They were not well received. For four years they were hounded from city to city as frauds, finally landing at Count Rosenberg's castle in Tribau in Bohemia. Kelly still possessed some of St. Dunstan's Philosopher's Stone, and he put on a show of making a transmutation for the count. He took one grain of the Stone and supposedly transmuted one-and-a-half ounces of MERCURY into nearly an ounce of GOLD. Kelly also supposedly made gold out of a piece of metal cut from a warming pan; he sent both to Queen Elizabeth as "proof" of his talent.

The beginning of the end of Kelly's relationship came in 1587 while they were still in Tribau. Kelly raised his effrontery to new heights when he reported that he saw a naked woman in the scrying crystal and that she ordered that Kelly and Dee should share their wives. Dee, who usually demurred to Kelly's demands, balked, and so did Dee's wife Jane. But Kelly prevailed, and Dee signed an agreement submitting to wife-sharing. It is not known whether any actual wife-sharing occurred, but violent quarrels did, and the Kelly-Dee partnership was torn asunder. The Dees returned to England in 1588, and Kelly went back to Prague.

Emperor Rudolf II still was unimpressed with Kelly and soon threw him into prison. Kelly languished there for four years and then was released. But a year later Rudolf imprisoned him again. In 1595 Kelly attempted to escape by making crude rope. He fell and sustained mortal injuries, dying several days later.

According to a diary of Dee's, Kelly successfully made gold on December 19, 1586, at the Rosenberg castle. In 1588 Dee wrote to the Elizabethan courtier Dyer about his travels with Kelly and that Kelly "had at last achieved the secret of the ages, that Kelly could indeed transmute base metals into gold." This startling news caused Dyer to leave England and go to Prague to investigate for himself.

Dee's diary for 1586 gives brief descriptions of some of the stages of the Great Work:

> March 24th, Mr K. put the glass in dung. . . . Dec 13th, Mr E.K. gave me the water, earth and all. . . . [on 19th December] E.K. made projection with his powder in the proportion of one minim upon an ounce and a quarter of mercury and produced nearly an ounce and a quarter of best gold; which gold we afterwards distributed from the crucible.

Dee's diary shows that he did not know exactly how this process worked. About a year-and-a-half later, Kelly allegedly revealed the secret to him. Dee cryptically recorded on May 10, 1588, that "E.K. did open the Great Secret to me, God be thanked."

Kelly later wrote to Dyer, "what delight we took together, when from the Metall simply calcined into powder after the usuall manner, distilling the Liquor so prepared with the same, we converted appropriate bodies (as our Astronomie inferiour teacheth) into Mercury, their first matter."

Alchemical texts that have been attributed to Kelly are *The Stone of the Philosophers* and *The Theatre of Terrestrial Astronomy*, which appear in *Tractatus duo egregii, de Lapide Philosophorum, una cum Theatro astronomae terrestri, cum Figuris, in gratiam filiorum Hermetis nunc primum in lucem editi, curante J. L.M.C.* [Johanne Lange Medicin Candidato], published in Hamburg in 1676.

FURTHER READING:
Halliwell, James Orchard. *Private Diary of Dr. John Dee and the Catalog of His Library of Alchemical Manuscripts.* Whitefish, Mont.: Kessinger, 1997.
Holmyard, E. J. *Alchemy.* New York: Penguin Books, 1957.
"The Stone of the Philosophers by Edward Kelly." Available online. URL: http://www.levity.com/alchemy/kellystn. html. Downloaded January 8, 2005.

Key of Solomon   See GRIMOIRES.

Khunrath, Heinrich (1560–1601 or 1604)

Influential German alchemist. Heinrich Khunrath's work blends phil-

Heinrich Khunrath at age 42, by Jan Diricks van Campen of Magdeburg, 1602. (Author's collection)

osophical elements of ROSICRUCIANISM, the KABBALAH, and Paracelsian thought.

Khunrath was born in 1560 in Leipzig. He obtained his medical degree in 1588 at the University of Basel, Switzerland, and entered the court of Emperor Rudolph II.

Khunrath believed that revelation comes through the "book of Nature." He saw the PHILOSOPHER'S STONE symbolized in Christ. His most important alchemical work is *Amphitheatrum sapientias aeternae* ("The Amphitheater of Eternal Wisdom"), printed in 1602. Khunrath never finished the manuscript.

Amphitheatrum is magical and mystical. It states that the path to understanding the mysteries of the macrocosm can be found through Christ, the Stone, and God. Khunrath gives 365 daily meditations, as well as alchemical interpretations of biblical texts, especially Proverbs, and also the Wisdom of Solomon, an apocryphal work.

One of the engravings in *Amphitheatrum* shows Khunrath, as an alchemist, kneeling in PRAYER in his laboratory. Another well-known engraving is of the EMERALD TABLET, depicted as an engraved triangular stone topped by a flame.

Different dates and places are given for Khunrath's death. He is said to have died in Antwerp in 1604. According to ARTHUR EDWARD WAITE, he died in obscurity and poverty on September 9, 1601, in Dresden.

FURTHER READING:
Klossowski de Rola, Stanislaus. *The Golden Game: Alchemical Engravings of the Seventeenth Century.* New York: George Braziller, Inc., 1988.
Waite, Arthur Edward. *Alchemists Through the Ages.* Blauvelt, N.Y.: Rudolph Steiner Publications, 1970.

Kirk, Robert   See FAIRIES.

Knights Templar   See ORDER OF THE KNIGHTS TEMPLAR.

knots   TOOL in folk MAGIC SPELLS. Knots are tied in cords, ropes, scarves, and so forth to bind magical power and are untied to release power. A spell is recited while knots are tied or untied.

Scandinavian sorcerers used knotted cords to control the weather at sea. The cords, which had three knots, would be untied in accordance with the desired weather. One knot yielded a breeze, two knots a violent wind, and three knots a tempest.

Knots are used in love magic to attract and bind love and to prevent someone from falling in love. A magical spell from ancient Egypt for securing love is as follows:

Take a band of linen of 16 threads, four of white, four of green, four of blue, four of red, and make them into one band, and stain them with the blood of a hoopoe [bird], and you bind it with a scarab in its attitude of the sun-god, drowned, being wrapped in byssus [woolen cloth], and you bind it to the body of the boy who has the vessel and it will work quickly.

Knotting a cord while reciting antilove CHARMS will prevent two people from falling in love. According to one spell, attend a marriage ceremony and secretly knot a cord—preferably THREE knots in a cord made of three colors—while the couple says their wedding vows. The couple will not be able to consummate their marriage and will fall out of love with each other. The spell can be broken by rubbing the threshold of the marriage chamber with wolf fat.

A man can make himself immune to antilove-knot magic before getting married by filling his pockets with SALT and urinating just before entering the church.

In Italian lore, the "witches' garland" is a rope tied into knots that is used for casting CURSES. With every knot that is tied, the curse is repeated, and a black feather is stuck into the knot. The best results are obtained when the garland is hidden beneath the victim's mattress.

In the Koran, Muhammad associated evil magic with women who blew on knots. According to lore, the prophet believed at one time that he was suffering from a SPELL of BEWITCHMENT cast by a man whose daughters tied the spell into a cord with 11 knots and hid the cord in a WELL. Muhammad fell seriously ill. God sent to him TWO surahs—verses of the Koran—about SORCERY—and also sent the archangel Gabriel to tell Muhammad how to use the surahs and where to find the magical cord. Muhammad had the cord brought to him. He recited the 11 verses of the two surahs over the cord, and as he spoke each line, one knot became untied. When all 11 knots were undone, the spell was broken and Muhammad recovered.

FURTHER READING:
Ashley, Leonard R. N. *The Amazing World of Superstition, Prophecy, Luck, Magic & Witchcraft.* New York: Bell Publishing Company, 1988.
Budge, E. A. Wallis. *Amulets and Superstitions.* 1930. Reprint, New York: Dover Publications, 1978.

Lam Entity contacted by ALEISTER CROWLEY.

In 1918 Crowley conducted a sex magic RITUAL called the Almalantrah working with Roddie Minor, known as Soror Ahitha. The working created a portal in the spaces between stars, through which Lam was able to enter the known physical universe. Since then, other entities are believed to enter through this widening portal and to be the basis for numerous contact experiences with UFOs and extraterrestrials.

One of the revelations of the working was the symbolism of the EGG. Crowley and Soror Ahitha were told, "It's all in the egg."

Crowley believed Lam to be the soul of a dead Tibetan lama from Leng, between China and Tibet. *Lam* is Tibetan for "Way" or "Path," which Crowley said had the numerical value of 71, or "No Thing," a gateway to the Void and a link between the star systems of Sirius and Andromeda. Lam was to fulfill the work initiated by AIWASS.

Crowley drew a portrait of Lam and said that gazing on the portrait enables one to make contact with the entity.

lampes de charm In Vodoun, "charm lamps" for casting SPELLS. *Lampes de charm* are small bowl or cups or are made from coconut shells or crab shells. They contain perfumed oil and two pieces of floating bones that form the shape of a CROSS. The lamps are burned to bring about a good desire or wish.

Hexing *lampes de charm* for evil purposes are painted black. Their oil contains *poudre de mort,* or powdered human bones, powdered lizard, and human sperm.

See also HEX; *WANGA.*

lapis See PHILOSOPHER'S STONE.

larvae Half-beings existing on either the ASTRAL PLANE or the MENTAL PLANE—usually astral—that are created from intense thought, especially over a prolonged period. Larvae are usually negative in nature and are associated with a person's preoccupation or obsession with a particular passion or habit. A person's thoughts and emotional energies nourish a larva and enable it to maintain its existence.

The form or shell of a larva depends on its created characteristics. It has enough intelligence to direct itself toward self-preservation; thus it is vampiric in nature, feeding off its human source. Larvae can gain strength over time and may be difficult to dislodge and destroy by MAGIC.

FURTHER READING:
Bardon, Franz. *Questions and Answers.* Salt Lake City: Merkur Publishing, 1998.

Lemegeton See GRIMOIRES.

Lesser Key of Solomon   See GRIMOIRES.

Levi, Eliphas (1810–1875)   French occultist who was a leader of the occult revival of the 19th century. Eliphas Levi has often been called the last of the magi. He is said to have coined the term *occult*.

He was born Alphonse Louis Constant in Paris in 1810. His father was a poor shoemaker and had no means to provide for his son's education. Young Constant was schooled at a local Catholic parish at the church of Saint Sulpice. He became a deacon and aspired to be a priest, even taking a vow of celibacy. But his tendency to speak his mind and not stick to teaching the doctrines of the church led to his expulsion.

Constant then became involved in radical politics, for which he was imprisoned several times. He married a 16-year-old girl named Madamoiselle Noemy, who gained fame in her own right as a sculptor. The couple had two children, who died in either infancy or childhood. After seven years Noemy left Levi and succeeded in getting the marriage nullified on the grounds that she had been a minor when they were wed.

In the wake of his marital breakup, Levi immersed himself in a study of the occult, teaching the KABBALAH, MAGIC, and ALCHEMY. He quickly became famous throughout Europe. His studies focused on the kabbalah, the TAROT, and the writings of Swedish mystic Emannuel Swedenborg. He was the first to draw a connection between the kabbalah and the Tarot. During this time, Constant called himself Abbé Constant and dressed in clerical garb, though it is doubtful that he was ever ordained a priest. He earned his living teaching magic. He was inspired by FRANCIS BARRETT's book *The Magus* (1801), which was a derivative of *Three Books on Occult Philosophy* by HENRY CORNELIUS AGRIPPA.

In the mid-1850s, he took the Hebrew equivalent of his name, Eliphas Levi, and wrote under the name Magus Eliphas Levi. His best-known work is *Transcendental Magic,* published in 1860, which presents his own system of magic, based in part on the GRIMOIRE known as the *Greater Key of Solomon.* Other significant works by Levi are *The History of Magic, The Mysteries of the Qabalah, The Great Secret,* and *The Book of Splendours.* Levi's works were a focus of the French occult revival, which gained momentum in the several decades following his death.

Levi's work so impressed and influenced other occultists that he was one of the few French experts to be translated into English. ARTHUR EDWARD WAITE, a principal in the HERMETIC ORDER OF THE GOLDEN DAWN, translated his works so that he could better study them himself. Waite called Levi a magus of light. Levi also influenced the English author Lord Bulwer Lytton, whom he met during a trip to London in 1853. Levi taught Lytton various magical RITUALS and procedures that Lytton incorporated into his fictional works, *A Strange Story* (1862) and *The Haunted and the Haunters* (1857), in which Levi served as the model for the magus.

ALEISTER CROWLEY, who was born in the same year that Levi died, claimed to be a reincarnation of Levi. Crowley translated Levi's book *The Key of the Mysteries.*

According to Levi, two things are necessary to acquire magical power: "to disengage the will from all servitude, and to exercise it in control."

FURTHER READING:
Levi, Eliphas. *The History of Magic.* 1860. Reprint, York Beach, Maine: Samuel Weiser, 2001.
———. *Transcendental Magic.* 1896. Reprint, York Beach, Maine: Samuel Weiser, 2001.

leys   Patterns of invisible lines of a complex power that seem to link sacred places and natural magical sites. These patterns and alignments are important for their connection to the forces of the elements, the basis of natural MAGIC. Leys also are called ley lines.

The original theory of leys was put forth in 1925 by a British amateur antiquarian, Alfred Watkins. Watkins observed that humanmade sacred places such as burial mounds, megaliths, churches, and pagan worship sites as well as natural peaks, magical springs, WELLS, and other earth features seemed to align with one another. The "leys," as Watkins named these alignments, were "old straight tracks" found by prehistoric ley hunters, or Dodman surveyors, who mapped the countryside to find power spots for sacred constructions, trade routes, and astronomical sites. Although the original mapping allegedly was done by prehistoric societies, Watkins included in his list of ley sites pre-Reformation churches. His theory was quite controversial. It was and still is rejected by scientists but has enjoyed a popular following. Public interest waned in the 1940s but has increased since the latter part of the 20th century.

Not all alignments are true leys. Modern ley hunters map leys by checking the alignments of various locations according to what else of significance lies in a sight line within a certain distance: a standing stone, church site, pagan sacred site, burial mound, mountain, and so on. Some alignments are astronomical, such as points where the sun rises at Beltane, the solstices, or the equinoxes. Some ley hunters say five alignments within 10 miles is required, while others maintain five within 25 miles is sufficient. Dowsers say that in addition, the alignment must be a dowsable energy line.

Ley centers, places charged with energy, radiate at least seven ley lines and are situated over magnetic fields or blind springs, a primary spiral of converging primary geodetic lines (the shortest lines between two points on a curved surface). It is possible that ancient pagans were aware of this energy radiating up from the earth and situated their sacred sites accordingly.

The energy charge is a vital force classed as either male or female depending on its rate of vibration and is present in all living material. In ley centers, the charge may be natural or artificial. Artificial charges may be induced in stones and metals by handling. Whether natural or artificial, the charge dissipates over time unless fixed by hammering, heating, or the presence of a magnetic field.

The stones used in the construction of meglithic monuments, churchs, holy wells, and temples were charged by handling and then fixed by being shaped with the blows of axes and chisels. The magnitude of the charge is thought to be related to the number of blows and the dimensions of the stones. Therefore, the charge of megaliths would be very great. Cremation pits and burials, such as those at Stonehenge; sacrifical pits and altars; and the burning of wood also fixed the charges.

The very ground itself may be charged and fixed with blows. British folklore tells of the ancient custom of "beating the parish bounds," in which the church priest and choirboys would go around the parish perimeter beating the ground with rods. Most likely, this was believed to erect a protective energy barrier around the parish.

The geomagnetic forces surrounding ley centers emit a beneficial energy, but the charge of stones themselves is sometimes found to emit a detrimental energy. This apparently is counteracted by the leys themselves, which redirected energy to other centers where it could be neutralized. Also, the charges may have been deliberately masked. Certain woods such as elm and elderberry; metals such as IRON; and mineral substances such as salt, quartz crystals, amethysts, jasper, and flint have been shown to mask charged stones. (Iron, salt, elm, and elderberry are all revered in folklore for their protective properties against bewitchment, illness, demons, and bad fortune.) The giant bluestones of Stonehenge contain flakes of quartz crystal. These stones were dismantled and reerected twice during the various construction phases of the monument; perhaps the builders recognized their beneficial properties. Also, quartz chips scattered among charged stones disrupts the power.

Lili Termed used by PARACELSUS for the PHILOSOPHER'S STONE.

lodges A system of organization and membership for magical, esoteric, and fraternal groups. Magical lodges have their roots in medieval trade guilds.

Traditionally, trade and fraternal guilds were economic and social organizations, intended to help members with wages, homes, health care, community support, and other needs. FREEMASONRY was the most significant movement to fuse the concept of these organizations with esoteric activities, creating a large system of exclusive and secret lodges open only to initiates. In the late 19th century, the HERMETIC ORDER OF THE GOLDEN DAWN established what became a model for magical lodges to come, emphasizing both RITUAL work within the organization and individual ritual work by initiates.

A magical lodge is a bridge between worlds, a place where the physical realm comes into contact with the spiritual realm. It is composed of individuals who share a common purpose or vision. It is organized around a chartered heritage or philosophy. The inner workings of a lodge—its rituals, SYMBOLS, and teachings—are secret.

Lodges have hierarchies, officers, by-laws, and rules governing the structure of their activities and the roles of initiates. Teachings are organized around grades of proficiency and knowledge, through which a member advances. A lodge has its own physical space, akin to a temple, where meetings are conducted and rituals are performed. The designs of lodges are planned and laid out to incorporate the important magical elements and symbols of the lodge.

Black lodges are said to be organized to serve the powers of darkness and evil. Belief in them was high during the late 19th and early 20th centuries, though evidence of their existence is scant.

See also BARDON, FRANZ; BROTHERHOODS.

FURTHER READING:
Greer, John Michael. *Inside a Magical Lodge: Group Ritual in the Western Tradition.* St. Paul, Minn.: Llewellyn Publications, 1998.

Lord of the Rings, The Author J. R. R. TOLKIEN's epic story of the destruction of the One Ring and the triumph of good over evil. *The Lord of the Rings* trilogy is considered one of the greatest literary achievements of the 20th century. It not only created the fantasy-story genre but spawned an entire industry of both serious research works and *LOTR* products that continue to appeal to the fans of Middle-Earth. Peter Jackson's film version of the trilogy (2001–03) introduced a whole new generation to the magic of J. R. R. Tolkien's world.

For all the wondrous creatures, places, and objects in *The Lord of the Rings*, perhaps the most fantastic is the author himself, John Ronald Reuel Tolkien. An eager student of languages and literature, Tolkien was one of the world's foremost philologists and an Oxford professor of Anglo-Saxon and English. To him, words and language *were* magic. He, his wife Edith, and their four children lived quietly in the country and counted another Oxford don, C. S. Lewis—author of *The Chronicles of Narnia*—as one of their closest friends. Lewis also wrote several books on religion and his conversion to Christianity, a choice inspired in part by Tolkien's deep Catholic faith. Tolkien never dreamed that his stories about hobbits and elves, WIZARDS and warriors would be so popular or make him such a public figure. He originally believed they were just for children.

His first published book, *The Hobbit, or There and Back Again* (1937), was a tale he told his three sons and one daughter. The story chronicles the adventures of Bilbo Baggins, a Hobbit about half the size of a man, who leaves the comforts of his home at Bag End in the Shire to travel with Dwarves and the wizard Gandalf the Grey to see the wider world. Along the way he meets Elves and Orcs, dragons and giant spiders, and most importantly Gollum: a type of Hobbit named Sméagol who murdered his best friend Déagol to possess the One Ring of Power made by the sorcerer Sauron—Gollum's prize possession that he calls his "Precious." But the Ring leaves Gollum, and Bilbo finds it in the Misty Mountains. The Hobbit does not understand the Ring's strength, but he intuitively senses something about the gold band, hiding it when he returns to the Shire. Even Gandalf does not realize until much later what a prize Bilbo has acquired.

The Hobbit, although published first, was not Tolkien's first book, however. Ever since returning from military service in France during World War I, Tolkien had been working on what he called a mythological identity for England to compensate for the legends he felt were lost as a result of the waves of barbarian invasions and the conquest of England by the Normans in 1066. With his extensive knowledge of languages, both modern and ancient, and his ability to create entire societies with their kings, their calendars, their histories, and their languages and alphabets, Tolkien invented a world where Elf-lords and larger-than-life Men from the Western Seas ruled during the First and Second Ages of Middle-Earth. When his publisher asked for more Hobbit tales, Tolkien submitted this early history—a prequel to *The Hobbit* and *The Lord of the Rings* which he called *The Silmarillion*—but with little success. Tolkien's son Christopher eventually edited his father's work and released the book in 1977.

Somewhat reluctantly, Tolkien began to work on *LOTR,* but World War II, paper rationing, his own penchant for perfectionist revision, and the enormity of the world of Middle-Earth postponed publication until 1954 and 1955 in England and slightly later in the United States. Tolkien never saw the stories as a trilogy but instead as one volume comprised of six books: The Return of the Shadow, The Fellowship of the Ring, The Treason of Isengard, The Journey to Mordor, The War of the Ring, and The Return of the King. His U.K. publisher, Allen & Unwin, however, was unsure of sales, and paper was still in short supply, so *LOTR* was divided into three volumes, and the story has been described as a trilogy ever since: *The Fellowship of the Ring, The Two Towers,* and *The Return of the King.* (Tolkien never liked the third title because he thought it gave away the story's end.)

Synopses of the Books
In Book I, *The Fellowship of the Ring,* Bilbo Baggins plans to leave the Shire for good to stay with his friends, the Elves in Rivendell. At the urging of the wizard Gandalf the Grey, Bilbo reluctantly gives his Ring to his nephew Frodo Baggins, who, like Bilbo, does not understand the Ring's power. Gandalf—who with a Ranger named Strider has started to see Black Riders in the Shire—convinces Frodo to take the Ring and leave Bag End. Gandalf realizes

that Bilbo's Ring was the One, long-sought by the sorcerer Sauron and that the Hobbit's life is in grave danger. The Hobbits Meriodoc Brandybuck (Merry), Peregrin Took (Pippin), and Samwise Gamgee (Sam) accompany Frodo on his journey, joined later by Strider and Gandalf.

Facing increasing danger from the ghostly Black Riders, also known as Ringwraiths or Nazgûl, the travelers make their way to Rivendell, home of the Elf-lord Elrond. Frodo discovers that wearing the Ring makes one invisible, but that the Wraiths still can sense the Ring's presence. The Lord of the Wraiths injures Frodo with his sword in an encounter at Weathertop, putting him at risk of becoming a Wraith. At Rivendell Gandalf reports that the wizard Saruman the White at Isengard has allied himself with Sauron. Elrond holds a council to decide the fate of the One Ring, for if found by Sauron, all will be lost. Frodo volunteers to be the Ring-bearer and throw the Ring into the fires of Mount Doom, thereby destroying it. Accompanying him is a Fellowship composed of Strider, now revealed to be Aragorn, Chief of the Dúnedain; Boromir of Gondor; Gimli the Dwarf; Legolas, the Elf-prince of Mirkwood; Gandalf; and the other three Hobbits.

Leaving Rivendell the company tries to cross the mountains but are turned back by the snow. Instead they go through Moria, the underground mines and halls of the Dwarves. No one dwells there any more, as all were defeated in battles with the Orcs. Making their way cautiously through the caverns, the travelers are nearly trapped as Orcs and trolls again try to gain the Ring. Fighting fiercely while running for their lives, they are stopped by a Balrog. Gandalf urges the others to cross the narrow stone bridge of Khazad-dûm and escape, for only he can possibly defeat the monster. During the struggle both are lost in a great abyss as the stone bridge cracks and breaks. The others escape but grieve for the loss of Gandalf, and they fear that their mission is doomed.

Turning south the travelers enter the land of Lothlórien, ruled by Celeborn and Lady Galadriel, the oldest of the Elves. Galadriel permits Frodo and Sam to look into her mirror to see what might be. Frodo is overcome by the appearance of Sauron's eye. He offers the Ring to Galadriel, but she already wears one of the Three Rings owned by the Elves, and she declines. Each of the travelers receives a magic Elven cloak fastened by a green-leaf brooch, and Galadriel gives Frodo a phial containing the light of Eärendil.

Book I ends with the dissolution of the Fellowship. Consumed by desire for the Ring, Boromir tries to take it from Frodo, but Frodo slips it on his finger and becomes invisible. Terrible visions show all Middle-Earth preparing for war. Becoming visible again Frodo tries to leave alone for Mordor, but Sam, who has promised to attend Master Frodo to the end, goes with him. They float noiselessly down the river, while the others, unaware of the Hobbits' departure, plan to head for Minas Tirith in Gondor.

Book II, *The Two Towers,* begins with the search for Frodo and Sam, interrupted by an Orc attack. Ordered to save the Halflings (Hobbits), the Orcs kidnap Merry and Pippin but kill Boromir. Aragorn, Legolas, and Gimli enter Rohan looking for the Orcs and Hobbits, where they meet Éomer, nephew of King Théoden, and the Rohirrim: the fabled horsemen of Rohan. By this time Merry and Pippin have escaped the Orcs and entered Fangorn forest, where they encounter Treebeard the Ent, an ancient tree shepherd. The Hobbits describe Saruman's treachery and destruction of the trees, and Treebeard musters the other Ents to march on Isengard. When Saruman sends his armies out to meet the men in Rohan, the Ents attack, tearing down the fortifications and flooding the area.

Meanwhile, Aragorn, Legolas, and Gimli pick up the trail of Merry and Pippin into Fangorn, but before they find the Hobbits, they are reunited with Gandalf, now the White, who survived the battle with the Balrog. He leads them to Edoras, home of King Théoden, who has become aged and ill through possession by Saruman. Gandalf breaks the spell, evicts Saruman's toady Wormtongue, and the men ride to the mountain fortress of Helm's Deep to fight Saruman's armies of Orcs and the even fiercer Uruk-hai. Many die, but the allies survive and ride to Isengard.

When they arrive, Isengard lies in ruins, but the friends are reunited with Merry and Pippin, discovered resting on the rubble. Saruman makes one last effort to recruit Gandalf but instead loses his crystal ball, called a *palantír:* Curious, Pippin dangerously gazes into the ball, nearly succumbing to Sauron. When Gandalf realizes that Sauron has released the Nine Nazgûl to seek the Ring again, the soldiers and friends return swiftly to Rohan.

Frodo and Sam, unaware of the others' trials, continue on to Mordor. All this time, Gollum has been following the Hobbits to try and regain his Precious, and when they meet he offers to guide Frodo and Sam to Mordor. Frodo takes pity on Gollum, a figure so warped from years of hiding in the dark that his two personalities—Gollum and Sméagol—talk and argue with each other. Warily the trio proceed to the Black Gate, past the faces of the corpses in the pools of the Dead Marshes, but the gate is shut fast. Trying another route, the three proceed through Ithilien. There they are captured by Faramir, captain of Gondor and Boromir's younger brother, and his men.

Book II ends with Gollum's treachery as he leads the Hobbits into the dark tunnels of the giant spiders, led by their queen, Shelob. Frodo raises the phial of light that he received from Galadriel and finds that they are trapped by giant webs. Holding the light and swinging his sword, Sting, Frodo tries to escape but is caught by Shelob, stung with poison, and bound. When Sam finally catches up to Frodo after fighting with Gollum and Shelob, he thinks that Frodo is dead and with regret realizes that he must finish their task. Taking the phial and Sting, he removes the Ring and its chain from around Frodo's neck and presses on. But Orcs are about, and Sam learns too late that Frodo is alive and captured by the enemy.

Book III, *The Return of the King,* opens with Gandalf and Pippin riding Shadowfax and entering Minas Tirith in Gondor. Pippin offers himself in service to Lord Denethor as small recompense for the death of his son Boromir. The others head for Rohan to muster the Riders (and where Théoden makes Merry his esquire) but are overtaken by a company of Dúnedain from the North and joined by Elladan and Elrohir, Elrond's sons. They remind Aragorn that he should travel by the Paths of the Dead. In the days of Isildur, a band of warriors broke their oath and retreated into the mountains rather than fight Sauron. They were cursed to remain as ghosts until one of Isildur's line called on them to honor their pledge. Minas Tirith is besieged by thousands of Sauron's forces. The city gate gives way under a battering ram, but the Witch-King of Angmar, chief of the Nazgûl, cannot get past Gandalf. The Rohirrim finally arrive, and the Battle of the Pelennor Fields commences.

King Théoden, accompanied by Merry, slays many before he is dealt a fatal blow. The Witch-King swoops down riding a horrible winged creature, prepared to take Théoden, when a knight named Dernholm orders him to depart. Confident that no man can kill him, the Witch-King moves forward. But to Merry's horror, Dernholm reveals herself to be Éowyn, Éomer's sister, and with the Hobbit's help kills the Nazgûl—for neither were men. The fighting is fierce, but just as hope fades, Aragorn arrives by sea with reinforcements, unfurling his standard as king of Gondor and Arnor, and spirits rise.

Meanwhile, Denethor, grieving for Boromir and the end of his reign now that Aragorn has come, has lost all reason and attempts to burn himself and his son Faramir—who had been injured in battle and is suffering from fever—on a pyre. Gandalf and Pippin save Faramir just in time, but Denethor dies. Faramir, Éowyn, and Merry are taken to the Houses of Healing to recover. The allies ride to the Black Gate where the Mouth of Sauron tries to ransom Frodo's things and scare the Fellowship into believing that the Hobbit is dead and that the Ring is with his Master. Sauron's armies surround them.

Stumbling through the dark, Sam discovers that the Orcs have gone, and he finds Frodo naked and wounded. They make their way out of Cirith Ungol tower and slowly cross Mordor. Crawling the last few feet toward the Crack of Doom, Frodo suddenly decides that he cannot part with the Ring. To Sam's horror Frodo puts on the Ring and disappears, but before Sam can act, Gollum attacks him and then follows Frodo to the very edge of the chasm. Desperate, Gollum bites off Frodo's finger and takes the Ring, but his dance of glee topples him over the edge, and calling out "Precious," he and the Ring disappear into the flames.

All of Mordor begins to tremble and blaze as the allies try to push back the armies of Sauron and avoid the Nazgûl. But with the Ring's destruction, the enemy falters and retreats. Gwaihir the Eagle Windlord arrives to carry Gandalf to rescue Sam and Frodo from the burning mountain. Days later Aragorn honors the Hobbits as true heroes at a ceremony on the Field of Cormallen. Sam and Frodo also learn what befell their friends after the Fellowship disbanded. Aragorn Arathornson takes the crown as King

Elessar Elfstone of Gondor and Arnor, and at Midsummer, Elessar marries Elrond's daughter, Arwen Undómiel or Evenstar, his heart's desire.

The rest of the book ties up the loose ends. Faramir and Éowyn marry. The Hobbits slowly ride back to the Shire, saying their goodbyes on the way. When they arrive, they find that Saruman and his bullies have taken over their homeland and terrorized the people. The Hobbits stage one last battle to clean the Shire, after which they confront Saruman and Wormtongue, who is with him. Wormtongue grovels until he can take the wizard's abuse no longer, then pulls out a knife, and slits Saruman's throat. Hobbit archers kill Wormtongue in turn. With peace restored, Sam marries Rose Cotton, and Frodo writes of the Fellowship's adventures in the Red Book begun by Bilbo so many years before.

But Frodo cannot resume the rhythm of Shire life. His wounds pain him, and he is sad and restless. So at the very end, he asks Sam to join him on a short journey, and Merry and Pippin come along. They travel to the sea, where a ship carrying Galadriel, Elrond, Gandalf, and Bilbo await Frodo to sail to the Grey Havens, where all who have struggled can finally rest. Tolkien also includes extensive appendices explaining the geneologies of the kings of Númenor and Rohan; the story of Aragorn and Arwen; the different languages and alphabets of the Elves, Dwarves, sorcerers, and men; the calendars of the Shire and elsewhere; and maps of all the lands of Middle-Earth.

Magical People, Places, and Things

Nothing in Middle-Earth can be considered ordinary, but some of the people, creatures, places, and things either possess magical powers or are so unusual that they stand out against the rest. It has been said that for Tolkien the words were the true agents of ENCHANTMENT and that he created his world to accommodate them. This idea has roots in the biblical notion of the Word and in ancient beliefs regarding the power of NAMES.

Middle-Earth itself comes from the Old English *middangeard:* the everyday world we live in between Heaven and Hell; the battleground for the forces of good and evil. According to his biography from the Tolkien Society, Tolkien was amazed to encounter the following couplet from the Old English poem, *Crist of Cynewulf:*

> *Eálá Earendel engla beorhtast*
> *Ofer middangeard monnum sended.*

> (Hail, Earendel, brightest of angels
> Over Middle Earth sent to men.)

The One Ring.   The most magical object in *The Lord of the Rings* has to be the One Ring itself (see RING). Sauron forged the One in the fires of Orodruin (Mount Doom) to control the other Rings: Three for the Elves, Seven for the Dwarves, and Nine for Men. The Three were made without Sauron's help and conferred the powers of wisdom and healing rather than conquest. The Elf Celebrimbor realized Sauron's plan for domination with the One and hid the Three Rings from his influence. Cirdan wore Narya (fire) and then gave it to Gandalf; Galadriel had Nenya (water); and Gil-galad wore Vilya (air) before giving it to Elrond.

Although the Seven Rings caused the Dwarves to lust after GOLD and precious metals—most especially the rare *mithril*—they did not succumb to the One Ring's control. For this reason Sauron particularly hated the Dwarves, and when he discovered the Ring of Durin's Folk (probably the greatest of the Seven), he used it against them. Sauron recovered three of the Rings, and dragons consumed the other four.

Sauron gave the Nine to the nine chiefs of men, who proved the easiest to corrupt with the lure of power. The Nine achieved an immortality of sorts but appeared only as black, ghostly apparitions, hence their name: Ringwraiths or Nazgûl. Sauron controlled them through the power of the One; their leader was the Witch-King of Angmar.

During the wars with Sauron, Isildur, Elendil's son, cut off Sauron's finger and claimed the One Ring. Elrond and Círdan urged him to throw it into the fires of Orodruin, but he kept it as treasure. During the Battle of Gladden Fields, Isildur lost the Ring in the Anduin river. It lay hidden in the mud until Déagol found it while fishing; his friend Sméagol, who became Gollum, murdered him for the Ring which he called his Precious. Gollum hid the Ring from Sauron, but it left him, seeking Sauron. Its next owner was Bilbo Baggins, who kept it for 50 years before giving it to his nephew Frodo. It became Frodo's mission to travel to Mount Doom and destroy the Ring, which he nearly kept as its power overcame him. In the end, Gollum bit off Frodo's finger to get the Ring, much as Isildur had cut off Sauron's, but Gollum's glee caused him—and the Ring—to fall into the fire.

Whereas the Three, the Seven, and the Nine Rings were each set with a jewel, the One was a plain gold band. When heated, these words in the evil Black Speech appeared:

> *Ash nazg durbatulûk, ash nazg gimbatul, ash nazg thrakantulûk*
> *agh*
> *burzum-ishi krimpatul,*

which translated to the most recognized couplet of the books:

> *One Ring to Rule them all, One Ring to find them,*
> *One Ring to bring them all and in the darkness bind them.*

The entire poem goes as follows:

> *Three Rings for the Elven-kings under the sky,*
> *Seven for the Dwarf-lords in their halls of stone,*
> *Nine for Mortal Men doomed to die,*
> *One for the Dark Lord on his dark throne*
> *In the Land of Mordor where the Shadows lie.*
> *One Ring to Rule them all, One Ring to find them,*
> *One Ring to bring them all and in the darkness bind them*
> *In the Land of Mordor where the Shadows lie.*

Magical People.   Those with special powers or abilities include:

Aragorn: Also known as Strider, Elessar Elfstone, king of Gondor and Arnor, and chief of the Dúnedain. After the death of his father Arathorn at the hands of Sauron, Aragorn's mother, the Elf Gilraen, took the boy to live with Elrond in Rivendell. Elrond named him Estel, meaning "hope," and did not reveal his true identity until Aragorn was 20. Aragorn possessed Elven-wisdom and the foresight of the Dúnedain and as the true king had the ability to heal. He spoke Elvish as well as Westron, the language of the men of the West. The Dúnedain lived longer than other men; Aragorn was in his eighties when he became king and married Arwen Undómiel; yet he was in the prime of life and fathered several children. His reign lasted 120 years.

Elrond: Elf-lord of Rivendell, Elrond was the widower of Celebrían, daughter of Galadriel and Celeborn, and father of sons Elladan and Elrohir and daughter Arwen Undómiel. Eärendil was his father. Elrond was very wise and possessed the gift of foresight. He lived through the First, Second, and Third Ages and possessed Vilya, the greatest of the Three Rings. Realizing the days of the Elves were ending, he sailed across the sea to the Grey Havens at the end of the War of the Ring.

Galadriel: Wife of Celeborn and queen of Lothlórien, Galadriel was a Noldorin princess. The oldest of the Elves in Middle-Earth, she possessed Nenya, one of the Three Rings given to the Elves. Her powers were great, enabling her to read Sauron's mind while keeping her thoughts closed to him. Galadriel possessed a large bowl that when filled with water became a mirror and device for seeing what had been and what yet could be.

Gandalf the Grey: Later Gandalf the White, he was called Mithrandir by the Elves and Grey Wanderer or Grey Pilgrim by men of the West. His given name was Olórin. Gandalf was the second-most powerful member of the Istari after Saruman, serving as an implacable enemy of Sauron for 2,000 years. He possessed one of the Three Elven Rings, Narya, which gave him special abilities with fire. Gandalf's powers increased markedly after he defeated the Balrog at Khazad-dûm; afterwards he was immune to injury and had more powers of foresight. As Gandalf the White, he could even undo Saruman's enchantments and was an ally of all who fought Sauron.

Gollum: Although he possessed no magical powers, Gollum's long ownership of the One Ring, obtained by murdering his friend Deagol, turned Gollum (first called Smeagol) into a wretched creature with black skin, long hands with clawlike nails, and large, pale eyes. He had lived in the dark caves of the Misty Mountains so long that while he had very poor vision, his hearing was acute. He hated and feared all things Elven. His only joy was the Ring, which he called his Precious, but died in Mount Doom when he carelessly stepped off a ledge after stealing the Ring from Frodo.

Saruman: The greatest of the Istari, Saruman was head of the White Council. His name comes from the Old English *searu*, meaning "treachery" or "cunning"; he was called Curunir in Elvish. He had tremendous knowledge of Elven lore and the ways of Sauron. Saruman's original friendship with Rohan deteriorated as he began to use the *palantir* of Isengard to communicate with Sauron and seek the One Ring. He cast a spell on King Théoden of Rohan to make him grow old and sick, but Gandalf returned Théoden to health. His pride grew along with his treachery until an attack by the Ents destroyed Isengard and all his plans. Homeless, Saruman and his toady Grima Wormtongue took over the Shire toward the end of the War of the Ring, where he was murdered by Wormtongue.

Sauron: Greatest evil sorcerer and shape-changer of the First through Third Ages. His name means "dung" or "filth" in Old Norse or Icelandic, and it means "abominable" in Quenya, Tolkien's High Elven language, and Gorthaur the Cruel in Sindarin (Low Elvish). Sauron could change shape at will, and he controlled many men and creatures. After his defeat by Isildur and loss of the One Ring, however, he could no longer assume a pleasing human form and most often appeared as a large eye. Just knowing that the Ring he had fashioned was out there gave him power, and he used it to control the Nazgûl. Sauron communicated with Saruman via the *palantir.* He lived in Mordor at the tower of Barad-dûr, but after the destruction of the One Ring was seen no more.

Witch-King of Angmar: Leader of the Nazgûl, he was also called the Captain of Despair. He wore a black cloak and cape and had a crown on his head, but there was no head or face visible, just two burning eyes in the blank darkness. He was impervious to the swords and strikes of Men and completely in thrall to the power of Sauron through the One Ring. Lady Éowyn of Rohan and Merry killed the Witch-King at the Battle of Pelennor Fields: Neither of the two were Men. The word *nazgûl* means "ringwraith" in Black Speech.

Magical Creatures.   Some of Tolkien's creature are noble; some are creepy:

Balrog: Translated from Low Elvish as "power-terror" or "demon of might," the Balrogs were monstrous spirits of fire with many-thonged whips of flame that lived in darkness. The Dwarves uncovered one near the *mithril* vein in Khazad-dûm, leading to their departure from the mines. When Sauron put Orcs in the mines to fight the Dwarves, the Balrog was their feared leader. Gandalf defeated the Balrog after a 10-day duel.

Dwarves: One of the speaking races, Dwarves were created by Aulë in the First Age to withstand Melkor and be hardier than any other race. They were short (about four-and-a-half to five feet in height), stocky, strong, and resistant to fire. They could not be dominated by evil, winning them Sauron's enmity, but proudly never forgot a wrong or slight and went off to battle frequently, usually wielding an axe. They were great miners, craftsworkers, and metalworkers. Dwarves were often wrathful, fair but stingy, and possessive. Their numbers dwindled as there were few Dwarf women (and they were bearded, just like the Dwarf men) and not all of them chose marriage. If they did marry, dwarves usually chose a mate at about 100 years; their lifespan was approximately 250 years. Tolkien derived many of the Dwarf names from the Icelandic epic poem _Poetic Edda_.

Gimli was a most unusual dwarf in that he had a life-long friendship with the Elf Legolas. He was generous of heart and not acquisitive.

Elves: The oldest speaking race of Middle-Earth, the Elves were the most comely, standing about six feet tall, slender and graceful, and resistant to weather and extremes of nature. They often appeared golden, having long, blonde hair. They had keener senses of sight and hearing than men and loved all things that were beautiful, especially in nature. Insatiably curious and good teachers, they taught the Ents to speak and valued communication. Elves called themselves _quendi_, meaning "speakers," in their High Elvish language of Quenya. They could be killed or die from grief but were unaffected by age or disease. They did not actually die but went to the halls of Mandos in Valinor.

Ents: TREES inhabited by spirits that shepherded the other trees of the forests. Ents are as old as Elves, who taught them speech. At some time during the First or Second Age the Entwives crossed the Anduin River and gave their attention to more agricultural pursuits rather than forestry; they taught farming and gardening to men. Eventually the Entwives disappeared, and the Ents did not search for them too long, preferring to remain in Fangorn. The word _ent_ is Old English for "giant."

Hobbits: Humans about half the height of men, Hobbits were a quiet race that lived fairly in the Shire or around the town of Bree. Although provincial and slow to anger, Hobbits were courageous, loyal, ingenious, and not easily ruffled. The word _hobbit_ comes from the Old English _Hob_ and refers to "hole-dweller": most Hobbits lived in burrows.

Oliphaunts or Mûmakil: Beasts similar to elephants but much larger and more ferocious. The Haradrim used the many-tusked animals in warfare, carrying towers and frightening the horses. They could be killed only by shooting them in the eye, but they were cumbersome and tended to run amok. These animals were used in the Battle of the Pelennor Fields. The singular of _mûmakil_ is _mûmak_.

Orcs: Evil and despicable descendants of the Elves, first bred by Melkor in his dungeons from captured Elves during the First Age. By the Third Age the Orcs served in Sauron's army but also served under Saruman and sometimes independently. They were fierce, tribal warriors, short and squat with bowlegs, long arms, dark faces, and little squinty eyes. Orcs had long fangs and liked BLOOD and raw meat, eating ponies, men, and each other. They grew weak in sunlight, preferring the dark, and were highly skilled tunnelers and armorers. Their weapons included spears, bows and arrows, and knives, but their favorite was a sword that was shaped like a scimitar. No mention is made of female Orcs.

Orc language was crude and profane and included words from Sauron's Black Speech. _Orc_ is an Old English word meaning "demon." They were _orch_ in Low Elvish and _uruk_ in Black Speech; Hobbits called them goblins.

Shadowfax: Gandalf's horse, who was swifter than the black horses of the Nazgûl and could run for 12 hours at a stretch. He was the leader of all the other horses. Shadowfax was silver-grey, and Gandalf rode him without saddle or bridle.

Shelob: Giant spider who lived in Cirith Ungol. Shelob ate men, Elves, and Orcs to keep travelers to Mordor from taking that route. Orcs referred to her as Her Ladyship, and they called Gollum Her Sneak because he would direct food her way. Sam stabbed her in the eyes and shone the bright light of Edrendil in her face, making her blind.

Uruk-hai: Larger species of Orc bred by Sauron and Saruman to be warriors and Orc commanders. Uruk-hai were almost as tall as men, had straight legs, and could withstand sunlight. They had black skin and slanted eyes and considered themselves superior to the average Orc. _Uruk-hai_ means "Orc race."

Places and Things. Anywhere the Elves lived was enchanted, as well as the clothes they wore, the food they ate, and the means by which they prophesied the future. The weapons of Middle-Earth were in a class by themselves.

Dead Marshes: Swampy area east of Emyn Muil that continued to spread outward during the Third Age, eventually engulfing the graves of men and Elves who died in battle. It was best not to look down at the faces that shone right below the surface or at the candle flames that seemed to light the corpses.

Elven clothing: Lightweight pieces in colors of grey that changed hues as the light and shadows shifted: the first camouflage. Each member of the Fellowship received an Elven cloak and hood that was held close by a green and silver leaf brooch.

Fangorn: Named for Fangorn the Ent, Fangorn was the eastern remnant of the great forests that originally covered Eriador. Many parts of the forest never saw light, making them forbidding, scary, and subject to SORCERY. All of the remaining Ents lived in Fangorn.

Grey Havens: Town and harbor of Cirdan, where Frodo resided until the last ship sailed over the sea in the Fourth Age. It is a place of peace for those who have struggled.

Lembas: Thin, tasty Elven bread wrapped in leaves designed to be the food of a traveler. One cake was enough for a day, and the slices stayed fresh for many days in their leaf wrapper. The word *lembas* means "journey bread" in Elvish.

Lothlórien: Elven realm west of the Anduin ruled by Lady Galadriel and her husband Celeborn. Lórien was founded by Galadriel in the Second Age, and it was the only place in Middle-Earth where the timelessness and beauty of the Elves still existed. Originally called Laurelindórinan, Lórien was also named the Golden Wood.

Mirkwood: Another dark forest, possibly enchanted. Legolas was prince of Mirkwood and fought tirelessly against the encroachment of Orcs and spiders into his domain. Most men and Dwarves avoided the area.

Mirror of Galadriel: Large basin filled with water that allows the viewer to see what has been, what might be now, and what might happen in the future. Galadriel warned Sam and Frodo when they peered into the water not to touch it and to remember that what is seen ahead can be changed. The phial of Eärendil's light Frodo received from Galadriel contained water from her magic mirror.

Mithril: Silvery metal prized by the Dwarves for its strength and lightweight beauty. In *The Hobbit,* Bilbo Baggins acquired a corselet and helmet made of *mithril* that had been fashioned for an Elf-prince. *Mithril* was supposedly the most valuable metal that the Dwarves mined in Moria. When Bilbo left the Shire, he gave the *mithril* corselet to Frodo, who wore it under his regular clothing.

Palantír: Crystal ball fashioned by the Elf tribe Noldor. The Noldor left the Master-stone in the Tower of Avallónë, but seven other stones were distributed throughout Middle-Earth by Elendil after the fall of Númenor. The main stone was in the Dome of Stars in Osgiliath, the first capital of Gondor. The others were taken to Minas Ithil, Minas Anor, Orthanc, Annúminas, the Tower Hills, and the Tower of Amon Sûl. The stones showed scenes far away in space and time, particularly of things near to another *palantír,* enabling them to be used for communication. The Elves controlled the stone in the Tower Hills, which went on the ship to Grey Havens with Elrond and Galadriel. The Nazgûl captured the *palantír* of Minas Ithil and gave it to Sauron. The stone of Minas Anor had not been used for many years until Denethor II consulted it; Sauron manipulated Denethor through the stone and drove him mad. Saruman used the stone of Orthanc to communicate with Sauron until Wormtongue threw the ball out of the tower, where it was given to Aragorn. As Elendil's heir, Aragorn had the right to use the stone, and he possessed the strength of will to bend the revelations to his control. The plural of *palantír* is *palantíri.*

Rivendell: Also called Imladris, Rivendell was the home of the Elf-lords Elrond, Gildor, and Glorfindel. A center of lore and wise counsel, Elrond used Rivendell to furnish help to the Dúnedain and to provide a safe home for Valendil, son of Isildur, and for Aragorn, son of Arathorn.

Swords: Most important piece of weaponry. In his book on warfare in *LOTR,* author Chris Smith notes that a sword has always been a weapon of priviledge and prestige, for unlike a spear, knife, or axe, it is not used for anything but fighting. The swords were carefully tended and cleaned like members of the family, for the soldier's life depended on his blade. And any cherished sword had a name since it was the man's valuable partner.

Aragorn's sword, Andúril, was reforged from the fragments of the sword Narsil that had belonged to Elendil. Only Elendil's heir could have authorized its rebirth. Other swords and their owners include Glamdring (also known as Orc Beater), the sword of Gandalf the White; Guthwine, blade of Éomer of Rohan; Hadhafang, Elrond's sword; Herugrim, the ancient sword of Rohan wielded by King Théoden; and Sting, Frodo's sword. If Orcs were about when Sting was drawn the blade emitted a blue light, as did Glamdring and Thorin's Sword Orcrist (or Goblin Cleaver). Frodo received Sting from Bilbo.

Weapons: Necessary equipment for nearly every male in Middle-Earth. Elves like Legolas carried a bow and arrows and two long knives housed in leather scabbards attached to the quiver. The blades were honed only on the downward side and had very sharp, tapered points, allowing the user to use the knives in fast, slashing strokes. The ash wood handles of these "white knives" were about eight inches long and decorated in Elven scroll patterns. Galadriel gave Elven daggers to Merry and Pippin. Orcs also used bows and arrows, usually identifiable by the arrows' black feathers. Dwarves, on the other hand, preferred axes. Durin's Axe was the one used by King Durin I. The axe lay in Khazad-dûm after the discovery of the Balrog but was found by Balin. When the Orcs killed Balin and his allies, the axe was lost again.

White Tree of Gondor: Central figure on the standard of Gondor, the White Tree was a Nimloth and represented the heirs of Elendil and the Dúnedain of the South. Isildur stole a fruit from the Nimloth in Numenor and planted the sapling in Middle-Earth at Minas Ithil. Sauron burned the sapling, but not before Isildur took a seedling with him to Arnor. After the overthrow of Sauron, Isildur planted the seedling at Minas Anor (Minas Tirith). The tree flourished until the Great Plague of the Third Age, when King Tarondor planted another seedling in the court of the Fountain of the Citadel. When that tree died there was no other, so the dead tree was left as a reminder of former greatness. After Aragorn became king of Gondor and Arnor he found a sapling on the slopes of Mindolluin and planted it in the Citadel, restoring yet another symbol of Isildur's heirs.

LOTR in Film

By the late 1960s, *The Lord of the Rings* had a huge following, and ideas for a film version began to emerge. Directors Stanley Kubrick and John Boorman each considered the project but found the story too big or too expensive. There was even talk of the Beatles doing a version of *LOTR*, but that fizzled as well.

In 1978 animated versions of *The Hobbit, The Fellowship of the Ring* and *The Two Towers* were released, but an animated *The Return of the King* never materialized. The conventional wisdom was that *LOTR* just could not be filmed.

But by the late 1990s, filmmaking techniques had improved. Using computer-generated imagery for situations like the battle scenes while hiring first-class actors for the live action, director Peter Jackson created a masterpiece. Shot on location in New Zealand, Jackson filmed all three movies at the same time so that the actors would not only remain in character but be committed to their parts for all three films. Elijah Wood played Frodo, Sean Astin was Sam, Viggo Mortenson played Aragorn, Ian McKellan was Gandalf, and newcomer Orlando Bloom played Legolas. Other actors included John Rhys-Davies as Gimli and Treebeard, Cate Blanchett as Galadriel, and Liv Tyler as Arwen.

Jackson released the films in order in December 2001, 2002, and 2003 to great critical acclaim—and reward: *The Return of the King* was the second movie after *Titanic* to earn more than $1 billion and be nominated for 11 Academy Awards. *The Fellowship of the Ring* won four Academy Awards in 2002, and *The Two Towers* took home two Oscars the next year. *The Return of the King* won all 11 of its nominated Oscar categories in 2004, including Best Picture, Best Director (Peter Jackson), and Best Song ("Into the West" by Annie Lennox). Although fans of the trilogy noted inconsistent details and the reordering of some scenes, Jackson's magnum opus introduced an entire new generation to the wonder—and the magic—of Middle-Earth.

FURTHER READING:

Foster, Robert. *Tolkien's World from A to Z: The Complete Guide to Middle-Earth.* New York: Ballantine Books, 2001.

"*The Lord of the Rings, The Return of the King:* Beyond the Movie." Available online. URL: www.nationalgeographic.com/ngbeyond/rings/language.html. Downloaded January 21, 2005.

———. "Myth and Storytelling." Available online. URL: www.nationalgeographic.com/ngbeyond/rings/myth.html. Downloaded January 21, 2005.

Smith, Chris. *The Lord of the Rings: Weapons and Warfare.* New York: Houghton Mifflin Co., 2004.

Tolkien, Christopher. *The History of The Lord of the Rings.* Part 1: "The Return of the Shadow." New York: Houghton Mifflin Co., 1988; Part 2: "The Treason of Isengard," 1989; Part 3: "The War of the Ring," 1990; Part 4: "The End of the Third Age," 1992.

Tolkien, J. R. R. *The Hobbit, Or There and Back Again.* New York: Houghton Mifflin Co., 1996.

———. *The Lord of the Rings: The Fellowship of the Ring.* New York: Houghton Mifflin Co., 1994.

———. *The Lord of the Rings: The Return of the King.* New York: Houghton Mifflin Co., 1994.

———. *The Lord of the Rings: The Two Towers.* New York: Houghton Mifflin Co., 1994.

———. *The Silmarillion,* Christopher Tolkien, ed. New York: Ballantine Books, 1999.

Lord's Prayer   An AMULET against evil; also an INVOCATION of the devil. The Lord's Prayer, the 23rd Psalm of the Bible, functions like a protective CHARM to ward off witches, BEWITCHMENT, DEMONS, and other supernatural evils. During the witch trials of the Inquisition, it was believed that a genuine witch could not recite the Lord's Prayer without stumbling or error.

Reciting the Lord's Prayer backward supposedly will cause the devil to appear.

Lucifuge Rofocale   See GRIMOIRES; PACT.

Lully, Raymond (c. 1235–c. 1316) Spanish philosopher whose works were important to ALCHEMY. Raymond Lully—also known as Ramon Lull—was well known in his time, and his name was borrowed for spurious alchemical works. Numerous legends ascribe to him a colorful life of high adventure.

Lully was born in about 1235 in Majorca. He had no formal education but gained attention as a poet and troubadour. He entered the court of King James I of Aragon, where he taught the royal family. He also worked as a missionary, inspired by a mystical vision in which he beheld the Creation as a hierarchy emanating from God. His missionary work was directed at Muslims.

Lully's vision also led to his development of what became known as "Lullian art." His complex cosmological scheme is represented according to the principles of NUMBERS and the numerical values of the letters of the Hebrew alphabet. Concentric disks inscribed with the Hebrew letters are revolved to make different combinations that represent the *Dinitates Dei,* or "Dignities of God," the causes of all phenomena. Alchemists appreciated this system and thought that it would aid them in their quest for the PHILOSOPHER'S STONE. Thus, a system of "Lullian alchemy" arose.

One story told about Lully is that he went to England, where King Edward III employed him to manufacture GOLD in the Tower of London. Supposedly, Lully made tons of base metals into rose nobles (a type of coin) on the condition that it be used only to finance the Crusades. The king refused and imprisoned Lully. He later escaped and then supposedly went to Westminster Abbey where he taught the secrets of alchemy to an abbot. The story, like others told about Lully, is probably fiction. There is no evidence that Lully ever visited England. It was King Edward II who was on the throne at the time, not King Edward III, and rose nobles did not appear until 1465 under the reign of King Edward IV.

FURTHER READING:
Waite, Arthur Edward. *Alchemists Through the Ages.* Blauvelt, N.Y.: Rudolph Steiner Publications, 1970.

lunaria/lunary See MOONWORT.

magic A superior power that arises from harnessing inner power and supernatural forces and beings to effect change in the physical world. The term magic is derived from Greek, either from megus, which means "great" (as in "great" science); from magein, referring to Zoroastrianism; or from magoi, a Median tribe in Iran recognized for its magical skills, and known to the Greeks. Many systems of magic exist, each with its own procedures, rules and proscriptions.

Modern perceptions of magic lean toward dismissal of it as fancy and fraud, even something to be ridiculed. But magic lies at the heart of all esoteric traditions and can be found in mystical and religious teachings.

The esteemed occultist FRANZ BARDON said in his book *The Practice of Magical Evocation* (1956), "Magic is the greatest knowledge and the highest science that exists anywhere on our planet. Not only does magic teach the metaphysical laws, but also the *metapsychical* laws that exist and which are applicable on all planes. Since time immemorial the highest knowledge has always been known as 'magic.'" Bardon said that knowledge passed on by religions is merely symbolic, but that true knowledge is contained within magic. The public often confuses magic with SORCERY. "Magic is the knowledge that teaches the practical application of the lowest laws of nature to the highest laws of spirit," he said.

Magic is as old as humanity and had its beginnings in humankind's attempts to control environment, survival, and destiny, either by controlling natural forces or by appealing to higher powers for help. Anthropologist Bronislaw Malinowski defined magic as having three functions and three elements. The three functions are:

- to produce
- to protect
- to destroy

The three elements are:

- spells and incantations
- rites or procedures
- altered states of consciousness accomplished through fasting, meditating, chanting, visualizing symbols, sleep deprivation, dancing, staring into flames, inhaling fumes, taking drugs, and so forth.

Magic is practiced universally by skilled individuals who are either born into their powers or train themselves to acquire powers. Magic is not inherently good or evil but reflects the intent of the magician. The ethical and moral uses of magic have always been ambiguous. Generally, evil magic is associated with sorcery and WITCHCRAFT. Throughout history, people and authorities have had an uneasy relationship with magic, depending on it and tolerating its practice while at the same time condemning it. Magic is both part of religion and a competitor of religion. It has been regarded as a science and has been discredited by science. In modern times, however, science is providing evidence in support of magic.

Magic and Liminality

Magical phenomena exist in a realm of liminality, a blurred borderland that is neither in the material world nor the spiritual world, but in both simultaneously. *Liminality* is a term coined by the anthropologist Arthur van Gennup to refer to the condition of being "betwixt and between." The word comes from *limen,* or threshold. Change, transition, and transformation are conditions that are conducive to psi and the supernatural. Magic ritual—and ritual in general—exposes the ordinary, predictable world to the instability of the liminal world. Strange things happen. The liminal realm is considered to be a dangerous, unpredictable one. Individuals such as magicians thus are dangerous because they work in this uncertain world. As adepts they are themselves the agents of change and even chaos.

Historical Overview

The Western magical tradition is rich and complex, evolving from a mixture of magical, mystical, philosophical, and religious sources. It incorporates the low magic of spellcasting and DIVINATION, the dark magic of sorcery and witchcraft, and the high magic of spiritual enlightenment that is closer to mysticism than to spell-casting. Some of the major streams of influence are:

Egyptian Magic. Magic played an important role in ancient Egypt, and the magic of the Egyptians became important in the development of Western ritual magic. Egyptian priests were skilled in magical arts of spell-casting, divination, NECROMANCY, the making of AMULETS and TALISMANS, the procuring and sending of dreams, the use of magical figures similar to POPPETS, and the use of magic in the practice of medicine. Illnesses were believed to be caused by a host of DEMONS who controlled various parts of the human body; thus cures involved EXORCISMS. The mummification of the dead was done according to precise ritual magic to ensure safe passage to the afterlife. The Egyptian *Book of the Dead* can be seen as a magical handbook of preparation for navigation through judgment into Amenti, the Underworld domain of Osiris, lord of the dead. In Hellenistic times, Egyptian magic was mixed with classical magic.

Especially important to Egyptian magic was the proper use of words and NAMES of power. Some INCANTATIONS involved strings of names, some incomprehensible, having been borrowed from other cultures. The use of such names evolved into the BARBAROUS NAMES of ritual magic.

The use of Egyptian magical elements in Western ritual magic gained favor during the peak of the HERMETIC ORDER OF THE GOLDEN DAWN in the late 19th century. Members of the Golden Dawn who were interested in Egyptian magic saw the *Book of the Dead* not just as a collection of funerary SPELLS for the dead but as a handbook of INITIATION. An Egyptian magical papyrus served as the basis for the Golden's Dawn's BORNLESS RITUAL, which is intended to bring deep contact with one's HOLY GUARDIAN ANGEL, or Higher Self. ALEISTER CROWLEY added his own elaboration to the bornless ritual. Crowley also brought increased attention to Egyptian magic in his *Book of the Law,* which he channeled while in Egypt and which proclaimed the dawn of the Aeon of Horus, the Crowned and Conquering Child.

Greek and Roman Magic. The Greek and Roman worlds teemed with magic. Power was channeled from a host of sources: deities, spirits called DAIMONES, celestial INTELLIGENCES, and the dead. Everything was connected by sympathetic bonds that enabled magical action at a distance. The Hermetic principle that the microcosm reflects the macrocosm ("As above, so below") was espoused in variations by Pythagoreans, Plantonists, and Stoicists.

All magical arts were practiced; the Greeks were especially interested in destiny and devoted great attention to the PROPHECY of ORACLES and to the fate forecast by the stars in a horoscope. Both Greeks and Romans practiced numerous forms of divination, especially lot casting and the examination of signs in nature. Dreams were consulted, especially for healing. Cursing one's competitors and enemies was routine in daily life. Incantations involved long strings of magical words, often nonsensical, which had to be precisely pronounced along with the correct gestures.

An exalted form of magic, *theurgia,* has religious overtones and is akin to ritual magic. The Neoplatonists favored *theurgia,* believing that they could bring divine powers to Earth and ascend their souls to heaven.

In *Natural History,* Pliny asserts that all magic originated in medicine in the search for cures. The magical workings of the heavens, especially the MOON, both caused and cured illnesses. In addition, demons flying through the air and shooting arrows stirred up poisonous vapors that caused plagues and pestilence.

Jewish Magic. The early Jews were steeped in magical lore, much of which was borrowed and adapted from the magical practices of the Canaanites, Babylonians, Egyptians, and later Hellenistic-Gnostic influences. Magic was not organized into systems but rather was a collection of beliefs and practices chiefly concerning protection from demons and the procuring of blessings. As early as the first century C.E., magical lore was attributed to the wisdom of King SOLOMON. This lore provided the basis for the later GRIMOIRE, the *Key of Solomon,* the most important of the old handbooks of Western magic.

According to Jewish lore, the magical arts were taught to humans by angels, chiefly the Watchers, who fell from God's grace when they departed heaven to cohabit with human women. The gift was dubious, for the Tanakh—the Old Testament—condemns sorcery, the use of spirits, and various forms of magic, such as ENCHANTMENT, SHAPESHIFTING, divination, mediumship, and necromancy.

Talmudic law reinterpreted sorcery. Magic requiring the help of demons was forbidden and was punishable by death. Magic that did not require the help of demons was still forbidden but received lesser punishments. The distinction between the two often was not clear. Natural magic involving the "Laws of Creation" was tacitly permitted. Later the use of mystical names of God and angels and verses of scripture were incorporated into incantations.

Magic was organized into systems in about 500 C.E., at about the same time as the development of Merkabah mysticism, a precursor to the KABBALAH. Merkabah mystics performed elaborate rituals of purification, contemplation of the sacred and magical properties of letters and NUMBERS, the recitation of sacred names, and the use of amulets, SEALS, and talismans. The trance recitation of long incantations of names was similar to the Egyptians' "barbarous names" in that many were corruptions of names of deities and angels.

By the Middle Ages, Jewish magic depended almost entirely on the use of names and interventions of spirits. The kabbalah, a body of esoteric teachings dating to about the 10th century and in full bloom by the 13th century, does not forbid magic but warns of the dangers of it. Only the most virtuous persons should perform magic and should do so only in times of public emergency and need, never for private gain. How strictly these admonitions were followed is questionable. A practical kabbalah of magical procedures developed from about the 14th century on. Kabbalists were divided on the issue of whether or not one could invoke demons as well as angels.

Black magic is called apocryphal science in the kabbalah. It is strictly forbidden, and only theoretical knowledge is permitted. Those who choose to practice it become sorcerers in the thrall of fallen angels.

By the Middle Ages, Jews were renowned among Christians as magical adepts. These adepts were not professional magicians, but were rabbis, doctors, philosophers, and teachers and students of oral transmission of mystical and esoteric knowledge.

Christian Magic.   Like Judaism, Christianity held paradoxical attitudes toward magic. In general, magic was looked upon with disfavor—the practices of non-Christians that interfered with the new religion. Manipulative "low" magic was forbidden, but helpful magic, such as for healing, was practiced within certain limits. Jesus performed magical acts, but they were called MIRACLES made possible by his divine nature. The early church fathers especially opposed divination, which took one's destiny out of the hands of the church.

Christian magic emphasized nature, such as herbal lore, and placed importance on mystical names. But the body of Christ, as represented by the Eucharist, held the biggest magic, as did the name of Jesus and relics (body parts and possessions) of saints.

Medieval Europe was rife with magic of all sorts: folk practitioners, wizards, cunning men and women, alchemists, and others. The practical kabbalah, Hermetic principles, Gnostic and Neoplatonic lore, Christian elements, and pagan elements came together in syncretic mixtures. A Western kabbalah emerged that became the basis for Western ritual magic. Magical handbooks called grimoires circulated.

The medieval church frowned upon magic of all sorts:

- divination of all kinds
- conjuration of spirits
- necromancy
- weaving and binding magic, in which spells were imbued into knots and fabric
- love magic and any other magic involving potions, poppets, and so forth
- magical medical remedies

The populace relied on the folk magic of local practitioners. Many possessed natural healing and psychic abilities and practiced home-grown magic that was passed down orally through generations. The church tolerated magic that was adequately christianized, such as through the substitution of the names of Jesus, Mary, and angels for pagan deities and spirits; the use of the CROSS, holy water, and the Eucharist; and incantations that were more like PRAYERS.

Folk magicians were often feared, and if their spellcasting or divination failed, they were persecuted. Any bad luck was liable to be blamed on the black magic or witchcraft of a rival or enemy.

The Inquisition capitalized on fear. In 1484 Pope Innocent VIII made witchcraft a heresy, thereby making the persecution of any enemy of the church easy. Witchcraft was not merely black magic but was devil worship, a servant to Satan's grand plan to subvert souls. A "witch craze" swept Europe and reached across the Atlantic to the American colonies. Thousands of persons were executed.

The witch hysteria died in the advance of the scientific revolution of the 17th century. Though many great scientists of the day were versed in alchemy and the principles of magic, the importance of the latter two declined.

Alchemy and Esoteric Orders.   ALCHEMY—the quest for perfection—entered mainstream Europe in about the 12th century. Western alchemy is based on Hermetic philosophy, that cosmic forces govern all things in creation and that the material world—the microcosm—reflects the heavenly world or the macrocosm. Thus all things in creation have the germ of perfection within them and evolve naturally from a base and impure state to a state of perfection. The Hermetic axiom of the EMERALD TABLET, "As above, so below," expresses this philosophy.

In medieval Europe, alchemy was part of medicine not only for cures but also for substances that would restore youth and lengthen life. Alchemists sought to speed the natural evolution of perfection through mysterious chemical processes that also involved magical concepts of the inherent magical properties both in natural things and in the magical workings of the cosmos. Perfection was accomplished through the production of the mysterious PHILOSOPHER'S STONE, an agent that had the power to transmute the impure to the pure.

Alchemy was corrupted by greed: the desire to create quick wealth by turning base metals into gold and silver. Certain alchemists were PUFFERS, men who labored with billows in their stinking laboratories trying to make treasure.

The Hierophant card in The Alchemical Tarot, *by Rosemary Ellen Guiley and Robert Michael Place. The hierophant is a master of occult mysteries. He wears a triple crown of the three kingdoms and holds an open book signifying access to secret knowledge. The Sun and Moon, man and woman, and light and dark candles signify the principles of opposites. Inspired by Senior's* De chemia *in Mangentus,* Bibliotheca chemical curiosa, *1720. (Copyright by and courtesy of Robert Michael Place)*

True alchemy was a more spiritual pursuit: the great work of perfecting the human being through enlightenment. Spiritual alchemy was practiced by esoteric orders and brotherhoods, most notably the Rosicrucians and the Freemasons, who in turn influenced the later development of ritual magic.

The 17th century ushered in the era of science and brought the decline of interest in magic. Science explained the workings of the world by new laws. The rise of cities and technology removed people from the magic of nature. By the beginning of the 18th century, magic was no longer a major force, except in personal folk practices.

The Occult Revival.   In the 19th century, a revival of interest in occultism and magic occurred, centered in and spreading out from France through ELIPHAS LEVI, "Papus" (Gerard Encausse), and others. Levi's works were particularly influential and were translated into English by ARTHUR EDWARD WAITE. Levi drew together the kabbalah, Hermeticism, and magic as the three occult sciences that lead to truth. He described the kabbalah as the "mathematics of human thought" that answers all questions through numbers. Magic is the knowledge of the secret laws and powers of nature and the universe. Of Hermeticism, he said in *The Book of Splendours:*

> Hermeticism is the science of nature hidden in the hieroglyphics and symbols of the ancient world. It is the search for the principle of life, along with the dream (for those who have not yet achieved it) of accomplishing the great work, which is the reproduction of the divine, natural fire which creates and recreates beings.

Levi and others could see the ideal marriage in magic and mysticism as the means to find perfection and God. But at the same time as the occult revival, the new world of science was taking the two realms apart. The Christian church continued to drive in its own wedge in its efforts to separate—and discredit—pagan magic from the magic–mysticism of the Christian faith. It would be left to secular esoteric and magical orders to keep the flame of real magic alive.

In the late 19th century, magical fraternities and lodges rose in prominence, the best known of which was the esoteric Hermetic Order of the Golden Dawn in England. The Golden Dawn was founded by Rosicrucians and Freemasons who were also familiar with the Eastern philosophy taught by the Theosophical Society. It was not originally intended to be a magical order—it taught only theoretical magic in its outer order—but eventually its inner order taught and practiced the magical arts as well as rituals of high magic. The rituals systematized by the Golden Dawn influenced much of the magical work that was yet to unfold.

Thelemic Magic.   A considerable contribution to ritual magic was made by Aleister Crowley, who was already well versed in the subject by the time he was initiated into the

Golden Dawn in 1898. Crowley's oversized personality could not be contained by the Golden Dawn, and he was expelled two years later. For a time he lived with ALLAN BENNETT, who introduced him to Eastern mysticism. Crowley incorporated Eastern techniques, especially for breathing, into his practices, along with sex and drugs. He expanded upon Golden Dawn rituals.

His most significant magical innovation is his Law of Thelema: "Do what thou wilt shall be the whole of the Law." The Thelemic law was dictated to an entranced Crowley in 1909 in Egypt by an emissary of the god Horus named AIWASS. *The Book of the Law* lays out the emergence of the New Aeon of Horus, for which Crowley was to be the chief prophet. Everything springs from the Thelemic law, and magic is the "art and science of causing change to occur in conformity with Will." The individual is sovereign and responsible only to himself. The proper use of will raises the individual to the highest purpose, not a selfish purpose.

Crowley preferred to spell *magic* with a *k* to distinguish it from the low magic of spell-casting and sorcery. He said that "the laws of Magick are the laws of Nature" and that better effect is obtained by a group than an individual: "There is no doubt that an assemblage of persons who really are in harmony can much more easily produce an effect than a magician working by himself."

Crowley understood that magic works forward and backward in time, which later would be demonstrated in quantum physics. Causality is complex, a force at play in a web of forces, he said. The projection of a magician's will does not necessarily precede the effect or result of the projection. In *Magick in Theory and Practice* he uses the example of using magic to induce a person in Paris to send him a letter in England. The ritual is performed one evening, and the letter arrives the next morning—impossibly soon, it would seem, to have been the effect of the ritual. However, the cause of doing the magical work is the cause of the action, and there is no reason why one should precede the other, Crowley said.

Modern Magic.   In the 20th century, occult teachings were carried on by adepts such as Bardon, ISRAEL REGARDIE, and WILLIAM GRAY. Participation in ceremonial magic went deeper underground. In rural areas practitioners of folk magic continued to work. Ritual magic was done increasingly behind closed doors. On a popular level magic was seen as illusory and superstitious, not "real"—Mickey Mouse in a wizard's hat commanding brooms to carry water. Magic was perceived as the equivalent of stage magic tricks, not a real power operating in the physical and spiritual worlds.

In the latter part of the 20th century, a renewed interest in spirituality and esotericism brought real magic back into the open. The new religions of Wicca and Paganism especially reacquainted the public with the concepts and principles of magic. In the media and arts, the image of magic has changed from negative to increasingly positive.

(See HARRY POTTER.) Novels, films, and television show feature characters who possess magical powers that are used for good. Witches, magicians, shape-shifters, gods, angels, demons, vampires, and others battle it out magically for control.

All things eventually come full circle, and it is science that has turned a new light on magic and its validity. Four areas are particularly important: psychical research, alternative healing, quantum physics, and chaos theory.

Psychical research: Scientific inquiry into paranormal phenomena began in earnest in the 19th century. In 1888 the Society for Psychical Research was founded in England with the object of finding evidence for survival after death. This object led researchers into telepathy, CLAIRVOYANCE, psychokinesis (PK), dreams, precognition, retrocognition, extrasensory perception (ESP), out-of-body travel, and mental and physical mediumship—in short, what magicians would consider the practical magical arts and what mystics would consider to be natural supernormal powers made accessible by enlightened consciousness. This research, which was furthered by similar organizations around the world, provided a new look into the powers of the mind and the ability of consciousness to act outside the physical body and outside of linear time. Although the protocols for hard scientific proof remain elusive, parapsychologists, as they are known today, have demonstrated repeatedly in controlled experiments that *psi*—a term for both ESP and PK—exists and that consciousness operates nonlocally. In addition, researchers noted the "experimenter effect": that the attitudes and beliefs of the experimenter and the subjects influence the outcome of experiments.

Alternative healing: The mind-body connection and the ability of the mind to influence matter has contributed to an increase in the research and practice of alternative, or complementary, healing and health therapies. Psychical researchers demonstrated the effects of prayer at a distance, and similar experiments were carried into the medical field. Stripped of its religious aspects, prayer is a magical act—a projection of THOUGHT, WILL, and IMAGINATION in a petition to higher (cosmic) power for change. Medical professionals have found that imagery—comparable in magic to the use of SYMBOLS—can play a significant role in health. Intentionality—the direction of one's thoughts, beliefs, and intents—became a focus of research. Intentionality has been shown to impact the course of healing. Mystical traditions have long taught that thought—in other words, our intentionality—creates reality. Call it intentionality or magic; the fundamental principles are the same.

Quantum physics: Newtonian physics holds that everything in the universe operates according to a set of laws and that space and time are linear. Newtonian physics defined the scientific world view until the 20th century when Albert Einstein demonstrated that space and time are curved. Quantum physics, of which Einstein was also a part, further dismantled the Newtonian view. In quantum physics the subatomic world seems a strange place. There is no such thing as discrete observation: The very act of observing changes the thing being observed. Everything is interconnected. Things exist as probabilities until they are observed. For example, an electron has no single "place" but exists in a cloud of probabilities, everywhere at once, until observation fixes it in a location. Particles can jump from one point to another without actually moving through the space between points—the so-called quantum leap. These behaviors in the subatomic world were thought not to apply to matter on a larger scale.

Chaos theory: According to fractals as found in chaos theory, which is the study of mathematical principles governing organic and complex phenomena, small-scale fractal patterns look the same as large-scale fractal patterns. This expresses the ancient Hermetic axiom of the Emerald Tablet, "As above, so below": The microcosm and the macrocosm reflect each other. Thus, large-scale phenomena involving teleportation, time travel, precognition, telepathy, psychokinesis, and other seemingly "magical" might indeed be explainable.

In the universe of the magician, everything in creation is interconnected. Consciousness affects matter, acts at a distance and moves backward and forward in time. Magic exerts forces on probabilities, manifesting or fixing them into the realm of matter.

Types of Magic

Though magic itself is neutral, practitioners often distinguish between good, or white magic and bad, or black magic—though such distinctions are subjective. Bardon divided magic into three types:

- Lower magic, which deals with the laws of nature and control of forces in nature, such as the ELEMENTS
- Intermediate magic, which deals with the laws of human beings in the microcosm, and how the microcosm can be influenced
- Higher magic, which deals with the universal laws of the macrocosm and how they can be controlled

Other types of magic are known by their distinguishing characteristics.

Black Magic.   Black magic is used for malevolent purposes—to harm or to kill. According to tradition, black magic is accomplished with the aid of demonic entities. Other terms for it are *goetic magic* or *goetia*. Levi said in *The History of Magic,* "Black Magic may be defined as the art of inducing artificial mania in ourselves and in others; but it is also above all the science of poisoning."

Waite termed black magic as the utterance of words and names of power for "unlawful purposes" and "the realm of delusion and nightmare, though phenomenal enough in its results." It involves communing with demons and evil spirits for materialistic gain or harmful purpose. In *The Book of Black Magic and of Pacts,* Waite said that black magic is not a profane rendition of religion, and:

> . . . it is not to do outrage to God in the interests of diabolism, but to derive power and virtue from above for the more successful control of Evil Spirits, and this obtains indifferently whether the purpose of the operator be otherwise lawful or not.
>
> . . . God acknowledged and invoked by Goetic Magic is not the Principle of Evil, as the myth of modern Satanism supposes, but the "terrible and venerable Deity" who destroyed the power of the rebellious angels, the Jehovah of the Jewish rituals and the Trinity of the Christian magical cycle.

Black magic is associated with sorcery and witchcraft. The Christian church associated pagan and folk magic as "black magic."

Ceremonial Magic.   Ceremonial magic is a term for ritual magic (see below) aimed at spiritual enlightenment.

Chaos Magic.   Chaos magic developed in the 1960s that dispenses with the pomp and ceremony of ritual magic and evocation of gods and spirits. AUSTIN OSMAN SPARE is considered the "father" of chaos magic for his emphasis on the power of the subconscious mind and his system of SIGILS. Chaos magic is not about disorder, as the name might imply, but rather focuses on order that is beyond conscious understanding. It combines elements of Eastern mysticism and Western ritual magic. The practitioner summons power from deep within the subconscious rather than calling upon the power of outside agencies. Ritual is used to evoke images from the subconscious and to release magical power.

Ray Sherwin developed chaos magic theory and early rituals. With Julian Carroll, Sherwin formed a "Circle of Chaos" for interested practitioners in England. Peter J. Carroll wrote *Liber Null* and *Psychonaut,* chaos magick training manuals, and was a leader in the formation of the Initiates of Thanateros in 1977, the primary chaos magic organization.

Liber Null—half of which is devoted to the black arts, a "natural inclination" of humans—teaches that magical abilities are attained through altered states of consciousness, which can be learned "without any symbolic system except reality itself." *Psychonaut* is intended for group magic and shamanic practice.

Carroll states that chaos is the life force of the universe and is not human-hearted; therefore, the wizard, or magician, cannot be human-hearted when he seeks to tap into this power. He must perform "monstrous and arbitrary acts" to push past his limitations, for only in extremes can the spirit, or Kia, discover itself.

Composite Magic. Composite magic combines various religious influences, for example, Christian and Jewish elements. Composite magic is found in some grimoires. Practical magic based on the Western kabbalah is a type of composite magic.

Gray Magic. Gray magic is a term sometimes applied to the morally ambiguous and subjective nature of magical power. For example, a curse might be black magic from one perspective, but if it is used to stop an evil, then it is considered justifiable and falls into the realm of gray magic, perhaps even good magic. In ancient times, the moral and ethical uses of magic were often quite ambiguous. Curses were regularly made against enemies and rivals of all sorts as supernatural means by which people sought revenge and tried to gain advantage.

High Magic. High magic is a term for ceremonial magic or ritual magic (see below) aimed at spiritual enlightenment.

Folk Magic. Local traditions of folk magic address casting SPELLS for healing, luck, protection, and so forth. Folk magic blends other forms of magic, often with mixed religious elements. Folk magic remedies and prescriptions are handed down in oral traditions and in small handbooks.

Natural Magic. Magic based on nature makes use of herbs, stones, crystals, the commanding of the elements and the influences of planets and stars. Natural magic draws on the inherent magical properties of things. Philters, potions, powders, OINTMENTS, and so forth are based on natural magic recipes combined with folk magic incantations and charms.

Practical Magic. Practical magic is a term used for applied magical and psychic arts, such as clairvoyance, divination and prophecy, ASTRAL TRAVEL, healing, and spell-casting. Practical magic makes use of many techniques in other forms of magic.

Ritual Magic. Also called ceremonial magic and high magic, ritual magic is a Western occult discipline that is part of the "Great Work"—spiritual enlightenment and self-mastery, and, in the highest sense, union with God or the Godhead. Through magical ritual, the initiate seeks to purify himself as a channel for divine Light dedicated to the service of the divine and humanity. In *Tree of Life,* Israel Regardie describes ritual magic as "a spiritual sci-

ence. It is a technical system of training which has a divine objective, rather than a mundane terrestrial one."

Ritual magic is highly disciplined. The initiate must become skilled in meditation, concentration, and visualization and the ability to focus thought, will, and imagination. Other necessary skills involve proficiency in rituals, with proper uses of magical tools, symbols, sigils and other accoutrements; and proficiency in at least some forms of practical magic. The initiate must develop inner plane contacts with gods, angels, and entities and learn how to access and navigate in the astral plane. With sufficient practice the magician can dispense with the physical and work entirely on the inner planes within an interior magic circle.

Performing rituals alone does not guarantee the success of ritual magic. A crucial ingredient is the ability of the magician to raise intense enthusiasm, even frenzy, that augments the release of magical power in a ritual.

Enthusiastic or frenzied energy can determine the success of any kind of magic. Francis Barrett observed in *The Magus,* "The reason why exorcisms, charms, incantations, etc. do sometimes fail of their desired effect, it is because the *unexcited* mind or spirit of the exorcist renders the words dull or ineffectual."

Ritual magic is practiced in groups, such as lodges, which have closed memberships; by fellowships; and in solitary form by individuals, usually with the help of a mentor. Most Western ritual magic follows the tradition honed by the Hermetic Order of the Golden Dawn.

Sympathetic Magic. Sympathetic magic is exerted at a distance through associations that establish a connection for the flow of power. One of the best-known sympathetic magic tools is the poppet, a doll, that substitutes for a person. The connection is strengthened by attaching to the doll photographs, hair, or personal objects of the victim.

Anything can be used to establish a sympathetic connection. The best items are from a person's body, such as HAIR AND NAIL CLIPPINGS. Personal possessions or any object handled by a person can be used. A gift can be magically charged and entered into a home or place as a magical Trojan horse.

Australian aborigines put sharp pebbles or ground glass in the footprints of enemies as sympathetic magic to weaken and destroy them. The Ojibwa use a straw effigy to drive evil away from their communities. If a member has a dream of disaster, a straw man is erected that substitutes for the trouble. The people eat, smoke tobacco, and ask for blessings. They attack the straw effigy, shooting it and clubbing it until it is in pieces. The remains are burned.

Transcendental Magic. Eliphas Levi used "transcendental magic" to describe ritual magic. "Magic is a science," Levi said. "To abuse it is to lose it, and it is also to destroy oneself." Waite said that transcendental magic is not the equivalent of transcendental philosophy, nor is it philosophical in nature. It does not involve black magic, or trafficking with evil spirits for evil purposes, except in cases of exorcism.

Transcendental rituals are divine and religious, with spiritual and moral counsels. The *Arbatel of Magic,* a grimoire, emphasizes meditation, love of God and adherence to the virtues as the best ways to practice magical arts.

White Magic.   White magic is used for positive goals, such as healing, blessings, good luck, and abundance. White magic can involve any form of magic when used for beneficence.

The Future of Magic

The powers called magic have never ceased to exist, despite the efforts to dismiss them as superstition, ignorance, fraud, and illusion. Magic has been rediscovered in new terminology, with words that are more comfortable in modern times, such as psi, intuition, and intentionality. The trappings may change, but the underlying principles remain the same. In its reinvented forms, magic has become more democratic, available to everyone and not a select few initiates. Inner powers are inherent, inborn in all humans. What was once magic will become more a part of daily life.

FURTHER READING:

Bardon, Franz. *Initiation into Hermetics: A Course of Instruction of Magic Theory and Practice.* Wuppertal, Germany: Dieter Ruggeberg, 1971.

———. *The Practice of Magical Evocation.* Albuquerque, N.Mex.: Brotherhood of Life, 2001.

Butler, E. M. *Ritual Magic.* Cambridge: Cambridge University Press, 1949.

Flint, Valerie I. J. *The Rise of Magic in Medieval Europe.* Princeton, N.J.: Princeton University Press, 1991.

Gray, William G. *Magical Ritual Methods.* York Beach, Maine: Samuel Weiser, 1980.

———. *Western Inner Workings.* York Beach, Maine: Samuel Weiser, 1983.

Hall, Manly P. *The Secret Teachings of All Ages.* 1928. Reprint, Los Angeles: The Philosophic Research Society, 1977.

Hansen, George. *The Trickster and the Paranormal.* New York: Xlibris, 2001.

Knight, Gareth. *The Practice of Ritual Magic.* Albuquerque, N.Mex.: Sun Chalice Books, 1996.

Kraig, Donald Michael. *Modern Magick: Eleven Lessons in the High Magickal Arts.* 2nd ed. St. Paul, Minn.: Llewellyn Publications, 2004.

Levi, Eliphas. *The History of Magic.* 1860. Reprint, York Beach, Maine: Samuel Weiser, 2001.

Luck, Georg. *Arcana Mundi: Magic and the Occult in the Greek and Roman Worlds.* Baltimore: Johns Hopkins University Press, 1985.

Malinowski, Bronislaw. *Magic, Science and Religion.* Garden City, N.Y.: Doubleday Anchor Books, 1948.

Maxwell-Stuart, P. G. *Wizards: A History.* Stroud, England: Tempus Publishing Ltd., 2004.

Pinch, Geraldine. *Magic in Ancient Egypt.* London: British Museum Press, 1994.

Radin, Dean. *The Conscious Universe: The Scientific Truth of Psychic Phenomena.* San Francisco: HarperSanFrancisco, 1997.

Regardie, Israel. *The Golden Dawn.* 6th ed. St. Paul, Minn.: Llewellyn Publications, 1989.

Thomas, Keith. *Religion & the Decline of Magic.* New York: Scribners, 1971.

magical attack   The use of MAGIC to harm or destroy a person. Magical attack is universal in SORCERY and the "dark arts."

There are two types of magical attack. One is the long-range attack, in which a victim is made to destroy himself. For example, the magician may influence dreams, telepathically implant commands, make POPPETS or FETISHES, or send FAMILIARS to cause a person to have a fatal accident. The magician casts the SPELL in a RITUAL in which he works himself up into a hateful state of rage. He may inflict pain on himself to intensify the CURSE. In some cases, he may first engage in a fast in which he directs the energy of fasting toward the victim in a negative way.

The second is a short-range attack, often requiring proximity or physical contact, in which a victim's energy is severely depleted. The latter is also called psychic attack or PSYCHIC VAMPIRISM. The magician sends out a powerful force from the solar plexus through his hands, eyes (see EVIL EYE), voice, or breath. The force is sent into the body of the victim, where it disrupts physical and psychological health.

Magical attack can be difficult to counter; sometimes it is best to have another person who is magically skilled intercede. Fear and paranoia only make magical attacks worse. Retaliating with the same attack is risky, for if it backfires or is repulsed, it will return to the sender.

Magical LODGES sometimes engage in magical attack and warfare.

See also CROWLEY, ALEISTER; DEATH PRAYER; FORTUNE, DION; HERMETIC ORDER OF THE GOLDEN DAWN.

FURTHER READING:

Carroll, Peter J. *Liber Null and Psychonaut.* York Beach, Maine: Samuel Weiser, 1987.

Fortune, Dion. *Psychic Self-Defence.* 1939. Reprint, York Beach, Maine: Samuel Weiser, 1957.

magical motto   In the Western esoteric tradition, a magical name taken upon INITIATION into a secret society or lodge. The magical motto usually expresses the initiate's spiritual goal and persona and is written in any language other than the initiate's own. This distinguishes the magical motto from the affairs and concerns of everyday life.

Latin is the most common language used for magical mottos, followed by Hebrew.

The magical mottos of some of the prominent members of the HERMETIC ORDER OF THE GOLDEN DAWN are:

NAME	MAGICAL MOTTO	MEANING
Allan Bennett	*Yehi Aour*	Let there be Light
Edward Berridge	*Resurgam*	I shall rise again
Algernon Blackwood	*Umbram Fugat Veritas*	Truth puts darkness to flight
Paul Foster Case	*Perserverantia*	Perseverance
Aleister Crowley	*Perdurabo*	I will last through
Florence Farr	*Sapienta Sapienti Dono Data*	Wisdom is a gift given to the wise
Dion Fortune	*Deus Non Fortuna*	By God not by chance
Annie Horniman	*Fortiter et Recte*	Bravely and justly
Moina Mathers	*Vestigia Nulla Retrorsum*	No traces behind
S. L. MacGregor Mathers (2)	*S'Rioghail Mo Dhream*	Royal is my race
	Deo Duce Comite Ferro	God as my guide, my companion a sword
Israel Regardie	*Ad Majorem Adonai Gloriam*	To the Greater Glory of Adonai
Arthur Edward Waite	*Sacramentum Regis*	The sacrament of the king
William Wynn Westcott (2)	*Sapere Aude*	Dare to be wise
	Non Omnis Moriar	I shall not wholly die
William Robert Woodman	*Magna Est Veritas Et*	Truth is great

FURTHER READING:
Cicero, Chic, and Sandra Tabatha Cicero. *The Essential Golden Dawn*. St. Paul, Minn.: Llewellyn Publications, 2004.

magic alphabets   Secret written languages that are used in various forms of MAGIC. Magic alphabets are used to invoke and communicate with ANGELS and spirits, and to translate and encode PRAYERS, CHARMS, texts, AMULETS, and TALISMANS. The alphabets are used in conjunction with SEALS, SYMBOLS, and MAGIC SQUARES.

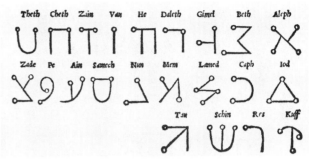

Celestial alphabet, in Oedipus Aegypticus, *by Athanasius Kircher, 1652.* (Author's collection)

Some magic alphabets—also called angel alphabets and celestial alphabets—are said to be the gifts of angels that are communicated to ADEPTS. One of the most common alphabets comes from the SEFER RAZIEL and is of unknown origin. Some alphabets resemble cuneiform, and some are related to early Hebrew or Samaritan script. "Eye writing" is a type of magical alphabet in kabbalistic literature, so-named because the letters are formed with straight and curved lines and circles resembling eyes.

Major magical scripts are:

Celestial Writing. Eye writing related to the stars.

Malachim. Eye writing inspired by the angelic order of malachim ("kings") and from the book of Malachi, whose proper name is derived from the Hebrew term for "my messenger." Of special significance in Malachi is verse 3:16:

> Then those who feared the Lord spoke with one another; the Lord heeded and heard them, and a book of remembrance was written before him of those who feared the Lord and thought on his name.

The Greater Key of Solomon refers to Malachim as "the tongue of angels." According to occultist SAMUEL LIDDELL MacGREGOR MATHERS, Malachim is formed by the positions of stars. The characters are shaped by drawing imaginary lines from one star to another.

Passing of (through) the River. A type of eye writing, but with more embellishments than the previous two. Also known as the Talismanic Script of King Solomon, this script is so-named from the four rivers that flow through the garden of Eden: Pison, Euphrates, Gihon, and Hiddekel.

Theban. A script of curved symbols. Also known as the Honorian Script, this alphabet is related to lunar energies and affects the lower astral and etheric planes. It is equated to English.

FURTHER READING:
Goddard, David. *The Sacred Magic of Angels*. York Beach, Maine: Samuel Weiser, 1996.

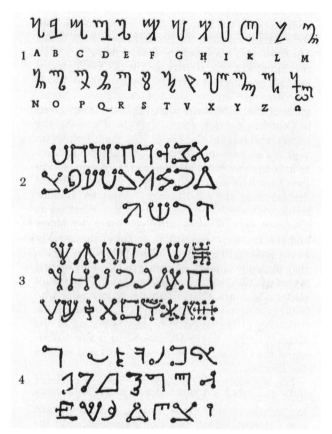

Magic alphabet scripts, from top: 1—Theban, credited to Honorius the Theban; 2—Writing of Heaven, based on Hebrew; 3—Writing of the Angels or Writing of the Kings; 4—Writing of the Crossing of the River. In Amulets and Superstitions, by E. Wallace Budge, 1930. (Author's collection)

James, Geoffrey. *Angel Magic: The Ancient Art of Summoning and Communicating with Angelic Beings.* St. Paul, Minn.: Llewellyn Publications, 1999.

Savedow, Steve. *Sepher Rezial Hemelach: The Book of the Angel Rezial.* York Beach, Maine: Samuel Weiser, 2000.

Three Books of Occult Philosophy Written by Henry Cornelius Agrippa of Nettesheim. James Freake, trans. Ed. and annot. by Donald Tyson. St. Paul, Minn.: Llewellyn Publications, 1995.

Trachtenberg, Joshua. *Jewish Magic and Superstition: A Study in Folk Religion.* New York: Berhman's Jewish Book House, 1939.

magic circle　A sacred, purified, and protected space in which magical RITUALS are conducted. The magic circle provides a boundary for reservoir of concentrated power and acts as a doorway to the realm of the gods. A circle symbolizes wholeness, perfection, and unity; the creation of the cosmos; the womb of Mother Earth; the cycle of the seasons, and birth-death-regeneration. Within the circle, it becomes possible to transcend the physical to open the mind to deeper and higher levels of consciousness.

Circles have had a magical, protective significance since ancient times when they were drawn around the beds of sick persons and mothers who had just given birth, to protect them against DEMONS. A magic circle protects a magician against negative spirits and influences and creates a symbolic barrier against the magician's own lower nature.

In ceremonial magic, the circle provides a defined space for the working of a ritual. It symbolizes the infinite and also the astral sphere or cosmos of the magician, outside of which nothing exists. The circle also corresponds to the *Ain Soph* of the kabbalistic Tree of Life. The center of the circle is the Self, and in the process of magical workings, the magician expands himself or herself to the circumference of the circle or to the Infinite.

The magician enters a magical circle in anticipation of uniting with God, the gods, ANGELS, and the forces of nature in a harmonious relationship of ecstatic union. If the magician performs a ritual calling for the CONJURATION of spirits which are dangerous and difficult to control, the circle provides protection against them. The magician must never leave the circle during a ritual nor even so much as swing his arm outside it, lest a conjured demon grab him and strike him down.

The Four Quarters
Each cardinal point of the magic circle is associated with an ELEMENT, a guardian spirit or an angel, a ritual tool,

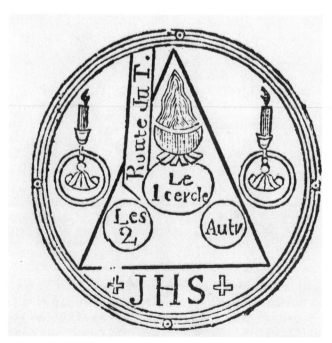

Magic circle, in the grimoire The Red Dragon, *1521. (Author's collection)*

colors, and attributes; correspondences may vary among traditions.

North. North, the cardinal point never touched by the SUN, is associated with darkness, mystery and the unknown, the spiritually unenlightened, the element of earth, the new phase of the MOON, the PENTACLE, secrecy, and the colors gold or black.

East. The quarter of enlightenment, illumination, mysticism, and the eternal, humankind's highest and most spiritual consciousness. The east is associated with the element of air and the colors red or white. In most traditions, the magical altar is aligned to the east.

South. Solar energy, the Sun, the element of fire, the colors blue or white, the WILL, the direction and channeling of the energy forces of nature, and the psychic. South is the halfway meeting point between the spiritual intuition of the east and the rationality of the west. It represents the zenith of intellectuality, as the Sun attains its zenith in the southern sky.

West. The element of water, creativity, emotions, fertility, reason, common sense, material-mindedness, and courage to face one's deepest feelings. The west is associated with the chalice, the symbol of female creative power and fecundity, and the colors red or gray.

Casting a Magic Circle

The circle is crucial to the magician's well-being and protection and must be cast carefully. GRIMOIRES and magical traditions give detailed instructions for casting the circle with a consecrated ritual TOOL such as a dagger, a sword, or a wand during certain astrological conditions and hours of the day or night. The traditional magician's circle is nine feet in diameter or may be a double circle of eight feet and 10 feet. The circle is inscribed with magical SYMBOLS and words and NAMES of power, which are appropriate to a particular ritual. A geometric figure pertaining to the nature of the ritual—such as a square, a tau cross, or a MAGIC TRIANGLE—is inscribed within the circle.

In casting the circle, the magician moves deosil, or clockwise, to the motion of the Sun, the MOON, and the stars through the sky. For black magic rituals, the magician moves widdershins, or counterclockwise. He leaves a small opening and then steps inside, carefully closing the opening to prevent clever demons from slipping inside. The magician consecrates the circle with the four ELEMENTS and invokes the guardian spirits who watch over the four quarters of the sky (the cardinal points) and the four elements. (See LORDS OF THE WATCHTOWER.)

The Astral Magic Circle

The physical circle is matched by a duplicate astral counterpart, which also must be fortified against the invasion of negative forces, including the magician's own lower THOUGHTS. In actuality, the real magical work is done on the ASTRAL PLANE within the astral circle. The physical circle is symbolic of the astral one. To prepare and fortify the astral magic circle, a banishing ritual should be done daily for months in advance of actual work (see PENTAGRAM). The magician also infuses the astral magic circle with a subtle spiritual essence and imbues it with a brilliant flashing light.

FURTHER READING:

Bardon, Franz. *The Practice of Magical Evocation.* Albuquerque, N.Mex.: Brotherhood of Life, 2001.

Cicero, Chic, and Sandra Tabatha Cicero. *The Essential Golden Dawn.* St. Paul, Minn.: Llewellyn Publications, 2004.

Regardie, Israel. *The Tree of Life: A Study in Magic.* York Beach, Maine: Samuel Weiser, 1969.

magic lights   See HAND OF GLORY; RAVEN STONES; THIEVES' LIGHTS.

magic square   A square made up of rows of letters or NUMBERS, used in making TALISMANS and CHARMS. There are different types of magical squares.

History

Magical squares have been in use since ancient times. It is not known exactly when or where they originated. The earliest known record of magic squares is in the Chinese *Lo Shu,* a scroll in manuscripts of the I CHING dating to the Chou Dynasty (951–1126 C.E.). According to the *Lo Shu,* a magic square showing the unity of all things was revealed to the Emperor Yu in about 2200 B.C.E. when he observed a divine tortoise crawl out of the River Lo with the pattern upon its shell.

Magic squares have been in use in India and elsewhere in the East; they are inscribed on AMULETS. Magic squares came into prominence in Western occultism in about the 14th century.

Squares Composed of Letters

The simplest magical square is composed of rows of letters which spell out the same words of power or names of power horizontally and vertically. Some squares are entirely filled with letters, while others have letters and voids or portions of the square left deliberately vacant. Squares are inscribed on magical TOOLS or talismanic objects or paper.

One of the best-known letter magical squares is the SATOR square that was used in ancient Rome for protec-

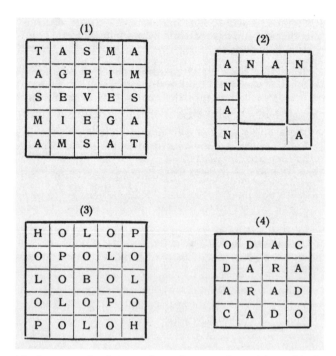

Magic squares for flying and traveling anywhere: (1) In a black cloud; (2) In a white cloud; (3) In the form of an eagle; (4) In the form of a vulture. In The Book of the Sacred Magic of Abra-Melin the Mage, translated by S. L. MacGregor Mathers. (Author's collection)

tion. It may have also been inscribed on sacred vessels. It was in use during early Christian times.

The book of ABRA-MELIN THE MAGE, said to be divine wisdom given from God to Moses and handed down through the patriarchs, contains many magical letter squares. Among them are squares to know the future, find hidden treasure, acquire magical abilities, raise the dead, divine by NECROMANCY, walk on water and operate under water, command spirits and have visions. One square is sort of alchemical in nature, for the instant manifestation of all the GOLD and SILVER one may desire for necessities and "to live in opulence."

Squares Composed of Numbers

Squares composed of rows of consecutive numbers are mathematically complex. The numbers are arranged on the cells in a square according to various formulae, for example, starting the number 1 in a certain cell, skipping to another line and position for number 2, and so on. When finished, the sum of any row of the square—vertical, horizontal, or diagonal—equals the same number. Squares are known by their "order," that is, the number of cells in a row. A three-cell grid, which has nine cells total, is an "order 3" magic square. The higher the order, the more permutations are possible. A permutation is the creation of another square by inverting, reflecting, or tipping the original square. There are no order 2 squares, only one order 3 square, but there are 880 order 4 squares

with 7,040 possible permutations. There are 275,305,224 order 5 squares.

The construction of a square depends on its class:

- odd squares, which have an odd-numbered order
- doubly even squares, which have four squares of an even order when they are divided into four equal parts by a cross
- singly even squares, which have four squares of an odd order when they are divided into four equal parts by a cross

In addition, there are pandiagonal squares, in which broken diagonals are the sum of the order of the square.

HENRY CORNELIUS AGRIPPA gave instructions for constructing the magical squares of the planets. Saturn has the lowest order of 3, and the MOON has the highest order of 9. None of Agrippa's squares are pandiagonal.

Magic squares are used in RITUALS to invoke the powers and spirits associated with specific planets. In addition, the magic squares of planets are used to create the SEALS of the PLANETS by connecting numbers in lines and circles according to mathematical formulae. Magic squares have within them magic circles, drawn according to numbers arranged magically in rays radially about a center point, and magic stars, created by the equal sums of numbers on the interstices or rays. Planetary SIGILS are created by tracing the name of a planet according to the number that is equivalent to the appropriate Hebrew letters spelling the name of the planet.

Magic squares are made with nonconsecutive numbers and primary numbers as well. A doubly magic square is magic for both its numbers and the squares of the numbers, and a trebly magic square is magic for its numbers, their squares, and their cubes. Furthermore, a magic cube is composed of layers of magic squares so that all columns and diagonals add up to the same number.

FURTHER READING:

Mathers, S. L. MacGregor. *The Book of the Sacred Magic of Abra-Melin the Mage*. Wellingborough, England: The Aquarian Press, 1976.

Three Books of Occult Philosophy Written by Henry Cornelius Agrippa of Nettesheim. James Freake, trans. Ed. and annot. by Donald Tyson. St. Paul, Minn.: Llewellyn Publications, 1995.

magic triangle In ceremonial MAGIC, an inscribed triangle into which a spirit or DEMON is evoked into physical appearance and is contained. The magic triangle, also called the Triangle of Art, is a symbol of manifestation of the invisible into the visible, or the powers of darkness and night into daylight. The points of the magic triangle are bounded by three great names of God.

As long as a spirit is inside a magical triangle, it is subject to the commands of the magician, who remains protected inside a MAGIC CIRCLE. The spirit must be discharged or dismissed from within the triangle. It is considered dangerous to allow a spirit to escape the triangle.

ALEISTER CROWLEY and his assistant and lover, poet VICTOR NEUBERG, performed a RITUAL in 1909 in the desert south of Algiers, in which the demon CHORONZON escaped from the magic triangle and attacked Neuberg. Neuberg managed to magically quell the demon.

FURTHER READING:
Regardie, Israel. *The Tree of Life: A Study in Magic.* York Beach, Maine: Samuel Weiser, 1969.

magie In Vodoun, a priest, priestess or sorcerer who is a practitioner of black MAGIC. *Magie* also refers to black magic itself.

magus See ADEPT; HERMETIC ORDER OF THE GOLDEN DAWN.

Maier, Michael (1566 or 1568–1622) Rosicrucian alchemist. Michael Maier is famous for his books of alchemical emblems, the best-known of which is *Atalanta fugiens,* published in 1618.

Michael Maier at age 49, 1617. (Author's collection)

Maier was born in Rendsburg (Ruidsburg), Germany; the dates of 1566 and 1568 are given in different sources. His father, Johann Maier, was an official in the duchy of Holstein. He studied medicine at the University of Rostock with the encouragement of Severin Goebel, a well-known physician who was a friend of Maier's mother. Maier became a physician, practicing in Rostock, and then with Goebel's son in Nuremberg and Padua, Italy. He took the post of *poeta Laureatus Casesarus* at the University of Frankfurt and published poetry in Latin under an anagram, Hermes Malavici.

Maier earned his doctorate in medicine at the University of Basel and went to Prague where he became the Imperial County Palatine under the favor of Emperor Rudolph II. He traveled extensively and may have engaged in spying and intrigue for the emperor. He pursued his interests in ALCHEMY. He probably became involved in ROSICRUCIANISM through his involvement with the Landgrave Maurice of Hesse and Prince Christian I of Anhalt, both of whom were associated with the Rosicrucian Fraternity. Maier became the private physician to Maurice of Hesse.

Rudolph II died in 1612, and Maier went to England where he met and became friends with ROBERT FLUDD; he also met William Paddy, physician to King James I. He translated THOMAS NORTON's *Ordinall of Alchemy* into Latin and wrote his own works. In 1616 he returned to Germany and had his works published. His first, *Arcana arcanissima* ("Most Secret Secrets"), published in 1614, is significant because it is the first Hermetic interpretation of Greek and Egyptian myths.

Maier's other works are *Lusus serius* ("The Serious Game"), 1616, about HERMES; *Examen fucorum* ("The Swarm of Drones"), about false alchemists; *Jocus severus* ("The Earnest Game"), 1617, about the PHOENIX; *Symbola aureae mensae* ("Symbols of the Golden Table of Twelve Nations"), 1617; *Tripus aureus* ("The Golden Tripod"), 1618, featuring three treatises by Norton, BASIL VALENTINE, and Abott Cremer; and *Viatorium* ("The Wayfarer's Guide") on the seven mountains of the PLANETS, 1618.

Maier died in 1622 in Magdeburg at the start of the Thirty Years' War.

FURTHER READING:
Klossowski de Rola, Stanislaus. *The Golden Game: Alchemical Engravings of the Seventeenth Century.* New York: George Braziller, Inc., 1988.
Waite, Arthur Edward. *Alchemists Through the Ages.* Blauvelt, N.Y.: Rudolph Steiner Publications, 1970.

malediction See BLASTING; CURSE; HEX; POINTING.

Maria Prophetess In ALCHEMY, one of the early and most esteemed Hellenistic alchemists. Maria Prophetess is also known as Maria the Jewess, Maria the Hebrew, Maria Hebraea, and Mary the Prophetess.

Little is known about the life of Maria Prophetess. She lived prior to ZOSIMUS, who lived in Hellenistic Egypt in about 300 C.E.; he quotes her as an ADEPT extensively in his own writings. It is not known where she was born, exactly where she resided, or how she acquired her alchemical wisdom. In medieval times she was associated with Miriam, the sister of Moses. In Arabic lore, she is called Mariya al-Qibityya, or Maria the Copt; "Maria the Sage, daughter of the king of Saba;" and also "the matron Maria Sicula." ARNOLD DE VILLANOVA called her "the daughter of Pluto." MICHAEL MAIER debated whether or not she was a fictitious person but concluded that she was genuine and was not the sister of Moses but another Jewish woman who possessed great knowledge. An early father of the church, Epiphanus (circa 315–402), cited

Maria Prophetessa in the Temperance card *in* The Alchemical Tarot, *by Rosemary Ellen Guiley and Robert Michael Place. Maria represents the process of distillation. Inspired by Michael Maier's* Symbola aureae mensae, *1617. (Copyright by and courtesy of Robert Michael Place)*

two works by Maria called *Great Questions* and *Small Questions,* of which he was critical. *Small Questions* relates a vision Maria allegedly had of Jesus in which he produced a woman from his side, had intercourse with her, and explained to Maria that this transfer of semen was necessary for things to live.

According to medieval lore, Maria said that the secrets of alchemy were revealed to her by God; the title *prophetessa* was appended to her name in about the early 16th century. Her most significant teachings are in a manuscript entitled *Dialog of Maria and Aros,* published in the late 16th century as a Latin translation of an Arabic work, which may in turn have been translated from a Greek original. Aros, a fictitious philosopher, comes to Maria to learn the secrets of the Great Work.

Maria is credited with inventing several alchemical apparatuses—whether she actually invented them or merely popularized them is not known. The best known of these is the *balneum Mariae,* a water BATH. The apparatus is a double vessel. The outer vessel is filled with water and the inner vessel contains whatever substance to be heated to a moderate degree by the surrounding hot water. Maria also gave the earliest description of a still, as well as a more complex alchemical still called a *tribikos,* made of copper.

Maria gave a formula for making the PHILOSOPHER'S STONE and was credited with inventing various alchemical procedures. She held that all things in nature are one, and she authored axioms about this fundamental concept of alchemy. The most famous axiom is "One becomes two, two becomes three, and by means of the third and fourth achieves unity; thus two are but one." CARL G. JUNG read a Christian interpretation into this axiom, saying that the even NUMBERS represent the feminine principle, the earth and evil, which are interwoven with the uneven numbers of Christian dogma.

FURTHER READING:
Patai, Raphael. *The Jewish Alchemists.* Princeton, N.J.: Princeton University Press, 1994.

marre corde In Vodoun, the ceremonial making of CHARMS, AMULETS, and other magical objects for the purposes of protection or SPELL-casting.

Martinism A spiritual, mystical, and magical organization that has been derived and fused into the Martinist Order from the system of Martinez de Pasqually and the philosophy of Louis-Claude de Saint-Martin.

The essential principles of Martinism are much older than any organizations bearing that name. Earlier organizations that embodied these principles practiced under other esoteric names. Martinism was forged out of the practical degree work and magical basis of Pasqually's Order of Elus Cohen, or Elect Priesthood, and the "inner way" or speculative mysticism of Saint-Martin. The modern form of Martinism was also greatly affected by PAPUS (Gerard Encausse) and his associates, and it evolved into the Martinist Order.

Martinism was influenced by the FREEMASONRY movement of France in the 18th century, and essentially was initiated by Pasqually through his Masonic connection. Pasqually was born in Grenoble, France, around 1727; his full name was Jacques de Livron Joachim de la Tour de las Case Martinez de Pasqually. His father held a Masonic patent delivered by Charles Stuart, king of Scotland, Ireland, and England. The powers of this patent were transferable at death to the son, Martinez. This occurred in either 1738 or 1758, marking the beginning of Pasqually's spiritual mission to develop further mystical orders. As a Master Mason, Pasqually held Freemasonry at the cornerstone of these efforts.

Pasqually developed and formed the Order of the Elus-Cohen in 1865. He introduced Saint-Martin into Freemasonry and became a teacher to him. Saint-Martin was initiated into the Elus-Cohen in October 1768.

Saint-Martin developed his own line of mystical thinking into a speculative mysticism. This "inner way" approach led him away from the Masonic method of the Elus-Cohen to Hermetic and esoteric circles, the teachings of JAKOB BÖHME, the Order of the Unknown Philosophers, and the Society of Initiates.

Saint-Martin acquired numerous followers in many countries. With the death of Martinez Pasqually in 1774, and the death of Saint-Martin in 1803, the framework of Martinism continued in the following manner:

- The Society of Initiates of Saint-Martin continued to be transmitted from person to person.
- The occult teachings of Pasqually were transmitted by the continuation of Elus-Cohen and some Freemasons of the Scottish Rectified Rite.

These set the stage for Martinism to incorporate both the Pasqually and the Saint-Martin work and philosophies into the degree or initiatory structure. This was accomplished in 1884 with the drafting of the Constitution by Papus in association with fellow Martinist Pierre Augstin Chaboseau and other initiates, establishing the Ordre Martiniste or Martinist Order. The Martinist Order has continued to evolve. There are several Martinist Orders; the present Ordre Martiniste incorporates much of the original work of the Papus Martinist Order. The degrees of present Martinist Orders consist essentially of the following groupings:

Associate
Initiate
Superior (SECRET CHIEF degrees)

These degrees convey and teach many mystical, magical, and Hermetic principles through their RITUALS, rites, lectures, and conventicles. The Martinist Order degree teachings contain the mystical meanings of the great universal truths, ALCHEMY, thoughts, NUMBERS, the KABBALAH, and symbolic practices. Upon completion of the three degrees, an initiate can advance to study the practices and workings of the Order of the Elus-Cohen.

FURTHER READING:
Waite, Arthur Edward. *Saint-Martin, the French Mystic.* London: W. Rider, 1922.

mask   An ancient and powerful magical mediator among the worlds of the living, the dead, and the spirits. Masks have been worn for magical, religious, and entertainment purposes since the beginning of recorded history. Masks actually reveal more than they conceal.

Ancient peoples understood well the power of the mask. Evidence of mask-wearing in prehistoric societies shows that masks may have been intended to transform the wearer magically to achieve or acquire something. Perhaps the first prehistoric masked dancer is the "Sorcerer," a Neolithic-Age cave painting at Trois Freres in France. The masked figure is half-human and half-animal, wearing stag antlers and poised in dance step. The image suggests a RITUAL for a successful hunt. His mask reveals and liberates the animal nature within the man, which would have enabled him to come into contact with supernatural forces or the spirit of animals and petition them for help.

Masks have been used throughout history in numerous rituals, liturgies, theater, and folk art. The mask has been revered as a sacred object of power, a living thing that either has its own persona or represents the persona of another being. It enables the wearer magically to bring to life, and even become, the persona or spirit being represented by the mask. While the mask is on, the wearer is no longer completely himself or herself but shares his or her identity with that of the mask. He or she has freedom—and permission within society—to act differently, even outrageously. The transformation has its limits and controls: The wearer cannot go beyond the bounds of the mask itself and is transformed only during the wearing of the mask. When the mask comes off, the wearer must return to ordinary reality.

The transformative power of the mask can be explained in Jungian terms. A mask connects its wearer to archetypal powers residing within the collective unconscious. The mask is a mediator between the ego and archetype, the mundane and the supernatural, the sacred and the comic. It connects the present to the past, the individual to the entire collective of race, culture, country—and humanity.

In cultures where the mask is treated with reverence, mask-making is a respected and skilled art. For example, in Bali, masks play major roles in rituals and performances. The masks are carved from wood. Before carving is begun, the sculptors meditate on the purpose of the mask, the persona in the mask itself, and the performer who will wear it. The performer also meditates upon the mask prior to wearing it. He or she may even sleep with it next to him or her to incubate dreams based upon its appearance and persona, which will inspire the performance to greater depth.

The challenge of the Balinese performer is to literally bring the mask to life—to make the wood seem elastic and capable of illuminating its fixed expression. Actors who have the gift to animate their masks are respected as "having *taksu*." *Taksu* means "place that receives light." Actors who have no *taksu* are called carpenters—they just push wood around the stage.

In most cultures, masks symbolize beneficient spirits: nature beings, deities, the ancestral dead, and the animal kingdom. North American Indians have used masks to represent evil spirits over which the medicine men are believed to have power. Similar attribution is made in Ceylon.

Masks play important roles in religious, healing, EXORCISM, and funerary rituals. Sri Lankan exorcism masks, for example, are hideous so as to frighten possessing demons out of bodies. Among North American Indians, bear masks invoke the healing powers of the bear, considered the great doctor of all ills. In funerary rites, masks incarnate the souls of the dead, protect wearers from recognition by the souls of the dead, or trap the souls of the dead.

The true intent of Halloween masks is to frighten. The practice of wearing masks and disguises on All Souls' Night stems from ancient beliefs that on this night the souls of the dead and unfriendly spirits walk the Earth. It is desirable to conceal your true identity from them so that they do not follow you home. Masks also frighten them away.

In the modern West, masks have lost much of their sacred and deep symbolic meaning. Once, they were integral to Greek drama, both secular and liturgical medieval ceremonies, the Renaissance court masque, and 19th-century mime and pantomine.

Contemporary masks are treated as entertainment props rather than as living things. They are used to disguise and conceal rather than reveal.

FURTHER READING:
Guiley, Rosemary Ellen. "The Truth Behind the Mask." Available online. URL: http://www.visionaryliving.com/paranormal.html. Copyright Visionary Living Inc., 2002. Downloaded December 13, 2004.

Mathers, Moina (1865–1928)

Occultist, artist, wife of SAMUEL LIDDELL MacGREGOR MATHERS, and influential member of the HERMETIC ORDER OF THE GOLDEN DAWN. Moina Mathers was an eccentric and flamboyant personality.

Mathers was born Mina Bergson on February 28, 1865, in Geneva, Switzerland. She was the fourth of seven children in a gifted but struggling Jewish-Irish family. Her father, Michel Gabriel Bergson, was a French musician, and her mother, Katherine Levison, was from Ireland. Her brother, Henri, became famous as a philosopher. When Mina was not quite three years old, her family moved to Paris in search of musical work for Michel. In 1873, the family moved to London.

Mina displayed an early talent for art and might have enjoyed a successful career as an artist had not the occult world intervened. In high school she met the wealthy tea heiress ANNIE HORNIMAN and became one of her best friends.

In 1888, Mina met Mathers while at the British Museum where she was studying Egyptian art. She was instantly captivated by him and perceived him to be a true soulmate, her other half. Mathers had no steady income, and her family and Horniman disapproved of him, but Mina defied them and married Mathers on June 16, 1890, in the library of the Horniman Museum. To accommodate Mathers's Scottish interests, Mina changed her first name to Moina.

From the beginning, Moina and Mathers agreed never to have sex, a promise which they kept. The reasons for this is not known; it is speculated that perhaps Moina had been abused early in life, and thus had a fear of, or aversion to, intercourse. The lack of sex did not seem to interfere in the relationship, which remained close and intimate in all other ways.

With the founding of the Golden Dawn in 1888, Moina surrendered her ambitions to be an artist and devoted her time and talent to the Order. At her INITIATION, she took the MAGICAL MOTTO *Vestigia nulla retrorsum*, "No traces behind" or "I never retrace my steps." She designed furnishings for the temples in London and Paris, TAROT card designs, costume designs, and color scales. She painted the vaults where ceremonial MAGIC rites took place, including the famous vault recreating the legend of CHRISTIAN ROSENKREUTZ. Moina possessed abilities for mediumship and SCRYING, and she used these abilities in teamwork with Mathers to produce materials for the order, especially the RITUALS and teachings of the Second Order.

Self-assured, Moina proved to be a gifted magician and performed well in ceremonial rites, especially when she incarnated the presence of the High Priestess of Anari in the Isis Rites, composed partially by Mathers.

The Matherses had always lived on the edge of poverty, but by 1892, they could no longer afford even a poverty lifestyle in London. They moved to Paris where they could live more cheaply, supported by Horniman. In 1894, they established a Golden Dawn temple there. Their absence from London was a major factor in the ensuing disintegration of the order. Horniman became displeased with Mathers and cut off her financial support. Mathers died in Paris in 1918; Moina is said to have blamed both PSYCHIC ATTACK from ALEISTER CROWLEY as a cause, as well as the drain of long-term contact with the nonphysical secret chiefs of the order.

Moina returned to London in 1919, where she established the Alpha et Omega Lodge, running it for nine years. She enlisted the help of a Frater X to continue her communication with the spirit planes, even though she now feared that it was at the risk of occult attack. DION FORTUNE claimed that Moina practiced black magic and was responsible for murdering a woman, Netta Fornario; however, Moina predeceased Fornario by 18 months.

In 1926, a new edition of Mathers's translation of the KABBALAH, *The Kabbalah Unveiled,* was published. Moina wrote the preface, in which she expressed "thanks to my occult masters, and the deepest gratitude to the memory of my husband, comrade and teacher, all of whom have shed much light upon my path."

In her final years, Moina was destitute and discouraged. She attempted to revive her art career by painting portaits but was only modestly successful. Her health declined. Near the end she refused to eat. She died on July 25, 1928.

FURTHER READING:

Greer, Mary K. *Women of the Golden Dawn: Rebels and Priestesses.* Rochester, Vt.: Inner Traditions, 1995.

Mathers, S. L. MacGregor. *The Kabbalah Unveiled.* London: Routledge and Kegan Paul, 1926.

"Moina Mathers." Available online. URL: http://www.golden-dawn.org/biomoinam.html. Downloaded June 29, 2005.

Mathers, Samuel Liddell MacGregor (1854–1918) English occultist, author, and founding chief of the HERMETIC ORDER OF THE GOLDEN DAWN. Throughout his life, S. L. MacGregor Mathers was a compelling, charismatic, colorful, controversial, and headstrong figure in occultism. He is responsible for the creation of much of the Golden Dawn RITUAL material which continues in use and is widely considered to be one of the finest and most powerful magical systems in the world. Some of his peers considered him to be the reincarnation of King James VI, the "WIZARD king" of Scotland.

Mathers was born in London on January 8, 1854, to a family of modest means. His father, William M. Mathers, a commercial clerk, died when S. L. Mathers was a child, and his mother took the family to live in Bournemouth. They lived there until Mrs. Mathers died in 1885. Poor, Mathers returned to London.

Mathers exhibited an early interest in warfare and the military. In his early twenties, he joined the First Hampshire Infantry Volunteers, intent on a military career. He never rose above the rank of private. He once took a self-portrait photograph dressed in the uniform of lieutenant—an early indication of his sizeable ego. In 1884, Mathers published his first book, a military manual, *Practical Instruction in Infantry Campaigning Exercise.*

Perhaps because his military aspirations never advanced, Mathers turned his attention to FREEMASONRY. He was initiated in Bournemouth in October 1877 and advanced to Master Mason on January 30, 1878. A fellow Mason, Frederick Holland, introduced Mathers to the KABBALAH, ALCHEMY, SCRYING, and other occult studies.

Mathers left the Masons in 1882 for ROSICRUCIAN-ISM, joining the *Societas Rosicruciana in Anglia.* He took the MAGICAL MOTTO *S'Rioghail Mo Dhream,* "Royal is my race," a reflection of his interest in his Celtic heritage. Mathers quickly developed a love for ceremonial MAGIC, and he pursued occult philosophies and esoteric languages. Within four years, he was a members of the Society's High Council. He formed close relationships with DR. WILLIAM WYNN WESTCOTT and DR. WILLIAM ROBERT WOODMAN, who later would become founders of the Golden Dawn with him. Westcott enabled Mathers to publish the first English translation of Knorr von Rosenroth's esteemed work on the kabbalah, *Kabalah Denudata (The Kabbalah Unveiled),* written in Latin in the 17th century. Published in 1887 the work quickly earned Mathers high regard in occult circles. The book remains in print today.

Mathers was familiar the with THEOSOPHICAL SOCIETY and met MADAME HELENA P. BLAVATSKY. He lectured to the society's members, as did Westcott.

By this time, Mathers had added *MacGregor* to his name, claiming it to be his real family name from Glenstrae in the Highlands of Scotland. He also said his grandfather was a military man whose heroics at Pondicherry, India, had caused King Louis XIV of France to give him the title of Count MacGregor de Glenstrae.

In 1888, Mathers, Westcott, and Woodman formed the Golden Dawn. At Mathers's insistence, the order was open to women, who were on a equal footing with men—virtually unheard of in Victorian times. Mathers had been influenced by Anna Kingsford, an occultist, champion of women's rights, and cofounder with Edward Maitland of the Hermetic Society. Westcott initially resisted but gave in when Mathers refused to otherwise participate. The three men established themselves as the chiefs of the Outer Order of the new organization, receiving guidance from nonphysical, superhuman ADEPTS called the Secret Chiefs. Mathers used two magical mottos for the Golden Dawn. For the Outer Order, he used the same motto as he had used in the Rosicrucians. His second motto comes from a TALISMAN for Mars: *Deo Duce Comie Ferro,* "God as my guide, my companion a sword."

Also in 1888, Mathers met artist Mina Bergson in the reading room of the British Museum where he spent much of his time. The two had an immediate rapport and were married on June 16, 1890, despite the opposition of Mina's family. Mina changed her name to MOINA MATHERS in honor of her husband's Celtic orientation. She was initiated into the Golden Dawn shortly after marriage. Mathers tried to convert her famous philosopher brother, Henri Bergson, to occultism and magic but failed to interest him. Through Moina, Mathers met ANNIE HORNIMAN, a wealthy tea heiress who helped him get a job at the Horniman Museum and who also joined the Golden

Dawn. Horniman became the Matherses' benefactor for many years.

Mathers set about the task of creating the rituals for the Golden Dawn. He reworked the ENOCHIAN MAGIC of JOHN DEE and EDWARD KELLY. Moina had psychic abilities, and the two worked together as a team, with Moina doing scrying and communication with spirits on the inner planes. Initially, the Golden Dawn was a theoretical organization, but with the establishment of the Second Order, more emphasis was placed on ritual and practical magic. Mathers and Moina developed the order's teachings on the TAROT and worked on the *Z Documents* concerning magical methods and techniques.

Eventually, Mathers's ego and imperious manner alienated members. He engaged in internal politics and fights. His argumentativeness cost him his job at the museum. In 1892, out of money, he and Moina were forced to leave London for Paris, where they lived on Horniman's charity. In 1894, they set up a Golden Dawn lodge there. Mathers was keen to revive Egyptian religion, and he and Moina performed rites of Isis and Egyptian masses. They performed their *Rites of Isis* publicly in theaters.

Mathers did not spend all of his time on the Golden Dawn, which irritated Horniman. In 1896, she cut off her financial support. Mathers declared himself initiated into the Third Order populated only by the invisible Secret Chiefs and demanded complete loyalty from all members. Horniman refused, and he retaliated by expelling her from the order. Mathers and his wife were left to live on whatever they could earn from their public ritual performances, as well as the charity of other friends.

Mathers was embarrassed by being taken in by two con artists, a husband-and-wife team who introduced themselves to him as Theodore and Laura Horos. Long working as occult scam artists doing fake mediumship, the two appeared in Paris in 1898 and established a relationship with Mathers. They stole ritual material from him and went to London, where they set up their own occult school.

In 1898, ALEISTER CROWLEY joined the Golden Dawn; he and Mathers had an uneasy alliance that disintegrated into PSYCHIC ATTACK upon one another. Mathers sent him to storm the London temple in an attempted takeover. Crowley failed, and both he and Mathers were expelled. Later, in 1910, Mathers lost a legal battle in London to prevent Crowley from publishing secret Golden Dawn material.

The debacle with Crowley was the final blow to an already fractured organization, and the Golden Dawn splintered into groups that aligned themselves by loyalty. Followers of Mathers joined his new Order of the Alpha et Omega Temple. The Mathereses remained in Paris.

Mathers retired and sank into obscurity. Little is known about his final years. He died on November 20, 1918; no record of his death has ever been found, nor has a grave ever been known. DION FORTUNE asserted—without basis—that he died in the Spanish influenza epidemic. Moina maintained that his health had declined because of the strain of dealing with the Secret Chiefs for so many years. She also felt that Crowley's psychic attack with an astral VAMPIRE had drained Mathers.

In later years, Crowley maligned Mathers in undeserving criticism.

Besides his scholarship on the kabbalah, Mathers also is especially known for his translations of two important GRIMOIRES, the *Key of Solomon* (from Hebrew, 1889) and *The Sacred Magic of Abra-Melin the Mage* (from French, 1889), as well as *The Tarot: Its Occult Significance and Methods of Play* (from French, 1888).

FURTHER READING:
Brodie-Innes, J. W. "Some Personal Reminisces." Available online. URL: http://www.controverscial.com/Samuel%20L iddell%20Macgregor%20Mathers.htm. Downloaded June 29, 2005.
Cicero, Chic, and Sandra Tabatha Cicero. *The Essential Golden Dawn*. St. Paul, Minn.: Llewellyn Publications, 2004.
King, Francis. *Megatherion: The Magickal World of Aleister Crowley*. New York: Creation Books, 2004.
"S. L. MacGregor Mathers." Available online. URL: http://www.golden-dawn.org/biomathers.html. Downloaded June 29, 2005.

mauvais   In Vodoun, an evil person, such as a sorcerer or a person who possesses the EVIL EYE. A *mauvais* has the ability to wreak havoc, death, and destruction.

medical astrology   See MOON.

mental body   A person's spiritual body. The mental body is immortal and exists beyond time and space. It consists of a subtle substance connected to the earth ELEMENT. Within the mental body is the ego, consciousness, and consciousness of self, which is comprised of WILL, intellect, and feeling.

mental magic   See MAGIC.

mental plane   The sphere of thoughts. The mental plane is timeless and spaceless and is the finest substance of the AKASHA, the source of everything. The mental plane draws into the conscious and subconscious mind ideas from the akasha, where they become thoughts, images, and impressions. Every thought has its own unique spiritual VIBRATION, color, and form. Everything created in the material world originates from the ideal world through thought and spiritual consciousness.

FRANZ BARDON said that the mental plane is inhabited with ideal forms, created by ideas, and by the dead whose astral bodies have been dissolved as part of their postdeath evolution. The dead are in regions of the mental plane that correspond to their development during incarnated life. The mental plane also is inhabited with ELEMENTALS that are created by humans either consciously or unconsciously through intense thought.

Communication among spirits on the mental plane is done through images, SYMBOLS, and gestures. More advanced beings communicate by CLAIRAUDIENCE.

In MAGIC, thoughts are focused, trained, and controlled through WILL, IMAGINATION, and VISUALIZATION.

FURTHER READING:
Bardon, Franz. *Questions and Answers.* Salt Lake City: Merkur Publishing, 1998.

mercury   One of the most important substances in ALCHEMY. The metal mercury is part of every stage of the Great Work of the creation of the PHILOSOPHER'S STONE and has numerous symbolisms. Mercury, or Mercurius, is the Roman name for the Greek god HERMES, the central mythological figure in the Hermetic arts.

The metal mercury, or quicksilver, is liquid at room temperature, lending it the qualities of substance and of liquid spirit. It is both volatile and fixed, masculine and feminine, and thus is symbolized by the HERMAPHRODITE. Alchemists believed that they could extract mercury from any metal, thus giving it great importance in the transmutation of base metals into GOLD and SILVER. Mercury also is a solvent and thus purifies.

As a spirit or vapor, mercury is associated with the biblical "spirit that moves upon the face of the waters," the breath of God. ZOSIMOS called mercury "divine water."

Mercury also is a SYMBOL for the *PRIMA MATERIA.*

See also CINNABAR; *TRIA PRIMA.*

The Mercury of the Philosophers, in Della transmutatione metallica, *by Giovanni Battista Nazari, 1589. (Author's collection)*

Merlin   Wizard in Celtic and Arthurian lore. Merlin, whose name is a Latinized version of the Welsh *Myrddin,* may be a composite of real and mythical characters. He may be in part a deity, perhaps derived from Mabon, or Maponos, the British Apollo who served as the divine ruler of Britain. He may have been a real prophet or a bard, or several bards. In modern times, Merlin has been interpreted as a Celtic mystic and shaman and as the archetypes of the Trickster (see TRICKSTER GODS) and the magician (see HERMES). In lore his consort is VIVIANE, the Lady of the Lake. In the Western magical tradition, Merlin and Viviane represent Jachin and Boaz, the male and female principles of the cosmos, force, and form.

The first written references to Merlin are in the Latin works of Geoffrey of Monmouth, a 12th-century Welsh cleric. In the early 1130s, Monmouth wrote *The Prophe-*cies *of Merlin,* verses of prophecies going into the future beyond the 12th century, which were attributed to a "Merlin" who lived in the fifth century. It is likely that Monmouth made up much of the book himself. Monmouth mentioned Merlin again in the *History of the Kings of Britain,* completed in about 1135–36, which provided the basis for the Arthurian legends. Monmouth described Merlin as a magical boy whose parents were a mortal woman and a *daemon (daimon),* a Greek-derivative term meaning "spirit" but which, later, Christians interpreted as an evil DEMON. According to Christianized legend, Merlin's father was the devil himself, sent to Earth to obstruct the works of Jesus. The devil assumed the shape of a DRAGON or a serpent (the symbol of wisdom and, in Christianity, of evil) and seduced Merlin's mother. However, the boy decided to devote himself to good and discarded all of the devil's powers that he inherited save two: PROPHECY and MIRACLE-making.

In Monmouth's account, Merlin possesses great powers of prophecy and MAGIC because of his half-supernatural nature of mortal and *daemon*. He arranges for the birth of Arthur through the seduction of Ygerna (Igraine) by King Uther Pendragon. After Arthur is born, Merlin drops completely from Monmouth's story. Monmouth also confused matters by placing Merlin in both the fifth and sixth centuries.

Monmouth wrote of Merlin the prophet in a third poetic work, *The Life of Merlin,* and composed Merlin's adult biography in *Vita Merlini,* written in about 1150. *Vita Merlini* has been interpreted as much more than a biography but as a text of Celtic mysticism. The *Vita* presents a series of questions such as why is there suffering, death, and love, which are answered in the form of cosmic visions that lead to greater questions, and reveal the small part humans play in a much greater cosmic landscape.

Merlin appears in other medieval works and in later chivalric tales and romantic poems. A French poetical version of *History of the Kings of Britain,* written in about 1150, tells of Merlin directing King Arthur on the establishment of his Round Table. Sir Thomas Malory's *Le Morte d'Arthur,* published in 1485, tells how Merlin raised Arthur, secured him the throne by having him pull the sword of Branstock from the stone, and served as his magical adviser. Merlin appears and disappears at will, possesses omniscient awareness, and casts the most powerful of SPELLS. Malory's work provides the modern popular conception of Merlin, despite the fact that Merlin disappears from his story early in Arthur's reign, after the Round Table is formed.

According to the *Mort Artu* by Robert Boron, part of the 13th-century Vulgate Cycle of French writing on Arthurian lore, Merlin gives magical instruction to MORGAN LE FAY but falls passionately in love with Viviane (also called Nimue). Viviane persuades Merlin to teach her all his magical arts, too, which she then uses to trap him in a tower of hawthorn, a spiny shrub or tree associated with FAIRIES and WITCHES. She weaves the hawthorn around him nine times while he sleeps in the Forest of Broceliande, a magical place where no one who enters comes out quite the same. When Arthur misses Merlin from his court, he dispatches Sir Gawain to find him. In the Forest of Broceliande, Merlin speaks to the knight from a cloud of smoke, tells him that he will never more be seen, and instructs him to tell Arthur to undertake without delay the quest of the Holy Grail.

There are other versions of the legend:

- Viviane traps Merlin in a tower of air.
- Merlin simply disappears into thin air, where he continues to exist as a shadow who has the power to communicate with humans.

- Merlin retires to a stone vault and seals himself inside.
- Merlin is buried alive under a stone in the Forest of Broceliande.

Merlin usually is portrayed as a wise, old man, tall and gaunt with a long white beard. He has in fact three aspects: youth, mature prophet, and elder. As the magician archetype, one who uses the powers of both Earth and sky (the microcosm and macrocosm) to transform, he serves as the model for many fictional characters, including Mr. Spock in *Star Trek* and Obi Wan Kenobe in *Star Wars.*

The deeper meanings of Merlin are the subject of ongoing research by Arthurian experts and conferences; the first international Merlin Conference was held in London in 1986.

FURTHER READING:

Hall, Manly P. *The Secret Teachings of All Ages.* 1928. Reprint, Los Angeles: The Philosophic Research Society, 1977.

Matthews, John (ed.). *At the Table of the Grail.* 1984. Reprint, London: Arkana, 1987.

Stewart, R. J. (ed.). *The Book of Merlin.* Poole, Dorset: Blanford Press, 1987.

———. *The Mystic Life of Merlin.* London: Arkana, 1986.

Mesmer, Franz Anton (1734–1815)   Austrian physician and Freemason whose method of "magnetic healing" was based on alchemical principles and led to the development of hypnotherapy. To many of his contemporaries, Franz Anton Mesmer's healing seemed magical. His use of magnets and the power of suggestion demonstrated the ability of WILL and consciousness to affect physical health.

Mesmer was born at Iznang on Lake Constance, Austria, in 1734. Initially he intended a career in the church, but he discovered that he had a gift for mathematics and science, and so he decided to pursue medicine at the University of Vienna. There he studied the works of PARACELSUS, JEAN BAPTISA VAN HELMONT, ROBERT FLUDD, and other scientist/alchemists. He also borrowed from the ideas of Richard Mead, an English physician who in 1704 published a treatise on the power of the SUN and the MOON on the human body.

Mesmer interpreted the prevailing theory of the times that a magnetic fluid permeates and links all things and beings, including people, on Earth and in the heavens. He believed that the human body has a natural magnetic bipolarity and that sickness and health were influenced by the balance of the vital fluid within the body.

Mesmer's thesis, *De Planetarum Influxu* ("On the Influence of the Planets"), caught the attention of Father Maximilian Hehl, a Jesuit priest, court astrologer to Empress Maria Theresa and professor of astronomy at Vienna University. Hehl also believed in a planetary magnetism that influenced physical health and used magnets with the shape of body organs to correct magnetic imbalances. He gave some magnets to Mesmer, who qualified as a physician in 1765 and used the magnets in spectacular healings in which he placed magnets on patients to end their pain. Mesmer surmised that his own body was a magnet, for he noticed that when once bleeding a patient, the flow of BLOOD increased when he approached and decreased when he left. He published his theory in 1775; the public reacted enthusiastically and patients began to seek him out.

A few years later, Mesmer observed the work of an exorcist, Father Johann Gassner, who maintained that all illness was caused by demoniacal POSSESSION and could be cured only by EXORCISM. This led Mesmer to the discovery that he could cure without the help of Hehl's magnets. The vital force or healing energy could be transmitted directly from healer to patient through touch or with the help of IRON rods or wands.

Mesmer called this universal life force animal magnetism. He envisioned the force as an invisible, fluidic, magnetic substance that permeates the universe and emanates from the PLANETS, the stars, and the Moon and from human bodies. The fluid links all things. An imbalance of the fluid in the body creates illness, which can be corrected with the application of appropriate magnetic forces. Animal magnetism may be transferred from a healer, who has an excess of it in his nervous system, to a patient.

Throughout the latter part of the 18th century and for part of the 19th century, the term *animal magnetism* referred to Mesmer's method of healing, which consisted of a laying on of hands, staring fixedly into the eyes of the patient, and making slow passes in front of the patient's face with hands or a wand. The healers themselves usually were called magnetists, sometimes mesmerists, who magnetized or mesmerized their patients. In addition to curing ailments, magnetists could put their patients into a magnetized sleep, which made operations painless.

The magnetized sleep produced certain side effects: CLAIRVOYANCE, telepathy, mediumistic ability, hallucinations, suggestability, and catalepsy. Mesmer left these phenomena largely unexplored, concentrating instead on the healing aspects of animal magnetism. The serious study of the side effects was taken up by hypnotists in the latter 19th century.

Mesmer fell out of favor with Hehl and the Viennese medical profession, but his esteem increased with patients, who sought him for cures. In 1778 he moved to Paris to set up a fashionable hospital that was more like a seance parlor than a medical facility. The rooms were lit with low light, perfumed, and decorated with MIRRORS, crystal objects, beautiful paintings, and handsome clocks. Mesmer himself seemed more like a WIZARD than a physician, dressed in purple robes and carrying an iron wand. While a chamber orchestra played soft music—Mesmer was a patron of Mozart—he and his assistants would move among the patients, waving hands and wands, stroking them and magnetizing them. Many phenomenal cures were effected, made all the more mysterious and awesome by the hysterics and convulsions of his patients as they were cured. Rich and poor alike descended upon the clinic. Mesmer entertained well, hosting coffee socials and carrying on lively conversations with his clients.

So many patients came to his clinic that Mesmer had to begin to treat them en masse. He created a device call the *baquet,* a round wooden bathtub that he filled with "magnetized water" and iron filings. As many as 30 iron rods protruded from the lid of the tub; they were placed on as many patients on whatever part of the body required healing. The patients were then tied to each other with moistened rope, forming a magnetic chain. Patients called the tub Mesmer's magic bath.

Mesmer's success earned him the animosity of the medical academy. Louis XVI was a supporter of Mesmer, but he agreed under pressure from the academy to establish two commissions to investigate mesmer and animal magnetism. The first, which published its findings in 1784, found no evidence to support the existence of animal magnetism and recommended that members of the Faculty of Medicine who practiced it be expelled. The second commission supported the first.

Mesmer's fortunes declined. A doctor consulted him with a phony illness, allowed Mesmer to "heal" him, and then accused him of fraud.

Mesmer fell into further discredit with his peers when one of his staunchest supporters, Antoine Court De Gebelin (see TAROT), died while sitting at a *baquet.* But the general public continued to patronize him, and Mesmer maintained his clinic until 1789 when the French Revolution forced him to flee the country. He went to Karlsruhe and then to Vienna in 1793. He was accused of being a French spy and was imprisoned for two months. Upon his release, Mesmer returned to Lake Constance, where he died in 1815.

FURTHER READING:

Douglas, Alfred. *Extrasensory Powers: A Century of Psychical Research.* London: Victor Gollancz Ltd., 1976.

Oppenheim, Janet. *The Other World: Spiritualism and Psychical Research in England, 1850–1914.* Cambridge: Cambridge University Press, 1985.

Seligmann, Kurt. *The History of Magic and the Occult.* New York: Pantheon Books, 1948.

migan   A magical liquid that is an important ingredient in Vodoun. *Migan* consists of BLOOD, rum, cane syrup, and spices. It is drunk during RITUALS and facilitates the casting of SPELLS. Any *migan* that is left over must be stored in a sealed container and hidden from sunlight.

miracle   An act often seen as caused by divine intervention. The word *miracle* comes from the Latin term *miracu-*

lum, which comes from *mirari,* or "to wonder." Miracles are "wonderful things." There is no one, all-encompassing definition of a miracle; rather, the meaning of what is miraculous is shaded by perspective and worldview. There are differences between Western and Eastern ideas of what constitutes a miracle and what distinguishes a miracle from MAGIC.

Western Views

To most Westerners, a miracle is an event that has no natural explanation according to the known laws of science and nature. Without a natural explanation, miracles then can only be possible by divine intervention: the reaching out of the hand of God.

Miracles play an important role in Judaism and Christianity. Both religions trace their origins to events viewed as both historical and miraculous: the Exodus of the Jews from Egypt in Judaism, and the Resurrection of Jesus in Christianity. Of all the great religions, Christianity, especially in the Catholic tradition, has developed the most systematic account of miracles.

In the Judeo-Christian traditions, miracles are seen especially as acts of God that signal his presence in the world and demonstrate his covenant with humanity. As creator of the world, it is expected that God will intervene in it when it suits his purpose.

There is no Hebrew word equivalent to *miracle.* The Old Testament tells many stories of "signs and wonders" by which God reveals his intentions. A pagan perspective on such signs and wonders would be as OMENS appearing in the natural world that are in need of DIVINATION by skilled priests. In the Old Testament, God's signs and wonders are almost all public events that are witnessed by many and are executed directly by God or by certain prophets of great holiness.

The most important wonder-worker of the Old Testament is Moses. God speaks to him initially through a burning bush. The book of Exodus, the liberation of the Israelites from captivity in Egypt, is full of magical acts called miracles performed by Moses and also his brother Aaron. They turn their staffs into snakes to defeat the magicians of the pharaoh. They turn the waters of the Nile into blood. Moses brings on plagues to force the pharaoh to set his people free. In the exodus he parts the waters of the Red Sea.

Perhaps most dramatic is the miracle of the revelation of the Ten Commandments directly to Moses on Mount Sinai, amid a formidable display of the elements. The people are awestruck by thunder, lightning, smoke, fire, and blasts of a divine trumpet. Moses speaks, and God answers him in thunder.

Other Old Testament prophets also are wonder-workers acting under the instructions of God. Joshua is instrumental in bringing down the walls of Jericho. On another occasion—a battle—he causes hailstones to rain down on the enemies and causes the Sun and the Moon to stand still. Elijah multiplies food and restores a dead child to life. Elisha cheats death and ascends directly to heaven.

In the New Testament, the central wonder-worker is Jesus, born of a miraculous virgin conception, who performs public and personal miracles. Among them are numerous healings by word and touch and also the casting out of DEMONS. At a gathering of 5,000 people, he multiplies a small amount of fishes and loaves of bread to feed to the entire crowd. He walks on water and shows his disciple Peter how to do it; Peter's fear causes him to sink. Jesus turns water into wine and raises the dead. Lazarus has been dead three days when Jesus calls him forth from his tomb. The greatest miracle of Jesus is his resurrection from the dead by God and his ascent into heaven.

Jesus performed his miracles to demonstrate the power of God in the world and also to show that this power flows through all of us if we but have the faith to accept it and use it. "According to your faith, be it done to you," he is quoted in Matthew 9:29. And "He who believes in me will also do the works that I do; and greater works than these will he do," he is quoted in John 14:12.

Following his resurrection, his apostles take up wonder-working as a way of spreading the gospel. The masses, however, do not take the mantle from them. The role of wonder-working is left to the holy.

Both Judaism and Christianity have strong traditions of miracles performed by persons of holiness. In Judaism, rabbis, sages, rebbes (itinerant preachers), and other pious persons perform miracles as a the result of leading righteous lives. In Catholic Christianity, saints are the primary wonder-workers—they are able to perform their miracles because of their purity and holiness. Saints act as intercessor figures who form a bridge between humanity and the awesomeness of God. Their relics—their body parts, clothing, and personal belongings—as well as objects that come into contact with relics become imbued with a mediating power for the manifestation of miracles. More about the miracles of saints will be explored in the next chapter.

Protestantism rejects the community of saints but allows for miracles to be performed both by God and certain persons whose holiness enables them to channel the power of God: evangelists, preachers, and spiritual healers.

Western religions accept the idea of a natural order of things and the laws of nature, which are considered the work of God; they hold that God can suspend or otherwise intervene in the natural order. Miracles always have a religious purpose. The New Testament miracles are presented as providing a divine sanction of the person and message of Christ. This stress on the meaning of the miracle sets the Judeo-Christian concept of miracle apart from miracle stories in other religious traditions. Miracles occur not because they can but because God manifests them specifically for the purpose of teaching and demonstration.

Eastern Views

To someone from the Eastern part of the world, miracles are seen differently. They are part of the natural and magical world—simply part of the way things are. The gods of Hinduism do perform miracles as a way of intervening in the affairs of people. The most significant of these is Krishna, an *avatar* (incarnation) of the creator god Vishnu who descends into human form to battle the forces of chaos. His miracles have the twofold purpose of maintaining the right order of things and inspiring human faith and devotion. He successfully battles demons and lifts a mountain aloft for seven days and nights.

Like Jesus, Buddha had a miraculous birth: he entered his mother in a dream in which her belly was pierced by a sacred elephant. Inside he had a special enclosure that protected him from the taint of flesh, and he emerged from his mother's right side possessing full memory and knowledge. Seven days later, his mother died.

Buddha develops miraculous abilities in the course of his spiritual development. These are considered a natural part of the spiritualization process. As he instructs his disciples, miracles are not to be performed for vanity or gain or for their own sake. To do so is to show that you are still attached to the material world.

In Eastern traditions, stories abound of holy persons who perform miracles similar to those of Western saints and holy ones.

Miracles through Yoga

The way of yoga enables a person to become godlike. Most Westerners are familiar with only one school of yoga, hatha yoga which features breathing techniques and body stretches and postures. Yoga is much more complex and consists of different schools of practices that involve meditation, mental disciplines, and the training of consciousness to experience union with the Absolute. Along the way, one naturally acquires miraculous abilities and powers. The Eastern adept strives to get past them. Miraculous abilities are distractions on the path to union with the Absolute.

Miraculous powers are called *siddhi* in Sanskrit, which means "perfect abilities" and "miraculous powers." According to the Yoga Sutra of Patanjali, the *siddhi* include such abilities as: CLAIRVOYANCE (the ability to know the mental states of others); knowledge of one's previous lives; levitation; miraculous transport (covering great distances in an instant); knowledge of and control over all bodily functions; shrinking and expanding the body; rendering one's self and other things invisible; projecting one's consciousness out-of-body; projecting one's consciousness into another body; possessing superhuman strength; knowledge of all languages; knowledge

of the sounds of animals; and knowledge of the moment when one will die.

The Buddhist traditions of yoga are similar. The extraordinary powers are called *iddhi* in Pali, meaning "wondrous gifts." The *iddhi* are the eight powers of mastery over the body and nature: invincibility, invisibility, fleetness in running, ability to see the gods, control over spirits and demons, the ability to fly, the preservation of youth, and the ability to make certain pills (such as for immortality).

The development of the *iddhi* is not considered harmful, but it is not encouraged, either. The *iddhi* are potential pitfalls that will turn the student away from the path to enlightenment. Attitudes toward *iddhi* have varied among schools of Buddhism. Shakyamuni Buddha, the historical Buddha, forbade the use and display of *iddhi*, especially to people who were not initiates. The same powers are possible through the use of magic—the manipulation of natural forces—and thus might not be a true demonstration of spiritual transformation. Some schools of Buddhism have continued that tradition.

One of the most famous ADEPTS of Tibetan Buddhism was Milarepa, who lived from 1052 to 1135. According to tradition, Milarepa learned black magical arts and then renounced them in favor of a spiritual path. He undertook intense training in yoga and developed the *iddhi*. He was witnessed flying. He traveled out-of-body at will not only anywhere on Earth but also to other planes and worlds where he would hold discussions with spiritual masters. He could shape-shift into a flame, a bird, or a running stream. Others wanted him to teach the powers to use them for material gain, but Milarepa stayed focused on his spiritual teachings.

Another adept is Sathya Sai Baba of India, who is regarded as a living avatar, an incarnation of God. His *siddhi* feats have attracted a huge following of devotees around the world. Sai Baba is renowned for his healing; materializations of precious gems, jewelry, devotional objects, and even hot foods and liquids; bilocation; mystical transport, or teleportation; levitation; precognition; and luminous phenomena.

Born in 1926, he began to exhibit miraculous gifts in his teens after being stung by a black scorpion. He lapsed into a coma for several hours and awoke a different person. On May 23, 1940, shortly after the scorpion incident, he left school and announced to his family that he was the reborn Sai Baba. *Sai* is a Muslim term for "saint," and *Baba* is a Hindi term of respect for "father." The original Sai Baba had been a middle class Brahmin fakir of the turn of the century, who had settled in Shirdi, about 120 miles northeast of Bombay, and had produced astounding miracles. Now reborn, he materialized for his parents flowers, sugar candy, and rice cooked in milk, all with a wave of his hand.

Although he quickly attracted devotees, not everyone loved him, and some denounced him as a fraud.

For decades, Sai Baba has used his miraculous abilities and has not been detected of fraud, even when studied by Western psychical researchers, albeit on a restricted basis.

Sai Baba materializes huge quantities of *vibuti,* holy ash made from burnt cow dung, which is smeared on the body; foods and liquids; religious statues and objects made of gold; precious jewelry; photographs; business cards; even stamps bearing his likeness that have not been officially issued by the government. He reportedly fills empty bowls with hot, steaming Indian food of most unusual flavors and produces enough to feed hundreds of people at a time. He opens his fist and drops sticky sweets into the palms of others; yet his own hands are dry. He also produces *amrith,* a honeylike substance. He has reached into sand and pulled out food free of sand. He has plucked apples, pomegranates, mangoes, and other fruits from a tamarind tree. All nonfood objects materialized are bright, fresh, and new. Jewelry includes valuable precious gems. Rings requested by followers fit them perfectly; if a person does not like a particular ring, Sai Baba takes it back and changes it instantly. Business cards bearing his name appear to be freshly printed. Many objects are inscribed with his name.

In his earlier days, he frequently fell into sudden, often convulsive, trances that lasted as long as one-and-a-half days and during which his body would be very cold to the touch. His explanation was that he had been called to another, often distant, location to help people in distress or illness. In these other locations he reportedly appeared as if in the flesh. If he had gone out of body to heal, he sometimes would return showing symptoms of the illness.

People who prayed to him for healing reported miraculous recoveries and sometimes said that he visited them in their dreams or came to their bedside.

In one reported instance during a trance, Sai Baba levitated. While in the air, the sole of his right foot split open, and an estimated two kilograms of vibuti poured out. In another trance incident he opened his mouth and out fell vibuti and golden plates that were a half-inch in width.

Sai Baba also appeared to teleport himself up a hill, disappearing at its base and appearing at the top of the hill within seconds. From the hilltop, he would produce luminosities so brilliant and blinding that others had to shade their eyes. Some witnesses collapsed from the brightness.

Other phenomena attributed to him include: the instant changing of the color of his loose robes; his appearance in the dreams of others, seemingly in answer to needs; weather control; unusual smells, often produced at a distance; the appearance of *vibuti* and *amrith* on pictures of him and on his apports; psychic surgery; the changing of water into gasoline and into other beverages; mind reading; and clairvoyance. Some of those who touched him experienced a mild electrical shock. During his early days, he forbade photographs and films to be taken of him. Those who attempted to do so surreptitiously found their film to be blank when developed.

Sai Baba is called a miracle worker, but in another era he might well have been called a magician or a magus.

Islam and the Sufi Tradition

Islam, which evolved from Christianity, has both Western and Eastern views about miracles. Islam acknowledges miracles as signs of the presence and the action of Allah in the world. The prophet Muhammad refused to perform them, however, reminding his followers that all things that were being made by Allah are signs of His power and goodness. Nonetheless, miracle stories are recounted of Sufi holy men, and some of the orders are known for extraordinary achievements, such as swallowing coals. Sufi saints perform miracles as a way of teaching people about spirituality. Some masters reject miracles as magical acts or tricks and teach that true mystics pursue a higher path.

Miracles in Other Traditions

In pantheistic religions, the divine is not separate from the world of nature. Magical or miraculous events are part of the broad spectrum of things that exist in the natural world. Access to that part of the natural world requires special skill or training, such as in shamanism. The shaman learns how to alter consciousness so as to perform miraculous tasks like those performed by saints and holy persons in other spiritual traditions.

The shaman has the power to see spirits and souls and to communicate with them—to know the language of other creatures. He is able to take magical mystical flights to the heavens where he can serve as intermediary between the gods and his people; he can descend to the underworld to the land of the dead. The flights are done by SHAPE-SHIFTING, by riding mythical horses or the spirits of sacrificed horses, by traveling in spirit boats, and the like.

The shaman's primary function is to heal and to restore the individual's connectedness to the universe. Shamans make no distinction among body, mind, and spirit; they are all part of the whole. Another important function is control of the ELEMENTS, especially the ability to make rain, for the life of the community may depend upon it. Shamans also prophesy.

Miracles versus Magic

Magic is an art or process that can produce the same things as miracles. Few people, however, consider magic to be an act of God or a grace of God. Miracles are perceived as happening when they need to, at God's discretion. Magic is performed by humans to bend the laws of nature according to their own WILL.

The difference between miracles and magic often is a matter of perspective. In the Bible the supernatural feats performed by the prophets are miracles, but when the same feats are done by those who worship other gods these actions are called magic. In the stories, the miracles of God always triumph over the magic of the heathen gods.

Moses and Aaron follow God's instructions to "perform all the wonders" that he has empowered them to do before the pharaoh to persuade the ruler to release the Israelites. Exodus tells how Aaron throws down his staff and it becomes a snake. The pharaoh summons his wise men and sorcerers. "They also, the magicians of Egypt, did the same by their secret arts. Each one threw down his staff, and they became snakes; but Aaron's staff swallowed up theirs." (Exodus 7:11–12)

The simplest definition of magic is that it is the art of effecting change with the help of higher forces. Higher forces can include spirit beings, such as ANGELS; intercessory figures such as saints; God; goddess; and a host of personifications of the godhead represented by various deities. Higher forces also include the inner powers within us as well: intuition; guidance from the Higher Self; WILL and determination; the creative power of IMAGINATION, THOUGHT and belief; and the power of love, which brings everything into balance.

Miracles and magic are facets of the movement of cosmic power. Personal, cultural, and religious beliefs provide unique and subjective frameworks for relating to this power. Attitudes shift with time. For example, 19th-century cultural anthropologists tended to classify all claims of miraculous events under the heading of magic.

Modern Personal Views of Miracles

In modern Western culture, miracles have acquired a wider popular definition than found in religious thought. A miracle is any unlikely, unusual, or unexplained event that has a significant impact on life. They do not need to happen on a grand scale, such as the parting of the Red Sea by Moses. Miracles can happen quietly and be intensely personal. In fact, most modern miracles are likely to be personal and not public. Most involve healing—any PRAYER service or circle receives more prayers for miraculous healing than any other situation.

A personal miracle occurs any time life takes an unexpected turn and a crisis or disaster is avoided, or fortunes suddenly improve in unforseen ways.

FURTHER READING:
Guiley, Rosemary Ellen. *A Miracle in Your Pocket.* London: Thorsons/HarperCollins, 2001.
Miller, Carolyn. *Creating Miracles: Understanding the Experience of Divine Intervention.* Tiburon, Calif.: HJ Kramer, 1995.
Woodward, Kenneth L. *The Book of Miracles.* New York: Simon & Schuster, 2000.

mirror A TOOL for DIVINATION and MAGIC. Mirrors train the inner eye to perceive the unseen. Throughout history, mirror gazing, has been used to look into the future, aid in healing, answer questions, solve problems, find lost objects and people, and identify or find thieves and criminals.

The power of mirrors—or any reflective surface—to reveal what is hidden has been known since ancient times. Gazing upon shiny surfaces is one of the oldest forms of SCRYING, a method of divination practiced by the early Egyptians, Arabs, the Magi of Persia, Greeks, and Romans. Magic mirrors are mentioned by numerous ancient authors, among them Apuleius, Saint Augustine, Pausanias, and Spartianus. According to Pausanias, divination for healing was best done with a mirror with a string attached to it. The string was dangled into water, and the diviner then was able to ascertain whether or not a sick person would be healed.

In ancient Greece, the witches of Thessaly reputedly wrote their oracles in human BLOOD upon mirrors. PYTHAGORAS was said to have a magic mirror that he held up to the MOON to see the future in it. Romans who were skilled in mirror reading were called *specularii*. Much later, Catherine de Medicis reputedly had a magic mirror that enabled her to see the future for herself and for France. Père Cotton, the confessor to King Henri IV of France, had a magic mirror that revealed to him the plots against the king.

In folklore, mirrors have a dark power—they are a soul stealer. A widespread folk belief calls for turning over the mirrors in a house when someone dies. If a dead person sees himself in a mirror, his soul will become lost or have no rest, or he will become a VAMPIRE. The power of mirrors to suck out souls is illustrated in the Greek myth of Narcissus, who sees his reflection in water and then pines and dies.

In Christian lore, mirrors enable DEMONS to make themselves known. This may have been part of the church's propaganda to discourage use of pagan folk magic. St. Patrick declared that Christians who said they could see demons in mirrors would be expelled from the church until they repented.

In Russian folklore, mirrors are linked to the devil because they have the power to draw souls out of bodies. In other lore, seeing a corpse reflected in a mirror puts the living at risk for having one's soul carried off by the ghost of the dead. Seeing one's own reflection in a mirror in a room where someone has died means one's own impending death.

Folklore also prescribes that mirrors should be removed from a sick room because the soul is more vulnerable in times of illness. It is considered unlucky for the sick to see their reflections, which puts them at risk of dying. Breaking a mirror is bad luck; since it holds the soul, a broken mirror will damage the soul.

In Vodoun, a magical mirror is called a *minore*. A *minore* is made of highly polished metal and is consecrated for the purpose of seeing visions. Only a priest or priestess can use a *minore.*

Applications of Magic Mirrors

Both flat mirrors and concave mirrors are used in magic. Other shiny and reflective surfaces work as well, such as crystal balls or crystals (see DEE, JOHN) and bowls of water or ink (see NOSTRADAMUS). FRANZ BARDON taught precise instructions for making magical mirrors that would be "loaded" or empowered with the help of the ELEMENTS, the AKASHA, light, and FLUID CONDENSERS. A charged magic mirror should be stored wrapped in silk to protect its energies.

Scrying is not done by the mirror itself but is accomplished by the astral and mental powers developed by the magician or scryer. The mirror serves as an aid for focusing those powers. The best success is obtained by those who have learned how to use their IMAGINATION to visualize images in detail. Without such skill, one is likely to see only distorted images in a magic mirror.

Bardon described major applications of magic mirrors:

A transit gate to other planes of existence. Imagining the body to be so small that it goes right through the mirror provides access to the ASTRAL PLANE. With repeated practice, more details become visible and meetings with the dead are possible. Eventually one perceives finer, more subtle spiritual vibrations, which enable access to higher planes and beings. By focusing on the spiritual vibrations of the elements, one can visit lower planes, such as the realms of gnomes, salamanders, sylphs and undines.

A link between the living and the dead. Visualizing a person in a magical mirror enables contact. The scryer goes to the astral plane to communicate with the dead. Living persons can be contacted through the mirror as well. The scryer visualizes the person intensely until the person seems to be drawn out of the mirror.

An aid to influencing other people or the self. The scryer loads the mirror with light from the universal ocean of light, allowing it to pass through the body into the mirror. The scryer focuses in meditation upon the desired goal, such as inspiration or the solution to a problem, and irradiates himself with the light vibrations stored in the mirror. Turning the mirror toward the bed will enable the rays to work on the subconscious in sleep. The scryer can influence others by using the imagination to direct the rays out into the universe.

A ray-emitter for room impregnation and the treatment of sick people. Similarly, a magic mirror can be loaded to emit rays that will anchor certain qualities in a room, such as peace, health, success, and so on. A magic mirror can be loaded to help a sick person; the person is exposed to the emanation of rays from the mirror's surface.

A transmitter and receiver. Thoughts, pictures, words, and sounds can be transmitted and received through magic mirrors regardless of distance.

An amulet against negative forces and influences. A magic mirror can be programmed to bathe a room in protective vibrations against the unwanted influences of spirits and people.

A projector of all powers, beings, and impressions. A magic mirror can be used to condense all astral and mental forces so that they can be perceived by persons with no magical training.

As a screen for clairvoyance and remote viewing. A skilled magician can gaze into a magic mirror and see distant scenes and activities. Bardon likened this to using the mirror as a television set.

As a tool for investigating the past, present, and future. A mirror helps a magician transcend time to see events. According to Bardon, this is one of the most difficult aspects of mirror work. Looking into the future, he said, deprives one of free will.

See also ARTEPHIUS; BACON, ROGER.

FURTHER READING:

Bardon, Franz. *Initiation into Hermetics: A Course of Instruction of Magic Theory and Practice.* Wuppertal, Germany: Dieter Ruggeberg, 1971.

Grillot de Givry, Emile. *Witchcraft, Magic and Alchemy.* New York: Houghton Mifflin, 1931.

Guiley, Rosemary Ellen. *The Encyclopedia of Witches and Witchcraft.* 2nd ed. New York: Facts On File Inc., 1999.

mistletoe   A an evergreen shrub plant that is believed to possess magical powers of fertility, healing, luck, and protection against evil. One of the most important plants of European magic lore, mistletoe is cut ceremonially at the summer and winter solstices. Throughout history, it has been used in potions, powders, and teas to control epilepsy, hypertension, and palsy, to enhance fertility and to cure sterility, to act as an aphrodisiac, and to protect against poisons. It has been hung in homes, barns, and stables as an AMULET to protect against WITCHCRAFT, fire, illness, and bad luck. A sprig of mistletoe over a doorway is said to prevent witches from entering.

Mistletoe, which bears white berries, grows parasitically on many deciduous trees in Europe and America. Its seeds are spread by bird droppings, and thus it had the appearance of springing to life from nothing. Some ancient peoples believed it descended from heaven on lighting bolts.

The Celts, who populated Britain and large portions of Europe circa 8000–2000 B.C.E., considered mistletoe sacred because it grew on their venerated oak TREES. It excited great wonder because it could grow without touching the earth, and it seemed to propagate itself magically. DRUID priests used it in fertility RITUALS. It was harvested in the following manner: Six days after the new MOON, white-robed priests cut its boughs with a golden sickle, the symbol of the SUN. The mistletoe was not allowed to touch the ground but was caught in a white cloth. If somehow the mistletoe touched ground, the Druids believed that it lost its magical properties. After the cutting, two white bulls were led to the oaks, and their throats were slashed while the priests recited prayers and incantations for blessings.

The Christmas (winter solstice) custom of harvesting mistletoe and kissing beneath it is a survivor of the ancient Druidic fertility rites.

Mistletoe appears in mythology. In Virgil's *Aeneid,* the hero Aeneus picked a "golden bough" of mistletoe at the gate of the underworld, which ensured his safety as he went through it. Balder, the Norse god of light and joy, was slain by spear of mistletoe that was thrown by Hodur at instigation of Loki, god of darkness and evil. In Sweden, mistletoe is sacred to Thor, the god of thunder.

In Ozark folklore, mistletoe is commonly called witch's broom, and is said to be used by witches in casting SPELLS. It is also used as an amulet, hung in homes and barns to keep witches away.

In folk medicine, mistletoe is called "allheal." It has been revered since the times of ancient Greeks for its ability to treat nervous conditions and disorders. Other applications include as a sedative, to lower blood pressure, and as a treatment of tumors. A powder made from the berries is believed to make fertile any man, woman, or beast.

Medical data on mistletoe is inconclusive. While the plant may have sedative effects, there is no certain evidence that it lowers blood pressure. In experiments with animals, it seems to treat tumors effectively. The U.S. Food and Drug Administration considers mistletoe toxic and unsafe for internal consumption.

mojo A SPELL or CHARM. The term *mojo* comes from Vodoun. Casting a spell is sometimes referred to as "working a mojo."

Mojo also refers to an AMULET carried on the person for protection.

Moon An important element in ALCHEMY, MAGIC, and DIVINATION.

The Moon has been regarded as a source of big magic since the earliest recorded history. Though both SUN and Moon have been worshiped and the Sun has been recognized as the giver of life, more magic has been based on the Moon. The ancients observed connections between the Moon's changing of phases and the natural rhythms of the

tides and nature. Thus, they believed that the Moon regulated body fluids and all life cycles as well. If one magically harnessed the mysterious force of the Moon, one could influence life. The waning moon was seen as a time of decrease and the waxing moon as a time of increase. The full moon represented plenty, and the new moon represented a dark, uncertain time.

The first characteristic early humankind observed about the Moon was its changing shape. The Sun appeared the same every day and never failed to rise; the Moon, on the other hand, grew larger and then smaller and for three nights in every cycle vanished completely from the heavens. This apparent death of the Moon was not permanent, however, for the Moon always resurrected itself anew.

Early humankind understood that the Moon had a rhythm that seemed to establish and govern the rhythms of all life cycles: the tides, the rain, fertility, women's menstrual cycles, plant life. It represented "becoming" and "being." The Moon established a unifying pattern for all living things, living and breathing in harmony, existing in an intricate and ineffable web of interconnectedness.

This magical power to regulate life was perceived as early as the ice age, long before the discovery of agriculture. The Moon was considered a force or power until about 2600 B.C.E. when it became personified as the Man in the Moon, who, in some beliefs, could incarnate on Earth as a king. The Man in the Moon gave way to gods and goddesses.

Early peoples believed that the Moon made all things grow and governed all life-giving moistures. Its changing phases were associated with the coming of rain, as well as with the torrents that produced floods. The Moon's fertilizing power governed not only plants and animals but human beings as well. It was believed that women who slept out beneath the rays of the Moon would become impregnated by them. Thus, as early humankind developed cosmogonies and mythologies, their deities associated with water, fertility, and fecundity were also associated with the Moon.

The earliest SYMBOLS of the Moon were the spiral, the lightning bolt, and the serpent, all of which are associated with change, regeneration, and fertility. The spiral relates to the phases of the Moon and to the shell, both a symbol of water and of the vulva. By way of association, the pearl became one of the earliest amulets for women to connect to the Moon's powers of fertility. Lightning heralds life-giving rain, which is ruled by the Moon. The serpent universally represents regeneration and the giver of all fertility, even to women. Snake-woman relationships abound in mythologies.

Other early symbols were animals who seemed to personify the Moon because they possess lunar characteristics: the snail, which periodically withdraws into its shell; the frog, a widespread fertility and rain symbol and which is seen by some peoples as residing in the Moon; the bear, which disappears and reappears on a seasonal basis; and the bull, a fertility symbol whose horns represent the crescent Moon.

With the discovery of agriculture and animal husbandry, the lunar cycle became a guide for the planting and harvesting of crops and the slaughtering of animals. The deities overseeing these activities invariably had lunar associations. Also, with the development of healing arts, deities ascribed healing functions also were associated with the Moon, for the Moon was perceived to govern all the moistures within the body as well as in the external world. RITUALS to influence all these aspects of life were addressed to the Moon, and to the Moon's representatives in the form of gods and goddesses.

Because of the Moon's apparent rebirth in the sky every month, the Moon became, in many cosmogonies, the repository of souls after death. Plutarch, the first-century Greek essayist and biographer, conceived of a lunar way-station for the going and coming of souls. Human beings had two deaths, he said. One occurred on Earth, the domain of Demeter, the goddess of fecundity, when the body was severed from the mind and soul and returned to dust. The soul and the psyche then went to the Moon, the domain of Persephone, the queen of the Underworld, where a second death took place with the separation of the two. The soul returned to the substance of the Moon where it was able to retain the dreams and memories of the life that had been lived. The mind, meanwhile, went to the Sun, where it was absorbed and then gave birth to a new soul. In rebirth, the process was reversed: The Sun sent mind to the Moon where it was joined with soul; then it traveled to Earth to join body and be born anew. Similarly,

the ancient Indians conceived of a "path of souls" and a "path of gods." As described in the *Upanishads*, the "path of souls" was to the Moon and was taken by the unenlightened where the souls would rest and await reincarnation. Those who had freed themselves of the need to reincarnate took the "path of gods" to the Sun, which was beyond becoming.

The earliest calendars were based on lunar cycles. Each day of the Moon's cycle through the heavens had its own influences for good and bad times for various activities. The Moon was personified as deities. The earliest moon gods were male, but later female moon goddesses predominated. The Moon was associated with feminine qualities: passivity, cycles, and life fluids.

Pliny the Elder, the first-century Roman naturalist, emphasized the importance of the Moon in his *Natural History*, a set of 37 volumes dealing with the nature of the physical universe, anthropology, zoology, botany, geography, and mineralogy. According to Pliny, the Moon was central to the rhythms of the Earth. He called the Moon "the star of our life" and said that "she" fills and empties all bodies, including the BLOOD volume in people, with "her" waxing and waning.

Pliny gave guidelines for planting, cutting, harvesting, and getting rid of things in accordance with lunar phases. He also included such lunar-based cures as the remedy for warts: Wait until the Moon is at least 20 days old; then lie in a footpath face up to receive its light and gaze at it. Then rub anything within reach. Variations of this "cure" call simply for rubbing one's hands under the moonlight or washing one's hands in moonbeams captured in a waterless but well-polished SILVER basin.

Pliny's work is among the earliest organized body of lunar magic lore. *Natural History* served as an important source for lunar magic that evolved over the centuries.

The Moon in Alchemy

In alchemy the Moon represents feminine forces and the feminine principle of the cosmos. According to the EMERALD TABLET, it is the archetypal Mother and is the supreme force known as the One Thing. It rules the Below, while the archetypal Father, the Sun, rules the Above. The Moon is mutable and volatile, a force that enables transformation to take place.

The creation of the PHILOSOPHER'S STONE is achieved by the marriage of the Mother and One Thing with the archetypal Father, the Sun, which is the One Mind. In alchemical art, the marriage is often represented by the physical union of the king (Sol) and the queen (Luna). Their offspring, a HERMAPHRODITE, represents the *PRIMA MATERIA*, the beginnings of the Philosopher's Stone.

The ELEMENT associated with the Moon is water, and the alchemical process is dissolution. Just as the Moon dissolves every month, dissolution dissolves ideas, thoughts, emotions, and attachments, thus making room for new things to come into being.

The Sun and the Moon, representing alchemical opposites, in Atalanta fugiens, by Michael Maier, 1618. (Author's collection)

In the alchemical stage of distillation, the Stone is purified in the rays of the Moon and the Sun.

The Moon in Ceremonial Magic

Ceremonial magic, a precise art in which the magician follows exact procedures to effect a spell or command spirits or the forces of nature, takes into account planetary influences and the positions of the Sun, the Moon, and the planets. Magic is the control of these influences, which in turn is the control of the basic forces which underlie all things.

The influence of a planet can be captured by a direct petition or by commanding the angel or spirit associated with the planet. In ceremonial magic the provinces of heaven are governed by seven ANGELS. The province of the Moon and everything pertaining to it is ruled by Phul, who has the power to transmute anything into silver, the Moon's metal, to cure dropsy, and to destroy the evil spirits of the water.

Another way to capture planetary magic is through the use of things connected to the PLANET—such as silver or moonstones in the case of the Moon—or by performing a ritual on the day or at the hour governed by the planet. Each day and each hour in the day are ruled by different planets. Each planet offers advantages for certain kinds of magical spells.

Monday, ruled by the Moon, is a day of peace and happiness. Medieval astrologers proclaimed it one of the week's luckiest days, along with Wednesday, Thursday, and Sunday. Monday is auspicious for raising the spirits of the dead, communion with spirits, SPELLS concerning love, emotions and reconciliation, CLAIRVOYANCE, becoming invisible, discovery of theft, learning the truth, attaining grace, and all activities concerning water, travel, the sea, and shipping, the home and family, agriculture, medicine, cooking, and dreams. The other days of the week are ruled as follows:

Sunday—Sun	*Thursday*—Jupiter
Tuesday—Mars	*Friday*—Venus
Wednesday—Mercury	*Saturday*—Saturn

Hourly influences follow a certain order. The ruling planet of the day commands the first hour after sunrise, and each following hour is ruled by planets in the following order: the Sun, Venus, Mercury, the Moon, Saturn, Jupiter, and Mars. A new progression begins at sunset. Thus the Moon's hours during day, marked from sunrise are:

Sunday—4, 11	*Thursday*—6
Monday—1, 8	*Friday*—3, 10
Tuesday—5, 12	*Saturday*—7
Wednesday—2, 9	

And the Moon's hours of the night, beginning at sunset are:

Sunday—6	*Thursday*—1, 8
Monday—3, 10	*Friday*—5, 12
Tuesday—7	*Saturday*—2, 9
Wednesday—4, 11	

(Note: these are not clock times. The fourth hour after sunrise, for example, might be 11 A.M., depending on the season.)

In addition to observing planetary influences, a magician always pays additional attention to the phases of the Moon. Spells involving increase, luck, prosperity, and gains of any sort should be done only when the Moon is waxing, and preferably when the Moon is full. Spells of vengeance, discord, hatred, unhappiness, and undoing should be done when the Moon is on the wane. The darkest of spells, involving death and destruction, should be done during the dark of the Moon. This period also is favorable for spells for invisibility. And no spells at all should be attempted when the Moon is new, for failure is guaranteed, according to love. At the new moon, the Moon and the Sun are in conjunction. A conjunction occurs whenever two planetary bodies are in the same sign of the zodiac or very close—within 12 degrees concerning the Sun and the Moon. This proximity causes the influences of the two bodies to combine and produce unpredictable side effects. Many folklore CHARMS exist to counteract these new moon influences.

A magician fashions his or her magical TOOLS under the proper lunar influences. Magical tools are most effective if handmade by the magician. This is done according to RITUAL, and the tools are purified and consecrated—imbued with the will of the magician—during rituals done under a waxing or full moon, as well as other planetary influences.

The wand is the primary magical tool and has an illustrious history: Moses and Aaron use wands to bring the plague to Egypt, and the Greek god, HERMES, wielded a wand entwined with snakes as his tool of power, wisdom, and healing.

Hazel is best all-round wood for wands. Ash and rowan also are excellent choices. For spells falling under the influence of the Moon, willow is best. Magical GRIMOIRES—textbooks of rituals, most of which were written in the 17th through 19th centuries—offer differing instructions for the making of a magical wand. According to one ritual, the wood is best cut at night, when the Moon is waxing or full, by either an "innocent child" or by a man who walks backward and reaches for the branch between his legs. The wand must be exactly 22 inches long.

The magical tools help the magician tap into the appropriate magical power. In addition, symbols, SIGILS, and SEALS are used. Fumigation—the producing of smoke or vapor—is used to harmonize with the planet that rules the spell being performed. The fumes are used to permeate the atmosphere and to bathe ceremonial objects and magical tools. (See PERFUMES.)

Moon fumes can be produced by burning the leaves of all vegetables, leaf indum, leaf of myrtle, and bay leaf. One 19th-century recipe calls for mixing together the dried head of a frog, eyes of a bull, seed of white poppies, frankincense, camphor, and either menstrual blood or the blood of a goose.

The Moon in Folk Magic

Folk magic—the use of simple charms, AMULETS, and spells for the enhancement of daily life—makes frequent use of the powers of the Moon. Most lunar folk spells call for performing an action or reciting a charm at a specific phase of the Moon. Many of these charms are still in use and form a body of superstitious practices involving the Moon. For example, to increase love and fertility, to protect yourself while you travel, or to avert the EVIL EYE, wear a crescent moon as an amulet or any object reminiscent of a crescent moon, such as the claws of a crab, the tusks of a boar, or any horns.

Certain spells must be done at different lunar phases to succeed.

Waxing and Full Moon.   Spells for luck, money, love, good business, good crops—any kind of bounty—benefit from the graces of the benevolent waxing and the full moon. According to farming and gardening lore, the waxing moon causes moisture and vital energies to flow up into the stalks of plants, while the waning moon causes energies to flow down into the roots.

Examples of lunar folk magic for increase of wealth are:

- Touch silver money in your pocket and say, "As you have found us in peace and prosperity, so leave us in grace and mercy."
- Turn the money in your pocket, and think about being lucky.
- Shake your pockets, take out all your money, and let the rays of the new moon shine on it.
- Count your money. It will increase.
- Stand on soft ground. Turn your money over, make a wish, and turn round three times.
- On the first day of the first new moon of the new year, put your hand in your pocket, shut your eyes, and turn the smallest silver coin in your pocket upside down. This will bring luck and prosperity all year long.

If you don't have any silver coins or money, you can capture the new moon's good luck in other ways:

- Turn your apron over to the new moon to bring a month of good luck.
- Bow three times to the new moon.
- Turn your apron three times to the new moon, and a present will arrive before the next new moon; or curtesy three times, and say with each curtsey, "Welcome, new moon; I hope you bring me a present very soon."
- Make a WISH, and it will be realized before the year is out.
- If you happen to live in a country ruled by a king, visit him when the new moon is one day old, and ask for what you want. He shall give it to you.
- Seeing the new moon, kiss the first person of the opposite sex you see without speaking. You will soon receive a gift.

The full moon is a good time for banishing evil and unwanted influences. A household magical formula for cleaning out negative energies calls for peeling nine lemons, placing the peels in a bucket of water, and squeezing them to release their oils. Visualize the lemon oil cleansing the evil away. Scrub floors, windows, and doorknobs. Pour some of the wash down each drain in the house. Repeat every full moon until the evil is gone.

Waning Moon.   Harvesting should be done during the waning moon. For herbal concoctions, folklore advises harvesting leaves, flowers, and seeds during the waxing moon when the vital juices are at their fullest and harvesting root crops during the waning moon. Most herbs should be picked on a clear, dry night after sunset. Cutting, pruning, and controlling pests, and culling herds are other good waning-moon activities.

The waning moon is the best time for medical procedures, especially those involving operations, for lore holds that the risk of too much bleeding will be less.

The waning moon also is the best time for cursing enemies and especially for getting rid of illnesses. The ancient Greeks had a powerful magical spell called *diabole*: slandering one's enemy to the Moon. The spell involved telling the Moon about the evils of the enemy and imploring the Moon to punish him. According to legend, the magician Pachrates was so successful with the *diabole* that the Roman emperor Hadrian doubled his salary. Pachrates is said to have brought a man to court within one hour magically, made him ill within two hours, and killed him within seven.

A waning moon counterspell to ward off any negative spell you consider has been cast on you by another person is as follows:

Take equal portions of myrrh and white frankincense, and crumble them into wine. Shave part of a jet stone into the wine. Fast at night, and then drink the mixture for three, nine, or 12 mornings.

New Moon. The most important time to cast many such spells is at the very start of the lunar phase cycle, the new moon. For example, when the new moon is seen for the first time, one should finger a silver coin in hopes that the increasing moon will increase one's fortune.

However, the new moon is unstable and unpredictable, and luck can be good or bad for an entire lunar month depending on the circumstances under which the new moon is first seen. It is lucky to first see the new moon straight on or over the right shoulder but unlucky to see it over the left shoulder. It also is unlucky to see the new moon through glass or the boughs of a tree. It is lucky to see the new moon with gold or silver money in one's pocket but unlucky if one is caught with no coins. In Ozark folk magic, seeing the new moon through the treetops means a month of bad luck. A housewife looking through a closed window will probably break a dish or a valuable household object before the Moon is new again. An instant folk magic remedy is to clasp the hands over the heart and say, "Bad luck, vanish!" A folk spell from England for vanquishing the bad new moon luck is to take a coin and spit on both sides of it immediately.

The new moon also is a propitious time to cast folk magic spells for love and for DIVINATION of the future.

Plants Ruled by the Moon. In folk magic herbal lore, certain plants are ruled by lunar influences; they are used especially in magic for lunar-based things such as love, fertility, sleep, and dreams. Some of the most common and their herbal magic uses are:

camphor—repel unwanted lovers; ward off colds; induce sleep

cucumber—cure headaches; enhance fertility

eucalyptus—general healing; colds and sore throats

gardenia—attract lovers

lettuce—induce sleep and relaxation; decrease lust

poppy—fertility; prosperity; prophetic dreams

sandalwood—air purifier; healing; protection

succulents—love and abundance

willow—healing; wishes; blessings of the Moon

See also MOONWORT.

The Moon in Witchcraft

The Moon has long been associated with the powers of WITCHCRAFT. It rules the night, the time when witches are said to be about; it rules the underworld and the dark powers, which are associated with witchcraft; and it regulates the rhythms of life, which witches disturb. The "witching hour" is midnight under a full moon, the moment when all the creatures of the night are at their fullest flower, the moment when witches have their greatest magical power. In ancient Greece, the feared witches of Thessaly were said to draw their power from the Moon, which they could command and bring down from the sky. Hecate, the terrible goddess of the dark of the Moon and the underworld, also is the patronness of witchcraft.

In vampire lore, vampire SORCERERS and witches, living persons who are vampiric in behavior, have their greatest power when the Moon is full and are at their weakest when the Moon is new. Vampires—the dead who rise from the grave—are weakest during the day and strongest at night under the influence of the Moon. The rays of the Moon have a resurrecting power on the dead.

The Moon in Wicca

Practitioners of the religion of Wicca, modern Witches who emphasize the positive use of magic, see the Moon as the symbol of the Goddess, who has a threefold aspect of Virgin (waxing moon), Mother (full moon), and Crone (waning moon). Wiccans practice rituals to draw power from the Moon. Spells are governed by lunar phases: benefit and increase during the waxing and full moon; banishment and decrease during the waning moon. While both gods and goddesses are recognized as aspects of the Supreme Being, goddesses, especially those with lunar associations, are given the most emphasis.

The regular meetings of a Wiccan coven, the "circle" or "esbat," traditionally takes place 13 times a year at the full moon, a time when magical forces are considered greatest. Some covens also meet at the new moon, a time of beginnings.

"Drawing Down the Moon" is an important Wiccan ritual. It is named after the Thessalian witches and is traditionally performed at full moons and at winter solstice. Drawing Down the Moon is a trance ceremony in which the high priestess invokes and channels the Goddess, thus drawing down divine feminine energies to Earth.

The Moon and Madness

As the ruler of moods, the Moon has long been associated with mental illness and aberration. The ancient Greeks associated the full moon with epileptic seizures. A widespread ancient belief held that exposure to the rays of the full moon would cause a person to go insane; the term *lunacy* is derived from this belief. PARACELSUS noted that the Moon had the power to tear reason from the head of a person literally.

In addition to insanity, the Moon is held to have the power to drive people to suicide and to go berserk and commit crimes. In occult lore, lycanthropy, the transfor-

In ancient times, scryers gazed into the still water of a lake or a pond at night. Their powers were enhanced if the light of the Moon—especially a full moon—fell upon the water. According to folklore, this method of divination can be used to learn when a person will marry. At a full moon, go to a stream or any body of water, and hold a silk square over the water with the Moon behind you. The silk will cause several reflections of the Moon to be cast on the water. The number of reflections is the number of months before you will marry.

Unscrupulous scryers used a trick invented by Pythagoras. They wrote a message in blood on a looking-glass in advance and then stood behind their client and turned the glass toward the Moon. The client was then invited to read the message on the mirror as though it were written on the Moon itself—a divine revelation.

Palmistry. PALMISTRY is based on the shape of the hands and the lines and mounds on the palms and fingers. The signs of the zodiac, the Sun, the Moon, and the planets are assigned locations on the hand. Each governs an aspect of life, such as longevity, health, love, career, money, and so forth. The mount of the Moon, the fleshy part of the outer palms, reveals psychic ability and "lightmindedness."

Tarot. The TAROT is a deck of 78 cards bearing symbolic images that must be interpreted intuitively. Lunar symbols representing the unconscious, intuition, creativity, emotions, and the nurturing forces of nature are threaded throughout the deck but are most dramatic in the High Priestess, which bears the number II, and the Moon, which bears the number XVIII.

The High Priestess is a lunar emissary, bringing the powerful forces of the unconscious into waking life. The great fertilizing, nourishing energies of nature emanate from her. Like the Moon, represented by the crescent at her feet, the High Priestess reveals little about herself. She appears tranquil and all-knowing; yet the source of her knowledge is kept hidden like the dark side of the Moon. Her silence exudes confidence and mystery. She gives part of the answers to questions, and her lunar glow encourages the rest to come through meditation and the intuitive voice within. The answers will emerge at the right time.

The Moon symbolizes a netherworld of dreams and illusions, as unreal as the light cast by the Moon herself. When the Moon rides high in the night sky, her silvery glow creates a dreamworld below, in which familiar shapes take on strange twists and shadows and things are not as they seem. The Moon steers its own course, changing shape and going somewhere, destination unknown. The traveler through this lunar world must be on guard.

The Moon card suggests being tested by illusion and distraction and points to the need to trust one's intuition.

The lunar goddess Diana on The Moon card in The Alchemical Tarot, *by Rosemary Ellen Guiley and Robert Michael Place. Diana's hounds represent the dark or passive principle and the light or active principle. The symbol of Cancer the crab, the moon sign, is in the sky. Inspired by Michael Maier's* Viatorium, *1618. (Copyright by and courtesy of Robert Michael Place)*

mation of a human into wolf form, is ruled by the Moon. At the full moon, certain people become werewolves and go berserk on rampages of killing and devouring humans and animals.

The Moon in Divination
Lunar influences are significant in various methods of divination.

Scrying. SCRYING is clairvoyance by concentrating on an object that has a smooth and shiny surface until visions appear. Clairvoyance and seeing into the future are powers ruled by the Moon.

The Moon in Astrology

The Moon plays a major role in natal ASTROLOGY, one of the most enduring and popular forms of divination since the time of the Greeks. Natal astrology, which foretells a person's destiny and prophesies events based upon the positions of the planets in the sky at the time of birth, is based on the ancient alchemical beliefs that the Earth is a microcosm of the heavens and that celestial bodies exert influences on people and events below.

Astrology is organized around 12 constellations of the zodiac. The horoscope is divided into 12 houses, each of which is ruled by one of the signs of the zodiac and governs an aspect of life, such as love, money, and career. The position of the Sun, Moon, and the planets at the time of birth determines the celestial influences that act on each of these houses, indicating a host of strengths and weaknesses.

Of the 12 signs of the zodiac, Cancer is particularly ruled by the Moon. Cancerians, or Moon Children, as they also are called, reflect the lunar influences more than any other sign. They are deeply in touch with their emotions and intuitions and are introverted, shy, and somewhat mysterious. It is often difficult for others to plumb and understand the full measure of their emotional depth. They are tenacious and loyal once they feel secure, but they also are prone to moodiness and easy to slight. When wounded, the Cancerian scuttles for cover and can remain in a funk for days. Thus, a marriage between two Cancerians courts disaster, for after a spat the partners may each retreat, wounded, into their own silent worlds, waiting to be coaxed out. Their ideal partner is their zodiac opposite, the Capricorn goat, whose practical sensibilities help keep the Cancerian grounded.

Home is very important to Cancerians—they must have a place where they can feel protected from buffeting by the external world. They are interested in domestic activities and tend to make good parents and good cooks, although at times their emotionalism can be smothering. Because they are in tune with their inner selves, they tend to be highly creative and make excellent writers and artists.

Moon Sign. Most people are familiar with their sun sign, the sign of the zodiac occupied by the Sun at the time they were born. Two other signs are important: the rising sign, which is the sign rising on the horizon at the time of birth, and the moon sign, the sign occupied by the Moon at the time of birth. The moon sign rules one's emotional makeup, outlook, and behavior.

The following list gives the major influences of the moon birth signs:

Aries Moon: Leadership and pioneering abilities, determination to be self-sufficient. Protective of family. Easy to anger and can be impulsive.

Taurus Moon: Conservative and stable with a tendency toward longevity. Must have security. Stubborn and tough but good nurturers.

Gemini Moon: Restless and full of energy, always on the move. Curious and quick-witted. Can be out of touch with emotions. Lack of interest in long-range planning for security.

Cancer Moon: Extreme sensitivity, easily wounded. Tendency to feel insecure, hang onto the past. Home and family very important, a refuge.

Leo Moon: Need to be at center of attention. Penchant for grand living. Showmanship can be tempered with dignity. Inability to let others run things.

Virgo Moon: Perfectionism, compulsive cleanliness, but well-meaning. Self-doubt. Emotions repressed in favor of sensibility, productivity.

Libra Moon: Selflessness, romanticism. Sense of balance creates good mediation skills. Comfortable with self but cannot be left out or ignored.

Scorpio Moon: Intense energy and concentration, bordering on obsession, for long periods of time. Secretive, tendency to brood. Money-driven, like to control things.

Sagittarius Moon: Dynamism, oriented to expansion and growth. Good teachers, but do not take well to being challenged. Enthusiastic but often insensitive to others.

Capricorn Moon: Self-discipline, organization, goal-setting, long-range planning abilities. Practical, material, and not emotionally demonstrative.

Aquarius Moon: Rebellion against authority, trendsetting, interest in fads. Intensely independent. Desire for frequent change in environment. Repression of emotions.

Pisces Moon: Mystical, spiritual leanings, great creativity. Not interested in the material. Emotional confusion. Compassion can be extreme.

Daily Lunar Auspices. In its travels through the zodiac, the Moon leaves one sign and enters another one every two to two-and-a-half days. In each sign, the Moon exerts unique influences on the processes of the unconscious, thus affecting certain undertakings. The influences wax and wane as the Moon enters each sign and takes its leave and are tempered by the Moon's phase and the signs on either side. The period in which the Moon is in transit and thus in no sign is called void-of-course and is particularly fraught with uncertainties. (See below.) The distance that the Moon traverses in any given day is called a Mansion of the Moon. The first Mansion begins at 0 degrees Aries, the second mansion at about 12 or 13 degrees Aries, and so on. Each mansion has its influences as well.

The travels of the Moon influence the daily favorable or unfavorable aspects for some activity. The general lunar influences within a particular sign of the zodiac are described below:

Moon in Aries: A time geared to action, enthusiasm, risk-taking, aggression, and independent decision-making. Things move quickly, but the energy is short-lived. Watch out for impulsiveness.

Moon in Taurus: The solidity and patience of the Bull yields caution, reserve, practicality, and protection of interests. A poor time for making changes, especially financial. Enterprises begun now have lasting value but will be hard to change.

Moon in Gemini: A highly changeable, fickle state. Avoid beginning new projects and concentrate on communication and exchange of ideas and wit. There's a playfulness in the air.

Moon in Cancer: The Moon is in its own home here, and sensitivities and emotions run high. Avoid stepping on toes. People who tend to be gullible need to be extra careful. Easy to overindulge on food, drink, and moodiness.

Moon in Leo: Entertainment, showmanship, and vitality reign. Take center stage, express yourself. Great opportunities to make good impressions and sell ideas, but do not go overboard.

Moon in Virgo: Emphasis on details, organization, concentration, routine tasks, research. A good time for intellectual matters, shopping for bargains, and attending to health.

Moon in Libra: Charm, eloquence, and artistic expression come to the fore. Good time for new friendships, romance, marriage, and partnerships. Give time to yourself. Avoid emotional conflicts.

Moon in Scorpio: People are likely to be critical and suspicious, especially concerning money matters. Heightened emotional sensitivity can lead to anger and malice. Habits, family loyalties strong.

Moon in Sagittarius: Honesty, optimism and imagination open up. Emphasis on intellectual, philosophical thought. Take a trip, have an adventure, break routine.

Moon in Capricorn: The establishment, authority, rules, and regulations are staunchly upheld. Practicality prevails, but progress can seem fraught with obstacles. A tendency toward depression, pessimism, and frustration. Good time for discipline and hard work.

Moon in Aquarius: Social activities and concerns and rational thought prevail. Good time for new ideas, planning the future. Excessive emphasis on ideals can bring disappointment.

Moon in Pisces: Urges to confide and seek advice, but confusion makes manipulation of others possible. Interest in the spiritual, a good time for oracles. Energies turn inward.

Void-of-Course.   The period that lasts from the Moon's departure from one sign of the zodiac to its entry into the next sign is a tricky little time known as the void-of-course. When the Moon occupies a sign, it exerts a certain influence but in transit between them has nothing to affect. And so, it seems, the Moon does not quite know what to do.

As a result, life below on Earth can turn topsy-turvy. Decisions made during the void-of-course go sour. Newly purchased objects break, are defective, or are left unused. Agreements made that seemed rock solid change at a later time. It is a time when crazy and odd things happen, behavior is erratic, objects are misplaced, mistakes are made, and we lose our way. Those who are accident-prone are likely to have a mishap. Travel is subject to delays, cancellations, and accidents.

Astrologers differ as to how significant the void-of-course influence is, but most at least advise caution during these times. If possible, it is best to stick to routine matters and projects already underway. Avoid launching new projects, signing contracts, making major decisions (especially financial ones), and traveling.

Void-of-course happens roughly every two to two-and-a-half days. Some voids last only for a few minutes, but most last several hours, and some for a day or more.

Black Moon.   The Black Moon is an imaginary point in the heavens that represents negative, consuming forces. It is said to spew black flames that absorb all light—a sort of astrological black hole. If the Black Moon is in one's sun sign, it portends an early death. In other houses of the horoscope, it indicates challenging forces that threaten to consume and annihilate.

Moon in Medical Astrology.   The signs of the zodiac correspond to different parts of the body. By reading a horoscope, a doctor trained in medical astrology can predict the likelihood that a patient will be afflicted with certain diseases, what the best treatment among a range of alternatives will be, as well as a good time in the lunar cycle for certain therapies. In addition, phases of the Moon are believed to influence certain medical procedures in positive or negative ways.

For example, according to lore, people bleed more during the waxing and full moons than at any other time, thus indicating that surgeries might best be performed during the waning moon. Ancient beliefs about the Moon's regulating powers suggest that the body's fluids, like the ocean tides, respond to the Moon's gravitational pull. In early times, those trained in the art of bloodletting were told to perform this medical therapy only when the Moon was at the proper phase, for the body's fluids were believed to be at a peak during the waxing and full phases and at an ebb during the waning and new moon. Other folk magic beliefs are:

- Do not operate on any part of the body when the Moon is in the zodiac sign representing that part. Wait until the Moon enters another sign, preferably one that is fixed and governs an area remote from the part to be operated on. Also, the Moon should not be on the ascendant.
- Do not operate when the Moon is in the patient's sun sign.
- Do not operate when the Moon approaches Mars, which increases the risk of inflammation and post-surgery complications.
- Do not amputate when the Moon is under the sun's beams and is opposed by Mars.
- Do not operate on the abdomen when the Moon is passing through Virgo, Libra, or Scorpio, which rule that area of the body. Instead, wait until the Moon is in Sagittarius, Capricorn, or Leo.
- Get dental fillings when the waning moon is in Taurus, Leo, Scorpio, or Aquarius.
- Have teeth pulled when the waxing moon is in Gemini, Virgo, Capricorn, and Pisces. Postpone extractions if the Moon is in Aries, Cancer, Libra, Taurus, Leo, Scorpio, or Aquarius.

FURTHER READING:

Guiley, Rosemary Ellen. *Moonscapes: A Celebration of Lunar Astronomy, Magic, Legend and Lore.* New York: Prentice-Hall, 1991.

———. *The Encyclopedia of Vampires, Werewolves and Other Monsters.* New York: Facts on File, Inc., 2004.

———. *The Encyclopedia of Witches and Witchcraft.* 2d ed. New York: Facts on File, Inc., 1999.

Hauck, Dennis William. *The Emerald Tablet: Alchemy for Personal Transformation.* New York: Penguin/Arkana, 1999.

moonstone   In MAGIC, a semiprecious stone linked to the supernatural forces of the MOON and that brings luck. Moonstone is a type of opaque feldspar ranging in colors, such as silvery gray, milky white, blue-white, pale yellow, pale pink, and brown. It is best known in its silvery gray form, which gives it the appearance of hardened teardrops formed from the moonbeams that fall to Earth, hence its alternate name *tears of the moon.*

The ancient Greeks and Romans wore AMULETS made of moonstone to protect against epilepsy, insanity, and "wandering of the mind." They also hung it in orchards, gardens, and among trees to assist the growth of all vegetation and to ensure an abundant harvest.

The Greeks associated moonstone with the lunar goddesses Aphrodite and Selene. In fact, another name for moonstone is selenite.

In Eastern lore, moonstone is considered one of the luckiest of stones. Along with the star sapphire and cat's eye, it possesses a moving light on its surface as it reflects the light falling on it, a sign of inhabitation by a powerful and beneficent spirit. In India, the stone is sacred and according to tradition must not be displayed for sale except on a sacred yellow cloth.

In European lore, one may divine the future by gazing into a moonstone during the waning moon. It is a gift for lovers and newlyweds, as it will help arouse tender passion. It will help the lovers foretell their future if it is placed in the mouth when the Moon is full.

Moonstones, along with pearls, are a birthstone for the month of June.

Moonstones are popular in Wicca.

moonwort   Magical and alchemical herb associated with the powers of the MOON. Moonwort, whose genus name is *Botrychium lunaria,* is a species of grape fern, so-named because the plants bear grapelike clusters of spore cases. Moonwort leaflets are shaped like crescent moons.

In English lore dating back as far as the 16th century, moonwort, found upon the heaths, has the power to open IRON locks and pull the iron shoes off horses. The country folk of the 17th century called moonwort Unshoo the Horse. A story goes that the Earl of Essex's horses, grazing on the White Down in Devonshire, lost 30 shoes after treading upon moonwort. Witches were said to love it, for iron repelled them, but with moonwort they could easily get past the iron AMULETS and locks of any home or stable that they wished to enter.

In ALCHEMY, moonwort is probably the "white herb" prized by alchemists in the belief that it possesses a celestial vitality. It represents the white, or *albedo,* stage of the Great Work. The "white herb growing upon small mountains" is cited in the writings of MARIA PROPHETESSA.

Morgan le Fay   One of the sorceress queens central to the legends of King Arthur. She is the daughter of Gorlois, duke of Cornwall, and his duchess Igraine. Morgan le Fay is either the sister to the witches Morgause and Elaine or their niece. She is Arthur's half-sister and sometimes is described as a mistress to the wizard MERLIN. *Morgan le Fey* means "Morgan the Fairy." She is also known as *Morgaine, Modron, Morgian, Morgan le Fee,* and *Fata Morgana.*

Sometimes described as a goddess, Morgan probably is a composite character derived from various Celtic myths and deities. In Welsh folklore, she is related to lake FAIRIES who seduce and then abandon human lovers; in Irish folklore, she lived in a fairy mound from which she flew out in hideous guises to frighten people. In English and Scottish lore, Morgan lived either on Avalon or in various castles, including one near Edinburgh that was inhabited by a bevy of wicked fairies. She also is related to the mermaids of the Breton coast, called Morganes, Mari Morgan, and Morgan who enchanted sailors. Depending on the story, the sailors either went to their deaths or were transported to a blissful underwater paradise. In Italy, mirages over the Straits of Messina are still called the Fata Morganas.

Morgan possesses the art of magic herbal healing and ENCHANTMENTS. According to Malory, she learned her arts in a nunnery.

Sexual betrayal lies at the bottom of the Arthurian tales, begun by the murder of Gorlois by Uther Pendragon, High-King of the Britons. Pendragon seduces Igraine, Gorlois' widow, and their union produces Arthur. Merlin raises the boy in secret, and his royal lineage remains a mystery until he pulls the sword from the stone, thereby identifying himself as Uther's heir. Morgan le Fay, swearing to avenge her father, bewitches Arthur and sleeps with him. Their son Mordred, born of incest and seething with hatred and ambition, brings about the destruction of Camelot and the deaths of both himself and the king. Morgan le Fay plots against Arthur's queen, Guinevere, as well, in return for Guinevere's interference in an affair between Morgan and the queen's cousin Guiomar.

Sometimes portrayed as a pagan healer, Morgan le Fay is most often depicted as a wicked enchantress and shape-changer who is well versed in Merlin's magical arts and is intent on sowing discord and chaos. She steals Arthur's magic sword, EXCALIBUR, and gives it to her lover, Sir Accolon of Gaul, son of her husband King Uriens. Accolon nearly kills Arthur in battle, but VIVIANE, the Lady of the Lake, returns Excalibur to Arthur just in time. Furious at the failure of her plans, Morgan le Fay throws the scabbard into the lake.

After years of intrigue and conflict, Arthur and Morgan apparently reconcile not long before the fatal Battle of Camlann against Mordred. Morgan le Fay, joined by the queens of Northgalis (North Wales) and the Wastelands, carry the dying Arthur to Avalon (also known as Appleland, or the Fortunate Isle or Isle of Apples), from where medieval listeners of the legends hoped that the king would someday return and reunite his people.

Later authors of the Arthurian legends have rebuked Morgan le Fay's wicked reputation and embraced her role as a priestess of the pagan Celtic Goddess. Worship of the Mother Goddess, known as Modron (one of Morgan's names) or as the Irish Morrighan, coexisted with the new Christian faith. Monks who recorded the Arthurian cycles painted Morgan as badly as possible, labeling her powers as a healer and leader of her people as blasphemous and diabolical.

Morgan was sometimes portrayed as an evil, old hag or crone, as in the stories of Sir Lancelot and the lake and in *Gawain and the Green Knight*. She is not the "Lady of the Lake" in the Arthurian legend by that name. Morgan was said to have a prodigious sexual appetite and was constantly capturing knights to satisfy her desires.

She may not have engaged in incest, either. T. H. White, in his novel *The Once and Future King,* makes Morgause the seducer, bewitching Arthur with a *spancel:* a long unbroken ribbon of human skin, carefully taken from around an entire body. To cast the SPELL, the spancel is tossed over the sleeping beloved and tied into a bow without waking him; if the intended awakes, he will die within a year. But in the novel *The Mists of Avalon,* by Marion Zimmer Bradley, Morgaine (Morgan) unknowingly sleeps with Arthur as part of the fertility rites of the Beltane festival (May 1).

Morgan le Fay was a popular subject for medieval and Romantic artists, who often showed her in a small boat carrying Arthur to Avalon, as an enchantress casting a spell, or as a beautiful lover. Her hair is either dark or auburn in accordance with her Celtic heritage.

FURTHER READING:
Bradley, Marion Zimmer. *The Mists of Avalon.* New York: Knopf, 1983.
"Morgan Le Fay." Arthurian Biographies: Ambrosius Aurelianus. Available online. URL: www.britannia.com/history/biographies/morgan.html. Downloaded October 17, 2004.
"Morgan le Fay: Based on Ancient Myth." Available online. URL: www.mythicalrealm.com/legends/morgan_le_fay.html. Downloaded October 17, 2004.
"Morgan le Fay." The Camelot Project at the University of Rochester. Available online. URL: www.lib.rochester.edu/camelot/morgmenu.htm. Downloaded October 17, 2004.
"Morgan le Fay." Other Characters in Arthurian Legend. Available online. URL: www.kingarthursknights.com/others/morganlefay.asp. Downloaded October 17, 2004.
White, T. H. *The Once and Future King.* New York: Berkeley Medallion Books, 1966.

Mormius, Peter (17th c.)   Alchemist and Rosicrucian. In 1630 Peter Mormius, a noted alchemist and author of Rosicrucian works, sought to introduce ROSICRUCIANISM into Holland by petitioned the States-General for a public audience. Mormius said that he had a plan to make Holland the richest and happiest nation on Earth with the help of the PHILOSOPHER'S STONE and ELEMENTARY SPIRITS. Unimpressed, state officials turned him away.

Mormius then thought that he could force this issue by publishing his alchemical book which he did during the same year in Leyden. *The Book of the Most Hidden Secrets of Nature* was comprised of three parts: perpetual motion, transmutation of metals, and universal medicine. This failed as well.

Title page of the Mutus Liber, *attributed to the authorship of Altus, 1677. (Author's collection)*

Johann Mylius at age 33, 1618. (Author's collection)

Mother   See SALT.

Mutus Liber (Wordless Book)   Anonymous alchemical text for creating the PHILOSOPHER'S STONE.

The *Mutus Liber* was first printed in France in 1677 and was reissued in 1702. Its origins and authorship are unknown. The content of the book consists only of 15 plates showing different stages of the Great Work, with no accompanying explanation. In true alchemical tradition, the images are meant to be interpreted and understood intuitively. Details missing from the images must come from a student's spiritual study.

See also VEGETABLE GOLD.

Mylius, Johann (16th–17th c.)   German philosopher and student of ALCHEMY, known for his books of alchemical emblems.

Johann Mylius's best-known work is *Philosophia reformata* ("Philosophy Reformed"), published in 1622, a 700-page illustrated book discussing the concepts, metals, and stages of alchemy. His last work, *Anatomia auri* ("The Anatomy of Gold"), was published in 1628 and discusses the physical and spiritual properties of GOLD.

names The identity of a person or being. Names convey and determine personality, power, essence, qualities, luck, destiny, and fate. The names of ANGELS, DEMONS, and gods are crucial to the success of MAGIC and spiritual practice. They are used in meditation to attain higher states of consciousness; in PRAYER to invoke assistance; and inscribed on AMULETS to protect, heal, and bring good fortune. Sacred names usually are spoken in magical practice, but some are meditated upon within the heart. The powers ascribed to names are limitless.

Historical Background

The ancient civilizations of Babylonia, Assyria, and Egypt developed cultures that ascribed great importance to the power of names because they hold the essence of a being or person. Thus, knowing the names of deities and spirits enables a person to invoke and command them. Great power can be unleashed simply by the vibration of speaking a name, especially that of a god.

Names were especially important in Egyptian religious and magical practice. God names had creative power. According to the story of creation, in the beginning the gods were not born but came into being by uttering a name. OSIRIS, the "germ of primeval matter," first formed a mouth. According to the *Papyrus of Nesi-Amsu:*

> I brought [fashioned] my mouth, and I uttered my own name as a word of power, and thus I evolved myself under the evolutions of the god Khepera [an aspect of Ra], and I developed myself out of the primeval matter which had

evolved multitudes of evolutions from the beginning of time. Nothing existed on this earth [before me], I made all things.

The power of a name to command others is seen in the story of how ISIS became a goddess. Isis was a woman who possessed a word of power, and she wanted to become a goddess. She made a poisonous serpent and caused it to bite Ra. When Ra yielded up his names to her, she healed him and thus became "the mistress of the gods."

The Egyptians believed that a person's name was an integral part of him, as important as his *ka,* or soul. The tombs of kings and royalty were inscribed with god names in the belief that as those names would be preserved, energized, and empowered, so would the name of the dead person, and thus his soul would prosper as well.

The Egyptian *Book of the Dead* emphasizes the importance of names in the underworld journey of the deceased. In one part of the underworld kingdom of Osiris are seven halls or mansions, each guarded by a doorkeeper, a watcher, and a herald. The deceased must know the correct names of all the guardians to pass through all halls. Success meant having freedom of movement and access through all seven Halls of Osiris. Many other passages in the underworld journey had to be navigated by using correct names.

In magical RITUALS, names were invoked with great precision and accurate pronunciation; anything less meant failure. Many gods and lesser spirits had numerous names and forms, any and all of which might be invoked to cover all bases. Wax figures of gods were inscribed with names; whatever was done to the figure was done to the god.

The associations of a person's name could affect the living. A name associated with a CURSE would bring evil upon the owner of the name. Similarly, a name associated with a blessing would bring good.

Egyptian practice, which borrowed names and gods and spirits from other cultures, evolved into the use of BARBAROUS NAMES. If the original name and language were not understood, a similar-sounding word, even nonsensical, was substituted. The substitutes were held to carry the same force. Many incantations carried strings of names and name substitutes.

The use of multiple and barbarous names passed into Jewish, Hellenistic, Gnostic, Essene, and Christian lore and magic. The Merkabah mysticism which preceded the KABBALAH (c. 100 B.C.E.–1000 C.E.) emphasized the importance of names of power—angels and God—as a way of ascending through the layers of heavens to the throne-chariot of God. Like the halls of Osiris, the levels of heaven were guarded by fierce angels. Only the correct names and codewords would allow entrance and passage through them.

By medieval times, names of power had acquired great importance, especially in Jewish mysticism. Texts such as the *SEFER RAZIEL* and The Sword of Moses underscored this importance and gave lists of names to use in INCANTATIONS. Angels, demons, and God all have secret names as well as their known ones. The secret names have the greatest power. Oral transmission of secret names led to a multiplication of unintelligible names. The more corrupted the word, the greater power it was held to carry.

The systems of GEMATRIA, *notarikon,* and *temurah* created sacred names of God and angels from the numerical values of letters and recombinations of Hebrew letters. Words evolved into names. Other names were corrupted versions of mystical names that were inherited from other cultures. A typical incantation could have dozens of angel and God names, the pronunciations of which were open to interpretation.

Names of power passed into the various magical texts or GRIMOIRES that flourished in Europe in the 17th–19th centuries and that drew upon a variety of esoteric sources. JOHN DEE and EDWARD KELLY employed barbarous-sounding names in their ENOCHIAN MAGIC angel language, such as in the following invocation:

> Eca, zodocare, Iad, goho. Torzodu odo kikale qaa! Zodocare od zodameranu! Zodoorje, lape zodiredo Ol Noco Mada, das Iadapiel! Ilas! hoatahe Iaida!

Modern magicians have made sense out of barbarous names by breaking them down into individual letters and syllables and associating them with gods and attributes. For example, ISRAEL REGARDIE demonstrates how the barbarous name *Assaloni* is a complete invocation for the HOLY GUARDIAN ANGEL with the following associations:

A—Harpocrates, the Lord of Silence, Babe in the Lotus, and The Fool of the TAROT; Parsifal in search of the Holy GRAIL.

S—the Tarot card depicting the angel wearing the SIGIL of the TETRAGRAMMATON on his breast.

Al—the Hebrew word for *God.*

On—a Gnostic name for God.

Oi—the Hebrew personal pronoun *my.*

In the INITIATION to one of the higher grades of the HERMETIC ORDER OF THE GOLDEN DAWN, the initiate pledges to use only the highest divine names that he knows, "for by names and images are all powers awakened and reawakened."

Using Names of Power in Magic

Sacred names can be uttered only when the magician has prepared and purified himself. In ceremonial magic, the proper use of names is key to the success of an INVOCATION. The power of a name is experienced when it is vibrated—spoken in a commanding and loud voice and felt throughout the body—with the knowledge and understanding of the full meaning and associations of the name and its kabbalistic implications. When God-names are properly vibrated, the upper ASTRAL LIGHT is stirred, and the summoned ones notice and respond.

The timing of vibrating the names is key to the success of a RITUAL. ALEISTER CROWLEY said:

> With all such words it is of the utmost importance that they should never be spoken until the supreme moment, and even then they should burst from the magician almost despite himself—so great should be his reluctance to utter them. In fact, they should be the utterance of the God in him at the first onset of divine possession.

The *Key of Solomon* (see GRIMOIRES) has an incantation for using the "Most Holy Names" to evoke and control spirits. It is to be spoken in a low but firm voice while the magician is enroute to the place of invocations. The incantation suggests that the conjuring and control of spirits is dangerous to the magician:

> ZAZAII, ZAMAII, PUIDAMON Most Powerful, SEDON Most Strong, EL, YOD HE VAU HE, IAH, AGLA, assist me an unworthy sinner who have had the boldness to pronounce these Most Holy Names which no man should name and invoke save in very great danger. Therefore I have recourse unto these Most Holy Names, being in great peril both of soul and of body. Pardon me if I have sinner in any manner, for I trust in Thy protection alone, especially on this journey.

The "Barbarous Names of Evocation," long strings of melodic names, are used in many rituals. The magician visualizes the names as pillars of fire in the astral light. He concentrates on propelling each letter into the ether and sends his consciousness, in a body of light, to follow along. Each successive name is magnified twofold so that by the time the invocation is completed, the magician is in a state of intense exaltation and ecstasy.

Personal Magical Names

In the Western magical tradition, a magical name is taken as part of the process of spiritual regeneration. The custom is said to be based on the practice of the ORDER OF THE KNIGHTS TEMPLAR, who in turn established the custom of name changes based on the biblical admonition of St. John, "You must be born again." For example, ELIPHAS LEVI is the magical name of Alphonse Louis Constant, and DION FORTUNE is the magical name of Violet Firth.

FURTHER READING:

Budge, Wallis. *Egyptian Magic.* 1899. Reprint, New Hyde Park, N.Y.: University Books, n.d.

Butler, E. M. *Ritual Magic.* Cambridge: Cambridge University Press, 1949.

Crowley, Aleister. *Magic in Theory and Practice.* 1929. Reprint, New York: Dover Publications, 1976.

The Old Testament Pseudepigrapha. vols. 1 & 2. James H. Charlesworth, ed. New York: Doubleday, 1983; 1985.

Regardie, Israel. *Ceremonial Magic: A Guide to the Mechanisms of Ritual.* London: Aeon Books, 2004.

———. *The Tree of Life: A Study in Magic.* York Beach, Maine: Samuel Weiser, 1969.

Scholem, Gershom. *Kabbalah.* New York: Dorset Press, 1974.

Trachtenberg, Joshua. *Jewish Magic and Superstition: A Study in Folk Religion.* New York: Berhman's Jewish Book House, 1939.

natural magic　See MAGIC.

nature spirits　See ELEMENTALS.

necromancy　The magical conjuration of the dead for the purpose of DIVINATION. Because they are no longer bound by the Earth plane, the spirits of the dead are believed to have access to information beyond the capabilities of the living. Conjured spirits are asked about the future and where to find buried treasure.

Necromancy has been practiced since ancient times. It was prevalent in ancient Persia, Greece, and Rome. During the Middle Ages in Europe, it was widely believed to be practiced by magicians, sorcerers, and witches. Necromancy is feared because of the dangers involved and is reviled as one of the ugliest and most repugnant of magical rites. It is condemned by the Catholic Church as "the agency of evil spirits. In Elizabethan England, it was outlawed by the Witchcraft Act of 1604.

FRANCIS BARRETT, author of *The Magus* (1801), said that necromancy "has its name because it works on the bodies of the dead, and gives answers by the ghosts and apparitions of the dead, and subterraneous spirits, alluring them into the carcasses of the dead by certain hellish charms, and infernal invocations, and by deadly scrifices and wicked oblations."

There are two types of necromancy: raising a corpse itself to life, and summoning the spirit of the corpse. The second type is more common.

The RITUALS for necromancy are similar to those for conjuring DEMONS, involving MAGIC CIRCLES, wands, TALISMANS, bells, and INCANTATIONS, as prescribed by various GRIMOIRES. In addition, the necromancer surrounds himself or herself by gruesome aspects of death: he or she wears clothing stolen from corpses and meditates upon death. Some rituals call for the eating of dog flesh, for dogs are associated with the Hecate, the Greek patron goddess of witchcraft, and also called for is the consumption of unsalted and unleavened black bread and unfermented grape juice, which symbolize decay and lifelessness.

Such preparations may go on for days or weeks. The actual ritual itself may consume many hours, during which the magician calls upon Hecate or various demons to help raise the desired spirit. The ritual customarily takes place

Edward Kelly conjuring the dead. The other person is thought to be Paul Waring, an associate, in Illustration of the Occult Sciences, *by Ebenezer Sibley. (Author's collection)*

in a graveyard over the corpse itself. The objective is to summon the spirit to reenter the corpse and bring it back to life, rising and speaking in answer to questions posed by the magician. Recently deceased corpses are preferred by necromancers, for they are said to speak most clearly. If the person has been dead for a long time, necromancers try to summon their ghostly spirit to appear. Once the ritual has been performed successfully, the necromancer should burn the corpse or bury it in quicklime, so that it will not be disturbed again. In the Middle Ages, many believed that necromancers also consumed the flesh of the corpse as part of the ritual.

Some necromancers summon corpses to attack the living. This practice dates to ancient Egypt and Greece. A version of it is practiced in Vodoun: the creation of a ZOMBIE.

One of the best-known necromancers is the Witch of Endor, whose conjuring of the dead prophet Samuel for King Saul is recorded in the Bible; Samuel foretold Saul's doom. APOLLONIUS OF TYANA gained a great reputation in first-century Greece as a philosopher and necromancer. The 16th-century English magician JOHN DEE and his partner EDWARD KELLY were reputed necromancers, though Dee never recorded such activities in his diaries. In the 19th century, ELIPHAS LEVI attempted to conjure the spirit of Apollonius, an experience that left him badly shaken and frightened.

Necromancy techniques were taught in medieval Spain, in deep caves near Seville, Toledo, and Salamanca. The caves were walled up by Isabella the Catholic, who considered them evil.

The numbers nine and 13 are associated with necromancy. Nine represents an ancient belief in nine spheres through which a soul passed in the transition from life to death. Thirteen was the number of persons who attended Christ's Last Supper, at which he was betrayed; Christ later rose from the dead.

Necronomicon, The

Necronomicon, The   A fictitious black magic GRIMOIRE, the idea of which was created by the American occult and horror fiction writer, H. P. Lovecraft (1890–1937). Lovecraft wrote about the book in his fiction and acquired a cult of followers who believe that it actually exists and that it is based, at least in part, on fact.

The Necronomicon was born of Lovecraft's fertile imagination in his 1936 essay, "A History of *The Necronomicon*." He said that the grimoire was originally titled *Al Azif* and was written by "the mad Arab Abdul Alhazred," a fictitious name that he derived from *Arabian Nights* and that he used to call himself. He claimed that a copy of the book existed in his fictitious city of Arkham. He referred to it in some of his stories but never produced an actual book.

The fantasy captured the imagination of some of Lovecraft's fans, and for years a belief persisted that a real grimoire titled *The Necronomicon* existed. Booksellers received requests for it. Different versions of the "real" *Necronomicon* have been published.

Neuberg, Victor (1883–1940)   Initiate of ALEISTER CROWLEY. Victor Neuberg, a poet and an editor, broke ground with Crowley in Crowley's development of sex MAGIC as the key to occult mysteries. He assisted Crowley with the publication of his magazine *Equinox* and for five years was an important figure in Crowley's magical activities.

Neuberg was born on May 6, 1883, in London to an orthodox Jewish family. He was educated at the City of London School and at Trinity College in Cambridge from 1906 to 1909. He rejected Judaism in favor of agnosticism.

Crowley read Neuberg's poetry and in 1909 arranged to meet him at Neuberg's rooms in Cambridge. They were immediately impressed with one another, though Crowley clearly had the upper hand. Crowley initiated Neuberg into his secret society, the Silver Star, and gave him the magical name Frater Omnia Vincam. Neuberg was infatuated with Crowley and looked up to him, referring to him as "my guru."

Crowley decided to give Neuberg a crash course in occult practices and invited him to Boleskin, his home in Scotland. For 10 days, Neuberg underwent intensive instruction and experiences, exacerbated in part by exhaustion, sleeping naked on a bed of gorse, lack of food, and sadomasochistic treatment by Crowley in the form of verbal abuse and beatings with gorse and stinging nettles. Neuberg recorded his experiences in his magical diary, including his performances of the BORNLESS ONE ritual and details of his long excursions of RISING ON THE PLANES, or ASTRAL TRAVEL, during which he had remarkable visions that were indicative of his natural ability for magic. He wrote of his disgust with Crowley's verbal abuse, which was anti-Semitic. At one point Crowley verbally abused Neuberg for being among the QLIPPOTH, negative entities that inhabit the kabbalistic Tree of Life, and beat him bloody with a gorse switch.

Crowley ultimately was satisfied with Neuberg's magical performance and later in 1909 took him to Algiers where they evoked the DEMON CHORONZON. Crowley was inspired during this experience to include sex as part of the RITUAL; for Crowley it was an illumination of the true workings of magic.

In 1910 Neuberg participated in semipublic rituals in which he invoked Bartzabel, the spirit of Mars, for PROPHECY and also performed a wild dervishlike dance that ended in his exhausted collapse. The performances began as a private ritual. Neuberg sat in a MAGIC TRIANGLE and allowed himself to be possessed by Bartzabel. The spirit accurately predicted the outbreak of the Balkan War in 1912 and World War I. Neuberg danced to the violin playing of Leilah Waddell, one of Crowley's mistresses. The ritual was received so enthusiastically by those in attendance that Crowley worked up seven rituals—the Rites of Eleusis—for public performance.

The rituals were staged in 1910 for paying audiences who were primed with a "loving cup," Crowley's mix of alcohol, fruit juice, heroin or morphine, and what he termed "the elixir introduced by me to Europe," which was probably buttons of mescaline. The potion tasted like rotten APPLES but had the desired effect on the audience. Neuberg was a vision in white, dancing in a spontaneous frenzy to the wild violin playing of Waddell.

The first press reports were glowing. A subsequent disparaging report, which implied that C. S. Jones, a member of the HERMETIC ORDER OF THE GOLDEN DAWN, was engaged in a homosexual relationship with Crowley and ALLAN BENNETT caused Jones to sue the newspaper for libel. The negative publicity may have been encouraged by SAMUEL LIDDELL MacGREGOR MATHERS, one of the founders of the Golden Dawn, who was suing Crowley in an effort to prevent him from publishing secret Golden Dawn material.

Neuberg's last significant magical involvement with Crowley took place in 1913–14 in 24 sex magic rituals known as "the Paris Workings." In them, Crowley was experimenting with sex magic that he was developing for the ORDO TEMPLI ORIENTIS and that he was coming to favor over the more sedate and traditional rituals of the Golden Dawn.

The primary purpose of the Paris Workings was to invoke the gods Jupiter and Mercury and to persuade the gods to bestow money. Neuberg was to play the active homosexual role. The workings began on December 31, 1913, and concluded on February 12, 1914. Neuberg became possessed by Mercury and answered questions posed by Crowley. Neuberg was not always able to perform sexually, and sometimes Crowley assumed the active role. Neuberg also became possessed after the close of the rituals; he gave some prophecies that failed to happen. During the workings, the two learned of previous incarnations in Crete. The final working was to obtain money for Neuberg. He soon received a sum from an aunt, but he angered Crowley by giving some of the money to others instead of all of it to Crowley.

The past-life recall inspired Crowley to commit to writing his thoughts on his relationship with Neuberg:

I am always unlucky for you, you know; you always have to sacrifice everything for my love. You don't want to in the least; that is because we both have hold of the wrong end of the stick. If only I could leave you and you could love me. It would be lucky. But that apparently has never happened. Mutual indifference and mutual passion, and so on.

The Paris Workings evidently proved too much for Neuberg—whose affections for Crowley may have been waning at that point, anyway—and he soon parted company with Crowley. Another likely reason for his departure was anger over the death of Joan Hayes, a professional dancer whose stage name was Ione de Forest and who had been hired to perform in the Rites of Eleusis. Neuberg became enamored with her, much to Crowley's dismay. In 1911 Hayes married but six months later left her husband and became Neuberg's mistress, angering Crowley.

Two months later, Hayes shot herself to death. Neuberg believed that Crowley had put a SPELL on her, thus magically murdering her.

In fall 1914 he informed Crowley that he had decided to leave the Silver Star, and he wanted nothing more to do with Crowley. Furious, Crowley ritually cursed him as a traitor. Neuberg suffered a nervous breakdown, thus upholding the prevailing lore that anyone who crossed Crowley either committed suicide or went into a mental institution.

Neuberg was drafted into the British army from 1916 to 1919, participating in World War I, and then went to Steyning, Sussex, where he wrote poetry and operated a hand printing press, the Vine Press. He published poetry under his own name and various pseudonyms. The press never made much money. Without his magic, Neuberg felt severed from his purpose in life and began a slow decline.

In 1921 he married an earlier mistress, Kathleen Goddard. It was not a love match but a favor to Goddard, who wanted to have a child but in marriage. In 1924 she had a son, and three months later openly took a lover, for Neuberg was psychologically and physically spent. He never fully recovered from the psychological wounds left by his relationship with Crowley.

In 1930 Neuberg met a woman and went to live with her in London. He brightened in the relationship, and his poetry benefited. In 1933 he became poetry editor of *Sunday Referee*. His last years were happy. He died of tuberculosis on May 31, 1940.

FURTHER READING:
King, Francis. *Megatherion: The Magickal World of Aleister Crowley*. New York: Creation Books, 2004.
Sutin, Lawrence. *Do What Thou Wilt: A Life of Aleister Crowley*. New York: St. Martin's Griffin, 2000.

Newton, Sir Isaac (1643–1727) English scientist, physicist, and mathematician who is credited generally with establishing modern science, paving the way for the breakthroughs of the 18th century and the eventual rise of the Industrial Revolution. His contributions to the fields of mechanics, physics, optics, thermodynamics, and mathematics, but most especially his discovery of the laws of gravitation, have earned him a place as one of the most influential people of all time.

Newton was also an avid alchemist, spending years on occult studies and searching for the PHILOSOPHER'S STONE. He pored over ancient manuscripts and tracts, looking for the secret codes that would explain how metals could be made to multiply. Ironically, it was Newton's acceptance of the Hermetic principles of sympathy and antipathy—attraction and repulsion—in ether that enabled him to discover the quantitative principles of what is known as Newton's Third Law: that for every action there is an equal and opposite reaction. Newton's reconciliation of empirical science and pseudo-science could be his greatest achievement.

Like many other geniuses, Newton's brilliant analytical mind was often overshadowed by his anger, insecurity, pride, obsessiveness, and vengeful nature. The infant Isaac was not expected even to live much less become famous. He was born on January 4, 1643, in Woolsthorpe, Lincolnshire, to Hannah Ayscough Newton; his father, Isaac Senior, died three months before his birth. Within two years the young widow married a well-to-do minister named Barnabas Smith and moved away to raise a new family. Newton was raised by his grandmother until Smith died in 1653 when his mother returned and tried to resume relations, failing miserably. Newton hated his mother and stepfather, and later biographers attribute his psychotic behaviors to his early abandonment.

A child prodigy, Newton attended Grantham Grammar School and in 1661 entered Trinity College, Cambridge, where his uncle William Ayscough had gone. Already fascinated by the work of Kepler, Galileo, Descartes, and Copernicus, Newton chafed under the traditional study of Aristotelian notions of the "natural" world as taught by not only Cambridge but also by every other major university in Europe. Newton began to study the new philosophers avidly on his own. But Newton also read the work of Henry More, a Cambridge Platonist and alchemist.

Newton received his degree from Cambridge in 1665, the same year he discovered the binomial theorem of mathematics, the precursor to calculus. He was forced to leave Cambridge and work at home, however, as the university had closed to avoid the Great Plague of 1665–66. Besides inventing differential calculus—a form of mathematical analysis that uses infinitesimal changes to find the slopes of curves and the area under those curves—Newton spent time alone in his laboratory, cooking up alchemical processes and reading occult lore. He also studied the refraction of white light into colors through a prism and worked on his theories of planetary orbits and how to calculate them.

When the university reopened in 1667, Newton became a Fellow. That same year he published the treatise *De methodis serieum et fluxionum (On the Methods of Series and Fluxions)* that alluded to his discovery of calculus but did not specifically explain it. Independently, German philosopher and mathematician Gottfried Wilhelm Leibniz had discovered the calculus, and most scientists found Leibniz's notation superior to Newton's (although German mathematicians prefer Newton's notation). Never one to share credit, Newton accused Leibniz of plagiarism and persecuted him for 25 years.

In 1669 Isaac Barrow, the Lucasian professor of mathematics at Cambridge, resigned and nominated Newton for the post. At that time one had to be an ordained minister to teach at Cambridge or Oxford; yet the terms of the Lucasian post required that the holder *not* be active in the church, supposedly leaving more time for scientific

endeavors. Newton, a secret Unitarian, petitioned King Charles II to excuse him from the necessity of ordination based on the requirements of the position, which he received. Newton was always careful to hide his true feelings about the Trinity for fear of reprisal.

By 1671 Newton had invented a reflecting telescope that eliminated the refraction of light into color, which interfered with observation. The Royal Society, purveyor of all the new scientific discoveries in England, asked for a demonstration, and Newton published his findings in a paper entitled *Opticks*. Society member Robert Hooke criticized some of Newton's findings. Newton was so offended that he withdrew from public debate about his work and counted Hooke his enemy until the man died. Newton published a second tract on colors in 1675, but Hooke claimed that Newton had stolen his ideas. Newton lashed out at Hooke again and also vented his spleen at a group of English Jesuits who questioned his theories. Angry, formal correspondence between Newton and the Jesuits continued until 1678, at which time Newton sent one last furious letter, suffered a nervous breakdown, and then said no more. Newton's mother died the next year, adding to the man's anguish. He retreated into his laboratory for six years.

His self-imposed isolation gave him more time to read occult tracts and practice his ALCHEMY, an often dangerous pastime in the 17th century because heads of state feared financial ruin from anyone who might actually create more GOLD than the king had in his treasury. The punishment was death. Newton was convinced that there were secret codes in the Bible or in the languages that had been used in ancient times that would allow him to predict the future. It was a strange course for someone who conducted empirical research to believe that esoteric evidence was merely waiting to be found and deciphered. Newton constructed a floorplan of King SOLOMON's temple that he claimed was really a template for esoteric knowledge. He read extensively from the works of "Eirenaeus Philalethes," also known as GEORGE STARKEY (1628–65), the first well-known American "chymist." Newton may have been a FREEMASON.

One of Philalethes's (his name means "peaceful lover of truth") alchemical discoveries that inspired Newton was "the Net," or a purple alloy of antimony regulus and copper whose surface was covered in a grid pattern of crystals separated by spaces. This alloy tied in with a story from Greek mythology, also believed to be code, as follows:

> Venus and Mars were found in bed by her husband, Vulcan. He made a fine metallic net and hung the lovers from the ceiling in it in front of all the other gods on Olympus.

The code is that in alchemy—a pursuit cloaked in mysterious symbols and metaphors—Venus is copper, Mars is IRON, and Vulcan is fire. Hence Venus is the copper in the alloy mixed with antimony regulus, itself reduced from antimony sulfide by the addition of iron (Mars) and then placed in intense heat (Vulcan). This is the recipe for the Net.

Newton continued working on gravitation and its effects on planetary orbits during his exile. In 1684 astronomer Edmond Halley visited Newton to solve the problem of orbital dynamics. Newton claimed that he knew the answer, giving Halley a small tract called *De Motu (On Motion)*. This paper became the germ for Newton's masterwork, the *Philosophiae Naturalis Principia Mathematica* (usually called the *Principia*), in which he laid out all his principles of math and physics and introduced Boyle's Law: a treatise on the speed of sound in air. The three Newtonian laws are:

1. That a body remains at rest (inertia) unless its state is changed by the exertion of force upon the body;
2. That change of motion is proportional to the force used, and
3. That for every action there is an equal and opposite reaction.

By analyzing circular motion using his laws, Newton developed a formula for the centripetal force necessary to change a body—in this case a planet or a MOON—from a rectilinear path to a circular or elliptical one. Newton named this force *gravity*, from the Latin *gravitas*. The law of gravity, therefore, establishes that every particle in the universe attracts every other particle with a force proportional to the product of their masses and is inversely proportional to the square of the distance between the particles' centers. Biographers now agree that the anecdote about the falling apple as the impetus for his theory of gravitation was invented to show how Newton could gain inspiration from everyday objects.

Publication of the *Principia* in 1687 brought Newton international prominence. During this period Newton formed a close relationship with the Swiss-born mathematician Nicolas Fatio de Duillier. Fatio lived in London and suggested Newton seek work there. Newton tried for several years, finally securing the position of Warden of the Mint in 1696 through the offices of Charles Montague, Lord Halifax. But by then he had broken off with Fatio, who had become ill and plagued with financial and family problems. Newton pleaded with Fatio via an intense flow of letters to move to Cambridge where he would take care of him, but in 1693 the letters and relationship abruptly ceased with no explanation. Newton sent wild letters to Samuel Pepys and John Locke, accusing them of trying to snare him with women; then he succumbed to a second breakdown. He briefly returned to science one last time with the publication of a treatise on rates of cooling in 1701.

Newton's later years were devoted to his duties at the Mint and study of the Bible. He also served in Parliament. As Warden of the Mint he oversaw the "great recoinage," and when he rose to Master in 1699 he also pursued counterfeiters and anyone debasing the currency. Seeking counterfeiters in the taverns and brothels of London gave

Newton a socially acceptable way to vent his rage, and he sent many to the gallows.

In 1703 Newton's nemesis Hooke had died, and he assumed the presidency of the Royal Society. Annoyed that John Flamsteed, the Astronomer Royal at the Observatory in Greenwich, would not give him all his data that he had collected on stars and planets, Newton began a campaign to form a group of "visitors" that would oversee the observatory. Newton, of course, was chairman and tried to force the immediate publication of Flamsteed's star catalogue, giving the task to Flamsteed's enemy, Edmond Halley. Nearly 10 years later Flamsteed succeeded in taking back his work by court order. Newton retaliated by removing any reference to Flamsteed in the *Principia*.

Queen Anne knighted Newton in 1705, the first scientist to be so honored. The end of his life was spent revising his earlier works and fighting with his enemies over slights and perceived plagiarisms. He never married nor had any known children. Newton died on March 31, 1727, and was buried in Westminster Abbey.

Dan Brown, author of *The Da Vinci Code*, used Newton's resting place as the last piece in the instructions for locating the Holy GRAIL. In the novel, Leonardo da Vinci had invented an encoded cylinder called a *cryptex* to carry secret messages. To open it the rotating components had to be correctly aligned, and the right order usually involved the answer to a riddle. The final puzzle piece in the search was to locate "the orb above the tomb of a knight a pope interred." The orb is Newton's legendary APPLE, and he is the knight buried and eulogized by A. (Alexander) Pope.

Until the 20th century, few scientists or biographers knew of Newton's alchemical efforts. But in 1936 a cache of Newton's papers and journals—described as having no scientific importance—were bought by the economist Lord John Maynard Keynes. Lord Keynes surprised the members of the Royal Society Club in 1942 with his revelations of Newton's search for the philosopher's stone and the ELIXIR OF LIFE. Lord Keynes commented in his now-famous assessment of Newton that, "Newton was not the first of the Age of Reason. He was the last of the magicians."

FURTHER READING:
"Isaac Newton's Hidden Agenda of Mysticism and Alchemy." Originally published in *The Wall Street Journal* Bookshelf, February 19, 1998, p. A20. Available online. URL: www.cftech.com/BrainBank/OTHERREFERENCE/ BIOGRAPHY/Newtonian.html. Downloaded January 2, 2005.
Newman, William. "Newton's Alchemy, Recreated." Available online. URL: www.indiana.edu/~college/William NewmanProject.shtml. Downloaded January 2, 2005.
"Sir Isaac Newton." Available online. URL: www.isaacnewton. utwente.nl/nieuw/sir_isaac_newton/SirIsaacNewton.htm. Downloaded January 2, 2005.
White, Michael. *Isaac Newton: The Last Sorcerer.* London: Fourth Estate, 1997.

nightmare In folklore, a bad dream caused by DEMONS, WITCHCRAFT, or SORCERY. The term *nightmare* comes from the Anglo-Saxon terms *neaht* or *nicht* (night) and *mara* (incubus or succubus, "the crusher"). Until the mid-17th century, the term *nightmare* was used to describe nocturnal attacks that were believed to be of supernatural causes.

In medieval lore, nightmares were thought to be caused by witches called hags who sat on a person's chest and "rode" him through the night, sometimes killing him from exhaustion. AMULETS against hag riding were a penknife placed on one's breast or a table fork placed under one's head. A sifter placed under the head also prevented riding, for the hag would be forced to pass through every hole in it, taking her all night.

Nightmares also are a form of PSYCHIC ATTACK in which magical means are used to summon and send demons to a sleeping victim. (See DREAM SENDING.)

In Filipino lore, *bangungut*, or "nightmare" is a killing illness caused by a CURSE. The victims suffers violent nightmares every night until he or she dies. According to lore, there is no antidote for the curse.

FURTHER READING:
Guiley, Rosemary Ellen. *The Encyclopedia of Vampires, Werewolves and Other Monsters.* New York: Facts On File, Inc., 2004.

Norton, Thomas (d. 1477) English alchemist who learned from GEORGE RIPLEY. Thomas Norton is the author of a noted alchemical work, *The Ordinall of Alchimy.*

Thomas Norton the alchemist is believed to be the same Thomas Norton as the privy councillor to Edward VI. He was born to a wealthy family in Bristol; his father was sheriff of Bristol in 1401 and mayor in 1413 and also was a member of Parliament.

Norton began his study of ALCHEMY early in life, writing letters to ADEPTS and asking for information. He was 28 when he sent a letter to Ripley, who answered by inviting him to meet face-to-face to discuss the secrets of the art. Ripley promised to make him "my heir and brother in this art."

Norton stayed with Ripley for 40 days. He had already studied both the occult sciences and natural philosophy; and he quickly learned alchemy. However, Ripley declined to give him the secret of the process of making the white elixir into red elixir (see ELIXIR OF LIFE; PHILOSOPHER'S STONE) because of his youth, and the danger of using it improperly. Only after Norton convinced him of his integrity did Ripley at last yield up the secret.

Norton returned to Bristol with the secret for making the Great Red Elixir. But his first elixir was stolen by a servant, sending Norton into such a deep depression that he nearly gave up alchemy altogether. He rallied and made more elixir, but once again he was robbed, this time by a woman who was said to be the wife of William Canning, the mayor of Bristol, who suddenly came into great wealth.

In 1477 Norton wrote *Of Alkimy the Ordinal, the* Crede Mihi, *the Standard Perpetuall,* which became known as *The Ordinall of Alchimy.* He gave a copy to George Nevill, the archbishop of York, to whom Ripley dedicated one of his major works. The *Ordinall* is written in verse, originally in Latin. It's first English translations was in 1652 in Elias Ashmole's *Theatrum Chemicum Britannicum.*

The *Ordinall* discusses alchemists and their equipment, especially their furnaces, and describes procedures in vague terms. Norton portrays alchemy as a holy art that should not be undertaken for "appetite of Lucre and Riches." He admonishes alchemists to learn how to discern honest and real alchemists from frauds and charlatans and says that most books of alchemical recipes are false. He holds that Nature can transmute minerals to metals under the Sun's rays but that alchemy is more modest and must deal with the transmutation of existing metals. Astrological aspects are important for carrying out the work in four successive stages: SUN in Sagittarius and MOON in Aries; Sun in Libra and Moon in Virgo; Sun in Virgo and Moon in Libra; and Sun and Moon both in Leo.

Norton gave no evidence of profiting from his alchemical labors, and friends who invested money with him took losses. He died in 1477. His grandson, Samuel, also became an alchemist and wrote treatises on the Hermetic arts.

FURTHER READING:
Holmyard, E. J. *Alchemy.* New York: Penguin Books, 1957.
Waite, Arthur Edward. *Alchemists Through the Ages.* Blauvelt, N.Y.: Rudolph Steiner Publications, 1970.

Nostradamus (1503–1566) French physician and prophet whose far-reaching prophecies have caused controversy for centuries. A gifted clairvoyant, Nostradamus made approximately 1,000 prophecies, many of which are interpreted as having a reach into the far future.

Nostradamus was born Michel de Nostredame on December 14, 1503, in St. Remy de Provence, the oldest of five sons in a well-educated Jewish family. His parents converted to Catholicism, which exposed Nostradamus to both the occult wisdom of the KABBALAH and the prophecies of the Bible. As a child, he experienced visions, which he believed were a divine gift from God.

At home Nostradamus was educated in Hebrew, Latin, Greek, mathematics, medicine, astronomy, and ASTROLOGY. In 1522 he was sent to Montpellier University to study medicine. He earned a degree and a license and went to work treating plague victims throughout southern France. He possessed an uncanny gift for healing and quickly became famous, despite opposition from fellow physicians to his unorthodox cures. He refused to bleed patients, and he made his own medicines. Some of his recipes, dating to 1522, have not survived.

In about 1534 Nostradamus settled in Agen, married, and fathered two children. He met Julius Cesar Scaliger, a philosopher and student of astrology who may have introduced Nostradamus to the art of prophecy. A few years later Nostradamus's life and medical practice fell apart when the plague claimed his entire family. In addition, the Inquisition sought him for questioning concerning a friend of Scaliger. Nostradamus left Agen and apparently drifted around Europe for about six years. According to legend, his prophetic vision began to flower during this time, and he delved further into a study of the occult.

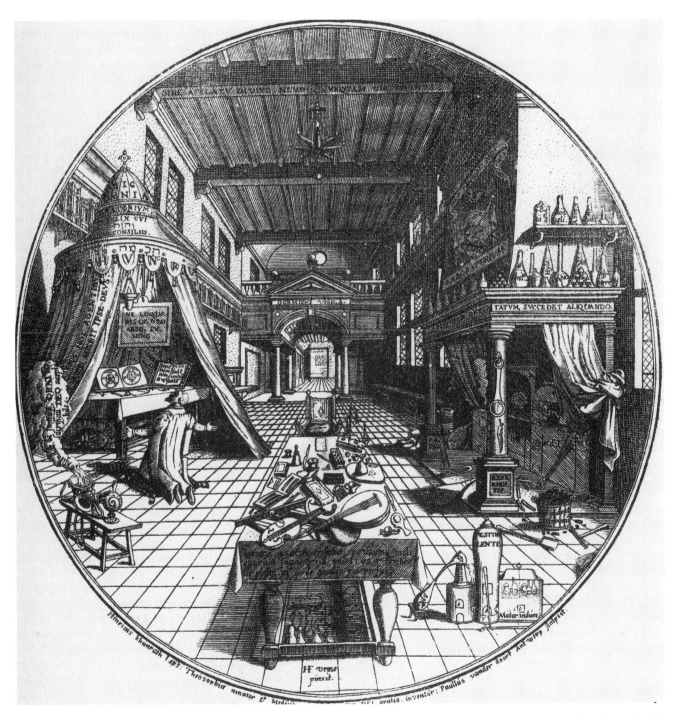

An alchemist in his laboratory, perhaps the one belonging to Thomas Norton. In Theatrum chemicum Britannicum, *by Elias Ashmole, 1652.* (Author's collection)

Nostradamus at age 59, 17th-century print. (Author's collection)

He settled down again, in Salon en Craux de Provence, where he married Anne Ponsart Gemelle, a wealthy widow who bore him six children. Sometime after 1550, he began to record his prophetic visions, which came to him by "the subtle spirit of fire," delivered in fragments and accompanied by a voice from limbo which he believed to be the "Divine Presence." He summoned the visions by SCRYING every night alone in his study, gazing into a bowl of water set in a brass tripod. He began his sessions with a magic RITUAL attributed to the ancient ORACLES of Branchus. He touched the tripod with a wand, then dipped the wand into the water, and touched the tip to his robe. He recorded the things he saw and heard, often not understanding them.

Nostradamus feared being accused of SORCERY and brought up on charges before the Inquisition, so he phrased the prophecies in rhymed quatrains written in a mixture of Greek, French, Provencal, and Latin; some words were further disguised in anagrams. He arranged the quatrains in groups of hundreds, or "centuries," which were not in chronological order.

The first prophecies were published in 1555 as *Les Propheties de M. Michel Nostradamus* and were an immediate success in aristocratic circles, gaining him the favor of Catherine de Medicis and cementing his reputation as a prophet. He published a second, larger edition of *Propheties* in 1558.

Once while traveling on a road near Anaconda, Italy, Nostradamus passed by a group of monks and suddenly knelt before one of them, Brother Peretti, a former swineherd. He addressed the monk as "His Holiness," the title reserved for the pope. Forty years later—and 19 years after Nostradamus died—Brother Peretti became Pope Sixtus V.

Nostradamus enjoyed fame and success until 1566 when his health declined due to gout and dropsy. He died during the night of July 1 of that year and was buried upright in a wall of the Church of the Cordeliers in Salon. In 1791 superstitious French soldiers opened his grave. His bones were reburied in the Church of St. Laurent, also in Salon.

Nostradamus wrote 10 volumes of centuries containing 1,000 prophecies, but he inexplicably left the seventh volume incomplete. At the time of his death, he had been planning to write the 11th and 12th volumes. Scholars have puzzled over the prophecies for centuries. Some seem clear, while others have been subjected to widely divergent interpretations. Among the many great events of history which Nostradamus is credited with having foreseen are the Napoleonic wars; the history of British monarchs from Elizabeth I to Elizabeth II, including the abdication of Edward VIII; the American Revolutionary War and Civil War; the rise and fall of Hitler; the assassinations of Abraham Lincoln, John Kennedy, and Robert Kennedy; and the rise of the Ayatollah Khomeini. He also foresaw air and space travel, including manned rockets to the MOON and submarines, that would be used for war. He is also said to have prophesied the development of the atomic bomb.

During World War II, Nostradamus's quatrains, including fake ones, were used by both Axis and Allied powers for propaganda purposes. The Germans airdropped over France selected quatrains that they claimed foretold victory by the Nazis. The British countered by air-dropping quatrains over Germany and occupied countries which foretold the Nazis' defeat. The U.S. government used quatrains in film shorts shown in movie houses that portrayed the United States as the torch of freedom for the world.

Nostradamus has been interpreted as predicting three reigns of terror created by what he termed three Antichrists. The first two have been identified by some as Napoleon and Hitler; the third remains open to interpretation, but the scenario is similar to the end times portrayed in the book of Revelation. New York City would be destroyed in a nuclear war that would take place from 1994 to 1999. This great war was to be presaged by famines, drought, earthquakes, and volcanic eruptions. After 27 years the Antichrist would be defeated and killed, followed by a 1,000-year golden age of peace. When the terrorist attack and collapse of the World Trade Center towers in New York City occurred on September 11, 2001, Nostradamians, as some students of his work are called, rushed to find validation for the event in his quatrains.

Nostradmus's predictions continue to be the focus of both controversy and scholarly study. Believers say he indeed could see several centuries ahead, while skeptics say that his veiled language, as well as translations of his language, enable the quatrains to be fitted to many events.

See also DIVINATION.

FURTHER READING:
Boesler, Knut, ed. *The Elixirs of Nostradamus.* Wakefield, R.I.: Moyer Bell, 1996.
De Fontbrune, Jean-Charles. *Nostradamus: Countdown to Apocalypse.* New York: Holt, Rhinehart and Winston, 1980.
Roberts, Henry C. *The Complete Prophecies of Nostradamus.* New York: American Book–Stratford Press, 1969.
Robins, Joyce. *The World's Greatest Mysteries.* London: Hamlyn Publishing Group Ltd., 1989.

notarikon See GEMATRIA.

numbers Ruling forces in MAGIC, ALCHEMY, and mysticism. All numbers are ascribed certain properties and energies, which are factors in RITUALS and SPELL-casting.

PYTHAGORAS observed that the musical intervals known in his time could be expressed in ratios between the numbers 1, 2, 3, and 4. Furthermore, the numbers 1 through 4 add up to 10, which begins the cycle of numbers over again, for all numbers larger than 9 may be reduced by a single digit by adding the digits together. Pythagoras reasoned that the entire universe could be expressed numerically, creating a mystical system expanded by other early Greek philosophers. He is quoted: "The world is built upon the power of numbers."

Each primary number is ascribed certain characteristics and values and a male or female aspect. Odd numbers are masculine, strong, and creative, while even numbers are feminine and either weak and evil or nurturing and stable.

In the Greek Mysteries, the number 888 represented the "Higher Mind." The Greek variation of "Jesus," "Iesous," equals 888. The number 666 represented the "Mortal Mind." In the New Testament, 666 is called the number of "the Beast."

The early Hebrews placed great importance on numbers, basing the letters of the Hebrew alphabet on them and relating them to cosmic forces. Each letter has a numerical value that enables forms and ideas to be expressed mathematically. In the Middle Ages, the teachings of the Merkabah sect of Judaism became intertwined with numerical mysticism. In the 13th century, German kabbalists developed the interpretation of the Scriptures through a system of number mysticism. (See GEMATRIA.)

In the 19th century when scientific discoveries were made about light, magnetism, and electricity, the theory that numbers were energy patterns of vibrations became popular. ELIPHAS LEVI said that the book of Revelation in the Bible comprises all of the secrets of the KABBALAH and is written in the code of numbers and SYMBOLS, the full meaning of which can only be understood by initiates.

Qualities of Individual Numbers

The following are some of the characteristics ascribed to the number 1 through 10:

One. One stands for beginnings, independence, strength, initiative, originality, leadership, the ego, one's self. It is the beginning of all things, unity, oneness, the source of all creativity and creation, and oneness realized with all good.

Two. Two symbolizes partnership, balance, cooperation, agreement, diplomacy, beauty, duality. On the higher planes, it is the joining of opposites, the descent of spirit into matter, the polarity of opposites, and the dawning of something new into consciousness.

Three. The number three plays a prominent role in myth, mysticism, the mystery traditions, folklore, alchemy, and the dynamics of spiritual growth and change. The product of 1+2, three is creation, growth, generation, forward movement, imagination, and artistic creativity. It is spiritual synthesis, harmony, and sufficiency; also prudence, friendship, justice, peace, virtue, and temperance. Three is the number that opens doors to the higher planes. It is a powerful number with a substantial presence in dreams.

Pythagoras said that three is "a triple Word, for the Hierarchical Order always manifests itself by Three." All the great religions recognize the expression of the Godhead in trinities. For example, in Christianity it is Father–Son–Holy Spirit. In Hinduism the trinity is Brahman-Shiva-Vishnu. There are three pillars to Zen Buddhism. The ancient Egyptians' holy trinity was Osiris-Isis-Horus. The Great Goddess has a threefold expression of Virgin-Mother-Crone.

The Greek philosopher Anatolius observed that three, "the first odd number, is called perfect by some because it is the first number to signify the totality—beginning, middle and end." Thus, we find in mythology, folklore, and fairy tales the recurrent motif of the triad: three wishes, three sisters, three brothers, three chances, blessings done in threes, and spells and charms done in threes ("thrice times the charm"). Three is also the number of wisdom and knowledge in its association with the Three Fates and the past, present, and future, and the ancient sciences of music, geometry, and arithmetic.

The Western mystery tradition and alchemy are based on the legendary teachings of HERMES TRISMEGISTUS, or "Thrice-Greatest Hermes." Three is the ascent of consciousness, represented by the upward-pointing triangle and the face of the pyramid. It represents the unification of body-mind-spirit and heart-will-intellect and eyes-ears-mouth (what we see, hear, and speak as products of our spiritual consciousness). The Three Wise Men of the Bible represent the enlightened consciousness. The Great Work of alchemy takes place in three main stages.

In the teaching of the kabbalah there are three pillars to the Tree of Life, which is a blueprint for the descent of the divine into matter and the return ascent to the God-head. The top three *sephirot,* or stations, of the Tree of Life are the mystical steps to unity: Understanding, Wisdom, and Humility. In the *Sefer Yetzirah* ("Book of Formation") of the kabbalah, three is expressed in the Three Mothers, Aleph, Mem, and Shin, which form the foundation of "all others." Aleph, Mem, and Shin are letters of the Hebrew alphabet that mean, respectively, "breath" or vital spirit; "seas" or water; and "life-breath of the Divine Ones" or "Holy Spirit."

The *Book of the Penitence of Adam* describes the origin of the kabbalistic triad. Seth, the descendant of Adam, is permitted to approach the entrance to Eden and behold the Tree of Life and the Tree of Knowledge, which he sees incorporated into a single tree. An ANGEL gives him three seeds containing the vital power of the combined trees. Seth places the seeds in the mouth of his father as a token of eternal life.

Saplings spring from these seeds, becoming the burning bush beheld by Moses and from which God revealed his sacred NAME. Moses took a triple branch of the bush and fashioned it into his magical wand (see TOOLS). The branch lived and blossomed and was preserved in the Ark of the Covenant. David planted the branch on Mount Zion, and his son King SOLOMON took wood from each section of the triple trunk to make the pillars of Joachim and Boaz, which were placed at the entrance to his temple. The two pillars were bronzed, and the third section was placed at the entrance of the main gate. The third section functioned as a TALISMAN to prevent unclean things from entering the scared space of the temple.

Four. Four represents solidity, stability, practicality, earthiness, responsibility, dependability, and industriousness. Four is a follower rather than a leader. It is the "eternal principle of creation," according to Pythagoras, since it is the final number that brings everything to unity (1+2+3+4). It describes the universe (four elements, four quarters, four directions). It is a principle number of alchemy and represents a transition or initiation of consciousness from the three-dimensional realm to the fourth dimension.

Five. Five is the number of energy, change, freedom, cleverness and resourcefulness, and the midway point. It expresses the fifth element of spirit, the QUINTESSENCE, and stands for the resurrected Christ (there were five wounds on the body of Jesus). It also stands for human-

kind (four limbs and the head) and the microcosm. Five represents the victory of the spirit over matter and the awakening of the I AM consciousness, the realization of God within.

Six. Six is the number of universal creation, equilibrium, and balance. Without six, there is formlessness. According to the *Zohar:*

> Through the conflict of unbalanced forces the devastated earth was void and formless, until the Spirit of God made for itself a place in heaven and reduced the mass of waters. All the aspirations of Nature were directed towards unity of form, toward the living synthesis of equilibrated forces; the face of God, crowned with light, rose over the vast sea and was reflected in the waters thereof. His two eyes were manifested, radiating with splendor, darting two beams of light which crossed with those of the reflection. The brow of God and His eyes formed a triangle in heaven, and its reflection formed a second triangle in the waters. So was revealed the number six, being that of universal creation.

(See SEAL OF SOLOMON.)

Six also symbolizes love and harmony in relationships, as well as generosity, domesticity, and humanitarianism. Esoterically, it pertains to the interrelationship of the human and the divine and is a working and building number aimed at illumination. Six relates to the beauty of the soul that emerges from the alternating light and shadow of life. It concerns the transmutation of physical love into spiritual love.

Seven. Seven is a number of great power: a magical number, a lucky number, a number of psychic and mystical powers, secrecy and the search for inner truth. Seven stands for investigation, research, analysis, discovery, philosophy, charm, and luck. It is the number of rest (God rested on the seventh day of creation) and spiritual realization. It is mysticism, the psychic and occult, introspection, intuition, magic, and the hero's quest for spiritual truth.

The origin of the power of seven lies in the lunar cycle of seven. Each of the Moon's four phases lasts about seven days. Thus, life cycles on Earth below also have phases demarcated by seven. Phul, the angel who rules the MOON, is the seventh angel of the heavens and rules over seven provinces.

The Sumerians, who based their calendar on the Moon, gave the week seven days and declared the seventh and last day of each week to be uncanny. Furthermore, there are seven years to each stage of human growth, seven colors to the rainbow, seven notes in the musical scale, seven petitions in the Lord's Prayer, and seven deadly sins. Diseases run their course in sevens, with the periods of gravest danger coming on the seventh, 14th and 21st days, according to occult lore. The seventh son of a seventh son is born with formidable magical and psychic powers. The number seven is widely held to be a lucky number, especially in matters of love and money.

Eight. Eight is material success, setting priorities, toughness, tenacity, executive ability, administration, judgment, supervision, and satisfaction with work. Eight is a cosmic number of regeneration and birthing into the new. It is cosmic knowing, exaltation, the essence of the life force, secret wisdom, and consciousness that spans the physical and spiritual.

Nine. Nine represents philanthropy, compassion, service, tolerance, broadmindedness, and the capability of living a largely divine life. It is spiritual and mental achievement and completion of a phase. Nine is the number of the spiritual evolution of humankind: the numbers 666 and 144,000, expressing spiritual opposites in the Book of Revelation, both reduce to a nine. Thus nine synthesizes the ego's entire journey or the PHILOSOPHER'S STONE of alchemy.

Ten. Ten is the number of completion and return to one. It is the number from which all things come and to which all things return. It is the divine inbreath and outbreath of creation. Both the Greeks and the Hebrews considered 10 the perfect number. Pythagoras said that 10 comprehends all arithmetic and harmonic proportions and, like God, is tireless. All nations reckon to it because when they arrive at 10, they return to 1, the number of creation. The Pythagoreans believed the heavenly bodies were divided into 10 orders. According to the kabbalah, there are 10 emanations of number out of Nothing. The emanations form the 10 sephiroth of the Tree of Life, which contains all knowledge and shows the path back to God.

FURTHER READING:

Levi, Eliphas. *The History of Magic.* 1806. Reprint, York Beach, Maine: Samuel Weiser, 2001.

Patai, Raphael. *The Jewish Alchemists.* Princeton, N.J.: Princeton University Press, 1994.

Scholem, Gershom. *Kabbalah.* New York: New American Library, 1974.

Three Books of Occult Philosophy Written by Henry Cornelius Agrippa of Nettesheim. Transl. by James Freake. Ed. and annot. by Donald Tyson. St. Paul, Minn.: Llewellyn Publications, 1995.

numerology A system of DIVINATION based upon the concept that the universe is constructed in a mathematical pattern and that all things may be expressed in numbers that correspond to vibrations. By reducing names, words, birth dates, and birth places to numbers, a person's personality, destiny, and fortune may be determined.

In numerological divination, all numbers are reduced to nine roots between 1 and 9. Each number corresponds to a letter of the alphabet:

1	2	3	4	5	6	7	8	9
A	B	C	D	E	F	G	H	I
J	K	L	M	N	O	P	Q	R
S	T	U	V	W	X	Y	Z	

To find the numerical value of a name, all the numbers of the letters are added together and reduced to a single digit; for example, if a name totals 45, it is reduced to 9 by adding 4 plus 5.

Certain numbers in numerology are not reduced to single digits. The numbers with repeating digits, such as 11, 22, and 33, are master numbers. People whose names correspond to these numbers are said to be highly developed spiritually. The number 33 is that of avatar, a rare occurrence. Twelve also has spiritual significance, as does 40.

Eleven

Eleven is the first master number that does not reduce to a single digit. It expresses a high level of humanitarianism, intuition, inspiration, prophetic ability, and illumination. It amplifies the power of the number one and is the resurrected lightbody demonstrated by Christ. Eleven brings the merger of the individual with the universal and the transmutation of earthly urges into the spiritual light of compassion, brotherhood, and universality.

Twelve

Twelve turns the wheel of the heavens and represents the cosmic order of things. It is the number of regeneration, representing the New Jerusalem. It concerns extension, expansion and elevation, and liberation from the bondage of time and space.

Twenty-two

Twenty-two is the second master number that does not reduce to a single digit. It is the mastermind, high capability, wisdom. Twenty-two is the spiritual master, a luminary. It is the number of the angelic kingdom and amplifies the power of the number two.

Thirty-three

Another master number, 33 is the level of avatar or bodhisattva, a human incarnation of the divine who functions as a mediator between humans and God and serves the spiritual evolution of humanity. Thirty-three is self-realization, the product of intense spiritual devotion and practice.

Forty

Forty is the number of spiritual incubation, trial, and initiation. The Bible makes references to 40: the period of the Deluge, the reign of David, the days Moses spent on Mount Sinai, the years the Jews wandered in the desert, the days Jesus spent fasting in the wilderness, and the elapsed time between the resurrection and the ascension. In alchemy, the initial phase of the work, the *nigredo,* the blackening, takes about 40 days to complete. Spiritual awakenings sometimes take place over a 40-day period.

The numerological value of a person's full name given at birth is the expression of the vibratory forces of the universe which determine one's character and destiny. Changing one's name can alter these factors, but several years supposedly are required for the vibrational patterns to readjust.

Adding up the values of vowels and consonants in a name yield additional information. Vowels reveal one's "heart's desire" or "soul's urge," while consonants reveal aspects of one's personality. The frequency of letters determines the karmic lessons to be faced in life. The sum of the month, the day, and the year of birth tells the birthpath, or the general direction of one's life. The sum of one's full name and birthdate equals a power number, which acts as a beacon to guide one through life.

All words may be converted to numbers to see how virtually anything complements or clashes with one's life, including one's career and city of residence. Numerology also is used to determine the propitious days for various activities, as a guide in health matters and in selecting business and marriage partners and friends, and to predict the future.

FURTHER READING:

Hall, Manly P. *The Secret Teachings of All Ages.* 1928. Reprint, Los Angeles: The Philosophic Research Society, 1977.

Heline, Corinne. *Sacred Science of Numbers.* Marina del Rey, Calif.: DeVorss & Co., 1991.

Scholem, Gershom. *Kabbalah.* New York: New American Library, 1974.

Odhar, Coinneach (17th c.) Scottish WIZARD and seer whose ability to prophesy by SCRYING may have led to his execution. Coinneach Odhar was known as the Brahan Seer and Sallow Kenneth the Enchanter.

Odhar was born Kenneth Mackenzie in the early 17th century on the Isle of Lewis in Scotland. Very little is known about his life. According to lore, he obtained his clairvoyant ability from the gift of a mysterious blue stone given to his mother by the ghost of a dead princess. The story goes that Mrs. Mackenzie was out one day herding her cattle near a graveyard. Several tombstones fell over, opening the graves. She saw ghosts float up out of their graves and fly away. Within an hour, all the ghosts returned to their graves but one. Mrs. Mackenzie blocked the grave by placing her staff over it. The ghost of a young woman appeared and demanded to be let back into her grave. Mrs. Mackenzie said she would do so if the ghost would explain why she had been gone so much longer than the others.

The ghost said she had much farther to travel—she was a Norwegian princess who had drowned while bathing. Her body was carried out to sea and then came ashore. She was buried there. Mrs. Mackenzie allowed the ghost to return to her grave, and in gratitude the ghost instructed her to search in a nearby lake, where she would find something of rare value, a small, round blue stone. She was to give that stone to her son, who would be able to see the future with it.

Mrs. Mackenzie found the stone, which had a hole in its center. Her son Kenneth discovered that when he looked through the hole, he could see the future.

Another version of the story says that the ghost of the princess told Mrs. Mackenzie to pick two white stones off her grave, which would bring good luck if they were used to help people. But when Mrs. Mackenzie did so, the ghost became anxious and proclaimed, "He will help a red-haired woman, and she will repay him with hell-fire." Mrs. Mackenzie threw the stones into a WELL, but Kenneth found them years later. She warned him never to help a red-haired woman. He eventually did, and it sealed his doom.

Yet another version says that Kenneth was cutting peat one day and laid down to sleep while he waited for his wife to bring him lunch. When he awakened, he discovered a small holed stone beneath his head. Looking through it, he saw his wife approaching with his lunch of curds that—unbenownst to her—had been poisoned by Kenneth's enemies. When Kenneth looked through the stone, he lost his physical sight in his left eye but gained second sight.

Kenneth adopted the Gaelic name Coinneach Odhar. He was called a *fiosaiche,* or "sorcerer." He achieved fame by making dire predictions that came true. Once while walking across a field in Drummoissie, he fell down and declared, "This black moor shall be stained with the best blood in the Highlands. Heads will be lopped off by the score, and no mercy will be shown or quarter given on either side." The field was the future site of a massacre of Scots during the rebellion of 1745–46.

Odhar's demise began with a summoning to Brahan Castle by Isabella, the wife of the third earl of Seaforth.

Isabella was concerned about her husband, who was overdue to return from a long trip to Paris. Odhar shocked her by informing her that her husband was in a Paris salon with another woman. Enraged, Isabella sentenced him to be burned on a pyre.

According to lore, the earl arrived home just as Odhar was being taken away to his execution. He tried to stay the execution. But Odhar sealed his own fate by delivering another PROPHECY to Isabella. "I see in the far future the doom of my oppressor," he is said to have stated. "I see a chief, the last of his house, both deaf and dumb. He will be the father of four sons, all of whom he will follow to the tomb. The remnant of his possessions shall be inherited by a white-coifed lassie from the East, and she is to kill her sister."

Isabella responded to this by ordering Odhar to be killed by having his head thrust into a barrel lined with spikes and filled with burning tar. The earl did not arrive in time to stop the execution.

Odhar's final prophecy came to pass but not for many years. An earl of Seaforth born in 1754 suffered scarlet fever at age 12 and lost his hearing. His four sons died young, causing the deaf earl to lose his ability to talk. He died on January 11, 1815. One of his daughters came home from India and inherited everything. One day she and her sister were out riding in a carriage; the older sister was driving. The carriage overturned and killed the younger sister.

Other prophecies of Odhar's also came to pass many years after his death.

In folklore, natural-holed stones possess magical powers for prophecy and also for healing.

FURTHER READING:
Gordon, Stuart. *The Book of Curses: True Tales of Voodoo, Hoodoo and Hex.* London: Brockhampton Press, 1994.

odic fluid   A term from 19th-century MESMERISM that refers to the universal life force. The odic fluid is approximately equivalent to the ASTRAL LIGHT of ELIPHAS LEVI and to the Akasha of Theosophy. In MAGIC and occult practices, odic fluid could be visualized as a protective barrier against negative or unwanted influences.

ointments   In MAGIC and ALCHEMY, special chemical and/or herbal salves that effect a transformation, a healing, or a CURSE.

During the WITCHCRAFT trials of the Inquisition, witches were believed to rub their bodies with magical ointments that enabled them to fly to their infernal sabbats. Some individuals who claimed to be WEREWOLVES said that they used magical ointments to achieve their SHAPE-SHIFTING from human to wolf form.

Such ointments most likely contained hallucinogens. Even as early as the 15th century, most demonologists believed the effects of magical ointments to be imaginary and not real. These conclusions were borne out by tests on accused witches whose ointments put them into deep sleeps—although they insisted upon awakening that they had been transported through the air.

In magic, ointments have been used to effect cures or BEWITCHMENT through sympathetic magic. For example, rubbing an ointment on an object owned by a person will have an effect on that person. Magical ointments have many purposes, such as inducing love, causing fear, and causing misfortune, illness, and death. A 16th-century recipe for a killing ointment, written as a CHARM, is as follows:

> Hemlock, juice of aconite,
> Poplar leaves and roots bind tight.
> Watercress and add to oil
> Baby's fat and let it boil.
> Bat's blood, belladonna too
> Will kill off those who bother you.

The alchemist PARACELSUS advocated a "weapon-salve" treatment that his critics considered to be nothing short of witchcraft. According to Paracelsus, wounds suffered in battle should be treated with a magical ointment applied both to the wound and to the weapon that caused the injury.

Paracelsus's ointment formula called for two ounces of moss taken from a buried skull, a half-ounce of embalmed human flesh, two ounces of human fat, two drams of linseed oil, and one ounce each of roses and bole armoniack (a type of acidic earth). The physician was to mix all of these ingredients together and add BLOOD of the patient. The wound would then be cleaned and treated with the ointment. It would be bound with bandages dipped in the patient's URINE.

Paracelsus also said that the ointment should be smeared on the weapon that caused the injury; it was sympathetic magic to his detractors. Paracelsus said that a mystical process of animal magnetism would draw on the sympathetic life spirit that flowed between wound and weapon.

Paracelsus was defended by the English physician and alchemist ROBERT FLUDD, who said that "the cure is done by the magnetique power of this Salve, caused by the Starres, which by the mediation of the ayre, is carried and adjoyned to the Wound."

Paracelsus's ointment was in use for a period of time and then disappeared.

The 17th-century English alchemist SIR KENELM DIGBY had a weapon-salve powder remedy. Digby claimed to have been given the secret for it by a Carmelite whom he met in Florence in 1622. The Carmelite had traveled in the East and claimed to learn the secret there. The powder was to be applied to a bandage stained with blood from the wound. The powder was green vitriol (ferrous sulfate). According to Digby, particles of the powder and blood found their way to the wound and healed it. He used this cure to heal a cut on the hand of Welsh author James Howell.

FURTHER READING:

Ashley, Leonard R. N. *The Amazing World of Superstition, Prophecy, Luck, Magic & Witchcraft.* New York: Bell Publishing Company, 1988.

Guiley, Rosemary Ellen. *The Encyclopedia of Witches and Witchcraft.* 2d ed. New York: Facts On File Inc., 1999.

Olympic Spirits   Spirits who dwell in the firmament and stars who govern the operations of the world. The Olympic Spirits are discussed in the *Arbatel of Magic,* a GRIMOIRE of anonymous origin and Christian influences dating to the 16th century.

According to the *Arbatel,* the universe is divided into 196 Olympic Provinces (the first edition of the grimoire gave 186 as the number, but this appears to have been a printer's error that was corrected in later editions). The provinces are ruled by seven governors who divide the number of provinces unequally among them. The governors preside over both operations in the natural world and also certain magical operations. The *Arbatel* states that correct pronunciation of the spirits' names is not necessary in magical work with them. Rather, the magician should call upon their offices and not use names at all, except for those given directly by the evoked spirits. Thus, different writers gave variations in the names of the Olympic Spirits, as well as variations in the details of their offices and other characteristics.

Governors

In the *Arbatel,* the seven governors and their offices, powers, functions, and characters (see SEALS) are:

Aratron.   Aratron rules 49 Olympic Provinces and governs things that are influenced by Saturn. He teaches ALCHEMY, MAGIC, medicine, and the secrets of INVISIBILITY. He confers FAMILIARS, fertility, and longevity. Aratron can transmute coal into treasure and treasure into coal and can change any living thing into stone. He reconciles subterranean spirits with humans (see ELEMENTS). He should be invoked on Saturday in the first hour of the day, using his character given and confirmed by himself.

Bethor.   Bethor rules 42 provinces and all affairs influenced by Jupiter. He comes quickly when evoked. He confers familiars and can extend life to 700 years, providing it is in accordance with the WILL of God. Bethor assists in finding large treasures. He reconciles the spirits of the air to humans so that they will give true answers in divination, transport precious stones, and concoct miraculous medicines.

Phaleg.   Phaleg rules 35 provinces and things governed by Mars. He is especially helpful in military matters and can help a soldier or an officer advance in his career.

Och.   Och rules 28 provinces and is a spirit of perfection. He extends life to 600 years with perfect health, confers excellent familiars, and concocts perfect medicines. He is the ultimate alchemist and is able to transmute any substance into the purest metals or precious jewels. He bestows GOLD and a purse "springing with gold." Whoever possesses his character will be worshiped as a god by the kings of the world.

Hagith.   Hagith rules 21 provinces and venereal matters. He confers faithful serving spirits. He converts copper into gold and gold into copper. Whoever possesses his character will be adorned with beauty.

Ophiel.   Ophiel rules 14 provinces and all things influenced by Mercury. He teaches all arts, including the ability to change quicksilver (mercury) instantly into the PHILOSOPHER'S STONE. He confers familiars.

Phul.   Phul rules seven provinces and all things governed by the MOON. He transmutes all metals into SILVER, heals dropsy, and confers spirits of water to serve humans in a visible form. He prolongs life to 300 years.

The governors are served by kings, princes, presidents, dukes, and ministers, all of whom have legions of inferior Olympic Spirits working for them.

Evocation and Dismissal

The *Arbatel* gives instructions for evoking the governors. The EVOCATION should be done on the day and in the hour of the planet associated with the governor and with the following Christianized PRAYER:

> O Eternal and Omnipotent God, who hast ordained the whole creation for Thy praise and Thy glory, as also for the salvation of man, I beseech Thee to send Thy Spirit N., of the Solar Race [or appropriate designation] that he may instruct me concerning those things about which I design to ask him [or that he may bring me medicine, etc.]. Nevertheless, not my will, but Thine be done, through Jesus Christ, Thine only-begotten Son, who is our Lord. Amen.

The spirit should be engaged for no more than an hour. It is discharged with the following:

> Forasmuch as thou camest in peace and quietness, having also answered unto my petitions, I give thanks unto God, in whose Name thou camest. Now mayest thou depart in peace unto thine own order, but return unto me again, when I shall call thee by thy name, or by thine order, or by thine office, which is granted from the Creator. Amen. [Then add:] Be not rash with thy mouth, and let not thine heart be hasty to utter anything before God: for God is in heaven, and thou art upon earth; therefore let thy words be few. For a dream cometh through a multitude of business, and a fool's voice is known by multitude of words.—Eccles. v. 3, 4.

FURTHER READING:

Waite, Arthur Edward. *The Book of Black Magic and of Pacts.* 1899. Reprint, York Beach, Maine: Samuel Weiser, 1972.

omen   In DIVINATION, a sign of a future event. An omen in and of itself is neither good nor bad.

Many omens are found in the natural world, such as changes in the ELEMENTS, the movements or appearances of animals and birds, and the movement of heavenly bodies. Unusual occurrences, such as monstrous births, eclipses, comets, meteors, novae, floods, storms, and earthquakes, have been considered to be omens of future disasters or of divine unhappiness with the state of human affairs. The ancient Babylonians, Sumerians, and Assyrians kept detailed records of such omens, interpreting nearly all events as portents of the future.

Other sources of omens are various methods of divination, dreams, and the appearance of apparitions and visions. In FAIRY lore, the banshee, or "fairy woman," is a spectral omen who wails to herald the impending death of members of old families and of great and holy persons. Joan of Arc's soldiers saw favorable omens in heavenly visions of the archangel Michael and of the Holy Spirit, which appeared as a dove perched on the Maid's shoulder.

See also PROPHECY.

FURTHER READING:

Seligmann, Kurt. *The History of Magic and the Occult.* New York: Pantheon Books, 1948.

Thomas, Keith. *Religion & the Decline of Magic.* New York: Scribners, 1971.

oracle   A person who practices DIVINATION and PROPHECY by allowing deities or supernatural beings to speak through them, often while in a trance. *Oracle* means "answer." Oracular divination is ancient and universal, and numerous techniques have been developed for its practice.

In ancient Greece and Rome, oracles were often sought by leaders for important political and military advice. The mediums were sibyls, women priestesses usually past child-bearing age, who resided in caves that were believed to be the thrones of deities. Major sibyls resided in Phrygia, Libya, Persia, Samos, Cumae, Cimmeria, Marpessa, Tibur, and Erythrae. The most famous was at DELPHI in a temple near Mount Parnassus, about 100 miles from Athens.

Zeus was oracle to the Romans, who believed that the god resided in the oak trees at Dodua and spoke through the mouths of the Peleiads (doves). The Peleiads may have been priestesses impersonating doves. The old Prussians believed that gods inhabited oaks and other high TREES and that they whispered answers to inquirers.

The ancient Babylonians consulted priestesses as oracles and also relied on the dream visions of deities. Major oracular centers were at Mani and in Sargonid Assyria. The goddess Ishtar was referred to as "She Who Directs the Oracles."

In the Old and the Middle Kingdoms of Egypt (2680–1786 B.C.E.), women of important families were known as prophetesses who had access to the goddesses Hathor and Neith. Other oracular consultation took place in the form of dreams. In the Middle Kingdom (2000–1786 B.C.E.), dreams were believed to be sent by the gods so that people might know the future. Oracular dreams were both induced and spontaneous. In the New Kingdom (1570–1342 B.C.E.), the first fully developed oracular procedure appeared with the use of cult statues. The statues—usually of Amun, the god of fertility, agriculture, and the breath of life—were carried in portable shrines on the shoulders of priests during festivals. The statues allegedly could nod and talk, perhaps due to surreptitious manipulation by a priest, or the priest indicated a "yes" answer by moving toward the enquirer and a "no" by recoiling. The statues were consulted by both commoner and royalty for predictions and dispensations of the law. A papyrus of magical SPELLS from the third century C.E. gives a RITUAL for transforming a boy into an oracle.

The primary function of ancient Hebrew priests was to divine and give oracles. The priests were consulted at sanctuaries where Yahweh, God, was believed to be present. Their procedure included the use of Urin and Thummin, of which little is known but apparently that were objects which the priests consulted. Answers were given by lots, though the oracle could give a "no-answer." Many answers required interpretation by the priests.

There is evidence that pre-Christian tribes of Germanic and Scandinavian peoples consulted oracles. The WIZARDS and village wise women of the Middle Ages who were consulted for their clairvoyant gifts were a form of oracle. The oracular practices were condemned by the Christian Church, even though a Christian priest functions as an oracle when he is consulted for advice, for he is expected to have a superior communication with God. Spiritualist mediums who consult the spirits of the dead also are a type of oracle.

In Welsh lore, the Awenydhon were a type of oracle who became inspired by spirit POSSESSION. They delivered answers to questions by violently roaring irrational and incoherent speeches that had to be interpreted.

The term *oracle* is rarely used in modern times, having been supplanted by such terms as *mediums, psychics, channelers,* and *intuitive consultants.*

FURTHER READING:

Brier, Bob. *Ancient Egyptian Magic.* New York: William Morrow, 1980.

Frazer, James G. *The Golden Bough: The Roots of Religion and Folklore.* New York: Avenel Books, 1981.

Marwick, Max (ed.). *Witchcraft and Sorcery.* Harmondsworth, Middlesex, England: Penguin Books, 2d ed., 1982.

Spence, Lewis. *The Magic Arts in Celtic Britain.* Van Nuys, Calif.: Newscastle Publishing, 1996.

Thomas, Keith. *Religion & the Decline of Magic.* New York: Scribners, 1971.

oraison A protective CHARM in Vodoun that is disguised as a Catholic PRAYER. The prayer is usually addressed to a saint such as Radegonde, Claire, or Bartholomew or to the archangel Saint Michael. It is written on paper and sewn into a pillow, pinned on a wall, or worn on clothing.

See also AMULET.

Order of the Knights Templar

Military arm of the Catholic Church during the Crusades and one of the most powerful monastic societies in Europe. The Order of the Knights Templar symbolized the holy struggle of Christians against the infidels. But the knights' enormous wealth, jealously coveted by kings and popes, and their secret RITUALS brought about their spectacular downfall and the establishment of SORCERY as evidence of heresy.

In 1118, about 20 years after the founding of the Kingdom of Jerusalem by Godefroy de Bouillon and a group of crusaders, French knight Hugues de Payns ("of the pagans") led a group of nine other French noblemen to the Holy Land, where they encamped next to the alleged site of King Solomon's Temple. Vowing to protect Christians traveling to the holy places, especially between Jerusalem and St. Jean d'Acre, the knights pledged chastity, poverty, and obedience. They called themselves the Order of the Knights of the Temple, or Templars.

Although led by de Payns, the real power behind the order was St. Bernard of Clairvaux, head of the Cistercian Order of monks and supported by Pope Honorius II. The Pope officially recognized the Templars as a separate order in 1128, giving it unheard-of sovereignty: It was exempt from local taxes; it could impose its own taxes on the community; it was immune from judicial authority; it could appoint its own clergy; and it answered only to the pope. Membership was restricted to men of noble birth who had to undergo various probationary periods and initiation rituals before acceptance. Attached to these noblemen were various artisans and manual laborers. The head of the order was the Grand Master, followed by his deputy the Senechal, the Marshal, and the Commander.

The Order's battle standard was a red eight-pointed cross on a background of black-and-white squares called the *Beauceant,* with the cross on a plain background of white as the official symbol. Their battle cry was *"Vive Dieu, Saint Amour"* ("God Lives, Saint Love"), and their motto was *"Non nobis Domine, non nobis, sed Nomini Tuo da gloriam"* ("Not for us, Lord, not for us, but to Thy Name give glory"). The Templar seal showed two knights sharing one horse, a sign of poverty and service.

By the beginning of the 14th century, the Templars had become one of the most powerful organizations in Europe and the Middle East, with branches in Scotland, England, Aragon, Castile, Portugal, Germany, and the Kingdom of Naples, all headquartered from the main temple in Paris. They had amassed huge wealth, and unlike the Order of Hospitalers of Saint John, supported no charities. They also lent money at rates lower than the Jews or Lombards.

For years stories circulated about the Templars' secret rituals and whether they were Christians or had become "Mahometans," or followers of Muhammad. The Templars had always maintained close ties with the Sufis, the mystic sect of Moslems, sharing their esoteric knowledge of ALCHEMY and the KABBALAH. The Templar battle cry, "God Lives, Saint Love," closely parallels the Sufi search for the Beloved as the symbol of God. The father of founder Hugues de Payns was a Moor from southern Spain and perhaps was heavily influenced by Sufi thought. Both Templars and Sufis admired each other's spiritual dedication and monastic determination.

Superstitious lore about the Templars claimed they worshiped a devil named BAPHOMET who appeared in various forms, including a huge black cat. These WITCHCRAFT rituals supposedly included kissing the cat's behind, bestiality, sodomy, kissing the Grand Master's genitals, roasting children alive, idol worship, denunciation of Christ and the Virgin Mary, intercourse with DEMONS and overall loss of their souls to the devil. All these rumors had been around since the Order's founding, but no one gave them much currency until 1307.

At that time, King Philip IV of France, called the Fair, was in debt to the Templars and was increasingly irritated at their protection from secular jurisdiction. He decided that the Templars' wealth was his last source of funds. On October 13, he seized the Temple in Paris and arrested Grand Master Jacques de Molay and 140 Templars, as well as every Templar his soldiers could find throughout France. Charged with heresy and blasphemy, the victims were hideously tortured to extract confessions. Needing the church's support, Philip bullied a weak Pope Clement V, the first Avignon pope, into signing a papal bull authorizing the Templars' trials and seizure of their properties.

The trials and tortures lasted for seven years, while the king and the pope bickered over jurisdiction and disbursement of the property. Few Templars could hold up under the severity of the tortures, and many went mad. Even de Molay at first denied Christ and confessed that the temple was seduced by Satan.

Philip's charges of heresy and witchcraft, supported by the tortured confessions, gave the Inquisition new evidence in its hunt for enemies, especially ones with valuable property. Such powerful arguments, preying on the deepest fears of the medieval mind, contributed to the eventual deaths of hundreds of supposed heretics and witches by the mid-1700s.

Pope Clement V officially abolished the order and all its branches in 1312 at the Council of Vienne, transferring the property to the Hospitalers. They, in turn, paid Philip IV money which he said the Templars had owed him. A great deal of the assets were seized directly by Philip and King Edward II of England for their own use or as gifts to friends. Resisting papal pressure, the kings of Spain and

Portugal transferred the remaining assets into new orders, allowing Templars to obtain membership.

In 1314, de Molay, completely broken during his seven years in prison, was promised life in prison instead of death if he confessed his crimes in public. In March, soldiers led the broken man and his chief lieutenant onto a scaffold in front of a packed crowd of clergy, nobility, and commoners. But de Molay, who had been Philip IV's friend and godfather to the king's daughter, frustrated the king's triumph by proclaiming his innocence and that of all the Templars. De Molay announced, "I admit that I am guilty of the grossest iniquity. But the iniquity is that I have lied in admitting the disgusting charges laid against the Order . . . to save myself from the terrible tortures by saying what my enemies wished me to say."

Enraged, Philip IV sentenced the Grand Master to be burned alive over a slow fire on March 14, 1314. As the flames took his body, de Molay supposedly cursed Philip's family to the 13th generation and called for Philip IV and Clement V to join him before God's throne within a year. Clement died within a month, Philip died in November, and Philip IV's Capetian dynasty withered within one generation, to be replaced by the Valois.

Although the truth probably died with Grand Master de Molay, temple tradition maintains that the order did not go with him. One persistent story says that some of the survivors of the persecutions fled to Scotland disguised as stonemasons. As a disguise, the Templars borrowed masonic symbols and called themselves Freemasons, giving birth to that secret society. The Templars were always known as builders, going back to the founding of the Order on the site of Solomon's Temple. One of the dearest wishes of their mentor, St. Bernard of Clairvaux, was to build cathedrals which would esoterically transmit the secret teachings that he carried from early church fathers. Sufi tradition also uses buildings as permanent repositories of esoteric knowledge.

Other lore holds that Geoffroy de Gonneville, a Templar, brought a message from de Molay before his death to a group of Templars meeting in Dalmatia, telling them of a resurgence of their order in 600 years. At the end of this meeting, or "convent," as it was called, the Supreme Council of the order remained in Corfu for three years and then dissolved. But before disbanding, the council supposedly launched the Order of the Rose-Croix, or Rosicrucians.

Later accounts insist that the 18th-century adept, the COMTE DE ST. GERMAIN, was a Templar. The comte also participated in Rosicrucian and Freemasonic rituals, and some Masonic scholars believe that he was attempting to reintroduce Templar secrets into those two organizations. Some believe that COUNT CAGLIOSTRO, another 18th-century occultist and a student of St. Germain's, was a Templar agent.

Regardless of whether the Knights Templar actually founded these organizations, their spiritual power lives on in the traditions of all secret societies and esoteric organizations.

See also CURSE; FREEMASONRY; ROSICRUCIANISM.

FURTHER READING:
Delaforge, Gaetan. "The Templar Tradition Yesterday and Today," *Gnosis*, No. 6, Winter 1988, pp. 8–14.
Gordon, Stuart. *The Book of Curses: True Tales of Voodoo, Hoodoo and Hex.* London: Brockhampton Press, 1994.
Hall, Manly P. *Masonic Orders of Fraternity.* Los Angeles: The Philosophical Research Society, 1950.
Mann, William E. *The Knights Templar in the New World: How Henry Sinclair Brought the Grail to Arcadia.* Rochester, Vt.: Inner Traditions, 2004.

Ordo Templi Orientis (OTO)   Quasi-Mason magical order founded in Germany in 1901 and focused on sex magic as the key to Hermetic and Masonic secrets.

The principal founders of the Ordo Templi Orientis (OTO) were Carl Kellner and Theodore Reuss. Kellner, born in 1851, was a wealthy Austrian industrialist and metallurgist and a high-ranking Freemason. He also was a member of the Hermetic Brotherhood of Light, which included sex magic in its RITUALS. In the 1890s, Kellner said he met three Eastern ADEPTS—a Sufi and two Hindu tantra masters—and received a "Key" to the esoteric mysteries.

Reuss, born in 1855, was a pharmacist, singer, and journalist also said to work as a spy for the Prussian police. Reuss joined FREEMASONRY in 1876. He also was Magus of the *Societas Rosicruciana* (Rosicrucian Society). Reuss was interested in reviving the defunct Bavarian Illuminati, a Masonic-based order founded by Adam Weishaupt in 1776, and he succeeded in establishing a new Order of the Illuminati in 1880. In 1886, he was a cofounder, along with Leopold Engel and Franz Hartmann, of the THEOSOPHICAL SOCIETY of Germany.

In 1895, Kellner approached Reuss about creating a Masonic rite for his secret Key. Kellner's idea was to do so through a reformed Hermetic Brotherhood of Light. In 1901, Reuss and Engel produced—but probably forged—a charter giving them the authority over the Bavarian Illuminati. The two, with Kellner, then founded a new and unnamed order. Initially, they relied on Masonic material for its rites. Reuss created a 10-degree system and wrote its original rituals. He became Grand Master of the Swedenborgian Rite, used in the first three grades of Masonry. By 1902, Reuss had acquired through his Masonic connections the 90th and 96th degrees of the Ancient and Primitive Rite of Memphis and Mizraim, and the 33rd degree of the Ancient and Accepted Scottish Rite. Kellner took the name Frater Renatus, and Reuss became known as Merlin and Peregrinus.

Kellner died in 1905, and Reuss assumed complete control as Outer Head of the still-unnamed order. After

Kellner's death, he named it the OTO. In 1906, Rudolph Steiner was chartered to found an OTO lodge; PAPUS was chartered in 1908.

ALEISTER CROWLEY joined the OTO in 1910 and was given an honorary seventh degree rank. According to lore, Reuss's attention was drawn to Crowley's *The Book of Lies*, published in 1912, in which Crowley described his ritual sex magic and ENOCHIAN MAGIC work with his initiate, VICTOR NEUBERG (see CHORONZON). Reuss contacted Crowley and told him that he knew the Key, the secret of the ninth degree, and therefore he must immediately take that rank. Crowley said he did not know the Key, but Reuss pointed it out in *The Book of Lies*. Crowley later said that instantly it flashed upon him that he indeed did hold the secret of the "future progress of humanity." (He did not, however, say exactly what the secret Key was, or which chapter of *The Book of Lies* contains it. Occultists have speculated that the Key lies in either chapter 36 or chapter 69). Crowley took the ninth degree and became head of the OTO in the British Isles. He quickly advanced to the 10th degree. He was invited to rework the OTO's ritual material. He removed most of the Masonic material and replaced it with his Thelemic magic.

In 1922, Reuss resigned and Crowley took over as Outer Head of the OTO. He continued to use the organization as a means for spreading his New Aeon gospel as dictated by the entity AIWASS in *The Book of the Law*. Some members of the OTO disapproved, and they withdrew to carry on their own versions of the OTO. Crowley's OTO continued on its own. The groups all expired under the Nazis during World War II but resurrected after the war.

Crowley named Karl Germer as his Outer Head successor, and Germer took over in 1947 when Crowley died. Germer, a German and a concentration camp survivor, emigrated to the United States. Under his leadership, the OTO languished; he initiated no new members, but he did charter a lodge in England, under the direction of Kenneth Grant. But when Grant started using his own material, Germer expelled him.

Germer did not arrange for a successor, and a vacuum was created with his sudden death in 1962. More than 1,000 persons claimed to be the new Outer Head. Grant continued the operation of his New Isis Lodge and called himself the only real Outer Head. In 1969, the OTO was reorganized by Grady McMurty in San Francisco, who assumed the title of "caliph." McMurty worked hard to rebuild the order, an effort that continued after his death in 1985. The OTO decided henceforth to keep the name of the caliph secret; he is referred to by his title, Hymenaeus Beta.

The OTO has lodges in more than 20 countries around the world. Crowley's material remains in the teachings and rituals.

JACK PARSONS was head of the Agape Lodge of the OTO, opened in Los Angeles in 1934 by his friend, Wilfred Smith.

FURTHER READING:
Carter, John. *Sex and Rockets: The Occult World of Jack Parsons*. Los Angeles: Feral House, 2004.

Osiris The Greek name for Ousir, the Egyptian god who enjoyed his greatest popularity as god of the dead. Originally, Osiris was a nature spirit, embodied in the crops that die in harvest and are reborn again each spring. According to the legend of his transformation as god of death, Osiris was a handsome king of Egypt who married his sister, ISIS. The SYMBOL of Osiris was the SUN, while the symbol of Isis was the MOON.

In a treacherous plot, Osiris's brother, Set, murdered him and hacked his body to pieces. Using MAGIC, Isis reassembled the body and breathed life back into him. In some versions of the story, Set murdered him again. Osiris preferred to remain in the domain of the dead rather than return to his throne. He served as king and judge of the dead; the *Book of the Dead* has approximately 100 litanies to him. Osiris is often portrayed with Isis and their posthumous son, Horus, in a trinity.

In the Egyptian mysteries of Osiris, his passion, death, and resurrection were reenacted in a fertility drama. The Romans absorbed Osiris's cult and spread it throughout the Roman Empire.

Osiris is a major figure in the magical rites of the HERMETIC ORDER OF THE GOLDEN DAWN, particularly for the grade of Adeptus Major. His myth is the foundation of an alchemical formula of transmutation to immortality and to magical power. The formula is expressed as I.A.O., Isis, Apophis, Osiris, birth, death, resurrection. Osiris died and then rose through the birth of Isis and the Higher Genius of THOTH to become the avenger son Horus. According to the mysteries, the initiate can only obtain true and lasting power when he submits the Self to the guidance of the Higher Self. Osiris reconciles the Lower Selfhood in which birth and death are unnecessary—the Bornless One (see BORNLESS RITUAL). The initiate becomes unified with Osiris.

ouanga A term used in Vodoun for TALISMANS, CHARMS, and so forth, especially FETISHES for love. An *ouanga* for an evil purpose is called a WANGA.

ouroboros (uroboros) Ancient symbol of a SERPENT biting its tail, forming a circle. The name *ouroboros* comes from the Greek terms *oura*, meaning "tail," and *boros*, meaning "devourer." The "tail-devourer" represents the eternal cycle of birth, death, and rebirth. The ouroboros is an important symbol in ALCHEMY and MAGIC.

Origins of the Ouroboros
The origins of the ouroboros can be traced to ancient MOON cults. The Moon served as timekeeper—especially

of the eternal, cyclical nature of time—and fertilizer of life on Earth below. Because the Moon waxed and waned, it became a symbol of birth, death, and regeneration. Lunar deities were often associated with a devouring snake or dragon, which, after swallowing the Moon, became the mother of the Moon's rebirth.

The ancient Egyptians depicted the goddess Buto as a cobra; in fact, the hieroglyph for *goddess* is a cobra. Buto protected ISIS and her son Horus, the sun god. Similarly, every individual in Egypt was protected by a personal snake spirit that symbolized their lifetime and their survival into the afterlife. In her form of the pharaoh's crown, Buto was called the *uraeus* and was the symbol of the pharaoh's power. She was most commonly depicted by the Egyptians as a serpent surrounding a solar disk. She was also depicted with the hieroglyph *shen*, a circle resting on a line that represents the Sun's orbit and thus eternal life. Perhaps the first true Egyptian depiction of the ouroboros comes from the tomb of Seti I, in which a carving shows the sun god lying on his back in a house surrounded by an ouroboros. Such art was intended to ensure the immortality of the deceased. The third shrine of the sarcophagus of Tutankhamen shows the deceased in a stylized profile with one ouroboros encircling his head and another encircling his feet.

The oldest Greek creation myth, the Pelasgian, says that Eurynome, the goddess of all things, emerged from Chaos; the north wind created Ophion, the great serpent. Mating with Ophion, Eurynome then took the form of a dove and created the world EGG, which Ophion encircled seven times. The egg hatched all things in creation.

The Orphics (sixth and seventh centuries B.C.E.), who believed in reincarnation, had variations of the Orphic egg myth. The Orphic cult, which strove to free the divine aspect of the soul that was imprisoned in the body, paved the way for Western mystery cults.

In classical times, the Greeks identified Chronos (Time) with the Earth-encircling river, Oceanos, that also encircled the universe in the form of a serpent with the zodiac on its back.

In the Hermetic philosophy that arose in Hellenistic Egypt, the ouroboros became a symbol of the underlying unity of spirit. The Gnostics, who believed the world to be at the center of the universe, believed that the ouroboros, or world serpent, marked the boundary between the world and the pleroma of heaven. Some Gnostics equated the world serpent with the evil demiurge (or Satan) who created the world and guards the gateway of escape. Gnostics equated the demiurge with the God of the Old Testament, the Alpha and Omega (the letter omega is similar in form to the Egyptian hieroglyph *shen*).

For the Naassenes and Ophite Gnostic sects, the ouroboros was equated with the serpent in the Garden of Eden. A hero rather than villain, the serpent helped Adam and Eve defy the demiurge Jehovah and obtain the first gnosis (knowledge) by eating the fruit from the Tree of Knowledge. Later, the serpent came to represent the guardian of the Tree of Life and therefore the gatekeeper to immortality.

Ouroboros on The Wheel of Fortune card in *The Alchemical Tarot* by Rosemary Ellen Guiley and Robert Michael Place. The winged crowned serpent represents the volatile, and the wingless serpent represents the fixed. Inspired by Abraham Eleazar's* Uraltes Chymisches Werk, 1760. *(Copyright by and courtesy of Robert Michael Place)*

In Roman mythology, the ouroboros was associated with Saturn, the god of time, who joined together the first and last months of the year like the serpent swallowing its tail. Saturn swallowed his children, and, with his scythe, symbolized the devouring of life or mortality.

In Renaissance Europe, Saturn continued to be associated with the ouroboros, and his scythe became the symbol of death. This association continued into more modern times, and the ouroboros came to decorate numerous Art Nouveau calendars.

The Ouroboros in Alchemy and Magic
In alchemy the fundamental message of the ouroboros is the changing of one thing into another, ultimately yielding

"All is One." It is a symbol for Mercurius and the union of opposites.

One of the oldest alchemical texts created in Hellenistic Egypt and included in the 11th-century Codex Marcianus, contains an image of the ouroboros. It symbolizes the underlying unity of the elusive PRIMA MATERIA, which exists in all matter and is simultaneously the beginning and goal of the Great Work. It is the PHILOSOPHER'S STONE, the vehicle for obtaining immortality, and it also represents the cyclical nature of the alchemical process, which is the union of the male and the female principles, their destruction, and their resurrection and reunification. The Codex Marcianus ouroboros is half black and half white, like the symbol for yin and yang in Taoism, thus depicting the sexual union of opposites that continually creates the world. Later alchemical imagery shows the ouroboros as two serpents devouring each other's tails, heightening the sexual symbolism. Another representation is two dragons fighting at each other's throats. The male and female principles are combined in their shared blood. An ancient Greek alchemical text says:

> Here is the mystery. The serpent Ouroboros is the composition in which our Work is devoured and melted, dissolved and transformed. It becomes dark green from which the golden color derives. Its stomach and back are the color of saffron; its head is dark green, its four legs are the four imperfect metals [lead, copper, tin, and IRON]; its three ears are the three sublimated vapors [SULPHUR, MERCURY, and SALT]. The One gives the Other its blood; and the One engenders the Other. Nature rejoices in nature; nature charms nature; nature triumphs over nature; and nature masters nature; and this is not from one nature opposing another, but through the one and the same nature, through the alchemical process, with great care and great effort.

On a higher level of the Great Work, the ouroboros represents the indistinguishable and eternal flow of sulphur and mercury into one another. The permanent fusion of the two creates the Philosopher's Stone.

From alchemy, the ouroboros was absorbed into European magical and mystical philosophies of such groups as the ROSICRUCIANS and the HERMETIC ORDER OF THE GOLDEN DAWN.

In dreams, the ouroboros often appears in variations such as the snake, the dragon, the egg, and the circle.

FURTHER READING:

Hauck, Dennis William. *The Emerald Tablet: Alchemy for Personal Transformation.* New York: Penguin/Arkana, 1999.

Jung, C. G. *Mysterious Coniuntionis.* 2d ed. Princeton, N.J.: Princeton University Press, 1970.

out-of-body experience   See ASTRAL PROJECTION; ASTRAL TRAVEL.

pact A binding agreement with a spirit, usually a DEMON, for services beyond the power of nature, such as procuring treasure. Informal pacts with demons and the devil exist in legend and folklore tales about individuals seduced into selling their souls. In ceremonial MAGIC, formal pacts are made enabling a magician to control a spirit for certain tasks and favors.

There are two types of pacts: a unilateral pact, in which a demon agrees to service without condition, and a bilateral pact, in which demon agrees to conditional service on penalty of forfeiture of the magician's body and soul. Pacts are dealt with in GRIMOIRES, handbooks of ceremonial magic. Regardless of type of pact, some spirits bind easily and some do not; the latter are dangerous and not to be trusted.

The most important grimoire, the *Key of Solomon*, mentions "penal bonds" and "pacts" only in connection with magic for love and favors but goes into no detail. Instead, the *Key* states that PENTACLES are sufficient to protect the magician from demons. Similarly, the *Grimorium Verum* has little to say about pacts and protection. The *Lemegeton* does not deal at all with the need for protection and pacts to armor the magician's soul from harm.

The *Grand Grimoire,* a book of black magic, emphasizes pacts as the means to secure demonic services. The book states that if the magician cannot master a kabbalistic circle (see MAGIC CIRCLE) and a BLASTING ROD (a wand feared by every demon), then a pact is an absolute necessity. Even with those two instruments of magic, a pact is advisable. Without the blasting rod and the kabbalistic

circle, a magician's prospects of success are slim, according to the grimoire.

A pact cannot be made with the top three demons named in the grimoire—Lucifer, Beelzebub, and Astaroth—but only with one of their lieutenants. It provides a written one between the magician and Lucifuge Rofocale, the prime minister of Lucifer. Lucifuge Rofocale is described as a reluctant and obstinate spirit who must be forced to appear with the use of the blasting rod and threats of CURSES.

The *Grand Grimoire* gives a Grand Conjuration of the Spirit for summoning Lucifuge Rofocale. When at last the demon appears, he demands that in exchange for his services, the magician "give thyself over to me in fifty years, to do with thy body and soul as I please." After more bargaining that involves threats from the magician to send him into eternal fire with the blasting rod, the demon agrees to appear twice a night except on Sundays and makes a written conditional pact with the magician. He recognizes the authority of the magician and his grimoire, agrees to provide requested services if properly summoned, and demands certain services and payment in return on penalty of forfeiture of the magician's soul:

> I also approve thy Book, and I give thee my true signature on parchment, which thou shalt affix at its end, to make use of at thy need. Further, I place myself at thy disposition, to appear before thee at thy call when, being purified, and holding the dreadful Blasting Rod, thou shalt open the Book, having described the Kabbalistic circle

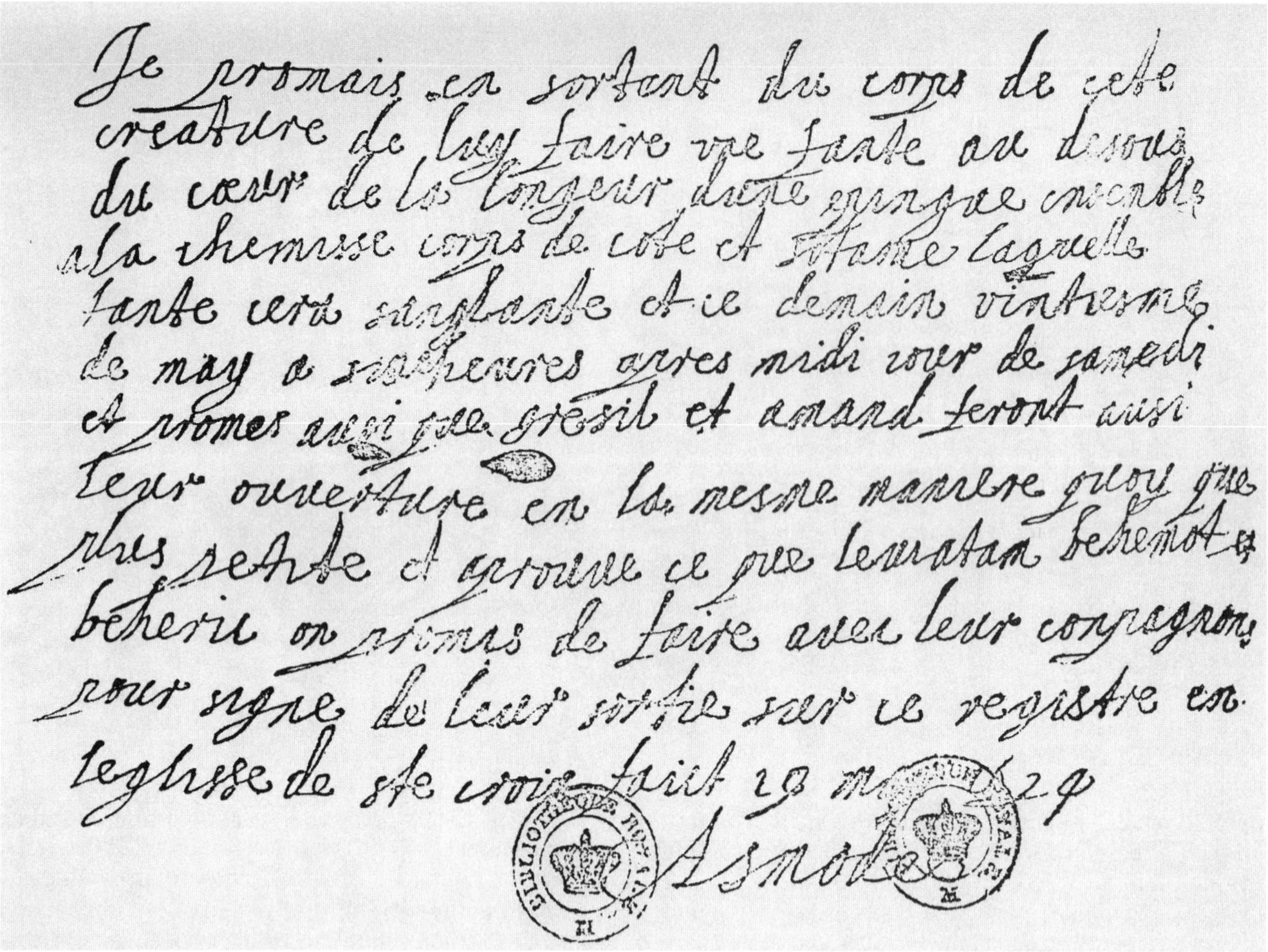

Pact signed by the demon Asmodeus, 17th-century manuscript. (Author's collection)

and pronounced the word Rocofale. I promise thee to have friendly commerce with those who are fortified by the possession of the said Book, where my true signature stands, provided that they invoke me according to rule, on the first occasion that they require me. I also engage to deliver thee the treasure which thou seekest, on condition that thou keepest the secret for ever inviolable, art charitable to the poor, and dost give me a gold or silver coin on the first day of every month. If thou failest, thou art mine everlastingly.

LUCIFUGE ROFOCALE

IMPRIMATUR

The reference to the "Book" is the spurious *Fourth Book*, a grimoire attributed to HENRY CORNELIUS AGRIPPA.

The *Grand Grimoire* tells how to make a pact with Lucifuge Rofocale, which must be signed by the magician with his own BLOOD. The magician collects the following TOOLS: a wand of wild hazel (not a blasting rod), a BLOODSTONE, and two blessed CANDLES. He goes to an isolated place either indoors or outdoors—the depths of a ruined castle are ideal. He makes a MAGIC TRIANGLE with the bloodstone

and enters it, holding his written pact, the Grand Conjuration of the Spirit, the hazel wand, the Clavicle (grimoire), and the discharge for dismissing the demon once business is concluded. He first conjures Lucifer, Beelzebub, and Astaroth to ask them to send Lucifuge Rofocale for the purpose of entering into a pact. When the demon finally appears, this exchange takes place:

Manifestation of the Spirit

Lo! I am here! What dost thou seek of me? Why dost thou disturb my repose? Answer me.

LUCIFUGE ROFOCALE

Reply to the Spirit

It is my wish to make a pact with thee, so as to obtain wealth at thy hands immediately, failing which I will torment thee by the potent words of the Clavicle.

The Spirit's Reply

I cannot comply with thy request except thou dost give thyself over to me in twenty years, to do with thy body and soul as I please.

LUCIFUGE ROFOCALE

Thereupon throw him your pact, which must be written with your own hand, on a sheet of virgin parchment; it should be worded as follows, and signed with your own blood:—I promise the grand Lucifige to reward him in twenty years' time for all the treasures he may give me. In witness thereof I have signed myself

N.N.

Reply of the Spirit

I cannot grant thy request.

LUCIFUGE ROFOCALE

In order to enforce his obedience, again recite the Supreme Appellation, with the terrible words of the Clavicle, till the spirit reappears, and thus addresses you:—

Of the Spirit's Second Manifestation

Why dost thou torment me further? Leave me to rest, and I will confer upon thee the nearest treasure, on condition that thou dost set apart for me one coin on the first Monday of each month, and dos not call me oftener than once a week, to wit, between ten at night and two in the morning. Take up thy pact; I have signed it. Fail in thy promise, and thou shalt be mine at the end of twenty years.

LUCIFUGE ROFOCALE

King James VI of Scotland, in his work *Daemonologie* (1597), agreed with the anonymous author of the *Grand Grimoire* that the need for a pact showed that a magician was too weak in power to secure the services of demons by magical means.

Pacts in Witchcraft

During the Inquisition, European witch hunters believed that witches entered into a "devil's pact," pledging to serve the devil or one of his satellite demons. The pact was said to be sometimes oral but traditionally was written on virgin parchment and signed in blood. The witch agreed to exchange allegiance and soul for the granting of magical power and all wishes and desires. Whereas the magician sought a pact for personal gain, such as finding treasure, the witch was believed to make a pact to obtain power to harm others out of pure malice. A witch's pact with the devil was either made privately, or was part of a ceremony conducted during a sabbat.

The devil's pact of the Inquisition was based on a long history of assumption among theologians that any practice of magic, SORCERY, or even DIVINATION had to involve a demonic pact. Such assertions were made by Origen (185–254) and by Saint Augustine (354–430), one of the most important fathers of the early church. In the 13th century, Saint Thomas Aquinas (c. 1227–74)—the church's greatest theologian, stated in *Sententiae*, "Magicians perform miracles through personal contracts made with demons."

Inquisitors tortured accused witches to force confessions of devil's pacts. There was no need to produce an actual document; an oral confession was sufficient to sentence the accused to death, often by burning at the stake. In two famous trials in 17th-century France, devil's pacts were produced, one orally and one in writing.

In 1611, Father Louis Gaufridi was tried on charges of causing nuns in Aix-en-Provence to be possessed. Under torture, he recited his pact verbally for the inquisitors:

I, Louis Gaufridi, renounce all good, both spiritual as well as temporal, which may be bestowed upon me by God, the Blessed Virgin Mary, all the Saints of Heaven, particularly my Patron St. John-Baptist, as also S. Peter, S. Paul, and S. Francis, and I give myself body and soul to Lucifer, before whom I stand, together with every good that I may ever possess (save always the benefits of the sacraments touching those who receive them). And according to the tenor of these terms have I signed and sealed.

One of Gaufridi's victims was a woman named Madeleine de la Paud, who also confessed orally to making a devil's pact:

With all my heart and most unfeignedly and with all my will most deliberately do I wholly renounce God, Father, Son and Holy Ghost; the most Holy Mother of God; all the Angels and especially my Guardian Angel, the Passion of Our Lord Jesus Christ, His Precious Blood and the merits thereof, my lot in Paradise, also the good inspirations which God may give me in the future, all the prayers which are made or may be made for me.

Father Gaufridi was convicted and burned alive at the stake. Sister Madeleine was convicted and was banished from the parish.

In 1633, Father Urbain Grandier, a parish priest of Saint-Pierre-du-Marche in Loudon, France, was brought to trial on charges of causing the nuns in Loudon to become possessed. A written pact was introduced as evidence. It was written backward in Latin and signed in blood. It read:

We, the all-powerful Lucifer, seconded by Satan, Beelzebub, Leviathan, Elimi, Astaroth, and others, have today accepted the pact of alliance with Urbain Grandier, who is on our side. And we promise him the love of women, the flower of virgins, the chastity of nuns, worldly honors, pleasures, and riches. He will fornicate every three days; intoxication will be dear to him. He will offer to us once a year a tribute marked with his blood; he will trample under foot the sacraments of the church, and he will say his prayers to us. By virtue of this pact, he will live happily for twenty years on earth among men, and finally will come among us to curse God. Done in hell, in the council of the devils.

(Signed by) "Satan, Beelzebub, Lucifer, Elimi, Leviathan, Astaroth.

"Notarized the signature and mark of the chief devil, and my lords the princes of hell.

(Countersigned by) "Baalberith, recorder.

Grandier was convicted and burned alive at the stake.

Pacts in Vodoun

A pact with a *loa,* or a god, in Vodoun is called an engagement. Such pacts usually are made only with evil *loas* and would be the equivalent of a demonic pact.

FURTHER READING:

Butler, E. M. *Ritual Magic.* Cambridge: Cambridge University Press, 1949.

Guiley, Rosemary Ellen. *The Encyclopedia of Witches and Witchcraft.* 2d ed. New York: Facts On File Inc., 1999.

Pelton, Robert W. *Voodoo Secrets from A to Z.* Cranbury, N.J.: A. S. Barnes and Co., 1973.

Waite, Arthur Edward. *The Book of Black Magic and of Pacts.* 1899. Reprint, York Beach, Maine: Samuel Weiser, 1972.

palmistry   A method of DIVINATION by studying the shapes of hands and lines on the hands. Palmistry is one of the oldest forms of divination. It is also known as cheiromancy or chiromancy, after CHEIRO, the pseudonym of "Count" Louis Harmon, a popular Irish fortuneteller of the 19th and early 20th centuries.

History of Palmistry

The exact age and origin of palmistry are not known. Prehistorical handprints found on cave walls in France, Spain, and Africa have a magical significance that may be connected with the earliest forms of palmistry. As a formal system of divination, palmistry was in use as early as 3000 B.C.E. in China and India. From the East, it spread through the Middle East and into Greek and Latin cultures. The ancient Greeks studied it, and Aristotle was interested in it. Among the early Hebrews, the Merkabah mystics read palms to determine if a man was fit to receive esoteric teachings.

Palmistry was widely popular during the Middle Ages, as were numerous other methods of divination that had an intellectual basis. In Hermetic thought, nothing in creation happens by chance. Humanity is a microcosm of the universe, and the body, in turn, is a microcosm of the person. Therefore, the lines on a hand are stamped by occult forces and will reveal character and destiny. Palmistry readers say that this view is reinforced by biblical scriptures:

- "Behold, I have graven thee on the palms of thy hands; thy walls are continually before me." (Isaiah 49:16)
- "He sealeth up the hand of every man; that all men may know his work." (Job 27:7)
- "Length of days in her right hand, and in her left hand riches and honor." (Proverbs 3:16)

In medieval Europe, hand readers were women: the village wise women, witches, and Gypsies. Among the kabbalists, rabbis were skilled at it, reading palms after Sabbath to foretell the future. Palmistry appeared in kabbalistic literature, including the *Zohar,* until about the 16th century.

Numerous medieval and Renaissance books and tracts were written about palmistry by the learned scientists of the day. The first textbook on palmistry, *Die Kunst Chiromantie,* was published in Germany in 1475, written by Johann Hortlich. In the 15th century, all such works were ordered confiscated by the Catholic Church, which forbade palmistry. The church was unsuccessful in squelching interest in it, as well as in other divination systems. In the 17th century, palmistry became a parlor art as scientific discoveries revealed that the universe operated according to immutable physical laws.

In the late 19th and early 20th centuries, palmistry enjoyed a revival of interest in the West, along with other divinatory arts. In 1889 the English Chirological Society was founded with the purpose of making the study of the hand a scientific pursuit. Cheiro, the pseudonym of "Count" Louis Harmon, an Irish fortune-teller (1866–1936), did much to popularize both palmistry and NUMEROLOGY. His books are still highly regarded.

Palmistry is practiced in modern times, though is not as popular as the TAROT and other methods. In India, China, and other parts of the East where the occult is more esteemed, palmistry has been treated more seriously and is part of some esoteric teachings. It is also a common divi-

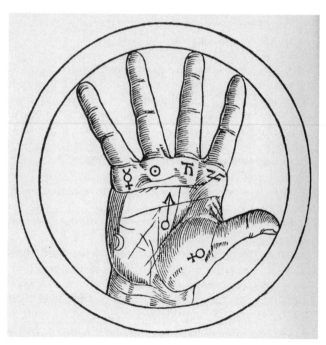

Planetary positions on the palm, in De Occulta Philosophia Libri III, *by Henry Cornelius Agrippa, 1533. (Author's collection)*

natory method used by Eastern fortune-tellers. As in all forms of divination, psychic and intuitive ability enhance the skill of the reader.

As a means of prediction, palmistry, like other forms of divination, reflects the conditions of the moment. Edgar Cayce once said that a palmistry prediction was about 20 percent absolute and 80 percent chance, depending on free will. Some palmists say choices can physically change the hands, within certain limits. In China, it is believed that the palm patterns can be improved through Zen and Yoga disciplines, especially in young children.

Elements of Palmistry
Palmistry is associated with ASTROLOGY. The signs of the zodiac, the SUN, the MOON, and the PLANETS are assigned spots on the hand. A palmist first looks at the shape of the hands, which indicates physical or artistic activities. The palmist then observes the lines, digits, fleshy mounts, and flexibility. The passive hand (usually the left hand) carries the imprint of destiny at birth and one's potential, while the dominant hand (usually the right) is a map of how that destiny has or has not been carried out.

Hand Shapes.   The shapes of the hands are associated with the four ELEMENTS and the characteristics that are in turn associated with those elements:

- Air hands have long fingers, square palms, and many fine lines. They indicate artistic talents, communication abilities, and emotional stability.
- Earth hands have short fingers and deeply lined square palms. They indicate a serious, practical nature and interests in physical activities.
- Water hands have long fingers, rectangular palms, and fine lines. They indicate sensitivity and a quiet personality who needs low-pressure jobs.
- Fire hands have short fingers, rectangular palms, and clear lines. They indicate an interest in high-risk, challenging occupations.

Palm Lines.   The palm has five major lines:

- The line of life, which rules longevity and stages in life
- The line of the heart, which rules emotions and intuition
- The line of the head, which rules the intellect
- The line of Saturn, which rules good fortune
- The hepatica line, which rules health.

In addition, marriage lines are on the outer palm, and numerous other small lines yield more details about a person.

Fingers and Thumbs.   The fingers and thumbs each are governed by a sign of the zodiac and thus rule certain characteristics. Finger shapes fall into four categories:

- Conic, which shows intuitive ability, sensitivity, impulsiveness, and a love of art and beauty
- Round, which shows a well-balanced disposition, adaptability, and openness to new things and change
- Square, which shows orderliness, clear communication, and confidence
- Spatulate, which shows independence, energy, enthusiasm, and a love of action and adventure

Thumbs—their length, shape, placement on the hand, and flexibility—reveal a person's personality.

Mounts.   Mounts are fleshy portions:

- The mount of Venus, at the base of the thumb, reveals emotions, sexual energy, compassion, warmth, and the ability to give and receive love.
- The mount of the Moon, located on the outer palm, reveals psychic ability, intuition, and imagination.
- The mount of Saturn, at the base of the middle finger, reveals one's introspective nature.
- The mount of Apollo, at the base of the ring finger, governs creativity and artistic ability.
- The mount of Jupiter, at the base of the index finger, rules self-confidence, leadership ability, and social sense.
- The mount of Mercury, at the base of the little finger, rules self-expression and disposition.
- The lower mount of Mars, located inside the thumb joint, governs assertiveness and perseverance.
- The upper mount of Mars, located beneath the mount of Mercury, rules determination, courage, and self-reliance.

The Palm Destinies of Napoléon and Josephine Bonaparte
Napoléon Bonaparte became interested in palmistry through his wife Josephine. Lunar aspects in the left hand of Josephine foretold that she would "enjoy boundless glory, have two husbands, amaze the world by her portentous fortune, and sadden her friends by her grievous and premature end," according to her palmist, Madame M. A. Le Normand. Her destiny was, for the most part, fulfilled.

Born Marie-Josephe-Rose Tascher de la Pagerie on June 23, 1763, Josephine was a comely but unsophisticated girl who aspired to the glittering courts of high society. In 1779 she married Alexandre, vicomte de Beauharnais, and bore him a son and a daughter. He lost his head to the guillotine in 1794 for his role in the revolution.

Josephine, by then quite sophisticated, caught the eye of Napoléon Bonaparte, a rising young general, whom she wed in a civil ceremony on March 9, 1796. He was madly in love with her, but she considered him primarily an entrée to the society she desired. During his Egyptian campaign from 1798 to 1799, she ignored his passionate love letters and instead amused herself by having an affair and running up stupendous debts with her lavish entertaining. The furious Napoléon threatened to divorce her but then relented. After he became emperor, Josephine persuaded him to marry her in a religious ceremony on December 1, 1804. However, she remained cool toward him and did not produce a male heir. Within a few years he decided to divorce her.

In 1807 Napoléon had his first palm reading with Le Normand, who astonished him by revealing secrets of his character, his tastes and desires, and, most important, his impending divorce of Josephine. The divorce had not yet been announced to either the public or Josephine. Fascinated, Napoléon ordered Le Normand to compile a complete record of her predictions. To ensure her discretion, he had her arrested and jailed for 12 days in 1809 until his split from Josephine was accomplished. He was able to nullify the marriage on a technicality—the absence of a parish priest at the religious ceremony. The marriage ended on December 14, 1809.

Napoléon then wed Marie-Louise, daughter of Emperor Francis I of Austria. Josephine, out of the limelight, retired to her private residence at Malmaison outside of Paris. She continued to throw lavish parties, however, and Napoléon continued to pay for them, perhaps out of guilt.

Soon after Napoléon's abdication, Josephine died quietly at Malmaison. She was 50, a respectable age for the times and certainly not premature in death, but her life ended in faded glory, which saddened her friends.

FURTHER READING:

Asano, Michael. *Hands: The Complete Book of Palmistry.* New York: Japan Publications, 1985.

Grillot de Givry, Emile. *Witchcraft, Magic and Alchemy.* New York: Houghton Mifflin, 1931.

Scholem, Gershom. *Kabbalah.* New York: New American Library, 1974.

Thomas, Keith. *Religion and the Decline of Magic.* New York: Scribner, 1971.

Papus (Gerard Encausse) (1865–1916) Physician, occultist, and author, known for his work on the TAROT and the KABBALAH and his leadership in MARTINISM. Papus was his pseudonym.

He was born Gerard Encausse on July 13, 1865, in La Corogne, Spain. His mother was Spanish and his father was a French chemist. When he was four, his family moved to Paris, where he was educated in medicine.

Papus was drawn to the occult and studied MAGIC and ALCHEMY. In the 1880s he joined the THEOSOPHICAL SOCIETY, but its emphasis on Eastern occultism failed to interest him, and he left. He was initiated into Martinism, and in 1884 he formed the Martinist Order with Pierre Augustin Chaboseau. Papus and Chaboseau also founded the

Supreme Council of the Martinist Order, which became the largest Martinist group in the world.

Papus gained fame for his occult knowledge. He evidently loved to found organizations, for he also helped create one of France's leading magical orders, *le Rose + Croix Kabbalistique* (The Kabbalistic Rose Cross) and the Independent Group for Esoteric Studies, which delved into ceremonial magic, ghosts, spiritualism, and folklore related to the occult.

Papus served in the medical corps of the French army during World War I. He died on October 25, 1916, of a lung infection.

Of his writings, the best-known is his book on the Tarot, *The Tarot of the Bohemians* (1889). The English translation was edited by ARTHUR EDWARD WAITE. Papus's other notable works are *Elementary Treatise on Occult Science* (1888), *The Divinatory Tarot* (1909), *The Qabalah,* and *Systematic Treatise of Practical Magic* (published posthumously in 1924).

paquet In Vodoun, special types of CHARM BAGS held to have great therapeutic powers. A *paquet* is a small flannel bag that contains mixtures of secret powdered ingredients, such as roots, herbs, spices, and flowers. The bags are made and consecrated in special RITUALS. RED bags are made for men, and black bags are made for women.

A *paquet congo* is a variation in which the powdered fillings are stuffed into a POPPET instead of a bag. A female *paquet congo* is distinguished from a male poppet only by the addition of earrings. A *paquet congo* is the most powerful type of magical doll and is used both for protective purposes (see AMULET) or as a WANGA.

Paracelsus (1493–1541) One of the greatest of alchemists and Hermetic philosophers, whose popular but unorthodox healing methods and supreme arrogance ran him afoul of the medical establishment. Paracelsus believed in natural MAGIC, a holistic approach to medicine, and the existence of the auric field as an influence on health. His contemporaries called him the Second Hermes and the Trismegistus of Switzerland. He is an important figure in the development of modern orthodox medicine and homeopathic medicine. MANLY PALMER HALL called Paracelsus a patron of forlorn causes who endured much ridicule in his lifetime but whose ideas have regained merit in modern times.

Paracelsus was born on either November 10 or December 17, 1493, (both dates are given in biographies) in Maria-Einsiedeln, near Zurich, Switzerland. He was the only son of a poor German physician; his mother died in childbirth or soon thereafter. He was christened Philippus Aureolus Theophrastus Bombast von Hohenheim. He was known as Theophrastus until he graduated from college, when he renamed himself Paracelsus, or "above Celsus," which reflected his egotistical belief that he was greater than the Roman physician Celsus.

Little is known of Paracelsus's early life. His father moved to Villach, near Klagenfurt, when the boy was nine. According to lore, Paracelsus learned ALCHEMY and medicine from his father.

Paracelsus probably studied at the university and Basel. In 1514 he went to work in the mines and metallurgical workshops in Tyrol, working for Sigismund Fugger, an alchemist. In just a year's time, Paracelsus learned a great deal from Fugger.

From then on, throughout the rest of his life, Paracelsus exhibited a restlessness that kept him on the move. He traveled throughout Europe and was even said to visit Russia and the Far East. He may have worked as an army surgeon. In Italy, he earned a medical degree at the University of Ferrara. He traveled for 12 years, amassing a great deal of knowledge from metallurgists, physicians, alchemists, and other occultists. According to lore, he learned the Hermetic secrets from Arabian adepts in Constantinople and learned about ELEMENTALS and other residents of the spirit world from the Brahmins of India. He was a devout student of the Bible and mingled his Christian beliefs with his esoteric wisdom.

Paracelsus settled in Strasbourg, where he quickly gained fame as a physician. He cured a prominent publisher in Basel of an unspecified illness that had resisted other therapies. Suddenly Paracelsus was famous, and he was named to the post of City Physician and Professor of Medicine.

As a doctor, Paracelsus was renowned for his gift of healing. However, his egotism antagonized his peers. His searing put-downs of colleagues were so offensive that he seldom lasted long in a post. In Basel, Paracelsus dedicated himself to reforming all of medicine. He scandalized his students and peers by publicly burning the revered medical texts of Galen and Avicenna.

His disdain for physicians was exceeded only by his alleged disdain for women. (There is no record of any romantic involvements in his entire life.) His *The Book Concerning the Tincture of the Philosophers* was subtitled *written against those sophists born since the deluge, in the age of our Lord Jesus Christ, the Son of God,* an example of his contempt for all physicians throughout history. He states in the text, "... I have been chosen by God to extinguish and blot out all the phantasies of elaborate and false works, of delusive and presumptuous words, be they the words of Aristotle, Galen, Avicenna, Mesva, or the dogmas of any among their followers."

Paracelsus's stay in Basel lasted only two years, for then he had thoroughly offended all of his professional colleagues. He was often drunk, rude, and loud and had a sharp tongue. He readily insulted the intelligence and practices of other physicians, calling them idiots, infants, sausage-stuffers, clownish concocters, ignorant sprouts, and wormy and lousy sophists. He was especially disdainful of the herbal remedies that were still in vogue at the time, calling them "loathsome and fulsome filthy potions." Furthermore, he bragged that he was first among physi-

Paracelsus, in Archidoxa, Munich 1570. (Author's collection)

cians and had made more cures than all physicians of Europe combined.

The last straw in Basel came when he publicly burned the works of IBN SINA (Avicenna) and Galen in a brass pan with sulphur and nitre to show his contempt for traditional medicine. Paracelsus proclaimed that these towering figures were "sticking in Hell." He proclaimed that his cap had "more learning in it than all the heads in the university," and his beard had "more experience than all the academies." He said he had no need to praise himself because Nature praised him, as exemplified in this passage from *The Treasure of Treasures for Alchemists:*

O, you hypocrites, who despise the truths taught you by a true physician, who is himself instructed by Nature, and is a son of God himself! Come, then, and listen, impostors who prevail only by the authority of your high positions! After my death, my disciples will burst forth and drag you to the light, and shall expose your dirty drugs, wherewith up to this time you have compassed the death of princes, and the most invincible magnates of the Christian world. Woe for your necks in the day of judgment! I know the monarchy will be mine. Mine, too, will be the honor and the glory. Not that I praise myself: Nature praises me. Of her I am born, her I follow. She knows me, and I know her. The light which is in her I have beheld in her; outside, too. I have proved the same in the figure of the microcosm, and found it in that universe.

His colleagues attempted to oust him from his post, but the city authorities supported him. However, his lectures were marred by catcalls and interruptions. The end came when the Canon Lechtenfels, a prominent citizen, became ill and offered a fee to anyone who could cure him. Paracelsus did so, but the canon refused to pay him. Paracelsus sued the man in court, but the sentiment against him was so great that he lost the case. He then heaped abuse on the magistrates. Threatened with severe punishment for contempt of court, he fled the city.

He roamed throughout Europe, plagued by increasing drinking problems. He borrowed money in taverns to pay for his drink. Lore holds that he always repaid the loans with handsome interest from some mysterious fund. He wore clothes until they were rags. He worked cures and revised old manuscripts, making a brief comeback with the publication of *Wundartzney* in 1536.

The prince-archbishop Duke Ernst of Bavaria invited Paracelsus to Salzburg in 1541. Within six months Paracelsus died, on September 24. He was 51 years old. The cause and circumstances of his death are not known. According to one story, his body was found on a bench at the White Horse tavern in Salzburg. Stories circulated that he had died during a drunken orgy or that he was poisoned or killed in a scuffle with assassins who were hired by his enemies. Some of his friends claimed that jealous physicians hired an assassin to push him off a cliff. After he was buried, his bones were dug up several times, moved, and reburied. A fracture in his skull was revealed to be caused by rickets. Paracelsus evidently sensed his impending demise, for he made out his will three days before his death.

Paracelsus was revered as a great healer by the public, who kept his memory alive. As late as 1830 when an epidemic of cholera swept close to Salzburg, people made pilgrimages to his grave and prayed. The cholera spared the residents of Salzburg but ravaged other parts of Austria and Germany.

During Paracelsus's time, the Hermetic wisdom was rediscovered and put to use. Paracelsus was the first man to write scientific books for the public. His writings comprise most of what is known about the ancient Hermetic system of medicine. His collected works were published in 10 volumes between 1589 and 1591.

Paracelsus's works attracted a growing following, and by 1570 a distinct Paracelsian school of thought existed. His work was a major factor in the inclusion of chemistry in university teachings.

Despite his bombast and lack of social graces, Paracelsus was unparalleled in his innovations in chemistry and medicine. He believed in a universal, natural magic that was bestowed on all things by God and that was manifested in physicians as healing ability. All things in nature served a good purpose, he said, even the midnight dew (see CELESTIAL DEW) that he collected on plates of glass.

His natural remedies often worked when the traditional wisdom of the day did not. While other doctors treated wounds by pouring boiling oil on them to cauterize them or simply by amputating flesh after it became gangrenous, Paracelsus maintained that wounds would heal naturally if kept clean and drained. He is credited with successfully treating syphilis, gout, leprosy, and ulcers with MERCURY. He also practiced an early form of homeopathy by treating plague victims with minute amounts of their own excrement. He practiced holism, believing that mind and body affected the other.

Paracelsus said that all things live in and radiate light that is different from ordinary light—it is the vitalizing force of the universe that creates health and well-being. Invisible light carries wisdom, and visible light, the light of Nature, nourishes the body. IMAGINATION, he said, is the route to self-discovery. When conscious WILL and the intellect are flooded with the light of Nature, one's destiny is fulfilled. There are three suns in the solar system:

- A physical sun warms and reveals the body of things and dissipates crystallization.
- An astral sun reveals the structure of the soul and dissipates the darkness of ignorance.
- A spiritual sun nourishes the human spirit and dispells the darkness of death.

Paracelsus believed the Hermetic principle that man has a vital body, an etheric double created and energized by the vital life force of the universe, and that when the vital body is depleted, physical ailment results. Paracelsus said the vital body could be reenergized by bringing it into contact with another vital body that had an overabundance of the vital life force. He is credited with having been the original discoverer of MESMERISM, a theory of magnetic healing put forward in the late 18th century by Franz Anton Mesmer. Paracelsus used concentrated mental energy to stimulate bodily functions in a patient. He was well aware of the dangers of this power, which if misused would degenerate into mental SORCERY. He said that only the most qualified physicians should use mental healing powers.

Like most alchemists and physicians of his time, Paracelsus believed in ASTROLOGY, that man was governed by the movements of heavenly bodies. He held that sickness and wellness are controlled by astral influences. The key to curing illness was secret remedies that restored the celestial harmony between the inner astrum, or star within man, and a heavenly astrum. The remedies were physical, but their healing components were spiritual. Paracelsus believed that all physicians should be knowledgeable about astrology and stellar influences. He used magical astrological TALISMANS in his work, metal disks inscribed with planetary SYMBOLS.

The careful preparation of medicines was crucial to their success, he believed. Substances possess a variety of spiritual powers, which affect one disease one way and another disease in another manner. Paracelsus believed strongly in the principles of sympathetic magic in healing. One of his most famous remedies was *mumiae*, a substance taken from Egyptian mummies. Later, other substances were used. The *mumiae* absorbed the vibrations of illness and also absorbed beneficial vibrations of other substances and things in nature, which could then be imparted into ill patients through physical contact.

In alchemy, Paracelsus regarded metal transmutation as secondary to the real, spiritual purpose of the art, especially as it pertained to medicine and healing. His primary tutor in the alchemical arts was a mysterious ADEPT named Solomon Trismosin, who taught Paracelsus how to obtain the PHILOSOPHER'S STONE in Constantinople. Paracelsus referred to the stone as the Tincture and the Lili of Alchemy and Medicine; he said that it was a "Universal Medicine, and consumes all diseases, by whatsoever name they are called, just like an invisible fire." Only small doses were necessary, he said. By this means, he claimed to have cured "leprosy, venereal disease, dropsy, the falling sickness, colic, scab, and similar afflictions; also lupus, cancer, noli-me-tangere, fistuals, and the whole race of internal diseases, more surely than one could believe."

He said that the PRIMA MATERIA is the essence of the world soul (see ANIMA MUNDI) and is key to creating spiritual GOLD. He said that MERCURY, SALT, and SULPHUR are the TRIA PRIMA buildings blocks of all things. He led the way in introducing chemical compounds into medicine and in describing zinc, a term he invented. He also invented the terms ALKAHEST (a universal solvent) and *spagyric*, a description of the art of alchemy. He applied the term *alcohol* (*al-kohl*), which referred to black eye-paint, to wine.

CARL G. JUNG considered the psychological aspects of Paracelsus's alchemy to represent the path of individuation or of becoming perfect and whole.

See also OINTMENTS.

FURTHER READING:

Hall, Manly P. *The Secret Teachings of All Ages.* 1928. Reprint, Los Angeles: The Philosophic Research Society, 1977.

———. *Paracelsus: His Mystical and Medical Philosophy.* Los Angeles: The Philosophic Research Society, 1964.

Holmyard, E. J. *Alchemy.* New York: Penguin Books, 1957.

Paracelsus. "The Book Concerning the Tincture of the Philosophers," in *Hermetic and Alchemical Writings of Paracelsus,* A. E. Waite, trans. 1894. Available online. URL: http://www.sacred-texts.com/alc/paracel2.htm. Downloaded January 10, 2005.

———. "The Treasure of Treasures for Alchemists," in *Hermetic and Alchemical Writings of Paracelsus* A. E. Waite, trans. 1894. Available online. URL: http://www.sacred-texts.com/alc/paracel1.htm. Downloaded January 10, 2005.

Seligmann, Kurt. *The History of Magic and the Occult.* New York: Pantheon Books, 1948.

Parsons, John Whitesides (1914–1952)

American chemist and magician and a follower of ALEISTER CROWLEY. John (known as Jack) Parsons was regarded as a brilliant physical chemist. He participated in the founding of the California Institute of Technology, where he worked as an expert in rocket propulsion.

Parsons was born on October 2, 1914, in Los Angeles. He was named Marvel Whiteside Parsons after his father, Marvel H. Parsons, and his mother, whose maiden name was Ruth Virginia Whitesides. He was their second child; their first died in infancy. Soon after Parson's birth, his mother left his father out of anger over an extramarital affair. It is uncertain whether they ever legally divorced. Ruth began calling her young son John but never legally changed his name. John favored the nickname Jack as he grew older.

As a boy, Parsons was fascinated by science fiction and rockets, and he and his friend Edward S. Forman experimented with small rockets, using dangerous combinations of black powder fuel. The two formed a lifelong friendship and working relationship.

In 1932 Parsons went to work for the Hercules Powder Company in Pasadena, where he refined his expertise on powder explosives. In 1933 he graduated from the private University School in Los Angeles. He and Forman attended Pasadena Junior College and went on to the University of Southern California, from which neither of them graduated. In 1935 Parsons married Helen Northrup.

Parsons and Forman were hired by the Guggenheim Aereonautical Laboratory, which became the Jet Propulsion Laboratory in 1936. With Frank Malina, they played key roles in the development of the United States's new rocketry program, as well as in jet projects for the U.S. Army Air Corps and the U.S. Navy.

In the late 1930s, Parsons discovered the works of Crowley and told friends that he was in correspondence with him. Parsons was strongly attracted to Crowley's sex magic, and soon a colleague introduced him to Wilfred T. Smith, the leader of the Agape Lodge of the ORDO TEMPLI ORIENTIS, located in Los Angeles. Parsons and his wife began attending meetings and the lodge's Gnostic Mass, Crowley's version of the Catholic mass that Crowley said was corrupted. Crowley had made the Gnostic Mass one of the OTO's central rites, and it was used to recruit new members. Parsons advanced in his occult knowledge and learned ASTRAL TRAVEL and other skills.

In 1940 Parsons met the actress Jane Wolfe, who had been initiated by Crowley at his Abbey of Thelema (Cefalu) in Italy. Wolfe considered Parsons to be "potentially bisexual" and the genuine successor to Crowley. Smith also saw great potential in Parsons, writing to Crowley that he was going to be valuable to the OTO. Jack and Helen officially joined the Agape Lodge on February 15, 1941. Parsons took the name Frater T.O.P.A.N., or Frater 210 for short; 210 was a number significant in Crowley's magic, the precise meaning of which Crowley said was "too holy" to reveal. T.O.P.A.N. had a dual meaning of "To Pan" and also

Parson's MAGICAL MOTTO, *Thelemum Obtentum Procedero Amoris Nuptiae*, or "The Obtainment of Thelema through the Nuptials of Love." Helen became Soror Grimaud.

Thus Parsons entered into a double life. By day he was a brilliant and successful rocket scientist, earning large sums of money, regarded as well educated and cultured by his peers. By night he was an occultist and magician, participating in rites that his peers would have found shocking and bizarre. Parsons became dedicated to bringing Crowley's New Aeon into manifestation. He was devoted to Smith. He and Helen turned their bedroom in their mansion into a temple and massed a library of occult works. Parsons rented out rooms in his mansion to occultists, offending the neighbors with frequent, loud parties involving strange RITUALS. A thrill-seeker, Parsons engaged in increasingly dangerous occult rituals, which he acknowledged might have undesirable side effects such as the creation of permanent haunting phenomena. He liked to evoke ELEMENTALS, some of which were lingering and troublesome in the bedroom temple. Banishing rituals were conducted frequently.

Rumors circulated that Parsons was leading a black magic cult. There were police investigations, but no action against Parsons was taken.

Parsons became one of Crowley's main sources of funding in the United States and funneled large sums of money to him in England through Crowley's named OTO Outer Head successor, Karl Germer. This arrangement lasted until Crowley's death in 1947.

Germer despised Smith and succeeded in influencing Crowley to retire him from the Agape Lodge. Leadership was taken over by Parsons. Meanwhile, Helen had become Smith's lover and bore him a son in 1943. Parsons divorced her the same year and entered into a relationship with her younger sister or half sister, Betty, whose real name was Sara. He told others that he had gotten rid of Helen by means of WITCHCRAFT. Betty was 18 years old, 11 years younger than Parsons. He encouraged her to take other lovers, and he engaged in affairs himself. He began to use drugs frequently in his magical work.

In April 1945, Parsons met L. Ron Hubbard, who became the founder of Scientology. Hubbard liked Parsons and moved in with him and Betty. Hubbard and Betty began an affair. In a letter to Crowley, Parsons enthused about Hubbard, noting that he had no formal training in magic but possessed a keen natural ability for it.

Despite Parson's sexual open-mindedness, he resented Hubbard's affair with Betty, and he conducted a ritual to overcome his jealousy. He told Crowley that, though he bore Betty and Hubbard no ill will, he desired to have a female magical partner on his own terms. He resolved to summon magically an elemental in a female form who would serve as his ideal companion and partner. The ritual was supposed to be performed alone, but Parsons performed it in the presence of Hubbard, who acted as scribe.

The Babalon Working, as the event became known, began on January 4, 1946, and was repeated several times until January 15. Babalon, Crowley's spelling for Babylon, is the ultimately desirable harlot inspired by the ENOCHIAN MAGIC of JOHN DEE and EDWARD KELLY. The elaborate working involved numerous invocations of spirits, Enochian calls, a wand TALISMAN magically charged with semen and BLOOD, and magical masturbation, that is, sexual arousal without release so that the energy is absorbed back into the body. Parsons specified that the manifested elemental would have red hair and green eyes.

As of January 15, the results were disappointing—only a violent wind storm. In February 1946, a woman artist from New York named Marjorie C. appeared, and Parsons recognized her as the result of his summoning. She was red-haired with green eyes. Parsons described her as "strong-minded and determined, with strong masculine characteristics and a fanatical independence."

Parsons and Marjorie performed sex magic for several weeks to invoke Babalon. Parsons informed Crowley in cryptic terms of his progress and impending success. Crowley dismissed it as an ill-intentioned effort to create a moonchild, a magical child. In late February, Marjorie split from Parsons and returned to New York, where she discovered she was pregnant.

Parsons performed a ritual alone to invoke Babalon. He said the presence of Babalon commanded him to write. The result was the 77-verse *Liber 49*, which Parsons viewed as the fourth chapter to Crowley's *The Book of the Law*. He also took it as further indication that he was to create a magical child into which Babalon would incarnate and fulfill Crowley's prediction of the birth of one "mightier than all the kings on earth." Only two chapters of Parsons's original book survive.

In March 1946, Marjorie returned to Parsons and began living with him. They resumed sex magic, and Hubbard served as the scryer to convey messages from Babalon. The rituals went on for some time. Crowley reacted to this with concern, warning Parsons not to become too attached to Marjorie. He quoted ELPIHAS LEVI, saying that "the love of the Magus for such things is insensate and may destroy him." The same month, Parsons stepped down as head of the Agape Lodge and turned it over to Roy Leffingwell.

The Babalon Working failed; Marjorie did not have a magical child. But nine years later, she claimed to be Babalon herself and to have given birth on the ASTRAL PLANE to a magical child.

While the Babalon Working was going on, Parsons, Betty, and Hubbard pooled money to purchase a yacht with the intention of reselling it for a profit; Parsons put up most of the funds. Betty and Hubbard deserted Parsons and left in the yacht. Parsons told Crowley he used magic to force them to return. Within the first few hours of their departure, Parsons said he performed a full EVOCATION to Bartzabel, the spirit of Mars, causing the yacht to be struck by a sudden squall. The severity of the storm ripped off the yacht's sails and forced a return to port. Parsons seized the damaged boat but lost most of the money he had invested.

Parsons retreated from magic and focused instead on his rocketry career. He was targeted by the Federal Bureau of Investigation and in 1948 lost his security clearance. FBI documents describe Parson's magical activities as a "mythic love cult," but the agency maintained that the real reason for their investigation was his ties to known Communists. His clearance was restored a year later in March 1949. In January 1952 Parsons permanently lost his security clearance. Meanwhile, on the magical front, he decided to pursue contact with his HOLY GUARDIAN ANGEL. His efforts, he told Germer in a letter, produced "acute psychosis . . . manic hysteria and depressing melancholic stupor."

With the loss of his security clearance, Parsons found part-time work for a powder company and did explosives consulting for films. On June 17, 1952, Parsons was working in his garage at home when two violent explosions ripped through it. Severely injured, he survived the explosions and was conscious when he was dragged out by neighbors. He died in a hospital about a half hour later, saying, "I wasn't done." Informed of her son's death, Ruth was shattered. Within a few hours, she committed suicide by overdosing on sleeping pills.

The explosion was said to be an accident due to Parsons's alleged mishandling of cordite and mercury fulminate, a sensitive detonator. But those familiar with his magical interests thought that the explosion resulted from his ongoing efforts to manifest Babalon.

FURTHER READING:
Carter, John. *Sex and Rockets: The Occult World of Jack Parsons.* Los Angeles: Feral House, 2004.
King, Francis. *Megatherion: The Magickal World of Aleister Crowley.* New York: Creation Books, 2004.

pelican See ALEMBIC.

pellar In English folk MAGIC and WITCHCRAFT, a country practitioner of magical arts. *Pellar* is probably a corruption of *expel,* as in the repelling or expelling of SPELLS. A pellar was considered especially skillful in breaking BEWITCHMENT, CURSES, and other negative spells.

Pellars were believed to acquire their gifts through heredity or supernatural means, such as bestowal of power by a spirit or fantastical creature such as a mermaid. Traditionally, people undertook annual trips to see a pellar, usually in the spring, for it was believed that the pellar's magical powers increased with the increasing rays of the SUN.

Pellars made CHARMS for their clients from herbs, powders, ointments, potions, stones, and perhaps teeth, bones, and dirt taken from graves. These were placed in little bags to be worn about the neck as an AMULET. Sometimes powders and earth from graves were to be thrown over children, cattle, or other livestock as a way of protecting them against bewitchment and the EVIL EYE, or the clients might be given bits of paper or parchment inscribed with mysterious words or astrological signs that were copied from magical texts such as BLACK BOOKS or GRIMOIRES. All magical prescriptions were to be kept secret by the clients, lest they lose their magical potency.

FURTHER READING:
Bottrell, William. *Cornish Witches & Cunning Men.* Kelvin I. Jones, ed. Penzance, England: Oakmagic Publications, 1996.

pendulum A rodlike instrument with a suspended weight used to tap into energy fields for purposes of DIVINATION. The pendulum appears to read energy patterns emanating from beings and objects, and it communicates the information to the user by swinging back and forth or in circles.

Pendulums are one of the TOOLS used in DOWSING for the detection and measurement of radiations that come from mineral, plant, animal, or human sources. The weight can be any object—a metal plumb, a button, a coin, for example—that is hung from a rod by a thread, string, or wire.

The precursor of the pendulum is the divining rod or wand, used for magical and practical purposes by various peoples since ancient times and referred to in the Bible as Jacob's Rod. Like the divining rod, the pendulum works on the principle that every organism is surrounded by various types of energy, some positive and some negative. Each living organism must develop a means by which it can sense these energies so that it can use the positive energies and avoid the negative. The pendulum serves as a tool that humans apparently can use to amplify the signals. It is not known exactly how this process takes place, but the user seems to be able to "tune in" intuitively or psychically to the frequency of whatever is being sought, including emotions. It is theorized that the nervous system and psychic sense are involved. Most persons are able to use a pendulum with success, but some individuals seem to have an innate gift for it.

Uses of the pendulum have been diverse throughout history, but the most common are the finding of water, minerals, and objects that are buried in the ground and the finding of lost objects, thieves, missing persons, and hidden treasure. Modern uses include medical diagnosis and treatment, geological prospecting, and military activities. In medical diagnosis the pendulum appears to pick up energies emanating from every cell, tissue, and organ. Negative energies are associated with disease, and positive energies with good health. In the military, the pendulum has proved useful. In the Vietnam War, U.S. Marines were trained in its use for finding underground mines, ammunition dumps, unexploded shells, and tunnels and to trace enemy movements. During World War II, British intelligence forces reportedly used a pendulum to divine Hitler's next moves. The pendulum also has been used in archaeological digs, and in police work to locate missing persons, bodies, and criminals.

A pendulum must be activated before first use by the asking of yes and no questions. For example, the pendulum may respond to a yes question with clockwise circular motions and to a no question with counterclockwise circular motions. Pendulum users say that one should ask the pendulum whether or not one can use it. The pendulum will affirm or reject.

The pendulum has become the dowsing tool of choice, perhaps due to its small size and convenience. It can be kept in a pocket or pouch. Some pendulums are fancy and expensive, made out of sterling silver chains and carved crystals or precious stones. Others are less elegant and costly but are equally effective. Many users feel they get the best results from pendulums they make themselves, which is in keeping with magical lore that one should make one's own magical tools.

There are different prescriptions for making pendulums. Here is one:

The pendulum should be onion or pear shaped, symmetrical about its vertical axis and about 2.5 to three inches at the largest diameter. It can be solid or hollow with a screw top. Another form of pendulum is cylindrical with two conical ends and about three to five inches long. The weight should be about 50 grams. Dowsers who work primarily indoors with documents can have a lighter weight from 15 to 30 grams. Pendulums for outdoor work are heavier, weigh up to 150 grams. Hang the pendulum from a cord which may be of thread, an antitwist nylon, or a chain. The cord should be held between the thumb and forefinger of either hand with up to about eight inches of cord between the thumb and the pendulum. Most dowsers determine their own ideal length of cord according to their experience.

T. C. Lethbridge, British archaeologist who became intrigued by dowsing, conducted considerable research with the pendulum following his retirement to Devon in 1957. A neighbor, an old woman reputed to be a witch, advised him that the pendulum is far more accurate than the forked-stick divining rods also used by dowsers. In his experiments, Lethbridge discovered that a pendulum appears to have precise responses to various substances. The responses are determined by two rate factors: the length of the string suspending the weight, and the number of times the pendulum rotates. For example, he found that the response for silver is 22 circular rotations of a pendulum on a 22-inch string.

Lethbridge discovered that the pendulum was astonishingly accurate. By creating rate tables, he was able to find a wide range of objects and things successfully, including truffles. He also discovered that the pendulum was sensitive to emotions and thoughts. He put forth theories that the pendulum could sense death, time, and other, nonphysical dimensions. Lethbridge determined that a pendulum on a 40-inch string registers death. Beyond that length, objects seem to response at their normal rate

plus 40, though the pendulum reacts not over them but off to one side. Lethbridge proposed that if 40 is death, then rates beyond 40 indicate a parallel dimension beyond death in which everything seems to continue to exist but not in the same position. Still another dimension appears to exist beyond the rate of 80. Lethbridge also determined that 40 is the rate for the concept of time. Between 40 and 80, time seems to exist in an eternal now and then begins to flow again between 80 and 120 when it stops again.

Lethbridge's theories about time and dimensions beyond death remain highly controversial. His widow, Mina, said that excessive work with the pendulum depleted his vitality and contributed to his death of a heart attack.

FURTHER READING:

Guiley, Rosemary Ellen. *Breakthrough Intuition: How to Achieve a Life of Abundance by Listening to the Voice Within.* New York: Berkley Books, 2001.

Lethbridge, T. C. *The Power of the Pendulum.* London: Routledge & Kegan Paul, 1976.

Nielsen, Greg, and Joseph Polansky. *Pendulum Power.* Wellingborough, Northamptonshire: Excalibur Books, 1984.

pentacle   Five-pointed star important in MAGIC. The pentacle is an ancient SYMBOL that represents the mastery of humans over all inferior beings and the significance of humans to superior beings.

The exact origin of the pentacle is unknown. The ancient Egyptians used a five-pointed star to represent spiritual education. Pentacles appear in relics dating to the ancient Babylonians, and were used as a secret sign by initiates of the Pythagorean mysteries. In the Middle Ages the pentacle was called the Druid's Foot, the Wizard's Foot, and the Goblin's Cross. It appears in the KABBALAH and in FREEMASONRY and ROSICRUCIANISM.

The pentacle forms part of a geometric constant called the Golden Section, designated by the Greek letter *phi*, which was used by the ancient Egyptians in the construction of the Great Pyramid and lauded by Plato as the key to the physics of the universe. The Golden Section, a constant of 1.618, occurs in the lines of a pentacle that is inscribed within a pentagon. The Golden Section was so named during the Renaissance when it was used by such artists as Michelangelo, Raphael, and Leonardo da Vinci. It is still used in modern architecture, including the design of the United Nations building in New York.

The five points of the pentacle represent different things:

- the four ELEMENTS of earth, air, water, and fire plus either human or God
- the points of a human with arms and legs outstretched
- the five senses
- the wounds of Christ

Pentacles serve as TOOLS in magical work and are used in RITUALS for the conjuring and control spirits and ELEMEN-

TALS, such as TALISMANS for invoking supernatural powers and astrological influences and as AMULETS for protection from evil forces. Pentacles are embroidered on magicians' clothing and etched into RINGS, jewelry, wands, and tools.

Pentacle also refers to other magical symbols: circles, semicircles, squares, and crosses that have been inscribed on disks of clay, metal, or wood with the names of God, angels, or demons. These are used for specific spells.

The *Key of Solomon,* the most important of the magical GRIMOIRES, places great importance on pentacles as a means of protection against spirits evoked in ritual and also as a means of controlling them:

> The Medals or Pentacles, which we make for the purpose of striking terror into the Spirits and reducing them to obedience, have besides this wonderful and excellent virtue. If thou invokest the Spirits by virtue of these Pentacles, they will obey thee without repugnance, and having considered them they will be struck with astonishment, and will fear them, and thou shalt see them so surprised by fear and terror, that none of them will be sufficiently bold to wish to oppose thy will . . . for the safety both of soul and of body, the Master [the magician] and the Companions [assistants] should have the Pentacles before their breasts, consecrated, and covered with a silken veil, and perfumed with the proper fumigations. By the which being assured and encouraged, they may enter into the matter without fear or terror, and they shall be exempt and free from all perils and dangers. . . .

According to the *Key,* the pentacles must be made of virgin parchment made from the skin of an animal that was sacrificed by the magician.

Inverted, the pentacle represents black magic and the dark forces, the opposite of God. According to HELENA P. BLAVATSKY, cofounder of the THEOSOPHICAL SOCIETY, it is the symbol of Kali Yuga, the present dark age of violence and materialism in Hindu belief. In occultism, it represents the infernal BAPHOMET or Goat of Mendes. The Church of Satan, formed in 1966, adopted an emblem of a Baphomet inside an inscribed inverted pentacle.

FURTHER READING:
Barrett, Francis. *The Magus.* 1801. Reprint, Secaucus, N.J.: The Citadel Press, 1967.

Butler, E. M. *Ritual Magic.* Cambridge: Cambridge University Press, 1949.

Cavendish, Richard. *The Black Arts.* New York: G.P. Putnam's Sons, 1967.

Guiley, Rosemary Ellen. *The Encyclopedia of Witches and Witchcraft.* 2d ed. New York: Facts On File Inc., 1999.

pentagram   In MAGIC, usually a PENTACLE enclosed in a circle. The pentagram is used in RITUALS and SPELL casting. Pentagrams are traced in the air with a magical TOOL, such as a dagger, for banishing unwanted energies and invoking desired spirit presences, and for opening and closing rituals.

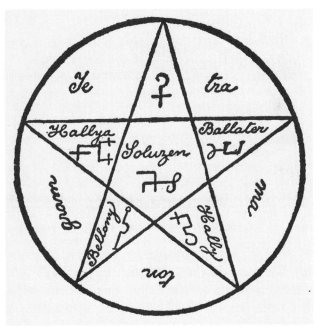

Pentagram of Solomon, in the grimoire Lemegeton. *(Author's collection)*

The pentagram also is the religious symbol of Wicca and represents the five senses and the four elements plus Spirit or Mind (see QUINTESSENCE).

GIORDANO BRUNO said that five is the number of the soul because the human form is bounded by five outer points. Thus magicians and sorcerers could cast spells by using a pentagram.

Perfume of Immortality   An occult perfume alleged to lengthen life and attract others magically. The perfume is said to be an old formula from Arabic lore. It has been correlated to the spiritual essences, or vibrations, of the *sephirot* of the Tree of Life (see KABBALAH).

The main ingredients of the Perfume of Immortality are one part ambergris, which corresponds to Kether; two parts musk, which corresponds to Chokmah; and three parts civet oil, which corresponds to Binah.

ALEISTER CROWLEY attested to the effectiveness of the Perfume of Immortality. He said that it must be rubbed onto the body, especially into the roots of the hair, in such a way that the subtle scent is not obvious to others. Said Crowley:

> The user is thus armed with a most powerful weapon, the more potent for being secret, against the deepest elements in the nature of those whom it is wished to attract. They obey, and they are all the more certainly compelled to obey; because they do not know they are being commanded.

FURTHER READING:
Ashley, Leonard R. N. *The Amazing World of Superstition, Prophecy, Luck, Magic & Witchcraft.* New York: Bell Publishing Company, 1988.

perfumes Scents used in magical RITUALS and SPELLS. Perfumes, also called fumigations, are combinations of herbs, incenses, and other substances made according to recipes in magical texts such as GRIMOIRES. The substances are burned in a container inside a MAGIC CIRCLE. Objects, such as magic RINGS, TOOLS, and POPPETS, are exposed to perfumes as part of their CONSECRATION or empowerment.

According to ISRAEL REGARDIE, perfumes have three purposes in rituals:

- They provide a means for spirits to manifest. The burning of a quantity of perfume creates smoke, which spirits can use to construct a temporary body.
- They provide a pleasant offering or sacrifice to a spirit or angel. Each entity has its own particular perfume that must be used.
- They can be used to evoke a particular spirit. A formula for perfumes is made from the letters in the spirit's name. Each letter of the Hebrew alphabet corresponds to a specific scent. A compound that is made based on letter correspondences can summon forth the spirit when used with IMAGINATION and the proper rites.

The PLANETS, days of the week, and individual ANGELS, DEMONS, and other spirits all have their own perfumes, as do different spells and CHARMS for specific purposes. A formula for causing ghosts of the dead to appear calls for sperm oil, aloes wood, pepperwort, musk, saffron, and red storax, all mixed with the BLOOD of a lapwing. Sweet and pleasant perfumes are used to attract benevolent entities, and foul-smelling perfumes are used to repel evil entities.

Some of the recipes provided in grimoires contain ingredients that have hallucinogenic properties and thus induce visions. Among such ingredients are henbane, poppy, hemlock, black hellebore, and hemp. For example, a formula for causing "visions of the Earth" to appear calls for cane reed root, fennel root, pomegranate skin, henbane, red saunders, and black poppy. Some formulae were dangerous, potentially causing stupor, delirium, convulsions, temporary insanity, and even death.

A curious case involving perfumes occurred near Jena, Germany, on December 24, 1715. Three men went to a hut to evoke a spirit they hoped would show them where to find buried treasure. They drew a magic circle and protected themselves with AMULETS of the TETRAGRAMMATON and various magical SYMBOLS. They used an INCANTATION from the *Arbatel of Magic*. They produced thick perfumes. During the ritual, all three fell unconscious. They were found the next day—two were dead, their bodies covered with weals, scratches, and powder burns, as though attacked by demons. The survivor was capable of making only guttural sounds. Three watchmen were placed at the site; one died during the first night. The other two said that they had been attacked by evil spirits and that they had seen the ghost of a small boy. Whether this tragedy was caused by the fumes produced or by an evil entity that was conjured has never been determined.

FURTHER READING:

Cavendish, Richard. *The Black Arts*. New York: G.P. Putnam's Sons, 1967.

Regardie, Israel. *The Tree of Life: A Study in Magic*. York Beach, Maine: Samuel Weiser, 1969.

Thompson, C. J. S. *The Mysteries and Secrets of Magic*. New York: Barnes & Noble, 1993.

Three Books of Occult Philosophy Written by Henry Cornelius Agrippa of Nettesheim. James Freake, trans. Ed. and annot. by Donald Tyson. St. Paul, Minn.: Llewellyn Publications, 1995.

Philalethes, Eirenaeus Pseudonym of an author of 17th-century alchemical works. Eirenaeus Philalethes probably was used by GEORGE STARKEY after his arrival in England in 1650. Starkey brought from America various alchemical tracts that he said were written by a New England ADEPT.

Philalethes claimed to be a friend of ROBERT BOYLE, an association that enabled the works to be circulated among members of the "Invisible College" of alchemists, occultists, and scientists.

THOMAS VAUGHN used a similar pseudonym, Eugenius Philalethes.

Philosopher's Stone In ALCHEMY, the mysterious substances that enables the transmutation of base metals into GOLD or SILVER. The Philosopher's Stone is said to speed a natural process of evolution in which minerals and base metals evolved to higher and purer states.

The stone was first mentioned by ZOSIMOS (c. 250–300), who described it as "a stone that is not a stone." It has never been described directly and has had hundreds of names (see below) and various descriptions, such as the elixir, the tincture, crystals, powder, lapis, and so forth. It is both the beginning, the PRIMA MATERIA, and the end of the Great Work.

Numerous recipes and formulae have been presented in alchemical literature for preparing the stone, some of them couched in heavy symbolism. One of the most famous recipes is attributed to MARIA PROPHETESS, said to be one of the earliest alchemical ADEPTS in Hellenistic Egypt. Her instructions are:

> Invert nature and you will find that which you seek. There exist two combinations: one pertains to the action of whitening, the other to that of yellowing; one is done by trituration [reduction to powder by grinding], the other by calcination [reduction to a friable state]. One pulverizes in a saintly fashion, with simplicity, only in the holy house; there takes place the dissolution and the deposition. Combine together . . . the male and the female, and you will find that which you seek. Do not be anxious to

know whether the work is on fire. The two combinations have many names, such as brine water, incorruptible divine water, vinegar water, water of the acid of sea salt, of castor oil, of horse radish, and of balsam. One also calls it water of the milk of a woman who gave birth to a male child, water of the milk of a black cow, water of the urine of a young cow or of a ewe, or of a male ass, water of quicklime, of marble, of tartar, of sandarac [realgar, arsenic sulphide], of schitose alum, of niter, of the milk of a sheass, of a goat, of the ashes of lime, water of ashes, of honey and oxymel [honey and vinegar mixed together], of the flowers of the arctium, of sapphire, etc. The vessels or instruments destined for these combinations must be made of glass. One must be aware of stirring the mixture with the hands, for the mercury is deadly, just as the gold which is found there is corrupted.

The Philosopher's Stone is ascribed great powers beyond the transmutation of metals; it is said to be the "universal medicine" that can improve health and lengthen life, even allowing some ADEPTS to achieve immortality.

The stone is often depicted in alchemical art as the HERMAPHRODITE, the product of the marriage of opposites, represented by the king and the queen. A florid description of the stone is given by HEINRICH KHUNRATH in *Amphiteahreum sapientias aeternae* ("The Amphitheater of Eternal Wisdom"), published in 1602:

> Thou shalt see the Stone of the Philosophers (our King) go forth of the bed-chamber, of his Glassy Sepulcher, in his glorified body, like a Lord of Lords, from his throne into the Theater of the World. That is to say, regimented and more perfect, a shining carbuncle, most temperate splendor, whose most subtile and depurated parts are inseparably united into one, with a concordial mixture, exceeding equal; transparent like crystal, compact and most ponderous, easily fusible in fire, like resin or wax before the flight of quicksilver yet flowing without smoke; entering into solid bodies and penetrating them like oil through paper, dissoluble in every liquor and commiscible with it; friable like glass in a powder of saffron, but in the whole mass shining red like a Ruby (which redness is a sign of a perfect fixation and fixed perfection); permanently colorating and tingeing, fixed in all trials, yea in the examination of the burning sulphur itself and the devouring waters and in the most vehement persecution of the fire, always incombustible and permanent as the Salamander.

From the 13th century onward, the stone possessed a spiritual significance; only an alchemist who observed a strict lifestyle of devotion and purification could attain it. BASIL VALENTINE, who called the stone the All in All, observed in *The Great Stone of the Philosophers*:

> Let me tell you, then, that although many are engaged in the search after this Stone, it is nevertheless found but by very few. For God never intended that it should become generally known. It is rather to be regarded as a gift which He reserves for those favored few, who love the truth, and hate falsehood, who study our Art earnestly by day and by night, and whose hearts are set upon God with unfeigned affection.

To acquire the Philosopher's Stone is to acquire full knowledge of God, a mystical union. The transmutation of base metals into gold int the alchemical furnace is likened to the purification and burning away of one's sins and imperfections by the burning fire of the love of God.

By the Renaissance, the Philosopher's Stone signified the force behind the evolution of life and the universal binding power of oneness. It also represented the purity and sanctity of the highest realm of pure thought and altruistic existence.

The World card in The Alchemical Tarot, by Rosemary Ellen Guiley and Robert Michael Place. The World card represents the culmination of the Great Work in the Philosopher's Stone. The Anima Mundi, holding the caduceus of Hermes the Magician and the rose of the quintessence, is wreathed by an ouroboros and framed by the four elements. (Copyright by and courtesy of Robert Michael Place)

The redemptive power of the stone led to its associations with Christ. CARL G. JUNG emphasized this association in his own alchemical works. Christ as the stone is mentioned as early as the works of Zosimus and is featured in the works of JAKOB BOEHME, RAYMOND LULLY, Khunrath, and others.

Names of the Philosopher's Stone
Common names for the stone are Lapis, Elixir, Elixir of Life, and Tincture. The following are some of the names of the Philosophers Stone, collected by William Gratacolle and published in 1652 in London:

Gold, Sol, Sun, Brasse of Philosophers, the body of Magnesia, a pure body, clean, ferment of Elixir, Masculine, Argent vive fixt, Sulphur incombustible, Sulphur red, fixed, the rubibe stone, kybrik, a man, greene vitrioll, burnt brasse, red earth: the water that is distilled from these things, is named of the Philosophers, the taile of the Dragon, a pure wind, ayre, life, lightning, the house, the afternoone light, virgin's milke, sal armoniack, sal niter, the wind of the belly, white fume, red water of sulphur, tartar, saffron, water, the white compound, stinking water, the filthiness of the dead bloud, Argent vive, a Cucurbite with his Alimbeck, the vessell of the Philosophers, a high man with a Sallet, the belly of a man in the midst, but in the end it is called the fot, or the feet, or on the which feet, or earth is calcined, rosted, congealed, distilled, or made still and quiet: the shaddow of the Sun, a dead body, a crowne overcoming a cloud, the bark of the Sea, Magnesia, black, a Dragon which eateth his tayle, the dregs of the belly, earth found on the dunghill putrefied, or in horse dung, or in soft fire, Sulphur, Mercury, secondly in number, and one in essence, name, in name, a stone, body, spirit and soule; it is called earth, fire, aire, all things, because he contains in him foure Elements; it is called a man or beast, that hath soul, life, body, and spirit, and yet some Philosophers do not thinke the matter to have a soule.

But as it is a stone, it is called the water of Sulphur, the Water of the world, the spittle of Lune, the shadow of the Sun, a denne, Sol, Elephas, white Jayre, eyes of fishes, Beyia, Sulphur, vine sharpe, water, milke, vineger of life, tears, joyning water, Urine, the light of lights, a marvelous Father, Father of Minerals, a fruitfull tree, a living spirit, a fugitive servant, certore of the earth, venome, most strong vineger, white gumme, everlasting water, a woman, a feminine, a thing of vile price, Azot, menstruous, Brazill, in nature Azot, water, the first matter, the beginning of the world; and mark this, that Argent vive, Mercury, Azot, the fulle moone, Hypostasis, white lead, or red, do all of them signifie but one thing, our stone, our brasse, our water, Iron, Silver, Lime, whiteness, Jupiter, Vermilion white, after divers times and degrees of operation.

And note, that the Philosophers washing is to bring again the whole soule into his body, wherefore you may not understand thereby, the common white washing is convenient to be done with vineger, and salt, and such like. Also note, that when blackness doth appeare, then it is called dispensation of the man and woman between them, and that the body hath gotten a spirit, which is the tears of the vertues of the soule upon the body, and the body doth revive the action of the soule and spirit, and is made an Eagle and the meane of natures. And note, that white earth, white Sulphur, white fume, Auripigmentum Magnesia, and Ethell, do signifie all one thing.

Also the Stone is called Chaos, a Dragon, a Serpent, a Toad, the green Lion, the quintessence, our stone Lunare, Camelion, most vild black, blacker than black, Virgins milke, radicall humidity, unctuous moysture, liquor, seminall, Salarmoniack, our Sulphur, Naptha, a soule, a Basilisk, Adder, Secundine, Bloud, Sperme, Metteline, haire, urine, poyson, water of wise men, minerall water, Antimony, stinking menstrues, Lead of Philosophers, Sal, Mercury, our Gold, Lune, a bird, our ghost, dun Salt, Alome of Spaine, attrement, dew of heavenly grace, the stinking spirit, Borax, Mercury corporall, wine, dry water, water metelline, an Egge, old water, perminent, Hermes bird, the lesse world, Campher, water of life, Auripigment, a body cynaper, and almost with other infinite names of pleasure.

FURTHER READING:
"Names of the Philosopher's Stone." Available online. URL: http://www.levity.com/alchemy/gratacol.html. Downloaded January 1, 2005.
Patai, Raphael. *The Jewish Alchemists.* Princeton, N.J.: Princeton University Press, 1994.
Waite, Arthur Edward. *The Hermetic Museum.* York Beach, Maine: Samuel Weiser, 1991.

Philosophical Research Society Educational organization founded by MANLY PALMER HALL in 1934. The Philosophical Research Society seeks to integrate the essential teachings of science, spirituality, and culture with the aim of "solving the personal and collective problems of modern man."

The PRS maintains a research library of more than 50,000 books and publishes books and other materials, especially the works of Hall.

philtre A magical potion that causes a person to fall in love. Philtres, also called love potions, have been used in MAGIC since antiquity. When drunk, a philtre is supposed to make the recipient fall in love with the giver.

Recipes for philtres are given in GRIMOIRES and books of SPELLS. A traditional formula calls for wine, tea, or water doctored with various herbs, drugs, animal parts, and other ingredients. The most common ingredient is mandrake root, also called "love apples," a small and poisonous member of the nightshade family. The bad smell and taste of mandrake root are neutralized with orange and ambergris. Other common ingredients are the vervain, briony, fern seed, human BLOOD, dragon blood (a red gum), and the hearts and reproductive organs of animals.

One medieval philtre recipe called for grinding into a powder the heart of a dove, the liver of a sparrow, the womb of a swallow, and the kidney of a hare. To that was added an equal part of the person's own blood, also dried and powdered. A 16th-century recipe called for "black dust of tomb, venom of toad, flesh of brigand, lung of ass, blood of blind infant, corpses from graves, bile of ox."

The best results are obtained with philtres made by a practitioner of the magical arts, such as a witch.

phoenix   In Egyptian mythology, a bird that embodies the Sun God. The phoenix, also called the fire bird, is said to live for 500 years and then burns itself to ash on a pyre. After three days, it resurrects itself by rising anew from the ashes. Thus it is a potent SYMBOL of sacrifice by death so that rebirth can take place. As a sun symbol, it represents the cycle of the Sun as it is born again every day.

In ALCHEMY, the phoenix is a symbol of the PHILOSOPHER'S STONE, the consummation of the Great Work.

In psychology, the phoenix represents the birth of a new personality.

physiognomy   See DIVINATION.

planets   In MAGIC and ALCHEMY, the seven heavenly bodies of ancient times have specific powers and influences over aspects of daily life. Each planet is associated with ruling spirits, ANGELS, and INTELLIGENCES and governs a day of the week, a metal, and a color. Planetary auspices are invoked and harnessed in RITUALS and in the making of TALISMANS, SIGILS, and CHARMS (see MAGIC SQUARE).

The influences of the planets are part of the action of the macrocosm upon the microcosm, and are the basis of ASTROLOGY. Magical and alchemical operations are best undertaken during certain planetary auspices.

Different angels and ruling spirits are assigned planets in various magical and alchemical texts.

Sun

Day: Sunday

Angel: Michael

Intelligence: Nakhiel

Associations: Leadership, justice, law, nobility, money management, reason, logic, fatherhood, enlightenment

Magical purposes: Promote health, self-confidence, virility, friendship, divination powers, harmony

Metal: Gold

Color: Gold

Moon

Day: Monday

Angel: Gabriel

Intelligence: Tarshism

Associations: Sailing, navigation, maritime trade, sea voyages, fertility, bodily and natural rhythms, intuition, dreams

Magical purposes: Promote good luck, success, fertility and childbirth, domestic stability, health, imagination, psychic ability, dream interpretation and sending

Phoenix resurrecting itself from its funeral pyre in the Ten of Staffs card in The Alchemical Tarot, *by Rosemary Ellen Guiley and Robert Michael Place.* (Copyright by and courtesy of Robert Michael Place)

Metal: Silver

Color: Silver

Mars

Day: Tuesday

Angel: Camael

Intelligence: Graphiel

Associations: War, sports, law enforcement, engineering, machinery, male sexuality, strength, aggression

Magical purposes: Victory in sports and war, enhance virility and potency, protect against enemies, increase physical strength and courage

Metal: Iron

Color: Red

Mercury

Day: Wednesday

Angel: Raphael

Intelligence: Tiriel

Associations: Travel by land and air, commerce, business, industry, science, mathematics, intelligence

Magical purposes: Promote eloquence, learning, good business, scientific innovations and discoveries; also aiding in theft

Metal: Mercury, zinc

Color: Purple

Jupiter

Day: Thursday

Angel: Zachariel

Intelligence: Lophiel

Associations: acquisition of wealth and power, legal and business deals, marriage, education, religion, philosophy

Magical purposes: Preserve health, promote friendship, protect in travel, eliminate anxiety

Metal: Tin

Color: Blue

Venus

Day: Friday

Angel: Haniel/Aniel

Intelligence: Hagiel

Associations: Love, marriage, relationships, personal and business partnerships, contracts, visual arts, female sexuality, personal income

Magical purposes: Promote and procure love and money, artistic creativity, sensuality and sexuality; also protect women against cancer and all poisons

Saturn

Day: Saturday

Angel: Orifiel

Intelligence: Agiel

Associations: Agriculture, archeology, mining, building trades, property deals, business and commerce, discipline, time

Magical purposes: Promote responsibility and discipline, patience and morality; also, protect women in childbirth and prevent death by poison or conspiracy

Metal: Lead

Color: Black

pointing In MAGIC and SORCERY, the ability to harm or kill others with a CURSE or a HEX directed at them by pointing a finger, stick, bone, or other magical implement. Pointing magic exists in many cultures and in European WITCHCRAFT lore. In tribal societies, it is used to mete out justice. The power of pointing is based on the belief that certain magically empowered persons can direct natural forces to affect other living things. North American Indian tribes have legends of the killing of animals by pointing. Pointing may have to be done repeatedly during a certain period of time before the curse takes effect.

Australian Aborigines have a custom of "pointing the bone" or "boning" as punishment for wrongdoing. In one case cited by anthropologist Ronald Rose, a man convicted of raping two girls was executed by boning. The tribal wise man hammered a point onto a wire and drew it through the flames of a fire while he recited curses. The wire was then pointed at the man. The wise man did this every night for a week. The victim grew progressively weaker, took to bed, and died on the final night of the RITUAL.

Pointing a finger while uttering a curse is considered to be especially malevolent. Deadly, magical energy streams from the finger toward the victim. Thus hatred and intent to harm or kill is "sent" into the victim. The only way to nullify a pointing curse is to prevail upon the sorcerer to lift it or to seek out another and more powerful sorcerer to make a counterspell.

One explanation of how pointing works is that the victim, who knows he or she has been pointed at, may help to bring about the curse by strongly believing in the power of the witch or the sorcerer.

Pointing itself is neither negative nor positive, but in magic and sorcery it is usually associated with cursing. A benevolent form of pointing is found in mystical and spiritual traditions, in which a teacher or a holy person sends spiritual power into an initiate for the purposes of advancing enlightenment. In yoga, *shaktipat* refers to a transmission of power (*shakti*) via pointing, looking, and even through the breath.

FURTHER READING:

Gordon, Stuart. *The Book of Curses: True Tales of Voodoo, Hoodoo and Hex.* London: Brockhampton Press, 1994.

Guiley, Rosemary Ellen. *Dreamwork for the Soul.* New York: Berkley Books, 1998.

Robins, Joyce. *The World's Greatest Mysteries.* London: Hamlyn Publishing Group Ltd., 1989.

popes and sorcery   Some of the highest authorities of the Catholic Church are associated with legends of SORCERY, PACTS with DEMONS, black MAGIC, and NECROMANCY. The legends probably were created out of jealousy and political intrigue, as all the "sorcerer popes" were involved in controversies. An accusation of sorcery was not uncommon in fights for control of the papacy.

The stories are as follows:

Leo I (r. 440–461)
Also called St. Leo the Great, Leo I was said to practice sorcery and black magic. He waged a power struggle against his bishops and attacked Manichaeism in Italy.

Leo III (r. 795–816)
Leo III was credited with writing a magical grimoire, the *Enchiridion of Pope Leo,* which was published in the early 16th century. The book claims to be based on a collection of PRAYERS that the pope gave to Roman emperor Charlemagne as a gift upon his coronation. Charlemagne reportedly had protected Leo III when he was physically attacked by the family of his predecessor. The CHARMS deal with various protections against evil and misfortune.

Sylvester II (r. 999–1003)
A learned man interested in science and the arts, Sylvester II also was a reputed necromancer who won the papacy through spells and a pact with the devil. He was said to have a lifelong demon mistress named Meridiana, who satisfied his carnal lust and provided him material wealth.

According to legend, Sylvester II sold his soul to the devil, who gave him a bronze head which gave oracular responses. The head predicted that Sylvester would not die, "except at Jerusalem," and so the pope decided that he would never visit that city.

While giving Mass one day at a church in Rome, Sylvester fell gravely ill. Remembering the PROPHECY, he asked for the name of the church and was told it was the Holy Cross of Jerusalem. He knew the prophecy had come true and resigned himself to his fate. He had a bed put in the chapel and then summoned his cardinals, confessing to them that he had dealt with demons. He instructed that his corpse should be placed on a chariot of green wood, drawn by one black horse and one white. The horses should be neither driven nor led. He was to be buried wherever they stopped. Then Sylvester died.

The horses stopped in the Lateran, and Sylvester was buried. According to Lore, his tomb sweats prior to the death of a prominent person. If a pope is going to die, the sweat is so heavy that it turns into a stream and creates a large puddle, and Sylvester's bones shake and rattle.

Gregory VII (r. 1081–1084)
The Synod of Bressanone pronounced Gregory VII a sorcerer on June 25, 1080, prior to his becoming pope. He was an austere reformer and was strongly opposed by cardinals.

Honorius III (r. 1216–1227)
Honorius III is the alleged author of a magical GRIMOIRE, the *Grimoire of Honorius* or the *Constitution of Honorius.* (In some early copies, Honorius II is credited as the author.) The grimoire was published in the early 17th century and was probably written strictly as a commercial venture with the pope's name added for authenticity. The book combines Christian and kabbalistic elements and deals especially with rites of EXORCISM. The tone of the book is aptly described by ELIPHAS LEVI:

> . . . the mystery of darksome evocations is expounded therein with a terrific knowledge concealed under superstitious and sacrilegious forms. Fastings, watchings, profanation of mysteries, allegorical ceremonies and bloody sacrifices are combined with artful malice.

Boniface VIII (r. 1294–1303)
Boniface VIII found his authority seriously challenged by the monarchies of Western Europe. He possessed a keen and superior intellect, which was tarnished by a short temper and impulsive nature. Philip IV of France, one of his main opponents and whom he intended to excommunicate, used defamation, forgery, and intimidation against him, including accusations of sorcery and heresy.

Boniface was charged with making a pact with demons and conjuring them regularly; keeping an imp in a ring on his finger; infidelity; and, when still a cardinal, sacrificing a cock in a black magic spell one night in a garden. Furthermore, it was said that when he died, he confessed his demonic pacts on his deathbed, and his moment of death caused "so much thunder and tempest, with dragons flying in the air and vomiting flames, and such lightning and other prodigies, that the people of Rome believed that the whole city was going to be swallowed up in the abyss." Boniface was exonerated of all charges posthumously in 1312.

Benedict XIII (r. 1394–1423)

An antipope, Benedict XIII was believed to hold continuous traffic with spirits, to keep two demons in a little bag, and to search out books on magic.

John XXIII (r. 1410–1415)

An antipope, said to be saved by magic. When John XXIII was deposed by the Council of Constance, he was saved by Abramelin the Mage, who helped his escape from prison.

Sixtus V (r. 1585–1590)

Sixtus V supposedly sold his soul to the devil to gain the papacy. Born Felice Peretti, he entered the Franciscan order and was sent in 1565 to Spain to investigate the alleged heresy of the archbishop of Toledo. He stirred up much animosity in Spain, and when he was named pope in 1585, the Spaniards accused him of entering into a pact with Satan.

The devil granted Sixtus a six-year reign. After five years, the pope fell gravely ill, and the devil appeared at his bedside one night to collect his soul. The pope protested that he still had another year remaining in his contract. The devil said he was reneging on one year because Sixtus earlier had sentenced to death a young man who was one year too young to be executed, according to law. The pope had no rebuttal and died.

During his papacy, Sixtus spent huge sums of money on public works projects, such as the completion of the dome of Saint Peter's Church in the Vatican. He also authorized Philip II of Spain to send his armada against England, but the armada was defeated by English witches who cast SPELLS to raise terrible storms at sea.

FURTHER READING:
Levi, Eliphas. *The History of Magic.* 1860. Reprint, York Beach, Maine: Samuel Weiser, 2001.
Waite, Arthur Edward. *Alchemists Through the Ages.* Blauvelt, N.Y.: Rudolph Steiner Publications, 1970.

poppet   A magical doll or effigy.

Poppets in Folk Magic Spells

In folk magic, a poppet substitutes for the person who is the object of a SPELL. The doll is carefully made in a state of concentration that focuses on the purpose of the spell. Things belonging to the victim, such as bits of clothing and snippets of hair and nail clippings, are attached to the poppet or are stuffed inside it. If no personal effects are available, a photograph can be pinned to the doll, or the person's name can be inscribed on it. These measures are a form of sympathetic magic that links the poppet to the person. Life is breathed into a poppet by blowing into the doll's mouth through a straw. Thus the poppet takes on a magical life of its own, attaches itself astrally to the intended person, and activates the spell.

If the spell is a CURSE, the poppet is pierced with pins, nails, or shards of glass or is bound with cord, covered with burning candle wax, or even hung by the neck. Sometimes poppets are buried after being activated.

Not all poppets have negative purposes. For example, a healing poppet might be attached with certain herbs, stones, or crystals that are intended to facilitate healing. Poppets also are made for good luck, love, any kind of goal-setting, and protection against harm and evil MAGIC.

Breaking Poppet Spells

To end the influence of a magically empowered poppet, the sympathetic astral link is severed between the doll and person. A clean, sharp knife is used to magically sever the astral cord, which is like an umbilical cord. All things pertaining to the person—hair, photos, personal effects, and so on—should be removed from the doll. Wooden and waxen poppets should be scrubbed under running water, and a cloth poppet should be washed and then taken apart while still under running water. The astral cords are broken to the personal objects by cutting, and then the personal objects are burned to ashes and scattered in running water or the ocean. Then the poppet itself is burned to ashes, which are scattered also in running water or the ocean.

If a person suspects he or she is the object of poppet magic or doll sorcery, he or she can self-protect without having access to the poppet—by taking a new knife and magically severing the astral cord between himself or herself and the poppet. This is followed by a bath and a change of clothes.

Other magical procedures can also break a poppet spell; they all involve ways of cutting the sympathetic connection.

Poppets in Ceremonial Magic

In ceremonial magic, poppets are substitutes for aspects of god and goddess. They are used in RITUALS and to activate certain energies. A common poppet for such purposes is the Biddy or Bridie Doll, made at Imbolc in honor of Saint Bride and to welcome in spring.

The Bridie Doll is made as much as possible from natural materials, such as twigs, straw, pine cones, and pebbles. When the doll is made, a bride song is sung to call in goddess energy for fertility and healing, especially of the land. The doll is then placed in a decorated carriage and taken to a home adjacent to her final destination, where she is given to the land.

FURTHER READING:
Denning, Melita, and Osborne Phillips. *Practical Guide to Self-Defense and Well-Being.* 2d ed. St. Paul, Minn.: Llewellyn Publications, 1999.
Guiley, Rosemary Ellen. *The Encyclopedia of Witches and Witchcraft.* 2d ed. New York: Facts On File Inc., 1999.

possession   The takeover and control by an outside influence, such as a spirit, a god, a dead person, or a DEMON. Possession is not the same as obsession, which is a heavy influence but not a complete takeover.

The belief that a person's mind and soul can be influenced by a departed spirit, whether of god, demon, or man, is ancient and universal. Possession happens in three dominant ways:

- Involuntary, in which a god or a spirit takes over a person (or animal) and causes them to act in certain ways to serve the spirits' purposes.
- Through WITCHCRAFT or SORCERY in which a person or animal is bewitched or cursed and thus suffers illness or misfortune.
- Voluntary, such as through magical RITUAL or an induced trance in which a god or a spirit is invited to make a temporary possession for purposes such as PROPHECY, empowerment, divine favors, enlightenment, and channeling.

In the first two ways, possession can end only by EXORCISM by a qualified person. In voluntary possession, the possession is brought to an end when its purpose is fulfilled.

Demonic Possession

Widespread beliefs about demons hold that they are capable of causing frequent upsets and mischief, as well as serious illness and trouble, by taking possession of a person. The unwary, the careless, and the vulnerable are particularly at risk as are people whose health is poor or who flout social conventions, mores, and laws. A troubled relationship might be caused by a pesky demon that has laid siege to a person, causing her or him to say and do things that she or he would not ordinarily do. Even problems such as alcoholism, gambling addiction, and drug addiction have been blamed on interfering malevolent spirits that become attached like leeches to the energy field of a person.

The Christian church recognizes demonic possession that is the result of witchcraft or sorcery under the aegis of the devil or else is the consequence of sin. In earlier centuries, a person who exhibited unusual behavior or expressed ideas radically different than those currently acceptable was often deemed to be demonically possessed. The devil claimed victims by passing directly into a person's mind and soul or by using a witch or a wizard to send a DEMON into the victim through BEWITCHMENT. Witches were said to transmit demons to the innocent victim through a CHARM, a PHILTRE, an AMULET, or, most likely, food. APPLES were especially popular since they seemed innocuous and were readily available.

As evidence of demonic possession, the victims may levitate, exhibit superhuman strength, forswear all religious words or articles, and speak in tongues. This last trait offers the strongest proof to the Catholic Church, allowing the attending bishop to permit an exorcism. The formal ritual is performed by a priest and done in the name of the Lord, sending the devil and his minions back to hell.

Epidemics of demonic possession occurred in Europe and even the American colonies from the 15th through the 18th centuries. Many of the afflicted were nuns, leading modern experts to theorize that repressed sexuality was a factor in the outbreaks, and hysterical children. The witch trials of Salem, Massachusetts, in 1692, were the result of fabricated stories by "possessed" children.

Spirit Possession

Voluntary possession serves as a means to communicate with spirits and deities and is a centerpiece of some religious worship. Possession by a god shows the possessed to be worthy of the god's notice and protection. For example, in Vodoun, the gods, or *loas,* possess entranced people who dance or perform superhuman feats.

Mediumship and channeling are forms of voluntary spirit possession in which spirits of the dead speak through a medium or entities (ANGELS, extraterrestrials, etc.) speak through a channeler. Communication takes place in deep trance during which the possessing agents use the human vocal chords, as well as in light trance, automatic writing, and so forth.

In ritual magic, voluntary possession can takes place when gods are invoked. In high magic, the magician seeks to become infused with divine energy, consciousness, and enlightenment, such as in the ritual of the HOLY GUARDIAN ANGEL. In Wicca, the ritual of Drawing Down the Moon involves a trance possession in which the High Priestess channels an inspirational message from the Goddess.

FURTHER READING:
Ebon, Martin. *The Devil's Bride, Exorcism: Past and Present.* New York: Harper & Row, 1974.
Guiley, Rosemary Ellen. *The Encyclopedia of Witches and Witchcraft.* 2d ed. New York: Facts On File Inc., 1999.
Rogo, D. Scott. *The Infinite Boundary.* New York: Dodd, Mead & Co., 1987.

Potter, Harry Boy WIZARD who is the heart of an immensely successful series of books by J. K. Rowling, as well as films based on the books. SPELLS and POTIONS, WANDS and witches, giants and fantastic beasts—all superimposed on the recognizable routines of an English public school education—have woven their magic on readers of all ages worldwide.

Introducing Harry Potter

Joanne Rowling (Kathleen, her grandmother's name, was added later) was born on July 31, 1965, in Chipping Sodbury, South Gloucestershire, England. She had written two books for adults that had never been published. One day, on a four-hour train trip, Rowling had the inspiration for a magical hero named Harry Potter, and by the time she reached her destination she had pretty much fleshed him out. She began to write at lunchtime breaks during a teaching stint in Portugal. When she divorced her Portuguese husband and moved to Edinburgh, she spent her days writing in a cafe about Harry's enchanted life while her infant daughter slept in the baby carriage. Several publishers rejected the manuscript before she finally sold it to Bloomsbury Publishing.

Although the plots are delightfully new to young readers, the series' premise is a time-tested one: A seemingly powerless child finds the strength to overcome adversity and eventually becomes wise, generous, loving—and empowered. English author Roald Dahl returned to this device many times, such as in *Matilda* and *James and the Giant Peach*. Frances Hodgson Burnette used the same idea in *The Secret Garden* and *The Little Princess*. Shirley Temple personified the plucky orphan in the film *Captain January*. And television sitcoms such as *Punky Brewster* or even *The Fresh Prince* highlighted the success of street kids who made it.

But it is the magic—the flying brooms sweeping through a Quidditch match, the wands emitting streams of spells, the murky potions, the baby dragons, the paintings of long-dead knights that come alive and speak, the special mirrors and prophesying bowls, the house elves and even owls that deliver mail and packages—that make the harrowing trials of Harry Potter so much fun.

The first book, *Harry Potter and the Philosopher's Stone* (called the *Sorcerer's Stone* in the U.S. edition published by Scholastic Books), introduces Harry and the Hogwarts School of Witchcraft and Wizardry. Harry lives with his Aunt Petunia and Uncle Vernon Dursley and their obnoxious son Dudley. The Dursleys shower attention and gifts on Dudley but force poor Harry to sleep in a cupboard under the stairs. He wears Dudley's too-large hand-me-downs and, like Cinderella, waits on the family like a servant. Any infraction and he is sent to bed without supper. Consequently, the 11-year-old is quite thin and gangly. His unruly dark hair covers his most distinguishing feature: a mark like a lightening bolt on his forehead.

When Harry was an infant, his parents, James and Lily Potter, were killed by the evil Lord Voldemort, a wizard so powerful and demonic that most members of the "wizarding community" refer to him as He Who Must Not be Named. Voldemort tried to kill Harry, too, but the sacrifice of his mother saved him, and Voldemort was temporarily vanquished by the magical power of such a selfless act. That is how Harry got his scar. Albus Dumbledore, headmaster of Hogwarts School, placed Harry with his aunt, Lily's sister, for safekeeping until his 11th birthday. The Dursleys are Muggles—humans with no wizarding blood or skills—and Dumbledore thought Harry would be safer there. And so young Harry bore the insults and suspicions of his relatives until the letter arrived to announce his entrance into the Hogwarts School. The Dursleys tried to hide the letter and keep Harry from attending, but the gentle giant Hagrid came to get him and to transport him to his new boarding school.

Hagrid took Harry to a parallel world where everyone was a wizard or a witch to some degree. In due course, Harry learned a little about his parents; discovered he had a sizable account at Gringotts Bank; bought textbooks with such titles as *Magical Drafts and Potions, The Dark Forces: A Guide to Self-Protection,* and *A Beginners' Guide to Transfiguration;* and selected a wand, a cauldron, a telescope, and black academic robes. New First Year students could bring an owl, a cat, or a toad as a FAMILIAR (Harry received a beautiful white owl named Hedwig), but they were not allowed their own brooms yet. The way to Hogwarts was by an express train that arrived and left from Platform Nine and Three-Quarters at King's Cross Station in London; one found the platform by magically passing through a brick barrier and exiting on the other side.

Once at Hogwarts, Harry marveled at his new home: a very old, medieval castle of a building with a great dining hall, paintings of long-dead knights and magicians who talk and even leave their canvases, and movable staircases that lead to the sleeping houses or to secret chambers. That first night the talking Sorting Hat assigned each First Year to one of four houses, meaning a designated part of the castle for those members of each group, with common gathering rooms. The four houses were named for the founding members of Hogwarts—Gryffindor, Slytherin, Hufflepuff, and Ravenclaw—and represented the virtues of each of those wizards, in order: bravery and chivalry, shrewd cunning, patience and loyalty, and wit and learning. Each house had its own colors and competed intensely against the others in sports and academics just as in ordinary English public schools. The Hat decided what characteristics each new student possessed and where they belonged. Harry received Gryffindor, as did his new friends Hermione Granger and Ron Weasley.

The most important sport at Hogwarts is Quidditch, sort of a combination of soccer, polo, and basketball played while flying on a broom. There are seven players on each side, three of whom are called Chasers. Their mission is to throw a bright red ball called the Quaffle through one of three hoops at the opponent's end of the field, while a Keeper protects his team's hoops and tries to prevent a score, which earns 10 points. Meanwhile, three black balls that fly on their own, called Bludgers, are trying to hit the Chasers and keep them from scoring. Those hijinks necessitate two teammates called Beaters to stave off the Bludgers. Finally, the team has a Seeker, whose job is to catch the Golden Snitch, a very small, very fast golden ball with fluttering silver wings. Scores with the Quaffle are good, but the Seeker who manages to catch the Snitch earns his house 150 points—and the game goes on until someone snares the elusive Snitch. Although First Years rarely make the house teams, Harry's natural flying ability earns him the coveted place as Gryffindor Seeker. To play, he receives a Nimbus Two Thousand flying broom (brooms in the wizarding world have model names and personalities, just as cars do for Muggles).

A good part of the story revolves around the rhythms of the school: the struggles to master classes in charms, potions, and protection against the Dark Arts; sessions in the library researching such great alchemists as NICHOLAS FLAMEL; the teachers who are popular (Professor McGonagall or Professor Flitwick) and those who are not (Professor Snape); the fierce competition among the houses. But the battle between good and evil, epitomized by Harry and his sworn enemy Voldemort, forms the climax of the *Sorcerer's Stone* and all the other books in Rowling's magical imagination. These are hand-to-hand, or rather wand-to-wand, encounters, for although Harry is much younger, his courage and quick thinking make him Voldemort's equal. But while Harry may win a round, Voldemort will return—in the next book.

The Story Continues

In *Harry Potter and the Chamber of Secrets,* Rowling follows the same format. Each book takes place in the next year of school, with Harry a year older each July. He can hardly wait to return after a dismal summer with the Dursleys. The friends resume their routines, struggling with classes and homework and defending Gryffindor House in Quidditch. But this year Ginny Weasley, Ron's little sister, joins Hogwarts, and Harry grows closer to all the Weasleys as his surrogate family. Ginny's insecurities provide an opening for Voldemort's evil genius. Readers meet Dobby, the House Elf who serves the Malfoy family (Draco Malfoy of Slytherin hates Harry), and Moaning Myrtle, the ghost of a shy student who lives in the girls' restroom. There is the Whomping Willow, which wrecks the Weasleys' Ford Anglia automobile (it also flies), and Aragog the giant spider.

Harry astounds everyone at Hogwarts with his ability to speak Parseltongue, or the language of snakes and serpents—a handy talent when he faces the Basilisk, a dreaded monster that inflicts instant death on all who return its stare. Voldemort returns in the persona of a student, revealing that, like Harry, he is half Muggle—a condition he derisively calls a Mudblood.

The third book, *Harry Potter and the Prisoner of Azkaban,* centers around the escape of Sirius Black from Azkaban, the wizard prison. Sirius was one of James Potter's closest friends, but he supposedly betrayed James to Voldemort, causing Harry's parents' deaths. Azkaban is a dark and despairing place, guarded by evil creatures called Dementors, ghostly wraiths who can draw out a person's soul with their deadly kiss. When Black escapes, he is believed to have come to Hogwarts, and the Dementors circle warily over the schoolgrounds, watching and waiting. Their presence aggravates the widening fissure between Dumbledore and the Ministry of Magic, headed by the officious Cornelius Fudge, for control of Hogwarts.

Book Three also features Professor Remus Lupin, another old friend of James Potter's and the new Professor of Defense Against the Dark Arts. Lupin teaches Harry, now thirteen, how to defend himself against the Dementors and reveals that he, like James and Sirius, were animagi: humans able to become animals at will. There was a fourth friend, Peter Pettigrew, who was an animagus also. Pettigrew, nicknamed Wormtail, became a rat; Lupin, called Moony, was a wolf; Black turned into a large dog

named Padfoot, and James had been a stag called Prongs. Ron's older twin brothers, Fred and George, give Harry a Maurader's Map that magically identifies the footsteps of whomever is moving nearby. By using the map, Harry learns the truth about Professor Lupin and who really betrayed his parents.

By the time the fourth book, *Harry Potter and the Goblet of Fire,* was published in the summer of 2000, the boy wizard had become a literary phenomenon. Adults as well as kids could not wait for the next installment of Harry's adventures; English publisher Bloomsbury even released the book with a cover jacket for children and one for grown-ups.

The Goblet of Fire features a Triwizard Tournament in which champions of three schools—Hogwarts, Beauxbatons, and Durmstrang—spend an entire school year in competition to see who is the best. Representatives from Beauxbatons and Durmstrang come to Hogwarts, where the contests will be held. The tasks, which can be dangerous and test the wits and cunning of the three wizards, are selected and approved by the Ministry of Magic. The Goblet impartially selects the names of the three winners—but there's a fourth name, and of course it is Harry. Bewildered at his selection—he is not old enough at 14 to enter—Harry undergoes terrible trials. Adolescent infatuation with the lovely Cho Chang—and his confusion over emotions he does not understand—only make his life more miserable. But none of those events come close to the epic battle he wages with Voldemort at the end. The Dark Lord has grown stronger and called his followers, the Death Eaters, to rejoin him. Harry and Dumbledore realize the urgency of a unified defense; yet the Ministry refuses to acknowledge the threat. When *The Goblet of Fire* ends, Harry knows that a war looms.

Summer at the Dursleys before Harry's fifth year in *Harry Potter and the Order of the Phoenix* drags on even worse than ever. At 15, Harry angrily broods about why he is the one chosen to fight Voldemort, why no one understands his fear and loathing, why he is treated like a child. He even turns on Dumbledore, who had always supported Harry, when the old wizard does not explain why he has apparently given in to the Ministry of Magic and its takeover of Hogwarts. And most especially, Harry hates the new professor of Defense of the Dark Arts, Professor Umbridge. A short, round woman with a treacly veneer, she directs particular hatred toward Harry. And on top of everything else, the Fifth Years are facing their Ordinary Wizarding Level (O.W.L.) examinations in the spring, a series of comprehensive tests that determine whether students will proceed to advanced work.

But all these tests of mind, character, and even friendship do little to divert Harry from the battle with Voldemort that he knows he can not escape. Believing himself alone in the struggle, not even aided by Dumbledore, he steels his will but nearly alienates everyone in the process. Harry's dark visions of Voldemort nearly overcome him. The confrontation exacts a terrible price, but *The Order of* the *Phoenix* ends with the expulsion of the ministry from Hogwarts and Harry's determination to accept his destiny.

The sixth book, *Harry Potter and the Half-blood Prince* (2005), finds 16-year-old Harry less rebellious but still resolute to confront Lord Voldemort. He spends most of the summer holidays at the Weasleys' home, called the Burrow, where he regains the friendship and trust of Ron and Hermione. The Ministry of Magic, finally acknowledging the return of Voldemort and his Death Eaters, has declared war on the Dark Lord and imposed stringent security procedures much like those enacted in the United States and Europe after September 11, 2001.

As Sixth-Years at Hogwarts, Harry and his friends begin lessons in Apparitions—passing through the time-space continuum. Otherwise, they only study the subjects in which they tested well the spring before. Although their O.W.L. scores in Potions were not Outstanding, Harry and Ron join the class, now taught by the officious but genial Horace Slughorn. The former Potions instructor, Professor Snape, has become the new Defense of the Dark Arts teacher. Since neither Harry nor Ron had bought books or supplies for Potions, Professor Slughorn allows the young men to use old manuals that are stored in the equipment closet. To his delight, Harry finds his manual to have been the property of an unnamed "Half-Blood Prince," whose tips and spells make Harry tops in Potions, much to Hermione's chagrin. Unfortunately, her enmity to the manual's former owner proves to be much more than jealousy over Harry's classroom success.

Through journeys in the Pensieve—Dumbledore's magic stone basin—Harry and the headmaster try to decipher the fragments of Voldemort's past, which are revealed in the captured memories of those who knew him, to learn his weaknesses and give Harry an advantage over his adversary. Readers no doubt welcome the explanations as much as Harry does. Dumbledore tells him that it is Harry's capacity to love that makes him dangerous to Voldemort. The most terrible revelation concerns the existence of the Horcruxes: horrors so great that nothing—not even Hogwarts—escapes their corruption. Nevertheless, Harry's love—for someone special, for Hogwarts, but especially for Ron and Hermione—provides the steel for him to pursue the Dark Lord to the end.

A Glossary of Potter Magic
Part of the appeal of Harry Potter for readers is the descriptions of the SPELLS, POTIONS, CHARMS, and the magical creatures and plants that define the non-Muggle universe. The following is a list of some of the magical terms in the world of Harry Potter:

Accio: a summoning charm

animagus: a person who can turn into an animal at will

apparate: the ability to transport oneself from place to place almost instantly

Avanda Kedavra: a curse to kill the unfortunate victim; one of the three unforgivable curses

basilisk: a huge mythological serpent that may live for hundreds of years. Besides its venomous fangs, it can kill with its murderous stare, causing instant death. Spiders fear the basilisk as their natural enemy, and the basilisk fears only the crow of a rooster, which is fatal to the monster.

bezoar: a stone taken from a goat's stomach that acts as a poison preventative

boggart: a shape-shifter that becomes whatever one fears the most

Crucio: also called the Cruciatus Curse, it causes excruciating pain; one of the three unforgivable curses

Diffindo: a charm to rip something in half

disapparate: the ability to instantly remove oneself from any place

Engorgio: a spell to enlarge something

Expecto Patronum: what one shouts to exact a Patronus spell; it places a silvery wall between the wand bearer and a Dementor

Expelliarmus: a spell to disarm someone wielding a wand

Floo powder: when thrown into a fire, it can transport one to any place in the Floo network

gillyweed: plant that allows one to breathe underwater

hippogriff: a creature that is half horse, half bird with a gleaming coat of many colors

howler: a letter that yells its arrival 100 times louder than usual

Hungarian Horntail: a species of dragon

Impedimenta: a spell to slow someone or something down

Imperio: also called the Imperius Curse, it gives the bearer total control; one of three unforgivable curses

mandrake: a plant that provides the essential part of most poison antidotes. The cry of a full-grown mandrake is fatal to the hearer

Morsmorde: the spell to send the Dark Mark to identify Voldemort's followers as a signal into the sky

Patronus: the animal form that appears as protection against the Dementors in the Patronum spell

Reducio: a spell to reduce the size of something

Stupefy: a spell to stun someone.

Is Harry Evil?

Despite the popularity of Harry Potter, he also engenders great controversy. Many conservative religious groups decry the young wizard's influence, claiming that the books teach their children the demonically inspired arts of witchcraft. Many schools have removed Harry Potter from their library shelves and language arts curricula. Scores of web sites allegedly demonstrate the evils of magic and the dangers of its practice. One web article, posted by a self-proclaimed former wizard, warns that the books teach sorcery, a very dangerous and tricky business. He says that casting a spell involves mastery over demons and could be fatal. Another posting equates Harry Potter with the Antichrist. Critics in France dismiss the books as just one more example of dog-eat-dog Western capitalism. The Catholic Church, however, gave its approval to the series, praising the books for their clear exposition of good versus evil and moral solutions to conflict.

Films and Wealth

Warner Brothers purchased the film rights to Harry Potter and by 2004 had released four films. According to *Forbes* magazine, all Harry Potter sales and rights has made Rowling worth more than $1 billion; she is the first person to achieve that status from writing. She is much wealthier than Queen Elizabeth II. Rowling planned to conclude Harry Potter's adventures in the seventh book (in honor of the seven books in the *Chronicles of Narnia* written by C. S. Lewis).

FURTHER READING:

Rowling, J. K. *Harry Potter and the Chamber of Secrets*. New York: Scholastic Inc., 1999.

———. *Harry Potter and the Goblet of Fire*. New York: Scholastic Inc., 2000.

———. *Harry Potter and the Order of the Phoenix*. New York: Scholastic Inc., 2003.

———. *Harry Potter and the Prisoner of Azkaban*. New York: Scholastic Inc., 1999.

———. *Harry Potter and the Sorcerer's Stone*. New York: Scholastic Inc., 1997.

Schnoebelen, William J. "Straight Talk No. 22 on Harry Potter." Available online at www.withoneaccord.org/store/potter.html. Downloaded July 5, 2004.

prayer A petition to a higher power for help. In essence, prayer can be considered a form of MAGIC. The word *prayer* itself means "to petition." It is derived from the Latin term *precarius,* which means "obtained by begging." Prayers are directed to deities, supernatural forces of nature, the ancestral dead, saints, ANGELS, and spirits. Most prayers are for divine intercession for one's self or for others.

The act of praying is a RITUAL. The most formal prayer rituals are conducted in religious services and may involve adoration and thanksgiving as well as petitions for assistance. Other forms of prayer confession, lamentation, meditation, contemplation, and surrender. Prayer may be done verbally, silently, or in writing.

Certain prayers are considered to be AMULETS against evil. For example, during the Inquisition, the Lord's Prayer was held to ward off DEMONS and SPELLS that had been cast by witches. It also was used in witch trials as a litmus test; true witches, who were believed to be in servitude to the devil, supposedly could not recite the Lord's Prayer at all or without mistakes.

In folk magic, a CHARM is a "little prayer," usually composed in verse, asking for a specific favor.

Prima Materia In ALCHEMY, the "First Matter," the substance from which the PHILOSOPHER'S STONE is created, or even the stone itself. The *Prima Materia* is the material beginning and end of all things. It holds the seed of perfection.

The exact nature of the *Prima Materia* is mysterious. It is disguised in alchemical writings and is referred to by hundreds of substitute names. According to Ruland in his *Alchemical Lexicon* (1612), "The philosophers have so greatly admired the Creature of God which is called the Primal Matter, especially concerning its efficacy and mystery, that they have given it many names, and almost every possible description, for they have not known how to sufficiently praise it." Ruland goes on to list 50 alternate names for the *Prima Materia*:

1. They originally called it Microcosmos, a small world, wherein heaven, earth, fire, water, and all elements exist, also birth, sickness, death, and dissolution, the creation, the resurrection, etc. 2. Afterwards it was called the Philosophical Stone, because it was made of one thing. Even at first it is truly a stone. Also because it is dry and hard, and can be triturated like a stone. But it is more capable of resistance and more solid. No fire or other element can destroy it. It is also no stone, because it is fluid, can be smelted and melted. They further call it the Eagle Stone, because it has stone within it, according to Rosinus. 3. It is also called Water of Life, for it causes the King, who is dead, to awake into a better mode of being and life. It is the best and most excellent medicine for the life of mankind. 4. Venom, Poison, Chambar, because it kills and destroys the King, and there is no stronger poison in the world. 5. Spirit—because it flies heavenward, illuminates the bodies of the King, and of the metals, and gives them life. 6. Medicine—the one most excellent medicine, for it speedily and marvelously heals all of the maladies and infirmities of mankind and of metals. 7. Heaven, for it is light and bright, indestructible, and is Heaven in operation. 8. Clouds—for it gives celestial water and rain upon its own earth. 9. Nebula, or Fog—for it ascends from the earth, and makes the air dark. 10. Dew—for it falls from the air and stimulates the soil, together with that which grows upon it. 11. Shade—for it casts a shadow over the earth and the elements, and causes darkness. 12. Moon—for she is in her nature and quality

cold and moist; her influence extends to the Under World; she receives her light from the sun; hence she ministers to the time of darkness, by means of the shade of the earth. 13. Stella Signata and Lucifer—the pre-eminent and morning star, for she gives the sign in operations, she shines first, then comes the sun, both evening and morning, which is a marvel to behold. 14. Permanent Water—metallic water of life, leafy water. It remains in fire, air, and earth, and cannot be destroyed by any element. 15. Fiery and Burning Water—for it is exceeding hot, melts up all metals more quickly than fuel and flame, yea, melts that which resists fire. 16. Salt of Nitre and Saltpetre—for it possesses their nature and kind. It also rises with greater strength and violence than any saltpetre whatever. It is, moreover, extracted from the earth. 17. Lye—for it washes and cleans the metals, and the garments of the King. 18. Bride, Spouse, Mother, Eve—from her royal children are born to the King. 19. Pure and Uncontaminated Virgin—for she remains pure and unimpregnated, notwithstanding that she bears children. She is a most extraordinary mother, who slays her husband and offspring, and revivifies them by means of her breasts. Assidous says: The Mother of our Stone, which is now perfected, is still a virgin, never having reclined in the nuptial couch, because this hermaphrodite and universal matter of the Sun and Moon, has intercourse only with itself, and is not yet impregnated in any special manner, such as the golden, silver, or mercurial process, etc. Consequently it is a pure, virginal birth. 20. Milk of Virgin, or of the Fig, for it renders things sweet, white, delicious, and wholesome. 21. Boiling Milk, for it warms, cooks, whitens, and matures. 22. Honey, for it sweetens, confers a pleasant smell, and renders things delicious and wholesome. 23. A Spiritual Blood—for it is like blood, and so remains, it reddens, vivifies, and has the spirit therein. 24. Bath—for it washes and cleanses the King, and metals, and causes them to perspire. 25. A Syrup—for it is acid, and produces strength and courage. 26. Vinegar—for it macerates, makes spicy, pickles, renders savoury, strngthens, preserves, corrodes, and yields a tincture. 27. Lead, for it is heavy, and is at first impure; gives colour and weight. Lead is made from the stone. 28. Tin—on account of its whiteness. 29. Sulphur of Nature, Lime, Alum, for it consumes and burns up. 30. Spittle of the Moon, incombustible saliva. 31. Burnt Copper, black Copper, Flower of Copper, i.e. Ore, as also is the Ore of Hermes. 32. The Serpent, the Dragon, for he devours and destroys. 33. Marble, Crystal, Glass—which is all clear and intelligible. 34. Scottish Gem. 35. Urine of boys, urine of the white calf, on account of its acrid nature. 36. White Magnesia, a Magnet, because it attracts gold, or the King, unto itself. 37. White Ethesia, a white Moisture. 38. Dung, for it manures the earth, which renders it moist, fat, and fruitful. 39. White Smoke, for it renders white and glistening. 40. Metallic Entity—for it is the true Essence and Quintessence of Metals. 41. The Virtue of mineral Mercury. 42. The Soul and Heaven of the Elements. 43. The Matter of all Forms. 44. Tartar of the Philosophers. 45. Dissolved Refuse. 46. The Rainbow—on account of its colors. 47. Indian Gold, Heart of the Sun, Shade of the Sun, Heart and Shade of Gold—for it is stronger than Gold; it holds the gold in its heart, and is itself Gold. 48. Chaos—as it is in the beginning. 49. Venus—On account of the fruitfulness of Nature. 50. Microcosmos—because it is a likeness of the great world, through heaven, the sea, and all elements.

Other names for the *Prima Materia* are:

Abzernad	The Bull	May Blossom
Adarner	Butter	Menstruum
Adrop	Caduceus	The Moon
Aevis	Cain	Mother
Agnean	Chyle	Orient
Alabar	The Cock	Philosophical Stone
Alartar	Dragon	
Alcharit	Eagle	Salamander
Alembroth	Ebisemeth	The Sea
Alinagra	Embryo	Shadow of the Sun
Alkaest	Euphrates	Silver
Almisada	Eve	The Son of the Sun and the Moon
Aludel	Feces	
Alun	Flower of the Sun	Sonig
Amalgra		Soul of Saturn
Anathron	The Garden	The Spouse
Androgyne	Golden Wood	Spring
Anger	Hermaphrodite	Sulphur
Animal Stone	Hyle	Summer
Antimony	Infinite	Tincture of Metals
Aremaros	Isis	The Tree
Arnec	Kibrish	Vapor
Arsenic	The Lamb	Vegetable Liquor
Asmarcech	Laton	
Asrob	Lead	Water of Gold
Azoth	Lion	Water of Life
The Belly of the Ostrich	Lord of the Stones	The West
Bird of Hermes	Magnes	Whiteness
Borax	Magnesia	The Woman
Boritis	Mars	

See also ALKAHEST; AZOTH; QUINTESSENCE.

FURTHER READING:
Hauck, Dennis William. *The Emerald Tablet: Alchemy for Personal Transformation.* New York: Penguin/Arkana, 1999.
"Ruland—On the Prima Materia." Available online. URL: http://www.levity.com/alchemy/ruland_e.html. Downloaded August 29, 2005.

projection In ALCHEMY, the successful transmutation of base metals into GOLD or SILVER. The projection is the ultimate goal of alchemy and requires the PHILOSOPHER'S STONE. Many famous alchemists labored much of their lives to accomplish only one or a few projections reportedly.

The Philosopher's Stone was sometimes called the projection or the Power of Projection.

psychic vampirism In occultism, the draining of one's vitality by persons, entities, or improper magical or occult activities. Psychic vampirism can be deliberate and intentional, as in PSYCHIC ATTACK, or it can be unintentional. A person victimized by psychic vampirism experiences depleted energy, inability to sleep and concentrate, deteriorating health, depression, and negative compulsions. In the severest cases, psychic vampirism can lead to death.

In the literature of the HERMETIC ORDER OF THE GOLDEN DAWN, Dr. Edward C. Berridge, a homeopathic physician whose occult name was Frater Resurgam, describes cases of different types of psychic vampirism and his remedies against them. In one case, he was repeatedly visited by an elderly man of "exhausted nervous vitality," who always made Berridge feel exhausted. It occurred to Berridge that the old man was preying upon him. "I don't suppose that he was at all externally conscious that he possessed a vampire organization, for he was a benevolent kind-hearted man, who would have shrunk in horror from such a suggestion," Berridge said. However, he believed the old man to be an "intentional vampire," for he had admitted that he was soon to marry a much younger woman in the hopes of revitalizing himself.

In another case, a woman sought his help concerning her failing health. In pursuit of spiritual development, she had become "passively mediuimistic," probably making her vulnerable to the draining influences of low-level entities. Berridge performed mesmeric passes over her (see MESMERISM) and placed a protective layer of odic fluid (universal life force) around her to shut out negative entities. The woman's health and strength improved and her mediumistic experiences stopped. However, she soon opened herself back up mediumistically and suffered a serious decline in health. After a lingering illness, she died. Berridge reported that he himself was attacked by an ELEMENTAL that he believed turned on him when he shut it off from the woman:

> I had not been initiated into the G.D. [Golden Dawn] then, or should have afterwards used the Banishing Pen-

tagram for my own protection. About two weeks after, I had a vivid dream that I was endeavoring to evoke an elemental, which attacked me, causing a sudden choking in the throat, and an electric shock in the body. The dream had an astrological meaning; and at the same time I believe it had a physical basis and that the same vampirizing spirit which had been preying on its victim, determined to attack me, in revenge for having thwarted its designs.

In another case, Berridge aided a woman who said she felt ill and exhausted whenever she was in the presence of a certain man who suffered from bad health. Berridge believed that the man was vampirizing the woman to try to improve his own health. He obtained a description of the man and then performed a magical RITUAL. Using the IMAGINATION, he visualized the woman and man facing each other, and he placed around the woman a shield of ODIC FLUID. He also made the sign of the Invoking Pentagram upon her for added protection. As a result, the vampirism stopped.

See also PENTAGRAM.

FURTHER READING:
King, Francis (ed.). *Ritual Magic of the Golden Dawn.* Rochester, Vt.: Destiny Books, 1997.

puffer Nickname for an alchemist who is preoccupied with transmuting base metals into GOLD and SILVER and who ignores the spiritual or philosophical side of ALCHEMY. Puffers earned their nickname from their penchant for the use of bellows and forges. They were scorned by "true" alchemists; however, their experiments sometimes led to discoveries in chemistry.

Puffers labored away in dirty laboratories, often killing themselves from careless handling of chemicals or from inhaling poisonous fumes. They hired themselves out to wealthy patrons who wanted easy riches, but their failure to produce precious metals landed them in prison or even on the execution block.

One puffer of note was Johann F. Bottiger, a German "pharmaceutical assistant" who in 1701, at age 16, reportedly transformed several 20-pfennig pieces of silver into gold in front of aristocratic witnesses in Berlin. The PROJECTION was aided by Bottiger's employer, who applied a dark red glass TINCTURE to the silver pieces.

Bottiger was vaulted to fame and caught the attention of Frederich I of Prussia, a gold-hungry ruler who executed alchemists who failed to make gold. Bottiger fled to avoid being forced to work for Frederich but fell into the employ of another greedy monarch, Augustus the Strong of Saxony, who hanged failed alchemists from a gallows decked out in tinsel to mock their failure. Augustus gave Bottiger everything he could want in the way of equipment—but made him a prisoner of the state.

Bottiger managed to spend 18 years working for Augustus, convincing the king that he could indeed make gold

Puffers, in Das Kloster, vol. I, *by J. Scheible, 1845.* (Author's collection)

and silver. What saved his life was his ability to imitate porcelain imported from China. In 1706 August ordered him to discover how porcelain was made, and it took Bottiger three years to do so. His success enabled August to establish a porcelain factory in Meissen in 1710. Bottiger oversaw the factory and carefully guarded his secret for making porcelain.

But Augustus still demanded gold and silver, and in 1713 he insisted that Bottiger demonstrate his ability or face execution. On March 13, Bottiger took copper and lead and made small buttons of gold and silver, according to witnesses. Bottiger's life was saved. In December 1717, again under pressure by the king, Bottiger swore that he would reveal his secret formula for making precious metals. But before he did so, he apparently inhaled poisonous fumes in his laboratory and died. Whether the death was accidental or suicide is not known.

FURTHER READING:
Secrets of the Alchemists. New York: Time-Life Books, 1990.

Pythagoras (sixth c. B.C.E.)   Greek philosopher and mathematician, best known for major contributions to astronomy, geometry, and music theory. His teachings influenced Socrates, Plato, Euclid, Aristotle, and thinkers in many disciplines down to the present day. Iamblichus listed 218 men and 17 women among the most famous of Pythagorean philosophers of ancient times. Pythagoras achieved such stature during and after his life that he was virtually deified, and numerous legends sprang up around him: He was said to be the son of God and had a gold shin bone. It is said that he was the first person to call himself a philosopher.

Pythagoras was born on the island of Samos. According to lore, he was named after the Pythia, the ORACLE at DELPHI, who prophesied his birth and said that he would be a great contributor to the wisdom of humankind. Little is known about his early life. Pythagoras left Samos about 530 B.C.E. to escape Polycrates' tyrannical rule. It is said that he traveled widely throughout the ancient world and

was initiated into the mysteries of Isis in Thebes and as well to the mysteries of Babylonia, Chaldea, Adonis, and probably Eleusis. He may even have gone to India and studied with the Brahmins.

He settled in the Dorian city of Croton, southern Italy, where he attracted a community of men and women followers, some of whom became organized as an order. He initiated followers with a sacred formula based on the letters of his name. Disciples were ranked by degrees, and only those of the higher degrees were allowed into the inner court of his temple, where Pythagoras revealed the most secret teachings. He was fond of lecturing at night.

At age 60, Pythagoras married one of his disciples, a young girl named Theano, and fathered either three or seven children; accounts vary. He wielded great influence over local politics. He believed in a scientific government similar to the priesthood of Egypt. Croton had an aristocratic constitution and was governed by a Council of One Thousand, comprised of representatives of the wealthy families. Over this body, Pythagoras organized the Council of Three Hundred, recruited from initiates who recognized Pythagoras as their leader. It was the goal of the Pythagorean Order to become the head of state throughout southern Italy. But in about 450 B.C.E. an antiaristocracy, anti-Pythagorean revolt forced out most of the Pythagoreans, including Pythagoras himself. He went to Metapontium, where he died, allegedly at the age of nearly 100.

The Pythagorean Order lasted for about another 250 years, with the founding of centers on the Greek mainland, and the influence of Pythagorean teachings has lasted to the present. Since individual Pythagoreans contributed to the order's philosophy and because contemporary records were not reliable, it is not possible to identify which of the order's concepts are specifically those of Pythagoras himself.

Neo-Pythagoreanism, a Hellenistic school of philosophy, was founded in the first century B.C.E. by Publius Nigidius Figulus and espoused by Apollonius of Tyana. Neopythagoreanism professed unbroken lineage from the Pythagorean Order and was absorbed into Neoplatonism in the third century C.E.

Major Teachings
Pythagoras is best known for fundamental geometric theorem named for him that states the square of the hypotenuse of a right triangle is equal to the sum of the squares of the sides containing the right angle. The theorem's corollary states that the diagonal of a square is incommensurable with its side.

Pythagoras conceived of the universe as a living being, animated by a great Soul and permeated by Intelligence. He called God the Monad, the Supreme Mind, the living and absolute truth clothed in light. Man is separate, save for his soul, which is a spark of the Monad that is imprisoned in a mortal body. Humanity's task is to purify itself in preparation for return to the Monad.

Pythagoras said all sidereal bodies are alive and have souls and that the planets are deities. According to Aristotle, Pythagoras also believed that the Earth had a dual rotation and circled the Sun, but this potentially sacrilegious teaching was saved for only the most trusted disciples.

The cosmos is a mathematically ordered whole. Everything in the universe and in nature is divided into threes. The universe has three worlds:

- The Supreme World, a subtle essence that was the true plane of the Monad
- The Superior World, the home of the immortals
- The Inferior World, the home of mortal gods, DAIMONES, man, animals, and all material things.

Living beings have a triune nature: body, soul (which Pythagoras related to mind), and spirit. He also said that all arts and sciences are based on three elements: MUSIC, mathematics, and astronomy.

Pythagoras described NUMBERS as an intrinsic and living virtue of the Monad. The Word is numbers manifested by form. He ascribed to each a principle, law, and active force of the universe. The first four numbers contain the basic principles of the universe, since adding or multiplying by them produces all other numbers. Besides three, Pythagoras gave special meaning to the numbers seven and 10. Seven, comprised of the numbers three and four, represents the union of humanity and divinity. It is the number of adepts and great initiates. Ten is a perfect number (1+2+3+4) and represents all the principles of the Monad. Pythagorean number theories survive in modern-day NUMEROLOGY.

In music, Pythagoras is credited with discovery of the diatonic scale and the reduction of all music to mathematical ratios. These ratios can be applied to the universe, he said, which gave rise to his theory of the Harmony (or Music) of the Spheres. The theory is based on harmonic relationships drawn among all heavenly bodies, which produces music as the bodies rush through space. This divine music cannot be heard by man, however (except perhaps by the enlightened such as Pythagoras), as long as man was in his fallen, material state.

Pythagoras believed in the healing power of music and composed "musical medicine." He favored stringed instruments, especially the lute; he said that songs sung to the lute purified the soul. He advocated avoidance of flutes and cymbals.

Pythagoras also taught herbal and medicinal plant lore. He opposed surgery. In other teachings, he said that friendship was the truest and nearest to perfection of all relationships. Anarchy was the greatest crime.

He told his disciples that once they were initiated, they had to allow the truth to descend into their beings and apply it on a daily life. To accomplish this, they had to bring together three perfections: truth in intellect; virtue in the soul; purity in the body.

To achieve purity in the body, Pythagoras advocated avoidance of beans and meat. Meat especially clouded the reason. He himself ate meat occasionally but said that judges in particular should not eat meat before sitting at trial.

The Pythagoreans believed in the immortality of the soul, the soul's ability to separate from the body, and in reincarnation.

FURTHER READING:

Dacier, Andre. *The Life of Pythagoras*. York Beach, Maine: Samuel Weiser, 1981.

Gorman, Peter. *Pythagoras: A Life*. Boston: Routledge & Kegan Paul, 1978.

Hall, Manly P. *The Secret Teachings of All Ages*. 1928. Reprint, Los Angeles: The Philosophic Research Society, 1977.

Schure, Edouard. *The Great Initiates: A Study of the Secret Religions of History*. San Francisco: Harper & Row, 1961.

Qabalah/Qabbalah See KABBALAH.

Qlippoth (Qlipoth, Qliphoth, Kelipot) In the KAB-BALAH, the evil, negative, and unbalanced aspects of the *sephiroth* on the Tree of Life. *Qlippoth* means "shells," and it also means demonic, infernal spirits, or fallen ANGELS. The singular form is *Qlippah*. The Qlippoth are sometimes symbolized by a red DRAGON.

In one sense, the Qlippoth represent materialism in the different spheres of life.

The Infernal Orders of Qlippoth correspond also to the PLANETS of the zodiac as well as the spheres of the Tree of Life. Qlippoth, their characteristics, and their respective correspondences are:

QLIPPAH	DESCRIPTION	CORRESPON-DENCE
Qemetiel	The Crowd of Gods	Ain
Belial	Without God	Ain Soph
Athiel	Uncertainty	Ain Soph Aur
Thaumiel	Twins of God	Kether
Ogiel	The Hinderers	Chokmah
Satariel	The Concealers	Binah

QLIPPAH	DESCRIPTION	CORRESPON-DENCE
Gasheklah	The Smiters	Chesed
Golachab	The Arsonists	Geburah
Tageriron	The Hagglers	Tiphareth
Oreb Zaraq	The Raven of Dispersion	Netzach
Samael	Poison of God	Hod
Gamaliel	The Obscene Ones	Yesod
Lilith	Queen of the Night	Malkuth
Beiriron	The Herd	Aries
Adimiron	The Bloody Ones	Taurus
Tzelilimiron	The Clangers	Gemini
Shichirion	The Black Ones	Cancer
Shalhebiron	The Flaming Ones	Leo
Tzaphiriron	The Scratchers	Virgo
Abiriron	The Clayish Ones	Libra
Necheshthiron	The Brazen Ones	Scorpio
Nachashiron	The Snakey Ones	Sagittarius

QLIPPAH	DESCRIPTION	CORRESPON-DENCE
Dagdagiron	The Fishy Ones	Capricorn
Bahimiron	The Bestial Ones	Aquarius
Nashimiron	Malignant Women	Pisces

See also NEUBERG, VICTOR.

FURTHER READING:
Godwin, David. *Godwin's Cabalistic Encyclopedia.* 3rd ed. St. Paul, Minn.: Llewellyn Publications, 2004.
Gray, William G. *The Tree of Evil: Polarities of Good and Evil as Revealed by the Tree of Life.* York, Maine: Samuel Weiser, 1984.

quatre yeux   A French term meaning "four eyes," used in Vodoun to describe the power of CLAIRVOYANCE. One cannot become a priest or a priestess without having *quatre yeux.*

quicksilver   See MERCURY.

quintessence (*quinta essentia*)   The fifth ELEMENT. Quintessence is a psychic spiritual energy that is superior to the other four elements of earth, air, fire, and water. It can bind the other elements together or dissolve them. According to PYTHAGORAS, the quintessence was the equivalent of the soul. PARACELSUS said the quintessence permeates and ensouls the body, enabling it to become a living being.

In ALCHEMY, the quintessence was held to heal any disease or condition and to rejuvenate the body. It was important in the process for transmuting base metals to GOLD and SILVER. *The First Book of the Secrets of Nature or the Fifth Essence,* a spurious work attributed to RAYMOND LULLY, describes the quintessence's alleged miraculous and adaptive powers:

> It preserves the body from corruption, strengthens the basic constitution (*elementativa*), pristine youth is restored by it, it unifies the spirit, dissolves the crudities, solidifies that which is loose, loosens the solid, fattens the lean, weakens the fat, cools the inflamed, heats up the cold, dries the humid, humidifies the dry; in what way soever, one and the same thing can perform contrary operations, the sole act of one thing is diversified according to the nature of the recipient, just as the heat of the sun has contrary effects, for it dries the mud and liquifies the wax.

Numerous recipes for miraculous medicines were written with the quintessence as a key ingredient.

The quintessence is associated with the ANIMA MUNDI, the PRIMA MATERIA, the PENTACLE and the PENTAGRAM, and the ROSE.

See also AKASHA.

FURTHER READING:
Patai, Raphael. *The Jewish Alchemists.* Princeton, N.J.: Princeton University Press, 1994.

Rasputin, Grigori Yefimovich (c. 1872–1916) Russian mystic, healer, and prophet who predicted his own death, the deaths of the czar Nicholas II and his family, and the downfall of the nobility in Russia. His unusual abilities were similar to those of WIZARDS and cunning men.

Grigori Yefimovich Rasputin was born in Pokrovskoye to Siberian peasant parents; he may have been the distant descendant of Siberian shamans. As a youth he worked as a carter and acquired an early reputation for fighting, drinking, and womanizing. He also was attracted to religion.

At age 20, he married a woman four years older than he and became a farmer. They had a son, who died as an infant. Not long after that, Rasputin experienced a vision of the Virgin Mary calling to him, and he set out on a two-year religious pilgrimage to Mount Athos in Greece. When he returned home, he was changed, possessing the ability to heal and cure by prayer. He set himself up as a *starets,* an unordained holy man. When his popularity threatened the village priest, Rasputin left town.

He was drawn to St. Petersburg, Russia's capital, where the nobility and high society was intensely interested in the occult and Spiritualism, due in large part to the 1871 visit by the famed English medium, Daniel Dunglas Home. The atmosphere was ripe for someone like Rasputin to be noticed.

Despite his scruffy appearance and odd ways, Rasputin gained quick fame with his healing ability. He attracted the attention of the royal family, Nicholas and Alexandra, whose sole male heir, Alexis, was threatened by hemo-philia. Rasputin was able to alleviate the boy's suffering. Alexandra became devoted to him, which aroused jealousy and enmity among others in court.

Rasputin's licentious behavior exacerbated his lack of popularity. He boasted of his early days of womanizing and preached that one must sin before one can be redeemed. He acquired numerous mistresses. By 1911 his behavior was considered a scandal and disgrace. Opposition to him grew, and in 1916 a group of nobles plotted to kill him.

Rasputin divined his own death, which he wrote down in a letter. He predicted that he would be dead by January 1, 1917. If peasants killed him, the monarchy would continue and prosper, but if the nobles killed him, the royal family would die within two years, and the aristocracy would be plunged into trouble for 25 years, after which it would be eliminated from the country.

The circumstances of Rasputin's death are bizarre. On the night of December 29, 1916, Rasputin attended a midnight tea to which he had been invited in the home of Prince Feliks Yusupov, one of his enemies. He allegedly was fed cakes and wine laced with cyanide, which did not kill him. Yusupov then shot him. Rasputin collapsed, then jumped up, and dashed into the courtyard. Yusupov shot him again and beat him with an iron bar. Still he remained alive. The desperate conspirators dragged him to the frozen Neva River, bound him, and pushed him through a hole in the ice. When his body was recovered, the cause of death was determined as drowning; no traces of poison were detected.

True to Rasputin's PROPHECY, the royal family was murdered within two years. The Russian Revolution and World War I plunged the country into chaos and threatened the old aristocratic order. The nobility finally came to an end 25 years later, in World War II, at the hands of Josef Stalin. See also CHEIRO.

FURTHER READING:

De Jonge, Alex. *Life and Times of Grigorii Rasputin.* New York: Dorset, 1982.

Wilson, Colin. *The Occult.* New York: Vintage Books, 1973.

raven   A messenger between God and humankind. In particular, ravens are also associated with death and the

A raven sits atop the skeleton of death in the Death card in The Alchemical Tarot, by Rosemary Ellen Guiley and Robert Michael Place. The raven and death represent the nigredo stage of alchemy: mortification and putrification. Inspired by Johann Daniel Mylous's Philosophia reformata, 1622. (Copyright by and courtesy of Robert Michael Place)

underworld and are often considered omens of death because they gather at battlefields and houses where someone is about to die and also as SYMBOLS of impurity because they feed on corpses. Thus, they are messengers of the dark side of God. However, ravens in mythology and fairy tales are neither good nor evil but express the blunt truth of the unconscious. Talking ravens are agents of PROPHECY.

In ALCHEMY, the raven, like the CROW, is the darkness that precedes the light. It represents the *nigredo,* the mortification that represents the dying to the material world that is necessary for spiritual purification and illumination to take place.

Other meanings of the raven are warfare and bloodshed and a magically empowered shapeshifter.

raven stones   In German folklore, magical lights made from the undigested eyes of executed criminals. Raven stones are so named because they are obtained from ravens that picked out the eyes of corpses hanging on gallows. According to lore, raven stones emit a light visible only to their owners and are used by thieves.

Rāzī (c. 850–925 or 932)   Islamic alchemist who also made important contributions to medicine. Rāzī, born Abū Bakr Muhammad ibn Zakarīyyā, was known as Rhazes, Rhasis, Rasi, and Al-Razi. He was called the man of Ray, a city that in his day was a major cultural center.

Rāzī was born near Teheran. He went to Ray to study and learned philosophy, logic, metaphysics, poetry, and his special love, music. When he was 30, he took a trip to Baghdad and there became interested in medicine. He helped to plan the rebuilding of the hospital in Baghdad, hoping for an appointment there, but he was sent back to Ray instead to take charge of a hospital. Soon, however, he was recalled to Baghdad and given the post of physician-in-charge of the hospital. Rāzī remained in Baghdad until his retirement when he returned once again to Ray.

Rāzī wrote encyclopedias on music and medicine, as well as books on other topics. Several of 12 books on chemistry attributed to him were probably written anonymously by others who used his name.

Rāzī is credited with writing numerous books on ALCHEMY, but only one survives, *The Book of the Secret of Secrets.* He believed that all substances are composed of the four ELEMENTS, but he did not accept JABIR IBN HAYYAN's theory of balances. He believed that alchemy could accomplish the transmutation of base metals into GOLD and SILVER and even transmute stones such as quartz into such precious jewels as rubies, sapphires, and emeralds. Transmutation could be accomplished with a master ELIXIR; Rāzī never used the term PHILOSOPHER'S STONE to describe such an elixir. His alchemical work led to contributions to medicine, chemistry, and pharmacology.

Later in his life, Rāzī presented a treatise on the transmutation of metals to Emir Almansour, prince of Khorassan, who was so impressed with it that he gave 1,000 pieces of gold to Rāzī. The prince wished to witness a transmutation, and Rāzī agreed to perform one provided that he had the proper equipment. The prince had Rāzī outfitted with a well-stocked laboratory. But Rāzī failed miserably in the transmutation, and the enraged prince beat him about the head. He soon went blind; some sources say as a result of the beating, while others attribute it to his long years of intense reading and writing.

FURTHER READING:
Holmyard, E. J. *Alchemy*. New York: Penguin Books, 1957.
Waite, Arthur Edward. *Alchemists Through the Ages*. Blauvelt, N.Y.: Rudolph Steiner Publications, 1970.

Rebis See HERMAPHRODITE.

red Color that offers protection against all evil acts and spirits, the EVIL EYE, and BEWITCHMENT. Red is used in the making of magical AMULETS and TALISMANS.

Regardie, Francis Israel (1907–1983) Magician, psychiatrist, and onetime companion of ALEISTER CROWLEY. It is said that no one person knew the Beast, as Crowley called himself, better than Israel Regardie.

Francis Israel Regardie (he later dropped use of his first name in favor of the middle name) was born in England on November 17, 1907. He was 13 when his family emigrated to the United States where he spent most of his life. He became fascinated with occultism and especially Crowley and in 1928 secured a position as the great magician's secretary. Regardie traveled around Europe with Crowley until 1934 when he met the eventual fate of most of Crowley's friends and associates and suffered a falling out with him.

Regardie wrote numerous books on occultism, the first of which were *The Tree of Life* and *The Garden of Pomegranates,* both of which were published in 1932. In 1934, the year of his falling-out with Crowley, he joined the Stella Matutina temple of the HERMETIC ORDER OF THE GOLDEN DAWN. He left after a few years and violated his oath of secrecy by publishing the complete rituals of the Golden Dawn, which appeared in a four-volume encyclopedia, *The Golden Dawn; an Encyclopedia of Practical Occultism,* between 1937 and 1940. The work has been revised and reissued several times, including a single-volume edition in 1986. Regardie said that he broke his oath because he believed that the teachings of the Golden Dawn should be revealed to the public. The Stella Matutina, no longer a secret society, went into decline. Golden Dawn material forms the foundation of most modern ceremonial MAGIC.

Professionally, Regardie became a chiropractor. He served in the U.S. Army during World War II and then set-

tled in southern California where he worked as a psychotherapist. He authored a definitive biography of Crowley, *The Eye in the Triangle,* and coauthored with P. R. Stephensen, another Crowley associate, *The Legend of Aleister Crowley,* both of which appeared in 1970. Regardie always acknowledged Crowley's faults, but he also defended Crowley as "a great mystic, sincere, dedicated and hard working."

Regardie's other books include: *My Rosicrucian Adventure* (1936); *Middle Pillar* (1945); *The Romance of Metaphysics* (1946); *The Art of Healing* (1964); *Roll Away the Stone* (1964); *What is the Qabalah?* (1970); *To Invoke Your Higher Self* (1973); and *Twelve Steps to Spiritual Enlightenment* (1975).

FURTHER READING:
Hyatt, Christopher S., ed. *An Interview with Israel Regardie: His Final Thoughts and Views*. Phoenix: Falcon Press, 1985.

Rhymer, Thomas the See FAIRIES.

ring In MAGIC, jewelry that possesses supernatural powers. Magical rings are made according to specific procedures and are engraved with magical SYMBOLS and NAMES.

Talismanic Rings
A magic ring can be a TALISMAN that confers special or supernatural powers on the wearer, such as invisibility, wisdom, and strength. King SOLOMON of the Israelites, the builder of the temple of Jerusalem, reputedly had a magical ring given to him by the archangel Michael that gave him power to command all DEMONS. The ring had a precious stone with a SEAL and the mystical word *Schemhamphorasch* engraved upon it. Different stories tell about the powers of the ring. According to one version, whenever Solomon looked at the ring, he saw whatever he desired to know on Earth or in heaven. One day he took it off prior to bathing, and it was stolen by a fury and thrown into the sea. After 40 days, Solomon found the ring in the belly of a fish that was served to him at a meal.

A talisman ring also can have the purpose of healing; they were used for that purpose as early as the first century C.E. Rings made of copper and zinc were worn to cure gout and rheumatism. In the Middle Ages, "cramp rings" blessed by a monarch were believed to have the power to relieve pain. Cramp rings also were used in love CHARMS, such as the following from the 16th century:

> Take two cramp rings of gold or silver and lay them both in a swallow's nest that buildeth in the summer. Let them lie there 9 days, then take them and deliver the one to thy love and keep the other thyself.

PARACELSUS had a talismanic ring made of antimony that he wore when he diagnosed patients. The ring was inscribed with sacred symbols. When he observed certain conditions in a patient, he placed the ring on their finger. He said the ring drew poisons out of the body.

Amulet Rings

Like the circle, a ring symbolizes protection. A magic ring can function as an AMULET to protect the wearer against disease, illness, bad luck, BEWITCHMENT, and evil spirits. Engraved magical rings supplanted amulet charms written on parchment, which were perishable.

Divination with Rings

Ring divination was popular among the early Romans. GOLD or SILVER rings were made at certain planetary auspices and were empowered with INCANTATIONS. For divination, the rings were moved about on a tripod (see TOOLS) in conjunction with incantations.

A type of ring PROPHECY involves taking a bowl, a vase, or a cylinder and inscribing the inside lip with the letters of the alphabet. Tie a consecrated ring on a thread, and use it like a PENDULUM. Hold the string in the right hand and a sprig of verbena in the left. Hang the ring into the cylinder. Ask a question. The ring will swing and strike the letters, spelling out an answer.

Making Magic Rings

According to lore, a magician's ring should be made of copper or lead and have the TETRAGRAMMATON engraved upon it. GRIMOIRES have RITUALS for making magic rings. According to one formula, wait until any star ascends in the horoscope with a fortunate aspect or conjunction of the MOON, and take a stone and herb associated with that star and make a ring of the metal that corresponds to the star. Put the herb or root under the stone in the ring, and inscribe the ring with the effect, image, name, and character of the talisman. Suffume properly by exposing the ring to certain rising PERFUMES.

A 16th-century formula for a magic ring for receiving an ORACLE calls for lead, the metal of Saturn:

> Write or engrave thereon ye name of ye angell Cassiel, then fumigate it. Then being so prepared, put it on thy finger as thou art entering into thy bed and speak no word to any person, but meditate thereon. If thou wilt complete the ring, truly, ye shall put a piece of ye roote of some especial herb governed by Saturn and put it under ye stone of a signet, as for example a little root of dragon or dragon-wort, or of black hellebore or hemp, upon which put some little onyx stone or sapphire, or lapis lazuli, but onyx is best, but let it first be made and engraved, and make ye mold to cast it, and all finished in due time with name of ye angel of Saturn.

Another formula for making a magic ring said to:

> . . . cast a ring of pure gold and engrave on it the name of an angel and the character of ye Sun. Then being made,

> fumigate it with masticke, red storax, benjamin and musk, or new sweet wine and rose water, all mixed with saffron. Forget not to first put a piece of root or yellow flower of marygold or some bay leaf, especially of angelica or root of bay tree. Then place either a carbuncle, hiacinth, chrysolite, or ye stone etites [sic] which is found in ye eagle's nest, over it.

See also LORD OF THE RINGS, THE.

FURTHER READING:
Hall, Manly P. *Paracelsus: His Mystical and Medical Philosophy.* Los Angeles: The Philosophic Research Society, 1964.
Leland, Charles Godfrey. *Etruscan Magic and Occult Remedies.* New Hyde Park, N.Y.: University Books, 1963.
Thompson, C. J. S. *The Mysteries and Secrets of Magic.* New York: Barnes & Noble, 1993.

Ripley, George (c. 1415–1490)   One of the most important English alchemists.

George Ripley was born in about 1415 in the village of Ripley, near Harrogate, England. Little is known about him. He is said to have studied ALCHEMY in Rome, Louvain, and Rhodes, where he was the guest of the Knights of St. John of Jerusalem.

In 1471 Ripley returned to England, where he became a canon at the Priory of Saint Augustine at Bridlington in Yorkshire. There he devoted himself to the study of the physical sciences, especially alchemy. The stench that emanated from his laboratory offended the monastic community.

Ripley traveled in France, Germany, and Italy in pursuit of more knowledge about alchemy. In Rome in 1477 he was made a chamberlain by Pope Innocent VIII. By 1478 he reportedly learned the secret of transmutation and returned to England. According to lore, he gave the knights an annual allowance of 100,000 pounds to finance their participation in the Crusades. The Augustinians did not approve of his smelly alchemical pursuits and expelled him from the order. He went to Boston, where he joined the Carmelites. He died in 1490 in Boston.

Ripley was among the first to champion the alchemical work of RAYMOND LULLY. He is credited with the authorship of numerous alchemical manuscripts, though some of these may be in doubt. He wrote in allegorical verse. His most important work is *Compound of Alchymy or the Twelve Gates* (1470–71). Dedicated to King Edward VI, it became one of the most popular alchemy texts of the time. In it Ripley stated that all of his experiments recorded between 1450 and 1470 should be disregarded because they were written from theory and because he found in practice later that they were untrue. He described the PHILOSOPHER'S STONE as a threefold microcosm and said that one astronomical year is required to make it. The PRIMA MATERIA exists in all things everywhere, he claimed.

His *Medulla alchimiae* (Marrow of Alchemy) was published in 1476, dedicated to George Nevill, the archbishop of York. His song *Cantilena* explains the alchemical mystery.

In *Compound* Ripley discusses the 12 "gates" or stages of the Great Work and especially describes the different colors that are observed in each stage.

His *Vision* uses the allegory of a toad to describe the Great Work:

> When busie at my Book I was upon a certain Night,
> This *Vision* here exprest appear'd unto my dimmed sight:
> A Toad full Ruddy I saw, did drink the juice of Grapes so fast,
> Till over-charged with the broth, his Bowels all to brast:
> And after that, from poyson'd Bulk he cast his Venom fell,
> For Grief and Pain whereof his members all began to swell;
> With drops of poysoned sweat approaching thus his secret Den,
> His Cave with blasts of fumous Air all bewhited then:
> And from the which in space a Golden Humor did ensue,
> Whose falling drops from high did stain the soyl with ruddy hue,
> And when his Corps the force of vital breath began to lack,
> This dying Toad became forthwith like Coal for color Black:
> Thus drowned in his proper veins of poysoned flood;
> For term of Eighty days and Four he rotting stood
> By Tryal then this Venom to expel I did desire;
> For which I did commit his Carkass to a gentle Fire:
> Which done, a Wonder to the sight, but more to be reheasrt;
> The Toad with Colors ran through every side was pierc'd,
> And White appear'd when all the sundry hews were past:
> Which after being tincted Ruddy, for evermore did last.
> Then of the Venom handled thus a Medicine I did make;
> When Venom kills, and saveth such as Venom chance to take:
> Glory be to him the granter of such secret ways,
> Dominion and Honor both, with Worship, and with Praise.

AMEN.

The toad is the *Prima Materia,* or First Matter. Fed the alchemical water, it bursts (*separatio*), and its body putrefies (*nigredo*). Reheated, it achieves the *cauda pavonis,* or Peacock's Tail of many colors, a sign that the Great Work is about the be accomplished. This occurs with the whitening and the reddening, the latter of which is the formation of the Philosopher's Stone.

The Ripley Scroll is a work of emblematic symbolism with allegorical verse describing how to perform the Great Work.

Ripley was the teacher of THOMAS NORTON.

FURTHER READING:

"George Ripley." The Alchemy Web Site. Available online. URL: http://www.levity.com/alchemy/ripley.html. Downloaded January 12, 2005.

Gilchrist, Cherry. *The Elements of Alchemy.* Rockport, Mass.: Element Books, 1991.

Holmyard, E. J. *Alchemy.* New York: Penguin Books, 1957.

Waite, Arthur Edward. *Alchemists Through the Ages.* Blauvelt, N.Y.: Rudolph Steiner Publications, 1970.

rising on the planes   Term in ritual MAGIC for ASTRAL TRAVEL, the ability to disengage consciousness from the physical body and travel throughout the levels of the ASTRAL PLANE.

The HERMETIC ORDER OF THE GOLDEN DAWN taught a technique for using the IMAGINATION to visualize one's ASTRAL BODY, to separate from the physical body, and to transfer consciousness to it. The astral body then serves as the vehicle for "rising on the planes." One imagines rising at right angles to the Earth up to the astral plane. Different beings and experiences exist on the various levels of the astral plane.

In Jungian terms, rising on the planes is comparable to "creative fantasy."

See also NEUBERG, VICTOR.

ritual   In MAGIC, a procedure for the transformation of consciousness to contact divine or supernatural forces, manifest something desired, and initiate important changes in life. Rituals are universal to all peoples and are used for all purposes: to create structure and meaning in daily life; to bring desired changes into being; to facilitate religious worship and spiritual growth; to secure luck, healing, love, and so forth. Rituals are neither inherently good nor evil but can be used for positive or negative purposes. Rituals are done both individually and collectively. Group rituals that combine mental and psychological forces can have great power.

Ritual has played an important role in the development of human consciousness since the beginnings of history. Rituals are not limited to religion and spirituality, but permeate all facets of life. Thomas Moore, author of *The Care of the Soul,* calls ritual the soul's work. Ritual helps the human consciousness tap into unseen forces: forces of the inner self, forces of nature, forces of the cosmos. Hsun Tzu, a Chinese philosopher of the third century B.C.E., said that ritual makes for harmony in the universe and brings out the best in human beings—it is the culmination of culture.

Rituals can be informal or formal. Lighting a CANDLE and saying a PRAYER are simple, informal rituals. Laying out sacred objects on an altar, wearing special clothing, using magical TOOLS, and reciting specific INVOCATIONS constitute more formal rituals, with procedures that must be followed exactly to prescription. A SPELL is a type of ritual as is an INITIATION ceremony.

According to anthropologist Arnold van Gennup, a ritual has three main parts. In the first part, a state of separation or withdrawal from the mundane world is achieved. In the second part, transformation occurs. In the third part, there is a return to the mundane world, and the transformation or change is integrated. Anthropologist Victor Turner described the phase of transition as "liminality," the "betwixt and between" worlds. He said rituals foster "communitas," or a bond that goes beyond words.

In magical and spell-casting rituals, the ritual opens and closes gateways to the spiritual realms. It focuses and intensifies the magician's WILL and enhances his ability to align his will with cosmic and natural forces. The projection of will is a significant element to ritual. In magical LODGE work, rituals are carefully constructed to incorporate the lodge's SYMBOLS, teachings, and group energies and to move energy throughout physical and psychic space with pattern movements.

ISRAEL REGARDIE states in *The Tree of Life: A Study in Magic* that ritual engages the lower self so that the soul is free to achieve an ecstatic union with the Higher Self, God or an ANGEL. He says that magical ritual:

> . . . is a mnemonic process so arranged as to result in the deliberate exhilaration of the Will and the exaltation of the Imagination, the end being the purification of the personality and the attainment of a spiritual state of consciousness in which the ego enters into a union with either its own Higher Self or a God. . . .
>
> When symbol upon symbol has affected his consciousness, when emotion beyond emotion having been roused to stimulate the imagination of the Magician, then the supreme orgiastic moment arrives. Every nerve of the body, every force channel of mind and soul is strained in one overwhelming spasm of bliss, one ecstatic overflowing of the Will and the whole of the being in the predetermined direction.

Regardie defines three types of ritual in ceremonial magic:

1. Union with a deity by means of love, service and devotion.
2. Union with a deity through identification with the deity, achieved by reciting sacred names, using magical tools, symbols and so forth, and intense projection of will and imagination.
3. A combination of both of the above working with a group rather than alone.

Rituals engage all of the senses, which is important for success. In ceremonial magic, all the senses are employed to engage the magician's will and imagination in order to alter consciousness and project the right energy toward purpose of the ritual. ELIPHAS LEVI described the controlled senses as "the golden gateway through which the King of Glory may come in." The senses are stimulated by the use of magical tools, walking, dancing, gestures, postures, chanting, recitation, incense, bells, drums, offerings, purifications, SACRIFICES, and so forth. Stillness, VISUALIZATION, fasting, and silence also are part of rituals.

Timing also is important to many rituals. In magic, certain rituals are undertaken during specific astrological times, hours of the day or night, phases of the MOON, and seasons of the year. Timing within the ritual also is important. For example, sacred NAMES should be vibrated at the precise moment of maximum psychic energy. Ritual must be dramatic to succeed. ALEISTER CROWLEY said that a ritual "should be constructed with such logical fatality that a mistake is impossible."

CARL G. JUNG said that rituals in general have lost much of their importance and power in modern Western society. Rituals have received new attention in the development of alternative religions such as Wicca and Paganism and in spiritual and personal growth groups.

FURTHER READING:

Crowley, Aleister. *Magic in Theory and Practice.* 1929. Reprint, New York: Dover Publications, 1976.

Driver, Tom F. *The Magic of Ritual.* San Francisco: HarperSan-Francisco, 1991.

Eliade, Mircea. *Patterns in Comparative Religion.* New York: New American Library, 1958.

Fortune, Dion. *Esoteric Orders and Their Work and the Training and Work of the Initiate.* London: The Aquarian Press, 1987.

van Gennup, Arnold. *The Rites of Passage.* Translated by Monica B. Vizedom and Gabrielle L. Caffee. Chicago: University of Chicago Press, 1960.

Gray, William G. *Magical Ritual Methods.* York Beach, Maine: Samuel Weiser, 1980.

Greer, John Michael. *Inside a Magical Lodge: Group Ritual in the Western Tradition.* St. Paul, Minn.: Llewellyn Publications, 1998.

Regardie, Israel. *The Tree of Life: A Study in Magic.* York Beach, Maine: Samuel Weiser, 1969.

———. *Ceremonial Magic: A Guide to the Mechanisms of Ritual.* London: Aeon Books, 2004.

Ritual of the Rose Cross A magical RITUAL of protection to ward off PSYCHIC ATTACK and interference from unwanted spirits and entities. The Ritual of the Rose Cross is important in the tradition of the HERMETIC ORDER OF THE GOLDEN DAWN.

Magical work itself is held to light up one's aura so that attention is drawn to the practitioner. Without adequate protection, entities and individuals who possess magical skills can invade a person's aura and create difficulties in daily life, even seriously jeopardizing health. The Ritual of the Rose Cross places a shield or a veil around the aura so that it cannot be penetrated. It cleanses a place.

The ritual also aids meditation work and helps a practitioner to withdraw consciousness to a higher level for problem solving or helping an individual in need.

The ritual can be performed in actuality, or it can be imagined and visualized by a skilled magician.

FURTHER READING:

King, Francis, and Stephen Skinner. *Techniques of High Magic: A Manual of Self-Initiation.* Rochester, Vt.: Destiny Books, 1976.

rose A SYMBOL of the true, archetypal Self, the highest expression of consciousness. The rose is a feminine symbol and thus is representative of fertility, passion, creation, life, beauty, love, and the eternal cycle of birth, death, and rebirth.

In ALCHEMY, the rose represents wisdom; red and white roses together are an alchemical symbol of the union of opposites. It also is similar in meaning to a mandala in Eastern mysticism.

Colors of roses have significance: A white rose represents purity and innocence, a red rose martyrdom and charity, and a blue rose the unattainable.

Roses in bloom indicate an opening to higher awareness, while withering roses indicate that a path to growth is being left untaken.

Rosenkreutz, Christian See ROSICRUCIANISM.

Rosicrucianism The Order of the Rosy Cross, called Rosicrucianism, is an esoteric society that traces its lin-

The rose, an alchemical symbol of perfection and the mysteries of life. Back design of The Alchemical Tarot, *by Rosemary Ellen Guiley and Robert Michael Place. (Copyright by and courtesy of Robert Michael Place)*

eage back to the Greek and Egyptian mystery schools. Much like FREEMASONRY, Rosicrucianism espouses Christian principles and ideals, claiming a long Western tradition, but the order also identifies itself with reincarnation and the mystical Great White Brotherhood of ADEPTS, ideas more closely associated with Theosophy and Eastern thought. Members also believe in alchemical transmutation of base metals into gold and the transformation of the spirit into higher consciousness.

History

According to Harvey Spencer Lewis (1883–1939), the first Imperator and founder of the Ancient and Mystical Order of the Rosae Crucis (AMORC) in the United States, Rosicrucianism began in 1489 B.C.E. during the reign of Pharaoh Thutmose III, a period of imperial expansion after the death of Thutmose's sister, Pharaoh Hatshepsut. Scholars from all over the kingdom, devout followers of the sun god Amon-Re, banded together to form a secret organization called the Order or the Brotherhood. Their search for occult understanding continued through the reigns of Amenhotep II, Thutmose IV, and Amenhotep III, reaching its zenith in the reign of Amenhotep IV.

But Amenhotep IV, also called Ahkenaton, upended Egyptian religion and society. Embracing the cult of Aton favored by his mother Queen Tiy's family, Amenhotep IV banished the old gods and instituted worship of Aton, which translates as heat or power, as the sole god of Egypt—thus his new name, Ahkenaton, or "one who serves the spirit of the Aton." He married his mother's niece, Nefertiti and by the seventh year of his reign had not only turned Egypt into a monotheistic state but had abandoned the capital of Thebes for a new capital city, Akhetaton, commonly called Amarna. Ahkenaton and his wife blissfully whiled away their days at the new capital, oblivious of the revolution outside.

Not 10 years later, Amarna lay empty. Ahkenaton's beloved mother, Queen Tiy, and his wife Nefertiti had died, and the pharaoh, slipping deeper into madness, had been forced by the priests of the old religion to name his half-brother Smenkhare as coregent. But that was not enough, and so Ahkenaton and Smenkhare were assassinated, and Tutanhkaton ascended the throne. The new pharaoh quickly changed his name to Tutanhkamun, but he was soon replaced by Nefertiti's father Aye. He ordered the obliteration of Ahkenaton's image, and when he was replaced by General Horemheb, all traces of any pharaoh since Amenhotep III were erased. The Brotherhood was forced underground. The surviving 296 brothers assumed the linen surplices and shaved heads of medieval friars.

Existing in secret, the brothers passed their knowledge down to succeeding generations. The legendary HERMES TRISMEGISTUS, a compilation of the gods HERMES and THOTH, supposedly led the order for more than 140 years. Imperator Lewis attributed the mystical proportions of King Solomon's Temple to the precepts of Freemasonry that were garnered from the order's knowledge. This period ended with the birth and death of the Great White Master Jesus Christ, whose life had been foretold by the Rosicrucian Essenes of Palestine.

For the next 500 years or so, the order disappeared, with instructions to each chapter, or Lodge, to determine its founding year then operate in 108-year cycles of activity and inactivity. In the years preceding "rebirth," members would advertise through symbolic pamphlets to notify the public that the allegorical "opening of the tomb to find C–R.–C. (Christus of the Rosy Cross)" would soon commence. Lewis explained that the advent of printing in the 17th century threw the 108-year cycle out of proportion, giving rise to the "real" start of Rosicrucianism: the discovery of the long-dead body of Christian Rosenkreutz.

The mysterious pamphlets announcing the legend of Christian Rosenkreutz appeared in Kassel, Germany, in 1614–15. Named the *Fama Fraternitatis dess Loblichen Ordens des Rosenkreutzes (The Fame of the Praiseworthy Order of the Rosy Cross)* and the *Confessio Fraternitatis*, the anonymous papers described a young man called Christian Rosenkreutz born in 1378. He was placed in a convent at age five to study the humanities and at age 16 accompanied one of his teachers to Damcar (perhaps Damascus) to continue his education. Three years later he traveled to Fez, Morocco, via Egypt, where he learned more secrets. Graduating in 1401, Rosenkreutz went to Spain to share his wisdom with the Moors, but they rebuffed him. Rosenkreutz returned to Germany and founded the Rosicrucian Fraternity.

The fraternity built its headquarters, called the Spiritus Sanctum, in 1409, and it taught an ever-larger circle of adepts and healers. Rosenkreutz died in 1484 at age 106 and was secretly entombed in the Spiritus Sanctum. In 1604, while making repairs to the building, the brothers encountered Rosenkreutz's vault. Across the door, in Latin, an inscription read, "After 120 years I shall open." Inside, the seven-sided vault was covered in magical symbols, the ceiling was lit by an artificial sun, and there were many ritual objects and books. But the most amazing item was Rosenkreutz's completely preserved body inside the coffin. The pamphlets told this story and offered invitations to membership, albeit that the names of current members and their whereabouts were secret. In 1616 a companion pamphlet supposedly written by Rosenkreutz himself in 1459 entitled *Chymische Hochzeit,* or *The Chymical Marriage of Christian Rosenkreutz,* describes a mystical wedding ceremony and the creation of a HOMUNCULUS.

These revelations created enormous interest within the burgeoning European occult community, but while hundreds applied for membership, the brothers remained in hiding. Current scholarship attributes the pamphlets to Johann Valentin Andreae (1586–1654), a young Lutheran pastor and reformer who used the propaganda to promote Protestantism and vilify the papacy. Most of the books and tracts promoting the Brotherhood of the Rosy Cross that appeared in the 18th and 19th centuries were actually treatises championing such causes as the free dissemination of knowledge,

universal brotherhood, support of the hermetic arts, and the unification of Europe. The millennialist followers of Johannes Kelpus (1673–1708), who settled in Pennsylvania in 1694, practiced occult and healing arts; according to Lewis, they brought Rosicrucianism to America.

In his book *Extraordinary Popular Delusions and the Madness of Crowds,* author Charles Mackay related a slightly different story of the brotherhood's founding. He acknowledged the legend of Christian Rosenkreutz but attributed the publication of the order's tenets and principles in 1615 to Michael Mayer, a renowned physician. Mayer asserted that:

> the meditations of the founding brothers surpassed any wisdom imagined since
> the Creation, not even excepting the thoughts of the Deity, and that they knew
> all that was ever known or ever would be known;
> that the brothers were destined to accomplish the peace and regeneration of man before the end of the world;
> that they possessed all the graces of nature and could distribute them to others, and that they were not subject to hunger, thirst, disease, old age or any other infirmity;
> that they controlled spirits and demons;
> that through their songs they attracted pearls and precious stones;
> that God gave them a thick cloud to hide behind, unseen by others, to protect their identities;
> that the first eight members had the ability to cure all ills;
> that the Pope would be eliminated and that only two sacraments would be permitted in the reorganized Church;
> that they knew at first glance who was worthy of membership into the Order; and
> that they recognized the Fourth Monarchy and Emperor of the Romans as the leader
> of the Christians, and that with their enormous wealth they would shower him with more gold and treasures than the King of Spain had ever taken.

Mayer went on to outline the rules of conduct for a brother:

> that wherever a brother traveled he must cure the sick;
> that wherever they were they should dress in the clothes of the people of that area;
> that they should meet at least once year in an appointed place or send a good excuse;
> that before death a brother should appoint his successor;
> that the words "Rose-Cross" would identify each one to the other; and
> that the Fraternity must be kept secret for six times twenty (120) years.

Mackay wrote that the fraternity made great inroads in Germany and other parts of Europe but that it was when the brothers arrived in Paris in 1623 that interest skyrocketed. Soon thereafter two books appeared claiming that the so-far invisible brothers were not protected by God but had instead made a pact with the devil to speak all languages, travel to the ends of the Earth as rapidly as thought, to have full purses, to infiltrate secret places by means of their invisibility, and to tell the past and future. Supposedly only 36 brothers existed, six of them in Paris. Rumors flew that mysterious, wealthy travelers enjoyed food and wine at inns and then did not pay; that chaste maidens often awoke to find men who resembled Apollo in their beds only to disappear when confronted; and that some people had found heaps of gold in their houses. No one was safe, and the police searched in vain for the Rosicrucian perpetrators. Many had opinions as to their identity; one man named Garasse, said Mackay, confidently called them drunken imposters who were really named for the garland of roses in the shape of crosses that were draped over tables in taverns all across Germany as emblems of secrecy—hence the saying that any secrets divulged there were said "sub-rosa."

Practitioners and Practices

All Rosicrucian orders incorporate the rose and cross into their logos, although colors, shapes of the cross, the numbers of roses, and the use of other occult symbols vary by organization. The Rosicrucian Fellowship places a gold CROSS with looped ends over a five-pointed star on a blue background; draped around the cross are seven roses. AMORC, the United States arm of Rosicrucianism, displays one red rose centered on a gold cross with looped ends or, alternatively, an equilateral triangle, point down, inscribed with a cross. Crosses represent death and suffering but ultimate resurrection, while roses—just as in medieval German taverns—stand for secrecy as well as love. Additionally, the family crest of Johann Andreae featured a cross of Saint Andrew with four roses between the arms, while the crest of Martin Luther was a rose with a cross in the center.

Rosicrucian ideals have changed little from the early manifestos, although by 1794 the pledge of initiation taken by Dr. Sigismund Bacstrom included a paragraph barring discrimination due to gender. Many 19th-century Rosicrucian lodges restricted membership to Freemasons, however, and Freemasonry remains open to men only. New initiates in 1794 also promised not to reward governments—or those wishing to overthrow them—with any monetary relief save paying taxes. No Rosicrucian was to donate funds to the establishment of churches, chapels, hospitals, or private charities, as there were plenty of those, "if they were only properly applied and regulated." And no member was to encourage laziness, public begging or debauchery, nor treatment of those infected with venereal diseases.

Alchemy has long been associated with the order, and Bacstrom's initiation pledge made reference to what members called the Great Work. Initiates promised never to use their knowledge of this work to support governments, to disseminate any new discoveries about the work to the membership, to never give the "fermented metallic

medicine for transmutation" to any but a brother (perhaps a solution with antimony; see ALBERTUS MAGNUS), and if mastery of the Great Work should ever be accomplished, to give praise and thanks to God. The German JAKOB BÖHME tried for years to prove the existence of the Philosopher's Stone in the Bible; some of his followers were tortured or killed for heresy.

To master the Great Work also required years of study and striving for spiritual improvement. Those who attained ultimate knowledge—true oneness with the divine—joined Christ, Buddha, Mohammed, Krishna, and the other invisible Masters in the Great White Lodge. While Lewis maintained that belief in reincarnation was not required, the progression of the spirit through each enlightened stage points to doctrinal acceptance. Men who appeared to be mere mortals could be Masters in disguise, such as the legendary COMTE DE SAINT-GERMAIN, an adept in 18th-century France. Other famous proponents of Rosicrucianism included the Elizabethan doctor ROBERT FLUDD and Joseph Balsamo, the flamboyant COUNT CAGLIOSTRO.

Modern Rosicrucianism

The United States organization AMORC, founded by H. S. Lewis in 1915, had its beginnings as the Rosicrucian Research Society of the New York Institute for Psychical Research (1904). In 1908 Lewis met Mrs. May Banks-Stacey, an avid Rosicrucian, who put him in touch with members in Europe. By 1917 AMORC held its first convention, during which Lewis organized the National Rosicrucian Lodge as a means for students to learn elementary teachings by correspondence with the eventual hope of joining a Lodge. By 1926 Lewis petitioned a Rosicrucian Congress in Belgium to allow those students who still had not found a Lodge to continue their correspondence

Rosicrucian allegory, in Summum Bonum, *by Robert Fludd, 1626. (Author's collection)*

courses and become part of the "Lodge at Home." These arrangements allowed materials to be distributed worldwide; there are currently approximately 250,000 members in more than 100 countries.

In 1927 Lewis moved AMORC's headquarters to San Jose, California. The Grand Lodge at Rosicrucian Park has become a tourist attraction, with a planetarium, research facilities, and the Egyptian Museum. Reputedly the only Egyptian museum in the world housed in authentic ancient Egyptian architecture, it contains the largest collections of Egyptian, Babylonian, and Assyrian art and artifacts on the West Coast.

Other major Rosicrucian orders include the Rosicrucian Fellowship, founded by Max Heindel (1865–1919) in 1909. Born Carl Louis Van Grasshoff in Denmark, his spiritual search first led him to the Theosophical Society and then to Germany in 1907, where Heindel claimed that the Elder Brothers of the Rosicrucian Order appeared to him and initiated him into their mysteries. Heindel studied under a Rosicrucian adept, believed to be Rudolf Steiner, founder of the Anthroposophical Society. Heindel returned to the United States and began to organize centers on the West Coast. He opened the Fellowship's headquarters on Mount Ecclesia in Oceanside, California, in 1910, where it remains; the compound features a 12-sided Temple of Healing that corresponds to the zodiac.

The Societas Rosicruciana in Anglia, England, and the Societas Rosicruciana in Civitatibus Foederatis in Scotland restrict membership to Freemasons of the 32nd degree, but the Societas Rosicruciana in America welcomes non-Masons. The Fraternitas Rosae Crucis, founded in 1858 by Pascal Beverly Randolph (1825–75), claims to be the oldest Rosicrucian organization in the United States and traces its lineage to the occultist Eliphas Levi. To combine the teachings of Heindel and Steiner, S. R. Parchment founded the Rosicrucian Anthroposophic League in the 1930s. In the 1970s R. A. Straughn founded the Ausar Auset Society, a Rosicrucian organization dedicated to meditation and healthy living within the African-American community.

Rosicrucian mysteries still entertain the popular imagination, such as in Umberto Eco's novels *The Name of the Rose* and *Foucault's Pendulum.* In the former a monk unravels a murder mystery involving the forbidden works of Aristotle, one of the Ascended Masters; in the latter computer hackers and historians stumble upon a Rosicrucian riddle that leads them to the lost treasure of the Knights Templar and the location of the Holy Grail. More recently, Dan Brown's book *The DaVinci Code* weaves a tale involving Rosicrucianism, Mary Magdalene, the Holy Grail, and the Priory of Sion as heir to the Knights Templar.

Charles Mackay, in his book *Extraordinary Popular Delusions and the Madness of Crowds,* said that the early Rosicrucians claimed that the earth, air, and water were full of demons and sprites, gnomes and undines, sylphs and salamanders, all bound to the will of the Rosicrucian adepts. Mackay observed that while those claims might be absurd, that the descriptions of such beings had so suc-cessfully entered the popular imagination that art and literature would be bereft without them.

See also HERMETIC ORDER OF THE GOLDEN DAWN.

FURTHER READING:

Bridges, Vincent. "Ahkenaton and the Myth of Monotheism." Aethyrea Books. Available online at www.vincentbridges.com/highweirdness/Akhenaten.htm. Downloaded July 8, 2004.

Guiley, Rosemary Ellen. *Harper's Encyclopedia of Mystical & Paranormal Experience.* San Francisco: HarperSanFrancisco, 1991.

Heindel, Max. *The Rosicrucian Cosmo-Conception.* Oceanside, Calif.: The Rosicrucian Fellowship, 1993.

Mackay, Charles, LL.D. *Extraordinary Popular Delusions and the Madness of Crowds.* New York: Farrar, Straus & Giroux, 1932.

McLean, Adam. "Bacstrom's Rosicrucian Society." Available online. URL: www.levity.com/alchemy/bacstrm1.html. Downloaded July 8, 2004.

Waite, Arthur Edward. *The Brotherhood of the Rosy Cross.* New York: Barnes & Noble, 1993.

runes   A magical alphabet of Norse symbols used for healing, DIVINATION, and in a variety of CHARMS and SPELLS. The runes were spread through Britain, Europe, and Russia by the Saxons, Norse, Danes, and Vikings and were in their height of usage during the Dark Ages (c. 400–1400).

The term *rune* desrives from the Old Norse term for "secret." According to Norse myth, the runes were created by the supreme god Odin (Woden or Wotan), the one-eyed chief of gods and the god of wisdom and war. Odin gained the forbidden, mystical knowledge of the runes by fatally impaling himself with his own spear to Yggdrasil, the World Tree, for nine days and nights. As he neared death, 18 runes appeared to him. Just as he grabbed them, he died. Odin was resurrected and decided to share the secrets of the runes.

Runic SYMBOLS have been discovered in rock carvings that date back to the prehistoric Neolithic and Bronze Ages (c. 8000–2000 B.C.E.) The early Druids may also have been familiar with runes, as evidenced in their own ogham alphabet of symbols. Runes formed the earliest German alphabet, Elder Fuhark.

In Western Europe during the Dark Ages and Viking era, runes were believed to possess potent magical power. They were the TOOLS of magicians, who passed on their knowledge to initiates by word of mouth. Spells composed of runic symbols were inscribed at night on wands made of hazel, ash, or yew; swords; chalices; and stone tablets to accomplish whatever the magician desired: victory in battle, healing, safe journeys, protection from the EVIL EYE, the opening of psychic power, cursing, love, fertility, or blessings for sacrifice. They were used in legal contracts and in pacts. As TALISMANS, runes were inscribed on swords to ensure more pain and death to the enemy.

As AMULETS, they were inscribed on personal jewelry, on swords for protection in battle, or on objects displayed in one's home to invoke protection against evil spirits and BEWITCHMENT. Runes inscribed on the foundation or walls of any building would protect it against destruction and evil WITCHCRAFT. Women inscribed runes on their palms to ensure safe childbirth. Runes could ward off grave robbers; however, they could not be inscribed on IRON for this purpose, for iron was believed to scare away spirits. Runes could both keep the dead in their graves or resurrect the dead. Runes also symbolized the forces of nature, the SUN and the MOON, and the names of the gods and goddesses.

One important use of runes was divination. Runes were cast in lots and their patterns were interpreted by readers. In that respect, the runes were associated with the Norns, the Norse Three Fates of past, present and future. Runic rods or stones were cast by tossing, in the fashion of the *I CHING,* and their patterns were interpreted by the adept.

During the slow conversion of Europe to Christianity, the use of runes coexisted with the new religion for centuries. Crosses, coffins, swords, and other objects show runic inscriptions with Christian elements. When the Inquisition began in earnest in the 14th century, runes along with other pagan practices were nearly snuffed out of existence. In 1639 a law was passed in Iceland that anyone using runes would be prosecuted as a witch.

Interest in runes was revived in the late 19th and early 20th centuries by German occultists who associated runes with racial supremacy. When the Nazis came to power, they adopted two runes that became the most feared and hated symbols on Earth: the swastika, the rune of the Earth Mother and the hammer of Thor, Norse god of thunder; and the sig or *S* rune, which was the trademark of Heinrich Himmler's Schutzstaffel, or SS.

In the 1980s rune stones became popularized as a means of divination, to be cast like the *I Ching* or laid out in spreads like TAROT cards.

Rupecissa, John de   See DE RUPECISSA, JOHN.

sacrifice In MAGIC, the RITUAL killing of a living thing to propitiate gods or spirits. BLOOD sacrifice is an ancient and universal custom. It is frowned on in modern Western magical rites but is still practiced in traditions around the world. Usually an animal or a bird is sacrificed, but human sacrifices are not unknown. Some sacrifice rituals call for a small amount of blood-letting but no actual killing. Blood consumed in ritual sacrifice is believed to give the drinker the soul and attributes of the blood of the deceased, whether it be human or animal.

Animal Sacrifice
In earlier times, the most common blood sacrifice was to secure bountiful harvests; it was believed that the land was fertilized by sprinkling upon it the sacrificial blood. A widespread custom in Europe called for the sacrificing of cocks in harvest festivals to ensure an abundant crop the following year.

The early Hebrews practiced blood sacrifices of animals, following instructions given in Leviticus in the Old Testament. The importance of a flesh and blood sacrifice is illustrated in Genesis: Cain offers the fruits of his harvest, which does not please the Lord, and Abel offers one of his flock, which pleases the Lord. Also in Genesis, God tests Abraham by instructing him to sacrifice his son, Isaac. Abraham is stopped at the last moment by an angel, who informs him that God was testing his faith. A ram was substituted for Isaac. In Christianity, Christ eliminated the need for blood sacrifice by shedding his own blood on the cross. The Eucharist and communion services are nonbloody sacrifices in which bread and wine or grape juice substitute for the body and blood of Christ.

Animals are sacrificed in various tribal religions and in Vodoun and SANTERÍA. The animal sacrifices of Santería—usually fowl and sometimes lambs or goats—have been protested by animal-rights groups.

Human Sacrifice
Practices of human sacrifice can look to mythologies for a model of divine sacrifice: for example, Osiris, Dionysus, and Attis are dismembered in sacrifice for rebirth.

The Celts and the DRUIDS drank the blood of their sacrificed human victims, whose throats were slashed over cauldrons; they also burned their victims alive in wickerwork cages. The Aztecs cut hearts out of human sacrifices with flint knives; the still-beating heart was held aloft by the priest and then placed in a ceremonial receptacle. The body was often dismembered and eaten in an act of ritual cannibalism. The Khonds of southern India impaled their victims on stakes and cut off pieces of their backs to fertilize the soil. The sacrifice of first-born children once was a common custom in various cultures, particularly in times of trouble. During the Punic Wars, the nobility of Carthage sacrificed hundreds of children to Baal by rolling them into pits of fire.

During the witch hunts of the Inquisition, witches were said to sacrifice unbaptized children to the devil and also to roast and cannabalize them. "Confessions" of such acts were largely the product of severe torture rather than "evidence."

Sacrifice in Magic

Blood sacrifice releases a flash of power, which the magician uses for an EVOCATION. The old GRIMOIRES call for killing animals, usually a young goat, in advance of the ceremony and using their skins to make parchment that was used in drawing the magical SYMBOLS needed to protect the magician and to evoke and control the spirits. The sacrifice may also be to God or spirits for the obtaining of favors. Sacrificial animals—called the Victim of the Art—offered to God or various spirits should be young, healthy, and virgin for the maximum release of energy. Sometimes the sacrifice is best performed at the peak of a ritual. The letting of blood and the fear and death throes of the victim add to the frenzy of the magician. The fumes of the sacrificial blood also enable the evoked spirit to become visible to the magician.

The *Grimorium Verum* specifies that the magician should cut the throat of a virgin kid goat with a single slash of his magical knife (see TOOLS) while saying, "I slay thee in the name and to the honor of N. [name of spirit or deity]."

According to the *Key of Solomon,* white animals should be sacrificed to benevolent spirits, and black animals should be sacrificed to evil spirits. The magician should cut off the entire head of the animal with a single blow while saying, "O high and powerful being, may this sacrifice be pleasing and acceptable to thee. Serve us faithfully and better sacrifices shall be given thee." Another version of the *Key* gives this INCANTATION: "I, N., slay thee, N., in the name and to the honor of N."

The *Red Dragon* gives instructions for evoking the devil by sacrificing a black hen that has never been crossed by a cock. Seize the throat so that it cannot make noise and thus dissipate life-force energy. Take it to a CROSSROADS, and at midnight draw a magic circle with a wand made of cypress (a symbol of death). Stand inside the circle, and tear the hen in two with your hands while saying, "Euphas Metahim, frugativi et appelavi." Turn to the east and command the devil to appear.

ALEISTER CROWLEY, in *Magick in Theory and Practice,* said that "The ethics of the thing [blood sacrifice] appear to have concerned no one; nor, to tell the truth, need they do so." Crowley sacrificed animals and fowl in his rituals within a MAGIC CIRCLE or MAGIC TRIANGLE, which prevented the energy from escaping. He condemned the practice of torturing the animal first to obtain an elemental slave, calling it "indefensible, utterly black magic of the very worst kind." However, he said that there was no objection to such black magic if it was "properly understood." Crowley noted that a magician could effect a blood sacrifice without the loss of life by gashing himself or his assistant.

According to ELIPHAS LEVI, when the grimoires spoke of killing a kid goat, they meant that a human child should be sacrificed. This is not likely, though records exist of human sacrifices in efforts to obtain something by magical means. For example, in 1841, treasure hunters in Italy sacrificed a boy to a DEMON in hopes of being led to buried treasure.

Crowley also said that "a male child of perfect innocence and high intelligence is the most satisfactory and perfect victim." His claim to performing such a sacrifice an average of 150 times a year between 1921 and 1928 is doubtful, however.

FURTHER READING:

Butler, E. M. *Ritual Magic.* Cambridge: Cambridge University Press, 1949.

Cavendish, Richard. *The Black Arts.* New York: G.P. Putnam's Sons, 1967.

Crowley, Aleister. *Magic in Theory and Practice.* 1929. Reprint, New York: Dover Publications, 1976.

Saint-Germain, comte de (c. 1710–1784)   A mysterious gentlemen believed by many to be an Ascended Master of the Great White Brotherhood and one of the greatest occult adepts that ever lived. He allegedly possessed the alchemical secrets of transmutation, was a Rosicrucian and Freemason, gave the appearance of surviving without food or drink, and played a role in 18th-century European politics. Saint-Germain was reincarnated as several famous historical men over the centuries; some said he was immortal.

Lives and Times

Very little of what has been written about the comte can be verified. According to lore, Saint-Germain's first appearance occurred about 50,000 years ago in a paradise that today is the Sahara. As high priest of the Violet Flame Temple, he led his enlightened people along the path of cosmic consciousness. Unfortunately, some of his followers succumbed to worldly pleasures, and he left them to their fates. In 1050 B.C.E., Saint-Germain returned as the Old Testament prophet Samuel. He anointed Saul as king of the Israelites but denied him when Saul disobeyed the Lord, choosing David to be king instead and establishing the lineage of the Messiah. Saint-Germain himself returned as Joseph, husband of the Virgin Mary and human father to the infant Jesus.

In the third century C.E., Saint-Germain appeared again, this time as Saint Alban, the first Christian martyr in Britain. Converted to Christianity by the monk Amphibalus, Saint Alban hid the holy man during the persecutions of Emperor Diocletian. When the saint refused to renounce his faith or reveal Amphibalus's sanctuary, he was beheaded in 303. In a happier role, Saint-Germain served as Proclus (410–485), the head of Plato's Academy in Athens. And in perhaps his most magical incarnation, Saint-Germain returned to Britain in the late fifth century as the wizard Merlin, counselor to King Arthur of Camelot.

Saint-Germain next appeared as ROGER BACON (1214–94), a scientist, alchemist, and contemporary of Saint ALBERTUS MAGNUS, reputedly the greatest mind of his age. Bacon believed so fiercely in the existence of the PHILOSOPHER'S STONE and the ELIXIR OF LIFE—and their alchemical potential—that others followed his example based solely on his passionate and learned arguments. His Franciscan brothers did not always share his enthusiasm, however, and kept him in confinement for 14 years as punishment for his heresies. Bacon predicted that India could be reached by sailing west from Spain; Saint-Germain, as Christopher Columbus, fulfilled that prophecy in 1492. Saint-Germain knew PARACELSUS (1493–1541), who studied his secret elixir composed of 777 ingredients.

In the 16th century, Saint-Germain returned as Sir Francis Bacon (1561–1626), English essayist, philosopher, statesman, and occultist. Reportedly a Freemason and a Rosicrucian, Sir Francis pursued alchemical transmutation as well as scientific experiment. Some scholars identified him as the real author of Shakespearean dramas. Saint-Germain also allegedly befriended JOHN DEE and EDWARD KELLY, assisting them in their work with ANGEL communications.

Accounts of Saint-Germain's life reported that the adept's incarnation as Sir Francis was to have been his last, ascending as Master on May 1, 1684. But desiring one last go-round, Saint-Germain arrived in Paris in the 1700s as the comte (Count) de Saint-Germain: alchemist, Rosicrucian, lover of jewels, politician, diplomat, and fascinating dinner guest.

The Historical Comte de Saint-Germain

Regardless of whether the comte really lived in earlier times, he is best known for his 18th-century identity as a historical figure, the comte de Saint-Germain. Some accounts say he was the third son of Prince Ferenc (Francis) Rokoczy II of Hungary and was under the guardianship of the emperor of Austria but was brought up by the Medicis in Italy. Others attribute his parentage to a Portuguese Jew from Bordeaux. To those most convinced of his immortality, his Semitic features identified him as the legendary Wandering Jew. No record exists of his first name; in a letter dated 1735 he signed himself as "P. M. de St. Germaine."

Although not handsome, he dressed well and wore jewels on every finger, cutting quite a figure at court. He was small and slight and always wore black satin and velvet, diamond studs, and the finest-quality linens and laces. He kept his hair powdered and tied in the back with a black ribbon. The comte claimed that his initiation into the Rosicrucian mysteries gave him the ability to call up diamonds, pearls, and other gems at will. He often carried a small casket of jewels when he called on ladies at court and was generous with his treasures.

Quite learned, the comte was an accomplished painter and musician, able to play both the harpsichord and the violin. He spoke and wrote Greek, Latin, Sanskrit, Arabic, Chinese, French, German, English, Italian, Portuguese, and Spanish fluently and without accent, making him invaluable as a diplomat and a statesman. King Louis XV of France trusted him implicitly—even allowing the comte to see his mistress, Madame du Pompadour, in her rooms—but the comte was no doubt spying for Frederick the Great of Prussia at the same time. Horace Walpole wrote that the comte lived in London until he was arrested as a Jacobite in 1743 but that he was seen dining and entertaining in Paris during that same period. He loved being a dinner guest but

never ate or drank anything in public. In 1762 he reportedly helped Catherine the Great become empress of Russia. Tragically, his warnings to King Louis XVI and Queen Marie Antoinette about the coming revolution were ignored.

But to the European intelligentsia, hungry to learn anything remotely esoteric, the comte's apparent knowledge of alchemy and the occult were more impressive than his political maneuvers. He seemed to have extensive financial means, but if they were obtained through alchemical transmutation, he wisely kept quiet. Before coming to France, the comte had made a small fortune selling bottles of age-defying elixir; one of his customers, the marechal de Belle-Isle, was so captivated with the solution that he convinced the comte to go to Paris. The comte gave the impression that he, too, had drunk the potion, allowing him to seem ageless. He described his meetings with King Henry VIII of England, Emperor Charles V, or other royal luminaries as if he had actually known them intimately.

In 1760 the *London Mercury,* an English newspaper, reported in all seriousness that the comte had given a vial of his elixir to a lady of his acquaintance who was concerned that she was aging too soon. The lady put the precious vial in a drawer, where it was accidentally discovered by her maid. The maid, not knowing the elixir's true nature, thought it was a purgative and drank some of the liquid. When the lady called for her maid's assistance, a young girl answered the summons.

Little is known of the comte's romantic life, save tales that he was charismatic to women. By some accounts, he was married more than once. He had a son by one unknown wife; Casanova reportedly poisoned him to death. Saint-Germain married a woman he met in Venice, Angioletta Bartolomeo, the daughter of a gondolier. He introduced her to King Louis XV as his sister. Later, she committed suicide following an affair with Casanova.

The comte's most famous students were COUNT CAGLIOSTRO and his wife, whom Saint-Germain personally initiated into the Lodge of Illuminists at his castle at Holstein in 1785. The ceremony was resplendent with thousands of candles, acolytes carrying perfumes, and countless diamonds and jewels. During the INITIATION, Cagliostro's future was read from a mysterious book: he would be persecuted, tried, dishonored, and imprisoned. Cagliostro introduced Egyptian rites of Freemasonry to France, although he was eventually discredited and charged with heresy, spending his last days imprisoned in solitary confinement in Italy.

Works

Occult manuscripts are attributed to the comte, but some exist only in legend. H. P. BLAVATSKY quoted Saint-Germain on the occult powers of NUMBERS but cited no reference. A manuscript owned by Cagliostro and confiscated by the Inquisition, *La Tres Sainte Trinosophie,* apparently was written by the comte; MANLY PALMER HALL translated it in 1933. Hall owned another Saint-Germain manuscript, *Ancien Membre du Conseil de Direction de la Societe Theosophique du France.*

A rare cipher manuscript called *La Magie Sainte* is attributed to Saint-Germain, who wrote it for an unknown person. The manuscript, printed on triangular paper around 1750, contains sacred Egyptian magic passed to Moses and is based on the GRIMOIRE the *Key of Solomon*. It provides instructions for preparing a MAGIC CIRCLE, consecrating magical TOOLS, and making PRAYERS to spirits.

Death and Resurrection

In 1784 the comte reportedly died at the castle of Count Karl of Hesse-Cassel in the duchy of Schleswig. While residing with Count Karl, the comte complained of feeling feeble, careworn, and melancholy. Although records indicated the count inherited all of the comte's secret Freemason papers and alchemical instructions, Count Karl provided no details about his friend's death. According to some reports, the comte was in excellent health until his passing; other stories tell of a lingering illness and severe melancholy that preceded his death. In either case, there are no funeral or burial records—remarkable for such an esteemed and important man.

But did Saint-Germain actually die? In 1785, in the presence of Count Cagliostro, FRANZ ANTON MESMER, and other ADEPTS, the French Freemasons elected him as their representative to that year's convention. He supposedly traveled to Russia in 1786. And the comtesse d'Adhémar swore she had talked with the comte at the Church of the Recollets in the summer of 1789 after the taking of the Bastille. She claimed she saw him again in 1815 and 1821.

His last official appearance was in 1822 when, according to occult lore, he retired to the Himalayas, secret home of the Ascended Masters. From there he reportedly helped Madame Helena Blavatsky found the Theosophical Society in 1875, aided by Masters Morya and Koot Hoomi. The comte administered the Seventh Ray in the theosophical universe, responsible for ceremony and ritual. Mysterious sightings continued, with rumored appearances in Paris in 1835 and Milan in 1867. Annie Besant, Madame Blavatsky's student, claimed she met the comte in 1896, while Theosophist C. W. Leadbeater swore he met the elusive comte in Rome in 1926.

Perhaps even stranger were the claims of Guy Ballard, who with his wife and son founded the "I AM" Religious Activity Movement in the 1930s. Ballard claimed that the comte had introduced him to visitors from Venus, which Ballard later channeled. More recently, Elizabeth Clare Prophet, cofounder with her late husband Mark of the Church Universal and Triumphant, embraced the comte as an Ascended Master and teacher of what each person must accomplish to bring about the Seventh Golden Age on Earth. The comte guides a variety of New Age organizations through psychics and channelers.

FURTHER READING:

Hall, Manly P. *Sages and Seers*. Los Angeles: The Philosophical Research Society, 1959.

———. *The Secret Teachings of All Ages*. 1928. Reprint, Los Angeles: The Philosophic Research Society, 1977.

Mackay, Charles, L. L. D. *Extraordinary Popular Delusions and the Madness of Crowds*. New York: Farrar, Strauss & Giroux, 1932.

Merton, Reginald. "Comte Saint-Germain: The Immortal German Alchemist." Available online. URL: www.alchemylab.com/count_saint_germain.htm. Downloaded July 8, 2004.

Seligmann, Kurt. *The History of Magic and the Occult*. New York: Pantheon Books, 1948.

salamander   A lizardlike amphibian that likes to live in moist places. In mythology the salamander is a poisonous

Salamander in fire in the Ace of Staffs card in The Alchemical Tarot, *by Rosemary Ellen Guiley and Robert Michael Place. Inspired by Michael Maier's* Atalanta fugiens, *1618.* (Copyright by and courtesy of Robert Michael Place)

creature that is able to live in fire. Pliny said that the salamander "seeks the hottest fire to breed in, but quenches it with the extreme frigidity of its body."

In ALCHEMY the salamander is a symbol of the PRIMA MATERIA. In the alchemical process, it plays the role of helping the substance under transformation to give up its secret fire, which will help the PHILOSOPHER'S STONE claim its final power, as this alchemical verse describes:

> [The Salamander] is caught and pierced
> So that it dies and yields up its life with its blood.
> But this, too, happens for its good;
> For from its blood it wins immortal life,
> And then death has no more power over it.

An emblem of the salamander in fire appears in *Atalanta fugiens* (1618) by MICHAEL MAIER. "As the Salamander lives in the Fire so does the Stone," says Maier. The salamander symbolizes SULPHUR and the Secret of the Fire. The Secret Fire, corporified as SALT, is the hidden Sulphur that is the "Philosophick Tincture."

salt   Mineral with magical and alchemical properties.

Because it is white and thus pure and is a preservative, salt is magical protection against evil, including DEMONS, WITCHCRAFT, the EVIL EYE, VAMPIRES, and anything unholy. Agents of evil as well as people and animals who are bewitched cannot eat anything salted, according to lore. In magical RITUALS, salt is used as a SYMBOL of the element of earth and also as a purifier. However, salt is avoided in MAGIC rituals for the CONJURATION of demons and in NECROMANCY.

In Christianity salt is symbolic of incorruptibility, eternity, and divine wisdom. A Catholic ritual of benediction with salt and water ensures physical health and the exorcism of evil spirits. Salted holy water is used in baptisms.

In magic rituals salt represents the earth element, spiritual purity, and the transmutation of consciousness to a higher level.

In alchemy salt is part of the *TRIA PRIMA* with MERCURY and SULPHUR that compose all things, including the four elements. Salt represents the body, female, and earth aspects. It is the Mother, or the feminine principle within matter. Salt is a preservative against the corruption of the body—the Egyptians used a form of it, *natron*, in mummification—and thus is a magical ELIXIR.

Salt, mercury, and sulphur also have spiritual properties in alchemy; salt represents the ultimate exaltation of matter—matter made aware—achieved through the union of opposites, including the fire and water, and the Above and Below. Salt is the ultimate PHILOSOPHER'S STONE, representing transcendence and ultimate knowledge.

Salt also represents lower consciousness in alchemy. In ancient times salt was associated with thought because of its ability to crystallize; in its purest form, thought was held to be a fluid, living substance in the higher realms that crystallized when it descended into human minds.

Thus salt symbolizes consciousness—thoughts, feelings, materialism, and so forth—that must be elevated through alchemical processes of dissolution and recrystallization.

Salt is identified with the OUROBOROS, the self-devouring SERPENT or DRAGON. The salt of metal is the lapis or Philosopher's Stone.

Salt is a crucial ingredient in alchemical recipes for making GOLD. A 17th-century formula for potable gold, believed to be an antidote for poison, a curative of heart disease, and a repellent of the devil, included gold, salt, red wine vinegar, the ashes of a block of tin burnt in an iron pan, wine, and honey.

CARL G. JUNG associated salt with lunar symbolism (see MOON) and the unconscious.

FURTHER READING:
Coudert, Allison. *Alchemy: The Philosopher's Stone.* London: Wildwood House Ltd., 1980.
Hauck, Dennis William. *The Emerald Tablet: Alchemy for Personal Transformation.* New York: Penguin/Arkana, 1999.

Santería   Animistic religion similar to Vodoun, brought by the West African slaves from Yoruba along the Niger River to the Spanish colonies in North and South America and the Caribbean islands. Similar beliefs and practices also accompanied the slaves taken to Portuguese colonies, principally Brazil, where the faithful practice *Candomblé* or *Umbanda.* Other names for Santería are Lukumí and Regla de Ocha.

Although both Vodoun and Santería are based on native African religions, in some communities Santería has merged nearly seamlessly into Catholicism. *Santería* comes from the Spanish word *santo,* meaning "saint," and can be translated as the "way of the saints." The term was originally a derisive epithet used by the white masters against their overly pious slaves; eventually, however, the slave owners became practicing *santeros* as well. Today any place with a large Hispanic population—like Miami, New York, or Los Angeles in the United states or Cuba, Jamaica, or the Dominican Republic—boasts as many *santeros* as Catholics, since many devotees practice both faiths.

The Ways of the Gods and Saints
In the ancient Yoruban tongue, the gods were called *orishas,* instead of the Fon term *loa,* and the name remains today. Like the Vodounists, *santeros* (female: *santeras*) acknowledge one supreme deity, Olodumare, but his distant greatness renders him incomprehensible. The *orishas,* with their more human frailties and failings, intercede with Olodumare on the worshipers' behalf. Or perhaps PRAYERS to the saint who most resembles the designated *orisha* might gain favors from the Christian God or Jesus. The African *orishas* have been completely syncretized into the Catholic canon.

Creation stories in Santería recognize Obatalá as the first man and father of the *orishas.* He married Oddudúa and had two children: a son Aganyú and a daughter Yemayá. The siblings married and had a son Orungán. The young man was so beautiful that his father Aganyú died of envy, at which time Orungán forced himself on his mother. Yemayá delivered 14 deities from their union, and when her waters broke the deluge became the Flood. She cursed her son, and he died; Yemayá died as well.

Although the 14 *orishas* and other ancestor gods are important, no *santero* can practice without the good offices of Elegguá (Legba in Vodoun; also called Eshu-Elegbara). Like Legba, he is the messenger, the door to the gods, the one who understands all languages and allows the *orishas* to descend upon the faithful and possess their hearts, minds, and bodies. Elegguá also governs the sexual side of life; he is quite well endowed and usually portrayed as such. Those possessed by the god exhibit overt male sexual behavior whether they are men or women.

Elegguá the TRICKSTER represents the CROSSROADS: choice and chaos, opportunity and disappointment. Like his Vodoun cousin Legba, he also gave his people the Table of Ifá, or system of DIVINATION, controlled by Orúnla. Only male *santeros* can aspire to be priests and diviners, called *babalawos*. A *babalawo* who specializes in the Table is called an *italero* and is probably consecrated to the service of Orúnla. To perform a reading, called a *registro*, the *italero* throws 16 seashells (*caracoles*) onto a straw mat. The shells, originally smooth, have been filed until their serrated edges appear, resembling tiny mouths with teeth: the "mouthpieces" of the *orishas*. The *ordun*, or pattern, is determined by how many of the shells land with their "mouths" on top. The *italero* interprets the *ordun*, repeating the procedure four times. Like the Chinese *Yijing* (I Ching), the proverbs and PROPHECIES associated with each *ordun* are vague and mysterious.

Petitioners may also request direct answers from Elegguá through a divination method called *darle coco al santo* ("give the coconut to the saint"). The diviner carefully breaks the coconut's shell with a hard object and then divides the meat—white on one side, brown on the other—into four equal pieces. The pieces are then thrown on the floor, yielding one of five patterns.

White and Black Magic

Babalawos wield enormous power. Besides controlling the interpretations of the Ifá, they perform animal SACRIFICE and are masters in the uses of herbs and plants for healing and MAGIC. If a *registro* indicates the petitioner is under an evil SPELL, or *bilongo*, the *babalawo* must place a contravening spell, or *ebbo*, on the victim's enemy. If the *ebbo* causes more damage than the original spell, the *babalawo's* prestige rises proportionately. Typical remedies for a spell range from herbal baths to complicated potions (see PHILTRES) of oils, plants, and intimate waste products. A *resguardo*, or small bag (see CHARM BAG; GRIS-GRIS) filled with herbs and FETISHES associated with a certain deity is often prescribed as an AMULET against further bad magic.

Most of these ingredients can be purchased at the local *botánica*, a shop dedicated to the sale of herbs, CANDLES, fetishes, and other supplies for those who serve the *orishas*. The herbs serve dual purposes as healing agents and components for spells. Garlic lowers high blood pressure; coconut water acts as a diuretic; anise seed alleviates indigestion; sarsaparilla cures rheumatism, nerves, and syphilis; and indigo helps epilepsy. The *higuereta* plant, which produces castor oil, has been used on cancerous tumors for centuries.

Cuttings from *escoba amarga* bushes purify a bath and also drive away the *abikus*: mischievous spirits that come from a child who has died young and reincarnate in another young child. When the first child dies, the priest makes a mark on the body, which he then claims to find on the next child born as a sign of *abiku* danger. To keep the *abikus* from claiming the next child, a small chain is placed on the wrist or ankle to keep the child "tied" to Earth and not at risk of being spirited away.

The five-leaf, silk-cotton TREE, or *bombax ceiba*, is sacred to *santeros* and is worshiped as a female saint. Devotees will not even cross the tree's shadow without permission. Teas made from the tree's roots and leaves cure venereal disease and urinary tract infections; the leaves help anemia. Tea from the bark helps cure infertility. The tree also aids in the casting of spells; if a *santero* wishes to cause a victim harm, he must walk naked around the *ceiba* several times at midnight and brush the trunk with his fingertips, softly asking for help against his enemy.

Followers describe Santería as African magic adapted to city life and to the West. It is a "sympathetic" system governed by the rules of similarity (that like produces like), and also "contagious," dependent upon contact. The *santero* can stage the outcome of a spell beforehand by acting out the future events or by substituting an item like a wax doll (see POPPET) to represent the victim and then sticking pins in it. To assure the success of a spell, the *santero* employs items that have touched the victim: HAIR AND NAIL CLIPPINGS or even dirt from his footprints or air from his home. Even santeros fear the EVIL EYE, however, knowing that the eye's black magic can come from anyone. *Babalawos* recommend that children wear a tiny jet hand or piece of coral to ward off the evil eye; adults may choose the same TALISMANS or wear a small glass eyeball pinned to their chest.

Most of the spells performed by the *santeros* come under the classification of "white" magic: healings, INCANTATIONS to reign in wayward lovers or attract them, tricks to get rich. But some of the *santeros* choose "black" magic (*brujería* or *palo mayombé*) and become *mayomberos*, a decision that is theirs alone and not connected to any of the *orishas*.

Becoming a *mayombero* requires great effort. First the supplicant must sleep under the sacred *ceiba* tree for seven nights and then take a new suit of clothes and bury it in a previously selected grave. While the clothing is buried, the novice takes a series of purifying herbal baths for 21 days or over three successive Fridays, then retrieves his clothes, puts them on, and returns to the *ceiba*. The candidate's teacher and other *mayomberos* join him there and invoke the spirits of the dead as well as of the *ceiba* to welcome this new witch into the brotherhood. The candidate receives a crown of *ceiba* leaves, symbolizing his surrender to the spirits; then the others present him with a lighted candle and his scepter, or *kisengue*: a human tibia bone wrapped in black cloth. The new *mayombero* can now call on the powers of darkness to make his *nganga*, the cauldron or sack that contains all his magical potions and powers.

Making the *nganga* begins with the new *mayombero* and an assistant returning to another preselected gravesite, one with a corpse possessing at least some brain matter. The witch sprinkles rum while making the sign of the cross over the grave, then exhumes the body, known to the *mayombero* and called the *kiyumba*, and removes whatever brain is left as well as the head, toes, fingers, ribs, and tibias. The *mayombero* wraps these treasures in black cloth and takes them home. Once there, the witch lies on the floor while his assistant covers him with a sheet and lights four candles, one at each corner, as if the witch were dead. The assistant places a knife near the witch with seven little heaps of gunpowder on the blade. As the *kiyumba* possesses the *mayombero*, rigidity sets in and then convulsions. If the *kiyumba* agrees to bend to the will of the witch, the gunpowder ignites; if the answer is no, it is back to the cemetery. None of these efforts will succeed if the MOON is in its waning phase.

If the *kiyumba* agrees, the witch places the *kiyumba's* name in a large IRON cauldron, along with a few coins for payment and a few drops of fresh BLOOD from either a rooster or the *mayombero's* arm. Further ingredients include wax from a burned candle, a cigar butt, ashes, lime, a piece of bamboo that contains sea water and quicksilver (the water represents the relentless tides and the silver is for speed) and that is sealed at both ends, the body of a small black dog to help the *kiyumba* stalk its victims, various tree barks, red pepper, chile, garlic, onions, cinnamon, rue, ants, worms, lizards, termites, bats, frogs, Spanish flies, a tarantula, a centipede, a wasp, and a scorpion. Then back to the cemetery, where the witch buries his *nganga* for 21 days (or again over three successive Fridays), digs it up, then reburies it for yet another 21 days. Finally, at the end of that period, the *mayombero* disinters the cauldron one last time and returns home. He adds peppered rum, dry wine, some cologne called Florida water, and more blood.

The *nganga* must pass two tests. The first one takes place at the sacred *ceiba*, where the *mayombero* buries the cauldron and then demands that the *kiyumba* prove its loyalty by drying all the tree's leaves within a certain time. If the *kiyumba* passes that test, it must then kill a specific animal. With that hurdle overcome, the *mayombero* can finally offer his services as a terrible—and terrifying—magician.

Portuguese Macumba

Santería as practiced among the slaves in the Portuguese colonies, particularly Brazil, split into two different religions: *Candomblé* and *Umbanda*. There is no Macumba; the word is an umbrella term for the African-based sects. The slaves who came to Brazil in the 16th century found many similarities between their African ways and the spiritual practices of the native Amazonian tribes. Forced to convert to Catholicism like the other slaves, the Brazilian blacks continued to worship secretly, deep in the jungles alongside the natives; by the time of emancipation in 1888, more than 15 generations of Brazilians had seen the magic of the *orishas*. Today, members of nearly all social classes practice some sort of spirit belief while nevertheless professing their Catholic faith.

Candomblé, the older of the two sects, most resembles the ancient Yoruban religion but with Portuguese spelling: The god Chango is Xango, Yemaya is Yemanja, and Olorún becomes Olorum. The term *candomblé* probably derives from *candombé*, a slave dance celebration held on the coffee plantations. The first *Candomblé* center opened in 1830 in Salvador, capital of the state of Bahia and the old capital of all Brazil. Three former slave women named themselves the high priestesses, claiming their magical skills sharpened their sexual prowess as mistresses to the white masters. These "Mothers of the Saints" trained "Daughters," excluding the men and ensuring their preeminence as leaders of the sect. Religious practices involve spirit possession and animal sacrifice, although neither Elegguá nor Papa Legba are called upon to open the door to the *orishas*. Instead the *candomblistas* call upon the Exus: gods of mischief, communication, crossroads, and chaos—in other words, tricksters.

Umbanda, with roots in Hinduism and Buddhism in addition to African religion, was founded in 1904. The Spiritism movements of the early 20th century also influenced the sect, with the result that much of *Umbanda* worship includes trance channeling. The most popular spirit guides are the Old Black Man (*Preto Velho*) and the Old Black Woman (*Preta Velha*), symbolizing the ancient wisdom of the black slaves and the native peoples along the Amazon River. *Umbanda* probably derives from the Sanskrit word *aum-gandha*, which means "divine principle." Worship focuses on healing, and *umbandistas* believe no healing of the body can be achieved without healing of the spirit and communion—ecstatic POSSESSION—by the spirit guides. The spirits offer enlightenment; each time a medium channels a spirit guide his mind rises to another level of consciousness.

Both *Candomblé* and *Umbanda* view the spirits as agents for good; even the more mischievous ones are merely misguided. But like the *mayomberos* and *bokors* of Santería and Vodoun, there are those that wish to ally themselves with the spirits of evil. Such persons practice *Quimbanda* (also known as *Cuimbanda*).

Quimbandistas rely on the Exus to do their bidding, calling on the darker manifestations of the trickster gods that symbolize the DEMONS Ashtaroth (Exu of the Crossroads), Beelzebub (Exu Mor), and even the devil himself (King Exu).

Exu of the Closed Paths inspires the greatest dread. Victims of this spell find themselves caught with no way out, with "all paths closed": no job, no friends, no help from family, no relief from pain and illness. Unless the *orishas* intervene, death is certain.

FURTHER READING:

Davis, Erik. "Trickster at the Crossroads: West Africa's God of Messages, Sex and Deceit." Originally appeared in *Gnosis,* Spring 1991. Available online. URL: http://www.techgnosis.com/trickster.html. Downloaded July 5, 2004.

Gonzales-Wippler, Migene. *Santería: African Magic in Latin America.* St. Paul, Minn.: Llewelleyn Publications, 1981.

Guiley, Rosemary Ellen. *The Encyclopedia of Witches and Witchcraft,* 2d ed. New York: Facts On File Inc., 1999.

Schweitzer, John Frederick   See HELVETIUS.

Scot, Michael (1175–c. 1235)   Reputed Scottish magician, alchemist, mathematician, physician, astrologer, and scholar. Michael Scot was outspoken in his condemnation of MAGIC and NECROMANCY; yet he seemed to know so much about these subjects that most of his peers considered him both a sorcerer and a necromancer. Legends described him as a magician with great supernatural powers.

Little is known about Scot's early life, including his exact birthplace. It is believed that he may have come from Balwearie, near Kirkcaddy in Fife. His family evidently was affluent, for he studied at Oxford.

After Oxford, Scot traveled to various centers of learning in Europe: the Sorbonne in Paris; Bolgna; Palermo; Toledo; and Sicily. According to ROGER BACON, he learned Arabic. He served Don Philip, an official in the court of King Frederick II. Scot took holy orders and was named the archbishop of Cashel, Ireland, by Pope Honorious III in 1224. This upset the Irish clergy, and Scot declined the office on the grounds that he did not know the Irish language, and he took an office in Italy instead. In 1227 he returned to Frederick's court in Sicily and became the court astrologer. Scot fit in well with the other court ADEPTS in magic, ALCHEMY, and the occult arts.

While in Sicily, Scot translated various works and wrote his own. His principal works include a four-part introduction to ASTROLOGY and a two-part work on alchemy, *Magistery of the Art of Alchemy* and *Lesser Magistery.* His alchemical works show that he conducted numerous experiments with Jewish and Muslim alchemists. He recorded elaborate and strange recipes, including one for making GOLD that is attributed to Scot and

that calls for "the blood of a ruddy man and the blood of a red owl," mixed with saffron, alum, urine, and cucumber juice.

In 1230 Scot went to England where he is erroneously credited with introducing the works of Aristotle, though he did translate Aristotle's works into English.

He wrote extensively, mixing science and the occult. His book on physiognomy, the study of the human face, held that the stars and the planets marked life events upon the face. His book on astronomy includes astrological PRAYERS and CONJURATIONS. As was typical of the time, Scot believed in alchemy, DIVINATION, and the magical properties of precious stones and herbs as sciences.

Scot is said to have predicted that Frederick would die in Florence, causing the emperor to avoid that city. However, Frederick did die in Firenzuola, or "Little Florence."

Scot also wrote extensively on magic and necromancy, fully describing practices and rituals. It was said that Scot performed them himself, disguising his magic rituals as scientific experiments.

According to legend, Scot commanded a retinue of FAMILIARS that he dispatched to raid the kitchens of the pope and French and Spanish royalty and to transport their food back to him by air. He also was said to ride through the sky on a demonic horse. He sailed the seas in a demonic ship or rode on the back of some fantastical seabeast. He could make the bells of Notre Dame ring with a wave of his magic wand.

The devil was said to help Scot in philanthrophic undertakings, such as the building of a road in Scotland within a single night.

Dante called Scot a fraud and placed him in eternal torment in the eighth circle of the *Inferno.*

Scot is said to have predicted that his own death would be caused by a small stone falling on his head. He started to wear a steel helmet, but one day he took it off in church, and a two-ounce stone fell from the roof onto his head and killed him. He is said to be buried in Melrose Abbey in Scotland along with his books of magic. According to legend, a "wondrous light" burns within his tomb to chase away evil spirits and will continue to burn until the day of doom.

FURTHER READING:

Guiley, Rosemary Ellen. *The Encyclopedia of Witches and Witchcraft.* 2d ed. New York: Facts On File Inc., 1999.

Holmyard, E. J. *Alchemy.* New York: Penguin Books, 1999.

scrying   A method of DIVINATION done by gazing on an object that has a polished and reflective surface, such as a CRYSTAL BALL or a MIRROR, until visions appear on its surface.

Scrying comes from the English term *descry,* which means "to succeed in discerning" or "to make out dimly." The TOOL of scryers, called a speculum, can be any object that works for an individual but usually is one with a polished or reasonably reflective surface. The oldest and most common speculum is still water in a lake, a pond, or a dark bowl. Ink, blood, and other dark liquids were used by ancient Egyptian scryers. NOSTRADAMUS scryed with a bowl of water set upon a brass tripod. His prepartory RITUAL consisted of dipping a WAND into the water and anointing himself with a few drops; then he gazed into the bowl until he saw visions.

Other common tools are glass fishing floats, polished metals and stones, precious gems, eggs, and mirrors. GYPSY fortune-tellers made crystal balls the stereotype of the trade. JOHN DEE, the royal magician to Queen Elizabeth I, used a crystal egg and a black obsidian mirror. In Arab countries, scryers have used their own polished thumbnails. Dr. Morton Prince, a medical psychologist of the 19th century, used electric lightbulbs in scrying experiments with his patients. Wiccans use rounded mirrors, the convex side of which is painted black, or small cauldrons that are painted black on the inside and filled with water.

Scryers have their own individual techniques for inducing visions. Some who use crystals focus on points of light on the surface. Others enter a state of altered consciousness and allow images to float into their inner awareness. Some scryers may actually see images appear on the surface of the speculum, while others see them in their mind's eye. Some images are couched in SYMBOLS, and the scryer must learn how to interpret them. In the Middle Ages, there was a belief that the images formed on a crystal ball or other tool were caused by demons that had been trapped inside by MAGIC.

A formal scrying ritual is given in *Crystal Gazing and Clairvoyance,* a book written by John Melville in 1896. Melville specifies the use of a crystal ball resting on an ivory or ebony stand that has been inlaid with magical words in raised gold letters. All of the tools must be consecrated by ritual. To begin, the scryer should recite a long and Christian INVOCATION. According to Melville, any scrying done with evil intent would rebound on the scryer "with terrible effect."

FURTHER READING:
Butler, W. E. *How to Develop Clairvoyance.* 2d ed. New York: Samuel Weiser, 1979.
Thomas, Keith. *Religion & the Decline of Magic.* New York: Charles Scribner's Sons, 1971.
Valiente, Doreen. *Witchcraft for Tomorrow.* Custer, Wash.: Phoenix Publishing, 1978.

Seal of Solomon   A six-sided star or HEXAGRAM made of two interconnected triangles with powerful magical properties of both AMULET and TALISMAN. The Seal of Solomon also is called the Shield of David and the Star of David. It appeared as early as the Bronze Age as a decoration on lamps, seals, and artifacts and on friezes along with PENTACLES and SWASTIKAS. In Arabic legend the hexagram and the real NAME of God were etched on the magic RING of

King SOLOMON, which enabled him to command an army of DEMONS, the djinn.

As an amulet the Seal of Solomon protects against the EVIL EYE and Lilith, the terrible demon who steals children during the night. The seal was not widely used in amulets until the early Middle Ages when it appeared in kabbalistic prescriptions for inscribed amulets, medallions, or pieces

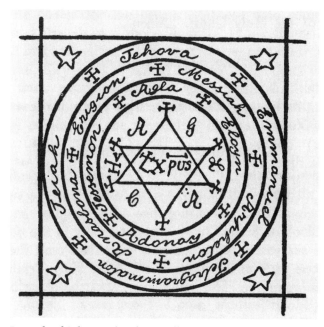

Pentacle of Solomon. (Author's collection)

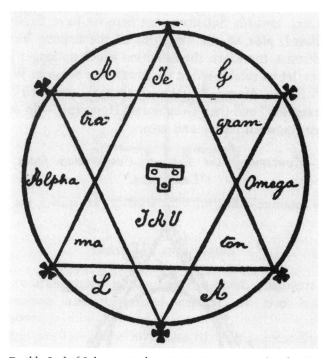

Double Seal of Solomon, in the grimoire Lemegeton. (Author's collection)

of parchment bearing the hexagram and various CHARMS, SPELLS, or PRAYERS. In the late Middle Ages, the symbol was popular as an amulet against fire.

In ALCHEMY the Seal of Solomon symbolizes the PHILOSOPHER'S STONE because it joined the symbol of fire, an upright triangle, with the symbol of water, an inverted triangle.

The most important use of the Seal of Solomon is in MAGIC, as a talisman to control the demons and spirits conjured by the magician. From the 14th to the 19th centuries, the magicians' GRIMOIRES, or handbooks, gave detailed instructions for drawing the Seal of Solomon inside or outside the magic circle. The TETRAGRAMMATON, or sacred name of God, was inscribed in the middle of the symbol.

The magician was to follow strict instructions for creating the seal. One formula in *The Magus* (1801), by FRANCIS BARRETT, said it should be made in the day and hour of Mercury on virgin kidskin parchment or pure white paper, with the letters written in GOLD. The magician then had to consecrate it and sprinkle it with holy water.

second sight   See CLAIRVOYANCE.

Secret Chiefs   In a magical LODGE or order, the most powerful and highest-ranking ADEPTS; also, discarnate adepts. Traditionally, the Secret Chiefs were living persons who provided guidance and direction and for the most part were hidden from others. In the late 19th century, the HERMETIC ORDER OF THE GOLDEN DAWN encouraged the idea that the Secret Chiefs were discarnate beings who could be contacted only by certain high-level initiates through magical and mediumistic techniques.

Sefer Raziel   In angel MAGIC, an important text of magical lore and RITUAL instructions. The *Sefer Raziel*—the Book of Raziel—is of Jewish origin and probably was written in the 13th century by different anonymous authors. The Jewish mystic Eleazar of Worms (1160–1237) is credited with being one of the authors. Other names for the *Sefer Raziel* are *Sefer ha-Raziel, Sefer Reziel, Sepher Rezial Hemelach,* and *Raziel ha-Malach.*

According to lore, the *Sefer Raziel* is first book ever written and is made of sapphire, or "angel's tears." It was given by God to the angel Raziel to give to Adam and the patriarchs, including the magically wise King SOLOMON, who was shown the book in a dream by Raziel. The book reveals secrets and mysteries of creation, the secret wisdom of the 72 letters of the name of God and its esoteric 670 mysteries, and 1,500 keys, which had not been given even to angels. Other important material deals with the five names of the human soul; the seven hells; the divisions of the Garden of Eden; and the types of angels and spirits who have dominion over various things in

creation. The book also gives angelic scripts (see MAGIC ALPHABETS), angel languages, magical INCANTATIONS for directing the *memunim* (deputy angels), and magical instructions for rituals and for the making of TALISMANS and AMULETS.

According to lore, the *Sefer Raziel* was so coveted by jealous angels that various intrigues and thefts were carried out. Raziel is said to stand on the peak of Mount Horeb every day and proclaim the secrets to humankind.

In the Middle Ages, the book was highly revered among kabbalists, alchemists, and magicians; it was thought that mere possession of it would prevent fire. By the 19th century, there were 25 editions of it. The *Sword of Moses,* a GRIMOIRE, makes reference to it.

FURTHER READING:
Guiley, Rosemary Ellen. *The Encyclopedia of Angels.* 2d ed. New York: Facts On File Inc., 2004.
Savedow, Steve. *Sepher Rezial Hemelach: The Book of the Angel Rezial.* York Beach, Maine: Samuel Weiser, 2000.
Trachtenberg, Joshua. *Jewish Magic and Superstition: A Study in Folk Religion.* New York: Berhman's Jewish Book House, 1939.

sending   In MAGIC and SORCERY, the dispatching of bewitched people, animals and insects, objects, spirits and DEMONS, FAMILIARS, THOUGHT-FORMS, and even animated corpses to carry out CURSES or perform magical duties. Sending, when used as a noun, refers to the entity that is sent.

Sending is universal to magical arts. It is especially common among tribal societies of the Pacific islands, Africa, Siberia, and North America and in the folk magic of Scandinavia, Iceland, and the Baltic countries. In medieval times European witches were believed to send their familiars—usually cats, dogs, toads, hares, or owls—to carry out evil spells against their neighbors.

In Maori lore, sorcerers send lizards as familiars on killing errands. If a person sees a lizard on the path in front of him, the person should recognize it immediately as a familiar sent as an *aitua* (evil omen). He should kill the lizard and cause a woman to step over it, thus neutralizing the SPELL.

Navajo and Hindu sorcerers send dogs, but if the curse calls for destroying crops, they will send grasshoppers, locusts, caterpillars, and other insects. The Chippewa lay a curse of starvation by stuffing an owl skin with magical substances and sending it to fly to the victim's home. New Guinea sorcerers favor snakes and crocodiles for sending, while in Malay, the familiar is usually an owl or badger passed down from generation to generation. New Guinea sorcerers also send disease-causing objects such as pieces of magical bone and coral to lodge in bodies. In Africa the Kaguru witches send anteaters to burrow under the walls of their victims' huts, and the Gisu send rats in pairs to collect hair and nail clippings of victims for use in black magic spells.

Sending usually is done for cursing but also is used for magical errands. In shamanism, familiars are sent to do magical battle, but if the familiar dies, so does the shaman.

The Zulus' familiars are said to be corpses dug up and reanimated with magic; they are sent out on night errands to scare travelers with their shrieking and pranks. Corpses also are sent in Vodoun (see ZOMBIE).

In the Haitian folk magic called "sending of the dead," Baron Samedi, god of the graveyard, possesses a *bokor,* or SORCERER, to go to a cemetery at midnight with offerings of food for the Baron. The possessed person must gather a handful of GRAVEYARD DIRT for each person the sorcerer wishes to see killed, a handful that he later spreads on the paths taken by the victim(s), or he can take a stone from the cemetery that magically transforms itself into an evil entity ready to do its master's bidding, like a familiar. The sorcerer throws the stone against the victim's house. The victim is expected to quit eating, spit BLOOD, and die.

FURTHER READING:
Guiley, Rosemary Ellen. *The Encyclopedia of Witches and Witchcraft.* 2d ed. New York: Facts On File Inc., 1999.

Sendivogius, Michael (1566–1646)   Moravian alchemist.

Born in Moravia, Michael Sendivogius—whose true last name was Sensophax—was an expert in mining and manufacturing of pigments who lived in Cracow, Poland. He led a lavish lifestyle. At age 37, nearly out of money, he rescued the imprisoned Scottish alchemist ALEXANDER SETON in hopes of learning the secret of making GOLD as a reward. Seton gave him only some of his PHILOSOPHER'S STONE powder. When Seton died, Sendivogius married his widow, but she did not know the secret of making the Stone.

Sendivogius tried to increase his existing supply of powder, but his experiments failed, and he wasted much of his stock.

To establish himself as an ADEPT, Sendivogius made several transmutations in public. He traveled about with a servant who wore a box that allegedly contained the secret powder on a gold chain around his neck. This was a decoy, as the real powder was hidden in the running board of Sendivogius's carriage.

Adopting Seton's name of Cosmopolita ("the Cosmopolite"), Sendivogius traveled about Europe in style. He fared considerably better than Seton. Rudolph II, an avaricious monarch who was known to torture and execute failed alchemists, invited him to court but accepted his demurral that he did not possess the secret of making the Stone. However, he did give some of Seton's powder to Rudolph

and coached him in making a transmutation in the presence of several of the king's nobles.

Sendivogius then departed for Poland, invited to court there by King Sigismond. In Moravia, a local lord had him ambushed and imprisoned, threatening to hold him until he released the secret of the stone. Fearing that he would suffer the same fate as Seton, Sendivogius cut through an iron bar in his cell window, made a rope of his clothes, and successfully escaped nearly naked. He boldly reported the incident to the emperor, who fined the lord and confiscated one of his villages to give to Sendivogius in compensation. The lord also was forced to give the hand of his daughter in marriage to the alchemist.

Sendivogius went to Varsovia and made transmutations. He performed two for the duke of Wurtemberg, who was so impressed that he gave him the territory of Nedlingen. A jealous alchemist planted the fear that the duke intended to imprison him to gain the stone, causing Sendivogius to flee. The alchemist, along with 12 armed men, arrested him, robbed him of his remaining stone, and cast him into prison. Though the rival alchemist enjoyed fame for a brief while with his ill-gotten treasure, word of the deed circulated, and soon Sendivogius was freed.

Sendivogius once again appealed to Rudolph, who forced a return of all of Sendivogius's stolen possessions. The one exception was the stone, which mysteriously vanished. Sendivogius had only a small portion left, which he used to dazzle the king of Poland, Sigismund III, with a transmutation of a crown piece into a porous gold. Thereafter, his stone gone, Sendivogius descended to the level of charlatan and managed to obtain large sums of money.

In his later years at his castle of Groverna, he was visited by two men who said they were from the Rosicrucian Society, which wished to initiate him. He declined.

Sendivogius died in 1646 at age 84 in Parma. His sole estate consisted of an unpublished treatise, *Treatise on Salt of the Philosopher's Stone,* to his only daughter. The treatise remains unpublished, though a spurious work attributed to him has a similar title.

FURTHER READING:
Waite, Arthur Edward. *Alchemists Through the Ages.* Blauvelt, N.Y.: Rudolph Steiner Publications, 1970.

serpent's egg   In DRUID lore, an oval crystal TALISMAN that enabled the casting of certain SPELLS and the counteracting of INCANTATIONS.

According to the Roman historian Pliny the Elder, the Druids wore their serpent's eggs suspended from their necks. The crystals were so-named because they were formed from the foam of slime of serpents having intercourse. The hissing of the serpents caused the ball of foam to rise into the air. The Druids, said Pliny, sought to capture them by catching them before they fell to ground. Pliny said they had to carry off their prizes on swift horses, for the serpents would pursue them. The trick was to cross running water, which stopped the serpents in their pursuit.

The serpent's eggs possessed magical powers that would enable the Druids to neutralize spells against them. Anyone who possessed a serpent's egg would be guaranteed to win lawsuits and be "well received by kings."

Serpent's eggs are also called Druidic eggs and Druid's glass, or *Glainnaider* or *Glain-nan-Druidhe*, in Celtic tradition. One description of them says they were small glass AMULETS about the width of a finger ring but much thicker, commonly colored green or blue, with some waved in blue, red, and white.

See also EGG.

FURTHER READING:
Spence, Lewis. *The Magic Arts in Celtic Britain*. Van Nuys, Calif.: Newscastle Publishing, 1996.

serpent/snake   A SYMBOL of great power indicating change, renewal, and transformation. The serpent, or snake, is a potent archetype of psychic energy, power, dynamism, instinctual drive, and the entire process of psychic and spiritual transformation. In dreams, the snake may indicate a transformative process already underway, or it calls attention to the need to move to a new level of consciousness.

In mythology, snakes are powerful magical and mystical creatures. They are universal symbols of renewal and rebirth because of their unique ability to shed their old skin for new. The OUROBOROS, the snake which forms a circle by biting its own tail, symbolizes the eternal cycle of life, death, and rebirth. The snake is a symbol of healing, which is part of the transformation process. In its carnal aspect, the snake represents a phallus and its associations of the life force, sexuality, and sensuality. As a phallic symbol, the snake often is associated with pregnancy in imagery and mythology. In dreams, such pregnancy also may refer to a state of psychic transformation: pregnant with ideas, possibilities, changes, events about to happen.

As a creature which crawls along the earth and lives in holes in the ground, the snake has connections to the underworld, the unconscious, and humankind's instinctual drives. Mythical snakes guard the sleep of both the living and the dead; thus, they are creatures at the gateway to new consciousness. The snake also is a universal companion to goddesses and thus can symbolize the feminine, the *anima*, the womb, the dark, intuition, emotion, and all the aspects of the Great Mother.

The coils of the snake represent the cycles of manifestation: life and death, good and evil, wisdom and blind passion, light and dark, healing and poison, protection and destruction.

In ALCHEMY, the snake is the *serpens Mercurii*, the MERCURY or quicksilver that represents the constant driving forward of psychic life forces: living, dying, and being reborn. The snake is the PRIMA MATERIA, the unformed and dark chaos, from which order and life spring. Alchemical art often shows the snake wearing a gold crown, gem, diadem, or light to depict its expanded spiritual consciousness, which arises from the same energy as sexuality.

Snakes also are associated with WATER, the symbol of the unconscious, and TREES, the symbol of wisdom and knowledge. A snake climbing up a tree represents the process of becoming conscious or going through psychic transformation.

Seton, Alexander (17th c.)   Scottish alchemist imprisoned and brutally tortured for his knowledge of how to make the PHILOSOPHER'S STONE.

Alexander Seton was probably born to a noble family. Little is known about his early life. For several years, he created a sensation in Europe, at tragic cost to himself.

In 1602 Seton began a tour of the Continent, starting in Holland. There he was hosted by a man named Jacob Haussen, a ship pilot whom Seton had rescued in 1601 when Haussen's ship ran aground off the coast of the village of Seton in Scotland. Seton impressed his host by turning a piece of lead into GOLD and giving it to him. Seton then traveled about Europe, allegedly making more transmutations. His fame spread quickly. His modus operandi was to volunteer to perform the art to convince skeptics or impress learned people and then mysteriously vanish from town. He called himself the Cosmopolite.

In Munich Seton fell in love with a woman and eloped with her to Krossen in 1603. There he came to the attention of Christian II, the elector of Saxony, who sent for him and demanded Seton's secret of transmutation. Seton refused. When persuasion failed, Christian had Seton severely tortured. He was put on the rack, scourged, pierced with pointed irons. and burned with molten lead. Seton still refused to talk. The tortures were stopped at the point of death, and Seton, broken, was cast into solitary confinement in a guarded dungeon.

News of Seton's fate reached MICHAEL SENDIVOGIUS, a wealthy Hermetic student in Moravia. Sendivogius was able to use his money and inluence at court to obtain visits to Seton. They discussed ALCHEMY, but Seton revealed little specific information. Sendivogius soon was able to bribe his way into living in the same prison, where he confided a plan to help Seton escape in exchange for some of Seton's secret powder. Seton promised to give him enough to take care of himself and his family for the rest of their lives.

One day Sendivogius got all the guards drunk and carried Seton out. They went to Seton's house to retrieve what was left of his powder, and, joined with Seton's wife, they fled to safety in Poland. Seton handed over some of his powder, but he disappointed Sendivogius by not revealing the secret for making it.

Seton never recovered from his torture, and died in either December 1603 or on New Year's Day 1604.

FURTHER READING:
Holmyard, E. J. *Alchemy*. New York: Penguin Books, 1957.
Waite, Arthur Edward. *Alchemists Through the Ages*. Blauvelt, N.Y.: Rudolph Steiner Publications, 1970.

seventh son   Man who inherits great magical powers, according to widespread folklore. Seven is a number that is important in folklore relating to MAGIC. A seventh son possesses natural abilities for CLAIRVOYANCE, PROPHECY, control of spirits, and healing. A seventh son of a seventh son is considered to be the most powerful of all. However, the supernatural ability then diminishes in reverse for the next seven generations.

Robert Kirk, a 17th-century minister who wrote about FAIRIES, was a seventh son and may have possessed natural psychic abilities that enabled him to see and comprehend the fairy realm.

Seventh daughters are valued among some Gypsies for their reputed fortune-telling abilities.

See also GREATRAKES, VALENTINE.

shadow   Container, shape, or essence of the soul. In folklore a person who has no shadow has no soul. In MAGIC a person's shadow can be used for sympathetic magic and other purposes. Numerous superstitions are associated with shadows.

A shadow can be sold to the devil for favor and gain. Loss of one's shadow results in death. For example, in ancient Greece it was believed that a person who entered the sanctuary of Zeus on Mount Lycaeus without proper authorization would lose his or her shadow and die within a year.

Seeing one's shadow cast by the MOON is bad luck, even fatal. In Arabic folklore, a hyena stepping on a human shadow will cause loss of speech.

In Romanian lore, a dead person will become a VAMPIRE if the shadow of a living person falls over him or her. A person's shadow can be secured by magic to strengthen a building—but the person is doomed to become a vampire after death. In the lore of Slavic Muslim Gypsies, vampires are a dead person's shadow.

Injury done to a shadow will cause the same injury to the person's body, according to widespread magical beliefs. A magician or a sorcerer must take great care not to involve his or her own shadow in casting a SPELL, lest the spell boomerang back on the magician or the sorcerer.

A shadow also is an astral THOUGHT-FORM that can be directed by a magician in a PSYCHIC ATTACK.

shape-shifting   The magical or supernatural ability to transform from one body into another, such as humans into the bodies of animals and birds. A human who transforms into an animal becomes a were-animal and acquires the powers of that animal and other supernatural powers as well. Witches, sorcerers, and other magically empowered persons are said to shape-shift at will. Gods and DEMONS have shape-shifting ability and can take on human form.

Shape-shifting is accomplished through magical RITUAL and perhaps the use of OINTMENTS or potions or the wearing of magical garments or animal pelts. In Navajo tradition, witches become skinwalkers, or were-animals, by donning animal skins, which enables them to travel about at night at great speed. The skill can be taught by a master magician or a sorcerer; for example, shamans use shape-shifting for traveling to the underworld.

In WEREWOLF lore shape-shifting may be involuntary, such as at the full MOON or as the result of a CURSE.

In parts of Southeast Asia, it is believed that the witchcraft/were-animal spirit resides within a person—often passed down through heredity—and can be transmitted to others through contagion. A person who lives close to a witch can contract the "witch spirit" without the direct action or intent of the witch.

During the witch trials of the Inquisition—the peak of which occurred in the 16th and 17th centuries—European demonologists debated whether shape-shifting could be conferred by the devil and his demons or was merely a demonically inspired illusion. Some demonologists accepted shape-shifting as a literal fact, while others said it was physically impossible and thus was a demonic illusion.

ALEISTER CROWLEY was reputed to have the power to shape-shift others. He was supposed to have once turned the poet VICTOR NEUBURG into a camel—not literally but in a magical sense.

FURTHER READING:
Baring-Gould, Sabine. *The Book of Werewolves*. London: Smith, Elder & Co, 1865.
Guiley, Rosemary Ellen. *The Encyclopedia of Vampires, Werewolves and Other Monsters*. New York: Facts On File, Inc., 2004.
Otten, Charlotte F., ed. *A Lycanthropy Reader: Werewolves in Western Culture*. New York: Dorset Press, 1989.
Watson, C. W., and Roy Ellen (eds.). *Understanding Witchcraft and Sorcery in Southeast Asia*. Honolulu: University of Hawaii Press, 1993.

sight   See VISUALIZATION.

sigil   In MAGIC, symbols that express occult forces, such as contained in a set of ideas, sacred NAMES, and the numerical essences of PLANETS. ISRAEL REGARDIE described sigils as "symbols representing either an inherent occult force in man or an Essence or principle obtaining as an intelligent moving force in the universe." The term *sigil* comes from the Latin *sigillum,* which means "seal."

A sigil itself does not call forth spirits, but it serves as a physical focus through which the practitioner achieves a desired state of mind. Its primary purpose is to stimulate the IMAGINATION of the MAGICIAN in accordance with the purpose of a RITUAL. A sigil is given energy via visualization, chanting, and intensity of WILL and then is "sent." The correct use of sigils is one of the factors that determines the success of the ritual.

Sigils can be likened to a form of shorthand that enable a magician to set in motion forces or to summon spirits into awareness and control them. Sigils are created from the NUMBERS in MAGIC SQUARES. They also can be SYMBOLS, astrological signs, RUNES, and even designs created by a magician. They can contain the entire essence of a SPELL or the magical properties of celestial forces, spirits, or deities. A magician might have a personal sigil that she or he engraves upon her or his TOOLS.

Sigils also can serve as the focus of meditation and contemplation.

The English occultist AUSTIN OSMAN SPARE developed his own system of sigils using ordinary letters of the alphabet, which he combined from affirmative statements concerning a goal. Spare said that "sigils are the art of believing, my invention for making belief organic, ergo, true belief." Furthermore, he described them as "monograms of thought" that find fulfillment from the subconscious. He preferred his system to ritual magic, saying that it did not require a person to "dress up as a traditional magician, wizard or priest, build expensive temples, obtain virgin parchment, black goat's blood, etc., etc., in fact no theatricals or humbug."

Spare's sigil process has four steps: formulation, creation, charging, and relinquishing. First the goal or desire must be formulated in a sentence that begins "It is my desire . . ." or "This my will . . ." or "This my wish. . . ." All repeating letters are removed, and the sigil is designed from the remaining letters, which are combined into shapes. The sigil is charged at a "magical time" of peak emotional intensity, in which it is energized and shot off into the void of deep space. The sigil is then consciously forgotten, relinquished to the powers of the subconscious.

In *The Book of Pleasure (Self-love): The Psychology of Ecstasy* (1913), Spare said that one must know exactly what the sigil is for and what it relates to. "If you use any form stupidly," said Spare, "you might possibly 'conjure up' exactly what you did not want—the mother of insanity, or what always happens then, nothing at all."

FURTHER READING:

Regardie, Israel. *The Tree of Life: A Study in Magic.* York Beach, Maine: Samuel Weiser, 1969.

Spare, Austin Osman. *The Book of Pleasure (Self-Love): The Psychology of Ecstasy.* Available online. URL: http://www.spirit.starlord.net/mystic/mx35.html. Downloaded July 14, 2005.

Tyson, Donald. *The New Magus.* St. Paul, Minn.: Llewellyn Publications, 1988.

silver   Important metal in MAGIC and ALCHEMY.

Silver has long and universal associations with the mysterious and magical powers of the MOON. It appears in nature in a pure state and is an excellent conductor of electromagnetic energy, thus making it a valuable metal. It was prized for its magical properties by the ancient Egyptians and Incas.

In folklore silver repels all evil, including spirits and malevolent SPELLS.

In alchemy silver is called Luna or Diana, the Roman goddess of the Moon. In alchemical formulae silver is represented by a crescent moon.

Simon Magus (first c. C.E.)   Gnostic wonder-worker who became the prototype of heretic and black magician. Simon Magus, also known as Simon the Sorcerer, came from Samaria, where he was worshiped as a god for his occult powers. He was attracted to Christianity and the miracles associated with it. He was converted to the faith by Philip the Deacon, whose MAGIC impressed Simon.

According to Acts 8:9–24, the apostles Peter and John were sent to Samaria to deliver the Holy Spirit into the population by a laying on of hands. When Simon witnessed their supernatural work, he offered the apostles money: "Give me this power, that any one on whom I lay my hands shall receive the Holy Spirit." The apostles, angry that Simon should expect to buy holy power, had him thrown out of the church. Peter told him, "Your silver perish with you, because you thought you could obtain the gift of God with money." Simon's name gave rise to the term *simony,* the sin of buying or selling a church office.

According to lore, Simon traveled to Rome, where he impressed people with his occult ability, and then to Egypt, where he allegedly learned such magic as INVISIBILITY, LEVITATION, and SHAPE-SHIFTING into an animal. He is said to have created a man out of thin air and boasted that he was part of the Holy Trinity. He conjured a woman who he said was Helen of Troy, but his critics claimed that the woman was a prostitute from Tyre. Simon said he was God and that Helen was his Thought of God.

In Rome again, Simon impressed Nero and was named court magician. His feats, which also included the moving of heavy furniture without touch (psychokinesis) and passing through fire unharmed, probably were illusions or the result of hypnosis. He convinced one of Nero's guards that he had cut off his own head, when actually he decapitated a ram. Thus, he claimed to Nero that he had risen from the dead.

Peter came to Rome to challenge Simon and to expose him of fraud. Simon conjured huge dogs and ordered them to attack Peter and tear him to shreds, but Peter made the dogs vanish by holding out a loaf of holy bread. Simon said that he would offer ultimate proof of his ability by ascending bodily into heaven. He went to the top of the Roman Forum and levitated. Peter fell to his knees and prayed to God to stop the deception, whereupon Simon crashed to earth, broke both legs, and died.

Simon is credited with founding a Gnostic sect that became known as the Simonians. The Simonians recognized Simon as the first God, sometimes worshiped as Zeus, and his consort Helen as the goddess Athena. Gnostics, who believed that spirit was good, that matter was evil, and that salvation lay in the attainment of esoteric knowledge (*sophia*), were branded heretics by the Catholic Church. Most of their records were destroyed.

In Celtic lore, Simon Magus is associated with DRUIDS; in Ireland *Magus* is translated as "Druid," and he is known as "Simon the Druid." He is said to have aided the Druid Mog Ruith in the making of the *Roth Fail,* the "wheel of light," a symbol of the SUN that enabled Druids to fly through the air. Simon is credited with using the *Roth Fail* to travel quickly to Rome.

FURTHER READING:
Spence, Lewis. *The Magic Arts in Celtic Britain.* Van Nuys, Calif.: Newscastle Publishing, 1996.

Sixth and Seventh Books of Moses Magical texts said to contain SPELLS and CONJURATIONS for all purposes. The *Sixth and Seventh Books of Moses*—also called the "Mystery of all Mysteries"—were published in 1849 in Stuttgart, Germany. They are credited to the authorship of Johann Scheibel (1736–1809). According to lore, the books were dicted by God to Moses on Mount Sinai. They were omitted from the Old Testament because of their power. The books were passed down to Aaron, Caleb, Joshua, David and then KING SOLOMON, who is credited with authoring his own powerful book of magic.

The *Sixth and Seventh Books of Moses* are based on Talmudic and practical Kabbalistic magic, and include CHARMS, TALISMANS, SEALS, sacred NAMES, the secret magic of the Psalms, and so forth. The spells are intended for luck, amassing wealth, NECROMANCY, healing, protection, CURSES and other magical purposes.

Folk tales about the books are similar to tales about BLACK BOOKS that confer powers but bring trouble to their owners.

In one German tale, an old master tailor who lived in Trent had a wife who inherited an unusual book from her mother reputed to be the *Sixth and Seventh Books of Moses.* Whenever the wife read in the book, deer, wolves, hares, and other animals would come to her, lie down at her feet, and play with her children. The animals vanished when she closed the book.

This disturbed the tailor, who decided he did not want the book in the house. One day while his wife was reading it, he grabbed it and threw it into the stove. To their astonishment, the fire went out, and the book remained undamaged. Some elders told the tailor that

he could successfully get rid of the book by having a boy born on a Sunday during the sermon throw the book into the stove. The tailor followed this advice. When the boy tossed the book into the stove, it was immediately burned up by the fire.

Like other folk tales about attempts to destroy magical books, this tale underscores the power of Christianity—the pure boy born on Sunday during a sermon—to defeat occult powers and pagan folk magic.

Another German folk tale holds that no more magic or WITCHCRAFT exist because the *Sixth and Seventh Books of Moses* are safely locked up in Wittenberg.

See also GRIMOIRES.

FURTHER READING:
Ashiman, D. L. (ed.) "The Hand of Glory and other gory legends about human hands." Available online. URL: http://www.pitt.edu/~dash/magicbook.html. Downloaded December 22, 2004.

Solomon (10th c. B.C.E.) King of the Israelites, son of David, and builder of the Temple of Jerusalem. According to lore, King Solomon was among the early great magicians. He possessed great powers and commanded an army of DEMONS called djinn. Numerous handbooks of magic are credited to him. (See GRIMOIRES.)

Solomon gained great wisdom and supernatural knowledge when he took the throne following his father's death. 1 Kings 3:5 tells how the Lord appeared to him in a dream and told him to "Ask what I shall give you." Solomon asked for an understanding mind for governing and for discernment between good and evil. Pleased that he did not asked for wealth, God granted his requests. The gift was not without a caveat, however. In another vision, the Lord said that Solomon's house would prosper as long as the commandments were kept and no other gods were worshiped. Otherwise, God would ruin the kingdom.

Solomon became famous for his great wisdom. In the fourth year of his reign, he built the Temple of Jerusalem. According to lore, he enslaved an army of demons with the help of a magical RING given to him by the Archangel Michael.

Forty years into his reign, Solomon had acquired 700 wives and princesses and 300 concubines. Some of his wives convinced him to worship pagan deities, especially the goddess Ashtoreth. God sent adversaries against him but decided not to take his kingdom away. Instead, God took it away from all but one of his sons.

Descriptions of Solomon's magical powers and feats are described in pseudepigraphal and apochryphal texts such as the Testament of Solomon, Odes of Solomon, Psalms of Solomon, and Wisdom of Solomon. Josephus's *Antiquities* credits Solomon with writing 1,500 books of odes and songs and 3,000 books of parables and similitudes, and he knew how to exorcize demons. The *SEFER RAZIEL,* a magical text based on Hebrew angel lore, says that Solomon received the book from the line of patriarchs and obtained his wisdom from it.

Solomon was popular among early Christians, who inscribed his NAME on AMULETS, TALISMANS, and lintels and in numerous incantations for protection against and removal of demons. His magical seal is a HEXAGRAM, called the SEAL OF SOLOMON.

FURTHER READING:

The Old Testament Pseudepigrapha. Vols. 1 & 2. James H. Charlesworth, ed. New York: Doubleday, 1983; 1985.

sorcerer   A professional practitioner of magical arts. In the Western magical tradition, a sorcerer is associated with low or black MAGIC, that is, SPELLS for power, money, love, and personal gain. The term *sorcerer* might be interchanged with *warlock, wizard,* or *witch.* The French word for *witch* is *sorcier,* which is derived from *sors,* or "spell."

In *The Book of Black Magic and of Pacts,* ARTHUR EDWARD WAITE gives a description of sorcerers:

> We have seen that the sorcerer of the Middle Ages was usually squalid and necessitous; hence he coveted treasures: he was usually despised, and hence he longed for mastery, for the prestige of mystery, and the power of strange arts: he was usually lonely and libidinous, and hence he sought, by means of spells and philtres, to compel the desire of women. To be rich in worldly goods, to trample on one's enemies, and to gratify the desires of the flesh—such are the ends, variously qualified and variously attained, of most Ceremonial Magic, and hence the Rituals abound in Venereal Experiments.

Outside of the Western magical tradition, a sorcerer might not be regarded in either a negative or positive light but rather as a magically empowered person who is consulted for spells for a variety of purposes.

See also WIZARD.

FURTHER READING:

Waite, Arthur Edward. *The Book of Black Magic and of Pacts.* 1899. Reprint, York Beach, Maine: Samuel Weiser, 1972.

sorcery   A magical art, usually associated with the low MAGIC of SPELL-casting. *Sorcery* is derived from the French word *sors,* which means "spell."

Sorcery is not a system of spiritual practice like ceremonial magic traditions but is mechanistic and intuitive. It involves the casting of spells or the use of CHARMS to influence love, fertility, luck, health, and wealth. Sorcery fulfills various needs in a society, such as protecting against disaster, outsiders, and enemies; redressing wrongs and meting out justice; controlling the environment; and explaining frightening phenomena. Sorcerers

The Abomination of the Sorcerers, *by Jaspar Isaac, 16th century.* (Author's collection)

are universally believed to have the power to harm and kill and to counteract spells cast by other sorcerers or practitioners of magic.

In the West, sorcery usually is associated with harmful black magic and demonic arts and with WITCHCRAFT. In other societies, however, sorcery is regarded more favorably than witchcraft, and in some others it is considered to be more evil than witchcraft.

DIVINATION is related to sorcery, although in some societies diviners are considered to be separate from sorcerers.

sound   In mystical and magical traditions, a formative and destructive power. Sacred sound both brings things into manifestation and destroys things. In creation myths, gods create by the power of sound.

The same power is employed in magical RITUAL, in which sacred NAMES and words of power must be spoken—or "vibrated"—with correct pronunciation and great force. According to ISRAEL REGARDIE, sound "connects with the law of vibration, whose forces are powerful enough to shatter or build anew whatsoever form the vibration is directed towards."

The correct pronunciation and intonement is of utmost importance, creating powerful vibrations which in turn affect the vibrations of all things in the universe, including deities and lower spirit beings. Mantric power is used to accomplish psychokinetic feats as weather control, teleportation, apports, and levitation.

All religions acknowledge the tremendous power of vibrating the names of God or a mantra—a Sanskrit term meaning "to protect"—such as "God is love." Repeating a name of God or a mantra aligns human consciousness with the highest spiritual consciousness possible.

ALEISTER CROWLEY created the mantra AUGMN, an expansion of Om which he said was the magical formula of the universe. Crowley believed the sound vibrations of AUGMN were so powerful that a magician using them would be able to control the forces of the universe.

The power of sound is found in the ancient Greek theory of music, in which the keynote of a particular organism, body, or substance can be used to cause it to disintegrate.

FURTHER READING:

Guiley, Rosemary Ellen. *Harper's Encyclopedia of Mystical & Paranormal Experience.* San Francisco: HarperSanFrancisco, 1991.

Regardie, Israel. *The Tree of Life: A Study in Magic.* York Beach, Maine: Samuel Weiser, 1969.

Spare, Austin Osman (1888–1956)   English magician who expressed his occult vision in strange and sometimes frightening art. Austin Osman Spare's talent for art was widely acknowledged and even called genius. He could have pursued a conventional artist's career but instead chose to devote himself to creating images of DEMONS and spirits that were raised up from deep levels of consciousness.

Spare was born on December 31, 1888, in London; his father was a City of London policeman. He left school at age 13 and worked for a time in a stained-glass factory. He obtained a scholarship to the Royal College of Art in Kensington and enjoyed success as an artist by 1909.

The seeds for Spare's occult life were sewn early in childhood. Alienated from his mother, he gravitated toward a mysterious old woman named Mrs. Paterson. She claimed to be a hereditary witch who was descended from a line of Salem witches who escaped execution during the witch trials in 1692—an unlikely claim considering that the Salem incident was a fraud perpetrated by hysterical children. The young Spare referred to her as his "witch-mother." Later he said that she possessed great skill in DIVINATION and had the ability to materialize her THOUGHTS.

Mrs. Paterson taught Spare how to visualize and evoke spirits and ELEMENTALS and how to reify his dream imagery. She also initiated Spare in a witches' sabbat, which he described as taking place in another dimension, where cities were constructed of an unearthly geometry. Spare said he attended such sabbats several times.

Under further tutelage of Mrs. Paterson, Spare developed his own system of MAGIC, based heavily on WILL and sex—his own sex drive was quite intense—and the works of ALEISTER CROWLEY.

Spare believed that the power of will is capable of fulfilling any deeply held desire. The formula, simpler than ceremonial magic, was in his unpublished GRIMOIRE, *The Book of the Living Word of Zos.* The formula called for creating SIGILS or TALISMANS in an "alphabet of desire." The desire is written down in full. Repeating letters are crossed out and the remaining letters are combined into a sigil like a sort of monogram. The sigil is impressed upon the subconscious by staring at it. The original desire is then let go so that the "god within" can work undisturbed toward the desired end.

According to one story, Spare once told a friend he would conjure freshly cut roses to fall from the air. His magic involved creating some symbolic drawings, which he waved in the air while repeating "roses." He got results, but they were unexpected—the plumbing in the room overhead burst, and Spare and his friend were dowsed by sewage.

In his strange art, Spare is best known for his atavisms, the reifying of primal forces from previous existences that were drawn from the deepest layers of the human mind. This, too, was a product of his education from Mrs. Paterson. According to another story, one of his atavisms caused the suicide of one witness and the insanity of another.

Despite his ability to paint the spirits and images he saw, Spare was occasionally at a loss for words to describe some of his more bizarre experiences. Some of his visions put him into a place that he was able only to describe as "spaces beyond space."

In 1956 Spare was contacted by the English witch GERALD GARDNER for his help in a magical war with Kenneth Grant. Gardner believed that Grant was stealing his witches for his own New Isis Lodge, and he decided to launch a magical attack on him and reclaim his witches. In particular, Gardner wanted back a self-proclaimed "water-witch" named Clanda. It was the last year of Spare's life, and by then he was living in dire poverty and obscurity, eking out a living by painting portraits in local pubs.

Using his "alphabet of desire," Spare created a TALISMAN for Gardner that would "restore lost property to its rightful place," which Spare himself described as "a sort of amphibious owl with the wings of a bat and talons of an eagle." Gardner did not give Spare specific information as to the exact nature of the "lost property"; he knew that Spare and Grant were on friendly terms.

During a Black Isis rite at the New Isis Temple, Clanda experienced the apparent negative effects of the talisman. Her role was to lie passively on the altar. Instead she sat up, sweating and with a hypnotized and glazed look in her eyes. She behaved as though in the grip of terror, convulsing and shuddering. Later she described what she experienced: the appearance of a huge bird that gripped her in its talons and carried her off into the night. She struggled and broke free, falling back onto the altar. The attending magicians saw none of this, but they did hear what sounded like the talons of a large bird scrabbling against the wind, and they felt a cold wind rush about the room. Physical talon marks were found on the window frame, and the window sill was covered with a strange, gelatinous substance that seemed to breathe on its own. A strong odor of sea permeated the temple for days.

As for Clanda, she failed to return to Gardner. Instead, she moved to New Zealand where she drowned.

Some of Spare's work appears in two quarterly art review magazines that he edited, *Form* and *Golden Hind*. He wrote three books that were published: *The Book of Pleasure (Self-love): The Psychology of Ecstasy,* (1913), and *The Focus of Life* (1921), both of which dealt with his magic system; and *A Book of Automatic Drawing*, published posthumously in 1972.

Spare spent most of his life as a recluse, living in poverty in London. He was remote and detached, preferring the company of his cats to that of human beings. He is considered a source of modern chaos magic.

FURTHER READING:
Cavendish, Richard, and Brian Innes, eds. *Man, Myth and Magic,* revised ed. North Bellmore, N.Y.: Marshall Cavendish Corp., 1995.
Guiley, Rosemary Ellen. *The Encyclopedia of Witches and Witchcraft.* 2d ed. New York: Facts On File Inc., 1999.
King, Francis. *Megatherion: The Magickal World of Aleister Crowley.* New York: Creation Books, 2004.

spell   A spoken or written magical formula. Spells are statements for desired goals or may take the form of CHARMS. Spells are cast for any purpose, positive or negative, on anyone or anything, including inanimate objects. They are intended to cause or influence a particular course of events; protect; bewitch, and enchant; increase and prosper; diminish and harm; and so forth. Spell-casting has been part of magical practices since antiquity.

Spells are related to PRAYER, which petitions gods or higher forces to bring about a desired outcome. In spell-casting, higher forces are invoked along with an intense projection from the spell-caster. Spells are cast in RITUALS, which in folk magic may be quite simple and in ceremonial magic quite elaborate.

A common type of spell is the diminishing word, which causes something to disappear, such as an illness or bad fortune. (See ABRACADABRA.) This spell is for curing a fever:

> Write this on a piece of bread and give it to the patient for eight days, specifically a piece each day, and on the ninth day, burn the last piece, which is C x.
>
> Colameris x, Colameri x, Colamer x, Colame x, Xolam x, Xola x, Col x, Co x, C x
>
> After doing this, the fever will be gone.

Diminishing words also are used in spells to cause something to happen at the end of the spell, such as this Norwegian folk spell for catching a thief who has burgled one's home:

> Write the following words over the door of the house which the thief has burgled. Auratabul—Auratabu—Auratab—Aurata—Aurat—Au ra—Aur—Au—A Write these words three times. The thief will come back and be caught.

The words of a spell can be spontaneous, or they may be taken from formulae given in many GRIMOIRES and BLACK BOOKS of magic. However, reciting spells and following the instructed steps do not alone guarantee success. To be effective, any spell-casting must employ VISUALIZATION, IMAGINATION, and projection of WILL. These, plus the activation of the senses through ritual, raise magical power that at its peak is "sent," or made manifest. The spell-caster visualizes and affirms the spell as already put into action. A similar attitude is cultivated in "positive thinking," when a person imagines a desired goal as already accomplished.

A spell should be spoken out loud to activate the magical force of SOUND. The ancient Egyptians believed that words were so powerful that merely speaking them would cause action. The power of sound and the correct pronunciation of sacred NAMES and words are important elements in Western magic. Many spells are written as well.

A spell can have a finite lifespan imposed by the spell-caster, or it can be in effect indefinitely. A spell can be broken by countermagic, usually a negating spell cast by another practitioner of magic.

Some modern practitioners of magic feel it is morally wrong to cast negative or harmful spells, and they believe that the ill effects of them will rebound on the spell-caster; Wiccans, for example, believe in a threefold return of magic cast. Some accept "binding spells" as a means of stopping negative or undesirable behavior. In the history of magic, however, negative spells are routine in the course of daily life and business: They are aimed at rivals and enemies.

See also BEWITCHMENT; CURSE; ENCHANTMENT; FASCINATION; HEX.

FURTHER READING:
Guiley, Rosemary Ellen. *The Encyclopedia of Witches and Witchcraft.* 2d ed. New York: Facts On File Inc., 1999.
Rustad, Mary S. (ed. and translator). *The Black Books of Elverum.* Lakeville, Minn.: Galde Press, 1999.

spittle   Ingredient in magical SPELLS. Spittle has been held to possess magical power since ancient times. It plays a role in sympathetic magic along with other issuances from the body and body parts, such as HAIR AND NAIL CLIPPINGS, BLOOD, URINE, and excrement. The principle behind the magical power is that something that is connected to the body makes a magical connection for a spell to take hold. Spittle also carries the intent in the casting of a spell.

Spittle is included in the making of magical objects such as POPPETS, FETISHES, CHARM BAGS, *GRIS-GRIS,* and other AMULETS AND TALISMANS, and imbues the essence and intent of the person doing the creating. A common magical technique of casting a BEWITCHMENT, HEX, or CURSE is to spit on an object, such as a doll, a stone, or KNOTS, while the spell is recited. Sometimes the object is ritually destroyed after being spit upon, which carries the magical power of destruction to the victim. Necromancers sometimes spit as part of their rituals for conjuring the spirits of the dead.

Widespread folk beliefs address the need to be careful about where and how one spits, for an evil sorcerer, a witch, or even a DEMON could capture spittle and use it against a person.

Spitting is a universal defense against the EVIL EYE, bad luck, illness, and WITCHCRAFT. Practices that date back to early Roman times include spitting in the right shoe every morning; spitting into the toilet after urination; spitting on the breast or on the ground three times; and spitting while passing any place where danger might exist. Pliny records the effectiveness of spittle against various disorders such as boils, eye infections, epilepsy, and leprosy.

Spittle is especially potent in protecting infants and children against FASCINATION. In Italy, persons who are suspected of overlooking children (the evil eye) are asked to spit in their faces to nullify the harm done.

The custom of spitting into the hands before a fight to make the blows stronger dates back to early Roman times.

Starkey, George (1628–1665)

American physician and alchemist. George Starkey became interested in ALCHEMY early in life. In the 1640s, he studied medicine at Harvard and then practiced as a physician in Boston. He experimented in alchemy to try to find cures for diseases. In 1650, he went to London to seek a better intellectual environment for his interests. There he found the activity he desired, inspired in part by the work of ROBERT BOYLE. Starkey quickly became allied with the Invisible College, and he partnered with Boyle to produce innovative medical remedies for fever, sweating, and vomiting.

Initially, the members of the Invisible College were enthusiastic about Starkey. He gave to them alchemical manuscripts that he claimed were given to him by an American alchemist named Eirenaeus Philathales. However, Philathales most likely was a pseudonym of Starkey for manuscripts that he wrote himself.

Starkey's standing with the Invisible College became tarnished. He gained a reputation for not paying his bills and often fell short of the promises he delivered. He was prone to deep depressions and was contentious. Starkey's debt grew to the point where he was sent to debtor's prison. He was allowed to conduct his alchemical experiments in his cell.

After his release from prison, Starkey attacked physicians in the Royal College of Medicine in his work *Nature's Explication and Helmont's Vindication: Being a Short and Sure Way to a Long Life,* published in 1657. He criticized physicians for clinging to the backward ideas of the Roman physician Galen and said that popular medicines were worthless and were intended only to make money.

In 1665, the bubonic plague hit London, and many doctors fled. Starkey denounced them as cowards. He also said that the plague was not determined by the cycles of the planets but by internal factors that could be treated chemically. He teamed with a fellow physician George Thomson to dissect the corpse of a plague victim publicly to prove his theory.

Thomson became ill with the plague, and Starkey treated him with medicines. Thomson recovered, but Starkey became infected and died. Thomson went on to dissect the corpse himself.

FURTHER READING:
Waite, Arthur Edward. *Alchemists Through the Ages.* Blauvelt, N.Y.: Rudolph Steiner Publications, 1970.

suffumigation See PERFUMES.

sulphur In ALCHEMY, a SYMBOL of the masculine principle. Sulphur coagulates liquid MERCURY (feminine), thus "fixing" it. It represents the fiery, active principle: the SUN, the DRAGON or OUROBOROUS, and also the *PRIMA MATERIA.*

PARACELSUS said that sulphur and SALT are the parents of mercury, which is the child of the sun and MOON.

See also *TRIA PRIMA.*

summoning See EVOCATION; INVOCATION.

Sun A SYMBOL of the active, volatile masculine principle. The Sun represents enlightenment, illumination, and GOLD. In ALCHEMY, it is sometimes depicted as the king who enters into a union of opposites with the queen to create the PHILOSOPHER'S STONE. The Sun also is sometimes itself a symbol of the stone.

swastika An ancient and potent sacred and magical SYMBOL. The swastika is a cross with bent arms of equal length that appear to rotate in the same direction. *Swastika* means something approximate to "fortunate."

The swastika probably was originated by the ancient Aryans. In the Iron Age, it symbolized the supreme deity. It was in use in ancient Troy, Greece, Egypt, China, India, Persia, Central and South America, and Scandinavia. The Chinese called it thunder-scroll, and the Hindus, in Sanskrit, called it All is Well. In China and Japan, it has symbolized Buddha since about 200 B.C.E. The Anglo-Saxons called it fylfot, or "many footed" cross. In the Middle Ages, the swastika was a solar wheel that represented the movement of the Sun across the heavens. Pagans associated it with the Mother Goddess; the Norse believed that it was the hammer of the thunder god, Thor.

The swastika appears among the symbols in Hermetic MAGIC and among Native American Indian tribes. The Navajo use it in the healing ceremonies of sand painting. Its division into quadrants has been interpreted as symbolic of the four directions on a compass and the four corners of the Earth; the center of the cross is sometimes viewed as symbolic of the center of the cosmos.

There are two kinds of swastikas, right-handed (and more common), which represents the vernal Sun, and left-handed (swavastika), which represents the autumnal Sun.

Prior to World War I, secret rascist groups sprang up in Germany and were attracted to the swastika as an emblem of might. They attached it to their occult philosophies of Germanic supremacy. The emblem of the *Germanen Orden*, created in 1912, was a bronze pin that was designed as a shield, on which two spears crossed a swastika. The bent cross was also the emblem of the Thule Society, whose purpose was to study the supposed occult meaning and symbolism of the German alphabet. The magical RUNE symbol of the Thule Society was Aarune (Aryan), associated with the Sun and the center of the universe. It was believed that the Sun dispersed rays of esoteric knowledge along with light and heat and that this knowledge could had by the initiates.

An occult ferment spread throughout Germany, fueled in part by interest in magical fraternities such as the HERMETIC ORDER OF THE GOLDEN DAWN and esoteric groups such as the THEOSOPHICAL SOCIETY. The swastika was an important symbol in the Golden Dawn, and ALEISTER CROWLEY wrote a pamphlet about it in 1910. Crowley later said the Nazis stole the idea for the swastika from him. The Theosophical Society was formed by H. P. BLAVATSKY, a Russian-born mystic, in 1875 in New York City and was dedicated to spreading Eastern esoteric thought throughout the West. The swastika was a mystical symbol to Blavatsky, who wore one as a brooch.

In 1920, as Adolf Hitler was nurturing his growing Nazi Party, he seized upon the swastika as the perfect emblem that would express what the party stood for and appeal to the masses. He put a black swastika inside a white circle against a red background. In his autobiography, *Mein Kampf,* he said, "A symbol it really is! In *red* we see the social idea of the movement, in *white* the nationalist idea, in the *swastika* the mission of the struggle for the victory of the Aryan man."

Hitler put the emblem on the armbands of his SS storm troopers and party members. By 1922 the swastika was on flags and standards displayed at all Nazi gatherings and meeting places.

By the end of World War II and the defeat of the Nazis, the swastika had become synonymous with horrific cruelties and barbarism. Some modern Pagan groups that worship the Norse and Teutonic deities have sought unsuccessfully to restore the swastika to its original symbolism.

sword   See TOOLS.

symbol   An object or visual image that expresses a concept or idea beyond the object or image itself. It translates the human situation into cosmological terms by both concealing and revealing with an element of mystery. Symbols are the language of the unconscious, especially the collective unconscious, where reside the accumulated archetypal images of humankind.

The beginnings of symbolistic thought date to the late Paleolithic Age, when nomadic hunter/gatherer societies expressed their magicosupernatural beliefs in rock carvings and paintings. As civilization developed, symbols became integral to MAGIC, ALCHEMY, and all esoteric teachings for they contain secret wisdom accessible only to the initiated. In all mystical, magical, and religious traditions, symbols play an important role in the alteration and transformation of consciousness.

Anything can become a symbol: natural and manufactured objects, numbers, the elements, animals, the Earth, the sky, the heavenly objects, deities, myths, folk tales, and even words. According to CARL G. JUNG, the whole cosmos is a potential symbol. The circle is a universal symbol of great power, representing the Sun, illumination, wholeness, the wheel of life-death-rebirth, the Word of God, Truth, the Christ, and the PHILOSOPHER'S STONE of alchemy. In Jungian thought the circle represents the Self, the totality of the psyche.

Philosopher MANLY P. HALL said that the human is the oldest, most profound, and universal symbol, as found in the ancient Mysteries, which taught that the macrocosm of the universe was symbolized by humans, the microcosm. Hall said symbols comprise the language of the Mysteries, and of philosophy, mysticism, and all Nature. Symbols both conceal (to the uninitiated) and reveal (to the initiated).

In magic, symbols are the keys to raising within the magician the qualities or abilities expressed by the symbols. The poet WILLIAM BUTLER YEATS, a member of the HERMETIC ORDER OF THE GOLDEN DAWN, said of the magical power of symbols, "I cannot now think symbols less than the greatest of all powers whether they are used consciously by the master of magic or half unconsciously by their successors, the poet, the musician and the artist." (See SIGIL.)

Alchemy cannot be pursued or understood without delving into symbols. Alchemists veiled the secrets of their work in symbolic images, the meanings of which must be interpreted and intuited by others. The *MUTUS LIBER* is perhaps the most famous example of an entire work in pictorial symbolism. Other such noteworthy works are *Atalanta Fugiens* by MICHAEL MEIER; the *Splendor Solis* by Saloman Trismosin; *The Book of Lambsprinck;* and the book obtained by NICHOLAS FLAMEL.

For the most part, alchemical symbols are allegorical and thus are open to broad interpretation. Beyond a few consistencies, alchemists often invented their own symbolic shorthand without regard for others. Planetary symbols are used for the primary metals of alchemy. The four ELEMENTS have fairly consistent symbols in downward-pointing triangles (earth and water) and upward pointing triangles (air and fire). The 12 steps of the Great Work are associated with the 12 signs of the zodiac and their symbols.

Alchemists also employed literary symbolisms, or "cover names," for aspects of the GREAT WORK. For example, the PHILOSOPHER'S STONE has well more than 100 cover names. *Crow* could mean lead, and *CELESTIAL DEW* could refer to MERCURY. Alchemical recipes sometimes were written entirely in such code, to the point where they were inscrutable to all but the original author.

Jung, who devoted a great deal of his life to studying symbols, said that objects and forms that are transformed into symbols become endowed with a great psychological and redeeming power. Jung said that the human mind has its own history, expressed in symbols, specifically archetypes, or models. Symbols surface in dreams, but some have become completely unfamiliar to many people. In his practice, he noticed that archetypal and alchemical symbols appear in dreams, even when dreamers are not knowledgeable about either.

He said that the religious dogma of the Christian Church tends to pull human consciousness away from its roots in the unconscious and that the symbols of ASTROLOGY help to keep the two connected.

Jung lamented the deterioration of the symbolic nature of Christianity. He said Christian symbols died of the same disease that felled the classical gods: People discovered that they had no thoughts on the subject. Jung also lamented Western efforts to adopt symbols from Eastern religions, which he did not think could be assimilated meaningfully into Western culture. Better to admit that Christianity suffered from a poverty of symbols than to attempt to possess foreign symbols to which the West could not be the spiritual heir.

Symbols become degraded if their original meanings are lost and replaced by lesser values. Jung said that symbols that are not constantly renewed lose their redeeming power. Symbols which become too well known also lose their power, becoming mere signs.

See also TAROT.

FURTHER READING:

Eliade, Mircea. *Symbolism, the Sacred, & the Arts.* Diane Apostolos-Cappadona, ed. New York: Crossroad, 1988.

Hall, Manly P. *The Secret Teachings of All Ages.* 1928. Reprint, Los Angeles: The Philosophic Research Society, 1977.

Holmyard, E. J. *Alchemy.* New York: Penguin Books, 1957.

Jung, C. G. *Psychology and Alchemy.* 2d ed. From *The Collected Works of C. G. Jung,* vol. 12. Princeton, N.J.: Princeton University Press, 1953.

Jung, Carl G. (ed.). *Man and His Symbols.* New York: Anchor Press/Doubleday, 1988.

sympathetic magic   See MAGIC.

T

taboo A system of magical prohibition in which certain people, animals, objects, actions, and words are untouchable, unmentionable, or not to be done. Taboo systems are universal. The term *taboo* comes from the Polynesian word *tabu*.

The effect of some taboos is a social CURSE: Something or someone is feared for their inherent and dangerous magical or spiritual power, and so they are made outcast. A taboo may be permanent or temporary; an example of the latter is the widespread taboo against touching or having social interaction with menstruating women.

Some things are taboo because they are sacred, and to tamper with them will desecrate them and incur divine wrath. It might be taboo to touch royalty or holy objects.

Some taboos are intended to purify, protect, and ensure success. For example, prior to a hunt, it might taboo to engage in certain practices, lest the spirits of the intended prey be offended.

FURTHER READING:
Gordon, Stuart. *The Book of Curses: True Tales of Voodoo, Hoodoo and Hex.* London: Brockhampton Press, 1994.

talisman An object that possesses magical or supernatural powers and transmits the powers to the owner. Talismans are different from AMULETS, which are objects that passively protect wearers from evil and harm. Talismans usually perform a single function and enable powerful transformations. The magic wand of a SORCERER or FAIRY,

King Arthur's sword EXCALIBUR, seven-league boots, and HERMES's helmet of INVISIBILITY are all talismans. Talismans draw to their owners luck, success, wealth, love, magical abilities, and cures for illnesses.

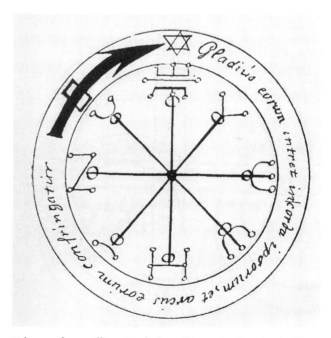

Talisman for repelling attacks by evildoers, in the grimoire The Key of Solomon, *18th century. (Author's collection)*

303

Any object can become a talisman. It may derive its powers from nature, such as a holed stone, or may be imbued with power by acts of ANGELS, spirits, or the gods. Magical handbooks known as GRIMOIRES give instructions for making talismans at auspicious astrological times. Magical TOOLS are engraved with SYMBOLS and SIGILS. Talismans for a specific purpose can be created and drawn or engraved on metal or paper. They are consecrated in RITUAL (see CONSECRATION).

Many Western talismans are based upon the principle of CORRESPONDENCES found in the KABBALAH, which holds that everything in creation is connected. For example, the PLANETS all have correspondences to aspects of daily life. Thus a talisman inscribed with the symbol of a planet can be empowered to influence that sphere of life.

Each planet has its own talisman, a disk engraved with NUMBERS and symbols that helps the magician obtain the magic virtue of the planet. According to a 19th-century formula, the talisman of the MOON bears on one side a magic square, a table of numbers arranged in a specific order. On the reverse side are the seals and signs of the Moon and its lunar spirits and INTELLIGENCES. If the talisman is engraved on SILVER during the Moon's fortunate aspects—waxing or full—it will make the bearer happy, cheerful, and pleasant and will bring security, esteem, health, wealth, and freedom from ill will and enmity. If engraved on lead during the waning or dark phases, the talisman will make the bearer unfortunate and unable to work. If it is buried, the spot itself will become unfortunate, and anyone who walks over it will become unlucky.

Alchemists followed elaborate rituals to make talismans that would facilitate their experiments. They waited for auspicious astrological signs and then recited INCANTATIONS to summon spirits who would imbue the talismans with power. The most sought-after talisman was the elusive PHILOSOPHER'S STONE, the agent of transmutation of base metals into GOLD and silver and of mundane consciousness into enlightened consciousness.

PARACELSUS, who held that illness is caused and cured by spiritual means, prescribed medical talismans for various ailments. He favored inscribed metallic talismans that were similar to saint medallions. They were cast from gold, silver, IRON, copper, and alloys under certain astrological conditions. Inscriptions were taken from sacred sources and magical grimoires; some were made to the specific and unique requirements of a patient. Paracelsus also kept ready-made talismans on hand as general prescriptions. The talismans were to be worn over the heart, which would attract stellar energies into the energy field of the patient.

Making a Talisman

Grimoires offer detailed steps and INVOCATIONS for making talismans. In general, a ritual incorporates the following elements:

1. Decide the purpose of the talisman
2. Identify appropriate planetary influences to determine best time for ritual
3. Undertake self-purification
4. Don ritual garments, and gather appropriate magical tools
5. Create a MAGIC CIRCLE to work within
6. Invoke appropriate divine, angelic, and spirit help
7. Inscribe a circle on a piece of metal, parchment, or paper
8. Inscribe symbols and sigils associated with the appropriate planet, as well as any sacred names, words, or charms, on one or both sides of the talisman
9. Focus intent, WILL, and emotional energy during inscription
10. Purify talisman by passing metal through fire (such as a CANDLE flame) or paper through smoke of incense
11. Charge talisman with magical power by consecrating it in a ritual on the appropriate day of the planet
12. Store or wear talisman in protective covering

Talismans made for specific short-term objectives are ideally done on paper so that they can be ritually destroyed by fire when the objective is accomplished. More permanent talismans—usually a tool such as for DIVINATION—can be inscribed on metal plates or disks.

See also ANGEL MAGIC; MAGIC; RING.

FURTHER READING:
Bardon, Franz. *The Practice of Magical Evocation.* Salt Lake City: Merkur Publishing, 2001.
Farrell, Nick. *Making Talismans: Living Entities of Power.* St. Paul, Minn.: Llewellyn Publications, 2001.
Hall, Manly P. *Paracelsus: His Mystical and Medical Philosophy.* Los Angeles: The Philosophic Research Society, 1964.
Kraig, Donald Michael. *Modern Magick: Eleven Lessons in the High Magickal Arts.* 2d ed. St. Paul, Minn.: Llewellyn Publications, 2004.

Tarot A deck of 78 cards bearing images and SYMBOLS that has been one of the most popular systems of DIVINATION since the 18th century. *Tarot* is a French derivative of the Italian term *tarocchi,* meaning "triumphs" or "trumps."

The Tarot is complex, and has been related to ALCHEMY, the KABBALAH, archetypes, and Jungian psychology. It has been reinterpreted in hundreds of decks with different themes.

The Tarot is divided into two parts, a Major Arcana, or Trumps, of 22 cards, and a Minor Arcana of 56 cards. The Major Arcana present images that mirror truths and stages of enlightenment in the soul's journey toward wholeness. The Minor Arcana is divided into four suits of 10 cards each and resembles today's playing cards.

Each Tarot card has its own meaning. For divination, Tarot cards are shuffled and laid out in various spreads. Each position in a spread holds a particular significance.

The archangel Gabriel sounds the trumpet of resurrection in the Judgment card in The Alchemical Tarot, *by Rosemary Ellen Guiley and Robert Michael Place. Judgment represents the reviving or healing powers of the Philosopher's Stone. Inspired by Michael Maier's* Tripusaureus, *1618. (Copyright by and courtesy of Robert Michael Place)*

Each card has a meaning whether upright or reversed. Though each card and its position has a unique meaning, the entire layout must be considered synergistically. Ideally, the Tarot is not consulted for "yes" or "no" answers but for insight into situations and forces in motion.

The Emergence of the Tarot

The exact origins of the Tarot are unknown. Some occultists have suggested that the cards are of great antiquity, the remnants of the fabled esoteric teachings of HERMES TRISMEGISTUS, the legendary Greco-Egyptian figure who gave humankind all its learning. More likely, the cards evolved out of the numerous decks of playing cards that spread throughout Europe as early as the 14th century.

It is likely that the Tarot emerged from Islamic alchemy and philosophy. Decks of four-suit playing cards existed in Islamic countries, and probably inspired Western playing cards. It is not known when the first playing cards were created, but in Europe a ban against them was decreed in Florence, Italy, in 1376. Official discouragement of playing cards did little or nothing to prevent their popularity throughout Europe, however.

At some point, a fifth suit of 22 allegorical figures was added to decks of playing cards. The original purpose of the fifth suit was to act as trumps in cards games. The creator is not known, but he was probably Italian. The first evidence of Tarot cards dates to 1442 in Ferrara, Italy, in court records. The first known deck dates to about 1445: a hand-painted set designed by Bonifacio Bembo for the duke of Milan, Francesco Sforza.

In the early 16th century, the *tarocchi,* as the cards were known, spread into Europe; they were manufactured in Lyon, France as early as 1507. Surviving decks from this period are hand-painted, and probably were commissioned by nobility as works of art. Wood-block printing on paper made the cards more available to the general population.

During the Renaissance, the allegorical images of the Tarot may have been used as tools in *ars memoria* (the art of memory), the use of meditation upon images as a way of acquiring and passing on knowledge. THOMAS AQUINAS advocated *ars memoria* as a devotional path, while the ex-Dominican friar GIORDANO BRUNO saw images more as a magical path. Images could be charged with WILL and emotion, and provide a way for connecting to divine power.

As usage of the Tarot spread, the allegorical cards changed too. The images changed names and orders. Today most decks follow nearly the same order. As artists express the Tarot through different themes, the names of the allegorical images vary as well. However, the trumps representing consistent qualities and ideas.

Here is a list of the 22 Major Arcana and their assigned numbers. This order is consistent in modern decks; however, sometimes the Justice and Strength cards, numbers 8 and 11 respectively, are reversed, with Justice being 11 instead of 8 and Strength being 8 instead of 11.

   0   The Fool

   1   The Magician

   2   The High Priestess

   3   The Empress

   4   The Emperor

   5   The Hierophant

   6   The Lovers

   7   The Charioteer

   8   Justice

   9   The Hermit

   10   The Wheel of Fortune

11   Strength

12   The Hanged Man

13   Death

14   Temperance

15   The Devil

16   The Tower

17   The Star

18   The Moon

19   The Sun

20   Judgment

21   The World

In alchemical terms, the cards can be seen as the path of the Great Work. The Fool is the PRIMA MATERIA, the beginning material. The subsequent cards represent different stages of alchemy. The culmination is The World, also a SYMBOL for the ANIMA MUNDI, or World Soul.

The False Egyptian Connection

Up to the late 18th century, Tarot cards were still used primarily for games. A revival in the interest of magic contributed to the reinterpretation of the Tarot as a secret book of esoteric wisdom. The most popular of these theories held that the cards originated in Egypt. At the time, the history of ancient Egypt also was enjoying a revival of interest throughout Europe.

The chief proponent of the Egyptian connection was Antoine Court de Gébelin (1725–84), a French archaeologist, Egyptologist, and high-grade Freemason. According to Gébelin, the Tarot was the surviving fragment an ancient Egyptian book, the *Book of Thoth,* supposedly authored by THOTH, the Egyptian god of magic writing, healing, arithmetic, astrology, and alchemy. The Greeks equated Thoth with HERMES.

Gébelin offered no proof for his claim. He told a story that an unnamed countess of his acquaintance possessed a Tarot deck, which he immediately recognized as of Egyptian origin. Gébelin said that the word *tarot* was derived from two Egyptian words, *tar,* meaning "road," and *ro,* meaning "royal." Thus, the Tarot was the "royal road" to esoteric wisdom. The 22 allegorical trumps were representations of 22 hieroglyphic stone tablets once hidden in a temple that once existed between the paws of the Great Sphinx. The tablets had told the story of the world. The Egyptians had created a card game containing this story and passed the cards along to the Romans. Gypsies had spread the cards throughout Europe.

It was all pure fabrication and speculation. No evidence existed of the mysterious temple. No one knew what Egyptian hieroglyphs meant; the Rosetta stone was yet to be discovered (1799) and deciphered (1821).

Nonetheless, this story had tremendous romantic appeal and was readily believed by others. Gébelin published his theory in his nine-volume book, *Le Monde Primitif* (1773–84). A popular Parisian occultist, Etteilla, created his own Tarot designed solely for divination. Suddenly the Tarot was quite in vogue as Egyptian wisdom.

The Kabbalah and Magic

In the 19th century, the magic revival spread, and occultists looked for other connections to the Tarot, such as the practical Kabbalah. ELIPHAS LEVI accepted Gebelin's theory and said the Tarot was a collection of symbolic "hieroglyphs" containing the inner truths of occultism. He was taken with the fact that there are 22 trumps, or "keys," as he called them, in the Major Arcana and 22 letters in the Hebrew alphabet, which in turn has a numerical value and corresponds to the 22 paths in the Kabbalistic Tree of Life. He corresponded each Tarot trump to a Hebrew letter and devoted 22 chapters to these correspondences in his book, *The Dogma and Ritual of High Magic* (1861). This correlation of symbols works at times, but in some cases is forced.

Levi described the Tarot as a miraculous book, the source of inspiration of all the sacred ancient books and a perfect tool for divination "on account of the analogical precision of its figures and its numbers. In fact, the oracles of this book are always rigorously true, and even when it does not predict anything, it always reveals something that was hidden, and gives the wisest counsel to those who consult it."

Levi delighted in the profound correspondences he saw. In his book, *Transcendental Magic, Its Dogma and Ritual* (1856), he said:

This Clavical [the Arcana] regarded as lost for centuries, has been recovered by us, and we have been able to open the sepulchres of the ancient world, to make the dead speak, to behold the monuments of the past in all their splendor, to understand the enigmas of every sphinx and to penetrate all sanctuaries . . . Now, this was the key in question; a hieroglyphic and numeral alphabet, expressing by characters and numbers, a series of universal and absolute ideas . . .

The symbolical tetrad, represented in the Mysteries of Memphis and Thebes by the four aspects of the sphinx—a man, eagle, lion and bull—corresponded with the four elements of the old world [earth, air, fire and water] . . . Now these four symbols, with all their analogies, explain the one word hidden in all sanctuaries. . . . Moreover, the sacred word was not pronounced: it was spelt, and expressed in four words, which are the four sacred letters, Yod . . . He[h] . . . Vau . . . He[h] . . .

The Tarot is a truly philosophical machine, which keeps the mind from wandering, while leaving its initiative and liberty; it is mathematics applied to the Absolute, the alliance of the positive and the ideal, a lottery of thoughts as exact as numbers, perhaps the simplest and grandest conception of human genius. . . .

An imprisoned person, with no other book than the Tarot, if he knew how to use it, could in a few years acquire a universal knowledge and would be able to speak on all subjects with unequalled learning and inexhaustible eloquence.

Levi opined that the Tarot was handed down by "certain wise kabbalists" who preserved their sacred knowledge "first on ivory, parchment, on gilt and silvered leather, and afterwards on simple cards, which were always the objects of suspicion to the Official Church as containing a dangerous key to its mysteries." He heaped praise upon Court de Gebelin for ferreting out the "truth," and he criticized Etteilla: "From these [simple cards] have originated those tarots whose antiquity was revealed to the learned Court de Gebelin through the sciences of the hieroglyphics and of numbers, and which afterwards severely exercised the doubtful perspicacity and tenacious investigations of Etteilla."

Levi also used another Kabbalistic letter-manipulation technique, *temurah,* to find meaning in the word *Tarot. Temurah* is the transposition of letters in a word to create new words. Thus, Levi found that *Tarot* could be transposed to *rota,* the Latin term for "wheel," and *Tora,* an incomplete spelling of Torah, the holy scriptures and law of Judaism. The *temurah* was corroborating evidence to him that the Tarot was indeed a wheel of life or spiritual evolution, and was founded on Kabbalistic wisdom.

Levi's work with the Kabbalah was expanded by another Frenchman, Gerard Encausse (1868–1916), a physician who went by the occult pseudonym PAPUS. As a leading Martinist and member of the Kabbalistic Order of the Rose-Cross, Papus, too, was steeped in occultism. He saw the Tarot as presenting the spiritual history of man: the emergence of the soul from the Source, descending to the material, then returning to the Source. In his most important work on the Tarot, *The Tarot of the Bohemians: The Absolute Key to Occult Science* (1889), he predicted that society was on the verge of incredible transformation and that materialism was on the way out. What was needed was synthesis, in the fashion of the wisdom taught by the ancients.

The Kabbalistic link was emphasized by the HERMETIC ORDER OF THE GOLDEN DAWN, which was probably the greatest esoteric order of modern times. The Golden Dawn flourished briefly in the late 19th and early 20th centuries and included as members some of the greatest occult and literary figures of the day, such as ALEISTER CROWLEY, WILLIAM BUTLER YEATS, SAMUEL LIDDELL MacGREGOR MATHERS, DION FORTUNE, and others. The Golden Dawn followed in Giordano Bruno's footsteps by using Tarot images in magical meditations and contemplations as gateways and guides to various levels in ASTRAL PROJECTION. Use of the images helped to avoid wandering along the astral byways and kept the initiate on track. Meditating on the Tarot also served to develop the important faculty of IMAGINATION.

Of great importance in the Golden Dawn were a set of Tarot papers called *Book T,* which was given to initiates. *Book T* set forth the Tarot as the key to the Hermetic Kabbalah and all Western esotericism and corresponded the Major Arcana to the Hebrew alphabet. According to Rosicrucian legend, *Book T* was found clutched in the hand of the perfectly preserved corpse of the legendary Christian Rosenkreutz when his secret burial vault was discovered in 1604. He supposedly had died in 1484 at 106 years of age. Golden Dawn Tarot teachings also corresponded the Major Arcana to the paths connecting the *sephirot* of the Tree of Life.

Another major—and modern—figure in the Kabbalistic Tarot was PAUL FOSTER CASE (1884–1954), a onetime member of the Golden Dawn and the founder of the BUILDERS OF THE ADYTUM. Case composed a thoughtful and detailed analysis of the Tarot-Hebrew alphabet correspondences in his work *The Tarot: A Key to the Wisdom of the Ages* (1947). His correspondences included not only the letters but the accompanying colors and musical tones associated with each letter and the astrological signs that fit each Arcanum. With the letter correspondences, Case probed the hidden, occult meanings of Hebrew words by spelling them out with the Tarot, with the greatest yield coming from many words in the Old Testament, divine and angelic names, and the names of the 12 tribes of Israel.

Tarot Interpretations

The most significant influence upon the meaning of the Tarot came from ARTHUR EDWARD WAITE, a Freemason and a member of the Golden Dawn. Waite reinterpreted the Tarot cards according to what he believed were their original mystical meanings. Waite thought the cards themselves were no older than the 14th century, but they portrayed much older esoteric symbols.

Waite drew upon his own extensive esoteric knowledge, including magic, the practical Kabbalah, and alchemy to design his own Tarot deck. He recruited another member of the Golden Dawn, artist Pamela Colman Smith, to execute his ideas. They named the allegorical trumps the Major Arcana (major secrets), and the four suits the Minor Arcana. Unlike all earlier Tarot decks, the Minor Arcana were presented by pictorial images, not pip signs. Thus, the entire deck was useful for occult meditation and VISUALIZATION. Only persons with sufficient esoteric knowledge would be able to read the true visionary secrets of the cards.

The Pictorial Key to the Tarot was published in 1910 by the Rider publishing house in London. The deck became known as the Rider-Waite deck. Nearly a century later, it is still considered one of the best renditions of the Tarot and is the universal standard by which other decks have been designed.

Waite's work was reinterpreted in 1995 with the publication of *The Alchemical Tarot* by the artist Robert Michael Place and author Rosemary Ellen Guiley. Place, an expert on alchemy, worked with inspirations he received through dreams and visions to restore deeper alchemical meanings to the cards that would have been limited only to initiates in Waite's time. He also drew upon alchemical drawings and woodcuts.

Two other noted members of the Golden Dawn created Tarot decks. Mathers, who claimed prodigious feats with the help of occult powers, designed a Tarot deck and his wife painted the finished product. Members copied the original. Decades later, the deck was reconstructed by artist Robert Wang, working under the direction of ISRAEL REGARDIE, onetime secretary to Crowley and a member of one of the Golden Dawn's offshoot lodges, Stella Matutina. It was published in 1978, marking the first time the deck was made public.

Crowley made his own interpretation of the Tarot, linking the cards to Thoth. The card designs in his deck, executed by the Lady Freida Harris, are erotic in theme, with Kabbalistic and astrological attributions. The cards have also been interpreted in terms of the I CHING, (Yijing) crystals and gems, and goddess concepts.

More recently, the Tarot field has seen an explosion of variations of deck themes and executions. Regardless of imagery, the alchemical content of the Tarot remains: the cards do serve as gateways to higher planes, and they light a spiritual path to cosmic consciousness.

FURTHER READING:
Case, Paul Foster. *The Tarot: A Key to the Wisdom of the Ages.* Richmond, Va.: Macoy Publishing Co., 1947.
Guiley, Rosemary Ellen, and Robert Michael Place. *The Alchemical Tarot.* London: Thorsons/HarperCollins, 1995.
Place, Robert M. *The Tarot: History, Symbolism and Divination.* New York: Jeremy P. Tarcher/Penguin, 2005.

taste   An important element in the success of a magical RITUAL. Taste, along with the other senses, must be fully activated to stimulate the MAGICIAN's IMAGINATION in accordance with the purpose of a ritual.

To activate taste, food or liquid is consecrated and charged with the essence of a spirit or occult force through INVOCATION. The food or liquid must be appropriate; for example, a wheat wafer or piece of bread has a CORRESPONDENCE to the Greek goddess Demeter, who rules grain and abundance of the land. When uncertain, a magician can study the Hebrew alphabet for appropriate correspondences, as each letter in the alphabet has its own correspondence.

In ritual, the food or liquid is consumed, which incarnates the divine essence within the being of the magician. When done repeatedly over time, this ingestion facilitates the union of the magician with higher forces.

This magical principle is expressed in Christianity in a mass or service in which a Eucharist, or holy wafer, and wine correspond to the body and BLOOD of Christ.

FURTHER READING:
Regardie, Israel. *The Tree of Life: A Study in Magic.* York Beach, Maine: Samuel Weiser, 1969.

tattoo   A pigmented marking etched into the skin which serves a variety of purposes: ornamental, religious, mystical, fertility, health, and magical protection against evil spirits and the EVIL EYE. The term *tattoo* comes from the Tahitian *tatau*. Tattoos were introduced to the West by Captain James Cook, following his exploration of Tahiti.

The custom of tattooing may be associated with the Arab proverb, "blood has flowed, the danger has passed." A tattoo serves as an initiatory means of identification and represents a sacrifice to an ideal, group, or order on the part of the wearer.

Tattooing was done in predynastic Egypt, circa 3500 B.C.E. The Egyptians of the New Kingdom (c. 1570–332 B.C.E.) tattooed their breasts and arms with names and symbols of deities. The priestess of the goddess Hathor tattooed three lines across her belly. Tattooing was known to the Greeks and Latins, who did not practice it, and to the Gauls, some of whom did. In Western culture, it died out during the Middle Ages. In modern times, it is done primarily for ornamentation, sometimes for luck and protection. In imitative magic a tattoo of a scorpion, for example, will ward off real scorpions.

Tattooing also has spiritual meaning. Tattooes are tribal marks of rank, scorecards for warriors, and badges of the rites of INITIATION. In Iraq, they are believed to enhance fertility for women. In Burma and elsewhere, they protect against evil spirits and DEMONS. In Polynesian lore, the gods tattoo themselves.

Tattooing traditionally is done by using a chisel or adzlike instrument to groove the skin, followed by rubbing in pigment, or by running a needle and soot-covered thread under the skin. Modern methods include the creation of scars by cutting, scratching, piercing, or burning the skin.

tattvas (tattwas)   Astral forms or qualities of the five ELEMENTS of Eastern yoga and ALCHEMY: earth, air, fire, water, and spirit (QUINTESSENCE). Tattvas are used in magical work and as meditation tools for developing CLAIRVOYANCE and ASTRAL PROJECTION.

The tattvic system was developed in Indian yoga around 700 B.C.E. The term *tattva* means "thatness," and is formed from two words: *tat* ("that") and *tvam* ("thou"). A general way of describing them is that they are qualities of *prana*, the vital life force that flows through the macrocosm and microcosm. In yoga, the tattvas correspond to the five lower chakra centers.

Each tattva has a shape, and each tattva can be incorporated as a subelement within all the other tattvas. Thus, there are 25 permutations altogether.

The five tattvas are

- *Prithvi* (earth), symbolized by a yellow square, representing solidity and physical manifestation
- *Apas* (water), symbolized by a silver crescent moon, representing all liquid activity on the planet
- *Tejas* (fire), symbolized by a red equilateral triangle, representing heat, expansion, and creation
- *Vayu* (air), symbolized by a blue circle, representing a mediation between fire and water
- *Akasha* (spirit), symbolized by a black or indigo EGG, representing the womb from which all things spring

Each subelement has its own shape, colors, and qualities as well. For example, the Vayu of Prithvi—air as a subelement of earth—is represented by a blue circle inside a yellow square. Earth alone is dense, but earth/air has movement and volatility.

The tattvas were introduced to Western esotericism primarily through the THEOSOPHICAL SOCIETY. The Theosophists added two tattvas, Adi and Anupadaka, so that there would be seven, to correspond with the seven primary chakras. Possibly the first mention of the tattvas in Western literature appears in Edward Bulwer-Lytton's esoteric novel, *Zanoni* (1842). The HERMETIC ORDER OF THE GOLDEN DAWN adopted the tattvas from Theosophy but eliminated the two that had been added.

In Western magic, the tattvas are ethers related to the five senses. They are carried out on the prana that streams forth from the Sun as solar wind becomes captured by the Earth's magnetic field. The waves of energy circulate around the Earth in waves that ebb and flow. Beginning at sunrise, the flow begins with Akasha and progresses to Vayu, Tejas, Apas, and Prithvi. Everything is vitalized by the continuing transits of tattvas, including the Earth's electromagnetic field and all ley lines. The tattvas are the basis of all forms and of the *PRIMA MATERIA*.

In magical work, attention is focused on the symbol of a tattva. Meditations upon them encourage visions that enable the magician to have a deep understanding of the true essences of the elements. Through active imagination and VISUALIZATION, the magician enters the actual element to experience its true, living form, which can take the shapes of beings. The tattvas serve as doorways through which the magician can enter the ELEMENTAL realms. The magician must use magical NAMES, questions, and perhaps the assistance of a spirit guide to discern the true forms from masquerading astral forms.

FURTHER READING:

Bardon, Franz. *Initiation into Hermetics: A Course of Instruction of Magic Theory and Practice.* Wuppertal, Germany: Dieter Ruggeberg, 1971.
King, Francis, and Stephen Skinner. *Techniques of High Magic: A Manual of Self-Initiation.* Rochester, Vt.: Destiny Books, 1976.
Melville, Francis. *The Secrets of High Magic.* Hauppauge, N.Y.: Barron's, 2002.
Wilson, Graeme. "An Introduction to the Tattvas." Available online. URL: http://www.magicalpath.net/articles/tattva.htm. Downloaded February 1, 2006.

Telesma   In ALCHEMY, the PHILOSOPHER'S STONE.

Rosicrucian alchemists viewed the Telesma as a self-perfecting substance that acts like genetic evolution. By working with the Telesma, alchemists hoped to quicken human evolution so that alchemical transformation could be part of the life process.

temurah   See GEMATRIA.

Tetragrammaton   The most powerful and personal Hebrew name of God. The Tetragrammaton is used in MAGIC as one of ineffable NAMES of power.

"Tetragrammaton" means "four-letter name." The Tetragrammaton consists of four Hebrew letters, *YHVH* (Yod, Heh, Vau, Heh). The exact pronunciation of the Tetragrammaton is not known; it is usually pronounced "Yahweh." A common variation is "Jehovah." These pronunciations are based on the addition of vowels to the original Hebrew name, which had none. According to tradition, *YHVH* is so powerful that it should not be spoken except by high priests on Yom Kippur. Other names are substituted for it, such as "Adonai" and "Elohim."

The numerical values assigned to *YHVH* add up to 10, which in Hebrew numerology represents the basic organizing principle in the universe. *YHVH* expresses the duality of the Godhead, the source of all things, in its union of masculine and feminine. Yod represents archetypal masculinity; the first Heh represents archetypal femininity; Vau represents physical masculinity; and the second Heh represents physical femininity.

Since the name of God could not be uttered, other names of God were substituted. During Talmudic times, these names multiplied, all derived from the original four-letter Tetragrammaton. Secret 12-, 22-, and 72-letter names were taught to only the most worthy. These names were joined by many other names of other numerical values.

In the seventh century, Isadore of Seville compiled a list of 10 names of God that were used frequently: El, Eloe, Sabbaoth, Zelioz, Ramathel, Eyel, Adonay, Ya, Tetragrammaton, Saday, and Eloym. Another commonly used name was Ehyeh Asher Ahyeh ("I Am That I Am," which MOSES heard from the burning bush).

The 12-letter name of God was out of use by Talmudic times. The 22-letter name of God first appeared in the *SEFER RAZIEL*, though probably has much older origins. The *Sefer Raziel* offers no interpretation of it. Anaktam Pastam Paspasim Dionsim quickly was incorporated into CHARMS and INVOCATIONS and was added to the reading of the Priestly Benediction in the synagogue in the 17th century.

The 42-letter name of God may have been derived from an old prayer, though medieval mystics held that it came from the first 42 letters in the Bible.

The 72-letter name of God is divided into triadic syllables. According to the *Sefer Raziel,* it cannot be surpassed in power, and no magic can be done without it. The name is derived from three verses in Exodus 14:19–21, each of which contains 72 letters. Different parts of the name have different uses. For example, the first part of the name will conquer evil and drive off evil spirits, while the second part will protect against the EVIL EYE and DEMONS and will help one acquire wisdom.

YHVH is sometimes appended to the names of the highest ANGELS around God to denote their power and stature.

JAKOB BÖHME analyzed the name *Jehova,* stating that it "is nothing else but a speaking forth, or expression of the Threefold working of the Holy Trinity in the unity of God." He noted that each letter "intimates to us a peculiar virtue and working, that is, a Form in the working Power":

J

For **I** is the Effluence of the Eternal indivisible Unity, or the sweet grace and fullness of the ground of the Divine Power of becoming something.

E

E is a threefold **I**, where the Trinity shuts itself up in the Unity; for the **I** goes into the **E**, and joineth **I E**, which is an outbreathing of the Unity itself.

H

H is the Word, or breathing of the Trinity of God.

O

O is the Circumference, or the Son of God, through which the **I E** and the **H**, or breathing, speaks forth from the compressed Delight of the Power and Virtue.

V

V is the joyful Effluence from the breathing, that is, the proceeding Spirit of God.

A

A is that which is proceeded from the power and virtue, namely the wisdom; a subject of the Trinity; wherein the Trinity works, and wherein the Trinity is also manifest.

ALEISTER CROWLEY considered the Tetragrammaton so powerful that it should never be uttered, even in thought, "until perhaps with it he gives up the ghost." Crowley said:

Such a Word should in fact be so potent that man cannot hear it and live.

Such a word was indeed the lost Tetragrammaton. It is said that at the utterance of this name the Universe crashes into dissolution. Let the Magician earnestly seek this Lost Word, for its pronunciation is synonymous with the accomplishment of the Great Work.

By "Great Work," Crowley referred to the alchemical or spiritual enlightenment of the magician, a process unique to every person.

FURTHER READING:

Bardon, Franz. *The Key to the Kabbalah.* Salt Lake City: Merkur Publishing, 1996.

Crowley, Aleister. *Magic in Theory and Practice.* 1929. Reprint, New York: Dover Publications, 1976.

The 'Key' of Jacob Boehme. Transl. by William Law. Grand Rapids, Mich.: Phanes Press, 1991.

Kraig, Donald Michael. *Modern Magick: Eleven Lessons in the High Magickal Arts.* 2d ed. St. Paul, Minn.: Llewellyn Publications, 2004.

Theosophia Pneumatica See GRIMOIRES.

Theosophical Society International, nonsectarian, esoteric organization founded in New York City in 1875 by MADAME HELENA PETROVNA BLAVATSKY, a Russian-born mystic; Colonel Henry Steel Olcott, an American attorney and federal government official; William Q. Judge, an American attorney; and others. The society espouses a philosophical system that teaches the acquisition of knowledge of a transcendent reality through revelation or through practice of the occult tradition.

The society derives its name from the term *theosophy,* originating from the Greek words *theos,* "god," and *sophia,* "wisdom." According to the society, all religions stem from the same roots of ancient wisdom, repeating myths and symbols, and that study of these secrets will lead to truth and spiritual oneness. Theosophy attempts to provide answers to the great imponderables of life by looking to the common denominators in all wisdom through the ages. The spiritual work involved is theurgy, or "divine work."

The Theosophical Society (TS) was strong in England, where it attracted the interest and participation of the leading occultists of the day, many of whom were members of ROSICRUCIANISM and FREEMASONRY. Some of the founders and principles of the HERMETIC ORDER OF THE GOLDEN DAWN attended TS meetings and gave lectures, among them SAMUEL LIDDELL MacGREGOR MATHERS and WILLIAM WYNN WESTCOTT.

Blavatsky preferred Eastern mystical approaches to esoteric study rather than Western ritual MAGIC, but a growing interest in magic among TS members led her to form a special Esoteric Section devoted to magic. However, the section emphasized only training in magical theory and principles and not in actual ritual skill. The training consisted of learning SYMBOLS, CORRESPONDENCES, NUMBERS, the ELEMENTS, and so forth.

To placate magically inclined members, the section engaged in magical "experiments" to attempt to produce occult phenomena: raising the ghost of a flower, evoking a dream by placing a symbol beneath a pillow, and so forth. Most of the experiments failed, probably because Blavatsky and those leading the experiments were not committed to magic itself. WILLIAM BUTLER YEATS was among those who left the TS because of these dismal results and found a more receptive environment soon in the Golden Dawn. The Esoteric Section was abandoned, and the TS returned to its original focus.

thieves' lights   In German folklore, magical lights made from the fingers of unborn children. Thieves' lights are similar in purpose to the HAND OF GLORY, enabling thieves to bewitch victims and steal their belongings.

Thieves' lights can be made only from unborn, innocent babies taken from the wombs of pregnant thieves or murderers. The RITUAL for harvesting them is grisly. According to a 19th-century account:

> When a female thief or murderer hangs or drowns herself, or is hanged or beheaded, and she is carrying a child inside her body, then you must go forth at midnight on the devil's roads, not on God's roads, with incantations and magic, not with prayer and blessings, and you must take an axe or a knife that has been used by an executioner, and with it you must open up the poor sinner's belly, take out the child, cut off its fingers, and take them with you.
>
> But this absolutely must all be done at midnight in the most perfect solitude and silence. Not even the softest sound, no "oh" and no sigh can escape the lips of the seeker. In this manner you obtain the lights, which you can burn whenever you want to. And however short they are, they will never burn up, but will always remain the same length.

Folktales tell of pregnant serving girls and others kidnapped by thieves who intend to kill them for their fetuses.

Thieves' lights ignite and extinguish themselves in response to the thoughts of their owners. They render their owners invisible to others, while enabling them to see everything in the dark. Like the hand of glory, thieves' lights will bewitch sleeping people into powerlessness so that thieves can carry off all their possessions. One candle is lit for every person sleeping in a house. The people will remain asleep as long as the candles burn.

Also, like the hand of glory, thieves' lights can only be extinguished by a person other than their owner who uses milk.

See also RAVEN STONES.

FURTHER READING:
Ashiman, D. L., ed. "The Hand of Glory and Other Gory Legends about Human Hands." Available online. URL: http://www.pitt.edu/~dash/hand.html. Downloaded December 22, 2004.

Thomas Aquinas   See AQUINAS, THOMAS.

Thoth (Toth)   The Egyptian god who created the universe and all mystical wisdom, MAGIC, learning, writing, arithmetic, and ASTROLOGY. Called The Lord of the Divine Books and Scribe of the Company of Gods, Thoth usually is portrayed as an ibis-headed man with a pen and ink holder. The exact symbolic meaning of the ibis has not been discovered, though it is believed to be associated with healing. Sometimes Thoth is portrayed as a baboon-headed man holding a crescent moon.

As a healer and magician, Thoth restored the eye of Horus, which was torn to pieces when Horus battled his evil uncle Seth (Set) to avenge the death of his father, Osiris. The eye of Horus became a funerary AMULET and magical, all-seeing eye. Because of his restoration of the eye, Thoth became the patron god of oculists in ancient Egypt. Thoth also was petitioned in many of the spells contained in the Egyptian *Book of the Dead,* such as the opening-of-the-mouth spell to reanimate a corpse, which was spoken over a mummy by the high priest.

The Greeks associated their god HERMES so closely with Thoth that the two blended together. Thoth/Hermes became identified with HERMES TRISMEGISTUS, a mythical figure who was patron of magicians and thaumaturgists and alleged author of the Hermetic books on occult, philosophical, and religious subjects.

According to legend, Thoth/Hermes gave to his successors the *Book of Thoth,* or the *Key to Immortality,* which contains the secret processes for the regeneration of humanity and for the expansion of consciousness that would enable humankind to behold the gods. *The Book of Thoth* was kept in a temple in a sealed golden box and was used in the ancient Mysteries. When the Mysteries declined, it was carried to another, unknown land, where, legend has it, it still exists safely and leads disciples to the presence to the Immortals.

ELIPHAS LEVI saw the *Book of Thoth* as the occult Bible. The TAROT has been called the *Book of Thoth.*

FURTHER READING:
Levi, Eliphas. *The History of Magic.* 1860. Reprint, York Beach, Maine: Samuel Weiser, 2001.

thought-form   A nonphysical entity or object created by thought that exists in the mental plane or the ASTRAL PLANE. Thought-forms are used in MAGIC and the casting of SPELLS. Thought-form structures, objects, and places can be created magically to exist in the astral plane for the purposes of visualization and workings. Thought-form entities can be created and summoned through EVOCATION to perform certain tasks, such as SENDING to carry out spells or even perform PSYCHIC ATTACK. Thought-forms are invisible to most people but can be perceived clairvoyantly.

Esoteric philosophy holds that thoughts produce two effects: a radiating vibration and a floating, colored form. The lifespan and endurance of a thought-form depends on the nature and intensity of the thought. Most thought-forms dissipate. Those imbued with sufficient energy, either through sustained intensity or through RITUAL, can become anchored on the astral plane and the physical plane. Thought-forms radiate out and attract sympathetic essences, thus forming the basis of the occult Law of Attraction, which holds that a person manifests on the physical plane what he or she thinks on the mental plane.

Characters in myth and legend and even deities can be thought-forms. They exist as long as they are energerized by collective thought. When they fade from interest, they return to formlessness on the astral plane.

Annie Besant and C. W. Leadbeater, Theosophists and clairvoyants, said that thought-forms are four-dimensional in nature and, therefore, are difficult to describe in three-dimensional terms. They classified thought-forms into three groups: (1) the image of the thinker; (2) an image of a material object associated with the thought; and (3) an independent image expressing the inherent qualities of a thought. Thoughts that are low in nature, such as anger, hate, lust, and greed, create thought-forms that are dense in color and form. Thoughts of a more spiritual nature generate forms that have greater purity, clarity, and refinement. Besant and Leadbeater said that well-sustained devotion could appear as a flower with upward-curving petals like azure flames. Devotional aspiration might appear as a blue cone, its apex pointing upward to the higher planes. On the opposite end, explosive anger appears as a splash of red or orange, and sustained anger as a sharp, red stiletto. Jealousy might appear as a brown snake.

Thought-forms build up in a person's energy field or aura, creating and influencing behavior and characteristics. Negative thoughts weaken a person, even facilitating the onset of illness, while positive and loving thoughts act as a protective, energizing shield. According to Besant and Leadbeater, selfish thought moves in a curve, eventually coming back on itself (and the person) and expending itself on its own level. On the other hand, unselfish thought moves outward in an open curve, expanding as it goes. It is capable of piercing higher spiritual dimensions and thus becomes a channel through which higher planes pour themselves into lower planes. This is how prayer functions.

Besant and Leadbeater stressed that regular meditation is important in cultivating positive thought-forms. The meditation sends out a stream of magnetism that continues to work long after the meditation is ended.

Some thought-forms occur spontaneously. "Group minds" are formed whenever a group of persons concentrates on the same thoughts, ideas, or goals, such as a team of employees or a crowd of demonstrators. To some extent, the group-mind possesses the group, as witnessed in the psychic bonding and power that coalesces in crowds and in the synergy of a close-knit working group. When the group disperses, the group-mind usually loses power.

Thought-forms may arise spontaneously out of the collective unconscious as archetypes that take on phantom or seemingly real form. This may explain reports of the devil, supernatural monsters, entities, nonphysical beings, and otherworldly beings.

Thought-forms in Magic

In the Western tradition, thought-forms are created on the astral plane with the TRIANGLE OF CAUSATION, a primary foundation of occult astral work. Thought-forms require intense concentration; otherwise they do not last. Thought-forms of things on the physical plane can be recreated in exact detail on the astral plane. Thought-forms of gods, angels, places, goals, and activities also can be created out of astral matter.

"Artificial elementals" are created by RITUAL to perform low-level tasks and errands and to be directed at individuals to protect, heal, or harm. To have an affect, thought-forms must be able to latch on to similar vibrations in the aura of the recipient. If they are unable to do so, they boomerang back to the sender. Thus, one who directs evil thoughts toward another runs the risk of having them return.

The duration of a thought-form, its strength, and the distance it can travel depend on the strength and clarity of the original thought. Thought-forms are said to have the capability to assume their own energy and appear to be intelligent and independent. Equally intense thought can disperse them, or they can simply disintegrate when their purpose is finished. Some may last years. In magical practice it is customary to charge a thought-form with a finite life span and at the end of it reabsorb the thought-form back into astral matter.

Thought-forms that are not dispersed, as well as some particularly powerful thought-forms, can go out of control. They wander about looking for energy sources and attaching themselves to people like vampiric entities, or they can turn on their creators, as in the case of ALEXANDRA DAVID-NEEL.

Tibetan Thought-forms

In Tibetan occultism, thoughts can create a phantom form called a *tulpa*. Of temporary duration, *tulpas* usually assume human shape and are created to be sent out on a mission. In her explorations of Tibetan thought, Alexandra David-Neel successfully created a *tulpa*, though it was not what she intended and for a time eluded her control.

David-Neel sought to create a lama who would be "short and fat, of an innocent and jolly type." After several months of performing the prescribed ritual, a phantom monk appeared. It assumed a lifelike form over a period of time and existed almost like a guest in David-Neel's apartment.

The *tulpa* tagged along with her as she went out on a tour. To her distress, the *tulpa* began to change. She wrote, "The features . . . gradually underwent a change. The fat, chubby-cheeked fellow grew leaner, his face assumed a vaguely mocking, sly, malignant look. He became more troublesome and bold. In brief, he escaped my control." The *tulpa* began to touch her and rub up against her. Others began to see him, but he did not respond to anyone's conversation.

David-Neel decided to dissolve the *tulpa*, according to certain Tibetan rituals, but the phantom resisted her efforts. It took her six months to eliminate him. The entire episode upset her, and she termed it "very bad luck."

Thought-forms in New Thought and Healing

In the 19th century, the New Thought movement emphasized the creative and spiritual power of thought. Science of Mind, founded by Ernest Holmes, teaches that we are surrounded by an Infinite Intelligence, or Mind (God), which functions upon our beliefs. If we let go of destructive thoughts and replace them with constructive ones, we enter into a cooperation with this Mind that enables us to be healthier, happier, more successful, and more spiritually fulfilled. To this end, daily affirmations, meditation, and PRAYER facilitate that objective. In magical terms, these activities create positive thought-forms that can manifest in the physical world.

Holmes taught that there is but one Mind and that everything is an aspect of it; each of us uses a portion of It. He taught, "My thought is in control of my experience and I can direct my thinking," and "the ability to control my experiences and have them result in happiness, prosperity, and success lies in my own mind and my use of it."

"Mind responds to mind," said Holmes. "It is done to you as you believe." In other words, do not *ask* for things, but *declare* them. This is the Law of Mind, which manifests the beliefs we speak into It.

To improve health and for healing, Holmes recommended meditation upon affirmations such as "God-life surges through my entire body," or "I am well and successful in everything that I do," followed by a period of prayer in which the pray-er does not ask for anything but declares desired results, accepts them as though they have manifested, and gives thanks for them. This method can be applied to any situation or need in life. One's thoughts and motives ideally should be Godlike. A key element is belief in the desired results; Holmes stressed that belief must be felt with the total being. He noted that the effective prayer is one prayed by a person whose faith has removed all doubt.

Similarly, a magician works with complete intensity of WILL, IMAGINATION, faith, and belief. A ritual declares manifestation.

In the field of complementary medicine, the term *intentionality* applies to the power of thought to affect the state of health and well-being. Intentionality corresponds to the creation of positive thought-forms.

See also FORTUNE, DION.

FURTHER READING:

Ashcroft-Nowicki, Dolores, and J. H. Brennan. *Magical Use of Thought Form: A Proven System of Mental and Spiritual Empowerment.* St. Paul, Minn.: Llewellyn Publications, 2001.

Besant, Annie, and C. W. Leadbeater. *Thought-forms.* Wheaton, Ill.: Theosophical Publishing House, 1969.

David-Neel, Alexandra. *Magic and Mystery in Tibet.* New York: Dover Publications, 1971.

Guiley, Rosemary Ellen. *The Encyclopedia of Vampires, Werewolves and Other Monsters.* New York: Facts On File, Inc., 2004.

———. *The Miracle of Prayer: True Stories of Blessed Healing.* New York: Pocket Books, 1995.

thumb of knowledge   See CLAIRVOYANCE.

Tincture   In ALCHEMY, a frequently used name for the PHILOSOPHER'S STONE.

toadstone   A gem alleged to be in the head of an old toad that possesses magical powers. According to lore, a toadstone detects the presence of poison, such as in food, by changing color. It functions as an AMULET in the protection of newborn children and their mothers from the power of FAIRIES.

Tolkien, John Ronald Reuel (1892–1973)   Oxford professor and author of the epic story *The Lord of the Rings,* considered by some to be the greatest literary achievement of the 20th century. J. R. R. Tolkien also wrote *The Hobbit, Or There and Back Again* and several other books about the lives and histories of all the people and magical creatures who live in Middle-Earth.

Arthur Reuel Tolkien and his wife Mabel Suffield, Tolkien's parents, emigrated to the Orange Free State, now part of South Africa, from England in the 1890s to help establish a branch of an English bank in Bloemfontein. J. R. R., called Ronald, was their first child, born January 3, 1892, followed by his brother Hilary Arthur Reuel, born February 17, 1894. In 1895, at the age of three, Mabel—exhausted from the South African climate—left with the two boys and returned to England to see her family. Arthur promised to join them in a few months, but before he could leave he died of rheumatic fever, leaving his young family in financial straits. Mabel and her sons briefly lived with her parents in Birmingham, in Warwickshire, and then took lodgings in the nearby town of Sarehole. Young Ronald loved Sarehole and the Warwickshire countryside, which he recalled in the descriptions of the Shire.

Tolkien's mother tutored her sons at home the first few years, introducing Ronald to the wonders of plants and gardening. But his favorite lessons were in languages, in which he excelled. Ronald could read by age four, learned to write fluently not long afterward, and already knew some Latin by the time he entered St. Edward's School, Birmingham, in 1900. That same year, his mother and her sister May converted to Catholicism, an event that estranged the family from their Protestant relatives on both sides. Ronald remained a devout Catholic for the rest of his life.

In November 1904, when Ronald was only 12 and Hilary 10, their mother died from diabetes, leaving the boys orphaned and destitute. Father Francis Xavier Morgan, parish priest of the Birmingham Oratory in the suburb of Edgbaston, became the boys' guardian and cared for them throughout the rest of their school years. Ronald studied the classics, Anglo-Saxon, and Middle English. Tolkien received a scholarship to Exeter College at Oxford University in 1911.

Unable to house the boys at the Oratory, Father Francis arranged for them to live in a boardinghouse run by a Mrs. Faulkner. When Tolkien was 16, he noticed a young woman named Edith Bratt, 19, who also boarded at Mrs. Faulkner's, and they struck up a friendship. Believing that Tolkien was too young and fearing that he would not continue his education, Father Francis forbade Tolkien from seeing or corresponding with Miss Bratt until he was 21. Stoically, Tolkien concentrated on his studies, immersing himself in Old and Middle English, Gothic German, Old Norse, Welsh, and Finnish as well as the classics, changing his degree program to philology. He even invented his own language, which he called Quenya, based on Finnish and Welsh. Quenya eventually emerged as High Elvish.

Tolkien turned 21 in 1913 and immediately tried to contact Edith Bratt. By this time she had accepted another proposal of marriage but broke it off. In 1914, Edith converted to Catholicism and moved to the castle town of Warwick. Tolkien finished Oxford with a first-class degree in June 1915. World War I had begun the previous August, and after graduation he enlisted as a second lieutenant in the Lancashire Fusilliers. When it appeared that he would be leaving for France, Tolkien and Edith married on March 22, 1916.

Tolkien saw active duty as a communication officer at the Battle of the Somme, but within four months (by the end of October 1916) he had contracted "trench fever" from the unsanitary conditions of the trenches and was sent back to England in November to recuperate. He did not return to the Front, which saved his life. Many of his comrades and friends from school did not survive the war. While he recovered, Tolkien began to write the stories that would someday form the basis of *The Silmarillion* (the lore of the Elves) and *The Lord of the Rings*. Tolkien described his tales as a mythology for England: legends that he believed lost due to barbarian invasion and conquest by the Normans in 1066. He undertook such an endeavor as a tribute to his fallen friends.

When Armistice was signed in November 1918, Tolkien already had feelers out to obtain academic employment. The Tolkiens' first child, John Francis Reuel, was one year old, born in November 1917. (John Francis later became Father John Tolkien.) His first job was as a lexicographer for the Oxford English Dictionary, then in preparation, but by 1920, he was the Reader in English Language at the University of Leeds. Their second son, Michael Hilary

Reuel, was born in Oct. 1920. While at Leeds, Tolkien collaborated with E. V. Gordon on a well-received edition of *Sir Gawain and the Green Knight*

Third son Christopher Reuel was born in 1924. In 1925, Tolkien returned to Oxford as the Rawlinson and Bosworth Professor of Anglo-Saxon, where his lectures on the En-glish epic poem *Beowulf* and the origins of the Welsh language cemented his reputation. Tolkien also helped found a group of Oxford friends who met to listen and comment on each other's work; besides Tolkien, the most prominent member of "The Inklings" was C. S. Lewis, author of *The Chronicles of Narnia* and Tolkien's closest friend. Tolkien's deep Catholic faith inspired Lewis to return to Christianity. The Tolkiens' last child, Priscilla Anne Reuel, arrived in 1929.

Tolkien continued writing his mythological stories. One day, while grading a student's exam, he found a blank sheet in the test booklet, and without thinking wrote, "In a hole in the ground there lived a hobbit." That led to research about what a Hobbit might be, why they lived in holes, their habits, and so forth and grew into *The Hobbit, Or There and Back Again,* told to his four children. Tolkien submitted it to his publisher, Stanley Unwin, who passed the manuscript to his then 10-year-old son, Raynor, for his perspective. Raynor loved it, and *The Hobbit* was published in 1937.

Allen and Unwin (now part of HarperCollins) asked for more Hobbit stories. Tolkien tried to submit his manuscript for *The Silmarillion,* but those tales concerned Elves and Men, not Hobbits. So in the late 1930s, Tolkien began to write *The Lord of the Rings,* but with the advent of World War II, paper rationing and Tolkien's own curious nature—leading him to research everything he could about any subject—the work was not published until 1954–55 in the United Kingdom and later in the United States. His son Christopher, who has been the editor of his father's papers, published a four-volume work entitled *The History of The Lord of the Rings* which explains his father's work and the various revisions of nearly every part of the books. Especially during the War, Tolkien wrote and rewrote on the same piece of paper. Christopher Tolkien told that his father was thrilled to find exams written on one side of the paper so that he could use the other side.

In 1945, Tolkien moved to Merton College at Oxford as the Merton Professor of English Language and Literature. He continued teaching and writing, each year promising his publisher that he was nearly finished with *The Lord of the Rings.* Tolkien never envisioned *LOTR* as a trilogy but instead as one large volume comprised of six books: "The Return of the Shadow," "The Fellowship of the Ring," "The Treason of Isengard," "The Journey to Mordor," "The War of the Ring," and "The Return of the King." But with paper still short and Stanley Unwin unsure of sales (Raynor, now an adult working at Allen and Unwin, was confident of success), the decision was made to release *LOTR* as a trilogy: *The Fellowship of the*

Ring, The Two Towers, and *The Return of the King.* Tolkien did not like the third title because he felt it gave away the plot.

In 1965, U.S. publisher Ace Books released an unauthorized version of the trilogy, capitalizing on a loophole that allowed them to forego paying royalties because the originals said, "Printed in Great Britain." Fans of the books, which had by then become cult classics, complained so loudly that Ace removed its edition and paid a small royalty to Tolkien. To regain copyright control, Tolkien began to reedit and revise the first editions; these resulted in a paperback edition from Ballantine Books in 1966. Typographical errors and mistakes in the minutiae of detail continued to plague Tolkien; every time a new edition was released something would be changed as something else was fixed. Later authorized editions include a slipcased edition in 1969, a Folio Society edition in 1977, and a one-volume "collectors' edition" from Houghton Mifflin in 1986. Christopher Tolkien continues to submit corrections even now.

The Lord of the Rings has been translated into many languages. More than one million Germans in 2004 voted the trilogy their favorite work of fiction, and polls in Great Britain and South Africa find Tolkien one of the top-100 people in both nations (he is the only person to be on both lists). Tolkien's saga expanded the demand for fantasy fiction and influenced the popularity of role-playing games like "Dungeons and Dragons." The success of Peter Jackson's film versions of the trilogy brings a whole new generation of travelers to Middle-Earth.

Tolkien the philologist, the lover of language and words, also changed Modern English. Prior to the publication of *The Lord of the Rings,* the plurals of "elf" and "dwarf" were "elfs" and "dwarfs," as in "Snow White and the Seven . . ." But due to Tolkien's insistence that the plurals he wanted were "elves" and "dwarves," they have become common usage; he also changed "elfin" to "elven" and "elfish" to "elvish."

After Tolkien retired in 1969, he and Edith moved to Bournemouth. Edith died on November 22, 1971, and Tolkien returned to Oxford where he took rooms in Merton College. Tolkien died on September 2, 1973, after a brief bout of pneumonia. Tolkien had often described the love he and Edith shared as being like that of Beren and Lúthien, the human/elven lovers in *The Silmarillion* and the models for the love of Aragorn and Arwen in *The Lord of the Rings.* To honor that love, Ronald and Edith were buried in a single grave in the Catholic section of Wolvercote cemetery outside Oxford under the following epitaph:

Edith Mary Tolkien, Lúthien, 1889–1971
John Ronald Reuel Tolkien, Beren, 1892–1973.

Other Works by J. R. R. Tolkien:

The Adventures of Tom Bombadil

The Road Goes Ever On

Farmer Giles of Ham

The Father Christmas Letters

Sir Gawain, Pearl and Sir Orfeo

Unfinished Tales of Númenor and Middle-Earth

FURTHER READING:
Doughan, David. "Who Was Tolkien?" The Tolkien Society. Available online. URL: www.tolkiensociety.org/tolkien/biography.html. Downloaded October 17, 2004.
"An Illustrated Biography of J. R. R. Tolkien, Together with an Interpretation of Some Ideas in His Stories." Available online. URL: http://home.freeuk.net/webbuk2/tolkien-biography.htm. Downloaded January 21, 2005.
"J. R. R. Tolkien: A Biography." Available online. URL: www.indepthinfo.com/tolkien/biography.shtml. Downloaded January 21, 2005.
Reynolds, Pat. "*The Lord of the Rings:* The Tale of a Text." The Tolkien Society. Available online. URL: www.tolkiensociety.org/tolkien/tale.html. Downloaded October. 17, 2004.

tools In MAGIC, certain objects used in RITUALS and the casting of SPELLS. Tools represent the divine forces of the masculine and the feminine and also the magical principles of the ELEMENTS. They are receptacles for higher forces and help the magician to connect to those higher forces as well. According to ISRAEL REGARDIE in *The Tree of Life: A Study in Magic,* a magician's tools—as well as SYMBOLS—are "the means . . . by which the Magician is able to understand himself, and commune with the invisible but no less real parts of Nature."

Western magical tradition holds that magicians should make their own magical tools in rituals performed under certain astrological auspices and/or phases of the MOON. The making of the tools imbues the magician's own energy into them. A great deal of time, energy, intent, WILL, and IMAGINATION goes into the tool-making. The tools need not be perfect works of art—the essence imbued into them is more important than the perfect form.

If a tool cannot be made—such as a steel dagger—it is acceptable to use one that has been purchased for magical purpose and never used for anything else.

Tools are inscribed with the magician's magical NAME and perhaps names of God or ANGELS, RUNES, or other magical SYMBOLS meaningful to the practitioner. Tools are consecrated in ceremony prior to their first use to charge them with magical power. When not in use, they are stored in the altar cupboard (see below) wrapped in colored silk. The GRIMOIRES give elaborate and precise instructions for the making of tools.

Specific tools vary according to traditions. In ceremonial magic, there are four tools—also called "elemental weapons"—considered basic to magical work. Each tool

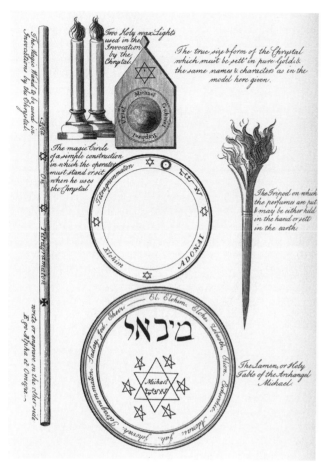

Magic tools, from left clockwise: wand, candles, invoking crystal inscribed with angel names, tripod for perfumes, lamen of the archangel Michael. In center is a magic circle. In The Magus, *by Francis Barrett, 1801. (Author's collection)*

corresponds to an element. There is no tool for the fifth element of spirit or askasa, which is invisible. Each tool also corresponds to characteristics of different gods or attributes of the sephirot of the Tree of Life; by using the tools, the magician takes on those authority and powers. (See CORRESPONDENCES.)

Dagger. Element: Air.   The dagger is made of iron or steel. It is associated with Mars and the color red. It is a weapon of Tipareth on the Tree of Life and symbolizes sacrifice, death, and resurrection. The dagger should never be used to cut any living thing.

Cup or chalice. Element: Water.   The cup corresponds to Netzach on the Tree of Life. It is a passive tool, representing the divine feminine forces, intuition, understanding, and receptivity. It is open to receive CELESTIAL DEW. The cup is made of SILVER, glass wood, or pewter and has a flared lip; it holds consecrated water or wine. In ceremonial magic, the cup is seldom used, except in the highest INVOCATIONS. It is not used in EVOCATIONS.

Wand. Element: Fire.   The wand is the WILL and the wisdom and spiritual presence of the creative self. The traditional wand is an 18-inch straight length of ash or hazel with the bark removed. Some wands are made of silver or crystal.

ELIPHAS LEVI prescribed specifics for wands in *Transcendental Magic:*

> [The wand] must be one perfectly straight branch of almond or hazel, cut at a single blow with the magical pruning-knife or golden sickle, before the rising sun, at that moment when the tree is ready to blossom. It must be pierced through its whole length without splitting or breaking it, and a long needle of magnetized iron must occupy its entire length. To one of the extremities must be fitted a polyhedral prism, cut in a triangular shape, and to the other a similar figure of black resin. Two rings, one of copper and one of zinc, must be placed at the center of the wand; which afterwards must be gilt at the resin and silvered at the prism end as far as the ringed center; it must then be covered with silk, the extremities not included.

Levi further specified the engraving of Hebrew words on the copper and zinc rings, followed by a CONSECRATION that would last seven days beginning at the new moon.

The wand is used for invocation and evocation and also to organize the forces of nature in spell-casting. The wand symbolizes manifestation; it unites the realm of spirit with the material world. It corresponds to Hod on the Tree of Life, the sephirah of Mercury and magic.

Pentacle. Element: Earth.   The pentacle is a medal or disk made of zinc, stone, wood, or wax. Like the cup, it is a passive tool of receptivity. It represents the body as a temple of the divine spirit. The border of the pentacle is inscribed, such as with the magician's magical name on one side and the archangelic and Godname of Earth on the other side. Inside the border on the side with the archangelic and God name is a HEXAGRAM or SEAL OF SOLOMON; on the other side is a PENTAGRAM. The pentacle thus symbolizes the union of humanity (pentagram) and the heavens (hexagram). The magician chooses which side to use depending on the nature and purpose of a ritual.

Other important magical tools are:

Altar. An altar anchors a sacred space. A traditional magical altar is a double cube—two cubes stacked one atop the other—and painted black or covered with a black cloth. In the kabbalistic tradition, the numerical value of the sides of the cubes add up to 10, which is the number of the Earth and also the TETRAGRAMMATON. Small tables also are used. Representations of the four elements as well as other magical tools are placed on the altar. The altar also functions as a cupboard for storage of other magical tools.

Bell. A bell clears and purifies the air, and sends away evil spirits. An 18th-century text, *De Mirabilis Naturae*

(1730), gives instructions for making a bell that will enable communication with the dead. A bell made of an alloy of lead, tin, IRON, copper, MERCURY, silver, copper, and GOLD should be inscribed with the magical names of Adonai, Jesus, and the tetragrammaton. The bell is to be placed in the middle of a ditch in a cemetery for seven days, after which communication with be possible. (See NECROMANCY.)

Knife. Some knives are used for cutting, preparing magical recipes, and fashioning magical objects.

Sword. A sword represents fire and Geburah, the sephirah of Mars. The sword represents the divine masculine forces analysis and separation, especially of good and evil. In some traditions a sword is used in place of a dagger. It is used in banishings. A sword is never used for cutting. It is considered to be more authoritative than a knife.

Brazier or Censer. A small dish or bowl, usually made of brass or earthenware, is used for the burning of incense, herbs, and PERFUMES for the purification of air and evocation of spirits.

Tripod. A tripod brings the brazier or censer up to chest level for the offerings of perfumes that are not done on the altar.

Bowl. In some DIVINATION rituals, a bowl is filled with ink or a mixture of water and olive oil. The shiny surface is used for SCRYING.

Talisman. A disk of metal, wax, clay, and stone that is inscribed with SIGILS, SEALS, a PENTACLE, or other magical symbols is often used in magical workings.

Lamen. A plate made of metal, wood, or cardboard that is inscribed with magical symbols or words, and is worn on a cord around the neck during rituals. A lamen is symbol of occult authority.

Bell. A bell—or a small gong—is used to mark the beginning and end of a ritual.

Candles. White CANDLES represent purity. Colored candles are used for different ritual purposes. The *Key of Solomon* specifies that the magician should make his own candles molded with virgin earth that he digs up himself or with wax taken from bees who have never before made wax.

Lamp. A lamp must always hang over the magician's head during workings and is never stored inside the altar cupboard. According to Regardie, it symbolizes "the undimmed radiance of the Higher Self, the Holy Guardian Angel to whose Knowledge and Conversation he [the magician] so ardently aspires."

Stylus. A sharp instrument for inscribing hard-surfaced objects with magical symbols and names.

Clothing. Traditional robes are the white or black "Tau" robe, so named because of the long and wide sleeves that create a tau-cross effect when the arms are outstretched. Robes are inscribed with magical symbols and names. A robe denotes a magician's inner concealed glory and also the shift from daily life to magical/spiritual work. Whatever the special ritual clothing, it should never be used for any other purpose.

In FREEMASONRY, masonic tools have symbolic significance. The compass represents virtue and the measure of a Mason's life and conduct. It is a symbol of the Sun and also represents light and illumination of one's duty. The square represents morality, propriety, and good conduct. The working tools of the Royal Arch Mason are the crow (for raising heavy stones), the pickaxe, and the shovel, which symbolize the removal of the rubble of corrupting influences, passions, and prejudices.

See also CONSECRATION.

FURTHER READING:
Bardon, Franz. *The Practice of Magical Evocation.* Salt Lake City: Merkur Publishing, 2001.
Cicero, Chic, and Sandra Tabatha Cicero. *The Essential Golden Dawn.* St. Paul, Minn.: Llewellyn Publications, 2004.
Flowers, Stephen Eldred, ed. *Hermetic Magic: The Postmodern Magical Papyrus of Abaris.* York Beach, Maine: Samuel Weiser, 1995.
King, Francis, and Stephen Skinner. *Techniques of High Magic: A Manual of Self-Initiation.* Rochester, Vt.: Destiny Books, 1976.
Kraig, Donald Michael. *Modern Magick: Eleven Lessons in the High Magickal Arts.* 2d ed. St. Paul, Minn.: Llewellyn Publications, 2004.
Mackey, Albert G. *Lexicon of Freemasonry.* Philadelphia: McClure Publishing, 1908.
Regardie, Israel. *Ceremonial Magic: A Guide to the Mechanisms of Ritual.* London: Aeon Books, 2004.
———. *The Tree of Life: A Study in Magic.* York Beach, Maine: Samuel Weiser, 1969.

Tree of Life   See KABBALAH.

trees   Reservoirs of immense life energy and longevity, trees are associated worldwide with spiritual, religious, and magical lore. Trees are the haunts of witches and FAIRIES and sometimes the ghosts of people who have met violent or tragic ends, such as a person hanged from a particular tree.

Since antiquity, trees have been associated with the beginning of all life, fertility, and mystical wisdom. Trees embody the universe: their branches represent the heavens, their trunks the earth, their roots the underworld. The immortal Tree of Life exists in the religions and myths of many parts of the world and is perhaps best known as the ash tree, Yggdrasil, in Scandanavian lore.

Sacred trees have been worshiped as the dwelling places of deities and nature spirits. In some cultures, trees are believed to be animated themselves and have souls. To cut a limb from them or fell them is to wound them and make them bleed. The person who injures a tree suffers the same wound or death in a form of sympathetic MAGIC.

The magical and sacred properties ascribed to trees varies according to culture and locale. Much of the lore surrounding trees comes from Europe, where peasants through the centuries practiced a wide range of tree-worship customs.

The ancient Celts, the DRUIDS, and the early Germans had a strong affinity with trees and used clusters and groves as sites of worship. The oak was sacred to the Druids. Greek deities are associated with various trees: Artemis with cedar, laurel, myrtle, hazel, and willow; Athene with olive; and Apollo with laurel. The ancient Romans revered the fig tree, whose roots entangled and saved the city's mythical founding twins, Romulus and Remus, and as they floated down the Tiber River.

As either animate beings with souls or the dwelling places of gods, trees have been regarded as ORACLES. Early Germans would go into the oak groves to ask questions and listen for the answers in the whispering and rustling of the leaves. Tribes in South Australia believe that the souls of the dead inhabit trees and may be consulted for their advice and wisdom.

With their magical power to bring forth fertility, trees play a central role in seasonal rituals and festivals throughout the world. In parts of Eurasia, folklore called for barren women to roll themselves on the ground beneath apple trees to conceive. An old Swedish custom called for pregnant women to hug a lime, ash, or oak tree to ensure an easy delivery. In parts of Africa, pregnant women dress in clothes made out of sacred tree bark to protect themselves against the hazards of delivery. Trees especially associated with fertility, such as cedar, sycamore, hawthorne, oak, birch, and fir, play prominent roles in traditional Beltane (May Eve) fertility festivals celebrated in Britain and Europe.

Certain trees are believed to repel witches, fairies, and evil spirits and are fastened on doors, about houses, and in stables: ash, rowan, birch, hazel, holly, oak, hawthorne, and bay. Oak, olive, bay laurel, elm, and holly offer protection against lighting. Birch and fir protect new construction from accidents.

In graveyards, yew and rowan are planted to keep spirits from wandering about at night. In Russia, aspen laid on the grave of a witch will prevent her spirit from riding out at night to terrorize people.

Witches are said to congregate around thorn and elder trees. The thorn is probably associated with witches because it grows alone, has an odd, gnarled shape, and is a bad-smelling wood. Witches are said to disguise themselves as elder trees. To burn one is to invite the devil or ghosts into one's home. If a person cuts an elder branch,

later he is likely to see an old woman walking about with her arm in a sling. In Scotland, elder branches are used to keep evil spirits out of houses, while in parts of the United States, burning an elder branch on Christmas Eve will reveal all witches in the locale. Elderberries make a strong wine, its flowers are used by herbalists in remedies for colds, and its branches are used in many charms, but to cut anything from an elder is bad luck without first asking the permission of the spirits which dwell in the tree. Elder wood also is sometimes used to make magic wands (see TOOLS) and is used as an AMULET against evil and WITCHCRAFT.

Some trees are believed to attract evil spirits, particularly cherry and blackthorn.

Fairies are said to congregate around elder and in copses that include oak, ash, and thorn.

In England, oaks are believed to have their own personalities. Oak groves are dangerous places at night because oaks that have been cut will revenge themselves on humans. In some areas, the oaks are haunted by oakmen spirits.

FURTHER READING:
Porteous, Alexander. *The Forest in Folklore and Mythology.* New York: Macmillan, 1928.

Trevisan, Bernard   See BERNARD OF TREVES.

Triangle of Causation   In the kabbalistic tradition of MAGIC, the foundation for work on the ASTRAL PLANE. The Triangle of Causation is used in the creation of THOUGHT-FORMS.

The Triangle's components and their correspondences to the TREE OF LIFE are (1) desire (*Kether*); (2) VISUALIZATION (*Chokmah*); and (3) IMAGINATION (*Binah*). The engagement of these qualities in RITUAL at high intensity and with projection of WILL builds the thought-forms. A fourth side is added to the triangle—organization (*Chesed*) to manifest the thought-form on the physical plane.

Tria Prima   According to the ALCHEMY of PARACELSUS, the three substances of SALT, SULPHUR, and MERCURY that make up all things. The *Tria Prima* are chemical substances that have similar properties to the three celestial, or archetypal, elements that flow out from the Mind of God into creation. These forces, or hypostatical principles, correspond to divine trinities and triads found in religions and mysticism; for example, in Christianity the triad is the Father, the Son, and the Holy Ghost.

The celestial elements comprise the four elements of the lower world, so that the *Tria Prima* is the basis for both macrocosm and microcosm. Paracelsus said:

> You should know that all seven metals originate from three materials, namely from mercury, sulphur, and salt,

though with different colors. Therefore Hermes has said not incorrectly that all seven metals are born and composed from three substances, similarly also the tinctures and philosopher's stone. . . . But that it be rightly understood what the three different substances are that he calls spirit, soul and body, you should know that they mean not other than the three *prinicipia,* that is, mercury, sulphur, and salt, out of which all seven metals originate. Mercury is the spirit, sulphur is the soul, salt the body.

The most important of the celestial elements is salt, which is born in the heating of fire and seawater. Its powers as a preservative, and thus a powerful force for the attainment of immortality, make it important to alchemical processes. Salt is passive/feminine and represents substance, Earth, and the body.

Sulphur is active/masculine, a transforming essence. It is associated with the SUN and the energy of nature.

Mercury is neutral and volatile, the agent of transformation. Its contradictory properties enable it to participate in all states of matter. It is liquid at room temperature and can dissolve GOLD. When heated it forms both white powder (highly poisonous) and red crystals (therapeutic).

Paracelsus held that disease arises from imbalances among the *Tria Prima.* For example, a excess of sulphur would cause fever and plague, while an imbalance would cause gout.

FURTHER READING:
Holmyard, E. J. *Alchemy.* New York: Penguin Books, 1957.

Trickster gods   Deities representing change, communication, opportunity, and mischief. Tricksters played major roles in the cosmologies of many cultures. The oldest evidence of these gods appeared in the ancient Middle East and Europe. Cave paintings in France dating back 18,000 years depicted tricksters, whereas drawings of warriors and kings appeared about 9,000 years later. They are creators, destroyers, inventors of language, gatekeepers, facilitators, scoundrels, thieves, and seducers. They could be old men walking with a staff, animals, musicians, winged deities, or very well-endowed lovers.

In Western tradition, the Greek god HERMES (Mercury to the Romans) symbolized the Trickster. With his winged feet Hermes performed the duties of messenger to the gods and communicator between gods and mortals. He escorted souls to the underworld and was the patron of magic and medicine, carrying a caduceus as his staff. The Ptolemaic Greeks in Egypt associated Hermes with the ibis-headed god Thoth, who also served in the underworld, keeping account of the judgments passed by OSIRIS on the souls of the dead. He brought writing to the Egyptians, while Hermes invented the alphabet for the Greeks. Merging the two deities created the legendary adept HERMES TRISMEGISTUS, supposedly the greatest philosopher and guardian of all occult knowledge.

Native American mythologies often identify spirits as animals that embody characteristics such as courage, strength, or resourcefulness. For many tribes, the Trickster is Coyote: shrewd and troublesome, but also a creator, teacher, lawgiver, and peacemaker. According to folklorists, the term *trickster* was not used by the native Americans but was coined to describe a recurring figure in myth for many different cultures. A story from the Chinook says that Coyote and Eagle traveled to the underworld to retrieve their dead wives. Every night, in a meeting lodge, an old woman swallowed the MOON, allowing the dead to appear, and every morning she vomited up the Moon and the dead disappeared. Coyote and Eagle built a large box, placed it at the entrance to the lodge, and then killed the old woman. Coyote ate the Moon, bringing out the dead, and then disgorged the Moon in the morning. But instead of disappearing, the dead souls were trapped in the box. Coyote begged to carry the box, but he opened it too soon, releasing death, and the souls of their wives disappeared.

According to the Montagnais tribe of Labrador, the god Messou received a box which his inquisitive wife could not wait to open; when she lifted the lid, man's immortal essence flew away, leaving humankind subject to death. Both of these stories appear similar to the Greek myth of Pandora, who opened the box and allowed the forces of death and destruction to escape.

For the tribes of the American Southwest, the Trickster appears as a hump-backed flute player called Kokopelli, dating back to about 200 B.C.E. in the pictographs (rock paintings) and petroglyphs (rock carvings) of the Anasazi, or Ancient Strangers, who lived in the Four Corners: the intersection of present-day New Mexico, Utah, Colorado, and Arizona. His image also appeared in murals, ceramics, and baskets of the Hohokam, Mogollon, Hopi, Zuñi, Acoma, and Pueblo tribes. *Koko* refers to his wooden flute, while *pelli* or *pilau* means his sack, in which he carried seeds and plants to make the crops grow and thrive. Like his brethren, Kokopelli was a magician, healer, musician, lover, and symbol of fertility. He also carried blankets and even babies in his sack to entice the maidens he wanted to seduce. For a young Hopi woman, to be chosen as Kokopelli's "dreamtime companion" was the highest honor. Kokopelli remains a popular figure, appearing on clothing, housewares, and decorative items designed to evoke the flavor of the Southwest.

But perhaps the gods most directly representative of the Trickster are those from West Africa. Known as *orishas,* they came to the New World on slave ships heavy with captives from the Yoruban, Fon, Mandingue, Iwe, Ibo, Congo, and other tribes of Nigeria, Dahomey, and Benin. Called the *Eshus* in the Spanish colonies and *Exus* in Portuguese Brazil, these gods again served as the messengers, the gatekeepers, the bringers of language, the facilitators, and mischief-makers. Eshu's sign is the crossroads (*carrefour*). Slaves taken to French colonies, such as Haiti, worshiped *loas* instead of orishas; yet practices remained very similar.

There could be no interaction between gods and the faithful unless Eshu was called upon first to intercede. For members of the Yoruban tribes, all prayers began by inviting *Eshu-Elegbara* into the temple of worship—anything from a special building to a hidden altar in the woods. Since slaves were forbidden to practice their religion on pain of death, they disguised the names, colors, and symbols associated with Eshu in the trappings of a Catholic saint. Such syncretization was not too difficult, incorporating candles, offerings, crosses, and pleas for intercession. The Fon called their Eshu *Legba;* he is Legba or *Eleggua* to the practitioners of Vodoun as well. In the Brazilian religions of Candomblé and Umbanda, the Exus facilitate communication between the orishas and the faithful but are principally divine Tricksters: the gods of opportunity and choice, life and death.

The common depiction of Eshu-Elegbara as an old, dark-skinned man sucking on a pipe or his fingers, walking with a staff, belies his true nature: Eshu is voraciously lustful. Worshipers possessed of his spirit often grope the women in attendance. Even while busy with other divine matters, Eshu seeks sexual conquest. He is exceptionally well endowed, and statues of the god feature an enormous phallus that may be used during worship. As the symbol of communication and interaction, Eshu's copulations become the ultimate connection. The results of such chaos lead to change, choice, and the success of the tribe.

Legba goes by many names, depending on the role he is playing. In Vodoun, he is the *grand chemin:* the way, the channel, symbolized by the center pole, or *poteau,* holding up the temple or *peristyle.* As such he is called Legba Ati-Bon, or Legba of the Good Wood. Legba is master of the crossroads, *Maitre carefour,* a position signifying magic as well as choice, since spells may be placed at an intersection or fork in the road.

Vodoun worshipers practice either "Rada" (from the Arada tribe) or "Petro" rites. Rada ceremonies follow more traditional African practice, whereas Petro embraces a more violent form inherited from the dances and ceremonies of the Caribe and Arawak natives on the island of Santo Domingo (now Haiti and the Dominican Republic). Most of the loas or orishas have a darker side; the sexual spirits called *Guedes* represent an Eshu's baser nature. The most famous Guede is Baron Samedi (Saturday, the day of death) or Baron Cimitiere (cemetery), master of graveyards, death, and black magic.

For Brazilian followers of Candomblé, Quimbanda provides spells of vengeance and retribution. King Exu, in company with Exu Mor (death, associated with Beelzebub and Ashtaroth) and Exu of the Crossroads, wield pain and destruction. Most feared is Exu of the Closed Paths. Calling this spirit involves taking a red satin cloth adorned with mystical symbols and placing it at a CROSSROADS. Four red and black crosses are placed on the cloth, accompanied by a cock that has been plucked and stuffed with red pepper and other devilish objects. Then the *quimbandista* lights 13 candles while intoning the name of the victim and invoking the aid of the powers of darkness. If the spell succeeds, the victim finds "all paths closed"—no choice, no job, no family, no way out: only death.

Modern occultists tolerate the Tricksters as by-products of contacting the spirits. Recommended methods of keeping the pranksters from taking control include burning incense, especially frankincense. In severe cases, dragon's blood incense should discourage Trickster activity, but the practitioner risks losing good spirits in the process. To invite Trickster spirits, use elemi, mastic, sandarac, white sandalwood, fennel, lavender, or wormwood.

FURTHER READING:

Davis, Erik. "Trickster at the Crossroads: West Africa's God of Messages, Sex and Deceit." Originally appeared in *Gnosis,* Spring 1991. Available online. URL: www.techgnosis.com/trickster.html. Downloaded July 5, 2004.

Guiley, Rosemary Ellen. *The Encyclopedia of Witches and Witchcraft.* 2d ed. New York: Facts On File Inc., 1999.

Hultkrantz, Ake. "Theories on the North American Trickster." Originally appeared in *Acta American,* Vol. 5, No. 2, 1997. Available online. URL: www.angelfire.com/realm/bodhisattva/trickster.html. Downloaded July 5, 2004.

Stafford, Greg, and Sandy Peterson. "The Trickster." Originally published in Questlines #1. Issaries Inc.: 1998. Available online. URL: www.glorantha.com/library/religions/cult-trickster.html. Downloaded July 5, 2004.

Trithemius, Johannes (1462–1516) German abbot, alchemist, magician, and historian. Johannes Trithemius authored numerous works on occult philosophy that influenced writers and artists, among them HENRY CORNELIUS AGRIPPA. The great French occultist ELIPHAS LEVI called Trithemius the greatest dogmatic magician of the middle ages.

Trithemius was born in Trittenheim near Trèves (Trier). His father, John Heidenberg, was a prosperous vine grower. His father died when he was young. He later took as his last name the place where he was born, a custom of the day.

An unhappy childhood with an abusive stepfather propelled him into deep study at an early age; he was fascinated by mysticism and the occult arts. Later, he said that an ANGEL had appeared to him in childhood and offered him two tablets with letters written upon them. After he chose one, the angel promised to fulfill his prayers and then vanished. After that, he had an insatiable desire to study and learn. He taught himself how to read German and engaged in secret lessons at night to learn Latin. This experience with the angel may have influenced his occult works, which were heavily couched in SYMBOLS.

Trithemius left Trittenheim for Heidelberg—a center of ALCHEMY and occultism—where he became the student of an unknown teacher. He went to Trèves and entered the university there.

In 1482 a seeming fluke incident altered the course of his life. While traveling back to Trittenheim, he was forced by a blizzard to seek shelter at the Benedictine monastery of Saint Martin at Sponheim. He was so taken by the life of the monks that he entered the order, and within two years—at age 23—he was named abbot. At the time of his visit, the monastery had fallen on hard times, but under his direction, it was restored to prosperity. One of his passions was building up the monastery's library from a mere 48 books to more than 2,000. He took on students, one of whom was Henry Cornelius Agrippa von Nettesheim.

Trithemius's knowledge eventually led to accusations that he was a SORCERER, and stories of his conjurations arose. He is said to have enabled Emperor Maximilian to see a vision of his dead wife, Mary of Burgundy.

Trithemius resigned his post in 1506, but soon he was named abbot at another Benedictine monastery, Saint Jakob at Würzburg. He remained there for the rest of his life. According to lore, he was often tormented by a spirit named Hudekin.

Johannes Trithemius, 18th-century engraving. (Author's collection)

Trithemius concealed occult secrets in PENTACLES. He wrote some 70 works. *Veterum sophorum sigilla et imagines magicae* is a history of magic written entirely in pentacles, containing TALISMANS and magical images. He explains the science of INCANTATIONS and EVOCATIONS in *Stenoganographia,* his original shorthand method for conjuring spirits, and in *Polygraphia,* on ciphers and MAGICAL ALPHABETS. *De septem secundeis,* on the planetary angels who rule the cycle of ages, includes one of his rarer pentacles: a white triangle and black triangle joined at the base. The white triangle contains a knight with the inscription of the TETRAGRAMMATON, and the black triangle contains a fool looking at his own reflection. This pentacle, said Levi, "is the distinction between miracles and prodigies, the secret of apparitions, the universal theory of magnetism and the science of all mysteries." The meaning of it is that the wise man rests in fear of the true God and the fool is overwhelmed by the fear of a false god made in his own image. By meditating on the pentacle, one will find "the last word of Kabbalism and the unspeakable formula of the Great Arcanum," said Levi.

According to legend, Trithemius discovered the secret of the PHILOSOPHER'S STONE, which was the real reason why the monastery prospered so much under his leadership. It was also said that he practiced forms of MAGIC, including NECROMANCY. *Stenoganographia* was denounced as magical and devilish.

Agrippa wrote his first version of his monumental work, *Occult Philosophy,* while studying with Trithemius and dedicated the work to him.

FURTHER READING:

Levi, Eliphas. *The History of Magic.* 1860. Reprint, York Beach, Maine: Samuel Weiser, 2001.

Mackay, Charles. *Extraordinary Popular Delusions and the Madness of Crowds.* New York: Farrar, Straus & Giroux, 1932.

Seligmann, Kurt. *The Mirror of Magic.* New York: Pantheon Books, 1948.

Three Books of Occult Philosophy Written by Henry Cornelius Agrippa of Nettesheim. Transl. by James Freake. Ed. and annot. by Donald Tyson. St. Paul, Minn.: Llewellyn Publications, 1995.

tulpa   See THOUGHT-FORM.

tutelary spirits   Indwelling spirits that provide guidance and influence. Tutelary spirits can be compared to intuition or wisdom from the Higher Self.

Plotinus, an Egyptian who taught neoplatonic philosophy in Rome in the third century C.E., rejected the idea of astral INTELLIGENCES influencing people but believed people to be guided by increasingly powerful higher forces—tutelary spirits—as they ascended to Divine Mind. Tutelary spirits keep the soul focused on God. In his treatise *On Our Tutelary Spirit,* Plotinus said:

> Our tutelary spirit is not entirely outside of ourselves, is not bound up with our nature, is not the agent in our action; it belongs to us as belonging to our soul, as "the power which consummates the chosen life"; for while its presidency saves us from falling deeper into evil, the direct agent within us is something neither above nor equal to it, but under it; man cannot cease to be characteristically man.

Tutelary spirits are mentioned in the *Arbatel of Magic,* a GRIMOIRE of magical instruction.

urine An important ingredient in magical CHARMS, SPELLS, and countercharms. The magical potency of human urine is attributed to its personal connection to an individual, thus providing a sympathetic link for MAGIC and to the belief that urine influences health.

By the 16th century, physicians knew that the condition of urine could be used in diagnosis. PARACELSUS wrote that urine, BLOOD, hair (see HAIR AND NAIL CLIPPINGS), sweat, and EXCREMENT retained for a time a vital life essence called mumia. These ingredients could be used to make a "microcosmic magnet," which, through the mumia, would draw off disease. Alchemists also used urine in their experiments for longevity.

Numerous folk magic remedies are based on urine. Boiling a person's urine helps determine if and how BEWITCHMENT has occurred. The victim's urine is then used to effect cures, usually by boiling, baking, burying, or throwing it into a fire. "Witch's cakes," containing urine and other magical ingredients, once were made to treat a host of ailments. In the early American colonies in the 17th century, witch's cakes were used to treat smallpox. Ingredients included rye, barley, herbs, water, and a cup of baby's urine. It was fed to a dog, and if the dog shuddered while eating it, the patient would recover.

A folk magic formula for killing someone by causing them to have jaundice calls for acquiring their urine and then buying a hen's egg without haggling. On a Tuesday or a Saturday night, take the egg and urine to a place where you will not be disturbed. Make a circular incision on the broad end of the egg, and extract the yolk. Pour the urine into the egg, and seal the hole with a piece of virgin parchment, saying the name of the victim as you do so. Bury the egg, and leave without looking back. As the egg rots, the victim will become ill and will die of jaundice within a year. The only way to break the spell is for the spellcaster to dig the egg up and burn it.

An effective countercharm against WITCHCRAFT prescribes securing the witch's own urine, bottling it, and burying it. The witch is then unable to urinate.

In ALCHEMY, urine, like water, represents the unconscious and creativity. Both urine and water are names for the *PRIMA MATERIA,* the basic material of the cosmos. In depth psychology, the *prima materia* is the state of conscious chaos at the beginning of the process of individuation.

uroboros See OUROBOROS.

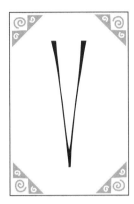

Valentine, Basil (c. 15th c.) Mysterious chemist, philosopher, and alchemist. Few details of the life of Basil Valentine are known; he has been placed in both the 15th and 16th centuries. His name may have been a pseudonym. Whoever he was, the writings attributed to him exhibit a profound knowledge of chemistry, medicine, and ALCHEMY.

According to some accounts, Valentine was born in Mayence, Germany, and by 1413 was a Benedictine monk at St. Peter's in Erfurt. He was made prior in 1414. Supposedly the city records of Erfurt verify this, but according to other accounts, Benedictine records have no information on a man by that name.

Valentine is said to have distinguished himself with his knowledge. Like PARACELSUS, he was openly contemptuous of the physicians of his time. He is credited with being the first to introduce antimony into medicine, and was the first to describe how to extract antimony from sulphuret.

Valentine's works are couched in allegories and kabbalistic SYMBOLS. They show Paracelsian influences and make references to the concepts expressed in the EMERALD TABLET. Numerous treatises have been credited to him, some without foundation. Some accounts attribute at least some of his works to Johann Tholde, a German metallurgist and owner of SALT mines at Frankenhausen. None of Valentine's alleged works were published prior to the late 16th century, and most appeared in the early 17th century.

According to legend, Valentine sealed 21 of his writings inside a stone pillar of his abbey. They were thought to be lost until a thunderbolt shattered the pillar. Supposedly heavenly powers wished the works to be made known. The pillar reportedly closed up again of its own accord when the manuscripts were removed.

However, no original copies of Valentine's alleged manuscripts exist. Among the most noted works attributed to him are *Triumphal Chariot of Antimony, The Great Stone of the Philosophers,* and *The Twelve Keys of Philosophy.*

In *Triumphal Chariot of Antimony,* Valentine discusses the medicinal properties of antimony and provides details of his experiments with it.

In *The Great Stone of the Philosophers,* Valentine says that after he spent some years at the monastery, he initiated a study of the "natural secrets by which God has shadowed out eternal things." At first he understood little, but he continued to apply himself to the works of the ancient philosophers, and at length God granted his prayer for understanding.

One of his convent brothers was seriously ill with a kidney disorder that no physicians could heal. Valentine spent six years treating the brother with herbal medicines, also to no avail. He then turned to the study of the powers and virtues of metals and minerals. He discovered the PHILOSOPHER'S STONE and extracted its spiritual essence, which he used to heal the brother successfully.

Valentine espouses the belief in the principal of evolution of all things to perfection. A seed exists in metals that is their essence and if properly treated can be caused to grow the perfect metal. He describes the Philosopher's Stone as a stone that is not a stone, composed of both white and red, to be used as a universal medicine to ensure good health and to lengthen life. Few ADEPTS ever achieve the stone and can only do so by intense study, PRAYER, confession of sins, and good works. They must understand "the truth of all truths":

> . . . that if there be a metalick soul, a metalick spirit, a metalick body that there must be a metalick Mercury, a metalick sulphur, and a metalick salt which can of necessity produce no other than a perfect metaline body. If you do not understand this that you ought to understand, you are not adepted for Philosophy or God concealeth it from thee.

At the end of *The Great Stone of the Philosophers,* Valentine provides a laborious procedure for preparing the Stone. Once accomplished, the alchemist can use it to transmute base metals into gold. Essentially, Valentine's secret is to coat (tinge) base metals with an amalgam of GOLD. When done repeatedly, the base metal itself becomes transmuted into genuine gold:

> . . . if this medicine after being fermented with other pure gold doth likewise tinge many thousand parts of all other metals into very good gold, such gold likewise becometh a penetrat medicine that one part of it doth tinge and transmute a thousand parts of other metals and much more beyond belief into perfect gold.

Fraudulent alchemists used the process of coating base metals with gold, many of them succeeding in fooling, at least for a time, gullible patrons.

The Twelve Keys was written as a follow-on companion to *The Great Stone of the Philosophers.* ELIPHAS LEVI lauded it as a work "at once Kabbalistic, magical and Hermetic." The work was first published in 1599 with no illustrations. In 1602 an edition with rough woodcuts was published. Twelve now-famous engravings were added when the text was included in *The Golden Tripod* (*Tripus aureus*), edited by MICHAEL MAIER and published in 1618. The plates probably were created by Merian and were added by the publisher, Lucas Jennis. Each key has its own allegorical emblem; the emblems themselves are referred to as the keys. They follow a geometry of three, with certain symbols and allegories appearing three times in different keys. The text for each key is couched in symbolism and allegory. The keys are studied for their philosophical and spiritual content by modern students of alchemy.

FURTHER READING:

Mackay, Charles. *Extraordinary Popular Delusions and the Madness of Crowds.* New York: Farrar, Straus & Giroux, 1932.

McLean, Adam. "Notes on the 'Twelve Keys of Basil Valentine.'" Available online. URL: http://www.levity.com/alchemy/twelve_keys.html. Downloaded May 17, 2005.

Thompson, C. J. S. *The Mysteries and Secrets of Magic.* New York: Barnes & Noble, 1993.

Waite, Arthur Edward. *The Hermetic Museum.* York Beach, Maine: Samuel Weiser, 1991.

————. *Alchemists Through the Ages.* Blauvelt, N.Y.: Rudolph Steiner Publications, 1970.

vampire   An entity or person who attacks the living, causing wasting away, misfortune, and even death. Folklore traditions describe different types of vampires, but they are most commonly associated with the restless dead who escape their graves to wreak havoc upon the living.

The origin of the word *vampire* is uncertain; it is thought to be of Slavic origin, with the root noun being the Serbian word *bamiiup.* The word *vampire* made its first appearance in Western literature in the early 18th century when news of the Eastern European "vampire cult" broke. According to the folklore of the vampire cult, certain persons became vampires after death and returned from the grave to attack the living. Causes were suicide, murder, sudden and especially violent death, sinful life, CURSES, death due to vampirism, improper handling of the corpse and improper burial, and failing to make a confession prior to death.

The vampires embodied the characteristics of restless ghosts, poltergeists, incubi and succubi, and nightmare DEMONS. Victims wasted away as though the life force were being drained from them. The remedy consisted of identifying the culprit by digging up bodies and looking for telltale signs of vampirism, usually BLOOD oozing from body cavities and insufficient decomposition. These indicated that the vampire was able to suck off the blood, or the essence of the blood, from the living. The corpse was staked, mutilated, hacked to pieces, or burned to stop the attacks. Vampires were thought to be the cause of plagues, epidemics, blighted crops, sick animals, and any other misfortune. Even animals could return from the grave as vampires.

The vampire entered Western Romantic and Victorian literature and performing arts, proving to be one of the most durable and alluring characters. Initially a creature of evil, the vampire mutated to more humanlike forms. Bram Stoker's Count Dracula set the prototype for the vampire as a reanimated corpse who lives in society and who possesses great occult and magical knowledge and skills and supernormal powers. The vampire evolved from villain to antihero and even hero, serving as a staple for modern romantic leads.

Other types of vampires are:

Supernatural Entities

Not all vampires are reanimated humans or animals. Some are demons who may have the ability to shapeshift into human form. Supernatural vampires are sexual predators or those who prefer to attack the living for their organs, blood, and entrails. Some, like the Greek *lamiae,* are childbirth demons, causing sudden death to newborns and their mothers.

In Japanese lore, the *kappa* is a horrible water imp who likes to drink human blood and eat entrails. The *kappa* is named after the river god Kappa, whom it serves as a messenger.

The *kappa* resembles a monkey. It is about the height of a 10-year-old boy and has webbed hands and feet, a monkey face, a long beak-like nose, and a tortoise shell on its back. On top of its head is a bowl-like indentation that contains a clear, jellylike substance which is the source of the *kappa's* power. Short black hair rings the indentation.

The *kappa* lives in swampy areas, ponds, lakes, and rivers, where it taunts its victims—men, women, and children—into treacherous or deep waters so that they drown. It also attacks animals. After the victims are dead, the *kappa* enters the bodies through the anus, drinks their blood, and sucks out their entrails. It is especially fond of livers. Sometimes it will devour some of the flesh.

Some vampire demons are created by MAGIC, such as the *polong,* a Malayan vampire in the shape of a tiny person, either male or female, about the size of a thumbtack and with the ability to fly. A polong is made magically by collecting the blood of a person who has been murdered. The blood is left in a bottle for two weeks, and magical INCANTATIONS are said over it. The polong grows in the blood and chirps when ready to emerge. Its human creator then must cut a finger daily for the polong to suck. The polong then can be dispatched as a FAMILIAR to attack enemies by burrowing into them and making them sicken and die. It travels with its own familiar, a *pelesit,* a cricketlike demon with a sharp tail. The *pelesit* burrows its tail into the victim, making a tunnel by which the polong enters the body to suck blood. The bite becomes infected, and the victim goes insane and raves about cats.

Vampire Sorcerers and Witches

Certain individuals are believed to be born as natural vampires, possessing the same powers as sorcerers and witches. Some are readily identified at birth by such physical oddities such as teeth already showing; a spine deformity that resembles a tail; or the presence of the caul, the inner fetal membrane of amniotic fluid, which at birth sometimes still covers the body, especially the head. If a child is the seventh child of seven children who are all the same sex, he or she is fated to be a living vampire. In Romanian lore, if a pregnant woman does not eat SALT—a protector against all things evil—her child will be born a living vampire.

In other folklore traditions, vampire sorcerers and witches are living persons who learn their evil trade from others and then pass their vampiric skills on to initiates.

Vampire sorcerers and witches use their powers to wreak havoc, destruction, and death among the living. They cast the EVIL EYE and BEWICTHMENTS on human and beast alike. They shapeshift into dogs, cats, horses, and other animals in order to frighten people. In Romanian lore female living vampires are dry in the body and red in the face before and after death. When they go out to work their evil, they leave their homes through their chimneys and return exhausted and in rags. Male vampires are bald, and after death they grow a tail and hooves.

In Russian lore, living vampire sorcerers have the power to take over the body of a person who is dying or who has died, preferably a villainous or insane person. The invaded body becomes a type of vampire called an *erestun.* The *erestun* maintains the outward appearance of a good peasant but carries on his vampiric activity among the people in secret. He stalks the family of the dead person and then others and devours them like a cannibal. The *erestun* is destroyed by whipping him to death with a whip that is used for heavily loaded horses. To prevent him from reanimating in the grave, a traditional method of vampire-killing is employed: a stake made of aspen is driven through his back between the shoulders.

In the lore of the Karachay, the *obur* is a shape-shifting vampire witch or wizard. *Oburs* recognize each other. They possess the knowledge to make magical salves. They take off all their clothing, smear their bodies with salve, and then wallow in the ashes on the edge of their fires. They mount brooms with whips in hand, run around the room in circles, and fly up the chimney in the forms of cat. They enter the houses of victims via the chimneys after all members of the household have gone to sleep. They drink their blood, especially of the children, and leave a black bruise at the wound. At dawn they return to their own homes, going back down the chimneys. They resume their normal human appearance. *Oburs* shape-shift into wolves and dogs to attack livestock out in pasture and drink their blood.

In lore found in Europe, vampire sorcerers and witches are not limited to the night hours for their evil activities but can come out in the daytime all year round. Their power is greatest during the times of the full moon and are weakest at the new moon. They meet with dead vampires and teach them magical incantations and spells and decide on their programs of evil.

Living vampire sorcerers and witches walk about the boundaries of villages, taking "power" from things, such as certain animals, bread, and bees—whatever is locally important to the sustaining of life and prosperity. "Taking power" zaps the life force. When the power is taken, the animals do not perform their natural functions: Hens do not lay eggs, cows do not give milk, bees do not make honey. A female vampire who has power over bread steals the taste from the bread of other women and puts it into her own bread. Some living vampires have power over rain and can prevent it from falling and nourishing crops.

Besides taking power for themselves, living vampire sorcerers and witches can take power from people and give it to others who pay them. They can take beauty away from women and give it to another, and they can take love away. They can take milk away from a nursing mother.

Although Native American lore does not include European-style vampires, some legends parallel European vampires and vampire sorcerers and witches. For example, in Cherokee lore there are old witches and wizards who live off the livers of the dead. When a person falls ill, the witches and wizards shape-shift into invisible forms and gather around the bedside, tormenting the person until he or she is dead. After the person is buried, they dig up his or her body and feast on the liver. In this manner, they gain strength and lengthen their own lives as many days as they stole from the dead person. Abenaki lore tells of witches who die and are buried in TREES and who attack the living at night to drink their blood.

In the lore of rural Tlaxcala, Mexico, one of the most feared vampire witches is the *tlahuelpuchi*, a shape-shifting human who can assume animal form and who sucks the blood of infants, causing them to die. The *tlahuelpuchi* epitomizes everything that is horrible, evil, and hateful. It can be either male or female but usually is female, considered to be the more bloodthirsty and evil of the two. At least 100 legends exist about the *tlahuelpuchi*.

Tlahuelpuchis are born into their fate; they cannot transmit or teach their powers to others. They are independent agents of evil but will do the bidding of higher evil forces, such as the devil. For example, they will act as intermediaries (in animal form) in transactions involving selling of the soul to the devil and making pacts with the devil. *Tlahuelpuchis* are more powerful than *nahuales*, a trickster type of supernatural agent.

When a *tlahuelpuchi* is born, it cannot be distinguished from an ordinary infant. Differences do not emerge until puberty, at which point their supernatural powers such as shape-shifting suddenly manifest. For females, this often occurs with the onset of the menses. When the powers manifest, the *tlahuelpuchis* of both sexes begin to have a lifelong, uncontrollable urge to drink human blood, especially that of infants. This causes a great deal of unhappiness and shame to their families, who go to great lengths to cover up their secret to avoid being stigmatized and ostracized by the community.

An attack by a *tlahuelpuchi* must be remedied by a *tezitlazc*, a helpful sorcerer and healer, called in to perform RITUAL cleansings of the corpse, the mother, and the space where the death took place.

See also PSYCHIC VAMPIRISM.

FURTHER READING:
Guiley, Rosemary Ellen. *The Encyclopedia of Vampires, Werewolves and Other Monsters.* New York: Facts On File, Inc., 2004.

van Helmont, Jean Baptista (1577–1644) Belgian alchemist and a disciple of PARACELSUS. Jean Baptista van Helmont was the first person to teach the chemistry of the human body and is called the Descartes of Medicine.

Van Helmont was born in 1577 to a noble family in Bois le Duc, Brabant, Belgium. He studied at Louvain and at age 17 became a medical doctor. He spent 10 years in a largely unsuccessful practice and then met a Paracelsian chemist. He became intensely interested in chemistry and its applications to illness. Van Helmont was the first to understand the chemistry of the digestive process. He is

credited with the discovery of carbon dioxide. He put forth the theory that all humans radiate a magnetic fluid, which can be used to influence the minds and bodies of others through will—an idea that later influenced the magnetic healer FRANZ ANTON MESMER.

In his early thirties, van Helmont retired to the castle Vilvord near Brussels. He lived in near seclusion and anonymity, studying ALCHEMY, writing and maintaining a limited practice of medicine. He left the castle only when necessary. Remarkably, van Helmont never asked for payment for his medical services. He died at the castle in 1644 at age 67, renowned throughout Europe as a learned man of good deeds.

Van Helmont was convinced that no scientific advancement could come without knowledge of alchemy—no one could ever know "radical knowledge of natural things without the fire."

He never claimed to make the PHILOSOPHER'S STONE himself, but in his treatise *De Natura Vitae Eternae*, he described his experiences with it:

> I have seen and I have touched the Philosophers' Stone more than once. The color of it was like saffron in powder, but heavy and shining like pounded glass. I had once given me the fourth of a grain—I call a grain that which takes 600 to make an ounce. I made projection with this fourth part of a grain wrapped in paper upon eight ounces of quicksilver heated in a crucible. The result of the projection was eight ounces, lacking eleven grains, of the most pure gold.

Van Helmont conducted his own search for the PRIMA MATERIA, rejecting Paracelsus's idea of the TRIA PRIMA and the four ELEMENTS of Aristotle. He undertook an experiment with a willow tree that convinced him that water was the *prima materia* for plants. Van Helmont planted a willow shoot, weighing both it and the soil. After five years of watering and tending it, he uprooted the willow and weighed it and the soil. The 164-pound gain of the tree led him to his conclusion about water. He further concluded that water was the *prima materia* for all things on the planet.

Van Helmont investigated claims of alchemical feats, including an Irishman named Butler who was imprisoned in the Castle of Vilvord in Flanders. Butler reportedly made miraculous cures with his alchemical knowledge and some stone (Red Powder) he had obtained in Arabia. Butler's story was that he had been traveling aboard a ship that was overtaken by pirates, and he was sold into slavery to a master of alchemy in Arabia. Thus he learned the art and stole some of the stone when he escaped.

At the Castle of Vilvord, Butler was said to cure another prisoner, a Breton monk who suffered from severe erysipelas, with almond milk in which he had dipped the stone. Intrigued, van Helmont and several noblemen visited Butler to investigate his abilities. They witnessed him cure an old woman of "megrim" by dipping the stone into olive oil and then anointing her head. They also relieve her abbess of paralyzed fingers and a swollen tongue—which she had suffered for 18 years—by rubbing her tongue with the stone.

See also BOYLE, ROBERT; STARKEY, GEORGE.

FURTHER READING:
"Alchemy in the Sixteenth and Seventeenth Centuries." Available online. URL: http://www.sacred-texts.com/alc/arr/arr09.htm. Downloaded December 31, 2004.
Waite, Arthur Edward. *Alchemists Through the Ages.* Blauvelt, N.Y.: Rudolph Steiner Publications, 1970.

Vaughn, Thomas (1621–1665)

Welsh alchemist and brother of poet Henry Vaughn. Thomas Vaughn contributed important metaphysical works to the field of ALCHEMY.

Vaughn was born in 1621 in Newton in the parish of Llansanffraid (St. Bridget), Wales. The lack of doctors in Wales inspired him to a career as a physician. In 1638 he entered Jesus College in Oxford, where he spent a decade pursuing medical studies. During the Civil War he was a Royalist, which caused him to be evicted from his parish in 1650.

In 1651 Vaughn married a woman named Rebecca. She died in 1658, and he went to live in London. Despite his university studies Vaughn never practiced as a physician but turned his interests to alchemy. He admired the work of PARACELSUS. He wrote under the pseudonym Eugenius Philalethes, not to be confused with EIRENAEUS PHILALETHES, another pseudonymous author. His first work, *Anthroposophia theomagica* ("A Discourse of the Nature of Man and his State After Death; grounded in his Creator's Promochimistry"), published in 1650, was a mystical-magical work that received favorable attention. His last work, *Euphrates or the Waters of the East,* was published in 1650.

Vaughn died on February 27, 1665, during one of his chemical experiments.

vegetable gold

An alchemical product made from plants, CELESTIAL DEW, and special peat. Vegetable gold was made in the 1960s by Armand Barbault, a famous French astrologer, and his wife Jacqueline.

Barbault was persuaded by his wife to be come involved in ALCHEMY after the couple moved to the French countryside in the 1940s. He read the MUTUS LIBER and modeled his own work on it.

The Barbaults' alchemical work began in 1948. At an auspicious astrological time, they collected four pounds of "philosopher's peat," living earth that they felt was specially charged with life forces. For 12 years, the Barbaults and their son, Alexandre, worked with this philosopher's peat until they transformed it into a golden liquid called vegetable gold. Barbault ingested this liquid, and his son—

who became a physician—credited it with prolonging his life.

To collect dew, the Barbaults dragged a canvas over grass before sunrise on a cloudless morning in spring. It took 50 yards of dragging to collect a quart of dew. According to Barbault, the dew contained valuable etheric forces. The wet canvas was wrung out into a container. It was not allowed to touch the ground, lest its etheric forces return immediately to the earth.

The alchemist harvested plants by selecting them one day and mentally ordering the plants to draw greater life forces out of the ground. The plants were harvested the next day before sunrise. The peat, the dew, and the plants were then left to ferment in an ALEMBIC for several months at 104 degrees Fahrenheit. The mixture was reduced to ash by burning at 1,500 degrees Fahrenheit, and the ashes were sifted. Ash, dew, and powdered GOLD were mixed in a circular oven, boiled for four hours, and cooled for four hours, a process repeated seven times. The vegetable gold, or "liquor of gold," was filtered out. Barbault said that when the ELIXIR was perfect, a symbolic star floated upon its surface.

FURTHER READING:
Secrets of the Alchemists. New York: Time-Life Books, 1990.

Villanova, Arnold de (ca. 1245–ca. 1310)

Theologian, physician, and alchemist. The dates of birth and death and the place of birth of Arnold Villanova (also Arnold de Villaneuve) are uncertain.

Villanova studied medicine for 20 years in Paris, after which he spent 10 years traveling around Italy visiting different universities. He served Frederick, king of Naples and Sicily, and was the physician to Pope Clement V.

As was common during the times, Villanova was accused of magical wizardy and learning all of his knowledge about ALCHEMY from DEMONS. He was careful of the Inquisition. On a trip to Spain he learned that a friend of his was being held by inquisitors, and he discreetly left the country.

Villanova was said by one of his contemporaries, John André, to have transmuted base metals into GOLD, which Villanova "submitted to all proofs."

Villanova's alchemical works were published in 1509 in a single volume, *Libellus de Somniorum Interpretatione et Somnia Danielis.* His most important treatises are *Rosario Philosophorum, Thesaurus Thesaursorum, Speculum Alchemiae,* and *Perfectum Magisterium.* Also significant are *Scientia Scientiae* and *Testamentum.*

Villanova said that *argent vive* (living MERCURY) exists in all things and is the medicine of all metals. Vulgar SULPHUR causes impurities in metals. He discusses all stages of the GREAT WORK. The PHILOSOPHER'S STONE, he said, must be dissolved in its own mercury to reduce it to its *PRIMA MATERIA.*

Among the spurious magical works attributed to Villanova is *De Sigillis duodecim Signorum* about the signs of the zodiac.

According to lore, Villanova died in 1314 during a storm. However, a letter written by Pope Clement V in 1311 asks for Villanova's "Treatise on Medicine," which he had promised to deliver to the pope but died before doing so.

FURTHER READING:
Waite, Arthur Edward. *Alchemists through the Ages.* Blauvelt, N.Y.: Rudolph Steiner Publications, 1970.

visualization   The use of mental imagery to realize and obtain goals. In a magical RITUAL, visualization facilitates the fulfillment of the ritual's purpose. A strong ability to visualize SIGILS, spirits and gods, SYMBOLS, and other aspects of ritual is a primary skill of the MAGICIAN.

In visualization, a mental picture of the desired result is held firmly and vividly in the mind, as if it were already real. Visualization is most effective when practiced in an altered state of consciousness, such as in meditation or in ritual, when the psychic forces of the mind flow more easily. In an altered state, the conscious mind connects with the Higher Self and aligns itself to the flow of cosmic forces in the universe.

The power of THOUGHT, IMAGINATION, and WILL to create reality has been known for centuries; it is an integral part of magical systems and religions throughout history. In modern times, visualization is a tool of psychology and is used for self-improvement, obtaining goals and healing.

In 1960 Maxwell Maltz, an American plastic surgeon, published *Pyscho-Cybernetics,* which discusses self-image psychology and the enormous influence of the imagination upon self-image. Maltz observed in his practice that plastic surgery often altered patients' self-image so that their personalities underwent positive transformations. Others whose poor self-image remained the same despite the surgery experienced little or no improvement in self-esteem.

In psychical research, mental imagery has been found to contain and convey extrasensory information, such as PRECOGNITION and telepathic messages. These skills are developed in the practice of ceremonial MAGIC.

Viviane, the Lady of the Lake   In Arthurian lore the lover of the wizard MERLIN and his most able pupil. Viviane is also called Nimue, Niviene, Eviene, or Vivienne. She served as foster mother to Sir Lancelot du Lac (of the Lake), raising him beneath the waters. Viviane gave the magical sword EXCALIBUR to King Arthur at the beginning of his reign and accepted the sword's return at the destruction of Camelot.

Origins of a Lady of the Lake go back to the Celtic goddesses Cerdwen and Brigid. The name *Viviane* or *Vivienne* derives from the Celtic *Vi-Vianna* or *Co-Viana,* which are other names for the Celtic water goddess Coventina. The Celts worshiped water deities, believing them to represent the essence of life. The spontaneous movements of the water illustrated the powers of the goddesses, nymphs, and FAIRIES that lived below the surface. Offerings to the water deities were common, especially gifts of swords and other metalware. Such practices continue today when someone throws a coin into the water and makes a wish or calls on "Lady Luck."

The sword Excalibur must have been such an offering to the water goddess. Following a battle early in his rule, King Arthur remarks to Merlin that he has no sword. Merlin confides that he knows the whereabouts of a great sword and directs Arthur's attention to a nearby lake. In the middle of the lake, a lady's arm holds a sword aloft. Presently a lovely woman rows a small boat across the lake to meet Arthur. Merlin explains that the woman is the Lady of the Lake, who comes from a place on a rock hidden in the lake's mists: in other words, Avalon. Arthur requests that the Lady give him the sword, but she demurs, saying that the sword, named Excalibur, belongs to her. But she will give it to Arthur if he will grant her a gift, which she will request at the right time. Arthur agrees to the bargain and boards a barge out to the middle of the lake where he claims the sword and scabbard, and the arm disappears.

According to the legends, Viviane returns Excalibur to Arthur after MORGAN LE FAY steals the sword and gives it to her lover, Sir Accolon of Gaul. Thwarted, Morgan throws the scabbard, which protected Arthur when he wore it, into the lake. After Mordred mortally wounds King Arthur at the Battle of Camlann, the king asks Sir Bedivere (Bedwyr or Girflet) to return Excalibur to the lake. Upon returning, however, Bedivere makes no mention of the Lady or the arm, and Arthur knows that he has not returned the sword. Ordered to try again, Sir Bedivere takes Excalibur to the lake and hurls it into the water, where the mysterious arm and hand catch it and then disappear.

As foster mother (perhaps stepmother) to Lancelot, Viviane gives the young knight the following advice: that a knight should have two hearts, one as hard as a diamond and the other as soft as wax. With his hard heart, the knight opposes treachery and cruelty, while the waxen heart allows the knight to follow people who can lead him to goodness and graciousness. Viviane also gives Lancelot a sword.

Another of Viviane's personae has been associated with Elaine, one of the three daughters of Igraine and Gorlois, duke and duchess of Cornwall and sister to Morgause and Morgan le Fay. As Elaine she is the mother of Sir Galahad, the knight who finds the Holy Grail. As Nimue she is Merlin's great love and tormentor who imprisons him in a cave or tree for many years. The name *Nimue* also relates to Mnemosyne, one of the water nymphs or Muses that gave magical swords to Perseus in Greek mythology.

FURTHER READING:
Ford, David Nash. "Excalibur: A Discussion of the Origins of King Arthur's Sword." Available online. URL: www.britannia.com/history/arthur/excalibur.html. Downloaded October 17, 2004.
"Lady of the Lake." Available online at www.angelfire.com/ma3/mythology/ladyofthelake.htm. Downloaded October 17, 2004

"Lady of the Lake." Available online. URL: http://csis.pace.edu/grendel/projs993a/arthurian/lady.htm. Downloaded October 17, 2004.
"The Lady of the Lake." Available online. URL: www.ancientspiral.com/ladylake.htm. Downloaded October 17, 2004.
"Welcome to Camelot, Home of King Arthur and His Court." Available online. URL: www.geocities.com/Athens/Acropolis/2025/art.htm. Downloaded October 17, 2004.

void of course   See MOON.

Waite, Arthur Edward (1857–1942) Author, mystic, magician, alchemist, and occultist/Arthur Edward Waite is probably best remembered as the cocreator of the popular Rider-Waite TAROT card deck. He was a member of the HERMETIC ORDER OF THE GOLDEN DAWN and was active in both ROSICRUCIANISM and FREEMASONRY.

Waite was born on October 2, 1857, in Brooklyn, New York, to Captain Charles F. Waite of the U.S. Merchant Marines and Emma Lovell, the daughter of a wealthy merchant involved in the East Indian trade. Captain Waite died at sea on September 29, 1858, leaving his wife with a baby and pregnant with their second child. After delivering Waite's sister Frederika, the three returned to London. Emma and Charles had never married, as her family objected to the match. They did not welcome her return with two illegitimate children, forcing Emma to live in the poorer sections of north and west London. As further renunciation of her parents' unyielding rejection, Emma converted to Roman Catholicism and raised her children in the faith.

Emma devoted her means to young Arthur's education, however, sending him to small private schools in North London then to St. Charles's College, a Catholic institution in Baywater. Waite worked as a clerk after graduation, writing poetry and editing a small magazine called *The Unknown World,* eventually pursuing writing and literary criticism full time. After his sister Frederika died in 1874, Waite began to spend even more time in the Library of the British Museum, reading and searching for the answers that he could not find in Catholicism. He eventually stum-

bled upon the writings of ELIPHAS LEVI and believed he had found his life's direction. In 1886 Waite published his first major work on the occult: *The Mysteries of Magic, a Digest of the Writings of Eliphas Levi.*

Waite married Ada Lakeman, known as "Lucasta," in 1883, and they had one daughter, Sybil. While at the Library Waite had met SAMUEL LIDDELL MacGREGOR MATHERS, a cofounder of the Hermetic Order of the Golden Dawn, but he did not like Mathers and was initially unimpressed with the order. However, in January 1891 Waite and Lucasta joined the order as neophytes at an initiation ceremony held in Mathers's home in Dulwich.

Waite never really agreed with Mathers; nevertheless, by April 1892 he had risen to the level of Philosophus. He left the order in 1893 but returned in 1896. By 1899 Waite had entered the Second Level of esoteric knowledge and was studying to receive the top degrees. The Golden Dawn, however, began a downward slide in 1897 with the resignation of Dr. WILLIAM WYNN WESTCOTT as head and the assumption of the order's leadership by actress Florence Farr. Controlled by Mathers from Paris and unable to manage effectively, Farr allowed standards to slip, precipitating the decline of the entire London order.

To compensate, Waite joined the Runymede Lodge of Freemasonry on September 19, 1901, becoming exalted to the degree of Holy Royal Arch on May 1, 1902. That same year he joined the *Societas Rosicruciana in Anglia.* Joining the Masons and the Rosicrucians was a canny move, as many of his new fraternal brothers had been former critics of his books and positions, and despite the internal haggling and splinter groups within Golden Dawn, Waite assumed the mantle of Grand Master in 1903.

Waite's first act as Grand Master was to change the group's name to the Order of the Independent and Rectified Rite. Many of the members objected to the name change and to Waite's preference for mysticism over MAGIC, leading to the formation of yet another group, the *Stella Matutina* (Order of the Morning Star), at the urging of poet WILLIAM BUTLER YEATS. After years of disputes, Waite dissolved what was left of the Golden Dawn in 1914.

Waite wrote more than 70 books, articles, lectures, and journal contributions during his lifetime, covering subjects from alchemy to Theosophy. He had been attracted to Theosophical philosophy early on but mistrusted the movement's founder, Madame HELENA P. BLAVATSKY. Some of his works are still in print, including *The Holy Kabbalah*, the *New Encyclopedia of Freemasonry*, and *The Book of Black Magic and of Pacts*. *The Book of Black Magic* remains one of the best examinations of magical GRIMOIRES.

He is best remembered, however, for the publication of the Rider-Waite deck of the Tarot. In 1909 Waite had published *The Key to the Tarot* and needed an illustrator for the book and cards. He persuaded artist Pamela Colman Smith, a member of the Golden Dawn, to illustrate the cards; they were the first deck to have illustrations for all 78 cards, including the Minor Arcana as well as the Major Arcana, and for using the drawings to suggest the DIVINATION meanings of the cards. Occultists embraced the deck when it appeared in 1910, and it remains a favorite Tarot deck today. Waite also popularized the 10-card Tarot divination spread entitled Celtic Cross.

By the start of World War I, Waite had separated from his wife Lucasta and lived with his secretary on Penywern Road in Earl's Court, London. He moved to Ramsgate, Kent, in 1920. Lucasta died in 1924, allowing Waite's marriage to Mary Broadbent Schofield in 1924.

Waite spent his remaining years in Kent. He died, relatively unknown, on May 19, 1942, during World War II. He is buried in the churchyard at Bishhopsbourne, where his grave is covered in a tangled growth of the deadly nightshade plant, a rather ironic ending for one whose early life as an occult celebrity ended in obscurity.

FURTHER READING:
Knowles, George. "Arthur Edward Waite." Available online. URL: www.controverscial.com/Arthur%20 Edward%20Waite.htm. Downloaded June 25, 2005.
Waite, Arthur Edward. *The Book of Black Magic and of Pacts.* 1899. Reprint, York Beach, Maine: Samuel Weiser, 1972.

wand   See TOOLS.

wanga   In Vodoun, a CURSE or HEX made with a POPPET. A *wanga* is negative and even vampiric in nature. It is used to cast an especially powerful SPELL or BEWITCHMENT that forces a person to do one's bidding, forces someone to fall in love, or causes accidents, illness, misfortune, and even death. A *wanga-mort* is a death hex, said to cause death in seven days.

Wangas are "placed" in poppets that are shapeless black or black and red dolls, the construction of which may include human hair and may be decorated with feathers. The feathers of a *frize* (owl) are considered to be the most potent and dangerous, for they represent danger, death, and destruction.

The poppets are stuffed with *poudres* (powders) made of dirt from an open grave (see GRAVEYARD DIRT), ashes from a RITUAL fire, SALT, the leaves of magical plants and herbs, cornmeal, gunpowder, flour, ground red and black pepper, and so forth. An especially lethal *poudre*, called *poudre de mort*, is made from human bone and is used in *wanga-morts*. Any *wanga* can be made even more powerful with the addition of human BLOOD or semen, both of which carry great magical powers.

Wangas are "planted" by being left in certain places in the victim's house or yard or even in a graveyard. The location depends on the nature of the hex.

Marie Laveau, the famed "Voodoo Queen" of New Orleans, was renowned for her *wangas*. One of the most potent reputedly was a bag made from the shroud of a person who had been dead nine days. Into the bag went a dried, one-eyed toad, the little finger of a black person who had committed suicide, a dried lizard, bat's wings, a cat's eyes, an owl's liver, and a rooster heart. It was hidden in bed pillows to cause victims to die. If they were mistreating their black servants, many white masters in old New Orleans found in their handbags or pillows some kind of *wanga* such as a little sack of black paper containing saffron, salt, gunpowder, and pulverized dog manure.

The results of a *wanga*—the sufferings of the victim—are called a *cambe*. A *wanga* can be broken with a counterspell or CHARM called a *piege*, which wards off evil influences.

FURTHER READING:
Pelton, Robert W. *Voodoo Secrets from A to Z.* Cranbury, N.J.: A.S. Barnes and Co., 1973.

warlock   A male sorcerer, WIZARD, or witch, especially of a malevolent nature. *Warlock* is derived from the old Anglo Saxon word, *waerloga*, which means "traitor," "deceiver," or "liar." According to lore, warlocks gained their supernatural power and knowledge through a demonic PACT. Like *wizard*, *warlock* is an outdated term.

washes   In folk MAGIC, an herb and water mixture with magical properties. Washes are applied to the floors and walls of homes, businesses, and other places to magically attract luck, money, tranquility, happiness, and other desired things. They are used to banish unwanted spirits and energies.

A wash is made with a pint of water in which herbs are steeped for several days in a dark place. As in the making of magical anointing oils and OINTMENTS, INCANTATIONS or CHARMS related to the purpose are said over the wash.

Watchtowers   In MAGIC, the four quarters of the Earth. The term *Watchtowers* was coined by JOHN DEE and EDWARD KELLY in their system of ENOCHIAN MAGIC. Dee and Kelley conceived that the four quarters of the Earth are guarded by ANGELS and ELEMENTALS.

Watchtowers are incorporated into the magical material developed by the HERMETIC ORDER OF THE GOLDEN DAWN. The Opening By Watchtower RITUAL, in which the guardians are invoked, is one of the most oft-used rituals in ceremonial MAGIC.

weapon-salve   See OINTMENTS.

wells   In occult lore, portals for spirits and the dead to enter the world, or the residences of guardian spirits. The water of certain wells is held to have magical or healing power.

Since pre-Roman times, wells have been associated with supernatural powers, used by diviners, healers, witches, and ordinary folk in the quest for various desires. In Bronze and Iron Age Europe, wells played an important role in water RITUALS and the worship of deities who were thought to live in or guard the well waters. Water, as a life source, was closely allied with fertility and healing. The Celts revered wells and erected shrines and altars at them. The Christian church absorbed many pagan beliefs about wells and replaced the deities and spirits with saints. Supernaturally endowed wells became "holy" wells.

Such wells acquired reputations for specialized powers. Some were strictly for healing, while others were for MAGIC, such as cursing (see CURSES), wishing, DIVINATION, or baptism. Some were multipurpose. Some wells were believed to be guarded by eels, DRAGONS, SERPENTS, monster fish, or vindictive spirits who had to be placated and protected, lest disaster or epidemic sweep the local population.

To invoke the powers of a well, rituals were necessary. The pilgrim usually tossed in coins, the idols of deities, pins, or other offerings while reciting PRAYERS, INCANTATIONS, or WISHES. In Ireland, it was common practice to decorate supernatural wells with yarn and ribbons, especially on certain holidays. Some magical rituals were elaborate, involving bathing in the well waters at certain hours, sacrificing animals, and circling the well a certain number of times.

One of the most renowned cursing wells was located at St. Elian's Church in Llanelian-yn-Rhos, Clwyd, Wales.

Pilgrims from all over the British Isles frequented this popular well until the late 19th century. The victim's name was written on a piece of paper, which was pierced with a crooked pin. Then the victim's initials were scratched onto a stone, which the well custodian—for a fee—tossed into the water. As long as the stone remained in the water, the curse was in effect, causing anything from aches and pains to illness to death. Victims could remove the curse by going to the well and paying the custodian a higher fee than was paid by the curser. The well was so popular that the church rector had it destroyed in the late 1800s to discourage "malicious superstition."

Methods of divination varied by well. For example, if a stone was tossed into the water, the appearance and quantity of bubbles that arose determined whether or not something would come to pass. At St. Gybi's Well in Llangybi, Gwynedd, Wales, maidens threw rags into the water to determine whether their lovers were faithful: If the rag floated south, the answer was yes; to the north, no. Other powers associated with wells are revealing the names of thieves and granting WISHES.

Supernatural wells acquired their reputations by either natural properties or by myth. Healing waters are rich in minerals, chemicals, and metals. In Celtic lore, Diancecht, the Irish god of leechcraft, treated a certain well with magical herbs that healed warriors of their wounds after they submerged themselves in the water overnight.

Other magic wells rise and fall in accordance—or in contradiction to—the tides. Some are said to be the sites where saints or kings were slain.

Witches were said to use supernatural well water in some of their charms, especially those for inflicting and curing disease. In 1622 in Eastwood, Scotland, one accused witch was said on Halloween to draw water from a well "which brides and burials passed over" for her SPELLS.

Mineral-rich wells and springs renowned for their curative powers, such as Our Lady of Lourdes in France, are still visited by thousands of hopeful pilgrims. The practice of tossing coins into fountains and making a wish is related to the ancient pagan beliefs of supernatural wells.

Westcott, William Wynn (1848–1925)   English occultist and founder of the HERMETIC ORDER OF THE GOLDEN DAWN. William Wynn Westcott was noted for his knowledge of the KABBALAH and for his translation of works by ELIPHAS LEVI.

Westcott was born on December 17, 1848, in Leamington, Warwickshire, England. His father was a physician. His parents died when he was 10 years old, and he was adopted by an uncle, who also was a physician. Westcott received a good education and graduated from University College in London with a bachelor's degree in medicine. He entered into his uncle's medical practice in Soberest. His peers described him as industrious and scholarly, with a special interest in histrionics and regalia, which may account for his interest in ceremonial MAGIC. His only relationships with women were platonic. His professional career advanced, and in the early 1881 he became deputy coroner for Hoxton. In the early 1890s he was named coroner for northeast London. Because of his professional standing, he kept his occult interests and activities secret.

In 1875 Westcott joined the Masonic Lodge at Crewkerne, England, and rose in its ranks. In 1878 he embarked on a two-year hiatus to Hendon, England, where he studied the kabbalah and other esoteric subjects. Sometime prior to 1878, he joined the ROSICRUCIANS in the Societas Rosicruciana in Anglia (S.R.I.A.), open only to high-grade FREEMASONS. In 1890 he became MAGUS of the S.R.I.A., followed by the positions of Worshipful Master of the Research Lodge and Quatuor Comati. He also joined the Theosophical Society, where he lectured, and became an honorary member of the Hermetic Society, a breakaway group that formed in 1884. The Hermetic Society may have served as the inspiration for Westcott to form his own group.

Westcott likely met SAMUEL LIDDELL MacGREGOR MATHERS at the Societas Rosicrucianas in Anglia (Rosicrucian Society in England), where they both were members, along with WILLIAM ROBERT WOODMAN. In 1887 Westcott recruited Mathers and Woodman to form the Golden Dawn, based (unknown to Mathers and Woodman) on a falsified occult legacy that probably was created by Westcott. Regardless of its origins, the Golden Dawn became, in its meteoric short life, the most influential magical order of the Western mystery tradition. Westcott's MAGICAL MOTTO was *Sapere Aude,* "dare to be wise."

Westcott became one of the three Chiefs of the Esoteric Order, and then one of the members of the Second Order.

He resigned from the Golden Dawn in 1897 when his esoteric interests became known in his professional circles and were problematic. At the same time, his falsification of documents authenticating the Golden Dawn's alleged esoteric heritage were being threatened for exposure to members and may also have influenced his decision to resign. However, he remained a member of the Rosicrucians and soon became supreme magus.

In 1918 Westcott retired from his career and moved to the Republic of South Africa, where he lived with his daughter and son-in-law. He became vice president of two lodges of the Theosophical Society there.

Westcott died in South Africa on June 30, 1925.

FURTHER READING:
Cicero, Chic, and Sandra Tabatha Cicero. *The Essential Golden Dawn.* St. Paul, Minn.: Llewellyn Publications, 2004.
"William Wynn Westcott." Available online. URL: http://www.golden-dawn.org/biowestcott.html. Downloaded June 30, 2005.

white book   A book of magical instructions and lore. A white book in principle is devoted to "good" magic and includes the names, SEALS, and characters of ANGELS. However, the distinction between a white book and a BLACK BOOK is often vague. Both types of books invoke both angels and DEMONS.

The *Key of Solomon,* the most important GRIMOIRE, provides instructions for a white book:

Make a small Book containing the Prayers for all the Operations, the Names of the Angels in the form of Litanies, their Seals and Characters; the which being done thou shalt consecrate the same unto God and unto the pure Spirits in the manner following:—

Thou shalt set in the destined place a small table covered with a white cloth, whereon thou shalt lay the Book opened at the Great Pentacle which should be drawn on the first leaf of the said Book; and having kindled a lamp which should be suspended above the center of the table, thou shalt surround the said table with a white curtain; clothe thyself in the proper vestments, and holding the Book open, repeat upon thy knees the following prayer with great humility:—

ADONAI, ELOHIM, EL, EHEIHEH ASHER, EHEIHEH, Prince of Princes, Existence of Existences, have mercy upon me, and cast Thine eyes upon Thy Servant (N.), whoe invokes Thee most devoutly, and supplictaes Thee by Thy Holy and tremendous Name Tetragrammaton to be propitious, and to order Thine Angels and Spirits to come and take up their abode in this place; O all ye Angels and Spirits of the Stars, O all ye Angels and Elementary Spirits, O all ye Spirits present before the Face of God, I the Minister and faithful Servant of the Most High conjure ye, let God Himself, the Existence of Existences, conjure ye to come and be present at this Operation, I, the Servant of God, most humbly entreat ye. Amen.

FURTHER READING:
Butler, E. M. *Ritual Magic.* Cambridge: Cambridge University Press, 1949.

Wicca   See WITCHCRAFT.

will   In MAGIC, the deliberate, organized direction of intent toward a goal. Without good execution of will, magic is not successful. Will works in equal partnership with IMAGINATION, the faculty that creates the goal.

Will not only marshals personal resources but also engages divine and supernatural forces toward manifestation. Through will, the help of spiritual entities such as ANGELS, religious figures, and spiritual masters is invoked and directed. Will commands unruly entities, such as DEMONS.

A highly concentrated will is necessary to succeed in ceremonial magic and also in the casting SPELLS. In a magical RITUAL, the magician uses TOOLS, sound, and SYMBOLS to change consciousness.

ALEISTER CROWLEY said that the projection of a magician's will should be done "without lust of result." That is, the use of will in and of itself should be done in accordance with the laws of one's own nature. Will affects a complex flow of forces in motion, working outside of time to bring desired results into being, sometimes without an obvious appearance of causality.

Celtic spells for SHAPE-SHIFTING assume that there is an underlying unity of all things in nature and that by sheer force of will, a magician can reassemble the basic factors of nature into any shape desired. Thus, the magician could focus the entire force of his will and shape-shift into another person, an animal, or even an object.

In ALCHEMY, the Red Lion is a SYMBOL of will and the highest powers of the ADEPT. The red represents perfect strength.

WILLIAM WYNN WESTCOTT, one of the founders of the HERMETIC ORDER OF THE GOLDEN DAWN, stated:

> To obtain magical power, one must strengthen the will. Let there be no confusion between will and desire. You cannot will too strongly, so do not attempt to will two things at once, and while willing one thing do not desire others.

ELIPHAS LEVIS said that "a strong and decided will can in a short space of time arrive at absolute independence." In ritual, said Levi, the will is determined by words and the words by acts. P. W. Bullock, another member of the Golden Dawn, whose occult name was Levavi Oculos, said that this state of independence is necessary to manipulate the will. He described the will as a kind of electric force that is the "executive of desire," more than the ascending of higher desires over lower desires. "It is through the agency of the will that the hidden becomes manifest, whether in the Universe or Man," said Bullock.

The magician must not be hasty or premature in the exercising of will, but must first cultivate spiritual knowledge and purity, and conquer ignorance and inner darkness. "Until we *know* we must refrain from *doing*," said FLORENCE FARR, whose Golden Dawn MAGICAL MOTTO was *Sapientia Sapienti Dona Data.*

The will should always be directed for higher spiritual purpose. To attempt to use it superficially, especially without adequate training, can result in problems. For example, it is difficult to truly control the will of another person to cause them to go against their natural tendencies. Farr said that "this once done the force you have set in motion becomes almost uncontrollable, the other individual seems sometimes to live in your presence, and the last state of that person is worse than the first."

Farr described a method for cultivating the will:

> . . . imagine your head as center of attraction with thoughts like rays radiating out in a vast globe. To want or desire a thing is the first step in the exercise of the Will; get a distinct image of the thing you desire placed, as it were, in your heart, concentrate all your wandering

rays of thought upon this image until you feel it to be one glowing scarlet ball of compacted force. Then project this concentrated force on the subject you wish to affect.

ISRAEL REGARDIE advocated yogic techniques for strengthening the will. For example, the magician chooses a minor activity and makes a commitment to not doing it for a specific period of time. It might be avoiding a commonly used word or crossing one's legs. Inadvertent violations should be punished, Regardie said, such as by cutting the arm with a razor, a practice advocated by Crowley. In that way, the will comes increasingly under conscious control. Another yogic technique is to practice *pranayama,* a regulated inhalation and exhalation of the breath that alters consciousness and energizes the body.

FURTHER READING:

Bardon, Franz. *Initiation into Hermetics: A Course of Instruction of Magic Theory and Practice.* Wuppertal, Germany: Dieter Ruggeberg, 1971.

Crowley, Aleister. *Magick in Theory and Practice.* 1929. Reprint, New York: Dover Publications, 1976.

King, Francis, (ed.). *Ritual Magic of the Golden Dawn.* Rochester, Vt.: Destiny Books, 1997.

Spence, Lewis. *The Magic Arts in Celtic Britain.* Van Nuys, Calif.: Newscastle Publishing, 1996.

Williamson, Cecil Hugh (1909–1999)

English researcher, occultist, and magical ADEPT. Cecil Williamson knew ALEISTER CROWLEY and GERALD B. GARDNER and was involved in British intelligence work during World War II to monitor Nazi activity concerning the occult. Williamson was born on September 18, 1909, in Paignton, South Devon, England. His father was in the Royal Navy and Fleet Air Arm. Williamson's interest in the occult was stimulated by incidents involving WITCHCRAFT. At age six, he witnessed an old woman reputed to be a witch being stripped of her clothing and beaten in North Bovey, Devonshire. He tried to defend her and was beaten himself. The grateful woman taught him about witches. Five years later, Williamson experienced his own magical power. He met an odd, elderly woman who taught him how to cast a SPELL against a boy who was bullying him at school. The bully soon had a skiing accident that left him crippled and unable to return to school.

For the remainder of his life, Williamson was involved in occult and magical activities. He worked with mediums and psychics in London. After graduating from Malvern College in Worcestershire, he was sent by his father to Rhodesia to learn the tobacco trade. His houseboy there was Zandonda, a retired witch doctor who taught him African magical skills.

In 1930 Williamson returned to London and went into production work for film studios. He collected information and artifacts related to folk MAGIC and witchcraft. In

1933 he married makeup artist Gwen Wilcox, niece of film producer and director Herbert Wilcox.

In 1938 he agreed to help the MI6 intelligence section of the Foreign Office collect information about Nazi occult interests. He founded the Witchcraft Research Centre as a cover for his activities. He identified and monitored high-ranking Nazis who were interested in ASTROLOGY, PROPHECY, NOSTRADAMUS, graphology, and so on. He played an instrumental role in using phony Nostradamus predictions to lure Rudolf Hess to Scotland. The predictions were planted in an old book in France that was made to find its way to Hess, who was arrested in Scotland.

Williamson took part in a famous "witches' ritual" to curse Adolf Hitler and prevent his forces from invading England. He said that the RITUAL, staged in Ashdown Forest, Crowbourgh, Sussex, was a hoax to fool Hitler. Crowley and Crowley's son, Amado, were part of the operation.

After the war ended, Williamson opened a witchcraft museum in Stratford-on-Avon. Public hostility caused him to move to Castletown on the Isle of Man, where in 1949 he opened the Folklore Centre of Superstition and Witchcraft and Witches Kitchen restaurant at the Witches Mill. He filled the center with the numerous magical objects and TOOLS he had collected over the years. He was renowned as a "witchcraft consultant" who could cast effective spells and make magical POPPETS.

He met Gardner in 1946 at the famous Atlantis occult bookshop in London. The two had an uneasy relationship—Williamson had a low opinion of Gardner—and their relationship eventually ended on bad terms. He took Gardner to meet with Crowley on several occasions. Crowley also did not care for Gardner and considered him a poor student of magic. Nonetheless, he gave Gardner magical material, which Gardner used in fashioning his witchcraft rites and tradition. The last time Williamson saw Crowley was in 1946, when Crowley was ill and living in Hastings. Williamson brought Gardner, who wanted to mend his relationship with Crowley. Crowley was wary and later privately warned Williamson to be careful of Gardner.

In 1952 Williamson sold his buildings on the Isle of Man to Gardner and took his collection to England, finally settling in Boscastle, Cornwall. In 1996 he sold the Museum of Witchcraft to Graham King and retired to Witheridge, Tiverton, in Devon. In April 1999, Williamson suffered a severe stroke and was permanently impaired, including his ability to speak and recognize others. He was moved to a nursing home in South Moulton. He died on December 9, 1999, not long after his 90th birthday.

During his life, Williamson amassed a huge database on witchcraft and magic for his Witchcraft Research Centre. According to his records, between 1930 and 1997, he took part as a spectator or operative in 1,120 witchcraft cases that produced beneficial results, and he had known, met with, and been taught by 82 wise women.

Crowley had always advised Williamson not to join any particular lodge, group, or order; because Williamson followed this advice, he could move with more freedom in magical circles. He said he valued folk witches as providing social and healing services to the masses, but he was critical of modern witches and pagans for knowing little about real magic and for "being nonproductive of results."

Crowley once offered Williamson his BAPHOMET magical ring for his museum but pawned it instead. Williamson redeemed it and gave it back to Crowley, but Crowley insisted that Williamson keep it. Williamson said he neutralized the magical power imbued into the ring.

FURTHER READING:
Guiley, Rosemary Ellen. *The Encyclopedia of Witches and Witchcraft.* 2nd ed. New York: Facts On File Inc., 1999.

wish   A simple form of MAGIC. A wish is not fanciful thinking but an intention that, if projected strongly enough, can set cosmic and supernatural forces in motion. Making wishes is not as structured as casting a SPELL, though certain observances should be made for best results.

Wishes are a common feature in folk and fairy tales. Usually a person is granted wishes—especially three (see NUMBERS)—by a spirit, a god, a magical animal, or even the devil. Sometimes wishes are obtained through a magical book. A lesson of some of these tales is that one must be careful what one wishes for. Wishes that are not well-thought out or correctly spoken will backfire.

Folklore provides the best timing and circumstances for making wishes on one's own. The most auspicious times to make wishes are:

- the night of the new crescent MOON
- the night of the full moon
- whenever a falling star is seen
- any Monday, the day ruled by the Moon
- birthdays
- anniversaries of significant events
- the changing of the seasons, marked by the equinoxes and solstices (March 21, June 21, September 21, and December 21)
- the appearance of rainbows, a sign of good fortune

Wishes should be stated three times to make them manifest. Lore also holds that wishes should never be divulged to others, for they then will not come to pass.

Ill Wishing

Ill wishing is a CURSE that is often made spontaneously in the heat of anger or deliberately due to resentment or envy. If two people argue and one soon suffers misfortune or illness, the other party may be blamed for ill wishing. Remarks such as "You'll be sorry" is a form of ill wishing. If someone enjoys good fortune or prosperity and then suffers a setback, they might believe themselves to be the victim of the secret ill-wishing of envious neighbors.

A widespread belief holds that wishing for a person's death makes one guilty of murder if that person dies. A 19th-century account of explorations in Africa relates how 60 wives of the late son of a king drank poison for wishing the son dead. Thirty-one of them died, thus proving thmselves guilty for ill wishing to their community. The 29 survivors vomited upon consuming the poison, which probably saved their lives.

Like other curses, ill wishing can be broken magically with a counter SPELL or CHARM.

See also BLASTING; HEX.

FURTHER READING:
Guiley, Rosemary Ellen. *Angel Magic for Love and Romance*. Lakewood, Minn.: Galde Press, 2005.

witchcraft A type of SORCERY. Beliefs about witchcraft are universal, but there is no universal definition of *witchcraft*. It involves the magical manipulation of supernormal forces through the casting of SPELLS and the conjuring or invoking of spirits. In most societies, witchcraft is considered a harmful branch of sorcery, with witches usually casting CURSES, HEXES, BEWITCHMENTS, and so forth. Witchcraft skills can be taught; some powers are said to be hereditary.

Anthropologists also define witchcraft as an innate condition involving the use of malevolent power by psychic means without need for RITUAL or CHARM. Witchcraft also involves the use of supernormal powers, such as INVISIBILITY, SHAPE-SHIFTING, flying, ability to kill at a distance, CLAIRVOYANCE, and ASTRAL PROJECTION.

Witchcraft was especially feared during the Middle Ages and during the Inquisition. In 1484 the Catholic Church—in a bull issued by Pope Innocent VIII—declared witchcraft to be a heresy, thus enabling inquisitors to persecute effectively any enemy of the church. The charge of witchcraft was nearly impossible to refute, and the accused usually were severely tortured until they confessed to having FAMILIARS, worshiping the devil, having sex with DEMONS, and casting malevolent spells. Witch hunting became a profitable pursuit and an easy way to take revenge on one's enemies. In the 16th century, the Protestant Reformation continued the campaign against witches; Martin Luther called them "the Devil's whores." The witch hysteria affected Europe, England, and America. It died down by the end of the 18th century, but prejudices against witches and fears of their malevolent powers remained. Nonetheless, "folk witches," people who possess magical skills especially for healing, fertility, luck, and DIVINATION, continued to function especially in rural areas. "White witchcraft"—good magic—flourished from the 18th century on.

The stain of the Inquisition was impossible to remove, however, and many people still perceived a "witch" as a malevolent person in league with the devil, and antiwitch sentiment continued. In England, Europe, and even America, there were outbreaks of violence against suspected witches all through the 19th century and into the early 20th century. The violence sometimes was turned on white witches whose magic failed to work. Stories in the press spread tales, about witches, magical charms, and rumors of nocturnal meetings in forests.

Wicca
After World War II, witchcraft was reinvented as a religion, a movement that started in England and gained popularity through the efforts of GERALD B. GARDNER and others. Gardner followed the work of British anthropologist Margaret A. Murray, who in the 1920s and 1930s had claimed that witchcraft comprised the remnants of an "Old Religion" based on pagan beliefs and practices centered around the Horned God, a Panlike deity. Gardner claimed to be initiated by a coven of "hereditary witches," followers of the Old Religion. He feared that Witchcraft—spelled with a capital W to distinguish it as a religion, not a sorcery—was in danger of dying out due to a lack of young members. He said his fellow witches had given him a framework of rituals, including INITIATIONS. He obtained additional rituals from ALEISTER CROWLEY, whom he met in 1946. Gardner never acknowledged Crowley's exact influence.

After the repeal of Britain's Witchcraft Act in 1951—which made witchcraft legal—Gardner formed his own coven. To flesh out his rituals, Gardner borrowed additional material from ritual magic practiced by such orders as the HERMETIC ORDER OF THE GOLDEN DAWN, the Freemasons, and the Rosicrucians, as well as sex magic rituals from the ORDO TEMPLI ORIENTIS, of which Crowley had been a leader in England. Gardner also mixed in Eastern mysticism and MAGIC. In 1953 he initiated Doreen Valiente, with whom he collaborated in writing and revising the rituals. Valiente deleted some of the OTO and Crowley influences and infused the rituals with an emphasis on Goddess. "Ancient Craft laws" and ethics—showing a Christian moral influence—were composed. The religion of Witchcraft was dedicated to good magic. Its main tenet, called the Wiccan Rede, "An' it harm none, do what thou will," reflects Crowley's tenet from *The Book of the Law*: "Do what thou wilt is the whole of the law." In other words, Witchcraft was meant to be used spiritually and magically for benefit, not for harm. (It was a good theory, but in practice, magical wars have been fought among witches as well as among magicians.)

The religion of Witchcraft was an immediate sensation and attracted adherents around the world. Murray's theory of the unbroken existence of an Old Religion was disproved, but did not discourage potential initiates from joining covens. For many, the new religion was a refreshing change from traditional faiths. The element of magical skills, taught to initiates, was especially appealing. Witchcraft itself split and divided into specialized traditions emphasizing different mythologies.

The word *witchcraft* proved to be problematic, however; the public and media were not willing to distinguish Witchcraft the white magic religion from witchcraft the malevolent, demonic sorcery. By the end of the 20th century, more witches were calling themselves Wiccans and their religion Wicca. *Wicca* is an Old English term for "witch." *Wiccian* means "to work sorcery" and "to bewitch."

Wicca continues to grow and evolve, a collection of religious traditions that reinvent themselves through reinterpretation of pagan customs, ritual magic, folk magic, and mainstream religious beliefs.

FURTHER READING:

Guiley, Rosemary Ellen. *The Encyclopedia of Witches and Witchcraft.* 2d ed. New York: Facts On File Inc., 1999.

Russell, Jeffrey Burton. *A History of Witchcraft.* London: Thames & Hudson, 1980.

witches' garland   See KNOTS.

wizard   A male witch or sorcerer. *Wizard* carries a negative meaning: The word comes from the Middle English terms *wys,* or "wise," and the suffix *ard,* which connotes "someone who does something to excess or who is discreditable." *Wizard* especially was originally used to describe men who were wonder workers or who produced illusions; they were often lumped in with "witches and necromancers."

Wizard continued in negative usage and was often applied to magicians who cast enchantments or who were believed to be in league with the devil. Nathaniel Hawthorne captured the essence of popular opinion of wizards in his fictional story, "Anne Donne's Appeal" (1835), in which he described a wizard as "a small, grey, withered man, with fiendish ingenuity in devising evil, and superhuman power to execute it, but senseless as an idiot and feebler than a child to all better purposes."

The term is seldom used in modern practices of magic. It has been rehabilitated in fiction, such as in the stories of HARRY POTTER and *LORD OF THE RINGS,* in which wizards possess magical skills and wisdom but are not necessarily evil in nature.

FURTHER READING:

Maxwell-Stuart, P. G. *Wizards: A History.* Stroud, England: Tempus Publishing Ltd., 2004.

Woodman, William Robert (1828–1891)   English occultist and a founder of the HERMETIC ORDER OF THE GOLDEN DAWN. William Robert Woodman is probably the least known among the early Golden Dawn principals, perhaps because he died before the order reached its zenith of power. Little has been written about him, despite the fact that he was active in ROSICRUCIANISM and authored numerous articles on Rosicrucian studies.

Woodman was born in England in 1828. He studied medicine in London and became a physician in 1851, practicing in Victoria Villas, Stoke Newington, outside of London. His occult interests attracted him to FREEMASONRY, and he became a Master Mason. He joined the Rosicrucian Society of England (Societas Rosicruciana in Anglia) when it was formed in 1866. The society was open only to Master Masons. In 1867 Woodman became secretary, and in 1878 he became Supreme Magus. He coedited a Rosicrucian magazine with R. W. Little, his predecessor as Supreme Magus.

In the Rosicrucian Society, Woodman met fellow members WILLIAM WYNN WESTCOTT and SAMUEL LIDDELL MacGREGOR MATHERS, with whom he shared interests in ceremonial MAGIC, ALCHEMY, and the KABBALAH. He became a mentor to the much younger Westcott.

When Westcott conceived the idea for the formation of the Golden Dawn in 1897, he enlisted the help of Woodman and Mathers. In particular, Woodman brought a desired air of respectable Victorian establishment to the new group. By then, Woodman was retired from his medical practice. With Mathers and Westcott, he was one of the three founding Chiefs of the Esoteric Order. His MAGICAL MOTTO was *Magna Est Veritas Et Praelavebit,* "Great is the Truth and it shall prevail."

Woodman stayed in the background of the emerging Golden Dawn due to his poor health and distance from London. He died in 1891 before the Second Order of the Golden Dawn was established and before the eruption of scandal and internal politics that ultimately led to the organization's downfall.

FURTHER READING:

"Dr. W. Robert Woodman." Available online. URL: http://www.golden-dawn.org/biowoodman.html. Downloaded June 29, 2005.

Yeats, William Butler (1865–1939)   Irish poet, playwright, Nobel prize winner, and member of the HERMETIC ORDER OF THE GOLDEN DAWN.

William Butler Yeats was born in Sandymount near Dublin on June 13, 1865, to a family with deeply divided religious beliefs. Yeats's grandfather was a devout Anglican, an orthodox rector in the Church of England, while his father was a skeptic. With no clear religious direction provided to him early in life, Yeats followed his natural interests to occultism, mysticism, and Eastern religions and philosophies. He spent some of his childhood in Sligo, Ireland, where he became fascinated by Irish tales of ghosts and FAIRIES. He studied in both Ireland and London.

As a young adult, he became intensely interested in black magic and devil worship, which prompted him to read widely in occult literature. He described one black magic RITUAL he attended in a darkened, small back room. The presiding magician, clad in a black hooded robe, sat at a table bearing a censer (see TOOLS), a skull decorated with magical SYMBOLS, crossed daggers, an empty bowl, a book, and tools that resembled grinding stones. A black cockerel had its throat slit, and its BLOOD drained into the bowl. The magician read an INVOCATION. For what seemed like a long time, said Yeats, nothing happened. Then the various magicians present exclaimed that they were seeing visions in the room: a great moving SERPENT, a ghostly monk, and moving black and white pillars. Yeats saw nothing, but felt a heavy oppression in the air, as though psychic black clouds were gathering about him in a threatening manner. Yeats felt in danger of being entranced by something evil. With great mental effort, he vanquished the clouds and asked for the lights to be turned on. After an EXORCISM, he felt better.

In 1885, Yeats was instrumental in the formation of the Hermetic Society in Dublin and presided over its first meeting. (The Dublin society was not affiliated with the Hermetic Society formed in London, which was associated with the Theosophical Society.)

In 1888, he joined the THEOSOPHICAL SOCIETY and met MADAME HELENA P. BLAVATSKY. When Blavatsky established the Esoteric Section of the society for members who wanted to learn the principles of MAGIC, he was among the first to join. But the section's dismal track record in magical experiments discouraged Yeats.

In 1890, Yeats joined the Golden Dawn and took the MAGICAL MOTTO *Demon est Deus Inversus* ("The devil is the reverse of God"), a reflection of his deep interest in the diabolic. He was much happier with the Golden Dawn's Western occultism, rather than the Eastern approach advocated by Blavatsky. He was especially impressed with the magical ability of SAMUEL LIDDELL MacGREGOR MATHERS, one of the three founders—although later he referred to Mathers as "unhinged" and "half lunatic, half knave."

Yeats became embroiled in the turmoil stirred up by ALEISTER CROWLEY, who was told by ALLAN BENNETT that he (Crowley) was under PSYCHIC ATTACK from Yeats because Yeats was jealous of his superior ability as a poet. Crowley and Bennett responded with a defensive psychic attack. Yeats was head of the Second Order when Crowley attempted to take control in 1900, and he called in the police to have Crowley removed from the premises of the

London temple. However, Yeats was unable to stop the disintegration of the troubled organization, and in 1901 he resigned from his position. He maintained an association with the Golden Dawn for another 20 or so years.

By his own account Yeats's interests in MAGIC and mysticism had a profound influence on his writing. He compiled a book on fairies, *Irish Fairy and Folk Tales* (1892). He took an interest in Spiritualism and lectured at the London Spiritual Alliance.

Yeats's accomplishments in the literary world are numerous. His first published work, the play *Mosada,* appeared in 1886. He was a founder of the Rhymers' Club in London and was a major figure in the establishment of the Irish Literary Theater in 1899. He served in the Irish Senate from 1922 to 1928. In 1923 he was awarded the Nobel Prize for literature.

Yeats was a great admirer of the actress and occultist FLORENCE FARR and wrote plays with her intended as the lead actress. He was married late in life, in 1917, to Georgia Hyde Lees. After they were wed, Yeats discovered that Georgia had mediumistic abilities and could do automatic writing.

Yeats died in Roquebrune on the French Riviera near Monaco on January 28, 1939. He was buried there, and nine years later his remains were moved to Drumcliffe, near Sligo.

FURTHER READING:

King, Francis. *Megatherion: The Magickal World of Aleister Crowley.* New York: Creation Books, 2004.

"William Butler Yeats." Available online. URL: http://www. goden-dawn.org/bioyeats.html. Downloaded June 29, 2005.

Yeats, William Butler. *Autobiography.* New York: Macmillan, 1938.

Zachaire, Denis (b. 1510) French alchemist who left behind a detailed autobiographical account of his alchemical adventures and his alleged discovery of the PHILOSOPHER'S STONE. In all likelihood, however, he died in extreme poverty.

Denis Zachaire is a pseudonym; the real name of the alchemist is not known. He writes in *The True Natural Philosophy of Metals* that he was born in 1510 to a family with old blood lines in Guienne. He went to Bordeaux to study with a tutor. The tutor, Zachaire said, was obsessed with finding the secret of transmutation and caused him to become obsessed with it as well. Zachaire's account provides a portrait of how numerous aspiring alchemists wasted their time, money and lives pursuing the secrets of making gold.

> I received from home the sum of two hundred crowns for the expenses of myself and master; but before the end of the year, all our money went away in the smoke of our furnaces. My master, at the same time, died of a fever, brought on by the parching heat of our laboratory, from which he seldom or never stirred, and which was scarcely less hot than the arsenal of Venice. His death was the more unfortunate for me, as my parents took the opportunity of reducing my allowance, and sending me only sufficient for my board and lodging, instead of the sum I required to continue my operations in alchymy.
>
> To meet this difficulty and get out of leading-strings, I returned home at the age of twenty-five, and mortgaged part of my property for four hundred crowns. This sum

was necessary to perform an operation of the science, which had been communicated to me by an Italian at Toulouse, and who, as he said, had proved its efficacy. I retained this man in my service, that we might see the end of the experiment. I then, by means of strong distillations, tried to calcinate gold and silver; but all my labour was in vain. The weight of the gold I drew out of my furnace was diminished by one-half since I put it in, and my four hundred crowns were very soon reduced to two hundred and thirty. I gave twenty of these to my Italian, in order that he might travel to Milan, where the author of the receipt resided, and ask him the explanation of some passages which we thought obscure. I remained at Toulouse all the winter, in the hope of his return; but I might have remained there till this day if I had waited for him, for I never saw his face again.

> In the succeeding summer there was a great plague, which forced me to quit the town. I did not, however, lose sight of my work. I went to Cahors, where I remained six months, and made the acquaintance of an old man, who was commonly known to the people as 'the Philosopher;' a name which, in country places, is often bestowed upon people whose only merit is, that they are less ignorant than their neighbours. I showed him my collection of alchymical receipts, and asked his opinion upon them. He picked out ten or twelve of them, merely saying that they were better than the others. When the plague ceased, I returned to Toulouse, and recommenced my experiments in search of the stone. I worked to such effect that my four hundred crowns were reduced to one hundred and seventy.

That I might continue my work on a safer method, I made acquaintance, in 1537, with a certain Abbe, who resided in the neighbourhood. He was smitten with the same mania as myself, and told me that one of his friends, who had followed to Rome in the retinue of the Cardinal d'Armagnac, had sent him from that city a new receipt, which could not fail to transmute iron and copper, but which would cost two hundred crowns. I provided half this money, and the Abbe the rest; and we began to operate at our joint expense. As we required spirits of wine for our experiment, I bought a tun of excellent vin de Gaillac. I extracted the spirit, and rectified it several times. We took a quantity of this, into which we put four marks of silver, and one of gold, that had been undergoing the process of calcination for a month. We put this mixture cleverly into a sort of horn-shaped vessel, with another to serve as a retort; and placed the whole apparatus upon our furnace, to produce congelation. This experiment lasted a year; but, not to remain idle, we amused ourselves with many other less important operations. We drew quite as much profit from these as from our great work.

The whole of the year 1537 passed over without producing any change whatever: in fact, we might have waited till doomsday for the congelation of our spirits of wine. However, we made a projection with it upon some heated quicksilver; but all was in vain. Judge of our chagrin, especially of that of the Abbe, who had already boasted to all the monks of his monastery, that they had only to bring the large pump which stood in a corner of the cloister, and he would convert it into gold; but this ill luck did not prevent us from persevering. I once more mortgaged my paternal lands for four hundred crowns, the whole of which I determined to devote to a renewal of my search for the great secret. The Abbe contributed the same sum; and, with these eight hundred crowns, I proceeded to Paris, a city more abounding with alchymists than any other in the world, resolved never to leave it until I had either found the philosopher's stone, or spent all my money. This journey gave the greatest offence to all my relations and friends, who, imagining that I was fitted to be a great lawyer, were anxious that I should establish myself in that profession. For the sake of quietness, I pretended, at last, that such was my object.

After travelling for fifteen days, I arrived in Paris, on the 9th of January 1539. I remained for a month, almost unknown; but I had no sooner begun to frequent the amateurs of the science, and visited the shops of the furnace-makers, than I had the acquaintance of more than a hundred operative alchymists, each of whom had a different theory and a different mode of working. Some of them preferred cementation; others sought the universal alkahest, or dissolvent; and some of them boasted the great efficacy of the essence of emery. Some of them endeavoured to extract mercury from other metals to fix it afterwards; and, in order that each of us should be thoroughly acquainted with the proceedings of the others, we agreed to meet somewhere every night, and report progress. We met sometimes at the house of one, and sometimes in the garret of another; not only on week days, but on Sundays, and the great festivals of the Church. 'Ah!' one used to say, 'if I had the means of recommencing this experiment, I should do something.' 'Yes,' said another, 'if my crucible had not cracked, I should have succeeded before now:' while a third exclaimed, with a sigh, 'If I had but had a round copper vessel of sufficient strength, I would have fixed mercury with silver.' There was not one among them who had not some excuse for his failure; but I was deaf to all their speeches. I did not want to part with my money to any of them, remembering how often I had been the dupe of such promises.

A Greek at last presented himself; and with him I worked a long time uselessly upon nails, made of cinnabar, or vermilion. I was also acquainted with a foreign gentleman newly arrived in Paris, and often accompanied him to the shops of the goldsmiths, to sell pieces of gold and silver, the produce, as he said, of his experiments. I stuck closely to him for a long time, in the hope that he would impart his secret. He refused for a long time, but acceded, at last, on my earnest entreaty, and I found that it was nothing more than an ingenious trick. I did not fail to inform my friend, the Abbe, whom I had left at Toulouse, of all my adventures; and sent him, among other matters, a relation of the trick by which this gentleman pretended to turn lead into gold. The Abbe still imagined that I should succeed at last, and advised me to remain another year in Paris, where I had made so good a beginning. I remained there three years; but, notwithstanding all my efforts, I had no more success than I had had elsewhere.

I had just got to the end of my money, when I received a letter from the Abbe, telling me to leave everything, and join him immediately at Toulouse. I went accordingly, and found that he had received letters from the King of Navarre (grandfather of Henry IV). This Prince was a great lover of philosophy, full of curiosity, and had written to the Abbe, that I should visit him at Pau; and that he would give me three or four thousand crowns, if I would communicate the secret I had learned from the foreign gentleman. The Abbe's ears were so tickled with the four thousand crowns, that he let me have no peace, night or day, until he had fairly seen me on the road to Pau. I arrived at that place in the month of May 1542. I worked away, and succeeded, according to the receipt I had obtained. When I had finished, to the satisfaction of the King, he gave me the reward that I expected. Although he was willing enough to do me further service, he was dissuaded from it by the lords of his court; even by many of those who had been most anxious that I should come. He sent me then about my business, with many thanks; saying, that if there was anything in his kingdom which he could give me—such as the produce of confiscations, or the like—he should be most happy. I thought I might stay long enough for these prospective confiscations, and never get them at last; and I therefore determined to go back to my friend, the Abbe.

I learned, that on the road between Pau and Toulouse, there resided a monk, who was very skilful in all matters of natural philosophy. On my return, I paid him a visit. He pitied me very much, and advised me, with much warmth and kindness of expression, not to amuse myself any longer with such experiments as these, which were all false and sophistical; but that I should read the good books of the old philosophers, where I might not only find the true matter of the science of alchymy, but learn also the exact order of operations which ought to be followed. I very much approved of this wise advice; but, before I acted upon it, I went back to my Abbe, of Toulouse, to give him an account of the eight hundred crowns, which we had had in common; and, at the same time, share with him such reward as I had received from the King of Navarre. If he was little satisfied with the relation of my adventures since our first separation, he appeared still less satisfied when I told him I had formed a resolution to renounce the search for the philosopher's stone. The reason was, that he thought me a good artist. Of our eight hundred crowns, there remained but one hundred and seventy-six. When I quitted the Abbe, I went to my own house, with the intention of remaining there, till I had read all the old philosophers, and of then proceeding to Paris.

I arrived in Paris on the day after All Saints, of the year 1546, and devoted another year to the assiduous study of great authors. Among others, the 'Turba Philosophorum' of the 'Good Trevisan,' 'The Remonstance of Nature to the wandering Alchymist,' by Jean de Meung; and several others of the best books: but, as I had no right' principles, I did not well know what course to follow.

At last I left my solitude; not to see my former acquaintances, the adepts and operators, but to frequent the society of true philosophers. Among them I fell into still greater uncertainties; being, in fact, completely bewildered by the variety of operations which they showed me. Spurred on, nevertheless, by a sort of frenzy or inspiration, I threw myself into the works of Raymond Lulli and of Arnold de Villeneuve. The reading of these, and the reflections I made upon them, occupied me for another year, when I finally determined on the course I should adopt. I was obliged to wait, however, until I had mortgaged another very considerable portion of my patrimony. This business was not settled until the beginning of Lent, 1549, when I commenced my operations. I laid in a stock of all that was necessary, and began to work the day after Easter. It was not, however, without some disquietude and opposition from my friends who came about me; one asking me what I was going to do, and whether I had not already spent money enough upon such follies. Another assured me that, if I bought so much charcoal, I should strengthen the suspicion already existing, that I was a coiner of base money. Another advised me to purchase some place in the magistracy, as I was already a Doctor of Laws. My relations spoke in terms still more annoying to me, and even threatened that, if I continued to make such a fool of myself, they would send a posse of police-officers into my house,

and break all my furnaces and crucibles into atoms. I was wearied almost to death by this continued persecution; but I found comfort in my work and in the progress of my experiment, to which I was very attentive, and which went on bravely from day to day. About this time, there was a dreadful plague in Paris, which interrupted all intercourse between man and man, and left me as much to myself as I could desire. I soon had the satisfaction to remark the progress and succession of the three colours which, according to the philosophers, always prognosticate the approaching perfection of the work. I observed them distinctly, one after the other; and next year, being Easter Sunday, 1550, I made the great trial. Some common quicksilver, which I put into a small crucible on the fire, was, in less than an hour, converted into very good gold. You may judge how great was my joy, but I took care not to boast of it. I returned thanks to God for the favour he had shown me, and prayed that I might only be permitted to make such use of it as would redound to his glory.

On the following day, I went towards Toulouse to find the Abbe, in accordance with a mutual promise that we should communicate our discoveries to each other. On my way, I called in to see the sage monk who had assisted me with his counsels; but I had the sorrow to learn that they were both dead. After this, I would not return to my own home, but retired to another place, to await one of my relations whom I had left in charge of my estate. I gave him orders to sell all that belonged to me, as well movable as immovable—to pay my debts with the proceeds, and divide all the rest among those in any way related to me who might stand in need of it, in order that they might enjoy some share of the good fortune which had befallen me. There was a great deal of talk in the neighbourhood about my precipitate retreat; the wisest of my acquaintance imagining that, broken down and ruined by my mad expenses, I sold my little remaining property that I might go and hide my shame in distant countries.

My relative already spoken of rejoined me on the 1st of July, after having performed all the business I had intrusted him with. We took our departure together, to seek a land of liberty. We first retired to Lausanne, in Switzerland, when, after remaining there for some time, we resolved to pass the remainder of our days in some of the most celebrated cities of Germany, living quietly and without splendour.

Most likely, Zachaire ended his days in poverty. Beyond this account, nothing further is known of his life, and his real name has never yet been discovered.

FURTHER READING:
Mackay, Charles. *Extraordinary Popular Delusions and the Madness of Crowds*. New York: Farrar, Straus & Giroux, 1932.

zombie   A person believed to be dead who has been "returned" to life, albeit in a very diminished state, through black MAGIC. Usually associated with Haitian Vodoun, the zombie blindly serves the sorcerer, or *bokor,* who made him or her. Zombies are physically identical to humans but have no conscious experience.

Fact or Fiction?

Folk tales about the "undead" or revenants—VAMPIRES, zombies, and other creatures of the night—have circulated for centuries. But the idea of bringing a human being back from the other side as an unthinking servant inspired particular fascination and dread among the black slaves of Haiti, who told stories of similar victims in their African homelands. The word itself most likely comes from the Congo word *nzambi,* which means "the spirit of a dead person." Several claimed to have seen one or to know of one, but no proof existed other than the likelihood that the secret societies—outlaws descended from bands of former slaves that hid in the mountains and intimidated the citizenry through the trappings of Vodoun and outright crime—were capable of anything.

Academics endlessly debated the possibility of the existence of what they called "philosophical zombies." In 1937 author Zora Neale Hurston was traveling in Haiti, collecting material for a book, when she heard about Felicia Felix-Mentor, who had died at age 29 in 1907. Yet 30 years later, villagers swore to Hurston that they had seen her walking the streets with a dazed expression. Hurston heard rumors that powerful drugs were involved but was unsuccessful in learning any hard facts. She speculated that if science ever were to unravel the mystery of zombie creation, that drugs would indeed be more influential than darkly dramatic ceremonies.

In 1982 a young Canadian ethnobotanist from Harvard named Wade Davis went to Haiti to try to prove his theory about the "zombi," as he preferred to spell it: that the creature only seemed dead, probably through the administration of powerful drugs, and was technically buried alive and then later disinterred. He interviewed two people, a man named Clairvius Narcisse and a woman who called herself Ti Femme, who claimed that they had died, witnessed their own burials, and then watched as the Vodoun *bokor* brought them back to life. Davis spent months in Haiti, undertaking a dangerous study of the *houngans* and *mambos* (priests and priestesses), observing ceremonies and talking to villagers, doctors, and government officials before confirming his suspicions—and Hurston's.

What Davis discovered was that zombies are made by the ingestion of highly toxic drugs either in the victim's food or through an open cut or wound. Chief among these poisons is *toxin tetrodotoxin* (TTX), or puffer fish poison. Puffer fish, of the species *Sphoeroides testudineus,* is considered a delicacy in Japan called *fugu,* but only certain parts are edible. Preparers must be certified by the government to serve *fugu,* and consumers tend to be reckless young men trying to prove their infallibility.

A tiny drop of tetrodotoxin kills instantly, but the poison exhibits two unusual characteristics: If the victim receives a less than fatal dose, his or her condition mimics death so closely that a doctor cannot tell the difference; yet full recovery is possible. The body becomes completely paralyzed, the eyes glaze over, and there is no organ response. Eerily, those few who survive report that they were aware inside their heads what was happening but could not communicate their state in any way. If a Japanese dinner guest appears poisoned from *fugu,* he or she remains hospitalized for three days to see if he or she will recover.

Making a Zombie

Convinced that he had proved making a zombie was not only possible but a reality, Davis analyzed the ingredients of the concoction:

First, the *bokor* buries a poisonous bouga toad (*Bufo marinus*) and a sea snake in a jar until they "die from rage"—in other words, the toad secretes venom in desperation. Next the sorcerer mixes ground millipedes and tarantulas with various plants and seeds, including *tcha-tcha* seeds from the *Albizzia lebbeck* tree to cause pulmonary swelling; consigne seeds from a type of mahogany tree with no known poisonous attributes; leaves from the cashew nut tree (*Anacardium occidentale*); and leaves from the *bresillet* (*Comocladia glabra*). The *bresillet* and cashew both come from the family of poison ivy and cause severe dermatitis. The *bokor* grinds these plant and animal products into a powder, places them in a jar, and then buries the jar for two days.

Next the preparer adds ground *tremblador* and *desmembre* (plants Davis could not identify) and four plants that also cause dermatitis: *maman guepes* (*Urera baccifera*) and *mashasha* (*Dalechampia scandens*), both members of the stinging nettle family, and *Dieffenbachia seguine* (dumbcane) and *bwa pine* (*Zanthoxylum matinicense*). The hollow hairs on the surface of *maman* and *mashasha* act as syringes, injecting formic acid into the skin. Eating the dumbcane's leaves is like swallowing ground glass, making breathing difficult and speaking nearly impossible. During the 18th and 19th centuries, masters forced their slaves to eat dumbcane to keep them mute. *Bwa pine* has sharp spines. Putting these agents into the victim's food assures that the poisons will enter the bloodstream.

To complete the recipe, the *bokor* now adds the skins of white tree frogs that have been ground with two species of tarantulas and then combined with a second bouga toad. Ground human skulls give the powder a dramatic touch. Finally the puffer fish, from four species (*Spheoroides testudineus, Sphoeroides spengleri, Diodon hystrix,* and *Diodon holacanthus*) complete the diabolical mixture.

After the *bokor* raises the victim from the tomb, he feeds the zombie a concoction of cane sugar, sweet potato, and *Datura stramonium* ("zombie's cucumber") which causes hallucinations and disorientation. The *bokor* announces the victim's new zombie name, and the victim, drugged and confused, follows the *bokor* to do his bidding.

While detailed knowledge and proficiency with poison is paramount to the success of zombification, the *bokor* also relies on the *belief* in zombies by the people for the spell to work. Just as frightening—and effective—is a "zombie astral," or a soul captured by the *bokor* and enslaved to serve him. Haitians believe that the soul—the *ti bon ange*, or "little good angel"—hovers over the body for seven days after death and is vulnerable to the *bokor's* magic. How the sorcerer takes the soul is unclear.

No antidote exists for zombie poison, but Vodoun practitioners claim that a cocktail made of various plants, the liquor clairin, ammonia, and lemon juice will work. Others swear by a combination of mothballs, seawater, perfume, rock salt, and a mysterious Vodoun potion called black magic. SALT, in particular, should be kept away from zombies if they are to remain in their subhuman state: Long considered a purifying agent, salt could cause the zombie to regain the ability to speak and could even function as a homing device that could lead the zombie back to eternal rest.

In his books *The Serpent and the Rainbow* (1985) and *The Ethnobiology of the Haitian Zombie* (1988), Davis not only gives his readers the components of zombification but also outlines his theories on why such a horrifying act exists: Making a zombie is a very effective method of capital punishment. Just as the slaves suspected more than 200 years ago, the members of the secret Maroon societies used zombification—or the threat of it—to control first the slaves then the superstitious Haitian citizens. Davis's conclusions have been clouded by allegations of fraud and questions about his sensational, rather than scientific, approach. *The Serpent and the Rainbow* movie, starring Bill Pullman and directed by Wes Craven, opened in 1988. Nevertheless, stories of people who rise from the dead to work for the *bokor* until eternity would give any lawbreaker pause.

Magical Resurrection

In Vodoun, zombie corpses are "raised" from graves in magical rituals in which appeals are made to Baron Samedi, the scarecrowlike god of graveyards and zombies. In Haiti, the rites take place in a graveyard at midnight. They are performed by the person who is the local incarnation of Papa Nebo, father of death, and a group of followers. A grave is selected and white candles are implanted at its foot and lit. A frock coat and a silk top hat, the symbols of Baron Samedi, are draped on the grave's cross (if the grave has no cross, one is made). A ritual is performed to awaken Baron Samedi from sleep. While the god makes no visible manifestation, he signals his presence and approval by moving or flapping the frock coat or hat.

The necromancers pay homage to the Baron and promise him offerings of food, drink, and money; then they send him back to sleep by tossing roots and herbs. The corpse is unearthed, and the incarnation of Papa Nebo asks it questions. The answers usually are "heard" only by the Papa Nebo representative.

Zombie Themes

The chilling idea of a robotic human raised from the dead to serve an evil master never ceases to entertain the public, and authors and moviemakers have created countless books and films. Perhaps the greatest classic zombie movie was George Romero's *Night of the Living Dead* (1968), with the sequel *Dawn of the Dead* in 1978 followed by *Day of the Dead* in 1985. Each spawned related spinoffs, such as John Russo's novelization of *Night* released in 1981, full of such scary prose as, "They are coming, rising rotten from their graves, filling the night with a furious howl, and staining the earth bloody red. . . ." Other items include novelizations of *Dawn* and *Return of the Living Dead,* a complete filmbook of *Night,* press kits and advertising materials from the original 1968 release of *Night,* board and video games, and even *Night of the Living Dead* barbecue sauce and accompanying T-shirt.

In 2005, Romero released *George Romero's Land of the Dead* after a 20-year hiatus. The zombies, who move in slow motion and feast on human flesh ("They kill for one reason. They kill for food."), have left the cemetery near the farm in *Night* and traveled into an urban setting ruled by actor Dennis Hopper, a nightmare scenario evoking the ninth round of Dante's *Inferno*. Little remains of humankind or the humanity they once possessed.

The first zombie film was *White Zombie* in 1932, in which the undead are portrayed as mindless henchman completely in thrall to an evil sorcerer. The 1943 movie *I Walked with a Zombie* gives the creatures limited control over their movements. But Romero's movies define most of the accepted zombie characteristics: cannibalism; zombification as the result of touching another zombie or through some terrible, toxic, ecological mistake or radiation emission; abundant gore; and the return of a zombie to his dead state only by a bullet to the head. Other favorite depictions or causes of a zombie infestation include pandemic infections, DEMONS, and evil spirits, the influence of aliens, implantation of computer chips, technology gone awry, completion of some event or unfinished business from the living days, or even a simple CURSE, as in Jerry Bruckheimer's Disney film *Pirates of the Caribbean: The Curse of the Black Pearl* (2003). Predictably, any phenomenon as popular as zombies invites parody, as in *Shaun of the Dead* (2004).

Zombies also have proved popular in toys and games.

FURTHER READING:

Dargis, Manohla. "Not Just Roaming, Zombies Rise Up." *The New York Times,* June 24, 2005.

Davis, Wade. *The Serpent and the Rainbow.* New York: Simon & Schuster, 1985.

Guiley, Rosemary Ellen. *The Encyclopedia of Witches and Witchcraft,* 2d ed. New York: Facts On File Inc., 1999.

Labaton, Stephen. "An Army of Soulless 1's and 0's." *The New York Times,* June 24, 2005.

"What Is a Zombie?" Available online at www.zombiejuice. com/whatisit.html. Downloaded June 12, 2005.

"Zombie Books." Available online at www.zombiejuice.com/ zbooks/index.html. Downloaded June 12, 2005.

"Zombie Stuff." Available online at www.zombiejuice.com/ zstuff/index.html. Downloaded June 12, 2005.

Zosimos (c. 250–300) Greek author of numerous alchemical texts and a self-professed disciple of MARIA PROPHETESS. Zosimos—also called Zosimos the Panopolitan, Zosimos the Theban, and Zosimos of Panopolis—lived in Hellenistic Egypt and was the earliest reliable author on alchemy. Little is known about his life. He probably was from Panopolis in Thebais, and he probably subsequently lived in Alexandria.

Among Zosimos's writings are 22 treatises, in which he extensively quotes Maria Prophetess. With his sister, Eusebeia, he wrote a 28-volume encyclopedia on ALCHEMY, the oldest text on the subject; only fragments survive. He was knowledgeable in Egyptian, Greek, Arabic, and Christian alchemical lore. He was the first alchemist to write about the PHILOSOPHER'S STONE and was the first to trace the origins of alchemy to the partriarchs and prophets of the Bible.

According to Zosimos, the Egyptians and the Jews possess the greatest science and wisdom, and that of the Jews is "rendered more sound by divine justice." He also held Greek alchemists in high esteem.

FURTHER READING:

Patai, Raphael. *The Jewish Alchemists.* Princeton, N.J.: Princeton University Press, 1994.

BIBLIOGRAPHY

Ackroyd, Peter. *Blake: A Biography*. New York: Alfred A. Knopf, 1996.

Asano, Michael. *Hands: The Complete Book of Palmistry*. New York: Japan Publications, 1985.

Ashcroft-Nowicki, Dolores, and J. H. Brennan. *Magical Use of Thought Form: A Proven System of Mental and Spiritual Empowerment*. St. Paul, Minn.: Llewellyn Publications, 2001.

Bardon, Franz. *Frabato the Magician*. Salt Lake City: Merkur Publishing, 1979.

———. *Initiation into Hermetics: A Course of Instruction of Magic Theory and Practice*. Wuppertal, Germany: Dieter Ruggeberg, 1971.

———. *The Key to the True Kabbalah*. Salt Lake City: Merkur Publishing, 1996.

———. *The Practice of Magical Evocation*. Salt Lake City: Merkur Publishing, 2001.

———. *Questions and Answers*. Salt Lake City: Merkur Publishing, 1998.

Baring-Gould, Sabine. *The Book of Werewolves*. London: Smith, Elder & Co, 1865.

Barrett, Francis. *The Magus*. 1801. Reprint, Secaucus, N.J.: The Citadel Press, 1967.

Besant, Annie, and C. W. Leadbeater. *Thought-forms*. Wheaton, Ill.: Theosophical Publishing House, 1969.

Blavatsky, H. P. *Isis Unveiled*. Pasadena, Calif.: Theosophical University Press, 1976.

———. *The Secret Doctrine*. London: The Theosophical Publishing Co., Ltd., 1888.

Boester, Knut, ed. *The Elixirs of Nostradamus*. Wakefield, R.I.: Moyer Bell, 1996.

Bradley, Marion Zimmer. *The Mists of Avalon*. New York: Knopf, 1983.

Brier, Bob. *Ancient Egyptian Magic*. New York: William Morrow, 1980.

Briggs, Katherine B. *An Encyclopedia of Fairies: Hobgoblins, Brownies, Bogies, and Other Supernatural Creatures*. New York: Pantheon Books, 1976.

———. *The Vanishing People*. New York: Pantheon Books, 1978.

Brown, Dan. *Angels and Demons*. New York: Doubleday, 2000.

———. *The Da Vinci Code*. New York: Doubleday, 2003.

Budge, E.A. Wallis. *Amulets and Superstitions*. 1930. Reprint, New York: Dover Publications, 1978.

———. *Egyptian Magic*. 1899. Reprint, New Hyde Park, N.Y.: University Books, n.d.

Butler, E. M. *Ritual Magic*. Cambridge: Cambridge University Press, 1949.

Butler, W. E. *How to Develop Clairvoyance*, 2d ed. New York: Samuel Weiser, 1979.

Carroll, Peter J. *Liber Null and Psychonaut*. York Beach, Maine: Samuel Weiser, 1987.

Carter, John. *Sex and Rockets: The Occult World of Jack Parsons*. Los Angeles: Feral House, 2004.

Case, Paul Foster. *The Tarot: A Key to the Wisdom of the Ages*. Richmond, Va.: Macoy Publishing Co., 1947.

Cavendish, Richard. *The Black Arts*. New York: G. P. Putnam's Sons, 1967.

Cavendish, Richard, and Brian Innes, eds. *Man, Myth and Magic*. Rev. ed. North Bellmore, N.Y.: Marshall Cavendish Corp., 1995.

Charlesworth, James H., ed. *The Old Testament Pseudepigrapha*. Vols. 1 & 2. New York: Doubleday, 1983; 1985.

Cheiro. *Mysteries and Romances of the World's Greatest Occultists*. New Hyde Park, N.Y.: University Books, 1972.

Christian, Paul. *The History and Practice of Magic I*. Secaucus, N.J.: Citadel Press, 1963.

Cicero, Chic, and Sandra Tabatha Cicero. *The Essential Golden Dawn*. St. Paul, Minn.: Llewellyn Publications, 2004.

Cooke, Grace. *The Illumined Ones*. New Lands, England: White Eagle Publishing Trust, 1966.

Coudert, Allison. *Alchemy: The Philosopher's Stone*. London: Wildwood House Ltd., 1980.

Crookall, Robert. *Out-of-the-Body Experiences: A Fourth Analysis*. New York: University Books, 1970.

———. *Psychic Breathing: Cosmic Vitality from the Air*. Wellingborough, England: Aquarian Press, 1979.

Crowley, Aleister. *The Book of Lies*. York Beach, Maine: Samuel Weiser, 1980.

———. *The Holy Books of Thelema*. York Beach, Maine: Samuel Weiser, 1983.

———. *Magic in Theory and Practice*. 1929. Reprint, New York: Dover Publications, 1976.

———. *777 and Other Qabalistic Writings*. York Beach, Maine: Samuel Weiser, 1973.

Dacier, Andre. *The Life of Pythagoras*. York Beach, Maine: Samuel Weiser, 1981.

David-Neel, Alexandra. *Magic and Mystery in Tibet*. New York: Dover Publications, 1971.

———. *My Journey to Lhasa*. 1927. Reprint, Boston: Beacon Press, 1986.

Davis, Wade. *The Serpent and the Rainbow*. New York: Simon & Schuster, 1985.

Dee, John. *True and Faithful Relation of What Passed for Many Years Between Dr. John Dee and Some Spirits*. Whitefish, Mont.: Kessinger, 1999.

de Fontbrune, Jean-Charles. *Nostradamus: Countdown to Apocalypse*. New York: Holt, Rinehart and Winston, 1980.

De Jonge, Alex. *Life and Times of Grigorii Rasputin*. New York: Dorset, 1982.

Denning, Melita, and Osborne Phillips. *Practical Guide to Self-Defense and Well-Being*, 2d ed. St. Paul, Minn.: Llewellyn Publications, 1999.

Douglas, Alfred. *Extrasensory Powers: A Century of Psychical Research*. London: Victor Gollancz Ltd., 1976.

Driver, Tom F. *The Magic of Ritual*. San Francisco: HarperSanFrancisco, 1991.

Dumas, F. Ribadeau. *Cagliostro*. London: George Allen and Unwin, 1967.

Duncan, Malcom C. *Duncan's Ritual of Freemasonry*. New York: Crown Publishers, n.d.

Ebon, Martin. *The Devil's Bride, Exorcism: Past and Present*. New York: Harper & Row, 1974.

Eliade, Mircea. *Patterns in Comparative Religion*. New York: New American Library, 1958.

———. *Symbolism, the Sacred, & the Arts*. ed. Diane Apostolos-Cappadona. New York: Crossroad, 1988.

Evans-Wentz, W. Y. *The Fairy Faith in Celtic Countries*. 1911. Reprint, New York: Carroll Publishing Group, 1990.

Fanger, Claire, ed. *Conjuring Spirits: Texts and Traditions of Medieval Ritual Magic*. Thrupp, England: Sutton Publishing Ltd., 1998.

Farrell, Nick. *Making Talismans: Living Entities of Power*. St. Paul: Llewellyn Publications, 2001.

Flint, Valerie I. J. *The Rise of Magic in Medieval Europe*. Princeton, N.J.: Princeton University Press, 1991.

Flournoy, Theodore. *From India to the Planet Mars: A Study of a Case of Somnambulism with Glossolalia*. New York: Harper & Bros., 1900.

Flowers, Stephen Eldred, ed. *Hermetic Magic: The Postmodern Magical Papyrus of Abaris*. York Beach, Maine: Samuel Weiser, 1995.

Fodor, Nandor. *Esoteric Orders and Their Work and The Training and Work of the Initiate*. London: The Aquarian Press, 1987.

———. *Freud, Jung and the Occult*. Secaucus, N.J.: University Books, 1971.

Fortune, Dion. *The Mystical Qabalah*. York Beach, Maine.: Samuel Weiser, 1984.

———. *Psychic Self-Defence*. 1939. Reprint, York Beach, Maine: Samuel Weiser, 1957.

Foster, Barbara, and Michael Foster. *Forbidden Journey: The Life of Alexandra David-Neel*. San Francisco: Harper & Row, 1987.

Foster, Robert. *Tolkien's World from A to Z: The Complete Guide to Middle-Earth*. New York: Ballantine Books, 2001.

Fox, Oliver. *Astral Projection: A Record of Out-of-the-Body Experiences*. Secaucus, N.J.: The Citadel Press, 1962.

Frazer, James G. *The Golden Bough: The Roots of Religion and Folklore*. New York: Avenel Books, 1981.

Gardner, Gerald B. *The Meaning of Witchcraft*. 1959. Reprint, New York: Magickal Childe, 1982.

———. *Witchcraft Today*. London: Rider & Co., 1954, 1956.

Gauquelin, Michel. *Birth-Times*. New York: Hill and Wang, 1983.

———. *Dreams and Illusions of Astrology*. Buffalo, N.Y.: Prometheus Books, 1979.

Gilbert, R. A., ed. *The Golden Dawn: Twilight of the Magicians*. San Bernadino, Calif.: Borgo Press, 1986.

———. *The Sorcerer and His Apprentice: Unknown Hermetic Writings of S. L. MacGregor Mathers and J. W. Brodie-Innes*. Wellingborough, England: Aquarian Press, 1983.

Gilchrist, Cherry. *The Elements of Alchemy*. Rockport, Mass.: Element Books, 1991.

Goddard, David. *The Sacred Magic of Angels*. York Beach, Maine: Samuel Weiser, 1996.

Godwin, David. *Godwin's Cabalistic Encyclopedia*, 3rd ed. St. Paul, Minn.: Llewellyn Publications, 2004.

Godwin, Joscelyn. *Robert Fludd: Hermetic Philosopher and Surveyor of Two Worlds*. Grand Rapids, Mich.: Phanes Press, 1979.

Goethe, Johann Wolfgang von. *The Autobiography of Johann Wolfgang von Goethe*. Vols. 1 & 2. Chicago: University of Chicago Press, 1976.

———. *Faust*. Ed. Cyrus Hamlin. Trans. Walter Arendt. New York: Norton, 1976.

Gonzales-Wippler, Migene. *Santeria: African Magic in Latin America*. St. Paul, Minn.: Llewellyn Publications, 1981.

Goodrick-Clarke, Nicholas, ed. *Helena Blavatsky*. Part of the Western Esoteric Masters Series. Berkeley, Calif.: North Atlantic Books, 2004.

Gordon, Stuart. *The Book of Curses: True Tales of Voodoo, Hoodoo and Hex*. London: Brockhampton Press, 1994.

Gorman, Peter. *Pythagoras: A Life*. Boston: Routledge & Kegan Paul, 1978.

Gray, Ronald D. *Goethe the Alchemist: A Study of Alchemical Symbolism in Goethe's Literary and Scientific Works*. Mansfield Centre, Conn.: Martino Publishing, 2002.

Gray, William G. *The Ladder of Lights*. York Beach, Maine: Samuel Weiser, 1981.

———. *Magical Ritual Methods*. York Beach, Maine: Samuel Weiser, 1980.

———. *The Tree of Evil: Polarities of Good and Evil as Revealed by the Tree of Life*. York Beach, Maine: Samuel Weiser, 1984.

———. *Western Inner Workings*. York Beach, Maine: Samuel Weiser, 1983.

Greer, John Michael. *Inside a Magical Lodge: Group Ritual in the Western Tradition*. St. Paul, Minn.: Llewellyn Publications, 1998.

———. *The New Encyclopedia of the Occult*. St. Paul, Minn.: Llewellyn Publications, 2005.

Greer, Mary K. *Women of the Golden Dawn: Rebels and Priestesses*. Rochester, Vt.: Inner Traditions, 1995.

Grillot de Givry, Emile. *Witchcraft, Magic and Alchemy*. New York: Houghton Mifflin, 1931.

Guiley, Rosemary Ellen. *Angel Magic for Love and Romance*. Lakewood, Minn.: Galde Press, 2005.

———. *Breakthrough Intuition: How to Achieve a Life of Abundance by Listening to the Voice Within*. New York: Berkley Books, 2001.

———. *Dreamwork for the Soul*. New York: Berkley Books, 1998.

———. *The Encyclopedia of Angels*, 2d ed. New York: Facts On File Inc., 2004.

———. *The Encyclopedia of Saints*. New York: Facts On File, 2002.

———. *The Encyclopedia of Vampires, Werewolves and Other Monsters*. New York: Facts On File, Inc., 2004.

———. *The Encyclopedia of Witches and Witchcraft,* 2d ed. New York: Facts On File Inc., 1999.

———. *Fairy Magic*. London: Element/Thorsons, 2004.

———. *Harper's Encyclopedia of Mystical & Paranormal Experience*. San Francisco: HarperSanFrancisco, 1991.

———. *A Miracle in Your Pocket*. London: Thorsons/HarperCollins, 2001.

———. *The Miracle of Prayer: True Stories of Blessed Healing*. New York: Pocket Books, 1995.

———. *Moonscapes: A Celebration of Lunar Astronomy, Magic, Legend and Lore*. New York: Prentice Hall, 1991.

Guiley, Rosemary Ellen, and Robert Michael Place. *The Alchemical Tarot*. London: Thorsons/HarperCollins, 1995.

Hall, Calvin S., and Vernon J. Nordby. *A Primer of Jungian Psychology*. New York: New American Library, 1973.

Hall, Manly P. *Masonic Orders of Fraternity*. Los Angeles: The Philosophical Research Society, 1950.

———. *Paracelsus: His Mystical and Medical Philosophy*. Los Angeles: The Philosophic Research Society, 1964.

———. *Sages and Seers*. Los Angeles: The Philosophical Research Society, 1959.

———. *The Secret Teachings of All Ages*. 1928. Reprint, Los Angeles: The Philosophic Research Society, 1977.

Halliwell, James Orchard. *Private Diary of Dr. John Dee and the Catalog of His Library of Alchemical Manuscripts*. Whitefish, Mont.: Kessinger, 1997.

Hansen, George. *The Trickster and the Paranormal*. New York: Xlibris, 2001.

Hauck, Dennis William. *The Emerald Tablet: Alchemy for Personal Transformation*. New York: Penguin/Arkana, 1999.

Heindel, Max. *The Rosicrucian Cosmo-Conception*. Oceanside, Calif.: The Rosicrucian Fellowship, 1993.

Heline, Corinne. *Sacred Science of Numbers*. Marina del Rey, Calif.: DeVorss & Co., 1991.

Helvetius, John Frederick. *The Golden Calf, Which the World Adores and Desires: In which is handled The most Rare and Incomparable Wonder of Nature, in Transmuting Metals; viz. How the intire Substance of Lead, was in one Moment Transmuted into Gold-Obrizon, with an exceeding small particle of the true Philosophick Stone. At the Hague. In the year 1666. Written in Latin by John Frederick Helvetius, Doctor and Practitioner of Medicine at the Hague, and faithfully Englished*. London, 1670.

Heywood, H. L. *The Newly-Made Mason: What He and Every Mason Should Know about Masonry*. Richmond, Va.: Macoy Publishing and Masonic Supply Co., 1973.

Holmyard, E. J. *Alchemy*. New York: Penguin Books, 1957.

Howe, Ellic. *Magicians of the Golden Dawn: A Documentary History of a Magical Order, 1887–1923*. York Beach, Maine: Red Wheel/Weiser, 1978.

Hyatt, Christopher S., ed. *An Interview With Israel Regardie: His Final Thoughts and Views*. Phoenix: Falcon Press, 1985.

James, Geoffrey. *Angel Magic: The Ancient Art of Summoning and Communicating with Angelic Beings*. St. Paul, Minn.: Llewellyn Publications, 1999.

Jung, Carl G. *Aion*. In *The Collected Works of C. G. Jung*, vol. 9, part II. Princeton, N.J.: Princeton University Press, 1959.

———. *Alchemical Studies*. In *The Collected Works of C. G. Jung*, vol. 13. Princeton, N.J.: Princeton University Press, 1967.

———. *The Archetypes of the Collective Unconscious*. In *The Collected Works of C. G. Jung*, vol. 9, part I. Princeton, N.J.: Princeton University Press, 1959.

———, ed. *Man and His Symbols*. New York: Anchor Press/Doubleday, 1988.

———. *Memories, Dreams, Reflections*. New York: Vintage Books, 1965.

———. *Mysterious Coniuntionis,* 2d ed. Princeton, N.J.: Princeton University Press, 1970.

———. *Mysterium Coniunctionis*. In *The Collected Works of C. G. Jung*, vol. 14. Princeton, N.J.: Princeton University Press, 1963.

———. *Psychology and Alchemy,* 2d ed. In *The Collected Works of C. G. Jung,* vol. 12. Princeton, N.J.: Princeton University Press, 1953.

———. *Synchronicity*. In *Collected Works*, vol. 13. 1952. Reprint, Princeton, N.J.: University of Princeton Press, 1973.

The 'Key' of Jacob Boehme. Trans. by William Law. Grand Rapids, Mich.: Phanes Press, 1991.

King, Francis. *Megatherion: The Magickal World of Aleister Crowley.* New York: Creation Books, 2004.

———, ed. *Ritual Magic of the Golden Dawn.* Rochester, Vt.: Destiny Books, 1997.

King, Francis, and Stephen Skinner. *Techniques of High Magic: A Manual of Self-Initiation.* Rochester, Vt.: Destiny Books, 1976.

Klossowski de Rola, Stanislaus. *The Golden Game: Alchemical Engravings of the Seventeenth Century.* New York: George Braziller, Inc., 1988.

Knight, Gareth. *Dion Fortune and the Three Fold Way.* London: S.I.L. (Trading) Ltd., 2002.

———. *The Practice of Ritual Magic.* Albuquerque: Sun Chalice Books, 1996.

Kraig, Donald Michael. *Modern Magick: Eleven Lessons in the High Magickal Arts,* 2d ed. St. Paul, Minn.: Llewellyn Publications, 2004.

Langley, Noel. *Edgar Cayce on Reincarnation.* New York: Castle Books, 1967.

Laycock, Donald. *The Complete Enochian Dictionary: A Dictionary of the Angelic Language as Revealed to Dr. John Dee and Edward Kelley.* York Beach, Maine: Samuel Weiser, 2001.

Legge, James, trans. *The I Ching.* New York: Dover Publications, 1963.

Leitch, Aaron. *Secrets of the Magical Grimoires: The Classical Texts of Magick Deciphered.* St. Paul, Minn.: Llewellyn Publications, 2005.

Leland, Charles Godfrey. *Etruscan Magic and Occult Remedies.* New Hyde Park, N.Y.: University Books, 1963.

Lethbridge, T. C. *Ghost and Divining-Rod.* London: Routledge & Kegan Paul, 1963.

———. *The Power of the Pendulum.* London: Routledge & Kegan Paul, 1976.

Levi, Eliphas. *The Book of Splendours: The Inner Mysteries of the Qabalah.* 1894. Reprint, York Beach, Maine: Samuel Weiser, 1984.

———. *The History of Magic.* 1860. Reprint, York Beach, Maine: Samuel Weiser, 2001.

———. *Transcendental Magic.* 1896. Reprint, York Beach, Maine: Samuel Weiser, 2001.

Long, Max Freedom. *The Secret Science Behind Miracles.* Los Angeles: DeVorss & Co., 1954.

Lowe, Michael, and Carmen Blacker. *Oracles and Divination.* Boulder, Colo.: Shambala, 1981.

Luck, Georg. *Arcana Mundi: Magic and the Occult in the Greek and Roman Worlds.* Baltimore: Johns Hopkins University Press, 1985.

Lukacs, Georg. *Goethe and His Age.* New York: Grosset and Dunlap, 1969.

Mackay, Charles. *Extraordinary Popular Delusions and the Madness of Crowds.* New York: Farrar, Straus & Giroux, 1932.

Mackey, Albert G. *Lexicon of Freemasonry.* Philadelphia: McClure Publishing, 1908.

Malinowski, Bronislaw. *Magic, Science and Religion.* Garden City, N.Y.: Doubleday Anchor Books, 1948.

Mann, William E. *The Knights Templar in the New World: How Henry Sinclair Brought the Grail to Arcadia.* Rochester, Vt.: Inner Traditions, 2004.

Martin, Malachi. *Hostage to the Devil.* New York: Harper & Row, 1976.

Marwick, Max, ed. *Witchcraft and Sorcery,* 2d ed. Harmondsworth, Middlesex, England: Penguin Books, 1982.

Masello, Robert. *Raising Hell: A Concise History of the Black Arts—and Those Who Dared to Practice Them.* New York: Berkley Books, 1996.

Mathers, S. L. MacGregor. *The Book of the Sacred Magic of Abra-Melin the Mage.* Wellingborough, England: The Aquarian Press, 1976.

———. *The Kabbalah Unveiled.* London: Routledge and Kegan Paul, 1926.

Matthews, John. *The Grail: Quest for the Eternal.* New York: Crossroad, 1981.

———, ed. *At the Table of the Grail: Magic and the Use of Imagination.* London: Arkana, 1987.

Maxwell-Stuart, P. G. *Wizards: A History.* Stroud, England: Tempus Publishing Ltd., 2004.

McCalman, Iain. *The Last Alchemist: Count Cagliostro Master of Magic in the Age of Reason.* New York: HarperCollins, 2003.

McDermott, Robert A. *The Essential Steiner.* San Francisco: Harper & Row, 1984.

Mead, G. R. S. *Thrice Greatest Hermes: Studies in Hellenistic Theosophy and Gnosis.* York Beach, Maine: Samuel Weiser, 1992.

Melville, Francis. *The Book of Alchemy.* Gloucester, Mass.: Fair Winds Press, 2002.

———. *The Secrets of High Magic.* Hauppauge, N.Y.: Barron's, 2002.

Meyer, Marvin W., and Richard Smoth, eds. *Ancient Christian Magic: Coptic Texts of Ritual Power.* Princeton, N.J.: Princeton University Press, 1999.

Michaelsen, Scott, ed. *Portable Darkness: An Aleister Crowley Reader.* New York: Harmony Books, 1989.

Miller, Carolyn. *Creating Miracles: Understanding the Experience of Divine Intervention.* Tiburon, Calif.: HJ Kramer, 1995.

Monroe, Robert A. *Journeys Out of the Body.* Garden City, N.Y.: Doubleday, 1971.

Morewedge, Parvis. *The Mystical Philosophy of Avicenna.* Binghamton, N.Y.: Global Publications at SUNY Binghamton University, 2001.

Muldoon, Sylvan, and Hereward Carrington. *The Projection of the Astral Body.* London: Rider, 1929.

Myers, F. W. H. *Human Personality and Its Survival of Bodily Death.* 1903. Reprint, New York: Longmans, Green and Co., 1954.

———. *Mysteries of the Unknown: Visions and Prophecies.* Alexandria, Va.: Time-Life Books, 1988.

Nielsen, Greg, and Joseph Polansky. *Pendulum Power.* Wellingborough, Northamptonshire: Excalibur Books, 1984.

Ogden, Daniel. *Magic, Witchcraft, and Ghosts in the Greek and Roman Worlds: A Sourcebook.* New York: Oxford University Press, 2002.

Oppenheim, Janet. *The Other World: Spiritualism and Psychical Research in England, 1850–1914.* Cambridge: Cambridge University Press, 1985.

Otten, Charlotte F., ed. *A Lycanthropy Reader: Werewolves in Western Culture.* New York: Dorset Press, 1989.

Patai, Raphael. *The Jewish Alchemists.* Princeton, N.J.: Princeton University Press, 1994.

Pelton, Robert W. *Voodoo Secrets from A to Z.* Cranbury, N.J.: A. S. Barnes and Co., 1973.

Peterson, Joseph. *John Dee's Five Books of Mystery: Original Sourcebook of Enochian Magic.* York Beach, Maine: Samuel Weiser, 2003.

Pike, Albert. *Morals and Dogma of the Ancient and Accepted Scottish Rite of Freemasonry.* Richmond, Va.: L. H. Jenkins, 1871.

Pinch, Geraldine. *Magic in Ancient Egypt.* London: British Museum Press, 1994.

Place, Robert M. *The Tarot: History, Symbolism and Divination.* New York: Jeremy P. Tarcher/Penguin, 2005.

Porteous, Alexander. *The Forest in Folklore and Mythology.* New York: Macmillan, 1928.

Radin, Dean. *The Conscious Universe: The Scientific Truth of Psychic Phenomena.* San Francisco: HarperSanFrancisco, 1997.

Regardie, Israel. *Ceremonial Magic: A Guide to the Mechanisms of Ritual.* London: Aeon Books, 2004.

———. *The Golden Dawn,* 6th ed. St. Paul, Minn.: Llewellyn Publications, 2003.

———. *The Tree of Life: A Study in Magic.* York Beach, Maine: Samuel Weiser, 1969.

Richardson, Alan. *Priestess: The Life and Magic of Dion Fortune.* Wellingborough, England: The Aquarian Press, 1987.

Richardson, Alan, and Marcus Claridge. *The Old Sod: The Odd Life and Inner Workings of William G. Gray.* London: Ignotus Press, 2003.

Roberts, Allen E. *The Craft and Its Symbols: Opening the Door to Masonic Symbolism.* Richmond, Va.: Macoy Publishing and Masonic Supply Co., 1974.

Roberts, Henry C. *The Complete Prophecies of Nostradamus.* New York: American Book–Stratford Press, 1969.

Rogo, D. Scott. *The Infinite Boundary.* New York: Dodd, Mead & Co., 1987.

Rowling, J. K. *Harry Potter and the Chamber of Secrets.* New York: Scholastic Inc., 1999.

———. *Harry Potter and the Goblet of Fire.* New York: Scholastic Inc., 2000.

———. *Harry Potter and the Order of the Phoenix.* New York: Scholastic Inc., 2003.

———. *Harry Potter and the Prisoner of Azkaban.* New York: Scholastic Inc., 1999.

———. *Harry Potter and the Sorcerer's Stone.* New York: Scholastic Inc., 1997.

Rudhyar, Dane. *The Astrology of Personality,* 2d ed. Garden City, N.Y.: Doubleday, 1970.

Russell, Jeffrey Burton. *A History of Witchcraft.* London: Thames & Hudson, 1980.

Rustad, Mary S., ed. and trans. *The Black Books of Elverum.* Lakeville, Minn.: Galde Press, 1999.

Savedow, Steve. *Sepher Rezial Hemelach: The Book of the Angel Rezial.* York Beach, Maine: Samuel Weiser, 2000.

Scholem, Gershom. *Kabbalah.* New York: New American Library, 1974.

Schure, Edouard. *The Great Initiates: A Study of the Secret Religions of History.* San Francisco: Harper & Row, 1961.

Secrets of the Alchemists. New York: Time-Life Books, 1990.

Seligmann, Kurt. *The History of Magic and the Occult.* New York: Pantheon Books, 1948.

Smith, Chris. *The Lord of the Rings: Weapons and Warfare.* New York: Houghton Mifflin, 2004.

Spence, Lewis. *The Magic Arts in Celtic Britain.* Van Nuys, Calif.: Newcastle Publishing, 1996.

Steiner, Rudolph. *An Autobiography.* Blauvelt, N.Y.: Rudolph Steiner Publications, 1977.

———. *The Secret Stream: Christian Rosenkreutz and Rosicrucianism.* Great Barrington, Mass.: The Anthroposophic Press, 2000.

Stephenson, P. R., and Israel Regardie. *The Legend of Aleister Crowley.* St. Paul, Minn.: Llewellyn Publications, 1970.

Stewart, R. J. *The Living World of Faery.* Lake Toxaway, N.C.: Mercury Publishing, 1995.

———. *The Mystic Life of Merlin.* London: Arkana, 1986.

———, ed. *The Book of Merlin.* Poole, Dorset: Blanford Press, 1987.

Stoudt, John Joseph. *Jacob Boehme: His Life and Thought.* New York: Seabury Press, 1968.

Sutin, Lawrence. *Do What Thou Wilt: A Life of Aleister Crowley.* New York: St. Martin's Griffin, 2000.

Symonds, John, and Kenneth Grant, eds. *The Confessions of Aleister Crowley, an Autobiography.* London: Routledge & Kegan Paul, 1979.

Thomas, Keith. *Religion & the Decline of Magic.* New York: Scribners, 1971.

Thompson, C. J. S. *The Mysteries and Secrets of Magic.* New York: Barnes & Noble, 1993.

Three Books of Occult Philosophy Written by Henry Cornelius Agrippa of Nettesheim. Translated by James Freake. Edited and annotated by Donald Tyson. St. Paul, Minn.: Llewellyn Publications, 1995.

Tolkien, Christopher. *The History of The Lord of the Rings.* Part 1, *The Return of the Shadow.* New York: Houghton Mifflin Co., 1988; Part 2, *The Treason of Isengard,* 1989; Part 3, *The War of the Ring,* 1990; Part 4, *The End of the Third Age,* 1992.

Tolkien, J. R. R. *The Hobbit, Or There and Back Again.* New York: Houghton Mifflin Co., 1996.

———. *The Lord of the Rings: The Fellowship of the Ring.* New York: Houghton Mifflin Co., 1994.

———. *The Lord of the Rings: The Return of the King.* New York: Houghton Mifflin Co., 1994.

———. *The Lord of the Rings: The Two Towers.* New York: Houghton Mifflin Co., 1994.

———. *The Silmarillion,* Christopher Tolkien, ed. New York: Ballantine Books, 1999.

Trachtenberg, Joshua. *Jewish Magic and Superstition: A Study in Folk Religion.* New York: Berhman's Jewish Book House, 1939.

Tyson, Donald. *The New Magus.* St. Paul, Minn.: Llewellyn Publications, 1988.

———, ed. *Three Books of Occult Philosophy Written by Henry Cornelius Agrippa of Nettesheim.* trans. James Freake. St. Paul, Minn.: Llewellyn Publications, 1995.

Valiente, Doreen. *Witchcraft for Tomorrow.* Custer, Wash.: Phoenix Publishing, 1978.

Vallee, Jacques. *Passport to Magonia: From Folklore to Flying Saucers.* Chicago: Henry Regnery Co., 1969.

van Gennup, Arnold. *The Rites of Passage.* Translated by Monica B. Vizedom and Gabrielle L. Caffee. Chicago: University of Chicago Press, 1960.

Waite, Arthur Edward. *Alchemists through the Ages.* Blauvelt, N.Y.: Rudolph Steiner Publications, 1970.

———. *The Book of Black Magic and of Pacts.* 1899. Reprint, York Beach, Maine: Samuel Weiser, 1972.

———. *The Brotherhood of the Rosy Cross.* New York: Barnes & Noble, 1993.

———. *The Hermetic Museum.* York Beach, Maine: Samuel Weiser, 1991.

———. *A New Encyclopedia of Freemasonry.* New York: Weathervane Books, 1970.

———. *Saint-Martin, the French Mystic.* London: W. Rider, 1922.

Watson, C. W., and Roy Ellen, eds. *Understanding Witchcraft and Sorcery in Southeast Asia.* Honolulu: University of Hawaii Press, 1993.

The Way of Hermes: New Translations of The Corpus Hermeticum and *The Definitions of Hermes Trismegistus to Asclepius.* Rochester, Vt.: Inner Traditions, 2000.

Weeks, Andrew. *Boehme: An Intellectual Biography.* Albany: State University of New York Press, 1991.

Whitcomb, Bill. *The Magician's Reflection: A Complete Guide to Creating Personal Magical Symbols & Systems.* St. Paul, Minn.: Llewellyn Publications, 1999.

White, Michael. *Isaac Newton: The Last Sorcerer.* London: Fourth Estate, 1997.

White, T. H. *The Once and Future King.* New York: Berkeley Medallion Books, 1966.

Wickland, Carl. *Thirty Years among the Dead.* 1924. Reprint, N. Hollywood: Newcastle Publishing Co., 1974.

Wilhelm, Richard, and Cary F. Baynes (trans.). *The I Ching.* Princeton, N.J.: Princeton University Press, Bollingen Series XIX, 1969.

Wilson, Colin. *The Occult.* New York: Vintage Books, 1971.

Woodward, Kenneth L. *The Book of Miracles.* New York: Simon & Schuster, 2000.

Wright, Elbee. *The Book of Magical Talismans/The Black Pullet.* Minneapolis: Marlar Publishing Co., 1984.

Yates, F. A. *Giordano Bruno and the Hermetic Tradition.* London: Routledge and Kegan Paul, 1972.

Yeats, William Butler. *Autobiography.* New York: Macmillan, 1938.

INDEX

Boldface page numbers indicate extensive treatment of a topic. *Italic* page numbers indicate illustrations.